MANAGEMENT INFORMATION SYSTEMS

A User Perspective

MANAGEMENT INFORMATION SYSTEMS

A User Perspective

James O. Hicks, Jr.

Virginia Polytechnic Institute and State University

West Publishing Company

St. Paul New York Los Angeles San Francisco

Copyeditor: Lawrence Synal
Designer: SOHO Studio, Inc.
Composition: Science Press
Artwork: J&R
Cover: Linda Benveniste
Production/Management Services: Cobb/Dunlop Publisher Services

50 West Kellogg Boulevard
P.O. Box 3526
St. Paul, Minnesota 55165

Printed in the United States of America

Library of Congress Cataloging in Publication Data

Hicks, James O.
Management information systems.

Includes index.
1. Management information systems. I. Title.
T58.6.H49 1984 658.4'0388 83-23293
ISBN 0-314-77912-4
ISBN 0-314-77914-0 (International ed.)
1st Reprint—1984

To my wife Eva
and
my son Kevin

CONTENTS

PREFACE

TO THE STUDENTS

Information systems is a dynamic and rapidly changing field that uses the electronic computer as its primary tool. Computers are a driving force in many areas of society but are particularly important in business. Students who learn to master this powerful tool to provide the information needed for their careers, whether they are in finance, marketing, management, accounting, economics, or some other business area, will have a great advantage over those who do not. In the field of information systems we study how computer hardware and software are efficiently combined to build effective information systems for business professionals.

Computer hardware and software, however, are only tools. Too often, people feel that the computer is mysterious, complex, and hard to understand, which is an unfortunate misconception. In this text, we take the view that information systems are logical, interesting, essential for a business career, and can be mastered with a reasonable degree of effort by any student.

The text deliberately takes a user orientation. Topics covered include those that are important for a manager, an accountant, a marketing person, and other business professionals to know. Although hardware and software for information systems are readily available, it is the application of these tools that is important. Accordingly, I have covered such topics as how you can develop applications without programming, how users can build decision support systems, and the structured development life cycle, which is a particularly user-friendly approach to developing applications. Also covered is how you can control information systems so that they operate properly, and how personal computers can be interfaced with a particular firm's information system to provide you with information you can directly control.

It is essential that users be directly involved in the process of developing information systems. The participation of information systems professionals such as system analysts and programmers is certainly important to this process because these people have technical expertise in the area. However, research has shown that the most successful information systems applications are those in which there is direct, heavy user involvement in development and maintenance. A business professional simply cannot afford to take the attitude that knowledge of information systems is not necessary and consequently leave application development to information systems professionals. Only *you* know what information *you* need from a system. If you do not understand information systems it will be impossible to translate this need for information into an operational information system.

This book contains several features which will assist you in learning and reinforcing the material it contains. Each chapter has the following sections:

1. A detailed chapter outline that provides you with an overview of the chapter so that you can see where we are headed as you read the chapter.
2. Within each chapter, there are short discussion cases that apply the material to real world situations. Your instructor is likely to use these cases for class discussion purposes.
3. At the end of the chapter there is a point by point chapter summary that summarizes major topics introduced in the chapter.
4. A list of key terms is included at the end of each chapter. I have found that learning the terminology is an important part of studying information systems. As with any new field, the terminology in this area is often unfamiliar. You should review these key terms, and for any that you don't understand you should refer back to the chapter or to the comprehensive glossary at the end of the text.
5. Review questions are provided so that you can independently test your knowledge of the chapter.
6. Several discussion questions, which often cover controversial topics, are provided for class discussion purposes.
7. The research projects provide ideas for out-of-class research that will enrich your learning experience in information systems. Your instructor is likely to assign some of these. If not, I hope you will find some of them interesting enough to pursue in greater detail.
8. Each chapter has an application case, an essay, or an MIS and management feature. These have been written by practitioners in the world of information systems. They provide unique insights into the applications, problems, and thoughts of managers and information systems professionals.

The first part of the book is designed to give you an overview of information processing and management information systems, including some examples of information processing systems. The second part of the book, Computer Resources, covers the hardware and software resources that are available to implement information systems applications. Topics covered in this area, such as data base management systems, personal computers, the automated office, and operating systems, are particularly important for an understanding of today's information systems. The next part, Conceptual Foundations of Information Systems, contains some very important concepts that must be kept in mind when designing and implementing information systems. It is for this reason that this material is covered just prior to the part on development of user applications. In the latter part, you will see two basic approaches to application development: 1) the structured development life cycle; and 2) application development by users without programming. The second approach is closely related to the building of decision support systems, which is also covered later in this part of the book. In the final part of the text, we cover the management of information systems, their relationship to society, and how information systems may affect you in your daily life and in your career.

I am sure you will find this an enjoyable and useful course. In fact, if you master the material in this course and apply it once you begin your career, there is no doubt in my mind that you will find this course to have been the most useful of any taken in your collegiate program.

TO THE INSTRUCTOR

This text takes a user approach to information systems. Its intent is to provide a business student with the information systems fundamentals necessary to operate effectively in a computerized business environment. In writing this text I had several basic objectives:

1. Since most of the students in the target course will in their careers be users of information systems rather than information systems professionals, the text should approach MIS from a user perspective.
2. The text should have good coverage of decision support systems, and this topic should be related to application development by users.
3. The personal computer and its relationship to distributed data processing, networks, and decision support systems should be covered.
4. The text should have application cases, essays, and MIS and management features at the end of each chapter to apply the material to real world situations.
5. The structured system development cycle, including structured analysis using data flow diagrams, should be covered. Most current texts cover structured design but often fail to cover structured analysis and show the logical transition between the two.
6. The end of chapter pedagogic material (review questions, discussion questions, research projects, application cases, etc.) should be more varied and of greater quality than those in current texts.
7. New tools are emerging that will assist users in developing their own applications without programmers. This area should be covered along with its relationship to the information center concept, data base management systems, and decision support systems.
8. The text should take a top-down approach, and therefore information processing, MIS concepts, and an overview of user applications should be covered first in the text. This ordering provides the student with a fundamental understanding of the subject and a basic framework that the student and the instructor can relate to as the course progresses.
9. There are many very effective approaches to the control of computer-based systems. Controls are an integral part of any good system and, as a topic it is particularly important to users. Therefore, at least one chapter should be devoted to controls.
10. Because of the increasing use of personal computers in business, more users will be directly involved in the evaluation and acquisition of hardware and/or software. A chapter should be devoted to this topic.

The text was specifically developed to cover material satisfying the AACSB requirement for MIS coverage in business programs. It also assumes that a student has little or no prior background in information systems. However, the text could easily be used at the sophomore level or beyond with students who have had a course in business data processing or computer literacy. If this is the case, I would simply skip some of the material covered in previous coursework, such as the chapters on hardware in the part on computer resources. I have attempted to include enough material in the text to facilitate skipping previously covered topics, but have also tried to provide ample subject matter for a full semester or quarter's work on information systems.

The teaching and learning tools included in each chapter are as follows:

1. There is a detailed outline at the beginning of each chapter to provide an overview.
2. Short discussion cases are inserted within the chapter body so the material can be applied to real world situations. These may also be used effectively for class discussion.
3. A chapter summary provides point-by-point summary of major topics in the chapter.
4. A list of key terms may be used for review of terminology.
5. A set of review questions may be used by the students on their own or in class to review the chapter.
6. Discussion questions describe sometimes controversial situations relating to the chapter material. I find these particularly useful for generating class discussion.
7. Research projects may be assigned as out-of-class research to the students. Class presentation and discussion of these topics may be used to cover particular areas in more depth.
8. At the end of each chapter is an application case, an essay, or an MIS and management feature. These relate the chapter material to real world applications and problems. They can provide unique insights into the thoughts of managers and information systems professionals concerning material presented in the text. If used properly they can help bring the material alive.

Each chapter in the text is written as independently as possible so that you may rearrange the sequencing of the material if you prefer. However, I think that it is important to explain the rationale for the organization of the text since the sequencing of part 3—Conceptual Foundations of Information Systems—and chapter 17—Decision Support Systems—may be different from what you are accustomed to. Quite often, organizational and behavioral aspects of systems theory are presented early in a text while the systems development material is presented later. In this approach the students learn systems, organizational and behavioral concepts but then must wait sometimes for weeks to apply them in systems development. Therefore, I think it is important to cover these concepts just prior to systems development. In this way the student can quickly see the importance of the concepts. The chapter on decision support systems is placed after the chapter on application development by users because the two are so closely related. I feel the student must have background in data base management systems, networks, personal computers, the structured development life cycle, and application development by users before he or she can really understand the implications and the development of decision support systems.

The end of text materials include the following:

1. A case appendix containing several classroom-tested cases. These may be used to generate classroom discussion or for term projects.

2. A comprehensive glossary. Understanding terminology is essential to understanding information systems. Quite often I have had students purchase a paperback dictionary of information processing terms. This should not be necessary with this text due to the comprehensive nature of the glossary, which offers standardized definitions. Where possible, I have used American National Standards Institute definitions from the *American National Dictionary for Information Processing*. Also used are definitions from the IBM publication *Data Processing Glossary*.

ACKNOWLEDGEMENTS

No one writes a textbook without the valuable contributions of others. For this book, many organizations gave permission to reprint their copyrighted material. These organizations are identified throughout the book as their material appears.

During various stages of the book's development, several graduate assistants have been very helpful in performing numerous clerical, proofreading, and research tasks associated with the book. These include Roy Smith, Connie Parks, Alan Jackson, Bob Collis, and Kih-yun Do. I am particularly indebted to two of my former graduate assistants who are now practitioners in the information systems field, Amer Mufti and Mike Bandy. These outstanding individuals made particularly significant contributions to the development of this book. I also thank Phyllis Neece and Sarah Kenley for the superb typing skills they contributed to the book's development. Along the way they have rescued me from several deadline crises with the speed and accuracy of their typing. I am also thankful for the environment at Virginia Polytechnic Institute and State University that encourages the commitment and provides the support for projects of this duration and size.

Several professors at other institutions were most helpful in providing review and criticism of the manuscript in its developmental stages. These include: Donald Ballou—Suny/Albany, Bob Bostrom—Indiana Univ., V. Thomas Dock—Univ. of Southern California, John Henderson—MIT, Nick Hopkins—Indiana Univ., Ronald Teichman—Penn State Univ., George Bohlen—University of Dayton, Robert Brown—University of Georgia, Dick Callahan—Middle Tennessee State University, William Cornette—Southwest Missouri State University, David Dougherty—University of Texas at El Paso, Joseph Farrelly—Palomar College, M. Jane Garvey—Loyola University of Chicago, Homer Gerber—University of Central Florida, Robert L. Gray—Virginia Commonwealth University, Rod Heisterberg—Austin Community College, Charlotte Hinson—Arkansas State University, Robert Keim—Arizona State University, Stephen Klotz—Onondega Community College, Ambrose Kodet—Mankato State University, Alden Lorents—Northern Arizona State University, George Mundrake—University of Tennessee, Wayne Ostendorf—Iowa State University, Steve Ruth—George Mason University, Albert Scandura—Riverside City College, Sharon Sipe—Prince Georges Community College, Sumit Sircar—University of Texas at Arlington, Philip Taylor—University of Nevada at Las Vegas. Many of their ideas have been included in the book.

Finally, I am grateful to my family for the support and encouragement they gave me in this project. The support of an author's family is crucial to a successful book. My family has contributed to this project in many ways. Even though on a day-to-day basis I may not have recognized all of these contributions. They are important and I am grateful.

PART ONE

INFORMATION SYSTEMS FUNDAMENTALS

CHAPTER 1

AN INTRODUCTION TO DATA AND INFORMATION PROCESSING

I. Introduction

II. What is a Computer?
- A. Definition
- B. Capabilities and Characteristics
- C. Stored Programs

III. Overview of a Computer System
- A. Input Devices
- B. Central Processing Unit
- C. Secondary Storage
- D. Output Devices

IV. Data Processing and Information

V. The Steps in Data Processing
- A. Input
  1. Originate
  2. Classify
  3. Edit
- B. Process
  1. Sort
  2. Calculate
  3. Summarize
  4. Compare
  5. Retrieve
- C. Store
  1. Protect
  2. Index
  3. Update
- D. Output
  1. Report
  2. Display
  3. Issue

VI. Qualitative Characteristics of Information
- A. Relevance
- B. Timeliness
- C. Accuracy
- D. Verifiability

VII. The Impact of Computer Data Processing on Business
- A. Easier Business Growth
- B. Fewer Clerical Workers
- C. Lower Costs
- D. Automation of Decisions
- E. More and Better Information

INTRODUCTION

The premier invention of this century is the computer. In a relatively short time it has affected many areas of our lives. For instance, computers help control our automobiles, are challenging adversaries in the form of electronic games, make possible very sophisticated medical diagnostic tools such as computerized axial tomography (CAT scanner), and even act as an ideal matchmaker through computerized dating services. But most importantly, computers have had a tremendous impact upon the way information is processed within various kinds of organizations. Although information has been processed manually throughout history, modern management information systems would not be possible without the computer. In addition, the basic foundation on which any useful management information system is built depends on a good data processing system.

This chapter will explore the nature of data and information processing. We will define the computer. A brief overview of a computer system will be presented. The steps in processing data and the qualitative characteristics that information should have will be explored, and finally the impact of data processing on business will be covered.

WHAT IS A COMPUTER?

Definition

In general, a *computer* may be defined as a data processor that can perform substantial computation, including numerous arithmetic or logical operations, without intervention by a human operator. The term "substantial" in the above definition is open to wide interpretation. For example, is a pocket calculator that performs a series of statistical computations without human intervention a computer? It may or may not be. In recent years there has been a substantial blurring of the distinction between calculators and computers—particularly with calculators that are programmable.

Capabilities and Characteristics

A computer should have the following specific capabilities and characteristics:

1. *Electronic*. A computer operates through the movement of electronic pulses through circuits rather than the mechanical movement of parts. This characteristic permits modern computers to operate at great speed. Electronic pulses flow through the circuits of today's computers at roughly the speed of light (about 12 inches in a billionth of a second). This is incredibly fast compared to any possible mechanical movement. Certainly a computer could be designed and built based on mechanical movement; however, such a machine would be useless because of its slow speed.
2. *Perform arithmetic operations*. A computer must be able to add, subtract, multiply, and divide.
3. *Compare*. The ability to compare one piece of data to another (to determine if they are equal, if one is less than the other, etc.) is essential to the operation of a computer. Comparison operations are also called *logical operations*.

4. *Internal storage and retrieval of data.* Today's computers have vast capabilities for storage and retrieval of data. Some computers can store several million characters of data within their central processing unit.
5. *Stored program.* The storage capability of the computer makes possible the storage of instructions to be performed during a run. This set of instructions for a particular run is called a *program.*
6. *Program modification at execution.* Computers can modify (branch) the execution stream of a program based on the values of the input data. For example, in a payroll program one series of steps would be executed if the employee is paid based on hours worked. A different series would be executed if the employee is paid a fixed salary. Therefore, the course of execution of a program may vary substantially depending on the input data that the computer is examining.

Although all of the above capabilities are important to the operation of a computer, the two most important are that computers are electronic and that they can execute stored programs. Prior to the computer there were machines, such as the mechanical calculator, that would perform arithmetic operations, and there were many ways to store and retrieve information, the most common being filing cabinets. However, the electronic basis for the computer gives it incredible speed and accuracy while the stored program capability enables this speed and accuracy to occur without human intervention. Essentially, humans are exceedingly slow in performing computational operations compared to the almost instantaneous computation that the flow of electronic pulses permits.

Stored Programs

Stored programs give the computer three advantages: 1) they enable the computer to operate at electronic speeds; 2) they provide tremendous reliability; and 3) they make the computer general-purpose. The electronic speed of the computer would be of little value if not for the stored program. For example, let's assume an operator had to sit at the console of a computer and manually enter an instruction for each step to be performed such as an addition, subtraction, or comparison. Obviously, such a machine would be of little more use than a basic pocket calculator. The speed of the machine would be limited by the speed of the human. Furthermore, the human would be making decisions on what sequence of operations would be executed next. This certainly would decrease the accuracy and reliability of such a machine because of the potential for manual errors.

Once a computer program is written to perform a task and is thoroughly checked out to remove all errors, the computer will execute it with extreme accuracy and reliability, producing results with essentially no error. Many experts would argue that this ability to mimic human decision-making and processing capabilities in a computer program is by far the most significant aspect of computers. In essence, once a task that was previously performed by humans is accurately captured by a computer program, the task can be performed repeatedly with very high accuracy and reliability by computer. In other words, society no longer has to train humans to perform that task. Humans are thus freed to perform tasks of which computers are not capable. This is indeed revolutionary! Man has long used machines and animals to lighten the burden of manual labor. However, the computer is the first machine that relieves man of the intellectual burden of storing, processing and retrieving data, and making decisions based on that data.

The stored program capability also makes the computer general-purpose because stored programs can be changed. A single computer can be used for many different tasks, which may be as varied as data processing, editing, formatting and typing the contents of this book, or controlling robots that weld the parts of an automobile body.

Computers are truly revolutionary machines. Because of the dramatic decrease in their cost, they are being used in many facets of daily life. To function in today's society, and especially in the business world, one must develop not only computer literacy, but also the ability to use the vast potential inherent in a computer.

OVERVIEW OF A COMPUTER SYSTEM

Figure 1-1 provides a basic overview of a computer system. Any computer system has four categories of devices: 1) input devices; 2) processing devices; 3) storage devices; and 4) output devices. We will briefly introduce these devices here and will explore them in greater depth in chapters 5 through 7.

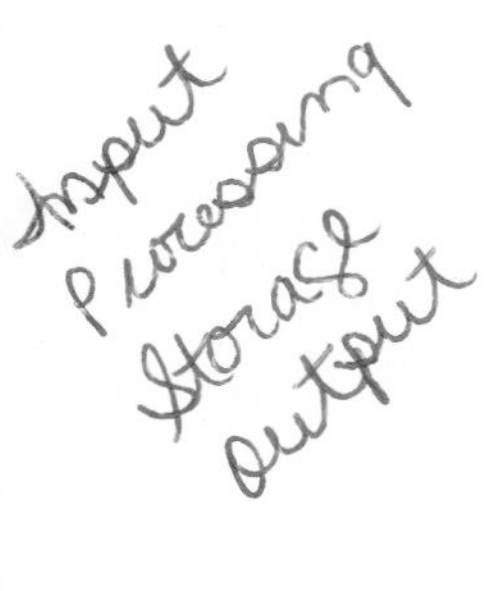

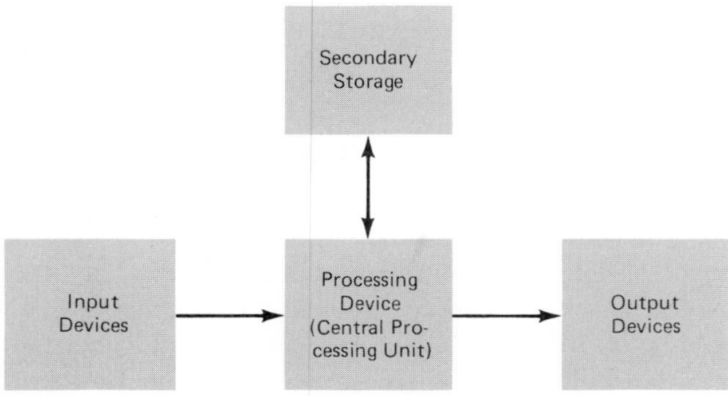

Figure 1-1 Overview of a Computer System

Input Devices

There are many different types of input devices. However, the most widely used are the cathode ray tube (CRT) and card readers. Currently there is a trend away from the use of cards for data processing towards input through CRT terminals. Other input devices include optical scanners, voice recognition devices, and various devices which will read a magnetically coded tape or disk. Many of these devices overlap into two or more of the four basic categories discussed above. For example, CRT terminals are both input and output devices.

Central Processing Unit

The processing role in a computer system is performed by the *central processing unit* (CPU). The CPU is the centerpiece of a computer system—strictly speaking, it is the computer. Its function is to interpret and execute the instructions provided by the program. Because of this, the CPU in effect controls the complete computer system. As shown in Figure 1-2 the CPU has three components: 1) the control unit; 2) the arithmetic-logic unit; and 3) primary storage unit. The control unit decodes program instructions and directs other components of the computer to perform the tasks specified in the program instructions. Arithmetic operations such as multiplication, division, subtraction, and addition are performed by the arithmetic-logic unit. The CPU also performs logical operations such as comparing the relative magnitude of two pieces of data. *Primary storage* stores the program instructions currently being executed and also stores data while they are being processed by the CPU.

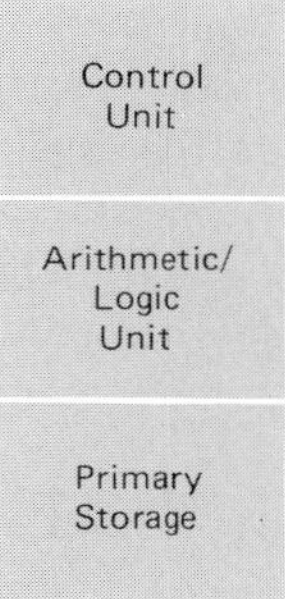

Figure 1-2 The Central Processing Unit

Secondary Storage

Secondary storage is used for relatively long-term storage of data. The most widely used secondary storage media are magnetic tape and magnetic disk. The bulk of data used by a computer application is stored in secondary storage, but data must be transferred to primary storage before it can be processed by the CPU. Therefore, data is continually being read into and written out of primary storage during the execution of the program. While the data is not being used by the CPU it is stored in secondary storage. The main differences between primary and secondary storage are that primary storage is a part of the CPU, allows very fast access to data, and is relatively more expensive than secondary storage.

Output Devices

Output devices record data either in forms readable by humans, such as printouts, or in machine-readable forms such as magnetic disks and tapes. Output devices include a wide variety of printers that use varying technologies such as impact, print chains, ink jets, and laser imaging to produce print. Other types of output include computer output microfiche (COM), which prints large volumes of output onto a small microfiche card, voice output, and graphics terminals, which will display computer-based data directly in graphic form such as bar charts and line graphs. Of course, many of the types of input and secondary storage already discussed, such as magnetic tape, disk, cards, and CRT terminals, also serve as output devices or media.

DATA PROCESSING AND INFORMATION

DATA VS. INFO

Data processing is the capture, storage, and processing of data for the purpose of transforming it into information useful for decision making. Note that a distinction has been made in this definition between data and information. *Data* are collected facts that are generally not useful for decision making without further processing. Conversely, *information* is directly useful in making decisions because it is based on processed data and is therefore the output of a data processing system. Although we have made a sharp distinction between data and information, in actual practice this distinction is often difficult to make. One individual's data may be another's information. For example, hours worked by individual employees are certainly information to a frontline supervisor. However, when the decision maker is the president of a company, hours worked by individual employees are simply data which can be further processed and summarized. This summarized data may then be information to the president. Therefore, to determine whether a particular fact is data or information, one must keep in mind the particular decision which is to be made.

MANAGEMENT CASE 1-1

Food Town is a medium-sized grocery chain located in the eastern seaboard states. John Wilson, the Chief Executive Officer of Food Town has become very concerned with the information he is able to get from his data processing system. He maintains that a large amount of data is gathered and stored in company disk and tape files. About all of the company's typical accounting systems such as accounts payable, accounts receivable, and general ledger are computerized. In addition, the company has computer-based inventory control systems, personnel systems, and sales/marketing systems. Wilson's primary question is: "with all this data being collected and stored, why can't I get better management information reports? My assistant should be able to sit down at a terminal and pull information from these various systems and integrate it in a way that would be meaningful. Sure I can get information from the personnel system or from the payroll system but whenever I need information from two or more of these systems, it seems to be a major undertaking to provide the information. More often than not, by the time I get the information, a decision has already been made and the information is not used. These computers just don't help me a great deal in my decision making." Does Mr. Wilson have a valid point? Is it possible to provide the type of information he is requesting?

THE STEPS IN DATA PROCESSING

In our review of a computer system earlier in this chapter, we found that a computer has four basic components: *input*, *process*, *storage*, and *output*. These components also relate directly to the basic steps in data processing as shown in Figure 1-3. Several data

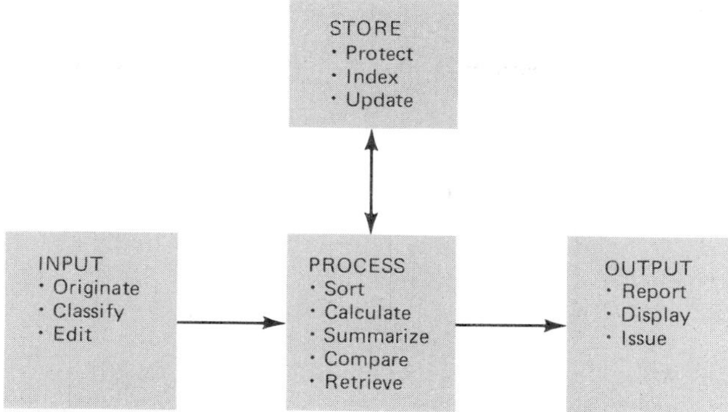

Figure 1-3 The Steps in Data Processing

processing operations occur within each of these basic data processing steps. These are discussed in the next four sections of this chapter.

Input

Originate

The occurrence of a business event or transaction often results in the *origination* of data that are input to a data processing system. For example, the event of your purchase of an airline ticket causes the origination of data that is input to the airline's reservation system.

Classify

The *classification* of input data is the identification of that data with a certain category. For example, your airline reservation input data would be classified when the reservation agent identified your flight number and the category of seat which you were reserving—either first class or coach. In this case, your reservation would be classified on a certain flight and perhaps classified first class.

Edit

Data is *edited* upon input to detect any errors that may exist in the data. Editing may also occur during any of the other three basic steps of data processing to detect errors that may have occurred during these steps. However, most editing occurs upon input of the data. There are many different ways to edit data, and a well-designed data processing system will edit data for all possible errors that might occur. Upon detection of an error, the individual who is performing the input is given the opportunity to correct the error.

Process

Several different data processing operations are performed within the process step. These include sort, calculate, summarize, compare, and retrieve.

Sort

Sorting is the placing of data in some order. Normally, it involves the arrangement of a file of records according to keys, which are used as a basis for determining the sequence of the records. For example, sorting may be used to arrange the records of a personnel file into alphabetical sequence by using employee names as sort keys.

Calculate

Calculation includes all standard arithmetic operations, such as addition, subtraction, multiplication, and division.

Summarize

To *summarize* is to aggregate data into totals or condensations that are more meaningful than the unsummarized data. Therefore, summarization in a data processing context is normally the addition of arithmetic data into meaningful totals.

Compare

Comparison is the process of examining two pieces of data to determine if they are equal, not equal, or if one is greater than the other. This is often called logical comparison.

Retrieve

The *retrieval* of data is its movement from secondary storage to the central processing unit so that other data processing operations may be performed.

Store

The *store* step in data processing includes three operations: 1) protect; 2) index; and 3) update. Some information systems professionals would place the retrieval operation discussed in the above paragraph under the store step, since a large part of the retrieval operation is performed by the storage unit in a computer system.

Protect

The *protection* of stored data is the safeguarding of data from unauthorized erasure, modification, or usage. Protection, or "control" of data systems, is becoming a very important area in data processing since such a large amount of sensitive and valuable information is now stored in computer systems.

Index

Indexing is the creation and maintenance of addresses indicating the physical storage location of a particular piece of data. Therefore, indexes are often used to find the storage location of a piece of data in a retrieval process. These indexes are the equivalent of a card catalog in a library.

Update

Finally, the *update* operation is the adding, deleting, and changing of stored data to reflect new events. For example, when an employee wage rate is increased, the payroll file is updated to reflect the new pay rate.

Output

The output step includes the operations of 1) report; 2) display; and 3) issue.

Report

To *report* is to print management information on a hard copy medium, normally paper. A report is often a summary of detail data and is used for management information needs.

Display

A *display* would contain similar or perhaps the same information as a report. However, the information would appear on a CRT terminal instead of a paper report. Most individuals refer to the information appearing on a CRT as a display rather than a report.

Issue

To *issue* is to prepare output documents (such as checks, purchase orders, or invoices) necessary to originate or complete a transaction. In contrast to these documents, a report contains management information that is often summary in nature and used in controlling the business operation. For example, a weekly listing that contains the total amount of purchase orders issued to various vendors would be a report whereas the purchase orders themselves would be transaction documents that are *issued* by the computer.

QUALITATIVE CHARACTERISTICS OF INFORMATION

Without quality, information loses its usefulness. A term often used in information processing to describe the lack of data quality is "garbage in garbage out" (GIGO). This term literally means that unless data meets qualitative characteristics upon input, the information output from the data processing system will be useless, or "garbage."

Information must meet four qualitative characteristics: 1) relevance; 2) timeliness; 3) accuracy; and 4) verifiability.

Relevance

Information is *relevant* when it is useful in making a decision. In other words, if information improves the decision, it is relevant. Obviously, if an airline reservation agent is making a decision whether or not to grant a customer a reservation on a particular flight, the number of empty seats on that flight is relevant information. On the other hand, personal characteristics of the potential customer, such as occupation or sex, would not be relevant information in an airline reservation decision.

Timeliness

Information certainly also has *time value*. In the context of most management information systems, as information becomes older its value decreases. Generally, lower-level decisions in an organization must have more current and timely information; as we move up the ladder to higher-level decisions the information can be somewhat older. For example, if we are making the very routine and low-level decision of whether to ship a customer the 150 shirts which have been ordered, we must know the number of shirts that are on hand at the current moment. The number of shirts that were on hand five days or two weeks ago is completely useless information relative to making this decision, so that information is not timely. Conversely, a high-level decision concerning whether to expand a company's capacity for making shirts by building an additional plant would depend partially upon the historical sales trends of shirts. These types of decisions may be based on information that is several years old.

Accuracy

Accuracy refers to information's freedom from error. The amount of error tolerable in information is related to other factors, especially timeliness and the dollar value of the decision to be made. If a decision maker must make a decision quickly, a larger amount of potential error can be tolerated than in a situation in which considerable time and resources are available to reduce data error. For example, if you smell smoke in your home you are likely to make a quick decision to call the fire department without taking the time to establish, without error, the location and actual existence of a fire. On the other hand, if you are reconciling your checkbook to a bank statement, you may want to base a decision to call the bank and accuse them of making an error on information that is accurate to the nearest penny.

Verifiability

Verifiability refers to the ability to confirm the accuracy of information. Information may be verified by comparison with other information that has known accuracy. However, quite often accuracy is verified by tracing information to its original source. The term *audit trail* is often used to describe the means by which summarized information can be traced back to its original source or by which detailed input data can be traced forward to summarized information. This audit trail is a very important part of any data processing system because without it the accuracy of information is usually impossible to determine. Consequently, the usefulness of such information is brought into question.

MANAGEMENT CASE 1-2

Western University is a large university with a well respected engineering college. All the departments within engineering and many departments in other colleges do a large amount of funded research. The manager of each research project is called a principal investigator (PI). In addition to assuring that the research is done properly the PI must be sure that the funds expended on a research project does not exceed the funds alloted for the project. Outside sponsors of research such as the National Science Foundation and the Department of Defense will not cover over-expenditures on these projects. Funds to cover over expenditures come directly from the university budget. Therefore, before committing to additional expenditures on a project, such as graduate assistants or equipment, the PI must be sure that there is enough remaining budget to cover the expenditures. The university has a central accounting system which allows a PI to retrieve the current budget balance through online computer terminals. Many academic departments in the university do not trust the central accounting system. Therefore they maintain their own separate accounting system for the department in various ways from manual ledgers to micro computer based systems. There are other departments who feel that the central system is perfectly adequate and therefore do not expend funds maintaining their own system. The major complaint of those who do not trust the central system is one of timeliness of data. All commitments to expend resources such as purchase orders for equipment are executed through manual forms which are processed through several administrative departments before being entered into the central accounting system on a daily basis. Often it takes four to five days for these expenditure commitments to be reflected in the central accounting system files. The vice president of finance of the university is considering a policy that would prohibit departments of the university maintaining their own accounting systems. Should departments be allowed to maintain their own accounting systems? Does the central system need improvements? If so, what would you suggest? Would a simple policy prohibiting departmental accounting systems be successful?

THE IMPACT OF COMPUTER DATA PROCESSING ON BUSINESS

Certainly all businesses large or small must perform data processing. They perform it either manually or with computers and other machines such as calculators and adding machines. Even the smallest business must perform data processing to keep records for income tax purposes. Federal tax law requires that taxpayers keep such records.

Often, though, small business managers depend less on a formal data processing system and more upon informal information sources for decisions. A small business manager is intimately familiar with all aspects of the business. Therefore, there is less need for a formal data processing system. However, as a business grows larger, managers depend much more upon data processing systems for their information. Imagine the managers of General Motors depending on informal sources for information about the operations of the company. Such an approach would be a disaster since the higher-level managers are not close enough to day-to-day operations to have the information necessary to make decisions.

Information is truly the lifeblood of a business. A business simply could not service its customers or make higher-level decisions without information to support customer service and decision making. The use of computers in data processing has had an impact on business in many areas. Among these are easier business growth, fewer clerical workers, reduced data processing costs, automation of some decisions, and the availability of different types and greater quantities of information.

Easier Business Growth

Once a data processing system is installed, most businesses find that they can expand their operations without substantial changes in the data processing system they have chosen. For example, if the data processing system is designed correctly it should have excess capacity. Therefore, it can easily accommodate a growth in the number of customers with perhaps only small changes, such as the addition of a more powerful central processing unit, or no changes at all. Furthermore, a significant factor in the growth of today's very large businesses is the very existence of computer-based data processing, which provides managers the information to control these very large enterprises.

Fewer Clerical Workers

The use of computers has reduced the need for clerical workers in business. These workers were the individuals who in the past did the data processing with a manual system. However, as the demand for clerical workers has decreased, computers have increased the demand for people who are technically oriented in the use of the computer, such as systems analysts and programmers. Demand has also increased for other information workers, such as accountants, whose discipline is closely linked with data processing.

Lower Costs

Computers can certainly process data at a much lower cost than humans can. Therefore, the cost of processing data in relation to the amount of output generated from the data processing system has drastically declined.

Automation of Decisions

Many businesses have used the computer to automate certain lower-level decisions. Examples of decisions which have been automated are the decision of when to reorder goods to replenish inventory stocks, the amount of fuel to carry on a specific airline flight, and the optimal mix of raw materials to produce paint that meets certain specifications.

More and Better Information

Computers have substantially increased the quantity of information available to management. Much information now available would have been impossible to produce in the past with manual systems simply because the amount of calculation necessary to produce it would have been prohibitive. Examples of this type of information include the output from linear programming, forecasting, and simulation models.

To illustrate this point, let's consider a simulation example. With simulation one can build a model (via computer program) of a real world system, such as an aircraft, through the use of mathematical formulas. The computer, through a large number of manipulations of these mathematical formulas, will simulate the performance of the real world system, in this case the aircraft. Specifically, if an aircraft manufacturer is considering the development and production of a new type of passenger aircraft, simulation of that aircraft prior to committing millions and sometimes billions of dollars to its development can be very useful. For example, we can simulate many factors concerning the aircraft, including fuel consumption and passenger load factors in relation to specific airline route structures. The output of such a simulation would enable the manufacturer to judge how profitable such an aircraft would be. This is obviously useful information considering the large amount of resources that would have to be committed to build the proposed aircraft.

Increased quantities of information are not always useful to managers. In today's environment, with computers producing large quantities of information, many managers suffer from information overload. That is, there is so much information available that they have difficulty sorting out and using information that is truly relevant. However, more sophisticated computer users have designed ways that managers can use the computer to select only the information that will be used in a specific decision.

SUMMARY

The premier invention of this century is the computer. In a relatively short time it has affected many areas of our lives.

A computer may be defined as a data processor able to perform substantial computation, including numerous arithmetic or comparison operations without intervention by human operators.

The primary capabilities or characteristics of a computer are that it must be electronic, be able to perform arithmetic and comparison operations, have internal storage and retrieval of data, have the ability to execute a stored program, and have the ability to modify the execution of a program stream during execution.

The electronic basis for the computer gives the computer incredible speed and accuracy while the stored program enables this speed and accuracy to occur without human intervention.

Stored programs have three advantages:

1. They enable the computer to operate at an electronic speed.
2. They provide very high reliability.
3. They make the computer general purpose.

Any computer system has four categories of devices: 1) input devices; 2) processing devices; 3) storage devices; and 4) output devices.

The processing role in a computer system is performed by the central processing unit (CPU). Its function is to interpret and execute the instructions of the programmer.

A computer system has two types of storage: primary storage and secondary storage. Primary storage is contained within the CPU and is used to store programs and the data they use during execution. Secondary storage is used for relatively long-term storage of data outside the CPU.

Data processing is the capture, storage, and processing of data to transform it into useful information for decision makers.

Data are collected facts generally not useful for decision making without further processing. Information is based on processed data and is directly useful in making decisions.

The four basic steps in data processing are: 1) input; 2) process; 3) storage; and 4) output.

The input operations are originate, classify and edit.

The processing operations are sort, calculate, summarize, compare, and retrieve.

The storage operations are protect, index, and update.

The output operations are report, display, and issue.

Information is relevant when it is useful in making a decision. If a piece of information improves the decision, it is relevant.

Information has time value. In the context of most management information systems, as information becomes older its value decreases.

Accuracy refers to information's freedom from error. The amount of error which we can tolerate in information is related to timeliness and the dollar value of the decision to be made.

Verifiability refers to the ability to confirm the accuracy of information.

The use of computers in data processing has had impact on business in many areas. Among these are: easier business growth, fewer clerical workers, reduced data processing costs, automation of some decisions, and the availability of different types and greater quantity of information.

KEY TERMS

Computer
Program
Stored Program
Central Processing Unit
Primary Storage
Secondary Storage
Data Processing

Storage
Output
Originate
Classify
Edit
Sort
Calculate

Protect
Index
Update
Report
Display
Issue
Relevance

Data	Summarize	Timeliness
Information	Compare	Accuracy
Input	Retrieve	Verifiability
Process		

REVIEW QUESTIONS

1. Define a computer. What is the difference between a computer and a programmable calculator?
2. What capabilities and characteristics must a machine have before it can be called a computer?
3. What advantages does the ability to store programs give the computer?
4. Why is the knowledge and ability to use a computer important in today's business world?
5. What are the four basic categories of devices in any computer system?
6. What are the functions of the central processing unit?
7. Distinguish between primary storage and secondary storage.
8. What are some of the ways that computers can produce output?
9. What is data processing?
10. Distinguish between data and information.
11. What are the four basic steps in data processing?
12. Identify the data processing operations which occur in each of the four basic steps in data processing.
13. Identify and discuss the four qualitative characteristics of information.
14. What kinds of impact has computer data processing had on business?

DISCUSSION QUESTIONS

1. Some people argue that computers are capable of making intelligent decisions and that the work that computers do are a form of intelligence. These people further argue that as time goes on, computers will be making higher levels of intelligent decisions. Others argue that computers are simply dumb machines that execute programmed instructions and therefore will never possess true intelligence as human beings do. Take one side of this argument and support your position.
2. If you are planning a career in the design and implementation of computer-based business systems, is it better to have an educational background in computer science or management information systems (MIS)? A typical computer science curriculum emphasizes the technological aspects of computing, whereas a typical MIS curriculum emphasizes business and how computers are used in the business area. Take one side of this argument and support your position.

3. Some people argue that personal computers will be used in the very near future in a majority of households to perform many different types of tasks, such as assisting in balancing bank accounts. Others argue that many of the tasks that have been advocated as good applications for personal computers in a household can be done more efficiently manually. Essentially they say that home computers are a passing fad. For example: Some would say that using a personal computer to balance your bank account to your check book is like using a Rolls Royce to go to the mail box daily to pick up your mail. Take one side of this argument and support your position.

RESEARCH PROJECTS

1. *Business Week*, *Forbes*, and *Fortune* often have articles discussing how computers are currently being used in business. Review recent issues of one of these magazines and report on computer-related articles.

2. Personal microcomputers are becoming a mass market item. Magazines such as *Time* and *Newsweek* often have articles concerning the use of these computers in the home. Review one of these magazines and report on articles which discuss the use of personal computers in the home.

APPLICATION CASE

Courts Side With Computers in Medicine

(Reprinted with permission from MIS Week, January 27, 1982, p. 4)

By Paul Ehrlich

NEW YORK—Physicians and hospitals that fail to acquire or use computer-based technology to help diagnose and treat patients may be subject to liability, based on recent court rulings. These rulings have gone against doctors whose failure to use available technology resulted in serious injury to the patient.

Furthermore, according to attorneys specializing in medical law, the rulings suggest that courts may begin to impose penalties if patients are injured by the absence of computers even if other medical facilities do not use such equipment.

Last year, for example, the District of Columbia General Hospital was found liable for failing to transfer a patient to another facility which possessed a computerized axial tomography (CAT) scanner.

"The courts have expanded the definition of a physician's responsibility regarding the care of the patient," said Bruce L. Watson, an attorney in Cambridge, Mass., who recently represented Boston University's Center for Law and Health Sciences. "This has led to the increased likelihood that courts will find liability where providers fail to make use of computers in medicine, given that such use would have reduced the risk to a patient's health."

In most hospitals, computers are as common as stethoscopes. They are used widely to assist or perform such medical tasks as monitoring a heartbeat during surgery, interpreting electrocardiograms and measuring a variety of laboratory tests.

Computers are also used to store the flood of information about new chemical therapies, and even to suggest the use of newly available drugs.

But many hospitals are also slow to take "full advantage" of current technology, claim many lawyers, and thus, where computer performance is superior to that of the physician, a finding of negligence is likely where the computer-assisted task would have affected patient outcome.

Discussion

1. Is it possible that a group of stockholders, in a publicly held corporation, could successfully sue corporate management for not using computers in an efficient and effective manner?
2. In what ways could the same computers used for medical tasks be implemented to provide information that would be useful in managing a hospital?

CHAPTER 2

MANAGEMENT INFORMATION SYSTEMS CONCEPTS

I. Introduction

II. What is MIS?
   A. Definition
   B. Components

III. Objectives, Decisions, and Information

IV. Levels of Decision Making
   A. Strategic Decisions
   B. Tactical Decisions
   C. Operational Decisions

V. Management Uses of Information
   A. Planning
   B. Control

VI. Types of Reports
   A. Scheduled Reports
   B. Demand Reports
   C. Exception Reports
   D. Predictive Reports

VII. The MIS and Business Functions

VIII. MIS and Data Base Management Systems

IX. Decision Support Systems and MIS

X. Basic Approaches to Systems Development
   A. Ad Hoc Approach
   B. Data Base Approach
   C. Bottom-Up Approach
   D. Top-Down Approach

XI. The Systems Development Cycle
   A. Survey
   B. Structured Analysis
   C. Hardware Study and Structured Design
   D. Implementation
   E. Conversion
   F. Post-Implementation Audit and Maintenance

INTRODUCTION

In the previous chapter we focused on data processing systems. Many firms with advanced computer systems have gradually evolved from a data processing system to a management information system (MIS). As we will see in this chapter, an MIS is a natural extension of a data processing system.

This chapter initially explores the relationship between MIS and data processing, including the ways that data processing applications support an MIS. Next, we will examine the close relationship between types of decisions managers make and the information required for those decisions. Third, we will look at the basic ways an MIS produces information through different types of reports. Fourth, we will briefly look at the relationship between the MIS and data base management systems (DBMS). Perhaps the single most important technological advance that has made MIS practical is data base management system software.

Next, basic approaches to the development of an MIS will be introduced. Finally, since the system life cycle is basic to understanding the steps in the development of application systems, we will briefly introduce it here, even though it is discussed in greater depth in chapters 14 and 15 of the text.

WHAT IS MIS?

Definition

A *management information system* is a formalized, computer-based system able to integrate data from various sources to provide the information necessary for management decision making. Figure 2-1 illustrates the relationship between data processing and management information systems. The data processing system supports management information systems. Much of the information which the MIS uses is initially captured and stored by the data processing system. To contrast the two, data processing is oriented towards the capture, processing, and storage of data whereas MIS is oriented towards using that data to produce management information. The data processing system performs transaction processing, in other words, it is very much involved with processing data related to orders, sales, payments on account, etc. In the course of processing these transactions, the data processing system collects and stores a large amount of detailed information. This information then provides the data base for the management information system.

Components

Management information systems must have the capability of integrating and summarizing detailed data to produce relevant management information. In order to do this, an MIS must include several components. There should be a data base management system (DBMS) to aid in the integration of information from various data processing applications. An MIS by itself is more a federation of functional information systems than it is a total system. Unfortunately, a myth has arisen that an MIS is a monolithic, all functions, online decision support system. In reality, such systems are not possible given

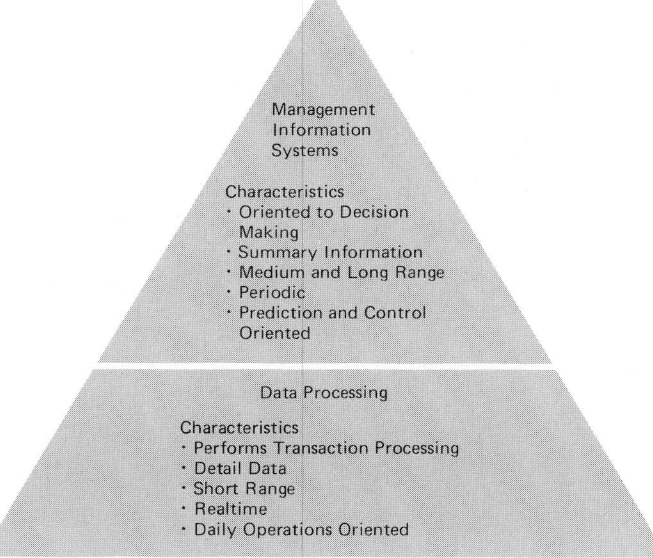

Figure 2-1 The Relationship Between Data Processing and Management Information Systems

the current level of technology and user sophistication. However, the DBMS does provide an integrating factor for an MIS. We will explore the relationship between MIS and DBMS in more detail later in this chapter.

An MIS should also include the typical models from management science, such as linear programming, regression, time series analysis, simulation, etc. These models enable management to predict the consequences of actions being considered for implementation.

OBJECTIVES, DECISIONS, AND INFORMATION

In this and the previous chapter, we have discussed the need for management information. We have also examined the relationship between data and information. But how does one determine what information a manager needs? Information needs are determined by what kinds of decisions must be made which, in turn, are determined by management objectives. This relationship between objectives, decisions, and information is illustrated in Figure 2-2. Having objectives implies a desire to achieve a set of goals. However, a problem arises when a gap is perceived between a desired goal and the current situation. To close the gap, decisions must be made based on information.

To illustrate these concepts, assume that a company has an objective of increasing net profit by fifty percent. Decisions would be necessary as to which products to push to reach the desired fifty percent increase in profits. Choosing a certain product might require further decisions concerning expansion of plants, or a decision to purchase the product from outside the company. All of these decisions would be based in part on

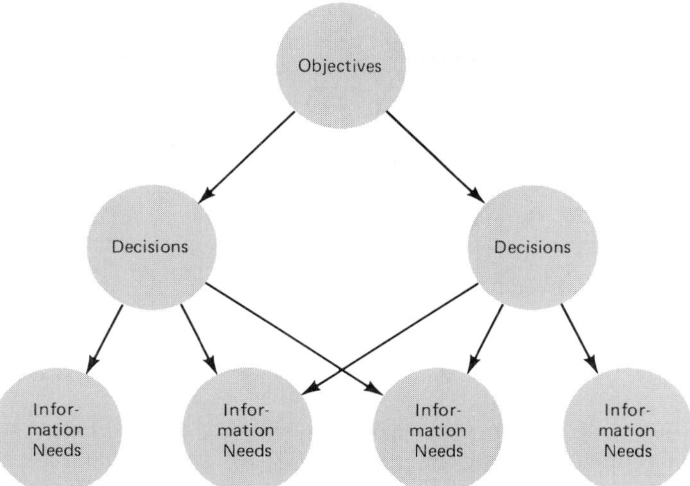

Figure 2-2 The Relationship Between Objectives, Decisions, and Information Needs

information from the management information system. As the company moves towards the fifty percent increase in net profit, reports showing how well each product is selling would be very important. These reports could indicate that a decision should be made to push an alternative product that is potentially more profitable. This approach to determining the information needs of management is very important to remember as we will see later in chapter 15 when the design of information systems is discussed. The systems analyst must always keep in mind the decisions and objectives the MIS supports.

LEVELS OF DECISION MAKING

Decisions may be classified on three levels: 1) strategic; 2) tactical; and 3) operational. These levels of decision making also correspond to management levels. Strategic decisions are made by top management; tactical decisions by middle management; and operational decisions by lower level management. As illustrated in Figure 2-3, all three of these levels of decision making rely on data processing for portions of their information.

Strategic Decisions

Strategic decisions are future oriented and involve a great deal of uncertainty. *Strategic decision making* primarily involves the establishment of objectives for the organization and long-range plans for attaining these objectives. Examples of strategic decisions include the location of plants, decisions related to capital sources, and decisions about which products will be produced.

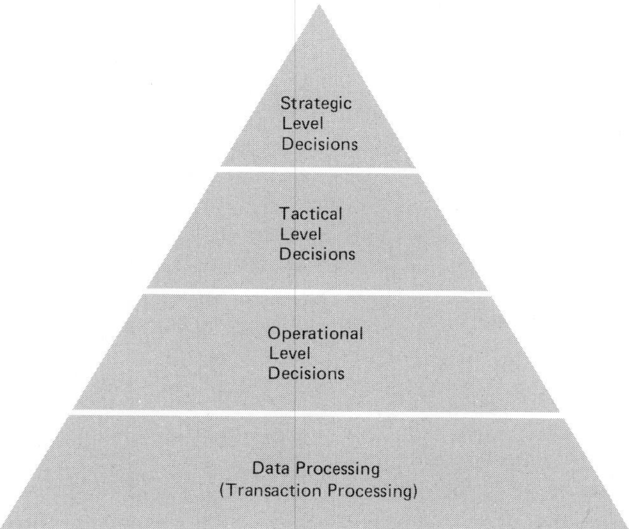

Figure 2-3 Levels of Decision Making—Data Processing Supports These Decisions with Information

Tactical Decisions

Tactical decision making is concerned with the implementation of decisions made at the strategic level. They include the allocation of resources to the pursuit of organizational objectives. Other examples of tactical decision making include plant layout, personnel decisions, budget allocation, and production scheduling.

Operational Decisions

Operational decisions concern the execution of specific tasks to assure that they are carried out efficiently and effectively. These decisions are made primarily by lower-level supervisors. Operational decisions are often programmed, with standards preset for execution. Managers and supervisors at this level are expected to make decisions keeping the operation in line with predetermined standards. Examples of operational decision making include acceptance or rejection of credit, determining inventory reorder times and quantities, and assignment of jobs to individual workers. Table 2-1 summarizes the characteristics of the three levels of decision making.

Programmable (or structured) decisions are those decisions for which policy standards or guidelines already exist. These decisions are routine in nature and can be made by reference to previously established policy. An example of a programmable decision is the credit granting decision based on income, years employed, etc. of the individual applying for credit. Note that programmable decisions do not necessarily have to be made by a computer-based system. Often these decisions are made by lower-level managers or supervisors. *Nonprogrammable decisions* are those dealing with ill-defined and unstructured problems. These decisions are future oriented and contain many variables whose impact on the outcome cannot be quantified. Such

Table 2-1 Characteristics of the Three Levels of Decision Making

	Levels of Decision Making		
Characteristic	**Operational**	**Tactical**	**Strategic**
Problem Variety	Low	Moderate	High
Degree of Structure	High	Moderate	Low
Degree of Uncertainty	Low	Moderate	High
Degree of Judgment	Low	Moderate	High
Time Horizon	Days	Months	Years
Programmable Decisions	Most	Some	None
Planning Decisions	Few	About half	Most
Control Decisions	Most	About half	Few

decisions require highly skilled managerial talent. Examples of these decisions include plant expansion, new product, and merger decisions.

In our discussion of levels of decision making, we have touched upon some characteristics of information required at each level of decision making. Table 2-2 summarizes these characteristics. Most of the entries in this figure are self-explanatory; but we should look closely at some of them. For example, consider the use of realtime information. Operational decision making depends heavily upon realtime information. Your school, for instance, probably uses a realtime system for course registration. The operational decision to allow you to sign up for a particular class depends on the realtime information of whether the class is full or not. On the other hand, strategic decision making depends much less on realtime information. For example, one important type of information used at the strategic level is income statements. These statements identify such factors as the profitability of plants and products, are generated periodically, and are not realtime. Strategic level decision making also tends to make great use of financial information. Decision makers at this level deal with capital requirements and profitability in dollars. On the other hand, a front line supervisor would be more concerned about the hours worked on a job, the number of orders shipped, the number of defective units produced, and other information of this type.

Table 2-2 Characteristics of Information Required at Each Level of Decision Making

	Levels of Decision Making		
Information Characteristic	**Operational**	**Tactical**	**Strategic**
Dependence on Computer-Based Information Systems	High	Moderate	Low to Moderate
Dependence on Internal Information	Very High	High	Moderate
Dependence on External Information	Low	Moderate	Very High
Degree of Information Summarization	Very Low	Moderate	High
Need for Online Information	Very High	High	Moderate
Need for Computer Graphics	Low	Moderate	High
Use of Realtime Information	Very High	High	Moderate
Use of Predictive Information	Low	High	Very High
Use of Historical Information	High	Moderate	Low
Use of What-If Information	Low	High	Very High
Use of Information Stated in Dollars	Low	Moderate	High

MANAGEMENT USES OF INFORMATION

Planning

Planning occurs prior to the execution of any organizational activity. As objectives are established in the planning process, actions that must occur to reach the objectives are identified, and resources necessary to support these actions are allocated. Although planning occurs at all levels of an organization, most of it occurs at the strategic and tactical levels of decision making. Planning depends mainly on predictive and external information. Past information is useful in planning only in the sense that it helps predict the future.

Control

Control is the process of comparing actual results to the objectives identified in the planning process. Figure 2-4 illustrates management control. Let us assume the system illustrated in Figure 2-4 is a factory. Management's plan for the factory is to produce $12 million in profit for the year. Inputs to the factory would be the factors of production—land, labor, and capital. Output will be net profit. For instance, an income statement which compares actual profit to planned profit provides feedback to management about the performance of the system (factory). If, during the year, management determines that the factory is not likely to reach the $12 million profit goal, this system is judged to be out of control. Management would attempt to gain back control of the system by making modifications to the inputs. These modifications might include reductions in the work force level or purchase of less expensive raw materials.

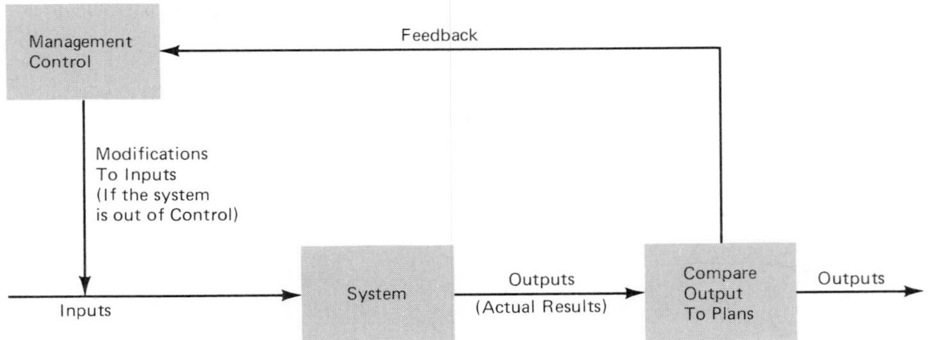

Figure 2-4 Management Control

A large percentage of the information produced by management information systems is of a feedback nature as illustrated in Figure 2-4. The information system monitors the system being controlled, compares the system outputs to plans, and provides the feedback information necessary for management control.

In summary, there are several variables that must be considered in designing a management information system. The designer must keep in mind objectives of the organization, decisions that must be made, and whether those decisions are of a planning or control nature. In addition, the type of information required would depend heavily on the level of the decision—whether it is operational, tactical, or strategic. Experience has shown that computer-based information systems are most successful in providing information for control decisions and less successful in providing information for planning decisions. They also decrease in success as we move up the levels of decision making to the strategic level. However, we must keep in mind that advancements in management information systems are increasing the applicability of computer-based systems to higher levels of decision making.

MANAGEMENT CASE 2-1

John Gilmer is a senior systems analyst for Montgomery Furniture Company. John has been assigned the task of developing an information system master plan which would govern the future direction of MIS development for Montgomery Furniture. Bill Harmon is manager of the system development office. John reports to Bill. Early one morning they are discussing the basic approach to developing the master plan. John feels that starting with objectives and deriving the decisions to reach those objectives is a waste of time. He feels that in interviews with the company executives the best approach is to ask them what information they need to perform their function. He states to Bill that, "executives just don't think in terms of objectives and decisions. It would be very difficult to get them to think in those terms and to take the logical steps from objectives to decisions to information". Furthermore, he feels that he should not suggest various types of possible information to the executives. He states, "I want to find out what information they feel they need and I don't want to contaminate their requirements with my own opinions." Evaluate John's positions.

TYPES OF REPORTS

We have thus far discussed management decision making and the need for information to support these decisions. But in what form is this information produced? There are four types of computer reports: 1) scheduled reports; 2) demand reports; 3) exception reports; and 4) predictive reports.

Although we have called these reports, which implies a hardcopy printout on a printer, they could just as easily be displayed on a CRT screen. In fact, as the use of CRTs becomes more widespread, many of these reports are being displayed on CRTs. The user thus interacts directly with the computer to obtain information on the CRT.

Scheduled Reports

Scheduled reports are produced on a regularly scheduled basis, such as daily, weekly, or monthly. These reports are widely distributed to users and often contain large amounts of information that are not used regularly. As the use of CRTs becomes more widespread, scheduled reports will diminish in importance. A manager will not feel compelled to ask for information on a scheduled report just in case he or she may need it in the future. With a CRT the information can be retrieved on demand.

Demand Reports

A *demand report* is generated upon request. These reports fill irregular needs for information. In the earlier days of computing, the contents of a demand report had to be previously anticipated or there was a delay of often weeks or months in receiving the data. It simply took time to modify programs to produce information that filled unanticipated demands. Today, largely through the query languages of data base management systems, we can fulfill unanticipated demands for information very quickly, often within minutes. This is possible because users and managers themselves can use the query languages to produce reports. Of course, if the data required to produce the information is not in the data base, then even query languages will not solve the problem of unanticipated demands for information.

Exception Reports

One of the most efficient approaches to management is the management by exception approach. Management by exception means that the manager spends his or her time dealing with exceptions, or those situations that are out of control. Activities proceeding according to plan are in control and therefore do not need the manager's attention. *Exception reports* notify management when an activity or system is out of control so that corrective action can be taken. An example of an exception report is a listing that
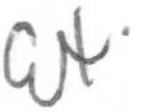
identifies all customers having overdue account balances. Another type of exception report is error listings, which identify input or processing errors that have occurred during the computer's execution of a particular application.

Predictive Reports

Predictive reports are useful in planning decisions. They make use of statistical and modeling techniques such as regression, time series analysis, and simulation. These reports assist management in answering "what if" questions. For example: What if sales increased by 10 percent? What impact would the increase have on net profit? The statistical and modeling techniques that produce predictive reports depend largely on historical data. Such data must be readily accessible by the MIS in a form that can be used by the models; otherwise, these models will be of little use to management.

THE MIS AND BUSINESS FUNCTIONS

An MIS is a federation of *functional information systems*. This concept is illustrated in Figure 2-5. Specialists within each of the functional areas, such as finance, production, or engineering, are much more familiar with the information requirements of that function than anyone else in the firm. These specialists can design systems to produce information required to manage their function. These functional information systems interact with one another and often share the same data. As we will discover in the next section of this chapter, data base management systems greatly enhance the ability of

these functional systems to share the same data. The important point to remember is that these integrated functional information systems *are* the MIS.

Each of the functional information systems are, in turn, made up of application systems as illustrated in Figure 2-5. The accounting information system includes several typical applications. Each application system is also made up of one or more programs. For instance, in the payroll system illustrated, there are five programs.

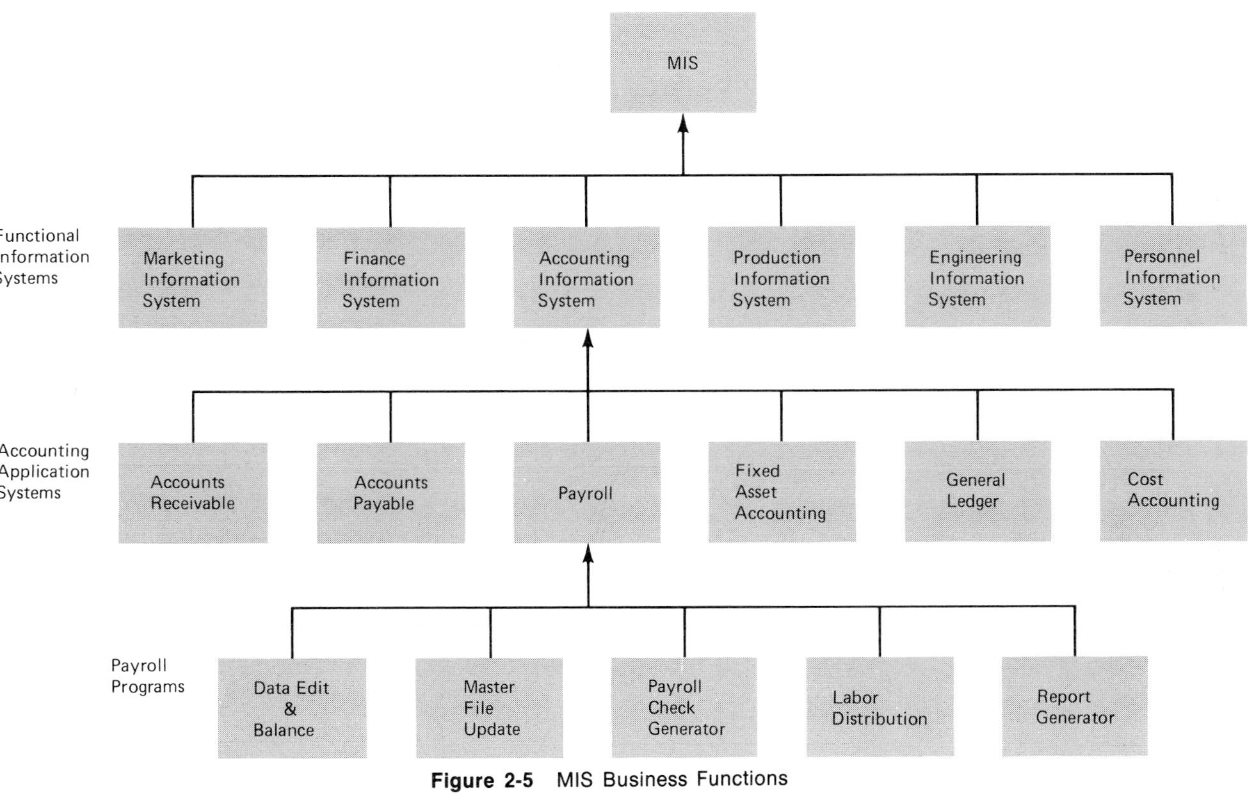
MIS
Functional Information Systems
Marketing Information System
Finance Information System
Accounting Information System
Production Information System
Engineering Information System
Personnel Information System
Accounting Application Systems
Accounts Receivable
Accounts Payable
Payroll
Fixed Asset Accounting
General Ledger
Cost Accounting
Payroll Programs
Data Edit & Balance
Master File Update
Payroll Check Generator
Labor Distribution
Report Generator

Figure 2-5 MIS Business Functions

MIS AND DATA BASE MANAGEMENT SYSTEMS

Data is the central resource of an MIS. The management of this resource is crucial. A *data base management system* is a program that serves as an interface between applications programs and a set of coordinated and integrated files called a data base. Prior to the use of DBMS there was little, if any, integration or data sharing among the functional information systems. However, there are now many opportunities for these systems to share the same data. For example, the payroll application within the accounting information system could share data with the personnel information system. Examples of data that might be shared are employee names, addresses, and pay rates.

Figure 2-6 illustrates the statement above that data base management systems are an interface between the functional applications and the data base. The DBMS allows the various functional systems to access the same data, and can pool together related data from different files as in the case of a personnel file and a payroll file. The DBMS is perhaps the most important tool in making an MIS possible. We will explore DBMS in greater depth in a later chapter.

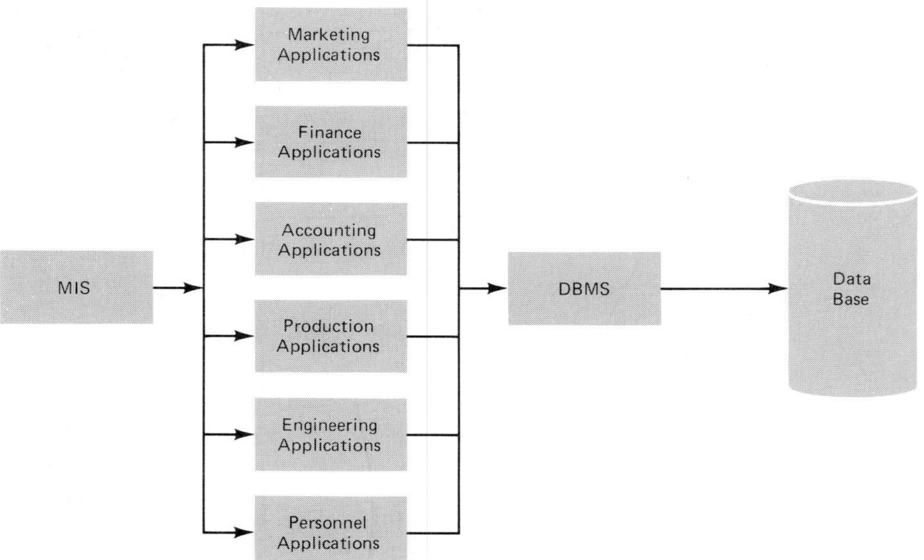

Figure 2-6 The Relationship Between a DBMS and an MIS

DECISION SUPPORT SYSTEMS AND MIS

Management information systems in the past have been most successful in providing information for routine, structured and preanticipated types of decisions. In addition, they have been successful in acquiring and in storing large quantities of detailed data concerning transaction processing. They have been less successful in providing information for semistructured or unstructured decisions, particularly unanticipated ones. A *decision support system* provides a set of integrated computer tools that allow a decision maker to interact directly with computers to retrieve information useful in making semistructured and unstructured decisions. Examples of these decisions include such things as plant expansion, merger and acquisition, and new product decisions.

A decision support system is an extension of an MIS. It provides user-friendly languages, data retrieval, data processing, and modeling capabilities for the decision maker's direct use.

BASIC APPROACHES TO SYSTEMS DEVELOPMENT

Systems analysts use several approaches when dealing with complex information systems. We will describe four of these approaches: 1) the ad hoc approach; 2) the data base approach; 3) the bottom-up approach; and 4) the top-down approach. This list is not exhaustive. Furthermore, analysts generally employ certain aspects of each approach. For example, a particular analyst's approach may be a combination of the data base, bottom-up, and top-down approaches.

Ad Hoc Approach

The *ad hoc approach* is directed toward solving a particular problem without considering other problems or the potential for integrating systems. In this approach an analyst may not deal with the overall information requirements of management, instead pinpointing only the trouble spots. In certain emergencies or in organizations undergoing rapid change, this approach might be appropriate. However, it is inconsistent with the concept of developing an information system that is integrated. Continually using this approach to meet additional demands for information produces a number of redundant and inefficient subsystems that cannot be linked together.

Data Base Approach

The *data base approach* emphasizes the development of a common data base in a computerized environment. Emphasis is placed on capturing, storing, manipulating, and retrieving data. Linkages are established in the data base to relate associated data. The underlying assumption of this approach is that since the analyst cannot anticipate the information requirements of management, it is necessary to maximize available data. It is very difficult to identify cost-effectiveness measures with this strategy because the design process is not linked to decision requirements. Another potential problem with this strategy is that users must have some sophistication to use the system. In many cases they must write short computer programs or execute a series of commands to retrieve information.

Bottom-Up Approach

The *bottom-up approach* produces an information system that satisfies the transactional processing needs of the organization. Initially the system is designed as a set of modules for processing transactions and updating files for each of the functional areas within the organization. This approach is also often called the *modular approach*. As managers' demands on the system become more complex, steps to integrate the modules can be undertaken. The advantage claimed for this approach is that it allows the system to be developed in a logical, evolutionary manner based on the expressed needs of management. However, with no overall model of the system there is no basis for incorporating features into the modules that will facilitate integration as the system evolves. Many of the modules may have to be redesigned in the development process. Problems can also arise if the development process is triggered only by the demands of management since these demands may not follow a logical development sequence.

Top-Down Approach

In the *top-down approach* the analyst first identifies the objectives of the organization. Then he or she identifies what information will be required to support management decisions related to these objectives. After the information needs are specified, systems are developed on the basis of priorities. A model of the flow of information throughout the organization serves to integrate the functional systems within the MIS. The major problem with this strategy is that it is very difficult to define the objectives of most organizations. It is also difficult to specify the decisions made by management, and this causes problems in specifying the required information. In some cases organizations are just too big for the top-down approach to be practical.

In summary, none of these four approaches to systems development is practical when used alone. Systems analysts use combinations of these approaches in a simultaneous fashion. Systems development is still very much an art, rather than an exact science. The analyst has to use many different techniques, combined with lots of common sense and professional judgement.

MANAGEMENT CASE 2-2

Fulton County Hospital is the largest hospital in a major southeastern city. Kevin Bohlin, manager of the system development group has called a meeting of the hospital's vice presidential level executives to discuss the establishment of a decision support system. After describing the concept of a DSS and explaining its benefits and costs, Kevin proposes that a new department be formed under his management. This department called the DSS Department would have at least one individual who is skilled in the discipline of each vice president's function. For example, there would be a marketing person, an accounting person, an operations person, etc. In addition there would be several individuals with MIS and quantitative methods backgrounds. After Kevin made this proposal, Ray Decker, vice president of operations, the most powerful of the vice presidents and an heir apparent to the president's position, was noticeably disturbed. He asked Kevin, "what's the difference between a data processing system, an MIS and a decision support system. As far as I'm concerned they're all the same. I'm afraid your proposal is simply an attempt at empire building. Furthermore if I'm ever convinced that I need a decision support system, I will establish it within my area and directly under my control." If you were Kevin Bohlin, how would you explain to Mr. Decker the difference between a DP system, an MIS, and a decision support system? Evaluate Mr. Decker's proposal for establishing a DSS for his vice presidential area under his direct control.

THE SYSTEMS DEVELOPMENT CYCLE

The development of a computer-based system typically goes through seven major phases. These seven phases are called the systems development cycle. Figure 2-7

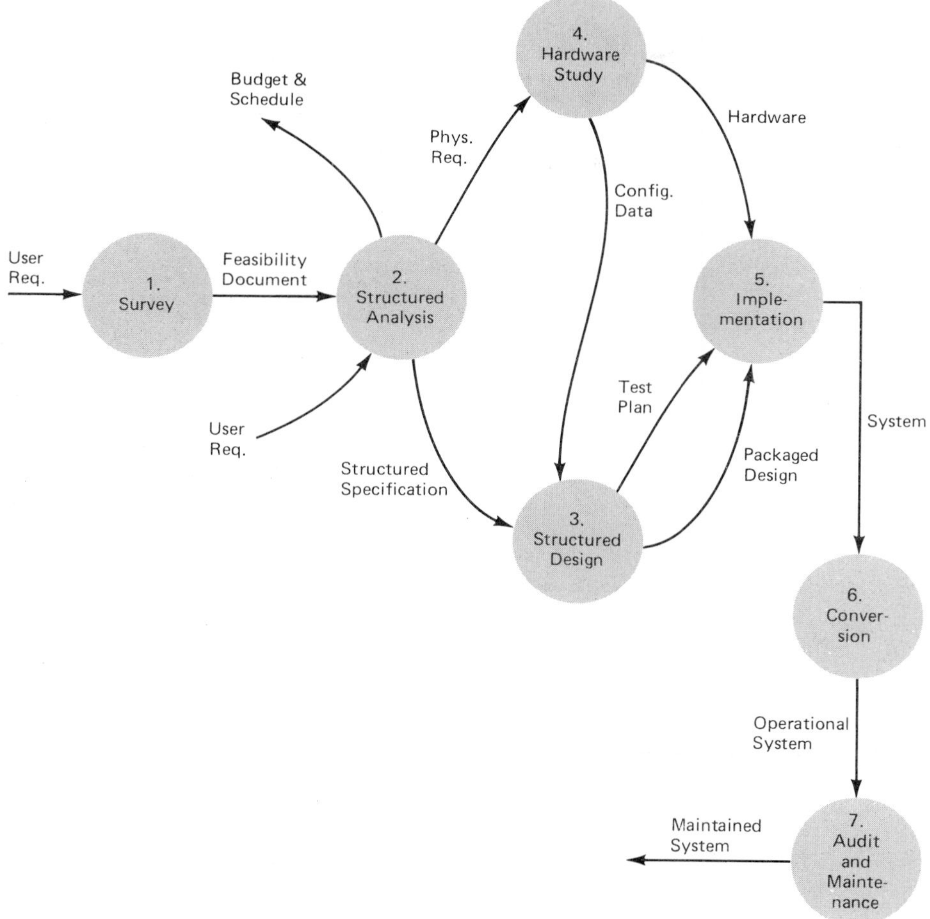

Figure 2-7 Structured Development Life Cycle

illustrates the seven major phases of systems development:

1. survey phase
2. structured analysis phase
3. structured design phase
4. hardware study
5. implementation phase
6. conversion phase
7. post-implementation audit and maintenance phase

Although these phases are consecutive, there is substantial overlap between them. For example, while programs are being written, changes may be made in the system design. Furthermore, the processes can be highly iterative. We will briefly describe each of the system development cycle phases. A more in-depth discussion of these phases will be presented in chapters 11 and 12.

Survey

The *survey phase* is, in effect, a miniversion of the later structured analysis phase. Analysts use interviews with user management as the primary source of information for the survey phase. It deals primarily with identifying the existing system's problems and determining whether there are feasible ways of solving these problems. Sometimes the survey is called a *feasibility study*. The primary purposes of the survey phase are:

PURPOSES

1. to decide whether there are feasible ways of improving the current system that would justify the expense of a system development project.
2. to identify the constraints within which a project must operate. For example, what are the funds available for a project?

The result of the survey is a feasibility document that identifies, on a preliminary basis, the feasible alternative solutions, estimated costs and benefits of the project, and a proposed time schedule for its completion.

Structured Analysis

The *structured analysis* phase has as its major inputs the feasibility document and additional interviews with users. This phase produces a budget and schedule for the design and implementation effort, the physical requirements (which are the major input to the hardware study), and a structured specification document. The structured specification document is basically a graphical statement of the requirements of the new system. It is analogous to a "blueprint," and system designers and programmers will use it to implement the new system.

The most important graphical tool the analyst uses is a data flow diagram which depicts the data flows and processes in a system. The diagram in Figure 2-7 is an example of a data flow diagram. The data flow diagram is an effective system development tool that we will discuss in considerable depth in later chapters.

Hardware Study and Structured Design

The *hardware study* and *structured design* are two phases that can go on concurrently. The hardware study should result in at least a tentative selection of hardware for the new system.

In the structured design phase the system design determines the number of individual program modules the system will contain. A *program module* is an individual, self-contained subroutine within a system that performs a particular task. For example, computation of an employee's gross pay in a payroll system would be performed by a program module. Additionally, the system designer would design the interfaces between program modules and develop the internal logic to be followed within each. During the design process the designer must also keep in mind the physical hardware on which the system will be implemented and package the design accordingly. These design outputs taken together are called the *packaged design*.

The other output of the design process is a *test plan*. The test plan is a set of test procedures, test data, and predicted test results used to assure that the system is working properly prior to its actual use.

Implementation

The primary activities that occur in the implementation phase are coding, testing, and procedure development. Coding is the process of writing a program module in a computer language. The programmer uses the packaged design generated in the structured design phase as the basis for a particular program.

After each program module is coded it is tested using the test plan. Testing includes all the procedures used to assure that the system is operating properly prior to conversion. One of the major ways that programs are tested is through execution of the programs using test data. Test data should be comprehensive, covering every possible type of valid and invalid input that could occur when the program is operational.

Systems analysts and user personnel normally develop manual procedures concurrently with module coding and testing. A complete written set of procedures must be developed that covers all manual processes to be performed both by users and data processing operations personnel.

Conversion

In the conversion phase the old system is replaced by the new system. Activities that commonly occur in this phase include 1) making physical changes such as site preparation; 2) training of personnel; 3) relocation of displaced personnel; 4) changing the organization structure; and 5) the actual conversion to the new system.

System conversion is a very critical step in the development of a computer-based system. Selling the new system to user personnel is a crucial factor in its future success. Any new system, especially one involving a computer, can be viewed as a threat to the security of user personnel. Resistance to change can be overcome if user personnel are more fully involved in the complete development cycle and if a good training and orientation program is implemented for all personnel who will have contact with the system. In essence, conversion is the management of change.

Post-Implementation Audit and Maintenance

A necessary step in the system development cycle is the *post-implementation audit.* Two general areas are included: 1) performance of the new system is evaluated in terms of objectives stated in the survey and analysis phases; and 2) performance of the system development cycle is reviewed. For example, budgets and schedules developed in the survey and analysis phases can be used to evaluate the performance of the system development team. The lifespan of an application system can be substantially extended through proper maintenance. Maintenance consists of promptly correcting errors discovered in programs, updating the programs to cover changed requirements, and maintaining the documentation to reflect system and program changes.

SUMMARY

The management information system is a formalized computer-based system able to integrate data from various sources to provide the information necessary for management decision making.

Information needs are determined by the decisions that must be made which in turn are determined by organizational objectives.

Strategic decision making primarily involves the establishment of objectives for the organization and long-range plans for attaining these objectives.

Tactical decision making is concerned with the implementation of decisions made at the strategic level.

Operational decisions involve the execution of specific tasks to assure they are carried out efficiently and effectively.

Programmable decisions are those decisions for which policies, standards, or guidelines are already established.

Nonprogrammable decisions are those dealing with ill-defined, unstructured problems.

Management uses information for two purposes: planning and control.

Planning is the establishment of objectives and the subsequent activities that must occur to reach these objectives.

Control is the process of comparing actual results to plans identified in the planning process.

Scheduled reports are produced on a regularly scheduled basis, such as daily, weekly, or monthly.

A demand report is generated upon request.

Exception reports notify management when an activity or system is out of control.

Predictive reports assist management in answering "what if" questions.

An MIS is a federation of functional information systems.

A data base management system is a program that serves as an interface between application programs and a set of coordinated and integrated files called a data base.

The ad hoc approach is directed toward solving a particular problem without considering other problems or the potential for integrating systems.

The data base approach emphasizes the development of a common data base in a computerized environment.

The bottom-up approach starts with the solution of individual problems at the subsystem level. These subsystems are then integrated into one large system.

The top-down approach first considers the overall objectives of the organization and then proceeds to a solution of specific problems within this larger framework.

The system development cycle is made up of seven phases: survey, structured analysis, structured design, hardware study, implementation, conversion, and post-implementation audit and maintenance.

KEY TERMS

MIS
Objectives
Decisions
Strategic Decisions
Tactical Decisions
Operational Decisions
Programmable Decisions
Nonprogrammable Decisions
Planning
Control
Scheduled Reports
Demand Reports
Exception Reports
Predictive Reports
Data Base Management System
Decision Support System
Functional Information Systems
Ad Hoc Approach
Data Base Approach
Bottom-Up Approach
Top-Down Approach
System Development Cycle
System Investigation
Feasibility Study
Review and Approval
System Design
Coding, Testing and Procedure Development
Implementation
Post-Implementation Audit and Maintenance

REVIEW QUESTIONS

1. What is the relationship between data processing and management information systems?
2. What is the relationship between objectives, decisions, and information?
3. Identify the three levels of decision making and discuss each one.
4. Differentiate between programmable versus nonprogrammable decisions.
5. Identify the characteristics of information required at each level of decision making.
6. What is the difference between planning and control?
7. What types of information are required for planning, and for control?
8. Identify the types of reports that an MIS can produce.
9. What is the relationship between MIS and functional information systems?
10. How does a data base management system support MIS?
11. What is systems development?
12. Identify and define the basic approaches to systems development.
13. Identify and explain the steps in the systems development cycle.

DISCUSSION QUESTIONS

1. Some have argued that an MIS, especially a total MIS, is a myth rather than a reality. Choose one side of this argument and support your position. Do you think a total MIS would be possible within the next twenty years?

2. A typical college of business offers undergraduate majors in several different areas, including management, marketing, finance, accounting, and management information systems. Many of you have already decided on one of these majors. Justify why knowledge from your chosen major would be necessary preparation for a career in systems analysis that would involve the design and implementation of computer-based information systems.

3. This chapter discussed several basic approaches to systems development. Although it is difficult to argue that one of these approaches should be used exclusively, one can argue that a certain approach should be used predominantly. Choose one of the approaches and build a case for its predominant use.

RESEARCH PROJECTS

1. Find an article which describes a company's philosophy or approach to the implementation of an MIS. Report on this article to the class.

2. Research decision support systems. What is the difference between an MIS and a decision support system?

ESSAY

Planning Prerequisite for Productive Data Processing
(Reprinted with permission from MIS Week, September 2, 1981, pp. 23–24)

By T. Cartter Frierson, (Certified Management Consultant) T. Cartter Frierson & Co., Consultants in Data Processing, Chattanooga, Tenn.

These last four years as a management consultant have given me a very different perspective on the state of business data processing from the view I held in the previous 11 years while working in data processing as a programmer, analyst and manager.

The opportunity to "climb over the DP manager's desk" and become a consultant has been tremendously interesting. It has been a chance to escape from the typical and necessary preoccupation with technical considerations of the DP manager job, as well as the heat of everpressing deadlines, and it has been an opportunity to think of the data processing group as another functional body of human beings within the overall enterprise.

Most importantly, perhaps, it has been a chance to identify principally with the chief executive officer in his concerns for the overall welfare of the firm, his challenge of developing a strong management team, the necessity of his contending with external business factors, and the ever-present challenge to allocate the capital and human efforts of his organization in the most constructive and profitable way.

The chief concern of executives today is the desire to understand data processing well enough to be able to develop a sensible direction for the systems development effort so that this new technology can play a major role in the conduct of the business. In other words, "How can I best use computing in my business?"

An additional concern of executives is how to develop a positive sense of direction for the use of computing in their organization. I call it MIS direction versus misdirection.

MIS is enjoying a respectable second birth. Most of you will recall that during the last decade MIS was abortive and perhaps premature. The Oxford Shorter English Dictionary defines misdirection as "the action of misdirecting or the condition of being misdirected; direction to a wrong address." Are we no longer misdirecting or are we no longer being misdirected? Do we have a right address?

These are very turbulent times for the chief executive. The day is gone when 90 percent of the factors determining the course of the business were internal in nature, and we find chief executive officers today having grave concerns about the ability of their company to meet the head-spinning changes of the 1980s.

Top management today is presented with a whole new set of complexities and the consulting profession seems to be in agreement that there are dangerous signs of a tendency for management to opt for the low-risk and the fast-return business decisions, substituting the short-term game plan for the long-term strategic plan.

This has dangers for our economy and for the firms which take this course, but it is also a very complicating factor for the data processing profession. That is because, as we all recognize, major systems cannot be developed in less than one year. No matter how many people work on a given project, the systems efforts which substantially contribute to corporate success take longer than a year and therefore must be developed within a planning environment.

And yet, the pressures on businessmen today are to go in the opposite direction. It is increasingly common to hear chief executives say, "Why should I do strategic planning when I don't even know what tomorrow is going to look like?" This phenomenon of our times is going to create special challenges for leadership in data processing. In the absence of a long-range plan, application development must proceed in an ad hoc fashion. We need to preserve a balance of long-term goals along with short-term objectives.

I have observed that most business leaders now accept the fact that computing should play a legitimate and vital role—even a strategic one—for their business. It offers a competitive edge they do not want to deny their companies. And yet, most executives are quite unsure how to proceed in harnessing this new technology and how to integrate this new function into their organization. They are reluctant to confide their confusion or uncertainty on how to proceed, especially to their own data processing employees.

Unfortunately, they are also convinced that they will never have time to learn enough about data processing to be able to play a constructive role in defining its direction. As a result, they almost universally over-delegate responsibility for computing to someone in the organization who knows more about computing than about the business itself. They too, often focus upon using the computer to eliminate an immediate bottleneck, instead of moving into computing as a long-term commitment.

Most capital decisions made by top management are reached with some explicit or implicit value in mind as to the contribution the investment should make to the success of the corporation. Unfortunately, this is not true in data processing. If the company that you work for is selecting applications by the ad hoc process, not cognizant of or integrated with a corporate plan, you may be truly missing something. You may be performing a magnificent job as the unsung hero simply because no one took the time in advance to quantify the value of your efforts.

There is universal agreement in data processing that the responsibility for establishing direction for data processing belongs to general management, not to DP management, and yet I would observe that, unwittingly for the most part, data processing managers tend to preempt management's ability to manage the overall systems development effort, by failing to make available to top management that limited body of information which they need in order to fulfill their role. Unfortunately, neither top management nor data processing seems to understand the whole problem sufficiently well.

Management does not typically understand what information it should require from data processing to enable it to actively direct the planning effort for applications. Data processing personnel, I find, too often do not really understand what information management needs. Most data processing personnel have a limited background in general management courses and do not understand the decision-making process of the chief executive officer. All too often, the academicians who taught the general management courses to the DP manager are not very business-oriented themselves.

The problem of getting management to accept that information, study it, and assume the proper decision-making role is educational. Perhaps due in part to the advent of personal computers, we now see business executives clamoring for more working knowledge of computing.

Perhaps times have never been better for the data processing industry. You are the envy of almost all other professions because of the critical shortage of programmers and systems development personnel, which is forecast to continue for at least half of this decade.

The point in this development that should not be overlooked by those of you in data processing is the fact that never before has the door been so open for data processing to seize the initiative of developing better communications and better inroads with management. There is much improved opportunity for you to obtain the active participation of management in planning the overall direction for data processing in your company.

To do a more effective job of drawing management into active participation in planning the direction of data processing, you have got to rise to the challenge of understanding the environment in which business executives live and the pressures upon them. You must achieve enough objectivity to see these data processing decisions facing the executive officer within the perspective of all the other major decisions facing him.

Finally, I would like to touch upon one of management's greatest concerns which, at the same time, for the leaders in data processing, can be one of your greatest opportunities. In a decade which will be typified by low growth, scarce capital and scarce programmers, the high cost of software versus hardware is becoming tremendously visible. We can anticipate extreme pressures on the systems personnel side of data processing budgets over the next five years.

The cry throughout industry is for increased productivity, and yet where is there an opportunity such as presently exists in data processing to double and triple productivity, by committing your organization to the development of competence in the latest software engineering methodologies such as structured design and structured programming. The opportunity exists for phenomenal productivity gains.

I view myself as being in the business of bringing general management and data processing management closer together. As I view pending developments in the data processing industry over the next five years, from a business perspective instead of a data processing perspective, I strongly suspect that the tough years ahead of us in our economy will bring increased emphasis upon packaged software products, more user-developed software, better software engineering methodologies and closer management concern over the cost of systems development efforts. In each of these areas there is substantial room for improvement and so we should look upon these considerations not negatively, but as a great opportunity.

Discussion

1. To what extent should top management be involved in defining a direction for information systems within their organization?
2. Why is planning so important to information systems development?

(This essay is excerpted from an address given at a meeting of the Data Processing Managers Association.)

CHAPTER 3

INFORMATION PROCESSING APPLICATIONS

- I. Introduction
- II. Basic Data Storage
  - A. The Data Hierarchy
    1. Bit
    2. Byte
    3. Field or Item
    4. Record
    5. File or Data Set
    6. Data Base
  - B. File Organization
- III. Processing Modes
  - A. Batch Processing
  - B. Immediate Processing
- IV. Overview of Information Processing Applications
  - A. Inventories
  - B. Order Processing
  - C. Accounts Receivable
  - D. Accounts Payable
  - E. Payroll
  - F. Other Applications

INTRODUCTION

The computer has been applied in many different areas of information processing. In fact, anywhere information is required or where data is processed computer application is likely. This chapter will first briefly introduce basic data storage and processing modes. An elementary understanding of these concepts will help you understand the information processing applications covered later in this chapter. In chapter 8 we will explain data storage and processing modes in greater depth. The remainder of this chapter introduces typical information processing applications. To further enhance your understanding of applications, summaries of real world applications have been included at the end of many chapters in the book.

BASIC DATA STORAGE

The Data Hierarchy

Listed below in ascending order of complexity are the components of the information system data hierarchy:

1. Bit.
2. Byte.
3. Field or item.
4. Record.
5. File or data set.
6. Data base.

Bit

The term *bit* is short for binary digit. It can assume either of two possible states and therefore can be represented by either a 1 or 0. Typically a bit represents data through the positive or negative polarity of an electrical charge on a magnetic recording medium such as a tape or disk. In the case of semiconductor storage, a bit is represented by an electrical circuit that is either conducting or not conducting electricity.

Byte

The ability to represent only binary information in a computer system is not sufficient for business information processing. Numeric, alphabetic, and a wide variety of special characters such as dollar signs, question marks, and quotation marks must be stored. In a computer system, a character of information is called a *byte*. A byte of information is stored by using several bits in specified combinations. One widely-used coding scheme is IBM's Extended Binary Coded Decimal Interchange Code (EBCDIC), an eight-bit code illustrated in Table 3-1. Each 1 or 0 in the Table corresponds to a single bit. The first four bits, called zone bits, are used in combination with the last four bits, called digit bits, for coding alphabetic and other special characters.

In the actual storage of data using EBCDIC or any other coding scheme, an extra parity or check bit is added to the scheme for checking purposes. Assuming an even parity machine, the computer expects the number of bits turned on in a byte always to be even. Refer to Figure 3-1, which illustrates how data is stored in EBCDIC on magnetic tape. Each bit within a byte is stored in a separate track on the tape. Note that the parity bit is turned on whenever necessary to produce an even number of "on" bits in a byte. Parity bits are an important control feature built into most computer hardware. With a parity bit, EBCDIC becomes a nine-bit code. Therefore, a nine-track tape is used whenever EBCDIC-encoded data is written onto magnetic tape. Each track contains one bit of data.

Another commonly used code for storing bytes of data is the American Standard Code for Information Interchange (ASCII–8) of the American National Standards Institute (see Table 3-1). This is also an eight-bit code and is used widely in the area of data transmission.

Table 3-1 EBCDIC and ASCII-8 Coding Scheme

Character	EBCDIC Binary	ASCII-8 Binary
A	1100 0001	1010 0001
B	1100 0010	1010 0010
C	1100 0011	1010 0011
D	1100 0100	1010 0100
E	1100 0101	1010 0101
F	1100 0110	1010 0110
G	1100 0111	1010 0111
H	1100 1000	1010 1000
I	1100 1001	1010 1001
J	1101 0001	1010 1010
K	1101 0010	1010 1011
L	1101 0011	1010 1100
M	1101 0100	1010 1101
N	1101 0101	1010 1110
O	1101 0110	1010 1111
P	1101 0111	1011 0000
Q	1101 1000	1011 0001
R	1101 1001	1011 0010
S	1110 0010	1011 0011
T	1110 0011	1011 0100
U	1110 0100	1011 0101
V	1110 0101	1011 0110
W	1110 0110	1011 0111
X	1110 0111	1011 1000
Y	1110 1000	1011 1001
Z	1110 1001	1011 1010
0	1111 0000	0101 0000
1	1111 0001	0101 0001
2	1111 0010	0101 0010
3	1111 0011	0101 0011
4	1111 0100	0101 0100
5	1111 0101	0101 0101
6	1111 0110	0101 0110
7	1111 0111	0101 0111
8	1111 1000	0101 1000
9	1111 1001	0101 1001

Field or Item

The next level in the data hierarchy is a field or item of data. A *field* of data is one or more bytes that contain data about an attribute of an entity in the information system. For example, an entity in a payroll system is an individual employee. Attributes are the employee's name, hourly rate, and so on. The hourly rate is a field or item of data. Figure 3-2 shows a payroll record with typical fields of data.

Record

A *record* is a collection of fields relating to a specific entity. For example, the payroll record shown in Figure 3-2 contains fields of data relating to a specific employee. An

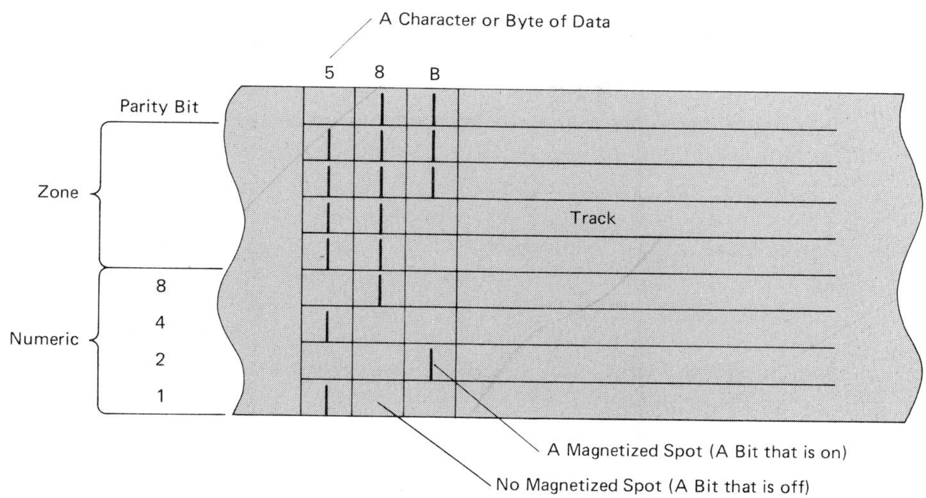

Figure 3-1 Data Coded in EBCDIC on Magnetic Tape

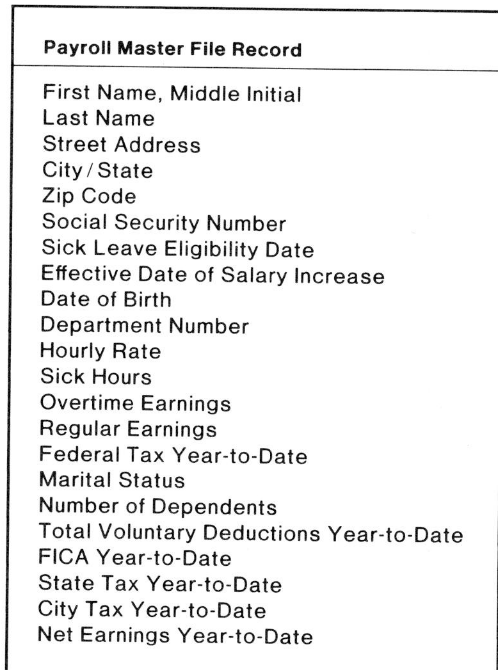

Payroll Master File Record

First Name, Middle Initial
Last Name
Street Address
City / State
Zip Code
Social Security Number
Sick Leave Eligibility Date
Effective Date of Salary Increase
Date of Birth
Department Number
Hourly Rate
Sick Hours
Overtime Earnings
Regular Earnings
Federal Tax Year-to-Date
Marital Status
Number of Dependents
Total Voluntary Deductions Year-to-Date
FICA Year-to-Date
State Tax Year-to-Date
City Tax Year-to-Date
Net Earnings Year-to-Date

Figure 3-2 An Example of Data Fields Contained in a Payroll Master File Record

analogy can be made between a computer-based record and the concept of an individual folder in a manual file. A folder in a manual employee file may contain much the same information as a record in a computer-based payroll file. The field that uniquely identifies a record from all other records in a file is the *record key*. For example, the record key in a payroll record is normally the employee's social security number.

File or Data Set

A *file* consists of a collection of related records. For example, all the payroll records for all of a company's employees are a payroll master file. There are seven basic types of files: 1) master files; 2) transaction files; 3) table files; 4) index files; 5) summary files; 6) program libraries; 7) and backup files.

Master files contain relatively permanent data. Examples include payroll, material inventory, finished goods, work in process, accounts receivable, and accounts payable. A typical payroll master file record might contain an employee's name, address, job description, pay rate, number of exemptions, and year-to-date totals of wages, FICA, and income tax withheld, as shown in Figure 3-2. A registrar's file containing student information such as name, address, courses taken, and grades is another example of a master file record. Business data processing revolves around master files, which are an organization's central files. They contain the information necessary for the organization to operate. All other types of files are auxiliary to and support the maintenance of master files or facilitate the retrieval and reporting of information from them.

Transaction files contain records used to change (update) master files. Any change to a master file is termed a transaction even though it may not be a transaction under the traditional accounting definition—that is, an exchange by the company with an outside party. For example, the change in an employee's address is a transaction to the payroll master file. Most transactions occur between the organization and external parties—for example, orders and payments on account. The data for these transaction records are taken from invoices, receiving reports, employee hiring and termination records, and the like.

Technically, transaction files are used only with batch systems. For example, a transaction file for a batch payroll system contains all the transactions that have accumulated between individual runs or updates of the system. These files usually contain several different record formats, since any system has several different types of transactions. For example, a payroll system can have the following types of transactions: the addition of a new employee, the deletion of an old employee, a change in pay rate, a change in address, and weekly hours worked. Codes within each record identify the record format. This enables the system to locate the data fields within each record format.

Although technically not a transaction file, the transaction log of an online realtime system is in effect a transaction file. This transaction log is created for the purpose of backup and as an audit trail, whereas under a batch system, the transaction file is created primarily as a vehicle to update the master file. Of course, the transaction file in the batch system also serves as a backup and audit trail.

Table files contain relatively permanent information that is used to facilitate processing. An example is the freight rate table used to assign freight charges to customer invoices.

Index files are used to indicate the physical address of records stored on secondary storage devices. They are analogous to a card catalog in a library, allowing computer systems to locate individual records without having to search the entire file.

Summary files contain data extracted and summarized from other files. Examples include temporary work files used by the computer in processing, and report files that contain the necessary information for specific management reports.

Program libraries are files containing the production copy of programs. These are the programs that are used in the day-to-day execution of data processing jobs. Program files contain both source and object copies of production programs. This is because it is wasteful to recompile a frequently executed program each time the program is run. Therefore, production program libraries actually used in the execution of jobs are kept in object form. When a production program is changed, the source copy of the program is changed, tested, and recompiled. The compilation produces an object module, which is then stored in the production program library.

Backup files are either copies of current files or the only copy of noncurrent files used to reconstruct current files in case they are partially or totally destroyed. Backup files should be kept for all the different types of files. In addition, they are sometimes kept for long periods of time to serve as archival files. Archival files contain information that is not on current files but which may be useful in the future for long-term studies or for support documentation, as in the case of income tax returns.

Data Base

A *data base* consists of all the files of an organization that are structured and integrated to facilitate information retrieval and update. The term data base has been used rather loosely by the data processing profession. Technically, a data base consists of the files that are part of a data base management system. However, the term data base also designates all the files of an organization. Data base management systems are discussed in chapter 9.

File Organization

There are basically two types of file organization: those that allow sequential access to the data and those that allow direct access. Under *sequential file organization* the computer typically begins searching for a record by examining the first record in the file and then examining the rest in sequence until the required record is located. Certain storage media like magnetic tape will allow only sequential file organization. To locate a record on a reel of magnetic tape, the tape must be read sequentially beginning with the first record.

On the other hand, *direct file organization* allows immediate, direct access to individual records in the file. There are several techniques that are used to accomplish direct file organization. These will be discussed in more detail in chapter 8. Magnetic disks are by far the most widely used device for storage of direct-access files. Direct-access file organization must be used whenever the application requires immediate access to individual records. It is widely used today whenever the computer configuration includes CRT (cathode ray tube) terminals, which will display management information upon demand.

PROCESSING MODES

In the preceding section we discussed two basic types of file organization—sequential and direct. These can be combined with two information processing modes—batch and immediate—to form three information processing approaches: 1) *batch sequential;* 2) *batch direct;* and 3) *immediate direct.*

Batch Processing

With *batch processing,* changes and queries to a file are stored for a period of time. Then a processing run is made periodically to update the file and to produce responses to queries. The batch runs can be made on a scheduled basis, such as daily, weekly, or monthly, or they can be made as needed. Figure 3-3 illustrates batch sequential

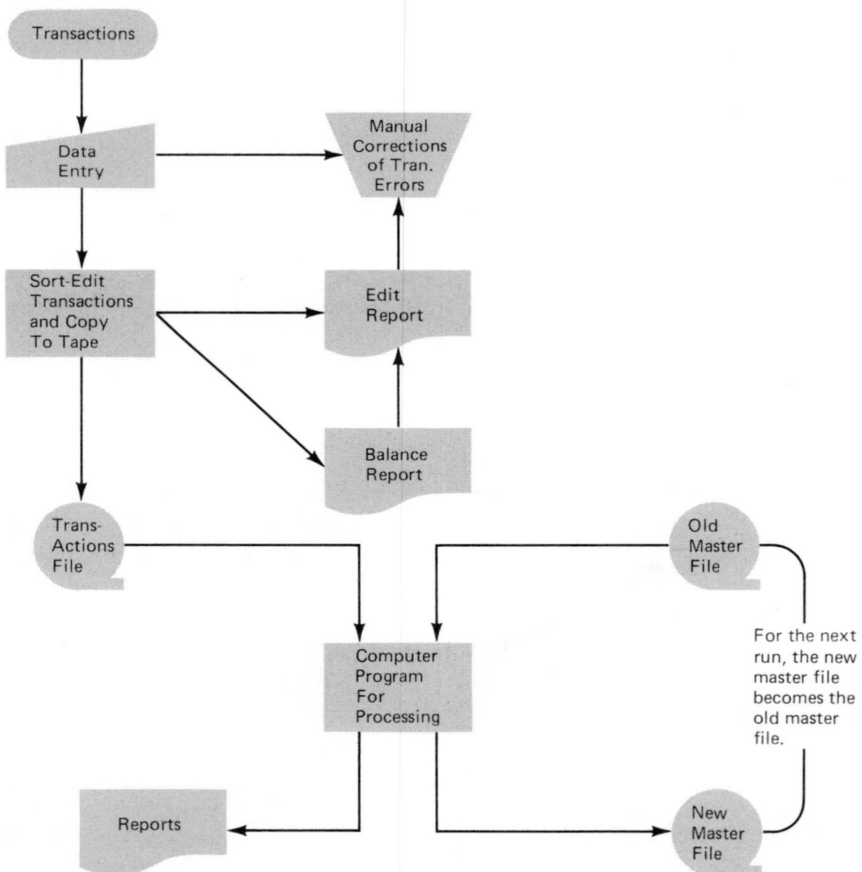

Figure 3-3 Overview of Batch Sequential Processing Using Tape Files

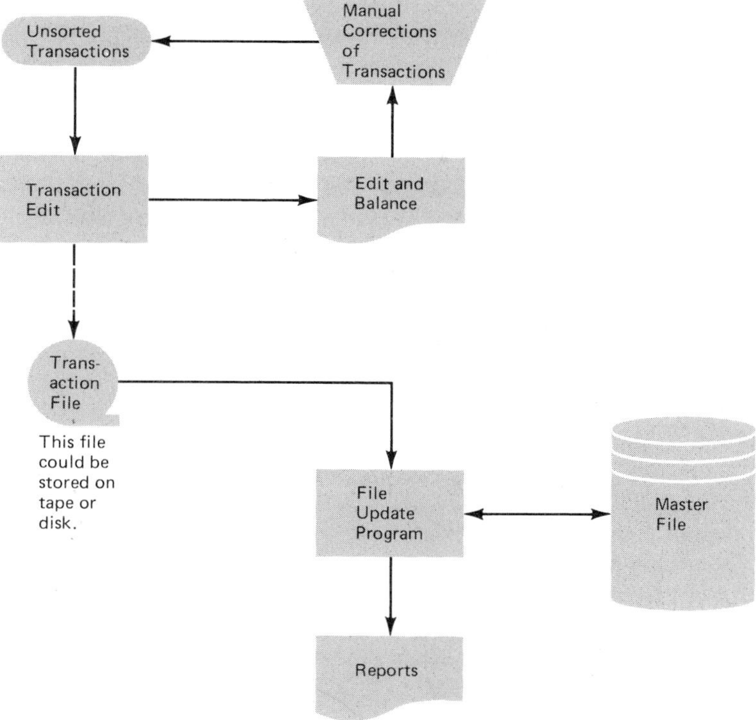

Figure 3-4 Batch-Direct Processing

processing with a file stored on magnetic tape. Batch processing can also be performed with direct organized files. Figure 3-4 illustrates batch-direct processing with a file stored on disk.

Immediate Processing

With *immediate processing,* transactions are processed to update the file immediately or shortly after a real-world event occurs. Immediate processing is illustrated in Figure 3-5. Quite often information processing applications using the immediate mode are

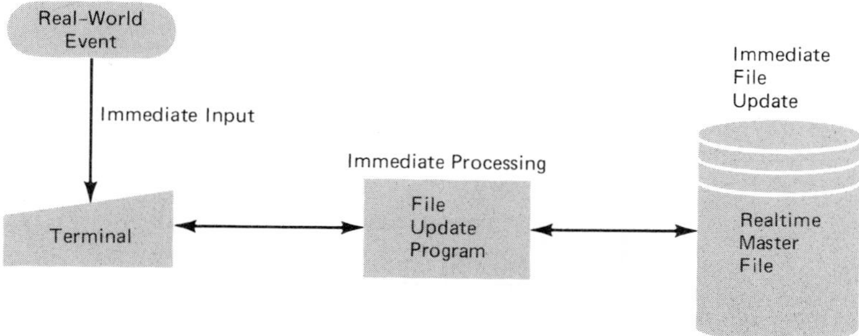

Figure 3-5 Immediate Processing

realtime applications. A realtime application can immediately capture data about ongoing events or processes and provide the information necessary to manage them. Examples of realtime systems are process control and airline reservation systems.

An essential component of a realtime system is realtime master files that are updated immediately after the event occurs. Consequently, at any point in time, the data in realtime master files should accurately reflect the status of the real-world variables that they represent. For example, when a customer reserves a seat on an airline flight, the reservations agent keys in that fact, and the inventory of nonreserved seats on the flight is immediately updated to reflect one less available seat. Immediate processing requires direct-access files—using sequential files would be impractical because of the time required to search for individual records. However, batch processing can occur either with sequential or direct files. Chapter 8 will cover these concepts in more detail.

MANAGEMENT CASE 3-1

Roanoke Power Company, an electrical utility, currently has a batch accounts receivable system. The system is updated daily on the night shift. Online terminals are available to inquire as to the status of the accounts. Of course, due to the batch update, an account could be out of date as much as a full day. The company is considering installing a realtime accounts receivable system. If you were a consultant to Roanoke Power, what would you advise them as to the advantages and disadvantages of a realtime accounts receivable system?

OVERVIEW OF INFORMATION PROCESSING APPLICATIONS

Figure 3-6 provides an overview of typical information processing applications in a business environment. The flow lines between the various applications in the figure illustrate the flow of data between applications. Arrows on the flow lines indicate direction of the data flow from one application to another.

Data needed for multiple applications should be shared between relevant applications in machine-readable form. This obviously eliminates much manual processing and recapture of data. In the remainder of this chapter we will discuss each of the applications illustrated in Figure 3-6.

Inventories

In a manufacturing firm, there are three types of inventories: 1) *raw materials;* 2) *work in process;* and 3) *finished goods.* Of course, in a merchandising firm there is only one type of inventory: finished goods or *merchandise inventory.* However, regardless of the type of inventory, an inventory system has two primary objectives: 1) minimize costs due to out-of-stock situations; and 2) minimize the inventory carrying costs.

At the finished goods level, out-of-stock situations can result in loss of sales; at the raw materials level, out-of-stock conditions may result in the unnecessary idling of production employees and facilities. However, a company cannot simply keep large quantities of inventory on hand to avoid out-of-stock situations. Such an approach

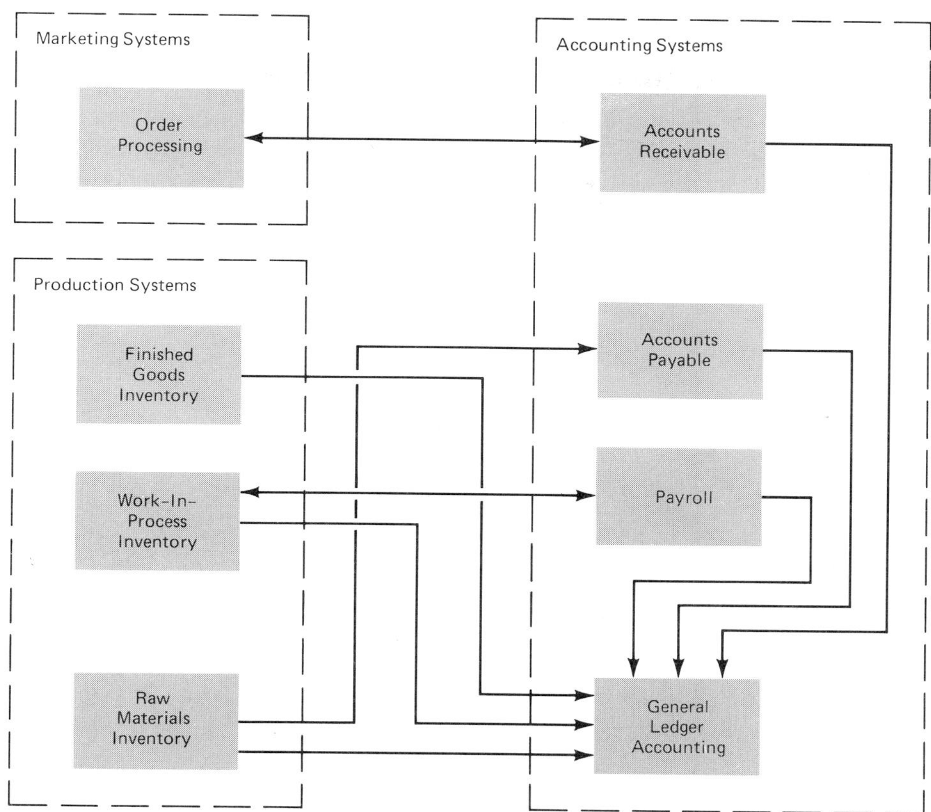

Figure 3-6 Overview of Typical Business Data Processing Applications

would certainly increase inventory carrying costs beyond acceptable levels. Inventory carrying costs include such things as the interest that could be made on funds invested in inventory, insurance costs, and warehousing costs. Obviously as the amount of inventory carried increases, carrying costs also increase. As you can see, these two objectives conflict. We could certainly minimize inventory carrying costs by not carrying any inventory. However, out-of-stock costs might then be unacceptable. Furthermore, we could avoid out-of-stock situations by carrying large amounts of inventory, but this would increase inventory carrying costs. Inventory must be closely monitored to minimize both costs. Computer-based inventory systems have been very useful in providing this close monitor. In fact, computers can be programmed to automatically make inventory reorder decisions that minimize these two costs. Such systems are based on mathematical economic order quantities (EOQ) formulas.

The work-in-process inventory system monitors goods while they are being produced. It has two important objectives in addition to the two discussed above: 1) to provide scheduling control over individual production jobs so that an accurate prediction of their completion date can be made; and 2) to accumulate the unit costs of individual products. In large companies these two objectives are often met by two separate applications that support the work-in-process system. These applications are a scheduling system and a cost accounting system.

Since there are many similarities between the three types of inventory systems, we will simplify our presentation of them in this chapter by using the example of a merchandising firm. Illustrating how a merchandise inventory system operates will give you a good idea of how all three systems are run. Figure 3-7 provides an overview of a merchandise inventory system, which maintains a merchandise inventory master file. Some of the data fields that could be contained in each record in this file are listed in Figure 3-8. At any point in time, the master file should accurately reflect the quantities indicated in Figure 3-8.

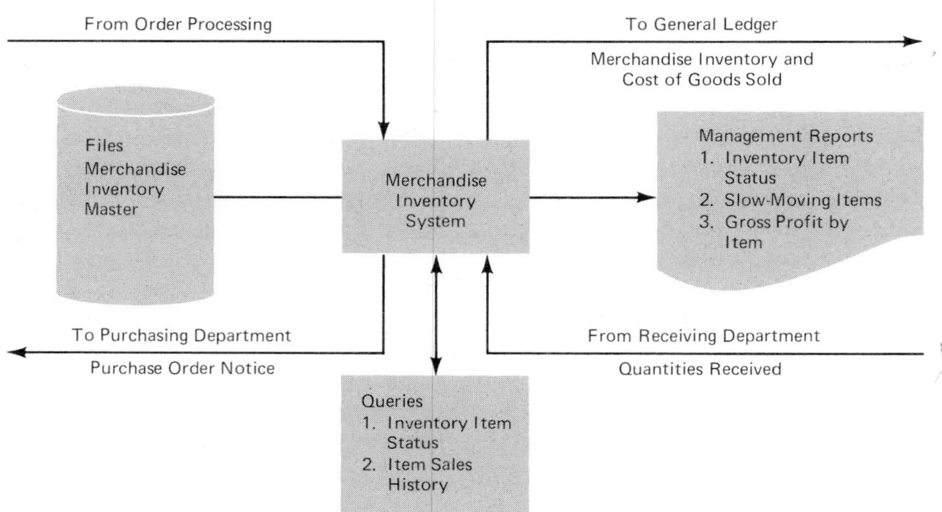

Figure 3-7 Overview of the Merchandise Inventory System

The two primary inputs that update the merchandise inventory master file are quantities of goods shipped (input from the order processing system) and quantities of goods received (input by the receiving department).

The merchandise inventory system produces outputs updating the general ledger system in the areas of current inventory on hand and the cost of goods sold. The system also provides the purchasing department with a purchase order notice. This notice identifies the items whose quantities are at or below the reorder level. Quite often the merchandise inventory system will produce a purchase order instead of a purchase

Inventory Item Number
Item Description
Location in Warehouse
Current Quantity on Hand
Current Quantity on Order
Quantity Sold—Year-to-Date
Quantity Backordered
Standard Cost

Figure 3-8 Typical Fields in a Merchandise Inventory Master File Record

PAGE 1
RUN DATE 11-5-8X

GROSS PROFIT BY ITEM
REPORT
MONTH ENDING 10-31-8X

ITEM NO	ITEM DESCRIPTION	SALES	QTY SOLD	GROSS PROFIT	QTY SOLD YTD
1003	PAPER,3H,LOOSE LEAF	187.50	250	40.00	3520
1004	PAPER,TYPING,BOND	7187.50	1250	1000.00	7500
1005	PAPER,MIMEO,8.5X11	2835.00	750	885.00	6000
7085	PEN,BALLPOINT	3185.00	3500	385.00	24500
4106	PENCIL,DRAWING 3H	1425.00	475	209.00	1900
8165	STAPLER REMOVER	675.00	1500	90.00	16500

PAGE 1
RUN DATE 11-5-8X

SLOW MOVING ITEMS
REPORT
AS OF 10-31-8X

ITEM NO	ITEM DESCRIPTION	STD UNIT COST	DAY OF LAST SALE	QTY ON HAND	QTY SOLD YTD
6405	BOOKCASE,37.5X55X5	133.03	041583	1000	250
6408	CHAIR,SWIVEL,ARMS	138.29	061083	75	20
8082	CUSHION,15X16	5.74	082383	60	15
3015	FAN,WINDOW	38.28	053083	25	10
6440	TABLE,MULTI-PURPOSE	121.68	072583	30	7
6017	TRANSPARENCY,8.5X11	20.93	072383	550	325

PAGE 1
RUN DATE 11-5-8X

INVENTORY ITEM
STATUS REPORT
AS OF 10-31-8X

ITEM NO	ITEM DESCRIPTION	WAREHOUSE LOCATION	QTY ON HAND	QTY ON ORDER	QTY BACK ORDER	QTY SOLD YTD	UNIT	STD UNIT COST
6045	BOOKCASE,37.5X55X5	7340	1000	500	0	350	EA	133.03
3403	CABINET FILE,8"	7340	400	0	0	150	EA	162.15
8002	CALENDAR,PAD,#SD 170	7428	75	60	0	25	EA	.98
3403	CLOCK,WALL,8",ELECT	7428	20	50	30	35	EA	27.88
9005	FOLDER,MANILA,LETTER	7419	50	750	250	950	BOX	3.78

Figure 3-9 Typical Inventory Management Reports

order notice. This purchase order is sent to the purchasing department for approval prior to sending it to a vendor. Figure 3-9 illustrates three typical kinds of inventory management reports. These reports may be printed on paper or displayed on a CRT screen.

Order Processing

Figure 3-10 provides an overview of the order processing system. The *order processing* system is the place of entry for customer orders and it initiates the shipping of orders. The system is also often called an order entry system. The primary objectives of an order processing system are: 1) to initiate shipping orders; 2) to maintain a record of backordered items (a backorder occurs when an item is out of stock and will be shipped later); and 3) to produce various sales analysis reports.

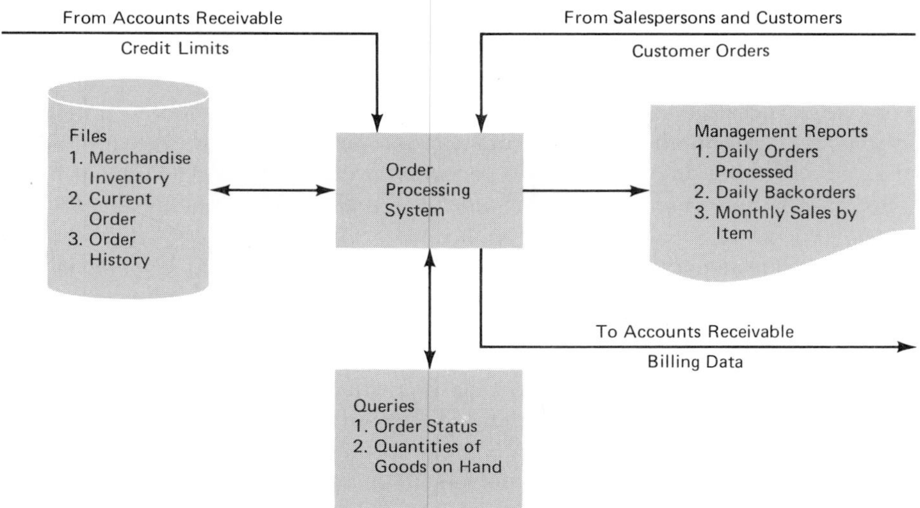

Figure 3-10 Overview of the Order Processing System

A shipping order is illustrated in Figure 3-11. The shipping order is issued in triplicate—a picking copy sent to the warehouse to tell the warehouse employees which goods are to be shipped, a packing copy put inside the box when the goods are shipped, and a copy to be kept on hand for record purposes. Some companies will also produce a fourth copy, which serves as a customer acknowledgment and is sent to the customer as soon as the shipping order is produced.

Most order processing systems access the merchandise inventory file to determine if particular goods are on hand prior to producing a shipping order. If given items are not on hand, they are placed on backorder. The inventory master file is updated to reflect quantities of goods that are actually shipped. Backorder quantities must be maintained on the current order file so that when the goods are available, the order processing system can initiate a shipping order.

```
                                                          PAGE 1
                                                 RUN DATE 11-5-8X

                        SHIPPING ORDER
                      ORDER DATE 10-31-8X

SHIP TO:

   NAME:    PERDUE PROCESSORS
ADDRESS:    104 LANDSDOWNE LANE
            BLACKSBURG, VA       24060

 PACKAGE NO:   764290
SHIPMENT NO:     1721
```

ITEM NO	ITEM DESCRIPTION	QTY ORDERED	QTY SHIPPED	UNIT	UNIT PRICE
1003	PAPER, 3H, LOOSE LEAF	100	100	PKG	.75
1004	PAPER, TYPING, BOND	500	500	PKG	5.75
1005	PAPER, MIMEO, 8.5X11	30	30	RM	3.65
9090	PAD, SCRATCH, 4X6	12	12	DOZ	1.69
8039	RUBBER BANDS, 1/8X3	10	10	BOX	.79
1035	STENCIL, 8.5X14	12	12	DOZ	3.10

Figure 3-11 Typical Shipping Order

In addition to the inventory file, the order processing file maintains a current order file and an order history file. The order history file is identical in format to the current order file. The typical fields within a record of these two files contain the same information that is displayed on the shipping order in Figure 3-11.

After a short period of time (for example, 3 months), records are deleted from the current order file and placed in the order history file. This procedure prevents the current order file from growing too large. Normally, the records in the order history file are maintained for at least a year to support various sales analysis reports that the system can produce.

Figure 3-12 illustrates representative order processing reports. The daily orders processed report is primarily a control report providing daily information concerning orders processed. Management can also use the totals on this report to monitor trends and the amount of orders processed. The daily backorder report is also a control report, enabling management to monitor the level of backorders. If the quantity of backorders

PAGE 1
RUN DATE 11-5-8X

DAILY ORDERS PROCESSED
REPORT
FOR 10-31-8X

ORDER NO	CUSTOMER NO	CUSTOMER NAME	ITEM NO	SHIPMENT NO	SHIPPING DATE
764290	25190	PERDUE PROCESSORS	1004	1721	12-31-83
764290	25190	PERDUE PROCESSORS	1005	1721	12-31-83
764290	25190	PERDUE PROCESSORS	9090	1721	12-31-83
889233	27300	KINKO'S	1005	2930	12-31-83
889233	27300	KINKO'S	1750	2930	12-31-83
931240	31790	POLYSCIENTIFIC	9005	3501	12-31-83

PAGE 1
RUN DATE 11-5-8X

SALES-BY-ITEM
REPORT
MONTH ENDING 10-31-8X

ITEM NO	ITEM DESCRIPTION	QUANTITY	CURRENT MONTHLY SALES	SALES YTD
1003	PAPER,3H,LOOSE LEAF	250	187.50	2640.00
1004	PAPER,TYPING,BOND	1250	7187.50	43125.00
1005	PAPER,MIMEO,8.5X11	750	2835.00	22680.00
7085	PEN,BALLPOINT	3500	3185.00	22295.00
4106	PENCIL,DRAWING 3H	475	1425.00	4864.00
8165	STAPLER REMOVER	1500	675.00	6435.00

PAGE 1
RUN DATE 11-5-8X

DAILY BACKORDER REPORT
FOR 10-31-8X

ITEM NO	ITEM DESCRIPTION	QTY ORDERED	QTY BACK ORDERED	UNIT	UNIT PRICE
3403	CLOCK,WALL,8",ELECT	50	30	EA	27.88
9005	FOLDER,MANILA,LETTER	750	250	BOX	3.78
6412	LETTER TRAY,LEGAL	50	20	EA	6.88
9090	PAD,SCRATCH,4X6	625	300	DOZ	1.04
4106	PENCIL,DRAWING 3H	200	150	DOZ	2.56

Figure 3-12 Typical Order Processing Reports

becomes excessive, relations with customers may be damaged. The monthly sales by item report is just one example of the many different types of sales analysis reports that can be produced. This particular report enables management to monitor sales trends by following the numbers of individual items sold.

Accounts Receivable

The objectives of the *accounts receivable* system are threefold: 1) to bill customers for orders shipped; 2) to maintain account records of the amounts which customers owe and records of payments on these accounts; and 3) to provide the information necessary to assist in the collection of past-due accounts. We are assuming here that the billing function is performed by the accounts receivable system. The billing function is the sending of the initial invoice to the customer. Actually, this function can be performed either by the order processing system, a separate billing system, or by the accounts receivable system.

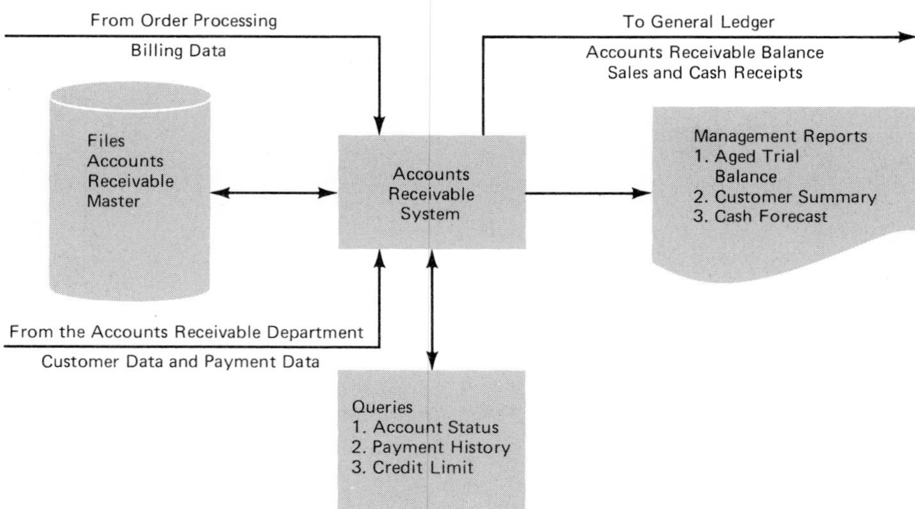

Figure 3-13 Overview of the Accounts Receivable System

Figure 3-13 provides an overview of the accounts receivable system. The accounts receivable system maintains one file—the accounts receivable master file. Typical fields contained within a record in this file are illustrated in Figure 3-14. This file is updated with billing data from order processing. All the other data in the file is input from the accounts receivable department.

Queries to the accounts receivable system display on a CRT screen information such as account status and payment history. The account status screen displays unpaid purchases and recent payments while the payment history screen would provide detailed information about the payment habits of a particular customer.

Figure 3-15 displays three typical kinds of management reports from the accounts receivable system. The *aged trial balance* is a very important and valuable report for collection purposes since it indicates the accounts that are past due and how far they are

Customer Number
Customer Name
Customer Address
Credit Rating
Average Days Late
Credit Limit
Purchase Date
Purchase Reference
Purchase Amounts
Payment Date
Payment Reference
Payment Amounts
Current Balance

Figure 3-14 Typical Fields in an Accounts Receivable Master File Record

PAGE 1
RUN DATE 11-5-8X

CASH FORECAST
REPORT
AS OF 10-31-8X

PROBABLE PYMT DATE	DUE DATE	INVOICE NO	CUSTOMER NAME	PYMT TERMS	DISC AMT	AMOUNT DUE	PYMT
010184	011584	23910	PERDUE PROCESSORS	2/10,N/30	10.00	490.00	490.00
011584	013184	24920	PERDUE PROCESSORS	2/10,N/30	9.00	441.00	441.00
013184	020584	39011	KINKO'S	3/10,N/30	7.50	242.50	242.50
013184	020584	39015	KINKO'S	3/10,N/30	2.25	47.75	47.75
013184	021584	39120	KINKO'S	3/10,N/30	1.50	38.50	38.50
020584	021584	45270	DORN,HC	*****	.00	125.00	75.00

TOTAL CASH FORECASTED $ 1334.75

PAGE 1
RUN DATE 11-5-8X

ACCOUNTS RECEIVABLE
CUSTOMER STATUS
REPORT
AS OF 10-31-8X

CUST NO	CUST NAME	CREDIT RATING	CREDIT LIMIT	AMNT DUE	AMNT REC'D	BALANCE
25190	PERDUE PROCESSORS	9	5000.00	2695.50	1500.00	1195.50
27300	KINKO'S	7	3500.00	1325.00	750.00	575.00
31790	POLYSCIENTIFIC	10	7500.00	5290.00	3900.00	1790.00
51230	BANDY,MW	* 0	.00	750.00	.00	750.00
61359	DORN,HC	6	1000.00	625.00	375.00	250.00
73401	JONES,LT	* 0	.00	100.00	.00	100.00

PAGE 1
RUN DATE 11-5-8X

AGED TRIAL BALANCE
REPORT
AS OF 10-31-8X

CUSTOMER NO	CUSTOMER NAME	AMOUNT NOT DUE	AMOUNT 1-30 DAYS OVERDUE	AMOUNT 31-60 OVERDUE	AMOUNT >60 DAYS OVERDUE	TOTAL BALANCE DUE
25190	PERDUE PROCESSORS	1000.00	195.00	.00	.00	1195.00
27300	KINKO'S	550.00	25.00	.00	.00	575.00
31790	POLYSCIENTIFIC	1500.00	200.00	90.00	.00	1790.00
51230	BANDY,MW	.00	350.00	400.00	.00	750.00
61359	DORN,HC	195.00	55.00	.00	.00	250.00
73401	JONES,LT	.00	25.00	75.00	.00	100.00

Figure 3-15 Typical Accounts Receivable Management Reports

past due, either 30–60 days, 60–90 days, or over 90 days. The *customer status* report provides detailed information concerning a specific customer. This information can be very valuable to the salesman assigned a given customer.

Since the accounts receivable system is the primary cash receipt system, it can provide very useful cash forecasts. This information is normally based on statistics maintained concerning customer payment habits, such as the average number of days the customer is late in making payments.

Accounts Payable

The accounts payable system tends to be a mirror image of the accounts receivable system. The accounts receivable system keeps records of the amounts owed to the firm whereas the *accounts payable* system keeps records of amounts owed to suppliers of the firm. The objectives of the accounts payable system are: 1) to provide control over payments to vendors of goods and suppliers of services; 2) to issue checks to these vendors and suppliers, and 3) to provide information for effective cash management.

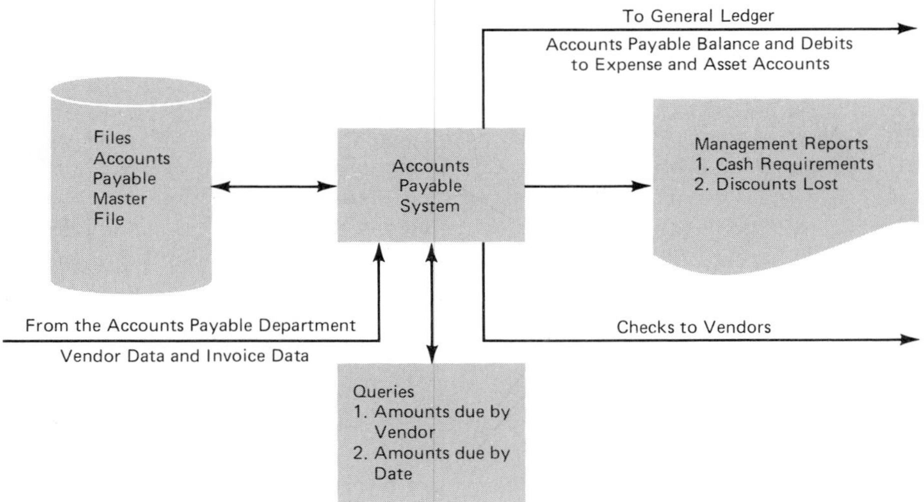

Figure 3-16 Overview of the Accounts Payable System

Figure 3-16 provides an overview of the accounts payable system. The accounts payable system maintains an accounts payable master file. Typical fields contained in an accounts payable master file record are illustrated in Figure 3-17. The accounts payable department provides the input to the accounts payable system. The primary types of input are data concerning vendors, such as vendor name, address, etc., and data from new invoices received from vendors and suppliers.

Representative accounts payable management reports are illustrated in Figure 3-18. They include a *cash requirements* report, which is based upon amounts owed and dates when these amounts are due. The *discounts lost* report is an important type of cash management report. Many vendors allow customers to take a discount on payments, say 2 percent off the invoice, if payments are made within 10 days. If enough cash is available, or can be borrowed, discounts generally should be taken. The discounts

Vendor Number
Vendor Name
Vendor Address
Payment Terms
Amounts Owed by Invoice
Payments—Year-to-Date
Discounts Taken—Year-to-Date
Discounts Lost—Year-to-Date

Figure 3-17 Typical Fields in an Accounts Payable Master File

lost report identifies payables where the discounts were not taken. These situations are usually deviations from management policy and therefore require investigation.

The accounts payable system also produces checks that are sent to vendors after review by the accounts payable department. Queries to the system normally are related to amounts due to be paid. Management may need to know the amout due a particular vendor or the amount due by a certain date.

MANAGEMENT CASE 3-2

James River Supply is a medium-sized hardware wholesaler. At any one time they have approximately 900 retail hardware stores as customers. Jim Richardson, vice president of marketing is dissatisfied with the current marketing information produced by his staff and computer-based systems. He has initiated a system development study to outline the major characteristics of an ideal marketing information system. Outline the characteristics of three or four reports or computer terminal screens that would be most useful in a marketing information system. Where would the data come from to support these reports or screens?

PAGE 1
RUN DATE 11-5-8X

DISCOUNTS LOST
REPORT
AS OF 10-31-8X

VOUCHER NO	VENDOR NO	VENDOR NAME	INVOICE AMOUNT	AMOUNT LOST	EFF APR	DAYS LATE
15270	25190	INTERNATIONAL PAPER	7500.00	150.00	24%	10
29563	31723	LLOYD'S MANUFACTURIN	1350.00	13.50	13%	5
14021	45310	ABDICK	1080.00	21.60	13%	4
83910	51377	IBM	2532.00	75.96	25%	9
85674	63784	PENTEL	950.00	9.50	15%	4
93201	72111	XEROX	1500.00	30.00	22%	6

PAGE 1
RUN DATE 11-5-8X

CASH REQUIREMENT
REPORT
AS OF 10-31-8X

DUE DATE	VENDOR NO	VENDOR NAME	PYMT TERMS	INVOICE NO	AMOUNT DUE	DISC AMOUNT	BALANCE DUE	PYMT
013184	25190	INTERNATIONAL PAPER	2/10,N/30	07519	450.00	9.00	441.00	441.00
021084	31723	LLOYD'S MANUFACTURIN	*****	21340	652.00	.00	652.00	200.00
021584	45310	ABDICK	2/10,N/30	17001	107.50	2.15	105.40	105.40
021584	51377	IBM	3/10,N/30	00910	963.00	28.89	934.11	934.11
022884	63784	PENTEL	*****	50003	93.00	.00	93.00	50.00
030184	72111	XEROX	1/10,N/30	43000	70.00	7.00	63.00	63.00

TOTAL CASH REQUIREMENTS 10-31-8X $ 1793.51

Figure 3-18 Typical Accounts Payable Management Reports

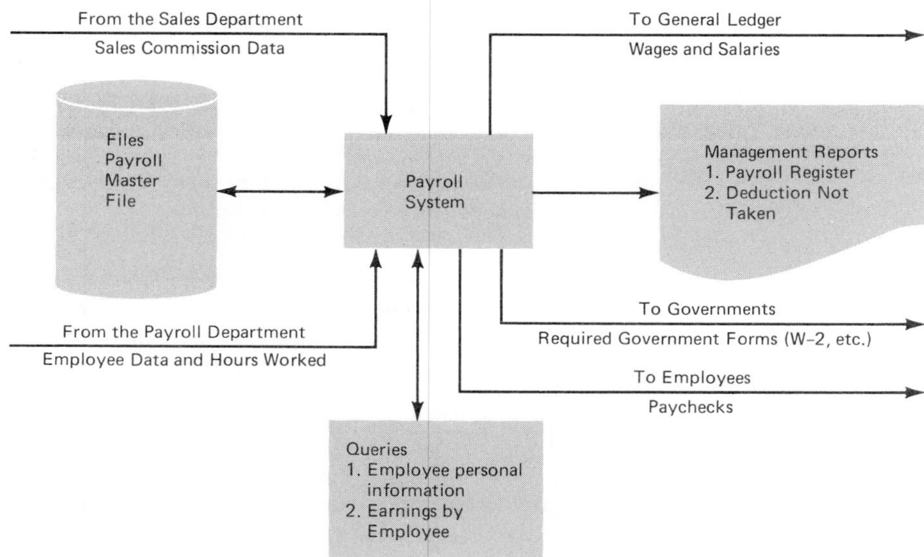

Figure 3-19 Overview of the Payroll System

Payroll

Payroll is often the first system that a company converts to computer processing because it is a relatively simple operation that does not interface with many other application systems. The primary objectives of the *payroll system* are: 1) to pay both hourly and salaried employees on a timely basis; 2) to maintain records of payments to employees and the taxes withheld from employee payments; and 3) to provide management with the reports necessary to manage the payroll function. Figure 3-19 provides an overview of a payroll system. This system maintains a payroll master file. Typical contents of a record within the payroll master file are illustrated in Figure 3-20. The payroll

Employee Number
Employee Name
Employee Address
Department
Occupation
Pay Rate
Vacation Time
Sick Leave Time
Gross Pay Year-to-Date
Federal Income Tax Withheld
State Income Tax Withheld
FICA Tax Withheld
Health Insurance Withheld
Credit Union Savings Withheld
Bank Code

Figure 3-20 Typical Contents of a Payroll Master File Record

department provides most of the payroll system input in the form of personal employee data, such as name, address, pay rate, and hours worked during a pay period. The sales department, in some cases, provides sales commission data for commission payments to salesmen. The output from the payroll system includes required government forms such as the W-2 form. This form is produced annually to report wages that have been earned for the year as well as other income tax information. The system also produces paychecks for employees. Management reports (illustrated in Figure 3-21) include the *deductions not taken* report and the *payroll register*, which is a record of wages paid and withholding amounts for each employee. The deductions not taken report shows payroll deductions not taken on schedule due to an employee's insufficient pay. Queries to the payroll system generally are for information concerning individual employees, such as personal information or earnings by the employee.

PAGE 1
RUN DATE 11-5-8X

PAYROLL REGISTER
REPORT
AS OF 10-31-8X

EMP NO	EMP NAME	RATE	REG HOURS	OT HOURS	TOTAL EARNINGS	FEDERAL TAX	FICA TAX	STATE TAX	EARNINGS YTD
00001	TURNBALL,JW	4.51	40	10	248.05	32.20	25.41	13.04	7840.21
00002	CLARK,TC	5.37	40	0	214.80	16.81	12.10	6.75	8250.00
00003	JONES,FL	3.35	21	0	70.35	6.91	4.21	2.10	2615.00
00004	SMITH,AJ	3.35	30	0	100.50	9.22	6.90	4.12	3700.12
00005	JAMES,CL	5.37	40	5	255.08	41.90	31.76	15.02	9215.91
00006	FREDERICKSON,JR	4.51	40	0	180.40	12.13	10.91	5.33	7651.00

PAGE 1
RUN DATE 11-5-8X

DEDUCTIONS NOT TAKEN
REPORT
AS OF 10-31-8X

EMP NO	EMP NAME	DEDUCTION DESC	AMOUNT TAKEN	AMOUNT NOT TAKEN	NOT TAKEN BALANCE
00001	TURNBALL,JW	UNITED FUND	.00	25.00	25.00
00001	TURNBALL,JW	CREDIT UNION	40.00	.00	57.00
00002	CLARK,TC	HOSPITALIZATION	26.00	.00	5.00
00003	JONES,FL	PENSION	45.00	.00	40.00
00003	JONES,FL	BONDS	.00	65.00	70.00
00005	JAMES,CL	CREDIT UNION	40.00	.00	40.00

Figure 3-21 Typical Payroll Management Reports

Other Applications

The general ledger is becoming a very common computer application. The *general ledger system* maintains the financial accounts of the business. It is responsible for producing such financial statements as the *income statement*, the *statement of financial position*, and the *statement of changes in financial position*. This application maintains a record of all assets, liabilities, owner's equities, revenues, and expenses of the firm.

Sometimes the general ledger system will also have the capability of maintaining a budget, especially for revenues and expenses. Reports can be prepared comparing actual revenues and expenses to budgeted amounts. Such reports are very valuable in maintaining control of a business organization.

Another application is the *manufacturing resource planning (MRP) system*. This system is closely related to our earlier discussion concerning inventory systems. However, an MRP system is a much more sophisticated approach to the materials inventory area than a simple inventory system. Based on production schedules and material requirements for individual products, the MRP system can efficiently order materials so that they will be on hand when required in production. Along with the MRP system, many manufacturing firms maintain a *production scheduling system*. This system helps control the flow of materials and production jobs through the factory.

Under order processing, we previously discussed the possibility of producing a few sales analysis reports from the order processing system. A separate marketing analysis system can go far beyond the scope of these few reports. In addition to providing information about past sales, the system can assist in estimating future sales and even help in optimizing the marketing strategy for certain products through a market research approach.

There are several other types of systems used by specialized industries. Examples of such systems are the reservation systems used by motels and airlines.

SUMMARY

The components of the information system data hierarchy, in ascending order of complexity, are: 1) bit; 2) byte; 3) field or items; 4) record; 5) file or data set; and 6) data base.

The two basic types of file organization, sequential and direct, are combined with two data process modes, batch and immediate, to form three data processing strategies: batch sequential, batch direct, and immediate direct.

Under the batch mode, changes and queries to a file are stored for a period of time and then a processing run is made periodically to update the master file, produce scheduled reports, and produce responses to queries.

Under the immediate mode, transactions are processed to update the master file immediately or shortly after a real world event occurs.

One type of application using immediate processing is a realtime system. A realtime application can immediately capture data about ongoing events or can process and provide the information necessary to manage them.

There are two primary objectives of an inventory system: 1) minimize costs due to out-of-stock situations; and 2) minimize the inventory carrying costs. These two objectives are in conflict with one another.

The primary objectives of an order processing system are 1) to initiate shipping orders; 2) to maintain a record of back ordered items; and 3) to update various sales analysis reports.

Objectives of the accounts receivable system are threefold: 1) to bill customers for orders shipped; 2) to maintain records of the amounts which customers owe and to maintain a record of payments on account; and 3) to provide the information necessary to assist in collection of past due accounts.

The objectives of the accounts payable system are: 1) to provide control over payments to vendors of goods and suppliers of services; 2) to issue checks to vendors and suppliers; and 3) to provide information for effective cash management.

The objectives of the payroll system are to: 1) pay both hourly and salaried employees on a timely basis; 2) maintain records of payments to employees and the taxes withheld from employee payments; 3) provide management with the reports necessary to manage the personnel function.

The general ledger maintains the financial accounts of the business and produces financial statements. Other typical applications include material requirements planning, production scheduling, and marketing analysis.

KEY TERMS

Bit
Byte
Field or Item
Record
File or Data Set
Data Base
Sequential File Organization
Direct File Organization
Batch Processing
Immediate Processing
Batch Sequential
Batch Direct
Immediate Direct
Inventory Systems
Raw Materials
Work in Process
Finished Goods
Merchandise Inventory
Order Processing
Backorder
Accounts Receivable
Accounts Payable
Payroll
General Ledger
Materials Requirements Planning
Production Scheduling
Marketing Analysis System

REVIEW QUESTIONS

1. What are the components of the information systems data hierarchy?
2. Define and explain each of the components in the information systems data hierarchy.
3. Identify the two basic types of file organization.
4. Outline the difference between batch and immediate data processing modes.
5. What are the similarities and differences between batch sequential, batch direct, and immediate direct processing approaches?
6. What is a realtime system?
7. What are the primary objectives of an inventory system?
8. For the merchandise inventory system, identify the following: primary inputs, typical data maintained on the master file, and some examples of output.
9. What are the primary objectives of the order processing system?
10. For the order processing system, identify the following: primary inputs, typical data maintained on the master file, and some examples of output.
11. What are the primary objectives of the accounts receivable system?

12. For the accounts receivable system, identify the following: primary inputs, typical data maintained on the master file, and some examples of output.
13. What are the primary objectives of the accounts payable system?
14. For the accounts payable system, identify the following: primary inputs, typical data maintained on the master file, and some examples of output.
15. What are the primary objectives of the payroll system?
16. For the payroll system, identify the following: primary inputs, typical data maintained on the master file, and some examples of output.
17. What is a general ledger system?
18. What is a manufacturing resources planning system?

DISCUSSION QUESTIONS

1. Of the applications covered in this chapter, which do you think could justify the use of realtime master files. Support your position.
2. Assume a company is installing a computer for the first time. The company plans eventually to computerize all the applications discussed in this chapter. However, they feel that it is impossible to implement all these applications simultaneously. Some applications must have priority over others. Rank the applications in the order in which you would implement them.

RESEARCH PROJECTS

1. Choose an application system in which you are interested. Identify a software vendor who has the chosen application system software for sale or lease. Contact this vendor. Obtain material describing the software and write a report describing the inputs, files maintained, outputs and capabilities of the application system. Vendors can be identified through the annual software ratings published in *Datamation* or through vendor ads in journals such as *Datamation*, *The Journal of Accountancy* and *Management Accounting*.

APPLICATION CASE

Now CAD/CAM + MIS = CIM

(Reprinted with permission from MIS Week, May 18, 1983, pp. 60–61)

By Kathryn Jones

DALLAS—As computer-aided design and manufacturing (CAD/CAM) move toward integration and give birth to a new buzzword, CIM, for computer-integrated manufacturing, MIS departments will emerge as key players in integrating every aspect of manufacturing and synchronizing the flow of information between MIS and the shop floor.

Consultants, MIS executives and CAD/CAM vendors interviewed agree that

CIM—which builds on CAD/CAM and merges it with other functions such as purchasing, inventory control and assembly—is the "next generation" of automation, one that will present new challenges to MIS.

CIM also is an expensive new direction that demands commitment from top management, farsighted coordination, a breakdown of barriers between MIS, engineering and manufacturing departments and a view of CAD/CAM beyond graphics to take in the "big picture" of manufacturing from design to assembly to distribution.

"CIM really doesn't work unless you take the slash out between CAD/CAM," said Glenn Palmer, vice president of engineering for Productivity International Inc., a Dallas-based CAD/CAM consulting firm specializing in CIM. Palmer used the equation "CIM = CAD + CAM + MIS" to illustrate that point.

In a recent interview with MIS Week, both Palmer and Warren Hastings, the firm's executive vice president, explained CIM and MIS's increasingly important role, particularly as custodian of the database.

"Ownership of data is going to become a very important issue," Hastings noted. "The tendency has been for data processing departments to say 'we own the database.' They really are custodians."

As custodians, one of the tasks that MIS departments face in manufacturing operations is getting updated information to the shop floor, the consultants said. Palmer noted about 30 percent of factory workers are idle or working on the wrong job with the wrong information because information wasn't synchronized.

Hastings cited the example of a change order that comes in for a product. "They'll continue making the bad product for another month because they can't get the information down to the shop floor," he said. "To succeed, CIM systems have got to take organization as a whole, looking at all functions and data-dependencies. The one constant thing about manufacturing is change—in processes, materials, products and technology."

While CIM is the objective most manufacturing companies are aiming for, its implementation still faces some hurdles. The cost ranges in the millions of dollars (most turn-key CAD/CAM systems range from $100,000 to $500,000 or more), requires an average 15- to 18-month implementation cycle and three to five years before integration is complete.

"One of the impediments in corporate America is that these things are three- to five-year implementations," Hastings said. "Companies cannot invest $3- or $4-million and not see a return for three or five years. It's not the way corporate America works today."

Foremost among the companies pioneering CIM and overcoming the obstacles is Ingersoll Milling Co., a Rockford, Ill, machine tool firm. Last year, the company won the Lead Award from the Computer and Automated Systems Association of the Society of Manufacturing Engineers for its role in developing and using CIM.

George Hess, Ingersoll's vice president of systems and planning, said the department was involved in the integration from the beginning in 1980, when Ingersoll decided to integrate after years of developing separate stand-alone "islands of automation" in CAD/CAM, bill of materials, production control, inventory control and accounting systems.

Ingersoll also had a unique manufacturing situation in that most of the thousands of component parts used in its heavy machine tool products are made in lots of only one, two and three, and require an enormous amount of information processing to track the products.

Starting with a bill of materials system in 1981, Ingersoll now has integrated master scheduling, engineering design, inventory control, accounts payable and purchasing, parts manufacturing and cost accounting, and assembly.

"We are the coordinating force," Hess said of systems and planning. "We pull together the long-range plans, the year-long plans, coordinate, design new systems. We're involved in all phases all the way to the actual manufacturing."

Employees use 115 alphanumeric terminals for main-line production management functions and 30 computer graphic display terminals for engineering design and numerical control programming. The terminals are connected to an International Business Machines Corp. (IBM) "3033U" central processor. On-line mainframe-based word processing is provided to all departments.

Echoing Hastings' observations, Hess said Ingersoll has been able to integrate because of its size, the fact that it is a privately held company and because top management believes CIM is essential to long-range planning to improve productivity and quality.

"A company of our size in the $100- to $200-million range is ideal. Two important ingredients are that we are privately held and are able to make long-range investments and we have a chief executive officer who is very much involved—and I don't mean with blank checks," Hess commented.

Although not so advanced in CIM, Bell Helicopter Textron Inc. in Fort Worth, has had integration in mind as its ultimate goal since the early 1960s.

"Our company was probably a little unique in that sense," noted Max Armour, supervisor, CAD/CAM systems, scientific and technical computing, in the MIS department. "Our aim was that there was no reason for the manufacturing people to redefine what the engineering people had done."

"We're still fairly early-on in CIM," he added.

Bell, which manufactures helicopters for the military services and commercial users, such as new organizations, police, rescue operations and offshore oil companies, has plans to integrate such functions as inventory, purchase, design and quality control under one computerized network. Minicomputers are located on the shop floor throughout the sprawling manufacturing plant, using tape containing designs to perform drafting and cutting of composite material, as well as to test cables electronically.

Due to Bell's integration of CAD/CAM, the company will add a new IBM "3033" mainframe soon and will add 21 graphic CAD/CAM terminals to the 34 it already has in place.

While MIS departments wrestle with justifying cost, implementing systems and coordinating the integration, CAD/CAM vendors also are developing CIM products, although users and consultants had more criticism than praise for vendors. The main criticism was that CAD/CAM turnkey systems don't go very far beyond graphics.

"Probably 85 percent of all CAD systems are installed in a drafting mode," said Carl Machover, president of Machover Associates, a CAD/CAM consulting firm in White Plains, N.Y. Machover gave a two day seminar on CAD/CAM in Dallas in March. "That's going to change. Certainly the trend is to expand the use of the system to these other areas."

The top two CAD/CAM vendors in terms of number of installations, Computervision and Applicon, both say future products will address CIM. Users, though, still are not completely satisfied with the systems from CAD/CAM vendors. In a study published last September by Merrill Lynch, Pierce, Fenner & Smith Inc., respondents were asked which CAD/CAM vendors most effectively fulfilled their needs. A third, 33 percent, replied that none did, with Computervision in second place with nine percent.

The users said the most common needs not being adequately addressed were better networking, more terminals per computer, interfaces with other CAD/CAM systems so that different brands could communicate, lower cost workstations and the ability to downstream tasks from the database—factors that will also affect CIM's development.

Ingersoll's Hess sees other factors driving CIM, such as the collapse of computer and mass storage costs, the explosion of on-line terminals and the evolution of practical database management software. These "prime movers," he said, could take CIM from "a promising development to an outright revolution."

Discussion

1. Why are CAD/CAM systems so important to manufacturing?
2. Does it make sense to integrate CAD/CAM systems with the traditional MIS applications of inventory, purchasing, accounts payable, and cost accounting?

PART TWO

COMPUTER RESOURCES

CHAPTER 4

THE CENTRAL PROCESSING UNIT AND STORAGE DEVICES

INTRODUCTION

The usefulness of a computer system for business purposes is largely determined by the characteristics of the central processing unit and the system's storage devices. The CPU is the centerpiece of a computer system; strictly speaking it is the computer (see Figure 4-1). Of course, as we will see later, software and input/output devices are also important considerations in a computer system. However, the characteristics of the CPU and storage devices, such as primary storage size, will determine whether certain business applications are feasible on a given computer system. Therefore, understanding these basic characteristics is crucial to business users of computers.

In this chapter, we will distinguish between digital and analog computers, cover the primary components of a CPU, and explore the differences between mainframe, mini, and microcomputers. In the storage area we will cover primary and secondary storage, including the current media used in these two types of storage and the storage technology likely be used in future computer systems.

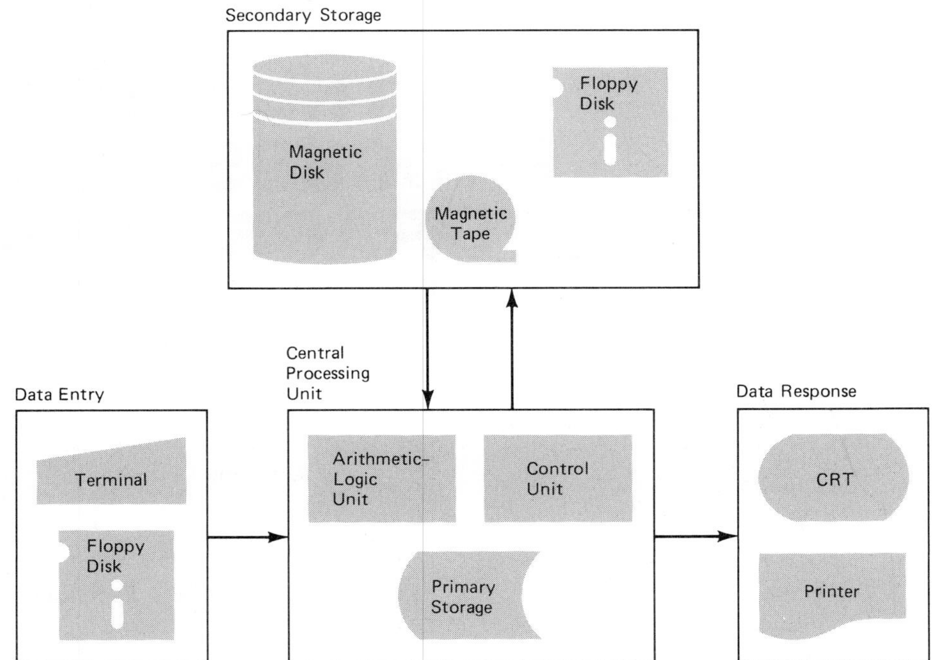

Figure 4-1 A Computer System

THE CENTRAL PROCESSING UNIT

Digital Versus Analog Computers

In a fundamental sense, all computers are symbol manipulators. They manipulate symbols such as numbers, alphabetic characters, names, amounts, and addresses. They can add two symbols together, move a symbol from one location to another, and compare symbols, among other operations. Digital and analog computers differ in the way they represent symbols internally. Table 4-1 illustrates the decimal numbers zero through nine as they are represented in a digital versus an analog computer. The digital computer represents decimal numbers through a string of eight bits. When the bit is on, it represents a one; when it is off it represents a zero. The complete string of eight bits, called a byte, is used to code a character or represent a decimal number. In the computer, an on bit can be physically represented by a positively charged magnetic domain such as a small spot on a tape or disk; it may also be represented by the fact that a circuit is conducting an electrical flow. An off bit would be represented by a negatively charged magnetic domain or the fact that a circuit is not conducting an electrical flow. Thus digital computers operate directly with digits either at the bit level, which is short for binary digit, or at the byte level where a nonbinary digit, such as a decimal number or an alphabetic character, is represented.

On the other hand, an analog computer does not operate directly on digits, but rather represents digits through a continuous physical magnitude, such as voltage level

Table 4-1 Digital versus Analog Number Representation

Decimal Number Representation	Digital Computer Bits On (1) and Bits Off (0)	Analog Computer Voltage Level
0	1111 0000	10
1	1111 0001	12
2	1111 0010	14
3	1111 0011	16
4	1111 0100	18
5	1111 0101	20
6	1111 0110	22
7	1111 0111	24
8	1111 1000	26
9	1111 1001	28

or the amount of rotation of a shaft. Table 4-1 illustrates the representation of the decimal numbers zero through nine through measurement of voltage levels.

Analog computers are used primarily in process control and scientific applications. For example, they may be used to monitor the thickness of steel coming out of a rolling mill and automatically adjust the mill to maintain the desired steel thickness. Digital computers may also be used for process control purposes. They are more accurate than analog computers and are the most widely used type of computer in business data processing. For this reason, in the remainder of the book, we will cover only digital computers.

Figure 4-2 illustrates the components of a CPU. These components are primary storage, the arithmetic-logic unit, and the control unit.

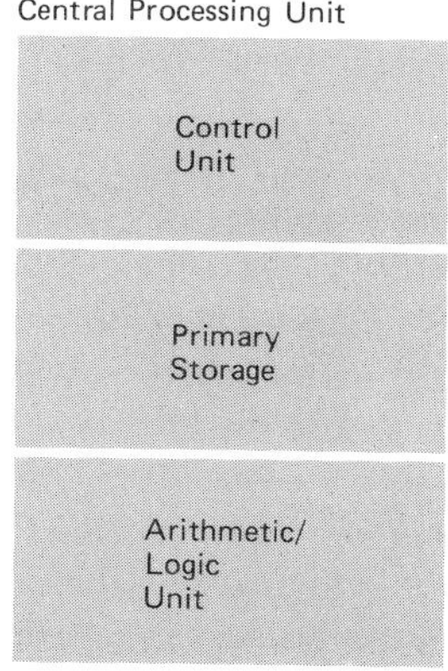

Figure 4-2 Components of a CPU

Primary Storage

Primary storage has three functions. First, it stores the complete program that is being executed. With the exception of virtual storage systems, which are discussed in chapter 6, primary storage must store the complete program while it is being executed. Second, primary storage stores operating system programs, which assist in managing the operation of the computer. Operating systems will be covered in chapter 6. Third, it stores data while they are being processed by the CPU.

The bulk of data used by a computer application is, of course, stored in secondary storage devices, but data must be stored in primary storage whenever the CPU is using them for processing purposes. Therefore, data are continually being read into and written out of primary storage during the execution of a program. For example, a complete customer record—that is, all the data associated with a particular customer—would likely be stored in primary storage while the CPU is performing operations pertaining to that customer.

Compared to secondary storage, primary storage allows fast access and is relatively expensive. Fast access primary storage is necessary because the other components of the CPU, the control unit and the arithmetic-logic unit, operate at electronic speeds. If the CPU had to depend on mechanical movement to retrieve specific pieces of data, as do disk and magnetic tape storage, the resulting slow primary storage access speed would then create a major bottleneck for the CPU, drastically decreasing the amount of work that could be performed by the CPU. Ideally, the CPU should have large amounts of very fast access primary storage. However, the relatively expensive cost of fast access memory may lessen its availability.

Early computer systems contained modest amounts of primary storage. For example, a CPU with 64,000 bytes (characters) of primary storage was a large computer in the 1950s and 1960s. Many computers had 16,000 bytes or less of primary storage. Today, large computer systems may contain 5 to 30 megabytes of primary storage. One megabyte equals 1 million bytes. In the 1950s and 1960s, primary storage was magnetic core storage as illustrated in Figure 4-3.

Magnetic cores are ferrite cores that can be polarized in two directions and can therefore represent a bit of data. Wires are strung through these cores both to write data on the cores and to read the data from the cores. Core memory must be assembled manually and is therefore very expensive. In addition, core memory is much slower than the semiconductor memory that is widely used today for primary storage.

Semiconductors are electronic circuits that can be reproduced photographically in a miniaturized form on silicon chips. They are often referred to as large-scale integrated (LSI) circuits or, in the case of advanced semiconductor technology, very large scale integrated (VLSI) circuits. The development of semiconductors has revolutionized the computer industry and many others as well. For example, the calculator that you can now buy at the grocery store for $7 would have cost over $1,000 in the late 1960s. Not only has the semiconductor replaced magnetic core for primary storage purposes, but a complete central processor can be placed on a semiconductor chip. These CPUs on semiconductor chips are the basis for the microcomputer industry. In fact, a CPU with the equivalent computing power of an early ENIAC computer, which required a large room to house it, can be placed on a chip approximately one-fourth of an inch square. Figure 4-4 illustrates such a chip in greatly magnified form. The actual size of this chip is about one-fourth of an inch square.

The semiconductor has two primary advantages when used in computer hardware. First, it can be produced in great quantity by mechanical means and is therefore inexpensive. A microprocessor CPU on a chip can cost less than $25 per copy. The second advantage of semiconductors is that the miniaturization of circuits has greatly enhanced the speed of the computer. Technically, the speed at which a CPU operates is

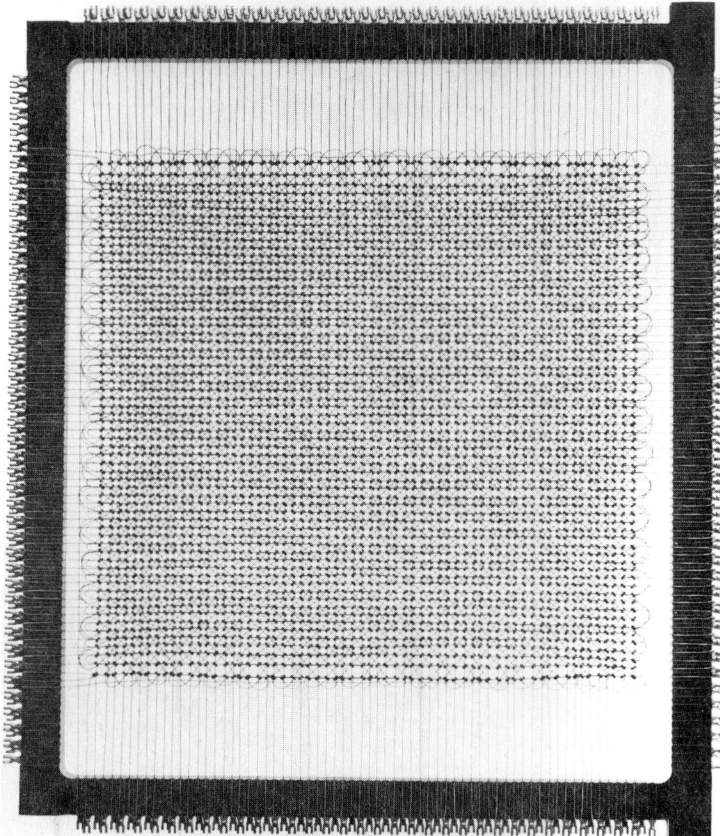

Figure 4-3 Magnetic Core Storage (Courtesy of IBM Corp.)

bounded by two factors: 1) the speed at which electrical currents flow (about the speed of light); and 2) the distance over which currents must flow. Computer designers have been able to greatly decrease current flow distance through miniaturization and thereby increase the speed of CPUs by factors of large magnitude. Improvements in semiconductor technology are the primary driving force behind improvements in computer hardware. Currently, it appears that semiconductor technology has not reached its theoretical limits. Therefore, we can expect additional, substantial improvements in hardware performance.

Semiconductors used for primary storage purposes represent a bit of data by means of an individual circuit that either does or does not conduct electricity. This fact points out the primary disadvantage of using semiconductors for primary storage. When the electrical supply to a CPU using semiconductor storage is interrupted, none of the circuits conduct electricity. Therefore, the CPU loses the data contained in primary storage, including any programs that are there. Semiconductor storage is *volatile;* that is, the storage loses its data representation when electrical power is interrupted. On the other hand, magnetic core storage does not lose its data representation when power is interrupted because the polarity of an individual core remains the same regardless of

Figure 4-4 Semiconductor CPU (Courtesy of Intel Corporation)

whether the power is on or off. This disadvantage of semiconductor primary storage can be overcome with an uninterruptible power source (provided by backup batteries and generators). It can also be overcome by backing up each program as it executes by using *checkpoints* in the program. This means that at certain points in the execution of a program, the data and status of the program can be written onto nonvolatile storage such as magnetic disks so that if a power interruption does occur, the complete program will not have to be reexecuted. Instead, the computer system will simply go back to the nearest checkpoint and begin execution at that point. The volatility of semiconductor storage is a relatively minor disadvantage compared to its advantages.

There are two basic types of semiconductor memory: 1) *random access memory* (RAM); and 2) *read only memory* (ROM). Actually, magnetic core is also RAM memory since access to a particular area of the memory can be performed on a random basis. However, the term RAM is normally used to refer to random access semiconductor memory. RAM and the term *primary storage*, as we have been using it thus far in this book, are synonomous. This kind of memory stores the user's program while it is being executed and stores the data while they are being processed by the CPU. The CPU can perform, read, or write operations on random access memory at any point in time.

Read only memory can only be read from and not written to. Therefore, ROM comes from the manufacturer with programs for functions already stored in it, which the user of the computer cannot modify. ROM is used to store program functions frequently used by many computer applications. An example of such a function would be computing the square root of a number.

This technique of placing software or programs in hardware (the ROM semiconductor) is often called *microcoding* or microprogramming. Microcoded functions in a computer can be changed simply by removing the old ROM and replacing it with another ROM. In this way computers can be tailored to meet the needs of specific users.

There are two subclasses of ROM: 1) *programmable read only memory* (PROM); and 2) *erasable programmable read only memory* (EPROM). PROM may be programmed (a program read into the PROM) one time by either the manufacturer or the computer user. Once PROM is programmed, it it essentially the same as ROM since it cannot be modified. On the other hand, EPROM can be programmed and then subsequently erased through a special process. Once erased, EPROM can be reprogrammed. Semiconductor (chip) memory is illustrated in Figure 4-5.

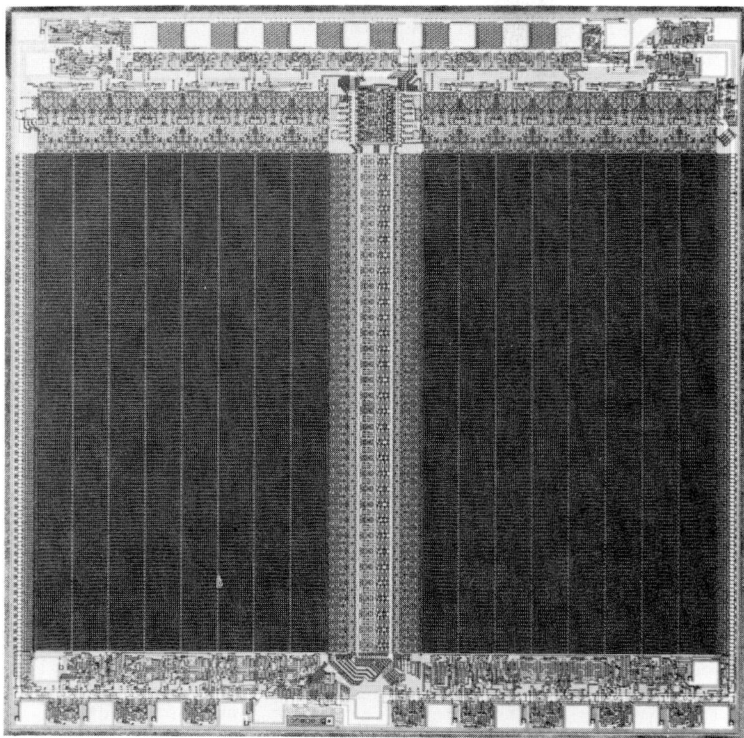

Figure 4-5 Semiconductor Memory (Courtesy of Intel Corporation)

Arithmetic-Logic Unit

The *arithmetic-logic unit* performs arithmetic operations such as multiplication, division, subtraction, and addition. It also performs logical operations, such as comparing the relative magnitude of two pieces of data. Arithmetic-logic operations are performed serially; that is, one at a time, based on instructions from the control unit.

Control Unit

The *control unit* decodes program instructions and directs other components of the computer system to perform the task specified in program instructions. Essentially, two cycles are performed for each program instruction: 1) the *instruction cycle;* and 2) the *execution cycle.* The program instructions are, of course, in machine language. They consist of an operation to be performed, such as addition, subtraction, move, or compare, and operands, which are the things used in the operation of the program such as data and input/output units. The process of executing an individual program instruction begins with the control unit reading and decoding the instruction. This process of decoding the instruction is called the instruction cycle. The execution cycle begins when the control unit causes the appropriate unit to perform the operation called for in the instruction. This unit may be the arithmetic-logic unit, or it may be an input/output unit. Input/output to or from the primary storage of the CPU is handled by channels. Channels are, in effect, small specialized CPUs that handle input and output of data so that the main CPU does not have to commit its time to the relatively mundane, standardized, and time-consuming task of handling input/output operations.

MAINFRAMES, MINIS, AND MICROS

Mainframe Computers

Computer systems are often categorized as mainframes, minis, or micros. *Mainframes* (Figure 4-6) are the large computer systems that typically have over one million bytes of primary storage as well as input/output units associated with a large computer system.

Minicomputers

Minis, or *minicomputers* (Figure 4-7), are medium-sized computer systems that typically have less than one million bytes but greater than 64K (K = 1024) bytes of primary storage. Minicomputers were first developed for use in process control applications. For example, they were used to monitor automated manufacturing processes such as steel rolling and to adjust the manufacturing equipment automatically so as to keep the output within specified tolerances. However, it was quickly seen that these medium-sized computers (when they were first developed they were the smallest of computers) had tremendous potential in the area of business data processing, especially for smaller companies. Minicomputer systems can be equipped with most of the input/output (I/O) devices and secondary storage devices that the large mainframe systems can handle, such as terminals and rigid disks. They are also now making

Figure 4-6 Mainframe Computer (Courtesy of NCR Corporation)

Figure 4-7 Minicomputer System (Courtesy of Digital Equipment Corporation)

possible the installation of distributed data processing systems (see chapter 10). Instead of a company having one large mainframe computer, it may distribute its data processing with a minicomputer at each of its remote locations, and connect them to each other through telecommunication links.

Microcomputers

The smallest of the computer systems are called micros or microcomputers (Figure 4-8). Microcomputer systems typically have between 16K and 256K of primary storage. They can handle peripheral devices like terminals, relatively slow printers, cassette tapes, floppy disks, and small hard disks, called Winchester disks. Microcomputer systems are used by even the smallest of businesses. However, the personal home computer market is also very important for microcomputer vendors. In the home these computers can be used for a wide variety of tasks—from keeping track of the family budget to storing recipes to monitoring the home burgler alarm system. Currently, a small microcomputer system can be purchased for approximately $500. A more sophisticated microcomputer system with a floppy disk and 48K of primary storage can be purchased for approximately $1,600. With high-quality printout and additional memory, these microcomputer systems can cost in the vicinity of $5,000 to $6,000. Because of the increase in power of microcomputers, minis are likely to become obsolete.

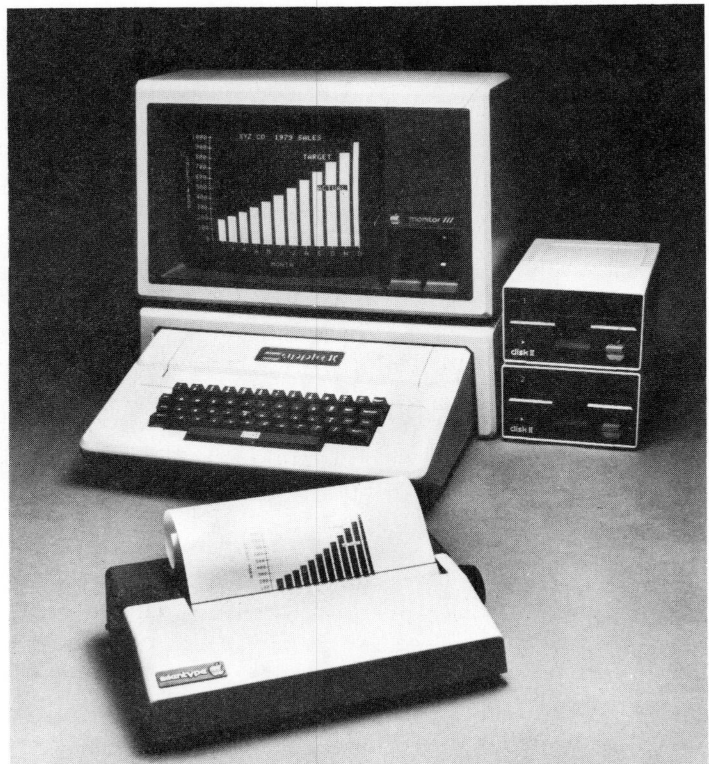

Figure 4-8 Microcomputer System (Courtesy of Apple Computer, Inc.)

Minis certainly overlap mainframes, and micros overlap minis. As minis become more powerful, they tend to perform the jobs mainframes were used for with equal efficiency. Therefore, there is no definite delineation among the three types of computer systems, and the lines of demarcation are constantly changing.

MANAGEMENT CASE 4-1

Lowes Incorporated is a medium-sized regional department store. The company currently has a medium-sized IBM mainframe at its central headquarters. Accounts receivables is run on this mainframe with terminals available in the various stores so that inquiries can be made concerning customer accounts. Some of the store managers feel that accounts receivable should be kept locally at each store. They have argued that a microcomputer such as the IBM PC could be used to keep up with the accounts receivable at each store. Individuals in the central data processing staff have argued that the volume of customers is too great for micros to handle accounts receivable. The store managers have countered this with the argument that two or more micros can be networked together to provide the necessary capacity. In addition, they argue that the micros in the various stores can be networked together. Which direction do you think Lowes should go? Should they maintain accounts receivable on the mainframe as they are currently doing or convert the system to microcomputers?

SECONDARY STORAGE

Primary Versus Secondary Storage

Earlier in this chapter, we covered primary storage and its characteristics. As illustrated in Figure 4-1, primary storage is part of the CPU and must allow very fast access in order to increase the speed at which the CPU can operate. Secondary storage, on the other hand, is physically separate from the CPU. Why do we have this distinction in types of storage? Why isn't the CPU designed with large amounts of primary storage so that all of the data would be randomly accessible at electronic speeds with no mechanical movement? The answer to this question is one of economics. Primary storage is expensive compared to secondary storage. Furthermore, the most widely used primary storage today, semiconductors, is volatile storage. Secondary storage must be nonvolatile; that is, the storage must be able to retain the stored data even when the electrical current is off. All widely used secondary storage media require mechanical movement for access to data. Therefore, it is relatively slow, but in contrast to primary storage it has the capability of storing large amounts of data at relatively lower costs.

Is it likely that computer systems in the future will use only one type of storage. In other words, will there be no physical distinction between primary and secondary storage? Probably not, since the technologically most advanced, fastest, and therefore most expensive storage will be used in the CPU. Secondary storage will continue to use less expensive media since there is always a requirement that secondary storage store large amounts of data. However, as we will see in chapter 6, some memory management systems now being used, such as virtual storage, blur the distinction between secondary and primary storage. With virtual storage, the user gets the impression that all data and programs are stored in primary storage, even though physically they are still being stored in secondary storage.

Magnetic Tape

Magnetic tape has long been an important medium for secondary storage. Supplied on reels in lengths up to 2,400 feet, the tape is normally one-half inch wide. It is similar in appearance to tape recorder tape, but is of higher quality. Figure 4-9 illustrates data encoded on magnetic tape using the EBCDIC coding scheme. As can be seen, there are nine horizontal tracks on the illustrated magnetic tape. A character of data is recorded in one column across the tape. Nine-track magnetic tape is by far the most common, although seven-, eight-, and ten-track tapes are available. They use different coding schemes for each character. Figure 4-10 illustrates a typical magnetic tape drive.

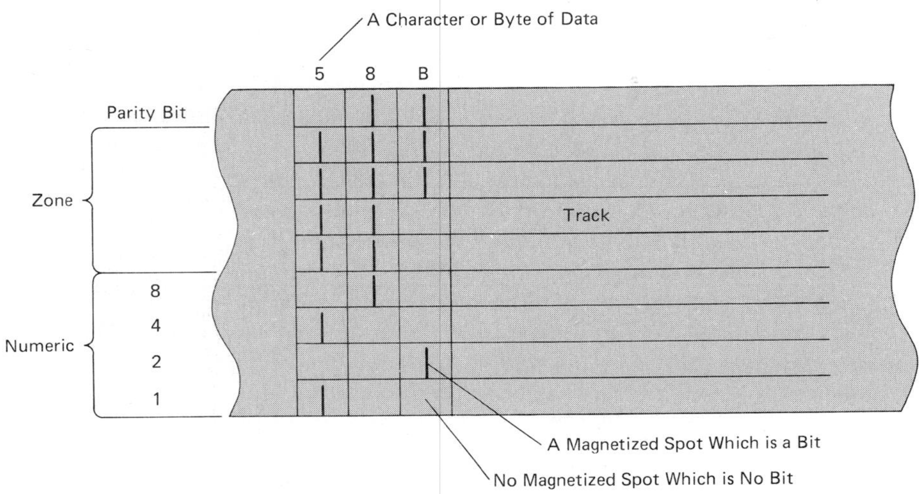

Figure 4-9 EBCDIC Coded Data on a Magnetic Tape

The *recording density* of magnetic tape refers to the number of bits per inch (BPI) or characters per linear inch that are recorded on a specific reel of tape.[1] The most common recording densities are 200, 556, 800, 1600, and 6250 BPI.

Another form of magnetic tape that is widely used on microcomputer systems is cassette tape (See Figure 4-11). Physically, these cassettes are identical to cassettes used in stereo sound systems, although the tape used with computers is often of a higher quality. These tapes are written to and read from by a standard audio tape recorder connected to the microcomputer. The primary advantage of cassette tape to the microcomputer user is its very low cost. Cartridges themselves are from $3 to $5 each, and the tape recorder typically costs from $50 to $70. A big disadvantage of cassette tapes is that they allow only sequential access to data. This can significantly increase the time it takes a microcomputer to perform an application.

[1]BPI is also equivalent to bytes or characters per inch of magnetic tape since a byte is recorded across the tape (see Figure 4-9.)

Figure 4-10 Magnetic Tape Drive (Courtesy of Hewlett-Packard Company)

Figure 4-11 Magnetic Tape Cassette (Courtesy of NCR Corporation)

The advantages of magnetic tape include:

1. Low cost compared to other forms of secondary storage.
2. Computer systems can use several tape drives simultaneously.
3. Compared to cards, the data transfer rate of tape is very fast.
4. As a storage medium, magnetic tape is very compact and portable.
5. Magnetic tape provides an ideal form of backup storage of data.
6. Magnetic tape devices have several self-checking features; therefore, the recording and reading of data on magnetic tape is highly reliable.
7. Record lengths on magnetic tape can be of unlimited size as long as they are within the limits of the individual computer system.
8. Magnetic tape can be used over and over for storage of different data simply by writing the new data over the old. This feature also allows mistakes to be corrected by simply writing over the old data.

Disadvantages of magnetic tape include:

1. Since magnetic tape is a sequential storage medium, to find an individual record stored on magnetic tape, the tape must be read up to the location of the desired record.
2. Damage to magnetic tape can result in the complete loss of data stored on a section of the tape near the damaged area. Therefore, critical data stored on magnetic tape should be backed up by storage on another tape or on another storage medium.
3. Magnetic tape is sensitive to dust, humidity, and temperature changes; consequently, the environment in which it is stored must be closely controlled.

•

Magnetic Disk

Magnetic disk (an example of which is shown in Figure 4-12) is currently the most popular form of secondary storage. There are two basic types of magnetic disk: 1)

Figure 4-12 Magnetic Disk (Courtesy of IBM Corp.)

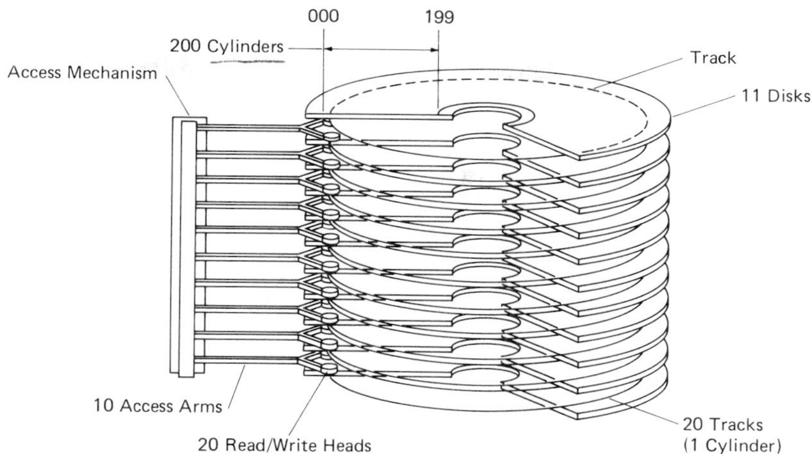

Figure 4-13 Disk Pack with Access Arms

floppy disk; and 2) *hard disk.* Floppy disk is a very important form of secondary storage for microcomputer systems. However, we will first discuss hard disk, which is the type used mostly with mainframe computers. Figure 4-13 illustrates a disk pack with access arms. This disk pack has eleven individual disks, each with two surfaces, top and bottom. In the illustrated disk, items are not stored on the top surface of the top disk or the bottom surface of the bottom disk. Consequently, there are twenty surfaces in the disk pack on which data can be stored. Within each surface, data are stored on concentric tracks. The same amount of data is stored on the outside tracks as on the tracks in the center of the disk, even though the circumferences of these tracks differ substantially. However, the time it takes for the disk to complete one revolution is the same for any track on the disk; and therefore, the amount of data written on each track is identical.

If we assume that our illustrated disk has two hundred tracks on each surface, then the access arms can position themselves in two hundred different track positions. When the access arm is positioned over one of these tracks, data can be read or written onto one track on each recording surface without moving the access arm. These twenty tracks at one position of the read/write access arms are known collectively as a cylinder. When data are stored sequentially on a disk, they are stored by cylinder. That is, all of the tracks in a cylinder are filled prior to filling any tracks in the adjacent cylinder. The cylinder approach improves read and write access speeds to the disk. The speed of access to data on a disk is a function of both the rotational speed of the disk and the speed with which the access arms move. Using the cylinder approach minimizes the need for moving the access arms.

Microcomputers can also use a form of hard disk, called Winchester disks. Winchester disk units contain a small (5¼ inch) nonremovable hard disk that can store up to 20 million bytes of data. These units costs approximately $2,500.

The advantages of magnetic disk include:

1. Magnetic disk is a direct access storage medium and therefore, individual records can be retrieved without searching through the entire file.

2. Although disks are more expensive than magnetic tape, their cost has steadily declined over the years.
3. For online systems requiring direct access, disks are currently the only practical means of file storage. Drum storage is too expensive, and other new types of storage, such as bubble storage, are not widely used yet.
4. Records can be readily updated by writing the new information over the area where the old information was stored.
5. With removable disk packs, a single disk drive can access a large number of disk packs. This method is especially economical with batch processing applications, which do not require frequent switching between disk packs. By using the same disk drive to access more than one disk pack, the cost of the disk drive is spread over a larger volume of stored data.
6. Interrelated files stored on magnetic disk can allow a single transaction to be processed against all of these files simultaneously.

The disadvantages of magnetic disk include:

1. Relative to magnetic tape, disk is expensive.
2. Updating a master file stored on disk destroys the old information. Therefore, disk does not provide an automatic audit trail and backup the way magnetic tape does. Subsequent to updating a master file stored on magnetic tape, there still exists the old master file, the new master file, and the transaction file on three separate reels of tape. When disk is used, equivalent backup and audit trail require that each old master file record be copied to another medium prior to update.
3. For periodic batch-type systems having no need for between-run data retrieval from the files, magnetic tape will serve just as well as disks for file storage purposes and will cost substantially less.

MANAGEMENT CASE 4-2

Randy Gilmer is the controller of Atlantic Industries, a conglomerate with several subsidiaries. Currently, each of the fifty subsidiaries has approximately 1,000 accounts in their accounting system. Data is stored by month for each of these accounts extending back over a 10 year period. This data is currently stored on online disks. The Management Information Systems Department would like to either purge some of the older data or store it on magnetic tape. The controller however, has argued that his staff needs historical data that can be called up on a terminal for unanticipated analysis purposes. Do you think that this large amount of data should be stored online? What about the alternative of storing some of the older data on magnetic tape?

Floppy Disk

Floppy disks (often called cassette disks) are flat 5¼- or 8-inch disks of polyester film with a magnetic coating. As illustrated in Figure 4-14, the disk is covered with a protective envelope, and reading/writing from or to the disk is performed through an access hole. Most disks have a capacity of 320K bytes, although some will store 640 or more K bytes.

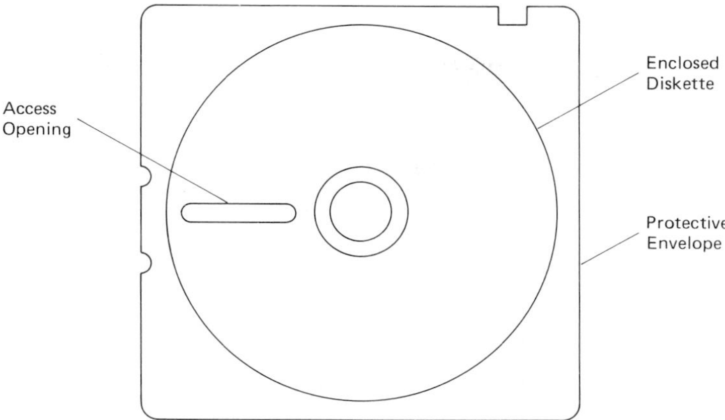

Figure 4-14 Floppy Disk

Floppy disks were originally developed by IBM in the early 1970s for use as secondary storage on minicomputers. However, they have also developed into a versatile medium for data input. In addition, they are widely used for secondary storage on microcomputers. The typical floppy disk used with microcomputers is 5¼ inches in diameter and can store up to 320K bytes of data. Drives for these disks cost about $500 each.

The primary advantages of floppy disks are their relatively low cost (since they can be reused over and over), their large capacity, and small size. The equivalent of 4,096 fully punched 80 column cards can be stored on a single floppy disk.

Other Forms of Secondary Storage

Another type of direct access storage is the mass storage device. These devices, such as the IBM 3850, can store very large amounts of data and access it without human intervention (Figure 4-15). The 3850 mass storage subsystem can store up to 472 billion bytes of data. This is approximately the amount of data that can be stored on 47,200 2,400 foot reels of magnetic tape. Data in this system are stored on small fist sized cartridges, which are in turn stored in honeycomb-like cells. Cartridge accessors can remove the cartridges from the cell and place them on a read/write unit. The data is actually stored within the cartridge on a 3 × 770 inch strip of magnetic tape.

Because of the relatively large amount of physical movement (even though it is machine movement), mass storage data systems provide much slower access to data than a magnetic disk unit. In fact, some users have found that data can be accessed just as fast using 6,250 BPI magnetic tape.

In the past, magnetic drums were an important form of secondary storage. In fact, the IBM 650 computer used them for primary storage. In drum storage, data are stored on the cylindrical surface of a large rotating drum. Although the access time to data stored on a drum is generally faster than for magnetic disk, drums are more expensive than disk. Also, they are not removable from the drum drive mechanism. Therefore,

Figure 4-15 Mass Storage Device (Courtesy of IBM Corp.)

their storage capacity relative to removable disks is limited. Drum storage is now approaching obsolescence.

FUTURE STORAGE TECHNOLOGY

Bubble Storage

As technology continues to advance, new forms of storage are likely to be used. In the late 1970s, bubble storage was expected to make magnetic disk storage obsolete (Figure 4-16). In a bubble storage system, data are stored through the polarization of microscopic bubbles that exist in certain crystalline substances. Bubble storage has potentially faster access time and vastly greater miniaturization than disk storage. For example, Honeywell ran advertisements claiming that it was developing a bubble storage device that would have the capacity to store all the data in the New York Public

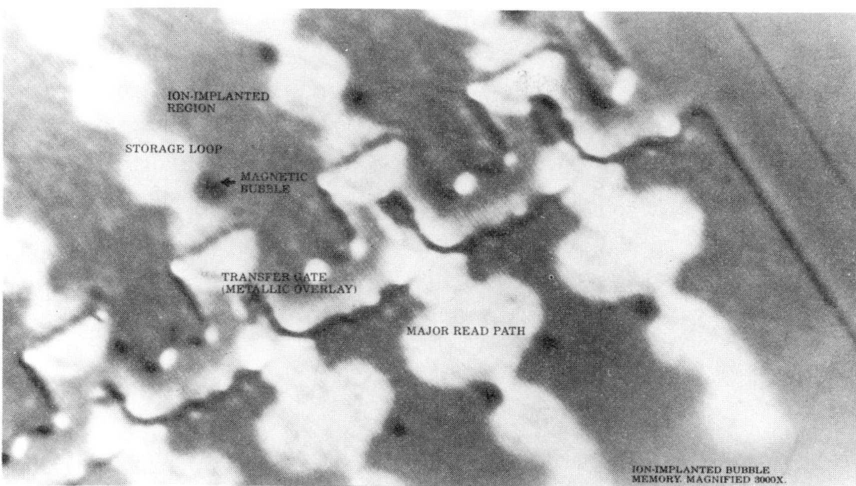

Figure 4-16 Bubble Storage (Courtesy of Bell Labs)

Library in an area the size of an average closet. Bubble storage is also nonvolatile. Initially, bubble storage appeared to be an almost ideal form of secondary storage. However, due to the fact that its production cost failed to decline at the same time it was being introduced, and because significant advances were made in disk storage technology, bubble storage has yet to be widely used. It is, however, being used today in limited applications, such as internal storage for portable computer terminals.

Laser Storage

Laser storage systems promise to store large amounts of data at economical costs. Laser beams can be used to form patterns, or in the case of printers—characters—on various surfaces. In the storage application of lasers, these patterns would be microscopic in size. They could be read by reflecting light off the surface, similar to the way the Uniform Product Code is read in a grocery store checkout lane.

Certainly new forms of secondary and primary storage will be developed. However, magnetic disks and semiconductors are likely to continue to be the major types of secondary and primary storage respectively even into the 1990s and perhaps longer simply because improvements in these two technologies continue to significantly reduce their cost.

SUMMARY

The central processing unit of a computer is its single most important component.

Digital computers represent information internally as strings of binary digits, i.e., zeroes and ones. These computers are used extensively in business applications.

Analog computers represent quantities in terms of physical attributes like voltage level. Such computers are used primarily for scientific and engineering purposes.

The primary storage unit stores the program that is currently being executed, along with data records being processed.

Primary storage must be on a fast access device in order for the CPU to be able to function at electronic speeds.

Magnetic core used to be a common storage device for primary memory. Today, however, semiconductors provide a cheaper and much faster medium for storage. Advances in semiconductor technology promise even better performance in the future.

Random access memory (RAM) allows the CPU to read any particular data or program instruction on a random basis.

Read only memory (ROM) can only be read from and not written to. It is used to store program functions widely used by many computer applications, which need not be modified.

The arithmetic-logic unit performs arithmetic operations and logical comparisons on data.

The control unit interprets program instructions and arranges for their execution. It typically calls on other units to actually execute the instructions.

Computers may be classified into three groups: 1) mainframes; 2) minis; and 3) microcomputers.

Secondary storage is an essential part of a computer system. It is used for storing the bulk of data as well as programs not currently being used. Secondary storage devices normally use some mechanical movement to access data, which makes them relatively slow.

Magnetic reel tape and magnetic cassette tape are widely used secondary storage media.

Magnetic tapes offer the advantages of being inexpensive, compact, fast, accurate, portable, and reusable. However, it is necessary to handle them carefully and protect them from dirt and humidity.

Magnetic disk is the most popular form of secondary storage. Its major advantage is its random access capability. Any piece of data on the disk may be accessed quickly with very little mechanical movement.

The cost of disk storage is steadily declining. It is a very useful direct access method for online systems. Its major disadvantage is that it does not provide an automatic audit trail or backup facility.

Other forms of secondary storage include mass storage and magnetic drums.

In the future, magnetic bubble storage and laser storage systems might also be adapted for secondary memory purposes. However, disk and semiconductor devices are expected to retain their importance for a long time yet.

KEY TERMS

Central Processing Unit (CPU)
Digital Computer
Analog Computer
Mainframe Computer
Minicomputer
Microcomputer
Bit
Byte
Control Unit
Primary Storage
Arithmetic-logic Unit
Secondary Storage
Magnetic Core
Semiconductor Memory
Volatile Memory
Nonvolatile Memory
Checkpoints
Random Access Memory (RAM)
Read Only Memory (ROM)
Microcoding (Microprogramming)
Operation Code
Operand
Distributed Data Processing
Memory Management Systems
Virtual Storage
Magnetic Tape
Recording Density
Magnetic Disk
Rigid Disk
Floppy Disk
Cylinder
Direct Access Storage
Audit Trail
Backup
Mass Storage
Magnetic Drum
Bubble Storage
Laser Storage

REVIEW QUESTIONS

1. What is the most important piece of equipment in a computer system?
2. Distinguish between a digital and an analog computer.
3. What is a "byte"?
4. List the three components of a central processing unit.
5. What are the major functions of the primary storage unit?
6. Why does primary storage have to be faster than secondary storage?
7. Describe the advantages of semiconductor memory.
8. Why is nonvolatile memory more desirable than volatile memory?
9. Describe random access memory (RAM) and explain its advantage.
10. Why is the arithmetic logic unit crucial to a computer's operation?
11. Describe the two cycles performed by the control unit.
12. How can we differentiate between mainframe, mini and microcomputers?
13. Why is a computer's memory divided into primary and secondary storage?
14. List four advantages of using magnetic tape for secondary storage.
15. Describe the concept of a cylinder in connection with magnetic disks.
16. What is the advantage of a direct access storage device?

DISCUSSION QUESTIONS

1. Small businesses are rapidly adopting mini and microcomputer systems to automate their record-keeping functions. Some data processing experts believe that these small systems are not a wise choice for the long run because business will soon outgrow them. It may be better strategy to rent computing power from an outside agency or to buy a large computer. What criteria should the business person use to decide whether to buy a small computer, a large computer, or to rent computer time?
2. A large primary storage unit enables the computer to retrieve and store data quickly, and thus operate at a high speed. However, primary storage is more expensive than secondary storage. What factors need to be considered when deciding on the amount of primary storage to be purchased? Identify two examples of business applications that would require large and small primary storage areas respectively.
3. Magnetic tape is a suitable storage medium for data that must be processed sequentially (e.g., printing of all the addresses that are on a mailing list). On the other hand, magnetic disk is more efficient for applications requiring random access (e.g., finding the quantity available for a specific inventory item). How would you go about deciding whether to use a sequential or direct access device for a particular application?

RESEARCH PROJECTS

1. Review a recent issue of *Personal Computing, Popular Computing* or *Byte* and report on some developments in the area of microcomputers.
2. Write an essay on progress in semiconductor technology and its implications for future data storage systems.

APPLICATION CASE

Thinking Small

(Wall Street Journal, Aug. 19, 1983, pp. 1–2)

By Erik Larson and Carrie Dolan, Staff Reporters of the Wall Street Journal

SANTA CLARA, Calif.—About a year ago, Matt Sanders got kicked out of his office.

His belongings were packed in boxes, and two new workers moved into the space at Convergent Technologies Inc., a Silicon Valley computer maker. Mr. Sanders hung around the building for a few days, borrowing desks, without a phone to call his own.

"If you get into trouble, call me," said his boss, Allen Michels, "and if you get some good news, call me, too. But I ain't calling you." Mr. Michels adds: "Let me tell you he was scared."

Mr. Sanders wasn't being fired, and he wasn't in trouble with his boss. On the contrary, he had been named leader of what Mr. Michels calls a "strike force" to build a new computer that would enable Convergent, which makes high-priced business computers, to enter the market for lower-priced personal computers in just one year. The idea was to tap into the entrepreneurial forces that energize so many Silicon Valley start-ups by cutting Mr. Sanders loose and letting him form his own "company-within-a-company." It's an approach that several large or maturing technology companies are turning to.

Quicker Reflexes

Companies say that small groups, given great freedom, can react better and more quickly to the abrupt changes in electronics technology that constantly buffet the valley. Unlike industries where change is more gradual, computer makers must regularly come up with new products or enhancements of the old, and for ever-lower costs. An electric-toaster model might sell for years, but a computer, particularly at the lower-priced end of the market, might have a life span of only 18 months before technology passed it by.

Apple Computer Inc. turned to a small group to help develop its Lisa, a $10,000 easy-to-use machine for business people. Timex Corp. did likewise to get into the computer business quickly with is Timex Sinclair 1000. Daniel Ross, the vice president and chief operating officer of the Timex Computer unit, says one virtue of the small-group approach is that responsibility gets pushed to lower-level employees. Also, he says, small groups can better focus their energies on a single goal. "Creativity is fostered in this kind of organization," he says.

Even giant International Business Machines Corp. has recognized the need for small working groups, especially in producing new products. It has formed 14 "independent business units" to capture the entrepreneurial spirit in work on such product lines as factory robotic systems. "The centralized organization just prevented innovation," says Peter Wright, a longtime IBM watcher and the director of research for the Gartner Group, a research concern. "They had problems because good ideas weren't getting out to the marketplace."

How to Beat the Japanese

Mr. Michels, the president and chief executive officer of Convergent, sees this approach as no less than the country's salvation in the electronics race with the Japanese. "The safety of the U.S. capitalist system relies on this," he says. "It's the only thing I know of that can keep us competitive with other companies and other systems." The use of small working groups is more productive for Americans, he argues, than trying to adopt Japanese management styles, which are dependent on the Japanese worker's intense loyalty to company and product.

"You keep things small so you can create a culture, the right culture," says Mr. Michels, a cofounder of Convergent (in 1979). "You inject a harmonious attitude. You give them the right amount of freedom so that there is no sense of futility."

And so the 30-year-old Mr. Sanders, who holds a master's degree in product design from Stanford University, was unceremoniously booted out of his office and left to wander the halls of Convergent. "The team consisted of me," says Mr. Sanders. "I was terrified." Mr. Michels, a portly cigar-chomper, watched Mr. Sanders. "I felt bad for him. It was awful," he says. "But tell me, does any little baby robin want to get kicked out of its nest?"

Mr. Sanders even had to find a new nest on his own. He settled on a slightly shabby one-story building that used to house a credit union. Employees call it the "vault," after a big safe in one corridor, and people still wander in to apply for loans. "I picked it out myself," beams Mr. Sanders. "It's a real dump."

The only help Mr. Sanders got was money. He wasn't allowed to take any Convergent employees with him. Armed only with a rough idea of what the machine would be, he set out to raid Hewlett-Packard Co., Texas Instruments Inc., Motorola Inc. and Atari Inc., promising recruits the chance to create a business and a product from the ground up. "Just starting at ground zero was very exciting," says Todd Lynch, the 34-year-old hardware engineering manager. He was hired away from Hewlett-Packard, where he had worked for 10 years.

Mr. Sanders says that when he was recruiting people he had to convince them that Convergent was serious about letting them build the machine and get it done fast. He also had to make them believe that their compensation would be comparable to what a true entrepreneur would reap for his risks. "The only thing they had to take on faith," he says, "was that Convergent would reward them handsomely when the product succeeds, not just chew them up for some selfish company goal." Most staff members were given Convergent stock when they signed on.

Mr. Sanders says that although the group resembles a start-up company in many ways, its creation obviously entailed less risk. "We had a healthy company behind us, with the financial resources to help things happen."

Convergent and the working group kept in close touch, says Mr. Sanders, with certain Convergent managers acting as "kind of an informal board of directors." He says he got advice from Mr. Michels and others at Convergent, but "all the decision making is done here. The day-to-day business decisions rest on our shoulders, as does the responsibility for the product's success."

He says Convergent gave the division a budget and let it decide how to spend money.

Secrecy is one of the advantages of setting up this sort of small group apart from the parent company, says Mr. Michels. The 50-member group assumed the code name "Ultra," after an Allied method of deciphering Nazi communiques during World War II. Convergent didn't even tell most of its parent-based employees what the group was doing. Members of Ultra typically clued in their families but swore them to silence. (One divorced software engineer gave his two teen-agers strict orders to say nothing—they live with their mother and her husband, an Atari executive.)

But in Silicon Valley, where even the apricot trees seem to have ears, rumors blossomed. Some had been planted by Convergent in a deliberate effort to mislead gossips. "If we became uncomfortable that somebody knew too much, we would vector it off," says Mr. Michels.

Enter WorkSlate

The rumors had Ultra building everything from a high-powered graphics work station to a $300 home computer. Mr. Lynch, the hardware manager, says he didn't mind stray gossip but got a little nervous when it came close to the mark.

Actually, the machine—to be unveiled formally on Tuesday—represents the convergence of many trends in the computer business: It is portable, it has a built-in speaker telephone, it has a voice and data tape-recorder. And it comes with a lot of functions already programmed in, including a spreadsheet that lets the user calculate, say, depreciation. The built-in programs also let one perform calculator functions, store phone numbers and dial them with the push of a button. Available software enables the user to do other tasks, including expense accounts and tax calculations.

Called "WorkSlate," the portable machine is about the length and width of a piece of typing paper and less than an inch deep. It costs $895.

It is, of course, just one of hundreds of new high-tech products that will hit the market this year, and the market's response to it is by no means certain. Still, its creators talk about it with an intense, parental devotion. "It's been an enormous physical and emotional commitment, which must be something like pregnancy," says Mr. Sanders. (Some employees note that the product's gestation period was about nine months.) "But at least when you're pregnant, you don't know how the child will turn out. Here, you see the 'child' being built every moment of every day. You have the chance to make it perfect. It's a hell of a burden."

The Man in the Machine

In Silicon Valley, it is the product that drives people—the chance to see their handiwork in a machine that people will use. That's what drew many of Ultra's crew from so many other larger organizations to such a risky small venture. "Everybody has a larger percentage of what we're doing," says Mr. Lynch. "When the machine goes out the door, they can point to pieces and say, 'That's mine.' " Bill Burnett, 26, an Ultra product designer, says, "All designers really like to see what they do turn into reality. Most places that's about a two-year, two-and-a-half-year cycle."

Karen Toland, who had 10 years of marketing experience with Savin Corp., is the marketing director and self-described "mother" of the machine (Mr. Sanders is considered the father). She says it could only have been produced by a small group. "I don't have to go through two department heads and write six memos if something needs to be changed. I just walk across the hall and say, 'Hey, Charlie, this space bar feels like . . . and then he fixes it."

She says that producing the product was an intense process of give and take, made easier because everybody knew everybody else so well. She recalls "lots of arguments" with engineers when she wanted to call a button on the computer a "Do It" key instead of the more standard, computer-jargon "Execute." "They thought I was nuts," she says. The matter was thoroughly thrashed out, and the machine now has a "Do It" key.

Perfection, however, is elusive. "It'll never be right," says Mr. Lynch the hardware manager. "There's always someone who'll say 'Gee, I like your machine, but I wish it could toast bread.' " John Powers, manager of software development notes, "A product is never ever done."

Having found a way of channeling this drive, Mr. Michels, Convergent's president, worries about how the Ultra people will cope now—how they will handle the "postpartum depression" he says will come once the group begins shipping its first machines to paying customers.

The people at Ultra haven't spent much time thinking about what will happen when it's all over. But most know there will be some kind of letdown. "I think we're all fearing that," says Charles M. Fiorella, the 33-year-old product-design engineering manager. "The fun on the big one will be over. The first one's always special."

Right now, however, there's a more pressing anxiety. What will people *say* about the machine? "I'll die when the reviews come out," says Miss Toland. "I'm so nervous. It must be how people feel when they make a Broadway play."

Discussion

The manufacture of computer hardware is a highly competitive and potentially lucrative business.

1. Do you think the information needs of management has driven the innovation in computers or vice versa?
2. In your opinion, has most of the innovation in computers come from small or large firms?

CHAPTER 5

DATA ENTRY AND INFORMATION RESPONSE

INTRODUCTION

In the previous chapter we covered the CPU and secondary storage devices. Data entry and information response devices link the CPU with human beings. Advances are continually being made in these links between the central processing unit and human beings, making it easier and more natural to communicate with the computer. The term *peripheral device* is often used as a name for any hardware device that is not the CPU. Therefore, data entry storage and output devices can also be called peripheral devices. As we discuss data entry devices you will note that quite often the same media (such as magnetic disks) are used both for data entry and secondary storage.

A distinction is usually made between the media and devices used for data entry, storage, or output. The medium is the material on which the data is actually recorded, such as magnetic tape, whereas the device is the complete unit that reads or writes on the medium, such as a tape drive. Similarly, a printer is an output device, and paper is an output medium.

Many data entry/information response devices of different types are currently available. This chapter will discuss various data entry/information response devices in widespread use, or that are expected to be in widespread use in the next five years. The chapter will not cover some of the more exotic devices, which are certainly useful in specific situations, but are limited in application.

DATA ENTRY

Punched Cards

The eighty-column punched card illustrated in Figure 5-1 is the original input, storage and output medium for computers. It was developed by Herman Hollerith for use in the 1890 census and was used in electronic accounting machine (EAM) equipment prior to the development of the computer in the 1940s. Early computer systems such as the IBM 650, which was introduced in the 1950s as one of the first commercial data processing computers, even used punched cards for secondary storage. The use of punched cards for computer-based systems is, in effect, a carryover from the EAM equipment that was used before computers were developed.

As can be seen in Figure 5-1, characters are coded in the punched card in each column by a combination of punches in twelve different punch positions. For example, the digit 4 is represented by a punch in punch position 4 and the digit K is represented by punches in punch position 2 and in the 11th or X position of the card.

Two primary advantages of the punched card are its simplicity and the fact that human beings can read the data on the card because the punches are interpreted on the top edge of the card. Punched cards can be used as original documents or as turn-around documents, as in the case of a bill being mailed out in punched-card form and being returned with the payment. In addition, a complete transaction record can often be contained in the eighty columns of a punched card.

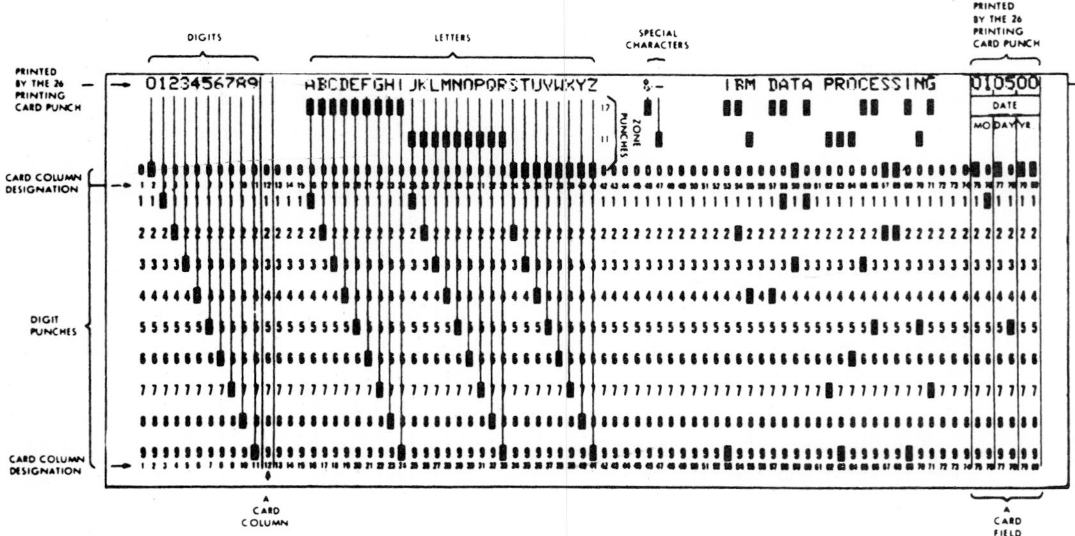

Figure 5-1 Eighty-Column Hollerith Coded Punched Card

The disadvantages of the punched card include the following:

1. They are expensive compared to other input media.
2. They are bulky, and input of information from punched cards is slow compared to input of data from other media, such as floppy disks.
3. Punched cards cannot be reused as magnetic media can.
4. Cards are easily damaged and are difficult to read into the computer whenever they are damaged or warped.
5. Each card is limited to eighty columns, so multiple cards are necesary to accommodate records that are longer than eighty bytes.

Punched cards are rapidly becoming obsolete because of the use of CRT terminals for data entry.

Key-to-Tape Data Entry

A *key-to-tape* device records data on magnetic tape, which are in the form of reels or cassettes (see Figure 5-2). The key-to-tape system normally has a small memory to store each record until it is completely keyed in and copied to the tape. A small TV-like screen allows the operator to view the data that has been keyed in for verification purposes. Key-to-tape systems may be either stand-alone or clustered systems. In a stand-alone system, each keying device is separate and is not interconnected with other keying devices. The data recorded on individual tapes from each of the devices are combined into a single magnetic tape for computer processing. Under a clustered system, several keyboards are connected to one or two magnetic tape drives; thus the combining of individual tapes for further computer processing is eliminated. Clustered systems tend to be less expensive on a per keyboard basis than stand-alone systems.

The concepts used in stand-alone and clustered systems also apply to key-to-disk and key-to-diskette systems, which we will discuss later in this chapter. The primary advantages of key-to-tape are that the tape is reuseable and that the keying operation is faster and much quieter than with punched cards. Furthermore, the magnetic tape is a compact data entry medium, and records of greater than 80 bytes length may be entered. Use of key-to-tape data entry is declining fast due to the advantages of the other methods of data entry to be discussed in this chapter.

Key-to-Diskette Data Entry

Diskettes (or floppy disks) are flat 5¼- or 8-inch disks of polyester film with a magnetic coating. As illustrated in Figure 5-3, the diskette is covered with a protective envelope, and reading/writing from or to the diskette is performed through an access opening. Each diskette has a capacity of approximately 160 to 1200 kilobytes. Key-to-diskette systems can be either stand-alone or clustered systems.

The primary advantages of diskettes are their relatively low cost (since they can be used over and over), their large capacity, and small size compared to punched cards. The equivalent of 6400 fully punched cards can be stored on a single 512 kilobyte diskette.

Figure 5-2 Key-to-Tape System (Courtesy of Inforex)

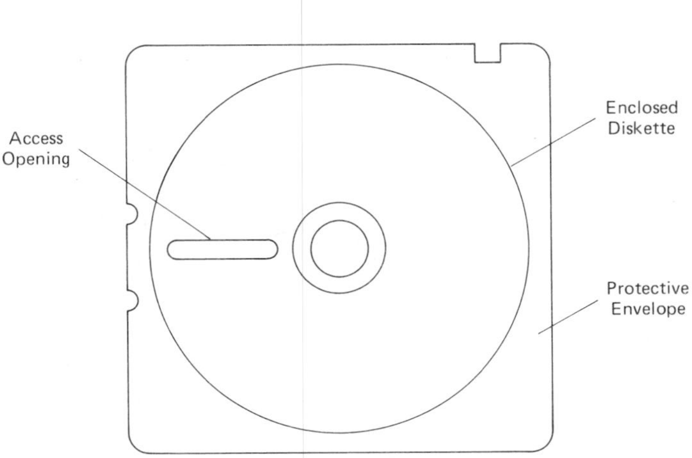

Figure 5-3 Floppy Disk

Key-to-Disk Data Entry

Many medium- and larger-sized companies are now using *key-to-disk* data input as shown in Figure 5-4. In this approach, a minicomputer is dedicated to the data entry function, and it supports a number of CRT terminals that are online to it. They are thus clustered data entry systems. Also online to the minicomputer is a hard disk unit that is used to store the data that have been keyed into the system. The typical procedure for use of a key-to-disk input system is to key the data initially from the source document onto the disk from a keyboard. As the data are keyed in, the minicomputer can execute edit programs to screen the data for errors that can be detected without reference to the master files to which the transaction data pertain.

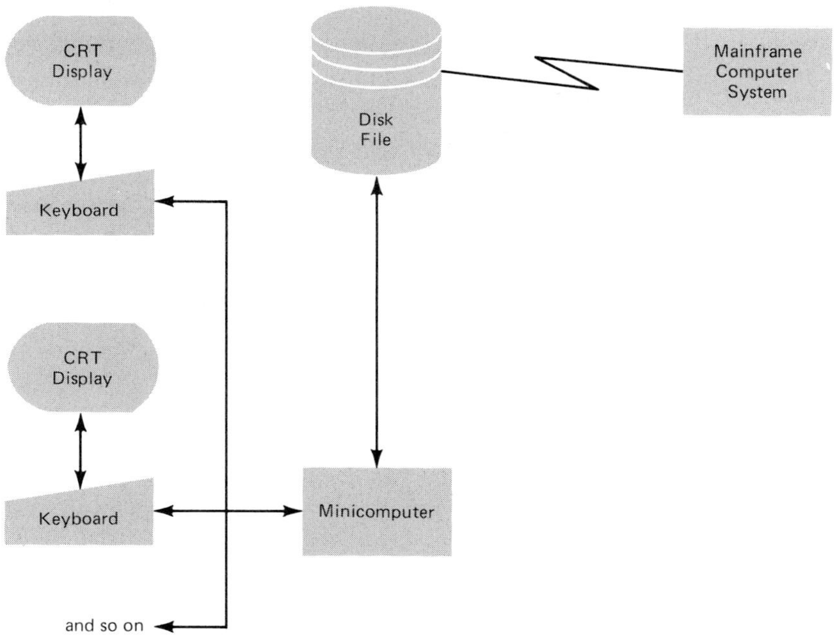

Figure 5-4 Key-to-Disk Data Entry

Once the data have been stored on the disk, key verification can be performed through the use of a key verification program executed by the minicomputer. Essentially, the data are keyed in a second time, and the key verification program compares the data that exist on the storage disk to the data that are keyed in the second time. After the data are verified, the minicomputer can produce control totals for balancing purposes. When the balancing step is complete, and any necessary corrections to the data have been made, the data are transferred to the mainframe CPU for processing. This transmission is usually performed through communication lines between the minicomputer and the mainframe CPU. However, the transmission can be performed by other means, such as magnetic tape.

We should emphasize that key-to-diskette systems (as discussed in the previous section) can operate like hard disk systems if the input device contains a microprocessor

Figure 5-5 Data Entry Stations (Courtesy of Inforex)

and can therefore execute input programs. The primary difference between the two systems is that the floppy disk system is for smaller-scale operations. Data entry stations that can be used for either floppy disk or key-to-hard disk are shown in Figure 5-5.

The advantages of a key-to-disk input system are as follows:

1. A large percentage of the editing and control total balancing can be performed at the time of data entry. Keying errors are often detected immediately when they occur, and therefore the operator has a much better chance of correcting them.
2. Key verification is easily performed on a key-to-disk system where a minicomputer is dedicated to the data entry system.
3. The minicomputer can execute various programs providing instructions, prompts, or input masks to assist the operator in entering data.
4. The minicomputer can compile and report various statistics concerning the data input operation, including operator productivity statistics and error rates. These statistics can be very valuable in determining which operators need additional instruction.
5. Input and verification with a key-to-disk system are considerably faster than with cards because the mechanical movement of cards is eliminated.

The primary disadvantages of key-to-disk data entry include:

1. The initial cost of a separate computer system dedicated to data input may be prohibitive for the smaller firm. However, the cost of computer hardware continues to decline.
2. A separate computer data entry system may not be necessary when a company's computer system has excess capacity and multiprogramming capability. In this case, the data can be entered directly to the mainframe system and processed immediately or stored in batches for later processing in a batch system.

Interactive Data Entry

Under *interactive data entry*, data are entered directly into the production CPU through a data entry terminal (Figure 5-6) with either immediate processing against the

Figure 5-6 A Data Entry Terminal (Courtesy of NCR Corporation)

master file or storage in batches on magnetic disks for later processing. A production CPU is the CPU that processes the application to which the input data pertain. If the system is a batch processing system, this type of data input is very similar to the key-to-disk discussed above except that, instead of a separate minicomputer for data entry, the production CPU handles the task that the minicomputer would handle. For a realtime system, interactive input is the only practical type of input since the master files must be updated when an event occurs so that they reflect real-world activities.

Essentially, interactive input has all the advantages discussed above under a key-to-disk system, since the production computer can perform any of the functions that the minicomputer can perform. Other advantages include:

1. Additional editing, which is not possible under a separate minicomputer data entry system, can be performed if the master files to which the transaction data pertain are online. Many edit checks depend on data stored in the master file. For example, under the assumption that all valid employees have a master file record, the input of weekly time data for an employee can be checked against the master file to see if the social security number being entered exists on the master file.
2. If excess capacity exists, the data entry function can use production CPU time that would otherwise not be used.

Disadvantages of interactive input include:

1. The production CPU may not have enough excess capacity to perform the data entry operation without degrading turn-around time on other jobs.
2. Unless master files are online and can be used for input data editing, a minicomputer can perform data entry operations for batch-type systems as efficiently and sometimes more efficiently than the mainframe CPU.

Interactive data entry can be performed by either intelligent or dumb terminals. An *intelligent terminal* contains a microprocessor that can execute small programs. Therefore, intelligent terminals can perform certain types of editing functions internally rather than relying on the minicomputer or the production CPU. This feature can reduce the load on the production CPU. *Dumb terminals* do not have microprocessors. Therefore, they are simply input devices that can also display output from the CPU to which the terminal is connected.

Source-Data Automation

Source-data automation is the capture of data, in computer-readable form, at the time and location of an event. This is often done through the capture of data as a by-product of some other operation usually not thought of as being part of a data entry operation. Perhaps the best example of source-data automation is the capture of data by a computer-connected cash register upon the sale of merchandise.

Figure 5-7 illustrates traditional keypunch data entry. As you can see, data entry

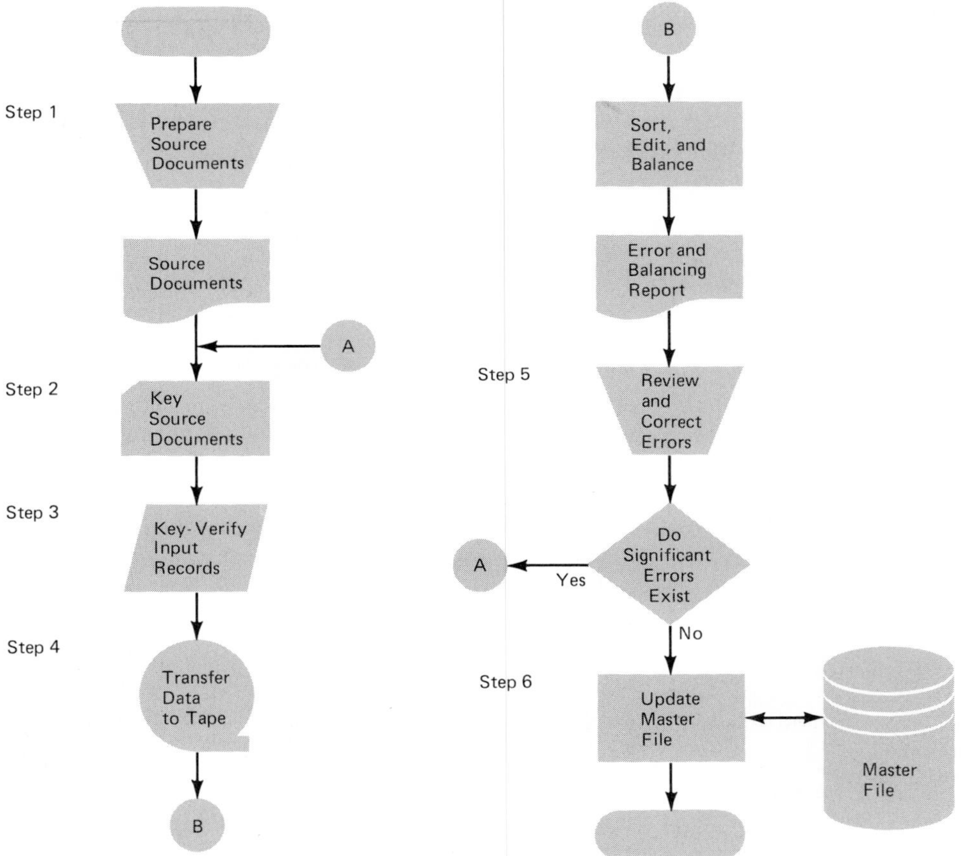

Figure 5-7 Keypunch Data Entry

editing and update of the computer files was a multistep process. Errors always occur in data entry regardless of whether you are using the keypunch approach or source data automation. However, the keying approach has significant disadvantages in error correction. First, if in step five we find that significant errors exist, the error corrections must be keyed and key-verified as in step two and three, and then combined with the original data entry cards, and steps four through five must be repeated. This process continues until no significant errors exist, then the file update can occur.

Secondly, the correction of these errors is more difficult than with source-data automation. Since the process depicted in Figure 5-7 is normally separated both in time and distance from the original event, we often must go back to those individuals who were involved with the original event to correct the data input. For example, if the event were customer payments on account, the payment and the filling out of the source document may have occurred several days ago in another office, perhaps in a

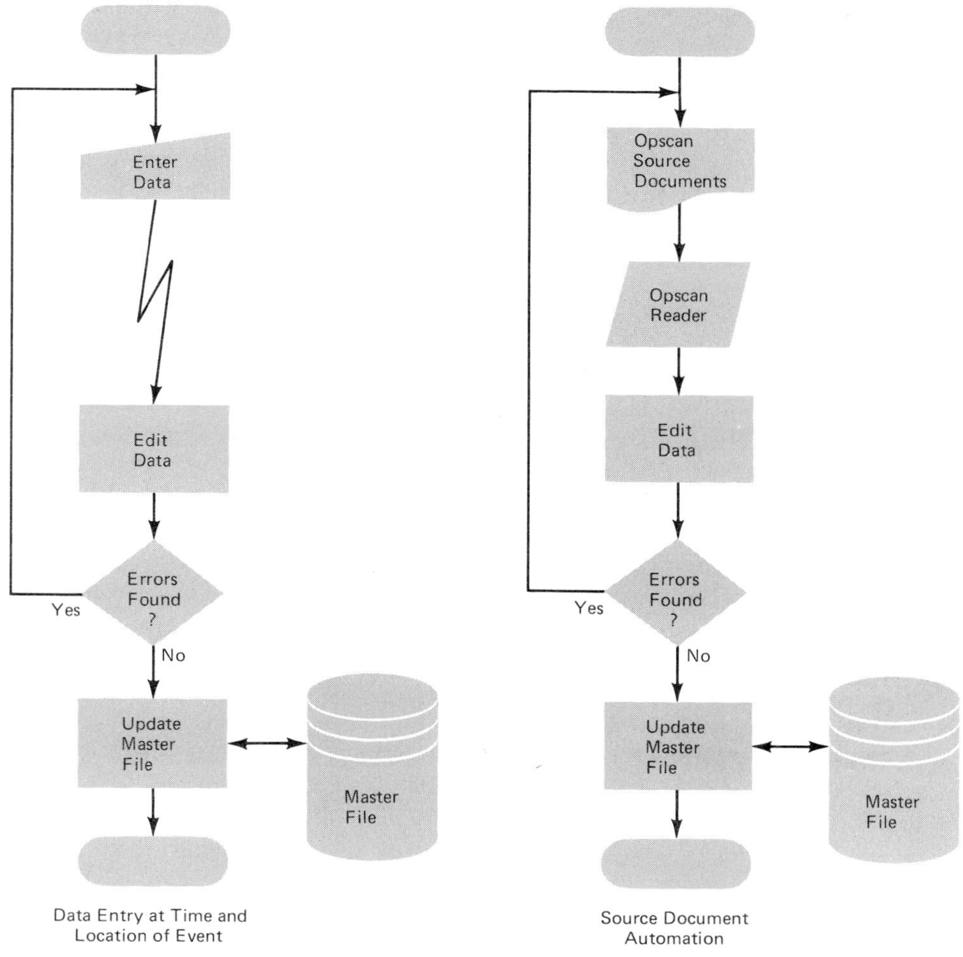

Figure 5-8 Source Data Automation

distant state. The individuals who completed the source document at the time of the event have the information to correct errors. It would be much more preferable to detect and correct errors at the time and place of the event, since the particulars of the event are then at hand. Most of these disadvantages concerning keypunch data entry also apply to key-to-tape, key-to-disk and key-to-diskette data entry.

Figure 5-8 depicts source-data automation. When data is entered through a terminal physically located at the site of an event, data can be immediately edited by the computer, and any errors sent back to the terminal screen for correction. Source data automation allowing immediate entry of data and correction of errors has very significant advantages. However, not all source-data automation allows for immediate correction of errors. For example, the opscan process depicted in Figure 5-8 is often a batch processing operation performed separately, both in time and distance, from the event. Therefore, it has many of the same disadvantages as keypunch data entry.

Regardless of the type of source-data automation used, there is a reduction of the number of times data has to be transcribed from one media to another, and therefore the chances of error are significantly reduced. Furthermore, all source-data automation reduces the human labor component of data entry.

Source-data automation is also often called *distributed data entry*. Essentially, what we are doing is changing from a centralized data entry function to a situation in which data entry is distributed out to particular locations where significant business events occur. In this way we can capture data about those events directly and immediately with on-the-spot error correction.

MANAGEMENT CASE 5-1

The Smith Company is a manufacturer of envelopes and paper products. Currently, initiation of a purchase of supplies or operating equipment is performed by filling out a paper form which is sent to the purchasing department for processing. Several managers have been complaining that the paper form slows down the purchasing process by as much as two to three days. They have recommended that a purchase be initiated through online computer terminals. Under this proposal the purchasing department would call up the purchase on their own computer terminal, verify the information, and assign the purchase to a vendor who can meet the requirements at the lowest price. Some individuals at Smith including the internal auditors have argued that with paper forms, an individual who is authorized to make the purchase can sign-off on the purchase with his or her signature. Therefore purchasing has assurance that each purchase is authorized. They further argue that with an online terminal input of purchase requisitions this vital control would be lost, since there is no way purchasing can be assured that the individual inputing the purchase is actually authorized to do so. Those advocating online terminal input of purchases have countered this argument with the fact that the person entering the purchase would first have to enter a password which has been uniquely assigned to him or her. The other group has argued that passwords are easily misplaced or discovered by those who are not authorized to make a purchase. They argue that signatures are unique to an individual and cannot be easily copied by someone else. Which side of this argument would you support? State your reasons why.

POS Data Entry

Source data automation has given rise to point-of-sale (POS) equipment. In a typical POS configuration, as shown in Figure 5-9, cash registers are online to a minicomputer, which is in turn online to disk storage files containing such data as product description,

Figure 5-9 Point-of-Sale Data Entry (Courtesy of NCR Corporation)

selling price, and collected sales statistics. The universal product code (UPC) illustrated in Figure 5-10 is imprinted on each item sold and is read by the cash register with either a light wand reader or a reader embedded in the checkout counter (see Figure 5-11). The UPC is transmitted to the minicomputer, which retrieves a description and selling price for the item and transmits them back to the cash register. Simultaneously, sales statistics are collected and stored on disk or tape. These are later used to update cash receipts and inventory master files.

Figure 5-10 Universal Product Code (UPC)

POS equipment is used most extensively by the grocery industry. However, it can be used in any merchandising operation. There are also other applications for POS equipment. For example, some libraries place a UPC sticker on each book and on each patron's library card. When books are checked out, the patron's identification number on the card and the code of each book are read by a light wand. Similarly, when books are returned, their code is also read with a light wand. Master files maintained by minicomputers contain book codes and the corresponding Library of Congress identification, titles, authors, and so on. Other files contain patron identification numbers, names, addresses, and information on checked-out books.

Figure 5-11 Light Wand Reader Attached to a Cash Register (Courtesy of IBM Corp.)

Magnetic Ink Character Recognition

Magnetic ink character recognition (MICR) was developed by the banking industry for use on checks. MICR equipment reads data according to the shape of each individual character printed with magnetic ink. Preprinted checks contain the bank's identification number and the depositor's checking account number in MICR code at the bottom of the check, as shown in Figure 5-12. When an individual check is processed, the amount of the check is also printed in MICR code on the lower right corner of the check. The MICR codes are used for sorting and routing checks to individual banks and for updating the depositor's account. The use of MICR is limited mostly to the processing of checks and credit card transactions.

101

MARY A. MORRISON
1765 SHERIDAN DRIVE
YOUR CITY, STATE 12345

19 00-6789/0000

PAY TO THE ORDER OF $

SAMPLE

DOLLARS

DELUXE CHECK PRINTERS, INC.
YOUR CITY, U.S.A. 12345

"Safety Paper" checks
SPECIMEN
All checks the same

MEMO

000067894 12345678

Figure 5-12 MICR Coded Check

Optical Character and Mark Recognition

Optical character recognition (OCR) devices are used to read printed characters optically. Such characters usually must be printed in a special font since most OCR equipment is capable of reading only certain fonts. An example of an OCR document is shown in Figure 5-13. Considerable effort is being made to develop an affordable OCR device that will read a relatively wide range of fonts. Essentially, this equipment would allow the direct entry of material that has been previously typed in a wide variety of type fonts, including standard typewriter fonts. Word processing would benefit most from such a development.

Figure 5-13 OCR Document and Input Device (Courtesy of NCR Corporation)

Optical mark recognition (OMR) equipment can detect marks on a specially prepared form. An example of an OMR form is given in Figure 5-14. OMR is widely used for academic testing purposes and is sometimes used on turn-around documents on which the recipient marks data to be subsequently read by OMR equipment.

Other Input Media and Devices

Voice recognition systems have some limited applications. In voice recognition, a computer recognizes the patterns of an individual's (or several individuals') speech. Essentially, a person speaks into a microphone capable of converting speech into analog electrical forms. These forms are converted to the digital signals of a digital computer system to represent individual words and characters. Several companies are working to develop a widely applicable voice recognition system. The potential market for such a system is enormous in the word processing area. Textual material could be dictated to a voice recognition system, and the computer would produce typed copy directly. There are currently on the market voice recognition systems that have very high accuracy (98 percent) over a very limited vocabulary. They are usually employed in a "hands busy" environment that prevents a production line worker from entering data through a keyboard. However, he or she can speak through a microphone.

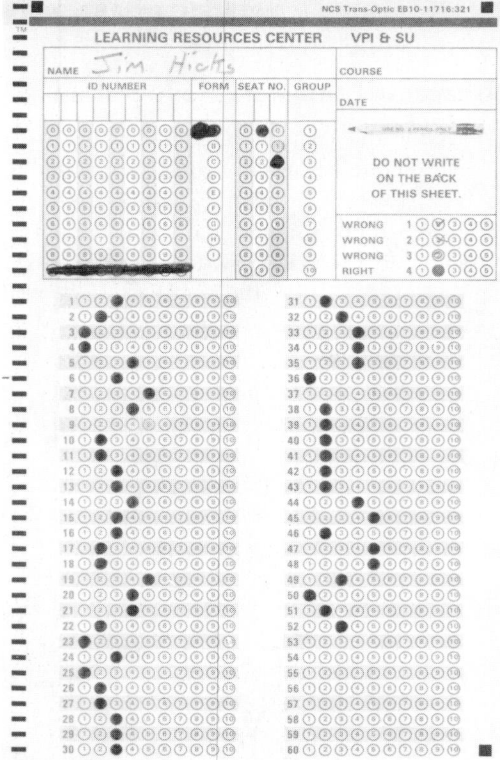

NCS Trans-Optic EB10-11716:321

LEARNING RESOURCES CENTER VPI & SU

NAME Jim Hicks

COURSE

ID NUMBER | FORM | SEAT NO. | GROUP

DATE

DO NOT WRITE ON THE BACK OF THIS SHEET.

WRONG 1
WRONG 2
WRONG 3
RIGHT 4

Figure 5-14 Optical Mark Recognition Form

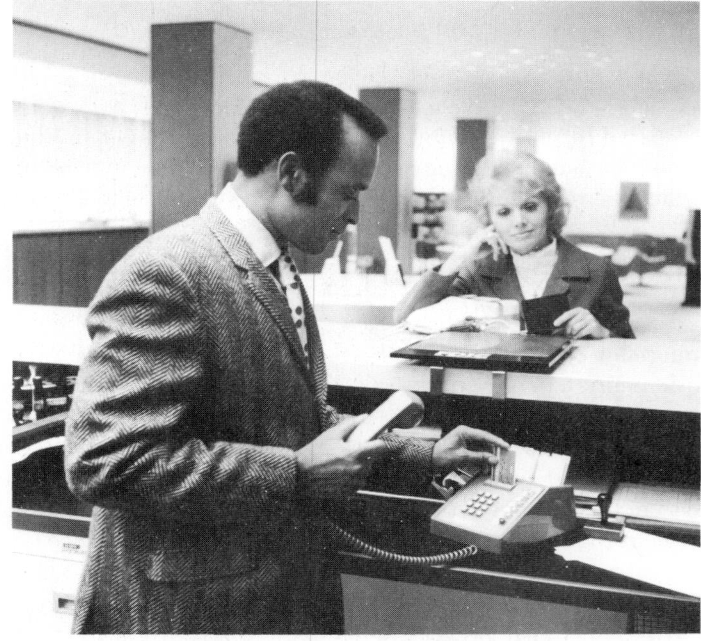

Figure 5-15 Telephone Touch Tone Device (Courtesy of AT&T)

Telephone line touch-tone devices, as illustrated in Figure 5-15, can be used to enter data directly over telephone lines into computer systems. There are many different variations of these devices.

Another data entry device that is becoming increasingly popular is the *portable terminal*, as illustrated in Figure 5-16. These terminals often have secondary storage capability, such as bubble storage, so that data can be entered when the terminal is off line from the computer, then stored and subsequently transmitted at high speed to the central computer. One application for these portable computers involves traveling salespeople. In a customer's office, perhaps using a toll free number, they can connect the terminal over regular telephone lines to their company's computer. The salesperson can inquire about the availability of goods the customer wishes to order and can enter the customer's order directly to the computer. This can reduce the delivery time of the goods to the customer by perhaps several days.

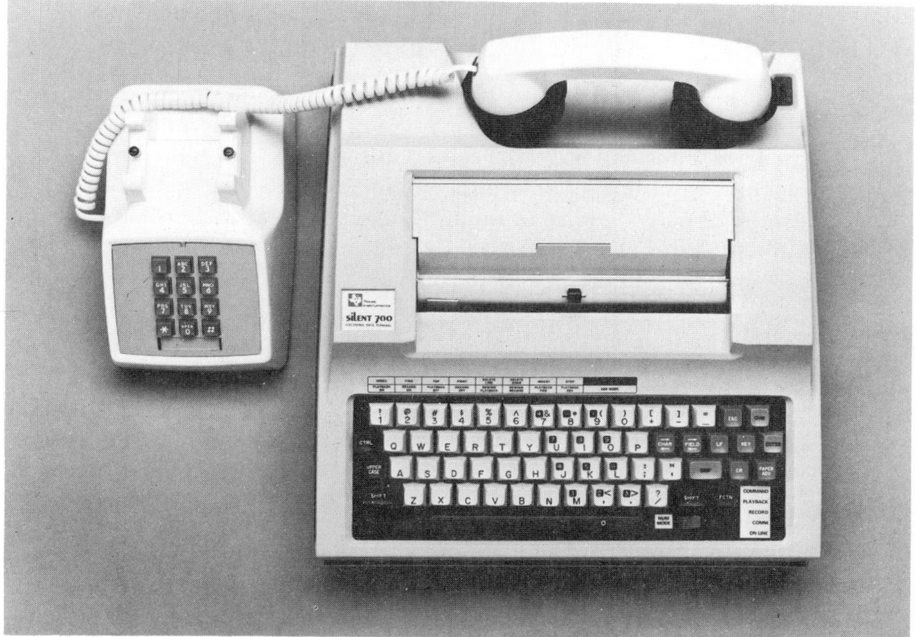

Figure 5-16 Portable Data Terminal (Courtesy of Texas Instruments)

INFORMATION RESPONSE

MANAGEMENT CASE 5-2

Lincoln Incorporated is in the process of developing a new budgetary control system. This system will produce information on a weekly and monthly basis which keeps the managers informed as to their spending in relation to their budgeted amounts for expenditures. Preliminary plans are to produce output from the system only on CRT terminals. Many managers already have terminals installed in their offices. When the new system is implemented, all managers will have a terminal and therefore can call up budgetary information at any time on the terminal. John Decker is manager of the manufacturing operations. John likes to play the role of a good ole country boy, but underneath he is a very sharp and astute manager and very valuable to the company. In a recent meeting, systems development presented the preliminary design of the system to the company's managers. When the plan to produce output only on terminals was discussed, John had this comment. "It seems that today the only thing anyone ever mentions as far as computer output is CRT terminals." He held up a piece of paper saying in his good ole boy country drawl that "one of these days somebody is going to discover paper and they're going to say, isn't this the best thing that has come down the pike, I can read it, I can write on it, I can put it in my briefcase, I can even take it to the bathroom with me." After the laughter died down, several managers joined with John in insisting that output be available in traditional paper form. System development countered with the arguments that many companies have in the past almost been choked to death with paper; that the trend is to a paperless business environment through the use of sophisticated computer technology; and that the sooner the company gets used to this environment the more competitive it will be. Which side of this argument would you support?

CRT Terminals

The CRT (cathode ray tube) terminal has quickly become the most popular form of information response. The same type of data entry terminal as shown in Figure 5-6 is used for information retrieval. A CRT usually has the capability of displaying 80 columns by 24 lines of data, although some will display up to 132 columns of data. Data can be displayed either in multiple colors or in a single color such as green, white or amber.

The advantges of CRTs include:

1. Information retrieval is simple and quick.
2. They eliminate or greatly reduce the need for paper output.
3. They are relatively inexpensive ($500 to $1500).
4. The information retrieval can be very up-to-date.

Printers

Printers are used to produce printed copy of information output. This printed copy is often called *hard copy.* A wide variety of printers are available. They may be categorized in two ways: line-at-a-time versus character-at-a-time printers (these are usually referred to as line printers and character printers respectively). The second way to categorize printers is impact versus non-impact printers.

Line printers (see Figure 5-17) print a complete line in one operation. Their speeds can range up to 2,000 lines per minute and they are typically used for high volume printed output. Line printers normally use print chains, print wheels or print drums to do the actual printing. A print chain is shown in Figure 5-18.

Character printers print one character at a time, similar to the way typewriters do. The technology used for printing is usually a print element such as those used in IBM Selectric typewriters, daisy wheel, or dot matrix printers (see Figures 5-19, 5-20, and 5-21). Dot matrix printers usually give lower quality output. Therefore, when high quality output is needed such as in word processing, daisy wheel printers are often used.

Figure 5-17 A Line Printer (Courtesy of IBM Corp.)

The printers that we have described thus far are all impact printers. That is, to print a character or line, the type font strikes the paper through an inked ribbon. Non-impact printers transfer characters to paper without physical impact. These printers include laser, xerographic, ink jet, electrostatic, and electrothermal printers. Some of the non-impact printers such as ink jet and lasers can produce very high

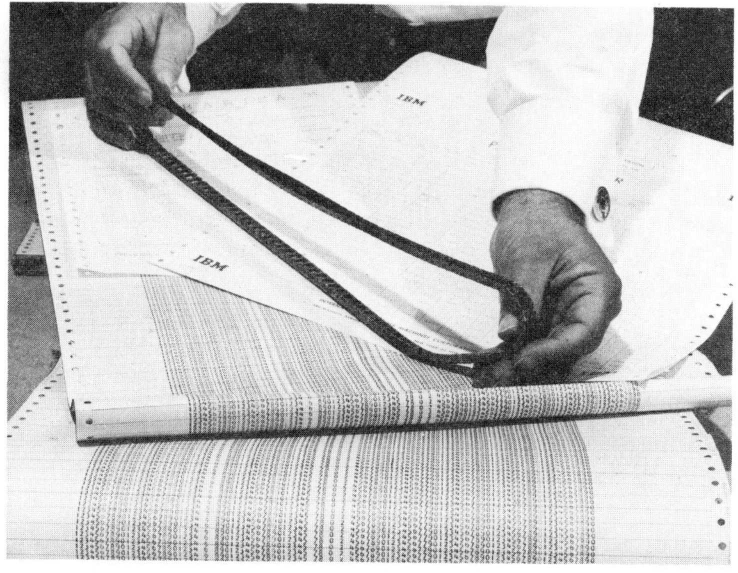

Figure 5-18 Print Chain (Courtesy of IBM Corp.)

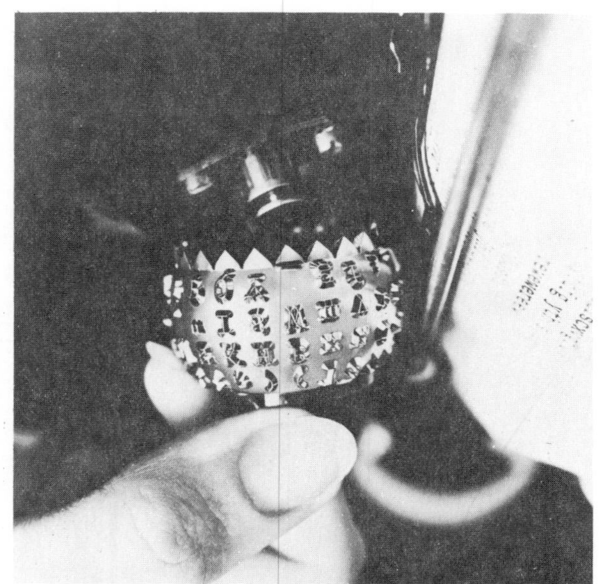

Figure 5-19 IBM Selectric Print Ball (Courtesy of IBM Corp.)

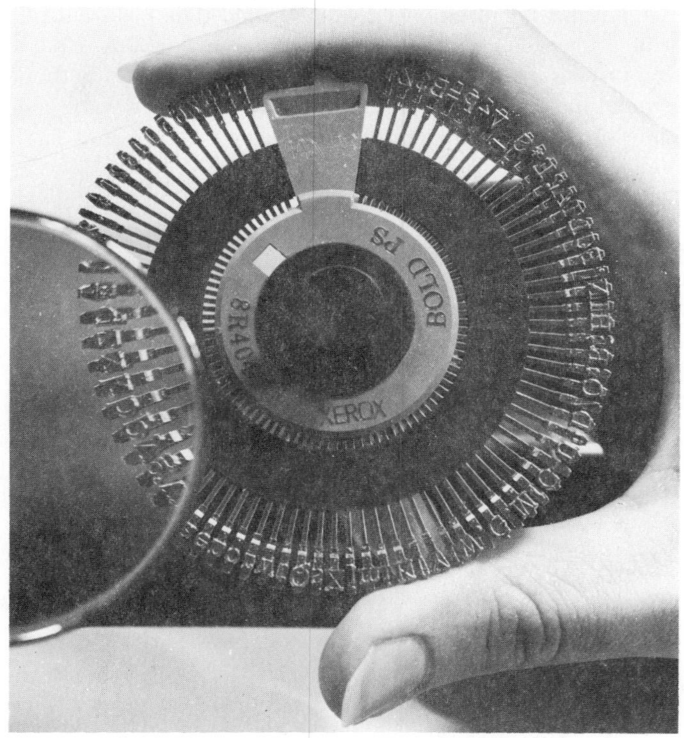

Figure 5-20 Daisy Wheel (Courtesy of Xerox)

A B C D E F G H I J K L M N O P Q R S T U V W X Y Z

a b c d e f g h i j k l m n o p q r s t u v w x y z

0 1 2 3 4 5 6 7 8 9 . , ; : ? ' " / ( ) { } + – / !

@ # $ % ⌒ & * ~ _ ` ¦ \ [ ] = ^^ ‾ (≤ ≡ ≥) ≠ ∨ ∧ ....

+ ÷ × $ ◊ ? ω ε ρ ↑ ↓ ι ⊙ * → ← ⊣ ⊢ α ⌈ ⌊ _ ∇ Δ ∘ K

□ ([ )] { } ⊂ ⊃ ∩ ∪ ⊥ ⊤ | A B C D E F G H I J K L

M N O P Q R S T U V W X Y Z

Figure 5-21 Dot Matrix Printer Character Set

quality, letter perfect printing. For example, laser printers are capable of producing a wide range of type fonts and quality approaching that of multilith printing, as illustrated in Figure 5-22. Laser printers are also very fast, producing output at up to 21,000 lines per minute. The primary disadvantage of non-impact printers is that they will not produce carbon copies. Extra copies must be produced by reprinting.

PAGE 1
RUN DATE 1- 5-84

GROSS PROFIT BY ITEM
REPORT
MONTH ENDING 12-31-83

ITEM NO	ITEM DESCRIPTION	SALES	QTY SOLD	GROSS PROFIT	QTY SOLD YTD
1003	PAPER,3H,LOOSE LEAF	187.50	250	40.00	3520
1004	PAPER,TYPING,BOND	7187.50	1250	1000.00	7500
1005	PAPER,MIMEO,8.5X11	2835.00	750	885.00	6000
7085	PEN,BALLPOINT	3185.00	3500	385.00	24500
4106	PENCIL,DRAWING 3H	1425.00	475	209.00	1900
8165	STAPLER REMOVER	675.00	1500	90.00	16500

Figure 5-22 Laser Printer Output

On the other hand, electrostatic and electrothermal printer output is of a lower quality since both depend upon dot matrix technology to produce an image. Other advantages of non-impact printers include their generally high speed and small amount of physical movement required for printing, which makes them more reliable and quieter than impact printers. A very significant advantage of laser, xerographic, or ink jet type printers is the ability to produce graphic output interspersed with text on the same page. Some of these non-impact technologies can also produce color output, which is especially important for graphics applications. Certainly, over the long run, non-impact technologies such as lasers will largely replace impact printers. For example, the same xerographic machines that are used for office copying and located in individual offices can be connected with a central computer so that high quality output can be directed from the central computer to local offices. Such a configuration could be an important part of an electronic mail system. If a high quality hard copy of a piece of mail is needed, it can simply be routed to the office copier/non-impact printer for printing. Table 5-1 provides a comparison of the speed and quality characteristics of various printing devices.

Computer Output Microfiche

Computer output microfiche (COM) is used by many companies that need large amounts of computer-based data printed in human-readable form. Figure 5-23

Table 5-1 Comparative Characteristics of Printing Devices

Device	Category	Speed	Quality of Printout
High Speed Line Printer	Impact Line Printer	High	Low / Medium
Decwriter	Impact Character Printer	Low / Medium	Low
IBM Selectric Print Ball	Impact Character Printer	Low	High
Daisy Wheel Printer	Impact Character Printer	Low	High
Laser Printer	Nonimpact Character Printer	Medium / High	Very High
Ink Jet Printer	Nonimpact Character Printer	Medium	Very High
Xerographic Printer	Nonimpact	Medium / High	High

illustrates a COM card. This single 4 × 6 inch card can hold up to 270 page-images of data with 99 lines per page. Some COM machines, like the one shown in Figure 5-24 read a reel of magnetic tape containing the data to be produced, while others are connected directly to the CPU. Both types, however, use a laser beam to image the data onto microfiche film. COM equipment can produce output at speeds of 10,000 to 20,000 characters per second and up to 10,000 pages per hour. The obvious advantages of COM are the compact size of its output, which reduces the size of the reports as compared to those produced by the print-to-paper approach, and the speed with which output can be produced. However, COM equipment is expensive, and microfiche is not

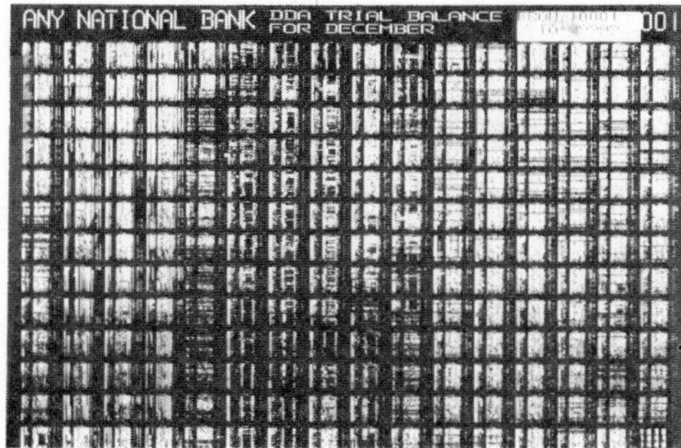

Figure 5-23 Computer Output Microfiche (Courtesy of Eastman Kodak)

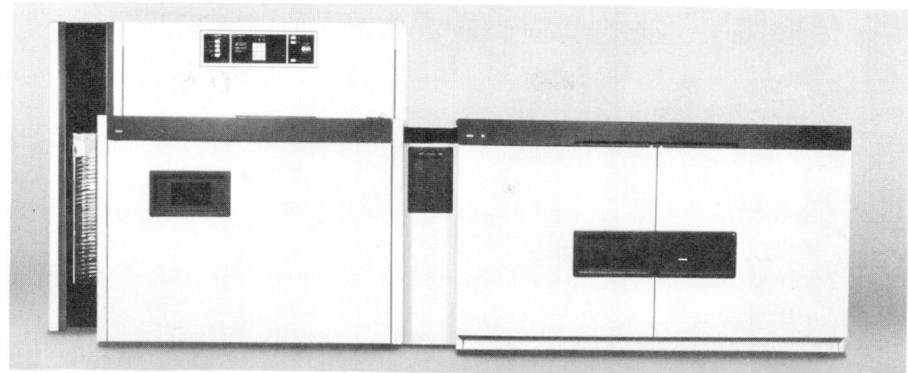

Figure 5-24 COM Equipment (Courtesy of NCR Corporation)

Figure 5-25 Electrostatic Plotter (Courtesy of Calcomp)

directly readable by humans, although microfiche readers are inexpensive and easy to operate.

Graphics

The ability to display computer-based data directly in graphic form is becoming an important business tool. Generally, the significance of data can be grasped much more easily in the form of bar charts and line graphs than by examining numerical data directly. Two types of graphics output equipment are available: 1) the plotter, which draws graphs directly on paper (see Figure 5-25); and 2) the graphics CRT terminal (see Figure 5-26). Both plotters and graphics terminals can be obtained in black and white or color models. Depending on the computer supporting the terminals and the communication lines available, graphics terminals can almost instantaneously display a complete graph on their screens. With this capability, management can quickly examine trends in sales, profits, and other areas.

Figure 5-26 Graphics Terminal (Courtesy of DEC)

Other Output Media

Many of the input and secondary storage media already discussed, such as magnetic tape, disk, cards, and hard copy or CRT terminals, can also serve as output media. In addition, audio response output devices are being used in limited situations. For example, certain railroads use audio response devices in conjunction with car locator systems. Through a touch-tone telephone, customers can access the railroad's computer system, key in a shipment code, and then receive an audio response that indicates where the customer's shipment is now and when the shipment is likely to arrive at the customer's siding.

SUMMARY

Data entry and information response devices provide a link between the central processing unit and the human beings that use it.

The punched card is the oldest medium used to enter and store data in a computer. The data punched on a card may also be typed on it, making it readable for human beings. For this reason, cards are often used as turn-around documents to accompany payments of bills.

Punched cards suffer from a number of disadvantages. They are expensive and cannot be reused. Their input speed is slow, and there is a high probability of data loss due to physical damage to cards.

A keypunch is used to transfer information from source documents to punched cards. A key verifier is a similar machine used to verify that data have been entered correctly.

Key-to-tape data entry systems have one or more keyboards connected to one or two tape drives. Key-to-tape data entry is fast and quiet. Moreover, magnetic tape is an economical, reusable input medium.

In a key-to-diskette data entry system, data is transferred from the keyboard to a floppy disk. Floppy disks are low-cost, reusable storage devices.

A key-to-disk data entry system allows some editing and verification of data upon entry. A minicomputer is used to perform the editing and verification functions. It may also provide other data input assistance like instructions, prompts, control totals, and error rates.

Interactive data entry allows the input of data directly to the production CPU. This kind of data entry is essential for realtime systems in which the master file must be updated immediately. Since data is entered directly to the master file, it is possible to execute a large variety of edit checks, including comparisons with existing data.

Source-data automation permits the capture of data as a by-product of a business event. Some source-data automation techniques in widespread use are as follows.

1. Point-of-sale data entry
2. Magnetic ink character recognition
3. Optical character recognition and optical mark recognition
4. Voice recognition, portable terminals, etc.

Printers are output devices providing information response in the form of hard copy.

Printers may be characterized as line versus character printers, or as impact versus non-impact printers.

Line printers print a complete line at once, while a character printer prints one character at a time, just like a typewriter.

The type font of an impact printer actually strikes the paper to create character images. Non-impact printers use techniques like laser beams, xerography, ink jets, and electrostatic printing to transfer information to paper.

Computer output microfiche can store large amounts of computer generated data in human-readable form. Although it requires some expensive output devices, computer output microfiche can be produced at a high speed and requires very little storage space.

Plotters and graphics terminals are becoming popular information response devices. They help summarize business data into an easy-to-understand pictorial format.

KEY TERMS

Data Entry
Information Response
Peripheral Device
Data Entry Device
Punched Card
Turn-Around Document
Key-to-Tape Data Entry
Stand-Alone Systems
Clustered Systems
Key-to-Diskette Data Entry
Key-to-Disk Data Entry
Data Editing
Control Batch Balancing
Interactive Data Entry
Production CPU
Intelligent Terminals
Dumb Terminals
Source-Data Automation
Opscan
Point-of-Sale (POS) Data Entry
Universal Product Code (UPC)
Magnetic Ink Character Recognition (MICR)
Optical Character Recognition (OCR)
Voice Recognition
Portable Terminals
Hard Copy
Line Printer
Character Printer
Impact Printer
Non-impact Printer
Daisy Wheel
Dot Matrix
Laser Printer
Computer Output Microfiche
Graphics Terminal
Plotter
Audio Response Ouput

REVIEW QUESTIONS

1. What is the primary function of data entry/information response devices?
2. Distinguish between data storage and data entry devices.
3. What are the advantages of using punched cards?
4. Why is the use of punched cards decreasing?
5. What is a turn-around document?
6. How does a clustered key-to-tape data entry system differ from a stand-alone system?
7. Enumerate the advantages of key-to-tape data entry.

8. Why is key-to-diskette data entry preferable over punched cards?
9. What are the major functions of a minicomputer in a key-to-disk data entry configuration?
10. Explain the significance of interactive data input for realtime systems.
11. How does an intelligent terminal differ from a dumb terminal?
12. What is the advantage of entering data at the time and place that the actual business event occurs?
13. What do the initials UPC stand for?
14. What are the two ways to categorize printers?
15. List the advantages and disadvantages of computer output microfiche.
16. What is the advantage of using graphics information response in business data processing?

DISCUSSION QUESTIONS

1. Data entry costs can be a significant portion of a business firm's total data processing costs. If you have to choose between a key-to-tape and a key-to-disk data entry system, what decision criteria would you use? How would you decide whether to use a stand-alone system or a clustered configuration?
2. Realtime data entry provides for up-to-date data files and powerful data editing facilities. Unfortunately, processing costs for realtime data entry tend to be high. On the other hand, batched data entry (such as key-to-tape and key-to-disk) is much cheaper, but involves a time lag between data entry, and updating of the master file. Which kind of data entry should a bank use for its deposits and withdrawals? Justify your answer by comparing the pros and cons of the suggested system.
3. While futurist writers predict paperless, computerized offices in the future, high speed printers continue to print tons of paper every hour. If we really do want to control the quantity of paper used in business enterprises, what would be some suitable alternatives to printed output? Is it possible to continue using paper, but in a more economical and efficient manner?

RESEARCH PROJECTS

1. Recently much concern has been expressed over the harmful effects that some data entry devices have on the health of data entry personnel. Search for some articles written on the subject of better human-engineered terminals and report on changes in hardware design to improve the work environment for data entry personnel.
2. Select some specialized information response technique, like graphic output or audio response, and research new developments in that area. Describe the technique and its current and expected applications.

APPLICATION CASE

Touch/Voice-Response Speeds Orders

(Reprinted with permission from MIS Week, Sept. 29, 1982, p. 21)

By Sanjay K. Jain, Consultant, Interface Technology, Inc.

The large soft-drink distributing company found itself plagued by the same administrative and financial woes that have troubled many businesses during the last four years of economic belt-tightening. Inefficient and labor-intensive internal systems were cutting deeply into shrinking corporate profit margins.

Previously ignored out-of-stock situations, late deliveries, order errors, hidden carrying costs and data collection equipment costs were forcing the company into a poor competitive position. The company's future market growth possibilities looked less than cheery. In the new and highly competitive struggle for economic survival, only the leanest and fittest companies stood to gain.

Fortunately, one of the latest developments in computerized telecommunications has helped several distributors—and other companies—avoid or escape from just this predicament. The development is an automatic touch-tone/voice-response (TT/VR) order processing system.

To use it, company salesmen and wholesale customers simply call the company's toll-free order number from anywhere in the nation, and then key-in orders and other information using the telephone's touch-buttons and a "codebook."

For dial phone users, inexpensive attachable keypads, and even alphanumeric keypads (with both numbers and letters), are now available. Once entered, order information is quickly processed by the system computer and then transmitted to the most convenient distribution center or shipping department.

The TT/VR system operates 24 hours a day, 7 days a week, thus making ordering easy and convenient. The system also saves labor and processing time, minimizes paperwork, frees personnel for other work, and shortens delivery time by speeding and organizing processing.

But, the unique feature of these new TT/VR systems is the computer voice response. Unlike other telephone order entry systems, the TT/VR system features a clear computerized voice that prompts and verifies all entries, thereby greatly reducing order errors.

The voice response can also help increase product sales. It enables management to record and transmit promotional messages and other important information to company salesmen and customers each time they call in. The voice response feature makes the TT/VR the first truly interactive automatic order and data processing system.

The Upjohn Co., a major pharmaceutical firm based in Kalamazoo, Mich., is typical of companies that are purchasing such systems. Faced with an increasingly competitive business environment, Upjohn purchased a TT/VR system late last year in hopes of improving customer service and cutting costs.

Its TT/VR system, designed by St. Louis-based Interface Technology, processes some 400 to 800 salesman and direct customer calls daily from a force of over 35,000 customers and 750 salesmen nationwide.

Upjohn's central TT/VR computer keeps track of all these orders, and breaks them down each hour for transmission to each of Upjohn's eight regional distribution centers. The computer also informs customers if a product is out of stock, or of other special circumstances.

The benefits of having the system have already been tremendous. Company officials report that the system has greatly reduced costly ordering errors, improved service through faster order processing, and improved office productivity.

The system "should also smooth over peak office workloads, such as after our monthly billing cut-off date, when a large number of orders come in," adds Kenneth Ellis, Upjohn's director of consumer services. Ellis expects to enlarge the TT/VR system to allow hospitals to place their orders on interactive teletype terminals before the end of the year.

"This project, when completed, will give our customers a number of options for their ordering," says Ellis.

The completed system is also expected to make Upjohn the first drug manufacturer to make TT/VR service available to all its representatives and customers.

Touch-tone data systems were originally developed in the late 1970s in response to technological advances coupled with changing social trends. The semiconductor "revolution" made it possible to design very compact high-speed telephone data entry systems, while a widespread desire for convenient and instantaneous communication coupled with sharply rising labor costs led a handful of companies to actually build such systems.

Voice-response systems, such as Interface Technology's Total Entry System (TOES) and Periphonics' Voicepac, arrived in the wake of the development of earlier non-audio touch-tone data systems. The voice feature was added both to reduce entry errors and to return a degree of personality to highly impersonal touch-tone systems.

Like the original non-audio systems, however, TT/VR systems have been slow to catch on. Mainly, this has been due to the newness of the technology and to the relatively small number of firms with experience in using TT/VR systems.

As with any new technology, it has taken time for people to become accustomed to the TT/VR concept.

Moreover, as with any new communications system, since a great deal of field data has not been gathered, it has not been easy for potential buyers to quantify and then weigh the costs and benefits of installing systems like TOES and Voicepac.

As labor and transportation costs—and thus the cost of competition—continue to rise, however, such calculations will become easier to make. Corporations will be forced to be much more imaginative and open-minded, especially in their utilization of advanced telecommunication technologies.

"Given the state of the art, and the state of the economy, we expect a big boom in these systems during the next three years," says Tony Koester, vice president of marketing at Interface.

Koester's firm seems to be already experiencing the first rumbles of this coming boom. In the last two years, Interface has installed 13 of its TOES systems for firms in businesses ranging from trucking to photography.

The king of breweries, Anheuser-Busch, purchased a TOES three years ago to allow the collection of weekly sales data from its 800 wholesalers throughout the country. The brewery felt that by knowing sales on a weekly level, it could project the deliveries that had to be made to insure that inventories were kept at previously established levels.

Its investment apparently paid off well: Anheuser-Busch recently purchased a second TOES system, this time to help in the collection of marketing research data. The system has allowed Busch to collect timely and accurate information at the lowest possible cost, with the optimal utilization of personnel and with a minimum of error.

Other firms that have recently installed similar TT/VR systems have reported similarly good results. Besides order-entry and marketing-data collection, successful applications have included cash management, credit authorization, engineering data entry, payroll time-sheet reporting, and sales quotations.

But perhaps the two most lucrative applications for the "talking computer" have yet to be fully developed in the United States.

Consumer shopping by phone, while available in some parts of Europe and Canada, has still to be developed in this country. And bank-by-phone systems, while already operative in many parts of the country, are still the exception rather than the rule.

Certainly as transportation costs continue to rise, and consumers as well as businessmen becoming more comfortable with automatic systems like TT/VR, their popularity will increase dramatically. We can be sure that the recent growth of interest in the technology will some day swell into a movement that will alter our lifestyles and firmly thrust us into the 21st century.

Discussion

1. What are some additional reasons beyond those mentioned, why TT/VR would be slow to catch on?
2. Suggest other unique applications for TT/VR beyond those mentioned. For example, course registration at colleges and universities.

CHAPTER 6
OPERATING SYSTEMS

INTRODUCTION

In most organizations the computer is a very important resource. Among the specific resources a computer has are processing time, storage space, printers, and terminals. Management of these resources is largely handled by a special set of computer programs called in their entirety an operating system. When users interact with the computer, much of this interaction is with the operating system. Operating systems will directly affect the ease with which users interact with a computer. Furthermore, operating systems are a very significant determinant of whether or not a particular computer's resources are optimally used. For these reasons it is important that users of computer systems have a basic knowledge of operating systems.

In this chapter we will first distinguish between systems software and application software. We will then explore the functions, components, and types of operating systems. Finally, we will see how operating systems make possible multiprogramming, virtual storage, timesharing, and multiprocessing computer systems.

SYSTEMS SOFTWARE VERSUS APPLICATION SOFTWARE

There are two broad categories of software: 1) systems software; and 2) applications software. The term systems software is synonymous with the *operating system*, which is a set of programs that manage the resources of a computer system (processing time, storage space, etc.) so that they are used in an optimal fashion. In effect, the operating system controls the operations of the computer.

Systems Software

Operating systems software began to be used extensively with the second generation computers in the early 1960's. Prior to this, the operation of a computer was controlled primarily by human computer operators. These operators monitored the processing of each job and, quite typically, when a job finished a ringing bell or a flashing light would indicate that another job should be read into the computer and started by the operator. If a job finished while the operator was having a coffee break, the computer might have sat idle for five or ten minutes or longer. In addition, the operator had to activate each peripheral device when that device was needed by the computer. Obviously this type of human intervention wasted computer time. In order to automate these functions, programs called operating systems were developed. These programs are stored partially in primary storage and partially in direct-access secondary storage so the computer can access them immediately when they are needed. With operating systems, a queue of jobs awaiting execution can be read onto a disk, and the operating system will start each job when system resources are available for its execution. By eliminating human intervention, idle computer time is significantly reduced.

Operating systems programs are written by both computer manufacturers and specialized software firms. The programmers who write systems software are called *systems programmers*. Most medium- and large-size firms have their own staff of systems programmers who are capable of modifying an operating system to meet the unique requirements of the firm.

Systems programmers are highly skilled computer professionals. Since many of the security features in a computer system, such as passwords, are executed by the operating system, it is critical that the work of the systems programmers be well controlled.

Application Software

An *application program* is a program written for or by a user that performs a particular job for the user. Examples of application programs are inventory control, accounts receivable, and marketing analysis. Programmers who write application programs are normally called *applications programmers*. The development of application programs will be covered in later chapters.

In summary, we may look upon operating systems programs as those general programs that assist the computer in the efficient execution of application programs. Application programs themselves perform specific tasks directly useful to the user of a computer.

FUNCTIONS OF AN OPERATING SYSTEM

Resource Management

In carrying out its responsibility for efficient operation of a computer, the operating system performs many different functions. One of its more important functions is the allocation of resources, such as primary and secondary storage space, to the application jobs being executed. The operating system also performs scheduling functions by examining the priority of each job awaiting execution. Jobs with higher priorities are executed first. Maintaining security is also a very important function of the operating system. This function is carried out through various password schemes that identify valid users and determine which data files they may access.

The operating system keeps track of computer resources—who is using them at what cost—and bills users accordingly. Most firms consider user billing for computer services an important part of controlling computer resources.

Compiling

Compilers are a part of systems software. *Compilers* translate programs from high level languages, such as BASIC or COBOL, into a machine language program that the computer can execute. This process is covered in more detail in a later chapter on programming languages.

COMPONENTS OF AN OPERATING SYSTEM

Figure 6-1 illustrates the storage of the operating system in primary and secondary storage. The device on which the complete operating system is stored is called the *system residence device.* Today this device is normally a disk unit. As portions of the operating system are needed for execution, they can be readily loaded into primary storage.

Since the operating system is constantly supervising and monitoring the computer system, a portion of it that is used very often, called the *resident supervisor*, is stored in primary storage at all times when the computer is operating. We will discuss the supervisor in more detail in the next section.

The copy of the operating system stored on nonvolatile disk is in core image form. *Core image storage* simply means that the programs are in binary form. They appear just as they would when stored in primary storage, and therefore can be directly transferred to primary storage without any conversion taking place.

The operating system can be divided into two main categories of programs: 1) control programs; and 2) processing programs. *Control programs* are the heart of the operating system. They are the programs that monitor and manage the operations of the

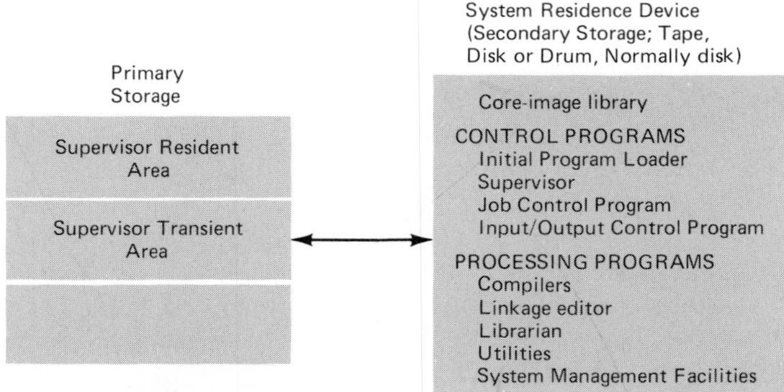

Figure 6-1 Storage of the Operating System

computer system. The *processing programs* assist computer users and programmers in the development and execution of application programs. For example, they do such things as compile procedural languages, for example COBOL, and perform operations involving sorting or merging of data. Some authors would not include processing programs as a part of the operating system. In fact, in a strict sense one can say that the operating system is only made up of control programs. However, in this book we are using a broader definition of the term *operating systems*, which includes both control and processing programs.

Control Programs

The control programs of an operating system generally consist of four different types of programs: 1) the initial program loader (IPL); 2) the supervisor; 3) the job control program; and 4) the input/output (I/O) control program. The purpose of the initial program loader is to start up the operations of a computer. It performs this function by reading the resident portion of the supervisor from secondary storage and then loading it into primary storage. Once the resident portion of the supervisor is loaded into primary storage, control is passed to the supervisor, and the operation of the computer begins.

Supervisor programs are the principal managing programs in an operating system. They are often also called *monitor* or *executive* programs. They organize and control the flow of work in a computer system by initiating and controlling the execution of other computer programs. The resident portion of the supervisor is used very often, and it is therefore stored continuously in the supervisor resident area of primary storage. Less often used parts of the supervisor are stored temporarily in primary storage only when they are in use. They are stored in the supervisor transit area of primary storage (refer to Figure 6-1).

As operating systems software replaced human operators in the control of computers, new languages were developed to enable users and programmers to communicate with the operating system. These *job control languages* (JCLs) require the user to include several job control statements along with a program. The statements identify the job and its steps, and specify the system resources to be used (for example, expected run time, input/output devices to be used, and memory space required). Job control languages also describe the data sets or files to be employed in the various job steps. Figure 6-2 shows how JCLs are employed to communicate with the operating system.

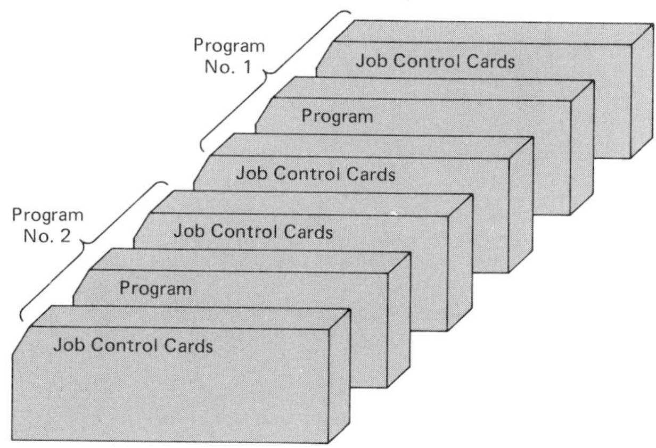

Figure 6-2 Relationship of Programs and JCL

Figure 6-3 illustrates how the supervisor and the job control program interact to stop the execution of one program and begin the execution of a second. Let us take a closer look at this job-to-job transition. After the job control program has identified the system resources required for the next job, the supervisor makes decisions prior to beginning the execution of program 2 based on several factors. For example:

1. Does program 2 have the highest priority among the jobs awaiting execution?
2. Are all the system's resources available that program 2 will need during execution (such as disk units, tape drives, etc.)?
3. Does program 2 have a valid password?

If the answer to these and other questions is yes, then program 2 is allowed to run.

Acting together, the supervisor and job control programs issue many instructions to the human computer operator. Examples of these instructions include whether to mount or dismount a tape or a disk pack. If special forms are needed for printing the output, the programmer specifies these forms through the JCL statements. When the job is ready to be printed, the computer sends a message to the operator to mount the particular forms needed on the printer. A large percentage of the work that a computer operator performs is in response to instructions from the operating system. Of course these instructions originate from the JCL the programmer includes with his or her program.

Input/output control programs manage the movement of data between primary storage and peripheral devices such as disk, tape, and card readers. These programs also perform many error-checking functions. For example, if a read error is detected while reading from a disk, the I/O control program will reread the data several times in an

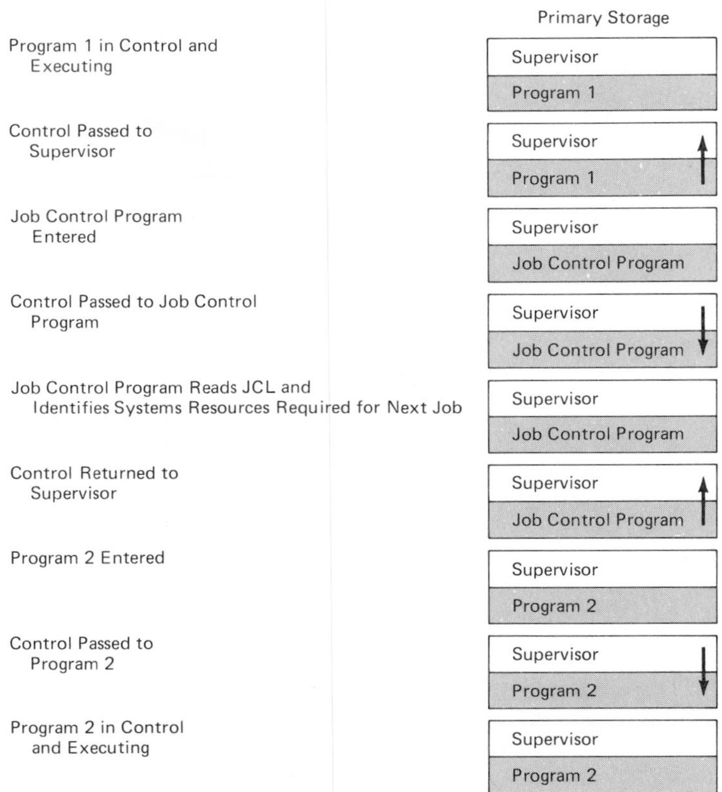

Figure 6-3 Program-to-Program Transition in Primary Memory

attempt to obtain error-free data. If the error continues to occur, an appropriate error message is written out.

Processing Programs

Processing programs assist a programmer or user in developing and utilizing an application program. Examples of processing programs are compilers, linkage editors, librarians, utilities, and systems management facilities.

A *compiler* is a computer program that translates a program written in a procedural language, such as COBOL, into machine language that is directly executed by the computer. There are many different types of compilers; in fact, one exists for each programming language. Programming languages and compilers will be discussed in more detail in chapter 7.

Quite often, in writing a program a programmer will call prewritten subroutines (or subprograms) stored on the system residence device to perform a specific standard function. For example, if a program requires the calculation of a square root, the programmer would not write a square root calculation program. He or she would simply call a square root subroutine to be used in the program. The function of the linkage editor is to gather all of these called subroutines and place them into the application program. The output from the linkage editor is called a load module (the term module is often used synonymously with program). A *load module* is a program that is suitable for loading directly into primary storage for execution.

Most computer systems have a processing system program known as a librarian. The primary function of the *librarian* is to maintain a catalog of the locations and usage of all program and data files. Librarians also often execute password controls.

There are many standard types of jobs that are executed by processing programs. Among these are sorting data, copying data from one storage medium to another, and copying from a storage medium to the printer. Programs that perform these standard functions are called *utility programs*. They are normally supplied by the computer manufacturer as a part of the operating system and may be called by any application program to be used by that program.

System management facilities (SMF), or similar programs, are a part of most systems software. They collect operating statistics, which can be a significant component in the control of a computer system. For example, SMF systems collect information about who used the system and for how long, the hardware employed, whether the job was successfully executed, and the amount of primary storage employed. This information is used in billing for use of the computer facility.

SMF systems also collect information about which files were used in performing a job. This provides an excellent audit trail concerning data and file usage. It is possible to determine, for example, which files were used when a particular program was run. It will also identify who the user was when the file access was made as well as the date and time of the access.

TYPES OF OPERATING SYSTEMS

Batch Systems

Operating in a *batch* mode, an operating system accepts jobs and places them in a queue to await execution. This process is often called *spooling*. Spooling is short for "simultaneous peripheral operations on line." Essentially, what happens is that jobs are placed in a queue on a disk unit. As execution time becomes available, the operating system selects jobs from this job queue based on preset priorities. Batch jobs may be executed on a serial basis, in which one job is executed at a time, or on a multiprogramming basis, in which several jobs are executed concurrently. Serial versus multiprogramming execution will be discussed in more depth later in this chapter.

Interactive Systems

Interactive operating systems allow users at individual terminals to interact directly with a computer. In effect, a user can interrupt a low priority batch job, causing the computer to perform his or her high priority work. Interactive operating systems must thus be multiprogramming systems. Also, realtime systems must be interactive since realtime files must be updated immediately after real-world events occur. This obviously requires an operating system to have an interrupt handling capability. An *interrupt* is the suspension of the execution of a computer program caused by an event external to the program. The interrupt is in such a way that the execution of the suspended program can later be resumed. Examples of such external events would be a request for data, or input of data, from an interactive terminal.

The remainder of this chapter will explore in more depth batch versus interactive operating systems, their respective relationships to multiprogramming, virtual storage, time sharing, interactive computing, and multiprocessing. These systems are the predominant computer systems today. Therefore, it is very important that computer users understand their operating systems.

MULTIPROGRAMMING

Multiprogramming is the capability of a CPU to execute two or more programs concurrently. It is accomplished through the operating system. Essentially, two or more programs are stored concurrently in primary storage, and the CPU moves from one program to another, partially executing each program in turn. Early computers systems executed programs on a batch-serial basis. That is, each program was executed in the order in which it was read into the system, and only one program was executed at a time.

MANAGEMENT CASE 6-1

Tieko, Inc. is considering two different microcomputers to adopt as the machine that the company will standardize upon. In other words, they have to decide which machine to use company wide. The company has narrowed its selection to two machines. One of the machines has available a multiprogramming operating system which allows the microcomputer to execute two or more programs concurrently. The alternative machine does not have a multiprogramming operating system, but otherwise it is somewhat superior to the first machine. Those in the organization that favor machine two, without the multiprogramming operating system, argue that a microcomputer can only have one user at a time, therefore there is no need for a multiprogramming operating system. How would you respond to this position?

Advantages of Multiprogramming

Increased Throughput

Several disadvantages associated with the batch-serial approach to program execution are overcome by the use of multiprogramming. First, throughput is not maximized under a batch-serial approach. *Throughput* is a measure of the total amount of processing that a computer system can complete over a fixed period of time. This disadvantage is due to the relative speeds of computer system components. The CPU operates without mechanical movement, depending only on the flow of electronic pulses that travel at about the speed of light. Therefore, it is very fast compared to the speed of input/output devices, which depend on mechanical movements or humans to operate them. Figure 6-4 depicts the elapsed time necessary to execute one job under batch-serial and three jobs under multiprogramming. Total throughput is significantly increased by the use of multiprogramming. Because the CPU is not waiting for input/output for the program it is executing, it simply rotates to another program and begins executing it. Of course, the address location of the next program step to be executed must be stored so that the CPU will know where to begin execution when it goes back to programs that have been partially executed.

Shorter Response Time

A second disadvantage of the batch-serial approach is its longer turnaround or response time. *Turnaround time* refers to the elapsed time between the submission of a batch job and the availability of output. *Response time* refers to the elapsed time between submission of a command on a remote terminal and the completion of that command as evidenced by a message on the terminal screen or printer. In a batch-serial environment, turnaround on small jobs normally takes longer than it does in a multiprogramming environment. Refer to Figure 6-4, and assume that jobs one and two are long, requiring 1.5 and 0.75 hours of CPU time respectively and that job three requires two minutes of CPU time. In the batch-serial approach, the turnaround time for job three could easily be four to five hours. With multiprogramming, the turnaround time for job three would be approximately 3–4 minutes, plus output printing time. Essentially, job three will execute completely in a short elapsed time by utilizing the CPU, which would otherwise be waiting for I/O for jobs one and two. Therefore, turnaround time for short jobs can be greatly improved under multiprogramming. However, the turnaround time for long jobs is usually lengthened since the CPU is devoting part of its time to short jobs. This is not a disadvantage, however, because long batch jobs usually have a lower priority. Multiprogramming systems normally have priority schemes whereby any job, including a long one, can be executed under a higher priority if necessary.

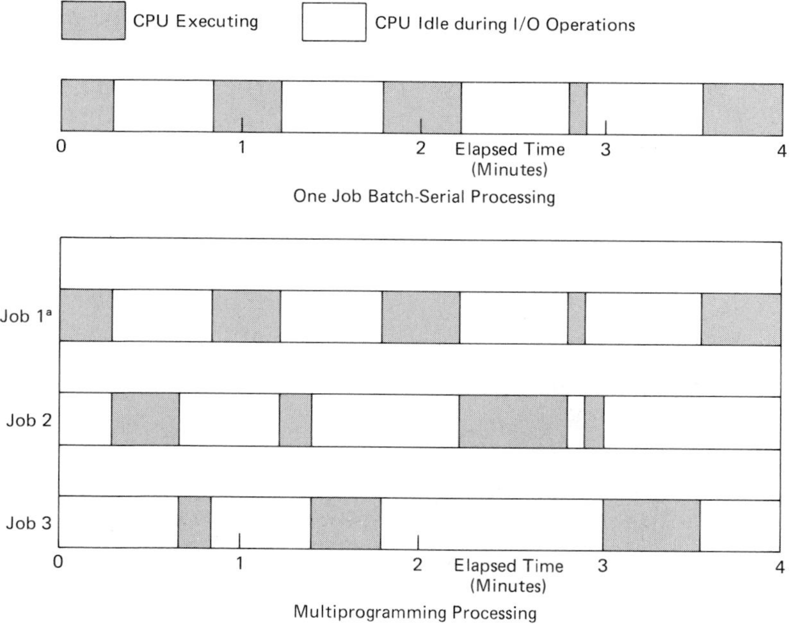

[a]Job numbers assigned in order of job submission.

Figure 6-4 Elapsed Time Under Batch-Serial and Multiprogramming Systems

Ability to Assign Priorities to Jobs

Most multiprogramming systems have schemes to set priorities for rotating programs. They specify when the CPU will rotate to another program, and which program it will rotate to. The user, through JCL specification of execution priorities for each job, can influence the priority under which a job will execute. Rotation can be initiated by natural program breaks, such as a request for I/O, or it can be initiated on the basis of both I/O breaks and CPU time slices. Under the latter approach, a program will execute until an I/O operation is required or for a fixed period of time, whichever, is shorter, before the CPU rotates to another program.

Multiprogramming with priority schemes improves system availability. That is, it increases the speed with which the system can respond to high priority, unanticipated requests on its resources. System availability under the batch-serial mode can be very poor when long jobs are executing. With multiprogramming, high priority jobs can be executed almost immediately. Online, realtime, or timesharing systems would not be practical without multiprogramming. The response time at terminals would be intolerable if all instructions from terminals and batch jobs were executed on a batch-serial basis. Instructions from terminals must be executed on a high priority basis. Timesharing and interactive computing will be discussed later in this chapter in more detail.

Improved Primary Storage Allocation

Using multiprogramming, programs being executed must in principle reside in primary storage until their execution is complete. Some operating systems, such as IBM's OS/MFT (Operating System with Multiple Fixed Tasks), divide primary storage into a fixed number of partitions. One program is stored in each partition and therefore, only a fixed number of tasks (programs) can be executed concurrently. Other systems, such as IBM's OS/MVT (Operating System with Multiple Variable Tasks), do not arbitrarily partition primary storage, and a variable number of tasks can thus be executed concurrently. The number of tasks executed depends on their individual size (main storage requirements). More small than large jobs can be executed concurrently since more small jobs can simultaneously fit into the limited total space of primary storage.

As can be seen, a constraining factor on the throughput of a multiprogramming system is the number of jobs that can reside in primary storage at a given point in time. If only two large programs will fit into main memory, the CPU may be idle a large percentage of the time while waiting for I/O. The greater the number of programs that primary storage can hold, the greater the probability that the CPU will be able to execute at least one program while waiting for I/O for the others. This line of reasoning led to the approach of rolling (writing) out to primary storage programs that were waiting for I/O, and rolling them back into primary storage when the I/O operation was completed, and the programs were ready for additional execution. When primary storage space is vacated, a program that is ready and waiting for execution is rolled in. This approach clears main storage of all programs that are waiting for I/O. Therefore, in principle, all the programs residing in primary storage are either running or awaiting execution. The roll-out technique helped develop the concept of virtual storage, which will be discussed later in this chapter.

Disadvantages of Multiprogramming

Multiprogramming does have disadvantages, which are generally minor compared to its advantages. First, multiprogramming is implemented through the operating system, which itself is a program requiring space in primary storage because it must be executed by the CPU. The operating system overhead (its primary storage and CPU execution time requirements) is greater under multiprogramming than with a batch-serial operating system.

Another potential problem with multiprogramming systems is *interprogram interference,* either intentional or accidental. While executing, a program can theoretically write to any area of primary storage. With multiprogramming, other areas of primary storage contain additional programs or their data. Therefore, a program could accidentally or intentionally modify another program while both are executing concurrently. To prevent this, operating systems assign each program a unique password while it is executing. Thus, in order to write to or read from, say, program A's assigned area of primary storage, the writing or reading program must present the proper password, which, in theory, is known only to program A. In effect, only program A has access to its area of primary storage.

VIRTUAL STORAGE

Virtual storage is primary storage that does not actually exist. It gives the programmer the illusion of a primary storage that is, for all practical purposes, unlimited. The computer system itself maintains this illusion through a combination of hardware and software techniques.

Before a program can be executed, each of its instructions must be resident in real primary storage, but not all instructions have to be resident at a given time. Essentially, virtual storage involves storing in primary storage only those program instructions currently executing, and storing the remainder on less expensive secondary storage, such as disks. Figure 6-5 illustrates the virtual storage concept.

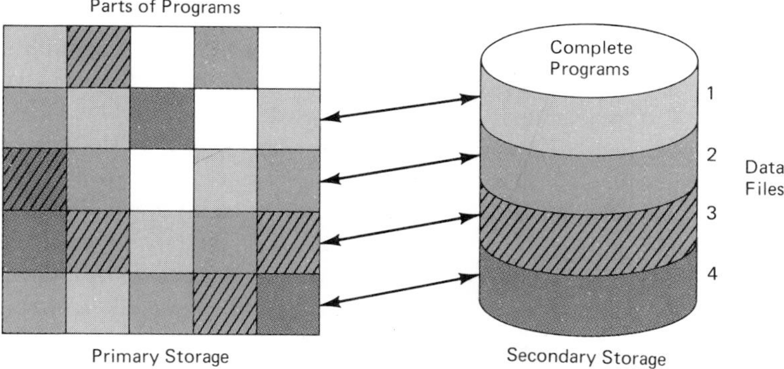

Figure 6-5 Overview of Virtual Storage

Memory Fragmentation

In order to explain the development of virtual storage, we will first explore some additional multiprogramming concepts. If several complete programs are stored simultaneously in main storage until the execution of each is completed, two problems arise. First, the number of programs that can be resident in primary storage at any point in time may be severely limited, thereby decreasing the probability that the CPU will always have a program available in primary storage ready for execution. For example, if primary storage consists of 512K bytes, the resident portion of the operating system requires 100K bytes, and the program currently executing requires 410K bytes, only 2K bytes of main storage will be available for a second program. If all the programs awaiting execution require more than 2K bytes, no other program can be read into primary storage. Thus, a multiprogramming system is executing only one program because of the program's large size (410K bytes).

The second problem is that of noncontiguous, unused primary storage. This problem will be illustrated with the example in Figure 6-6. There are three programs in primary storage: 1) program one requires 200K of primary storage; 2) program two requires 40K; and 3) program three requires 142K. With the 100K required by the operating system, a total of 482K of core is utilized. However, 30K is not utilized since none of the three programs awaiting execution will fit in 30K. Assume that program two has completed executing, thereby freeing an additional 40K of main storage. We now have 70K of unused primary storage. This is enough to read in program four and begin its execution, but we cannot do it because the two unused areas of primary storage are not contiguous. Essentially, primary storage becomes fragmented, with unusable portions of main storage becoming interspersed among executing programs.

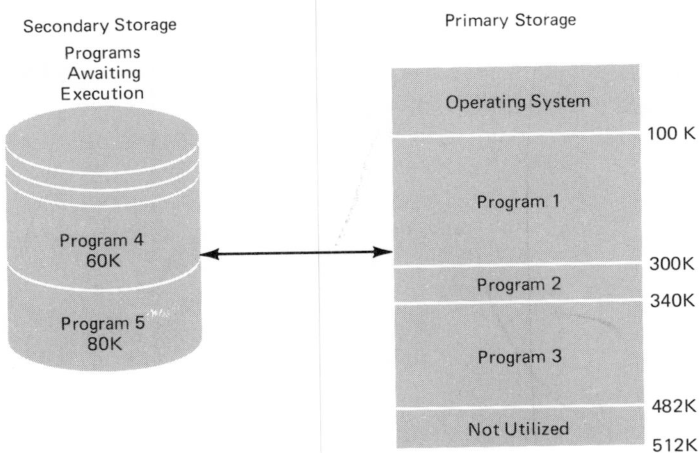

Figure 6-6 Memory Fragmentation

Program Segmentation and Paging

The solution to the above problem of fragmentation is to break program four into two segments, storing one segment in the 40K area and the other in the 30K area. This approach is called *program segmentation*. The breakpoint between one segment and another can either be predetermined by the programmer or left to the operating system to decide. Normally, segments are determined by natural program breaks—for example, a complete subroutine would constitute one program segment.

However, program segments (subroutines) themselves can be rather large. If the largest segment of a program is larger than the largest unused portion of primary storage, we still cannot read in the program. To solve this problem, the *paging* approach was developed. In this approach, every program is divided into pages, each of which has a size of say, 4K. Consequently, all unused portions of primary storage will be at least 4K in length since every program is paged. With paging, any program can utilize any noncontiguous, unused 4K portion of primary storage as long as the total of the unused portions of core is at least equal to the primary storage requirements of the program. Recall that we are still assuming that the complete program must be resident in primary storage prior to beginning its execution. Utilizing both paging and segmentation, the operating system maintains tables that tell the CPU where in primary storage each page of a program is located.

Virtual Memory

Once the program has been broken down into pages or segments, the idea of virtual memory logically follows by relaxing the assumption that the complete program must be stored in primary storage during execution. In fact, with virtual storage, only the page of the program currently executing must be stored in primary storage. All other program pages can be stored on a peripheral disk unit until each is required for execution. Figure 6-7 illustrates paging in a virtual memory system.

Virtual storage provides two primary advantages. First, the CPU is utilized more fully. Pages of many different programs can reside in main storage simultaneously

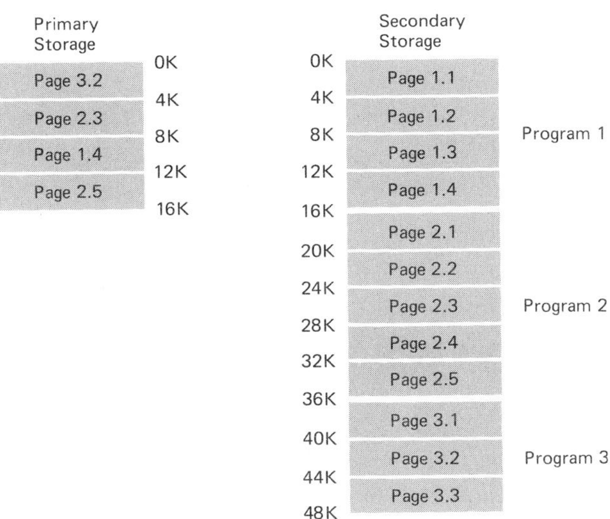

Figure 6-7 Paging in a Virtual Memory System

because only one page of each program is resident in primary storage at any time. Thus primary storage can contain pages of many different programs before encountering size constraints.

The second advantage of virtual storage is that programmers no longer need concern themselves about primary storage size constraints when writing programs. When the complete program had to reside in primary storage, an individual program's primary storage need could not exceed what was left of primary storage after provision for the operating system's requirements. With virtual storage there is practically no limit on a program's primary storage requirements.

Current developments in virtual storage tend toward a single level storage concept. Single level storage treats all storage—both primary and secondary—as a single unit or level. Therefore, the real difference between primary and secondary storage becomes transparent to the programmer.

Disadvantages of Virtual Storage

As one might expect, there are disadvantages to virtual storage. Overhead costs increase. CPU time is required to page (read/write) all those pages in and out of primary storage. Additional primary storage is required to hold the tables that keep track of the pages, and to hold the virtual storage operating system itself, which is inherently large and complex.

Another potential problem is *thrashing,* which occurs when one or more pages of a program have to be paged in and paged out of primary storage frequently during execution of the program. Obviously, thrashing could reach a point where the CPU is spending too much time on paging in and out compared to time spent on program execution.

Program structure can have a significant positive or negative impact on the problem of thrashing. Consider the segment of a FORTRAN program illustrated in Figure 6-8. If, as illustrated, page two of the program ends at statement number forty

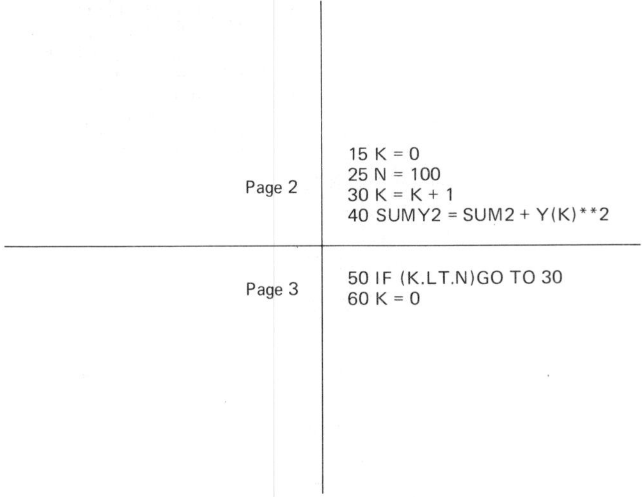

Figure 6-8 A Program Which Can Cause Thrashing

and page three begins at statement number fifty, significant thrashing is going to occur when this program is executed. Pages two and three will have to be paged in and out as many as one hundred times each, as the program branches from statement fifty to statement thirty. Therefore, when writing a program to be executed many times on a virtual storage system, the programmer should minimize branching within the program. Structured programming (which is sometimes called GO TO-less programming) is a technique that can minimize program branching. As a bonus, if a program has a minimum of branching, its logic is easier to follow and understand.

TIMESHARING AND INTERACTIVE COMPUTING

A *timesharing* system allows access to a CPU and data files via many remote terminals. The central computer system is owned by a timesharing vendor, and the users pay for the service monthly. The cost is based on a fixed charge plus a usage charge. From the user's point of view the computer system appears to be dedicated exclusively to his or her terminal because of the fast response by the CPU to commands from the terminal. In reality the CPU is servicing many terminals and perhaps one or more batch jobs. Obviously, multiprogramming is the preferred method of implementing timeshared operations, since fast response to terminal commands is necessary.

One of the major concerns in a timesharing system is the scheme for distributing the processing time to various users. Distribution is accomplished in most systems by using a combination of natural breaks and time slices. That is, the CPU executes a program until a natural break occurs or until a given time period has elapsed. A user can typically obtain priority processing for a job through a terminal request. Priority processing is charged to the user at a higher rate than normal processing.

Many timesharing systems are structured so that commands from a terminal can interrupt the CPU's processing. Upon any interruption, the CPU immediately stores the status of the program it is presently executing and begins to process the interrupt command. Different types of interrupts are usually assigned different priorities. Interrupt commands assigned high priority usually require negligible CPU time. Examples include log on, edit, and log off commands. Lower priority interrupts might include a command to compile and execute a program. Low priority commands do not interrupt the processing of high priority commands, but high priority commands always interrupt low priority processing.

Small businesses have readily accepted timesharing as a means of automating information processing. Before timesharing, a decision to automate involved a choice between investing in an in-house system or using a batch service bureau. Timesharing traditionally has been suitable only for areas where a minimum of input or output was involved. It was not suitable for high-volume, batch-type operations because of the high cost and time involved. Beneficial changes have occurred in the technology, however. The proliferation of low-cost terminals has enabled users to prepare numeric data as easily as running an adding machine tape. Much preparation can be done offline, which does not involve a usage charge. Timesharing now also has the capability of sending or receiving large amounts of data.

Unnecessary costs are incurred if an interactive timesharing mode is used when some processing could be carried out in the batch mode. A relatively new service, called remote computing services, involves the use of both timesharing and batch processing.

It is also referred to as an interactive batch. Such a system could increase operating efficiency and hold the line on operating costs. The system permits a user to have an application program, originally developed for interactive processing, to be run in a batch mode. The computer accepts data commands from a file in the program as if the latter were the user at the terminal. Programs most likely to be entered for interactive batch are long ones that come up at a busy time of day or at the end of the day.

MANAGEMENT CASE 6-2

The First Federal Savings and Loan Association is a local and relatively small association. Currently the record keeping is done through timesharing with a computer service bureau. The association is well satisfied with the timesharing service they are now getting. However, several software firms have recently called upon the association and presented a complete package including software and microcomputers that could perform the association's information processing needs locally. One of the major points that these software firms have made is that their systems are flexible and can produce a wide variety of information for management needs. They also maintain that processing customer records locally would improve the confidentiality of the association's records. They argue that there have been instances of customer data being divulged to unauthorized persons at service bureaus. Which direction do you think the savings and loan association should take?

MULTIPROCESSING

As explained earlier in this chapter, a multiprogramming system executes two or more programs concurrently on a single CPU. In contrast, under *multiprocessing*, a single program is processed by two or more CPUs. The most typical kind of multiprocessing occurs in systems supporting both a batch mode and many remote terminals. Figure 6-9 illustrates such a system. When a system has only a few remote terminals to support, the main CPU can handle all terminal interrupts and trivial jobs, such as editing. However, the processing requirements of a large number of remote terminals can overload the main CPU. In this case, terminal interrupts and trivial jobs can be handled by a mini CPU which, in the configuration shown in Figure 6-9, is called a front-end processor. The main CPU processes batch jobs and executes programs that the front-end processor cannot handle.

Multiprocessing systems can take many forms. For example, a third CPU, equivalent in processing power to the existing main CPU, could be added. The new CPU would handle all timesharing processing not handled by the front-end processor. The existing CPU would be used for batch processing and would be able to accept and execute batch jobs from the timesharing CPU that were originated by the terminal. These jobs would typically have long run times, and the output could be directed to the high-speed batch printer rather than back to the originating terminal.

Multiprocessing systems substantially increase the throughput capabilities of a system with an overloaded CPU. Another advantage of multiprocessing is the backup CPU capability provided by two or more CPUs which are, in some configurations, identical.

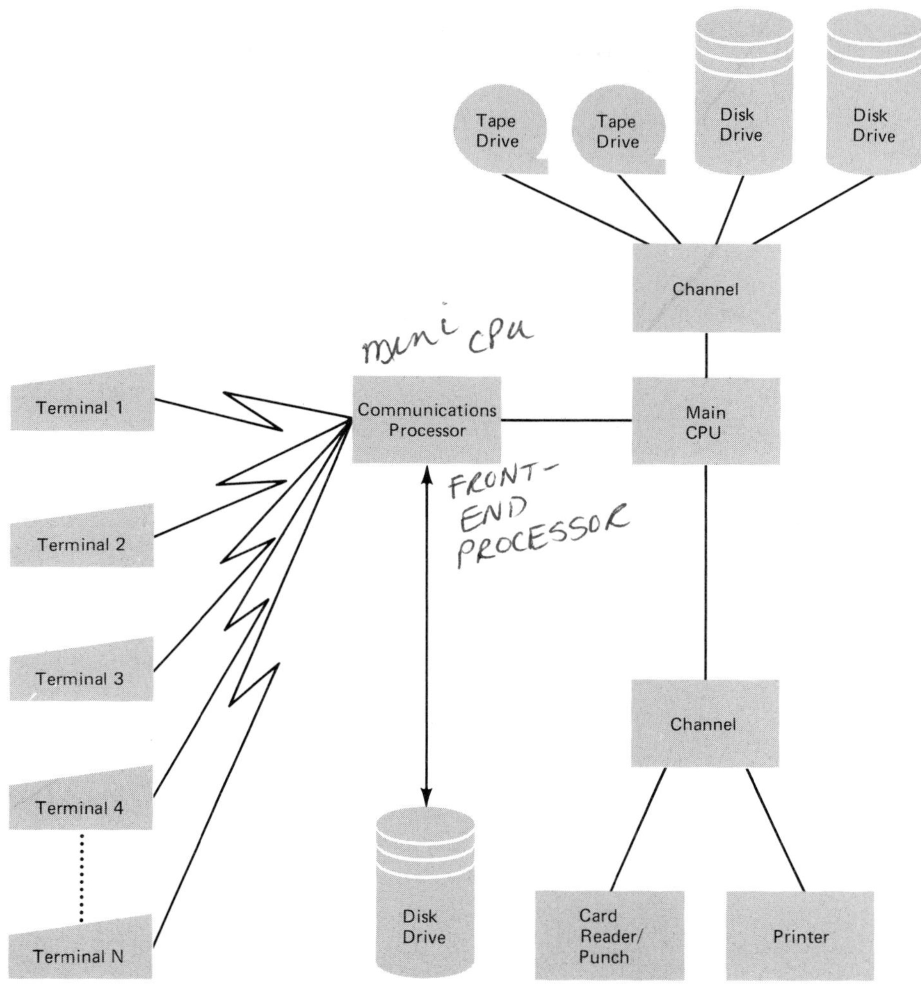

Figure 6-9 A Multiprocessing System

SUMMARY

Systems software is a set of programs controlling the operations of the computer. These programs, collectively known as the operating system, are written and maintained by systems programmers.

Application programs are written to perform specific jobs for computer users.

The major functions of an operating system include the allocation of resources to different jobs and the compilation of high level language programs.

The control programs in an operating system start up the computer, schedule the execution of various user programs, supervise the allocation of resources to these programs, and facilitate interaction between the CPU and I/O devices such as terminals and printers.

The processing programs in an operating system assist in compiling and linking application programs. They also provide facilities to catalog programs and data files.

Batch-type operating systems line up jobs as they are received and then process them when time is available. In contrast, interactive systems start executing a job as soon as it is received, so that a user does not have to wait at the terminal.

The major advantages of multiprogramming are improved throughput, and better turnaround and response time. These advantages are achieved primarily through the use of job rotation and priority schemes.

Primary storage space may be underutilized because of memory fragmentation. By breaking a program down into segments or pages we can utilize these fragmented blocks of memory.

The concept of virtual memory refers to storing only the active segments or pages of a program in primary storage. The rest of the program is stored in secondary storage, and parts of it are rolled in when required.

A timesharing system allows many interactive users to utilize the CPU concurrently. It is made possible through the use of multiprogram operating systems. CPU processing time is distributed among users by a sophisticated job rotation and priority allocation system.

Multiprocessing systems allow the same job to be run on two or more CPUs. This improves system throughput by letting the different CPUs specialize in those functions they can perform best.

KEY TERMS

Operating System
Systems Software
Application Software
Multiprogramming
Virtual Storage
Multiprocessing
Timesharing
Systems Programmers
Passwords
Application Programmers
Resource Management
Job Scheduling
Job Priority
Compiler
System Residence Device
Resident Supervisor
Core Image Storage
Control Programs
Processing Programs
Initial Program Loader
Job Control Program
I/O Control Program
Monitor Program
Executive Program
Job Control Language (JCL)
Linkage Editor
Librarian
Utility
Load Module
Audit Trail
Simultaneous Peripheral Operations on Line (SPOOL)
Interrupt Handling
Throughput

Job Rotation
Turnaround Time
Response Time
Memory Partitions
Memory Fragmentation
Program Segmentation
Paging
Thrashing
Front-end Processor

REVIEW QUESTIONS

1. What is systems software? How is it different from application software?
2. Describe the major functions of an operating system.
3. How can we categorize the programs in an operating system?
4. What is a JCL? What functions does it perform for an application program?
5. For what kind of job would you use a utility program?
6. Briefly describe the two types of operating systems.
7. Why is an interrupt handling capacity necessary for an interactive operating system?
8. What are the disadvantages of the batch-serial approach to computer job execution?
9. How does multiprogramming overcome the disadvantages of the batch-serial approach to computer job execution?
10. Explain the concept of job rotation in a multiprogramming system.
11. What is memory fragmentation?
12. Distinguish between program segmentation and paging.
13. What are the advantages of virtual memory?
14. How are timesharing, interactive computing, and multiprogramming related?
15. Give an example of a multiprocessing system.

DISCUSSION QUESTIONS

1. Assignment of processing priorities to different users can often be a difficult task. Operating level personnel may desire a higher priority because they need a short turnaround time to keep the production process moving. Middle managers might feel that precious executive time is wasted waiting for computer output because the operating level people overload the CPU with long routine jobs. How would you approach the problem of assigning user priorities in a large business firm? Is it feasible to allow the same user to use different priorities depending on the importance of the job? How would you control the abuse of such a system?
2. Electronic Games, a small manufacturer of simple electronic games, has decided to purchase a computer system. One vendor is recommending a system with multiprogramming capability. Karl Spear, the owner, does not understand what multiprogramming means. Briefly explain multiprogramming to Spear. Include in your explanation

what factors he should consider before making a decision on whether to buy the system or not.

3. The Getrichquick Co. is overhauling its information and computer systems. The president is considering installing a realtime system to obtain quick answers to company problems (he feels the present batch system is outdated). He is even considering having a CRT terminal installed in his office. The Getrichquick Co. sells construction materials and supplies to commercial contractors. The construction materials are usually heavy steel and equipment, normally ordered so far in advance that only nominal inventories are maintained on this line. Smaller orders and orders for supplies have been a real headache. An extensive inventory is maintained for supplies, but many stockouts occur due to unpredictable demand and supply problems. Sales personnel have long advocated a better computer system to help ordering and shipping problems and to reduce stockouts. Describe how you would advise the president about a realtime system. If a realtime system is not recommended, what type of system would you recommend? If a realtime system is recommended, what information should be handled on a realtime basis? What misconceptions does the president have? How would you advise him about these misconceptions?

RESEARCH PROJECTS

1. Although batch-serial type operating systems are not widely used on mainframe computers any more, they are still used by most microcomputers. Identify one popular operating system for small computers and analyze its capabilities. *Byte* and *Personal Computing* are good sources for information on small systems.

2. Trace the historical development of systems software and write an essay entitled "Systems Software—The Unsung Hero of Management Information Systems."

ESSAY

Standards Needed for Development of Micro Industry

(Reprinted with permission from MIS Week, January 20, 1982, p. 36)

By Eddie Currie, Director, Marketing/Business Development, Lifeboat Associates

Imagine this. You walk into your favorite record store to pick up the latest Jane Olivor album you've been so anxious to hear.

You put the album on your stereo, but something is immediately wrong. Suddenly, Jane Olivor sounds just like John Denver. The reason—the album, instead of being produced at 33⅓ revolutions per minute, was recorded at 37½. The only way to hear Jane correctly is buy another stereo designed to play at 37½ rpm.

Ridiculous, you say. Well of course it is. But that doesn't mean the same situation doesn't apply daily to the microcomputer industry, where the current lack of industry standards for hardware, software and, most importantly, operating systems drastically restricts programs available to end-users.

Microcomputers today are on the verge of a tremendous explosion in sales and interest—interest from business, professional and personal users. Much of this interest stems from IBM's entry into the personal computer market. IBM is giving the industry a validity it never had before, for the name IBM connotes "standards."

Of course calling them "microcomputers" hasn't helped industry development at all. The choice of the prefix "micro" is an unmitigated public relations disaster since it leads people to think the machines are limited in capabilites rather than simply small in size.

Historically, hardware manufacturers have cared little about software, understood it even less and thought virtually nothing about it in the construction of their machines. Hardware manufacturers sought to keep their machines "special" and "proprietary" and assumed that software would be designed especially to serve their machine—and most particularly their machine. It was as though you needed one stereo to play Bach and a second if you wanted to hear the Rolling Stones.

The need to establish standards is unquestionable. Standards regulate virtually everything we buy and use today—from the size of garden hoses, to the width of candles, to the height of the inside open area of automobile tires.

All microcomputer standards to date have simply been de facto adoptions of systems which—for whatever reason—became temporarily popular. As a result, control of industry development has often fallen into the hands of select vendors who can—and do—arbitrarily make alterations in their systems sending reverberations throughout the industry and frustrating users time and again.

For 8-bit microcomputers only, de facto standards have emerged. But the entry of IBM into the market has speeded up the process of establishing industry-wide standards that are stringent, firmly established and reliable.

While every industry likes to control independently its own development and future, the need today is for the microcomputer industry to turn over decision-making on standardization to respected, qualified, outside agencies. Of various possibilities, two spring quickly to mind: ANSI (American National Standards Institute) and IEEE (Institute of Electrical and Electronics Engineers). The latter has already studied, and appears ready to adopt, an S-100 bus standards.

The history of the S-100 standard clearly spells out the dangers of failing to develop standardized microcomputer systems. Basically, a de facto standard widely accepted in the industry, S-100 was developed by MITS, a popular company which shocked the industry when it went out of business in the late 1970s. The de facto standard was virtually lost with the failure of this one company.

The reasons for standardization are manifold and they offer benefits to software companies, original equipment manufacturers (OEMs) and program authors, as well as information managers.

The most important need for standardization among information managers and end-users is to be able to transfer data and programs between machines of the same generation and between machines of current and future generations of technology. Most users today are professionals with strict requirements for computerized aids to help them with everything from report-writing and billing to appointment-scheduling and sales-trends projections.

These users have a tremendous need not only to store information but to be able to transfer it and exchange it from one machine to another and from one office or company branch to another whenever necessary.

Take the company whose accounting department uses a Xerox to process and handle billings, but whose purchasing department uses Hewlett-Packard microcomputers to do its work. Transference of data from one machine to the other is greatly facilitated by the use of a standardized operating system that has been adopted for both.

Suppose your company has purchased hardware from a manufacturer who later goes out of business. Without standardization, all the stored information may become locked into a system which may not be compatible with any future hardware purchases made by your company.

Or take the business executive who has one manufacturer's computer in the office and another manufacturer's computer at home. With standardized operating systems serving both machines, that professional may easily transport work from one machine to another.

While operating systems that make software transportable do exist today, standardization does much to assure users of transportability of programs and data. Standardization would allow, for example, any microcomputer user to walk into a store and purchase a particular piece of software without concern, provided the package carried the marking. "This program complies with the ANSI-adopted standard for 16-bit microcomputers."

While standardization provides obvious aid to users, standardized operating systems offer additional benefits to manufacturers and program authors.

Some manufacturers continue to feel they need not get involved in software development which is time-consuming, costly and exacting. They feel they are supplying hardware and how it is utilized is of little concern as long as it functions. Other companies have come to believe that the best way to keep customers is to lock them into their own system.

Of course, such reasoning is fallacious. The way to keep customers happy is to help them in every way possible. Supporting the adoption of standards and thereby opening the floodgates of available software to service them is the safest way of assuring that an end-user will have no reason to switch to another machine simply to be able to use particular programs.

The adoption of standards would also free OEMs and manufacturers from concerns about software development and availability and would allow them to focus on introducing new systems without having to wait for software to be developed. It was the proliferation of software for 8-bit machines that led to the adoption of the current de facto operating system standard for microcomputers.

And standardization promises to be a boon for software development because it will allow software authors—the people who develop and write software programs—to serve the largest base of microcomputer users possible. Today an author writes software for a specific operating system hoping to be able to judge who uses it, how long it will be popular and what other programs will be available for it.

However, an author writing a program to fit an established standard can be sure it will be available to the largest possible market.

To some people the term "standardization" creates a fear that the word means the adoption of a less than satisfactory system or perhaps "the lowest common denominator" of those systems now available. Such a fear is unfounded. Standards are adopted to establish a foundation upon which others may build.

Standardization does not necessarily mean all systems will be the same. Manufacturers are free to make improvements and alterations and the hardware will retain its own unique qualities. All LP albums play at 33⅓ rpm, but they sound quite different on different stereo systems. All light bulbs fit standard lamp sockets, but some still burn longer, or provide better light, than others.

As microcomputer hardware prices continue to drop or stabilize, software costs (because software is labor-intensive to develop and support) will continue to increase. Software considerations, therefore, will become increasingly more important to end-users.

The microcomputer industry has a chance to turn over to unbiased experts the responsibility of establishing criteria which will give the industry's future a clear and usable path to follow. Failure to do so will simply force microcomputers to continue to live under the specter of being devices that, lacking a universal medium of information exchange, are immersed in a sea of incompatibilities, and have no long-lasting place in the business world.

Let ANSI or IEEE or other official organizations examine the multitude of operating systems available today—particularly for 16-bit machines.

Discussion

1. What functions would an operating system perform on a microcomputer?
2. How do operating systems help to alleviate the problem of lack of standardization?
3. Assume IBM's Disk Operating System (DOS) becomes the de facto standard operating system for 16-bit microcomputers. Does this solve the standardization problem? If this were to occur, are any additional problems created?

CHAPTER 7
PROGRAMMING LANGUAGES

INTRODUCTION

The computer is a resource whose business uses include information processing, communications, and automated office systems. Users of computers are a diverse group, but can be broadly classified as end-users (secretaries, executives, managers) and applications programmers. The end-user generally enters data into the computer via an application program that accepts commands or data from a CRT, cards, tape, or any other input media, and the computer then generates the desired results. The end-user usually has limited knowledge of how the computer operates, and is concerned primarily with obtaining specified results and solutions.

Software was developed as one of the necessary communication links between a computer and its users. Software provides a way for the users of the machine to enter, manipulate, and obtain output from data without having to alter the machine's hardware. This level of software serves as a buffer between the machine and its users.

Software packages can be bought from vendors of the hardware or from a software development house. It may also be developed directly by a user or applications programmer to suit a particular user or application. If the latter method is chosen, the development of the application software should be performed using structured methodology as discussed in chapters 14 and 15 of this text. Before any coding (programming) is started, the application must be analyzed and a structured physical design developed. This two-step process forms the programmer's blueprint for coding the application. Using the structured design specification, a suitable language is chosen to code the program(s). A *program* is a set of instructions executed by the computer.

The selection of a particular language depends primarily on the nature of the problem or application, as well as upon the individual programmer's preference.

This chapter will introduce you to different types of programming languages, including the most widely used high-level languages. In addition, factors influencing the selection of a language will be discussed in the last section of the chapter.

TYPES OF PROGRAMMING LANGUAGES

Machine Language

As with hardware, the evolution of software has been characterized by various stages or generations, beginning with the tedious machine language, and later evolving to the present day high-level languages and user-friendly languages. Machine language, as the name implies, is a machine-oriented language. Programmers using such a language must be extremely familiar with the design, operation, and peripherals of a particular computer. In addition, using machine language creates a "semantic gap" between the application and the programming language. In other words, a programmer cannot write a machine language program directly from the structured design specifications developed for the application, and expect any similarities between the program and the specifications. In fact, the machine code would be unintelligible to most users. For example, a program written in machine code to compute taxes is in no way similar to the description in everyday language of the computation.

A machine language program, being machine-oriented, is a set of instructions having a one-to-one correspondence to each and every operation that must be performed. It is the only language that a computer can understand. All programs written in other languages must be compiled or translated into machine language for execution. A machine language program is also known as *object code*. Object code is machine-readable and requires no translation process before execution. This feature allows for extremely fast processing time and more efficient use of primary storage.

However, programming in machine code is very tedious because the programmer is not only concerned with problem definition but also with the "clerical" tasks such as manually assigning storage locations and registers. The programmer must keep track of each location throughout the programming task by building symbol tables for the variables and storage locations. This task makes writing and debugging a machine language program extremely difficult. The probability that the programmer may inadvertently write data or instructions into locations containing other data or instructions, thereby destroying them, is very high. Clerical overhead is very high when writing in machine code. Changes in instructions are extremely difficult to make because the programmer must reassign all references to storage locations manually, thus making the program inflexible.

Symbolic Languages

As the evolution of software continued, symbolic languages were developed, such as assembly language that uses mnemonics or symbols for each machine language instruction. Like machine language, an assembly language is designed for a particular machine. Therefore, the program still makes efficient use of the CPU's time and resources. In general, there is still a one-to-one correspondence between instructions and operations. Each symbol corresponds to one machine operation, and is descriptive of that particular operation. Assembly language also allows the programmer to specify constants and storage locations symbolically. These features take some of the tediousness out of programming in machine language and relegate it to a program called an assembler. The assembler translates the assembly language program into machine code, and then references and assigns all addresses and storages locations. An assembly, or higher level language program is known as *source code*. It is written by an applications programmer, and must be translated or compiled into object code (machine language code) before it is executed.

Since machine language code and assembly languages are difficult to comprehend, a simple example will be used to illustrate the nature and complexity of programming in these languages. Figure 7-1 illustrates a simple program which adds two variables, X and Y, and then places the result in a third variable, SUM. In *pseudocode*, the program would be expressed as follows:

```
program ADD;
    declare X        real initial (1),
            Y        real initial (2),
            SUM      real;
```

```
Machine Code                                    | Assembly LANGUAGE                  Explanation
                                                |
MEMORY                                          |
LOCATION  OBJECT CODE  ADDR1  ADDR2             | STMT    SOURCE STATEMENT
0000000                                         |    1 ADD       CSECT              ;IDENTIFIES BEGINNING/NAME OF PGM
                              00000             |    2           USING  *, 15       ;IDENTIFIES R15 AS BASE REGISTER
000000    5820 F010    00010                    |    3           L      2,X         ;LOAD '1' INTO R2
000004    5A20 F014    00014                    |    4           A      2,Y         ;ADD '2' TO CONTENTS OF R2
000008    5020 F018    00018                    |    5           ST     2,SUM       ;STORE CONTENTS OF R2 IN SUM
00000C    07FE                                  |    6           BR     14          ;RETURN CONTROL TO CALLER PGM
00000E    0000                                  |
000010    00000001                              |    7 X         DC     F'1'        ;RESERVE MEMORY LOCATION FOR X, INIT TO '1'
000014    00000002                              |    8 Y         DC     F'2'        ;RESERVE MEMORY LOCATION FOR Y, INIT TO '2'
000018                                          |    9 SUM       DS     F           ;RESERVE MEMORY LOCATION FOR SUM
                                                |   10           END
```

Figure 7-1 A Program Coded in Machine and Assembly Language

To illustrate the complexity of the machine code, we will look at only the LOAD instruction. The LOAD instruction in the example is broken down as follows:

58 2 0 F 010

where 58 is the hexadecimal representation for the LOAD operation code,

- 2 is the hexadecimal representation for "register 2",
- 0 is the hexadecimal representation for the index register (not used in this example),
- F is the hexadecimal representation for the base register,
- 010 is the hexadecimal representation for the relative location of contents to be loaded.

This example shows the clerical detail involved in coding this program. The programmer must determine which storage areas or registers will be used in the program. Looking at statement two of the assembly language program, register fifteen is designated as the *base register* from which all storage locations associated with the program will be determined. The base register contains the relative address of the next instruction, which is the LOAD instruction (statement three) at relative location 000000. Statements three through five use register two for temporary storage during the addition process. Statement three is the instruction which will "load register 2 with the contents of the memory location (000010), designated X." Statement four will "add to register 2 the contents of the memory location (000014), designated Y." Statement five "stores the contents of register 2, the sum of X and Y, in the memory location (000018), designated SUM."

You should now have some appreciation for the tediousness a programmer must endure when programming in these machine-oriented languages. Today, applications programmers seldom write in machine or assembly languages. Some applications programmers use assembly language to write programs that are executed many times (e.g., arithmetic functions, specialized I/O routines). Because assembler programs are efficient in terms of processing time and primary storage utilization, assembly language is generally used by a systems programmer who writes operating system programs. For these programs, execution time is a primary consideration.

Macro-instructions, which combine many repeated assembler instructions into a one-line reference to the particular sequence of instructions, are often used when programming in assembler languages. Macros, when executed, enable the assembler to insert a set of instructions into the program that replace the macro-instructions. This is known as macro-expansion. These macros, or sets of instructions, are stored in a macro-library for future referencing. Macros are very convenient for a programmer in that they make the programming task less tedious.

High Level Languages

The next stage of software evolution brought about the development of procedure-oriented high level languages (e.g., FORTRAN, COBOL, PL/1, etc.) and problem-oriented high level languages (e.g., RPG). A procedure-oriented language is a language in which the programmer gives step-by-step instructions to the computer. Using a problem-oriented language, a programmer needs only to describe the functions the computer must perform. The compiler for the problem-oriented language generates the necessary machine language instructions for the computer. These languages help bridge the "semantic gap" between problem definition and the computer language. They are descriptive in nature and machine independent.

A programmer needs to know very little about the machine on which the program is executed. Programming is now simpler because there is a buffer of software, the compiler, which handles all cross referencing and storage allocation. However, processing speed and efficient use of computer memory is sacrificed for the advantage of simplified programming. The high level language program must go through three processes before it is ready to be executed:

1. Translation: The translator program translates the source code into object code.
2. Linking: The linkage editor appends any necessary instructions or library routines referenced in the program.

3. Loading: The loader program loads the object code and its appended library functions/instructions, with all addresses resolved, into main memory for execution.

Figure 7-2 illustrates these processes, which are performed for most high level programming languages.

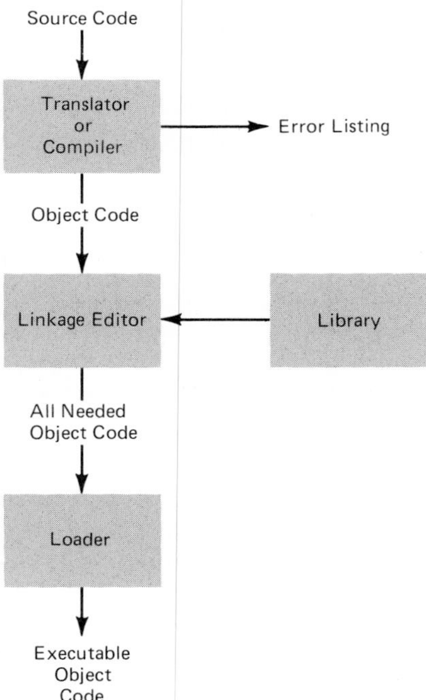

Figure 7-2 Translating Source Code into Executable Object Code

Our discussion will include six procedure-oriented languages—FORTRAN, COBOL, PL/1, BASIC, PASCAL, and ADA—and one problem-oriented language—RPG. We will illustrate selected languages with an example that calculates and prints a payroll register. A description of the algorithm is as follows:

1. Print the header for the payroll register.
2. Read in a record for each employee containing the object code describing the type of job, the employee's social security number, the number of hours worked, and his or her current hourly wage.
3. If the object code is equal to 1111, the employee is part time and no deductions are taken except for federal and state income taxes.
4. If the object code is equal to 1120, the employee is full time and all deductions are taken except for credit union dues.
5. If the object code is equal to 1122, the employee is full time and all deductions are taken.

6. Calculate the payroll for each employee with a valid object code, or else print an error message.
7. Finally, when the end of the input file is reached, print the totals for the payroll register.

This algorithm is designed to process any number of employees and print the total of their net earnings. A sample of the output, the payroll register, is illustrated in Figure 7-3.

PAYROLL REGISTER

Object Code	Employee Number	Hours Worked	Hourly Wage	Gross Pay	Social Security Tax	Federal Income Tax	State Income Tax	Credit Union	Retirement	Net Pay
1111	400941648	33.00	4.51	148.83	0.00	1.04	1.19	0.00	0.00	146.60
1122	224949460	40.00	5.10	204.00	13.67	23.05	6.12	10.20	10.20	140.76
1120	900221792	44.00	4.51	207.46	13.90	23.44	6.22	0.00	10.37	153.52
1122	224885493	45.00	7.25	344.38	23.07	38.91	10.33	17.22	17.22	237.62
1111	900120001	25.00	3.25	81.25	0.00	0.57	0.65	0.00	0.00	80.03
									Total Earnings:	758.53

Figure 7-3 Payroll Register

MANAGEMENT CASE 7-1

The Hercules Company recruits a large number of business majors such as management, marketing, finance, management science, and accounting each year. Ray Foy is director of personnel for the Hercules Company. Several operational managers in the company have suggested to Ray that all potential new hires of the company should have taken at least one programming course in their collegiate career. They argue that a person must understand programming to be able to use computers effectively and really understand what the computer is doing. However, Ray maintains that programming is becoming an obsolete skill. He states that certainly business personnel who are not programmers can utilize the computer in many effective ways without knowing how to program. For example, he states that there are many user-friendly packages available for microcomputers and personal work stations such as electronic worksheets, report generators, data base management systems, and graphics packages. All of which can be used without programming. Do you think that learning at least one programming language is useful to a business student?

FORTRAN

FORTRAN (FORmula TRANslator) is considered one of the oldest high level languages, dating back to the 1950s. Before the advent of FORTRAN most programming was done in machine or assembly language. FORTRAN, created in 1954, was developed for use in coding scientific and mathematical expressions. Therefore, algorithms dealing with processing of numbers or arrays of numbers can easily be coded in a FORTRAN program. Several versions have been released beginning with the original version, FORTRAN I. In 1958, FORTRAN II was devised, and FORTRAN IV was developed in 1962. In 1966, FORTRAN was standardized, bringing about the ANS FORTRAN version. Finally, in 1978, a new version called FORTRAN 77 was developed, which provides for structured, modular programs enhancing readability and overall writing. An instructional version of FORTRAN was developed at the University of Waterloo in Canada, and is called WATFIV.

A FORTRAN program is a sequence of *statements*. All statements are composed of keywords, variable names, and symbols. Keywords are verbs telling the computer which operations to perform, such as READ, WRITE, STOP, DO, and IF. Variable names are used to designate storage locations. Symbols, such as +, −, ×, etc., are used primarily for arithmetic operations. Figure 7-4 is an example of a FORTRAN 77 program.

There are two types of FORTRAN statements: 1) executable; and 2) nonexecutable. Nonexecutable statements are used to declare various characteristics of the program, such as data types or input/output formats. These statements are known as *specification statements*. They tell the computer how data is to be arranged when it is transferred between the computer and an I/O device. Examples in Figure 7-4 would be statements forty-seven through fifty-three. A specification statement can also tell the computer the data type of a particular variable. Examples are statements one and two. In FORTRAN, a real variable may have fractional values, while an integer variable can take only integer values. Statement five tells the computer to initialize the variable TOTAL to zero.

Executable statements tell the computer which operation to perform by the use of keywords and symbols. Executable statements can be further divided into the following classifications:

1. *Assignment statements* perform a series of arithmetic operations, placing the results of the operation into a storage location designated by the variable name to the left of the equal sign. Examples are statements sixty through sixty-seven in Figure 7-4.
2. *Control statements* control the order of execution within the program. The example illustrates the use of the IF-THEN-ELSE statement. Statement eighteen determines if the object code of the present time card is equal to 1111. If yes, deduct only 7 percent for federal withholding and 8 percent for state withholding. Else, if the object code equals 1120 or 1122, then . . . The END IF, at line forty, signals the end of the IF-THEN-ELSE statement.
3. *Input/output statements* instruct the computer from which input device or to what output device data is to be transferred. In our example, statement ten will read in the input values, using statement forty-seven to describe how the input data will be arranged. Statement forty-four will transfer data to an output device, the printer, using statement fifty-one to describe the layout of the data.

FORTRAN has the major advantage of a vast amount of experience behind its design, implementation, and standardization. Even though FORTRAN was primarily designed for scientific applications and efficient mathematical manipulations, it has been used for business data processing and file handling applications. However, before the advent of FORTRAN 77, which allows for structured programming, logical problems were difficult to express in FORTRAN. The FORTRAN 77 version has made writing and debugging programs easier and faster. FORTRAN processes large volumes of mathematical calculations efficiently and has good input/output facilities. However, FORTRAN can be expensive in terms of memory allocation for variables and constants. Another disadvantage of FORTRAN is that the language is "non-English-like" and requires extensive internal documentation.

FORTRAN has also been implemented on microcomputers. However, the standardization level of microcomputer FORTRAN varies, from having additional nonstandard features to lacking some very basic features. The most common version on microcomputers is FORTRAN IV.

```
      REAL EXTRA,OTIME,TOTAL,FCRATE,FTRATE,STRATE,CURATE,RTRATE,
     1     HOURS,RATE,GROSS,FICA,FIT,SIT,RETIRE,CUNION,NET,WHRS
      INTEGER EMPNO,OBCODE
      COMMON WHRS,OTIME,FCRATE,FTRATE,STRATE,RTRATE,CURATE,TOTAL,
     1       HOURS,RATE,GROSS,FICA,FIT,SIT,RETIRE,CUNION,NET
      COMMON OBCODE,EMPNO
      DATA TOTAL/0.0/
      WRITE (6,300)
      WRITE (6,500)
      WRITE (6,400)
   10 CONTINUE
      READ (5,200,END=100) OBCODE,EMPNO,HOURS,RATE
      OTIME=0.0
      WHRS=HOURS
      FCRATE=0.0
      FTRATE=0.0
      STRATE=0.0
      RTRATE=0.0
      CURATE=0.0
      IF (OBCODE.EQ.1111)THEN
         FTRATE=0.007
         STRATE=0.008
         CALL CALC
      ELSE
         IF ((OBCODE.EQ.1120).OR.(OBCODE.EQ.1122))THEN
            FCRATE=0.067
            FTRATE=0.113
            STRATE=0.03
            RTRATE=0.05
            IF (OBCODE.EQ.1122)THEN
               CURATE=0.05
            END IF
            IF (HOURS.GT.40.0) THEN
               EXTRA=HOURS-40.0
               OTIME=EXTRA*RATE*1.5
               WHRS=40.0
            END IF
            CALL CALC
         ELSE
            WRITE (6,900)
         END IF
      END IF
      GO TO 10
  100 CONTINUE
      WRITE (6,500)
      WRITE (6,700) TOTAL
      WRITE (6,800)
      STOP
  200 FORMAT (I4,I9,F5.2,F4.2)
  300 FORMAT ('1',50X,'Payroll Register')
  400 FORMAT (' ',56X,'Social',5X,'Federal',5X,'State'/
     1         ' ',1X,'Object',5X,'Employee',5X,'Hours',4X,'Hourly',5X,
     2         'Gross',5X,'Security',5X,'Income',4X,'Income',4X,'Credit',
     3         20X,'Net'/
     4         ' ',2X,'Code',7X,'Number',5X,'Worked',5X,'Wage',7X,'Pay',
     5         8X,'Tax',9X,'Tax',8X,'Tax',6X,'Union',4X,'Retirement',
     6         6X,'Pay'/)
  500 FORMAT (' ',1X)
  700 FORMAT (' ',95X,'Total Earnings: ',F8.2)
  800 FORMAT ('1',1X)
  900 FORMAT (' ',2X,'Invalid Object Code.')

      END
      SUBROUTINE CALC
      REAL EXTRA,OTIME,TOTAL,FCRATE,FTRATE,STRATE,CURATE,RTRATE,
     1     HOURS,RATE,GROSS,FICA,FIT,SIT,RETIRE,CUNION,NET,WHRS
      INTEGER EMPNO,OBCODE
      COMMON WHRS,OTIME,FCRATE,FTRATE,STRATE,RTRATE,CURATE,TOTAL,
     1       HOURS,RATE,GROSS,FICA,FIT,SIT,RETIRE,CUNION,NET
      COMMON OBCODE,EMPNO
      GROSS=(WHRS*RATE)+OTIME
      FICA=GROSS*FCRATE
      FIT=GROSS*FTRATE
      SIT=GROSS*STRATE
      RETIRE=GROSS*RTRATE
      CUNION=GROSS*CURATE
      NET=GROSS-(FICA+FIT+SIT+RETIRE+CUNION)
      TOTAL=TOTAL+NET
         WRITE (6,600) OBCODE,EMPNO,HOURS,RATE,GROSS,FICA,FIT,SIT,
     1                 CUNION,RETIRE,NET
  600 FORMAT (' ',2X,I4,5X,I9,4X,F6.2,4X,F6.2,4X,F7.2,5X,F6.2,6X,F6.2,
     1        4X,F6.2,4X,F6.2,6X,F6.2,6X,F7.2)
      RETURN
      END
```

Figure 7-4 Payroll Program Written in FORTRAN

COBOL

COBOL (Common Business-Oriented Language) is considered one of the leading and most widely used languages today. This language is considered to be the standard for business-oriented languages. COBOL was first conceived in 1959 by a group of users, programmers, and manufacturers from the government and business sectors, referred to then as the CODASYL Committee (Conference On DAta SYstems Languages). The goal of this committee was to design and implement an English-like common business language (COBOL). In December, 1959, the initial specifications for COBOL had been drafted, with the basic objective of making COBOL highly machine independent and self-documenting.

The first version of COBOL was published in 1960, and was known as COBOL-60. The second version, released in 1961, included many changes to the procedure division. An extended version of COBOL-61 was released in 1963 that included sorting and report writing routines. ANSI (American National Standards Institute) formed a committee to standardize COBOL. Several versions of COBOL had been developed so this committee used COBOL-68 as a basis for COBOL standardization. The standardization process was a very strict one, thereby solving the portability problem of having too many dialects of the language. COBOL became a truly common language. The CODASYL committee, in an effort to update the language, meets on a regular basis every year.

COBOL is English-like, making it easier to read and code. Therefore, COBOL can best be described by loosely comparing it to an English composition consisting of headings, sections, paragraphs, and sentences. Looking once again at our payroll problem, we will illustrate the various aspects of the COBOL language (refer to Figure 7-5).

The COBOL program is divided into four major parts, which are called *divisions*. Each division and its function is listed in the order they must appear within a program:

1. The *identification division* identifies the name and various documentary entries of the program.
2. The *environment division* identifies the input/output hardware needed to support the program.
3. The *data division* identifies the storage record layout for input, output, and the intermediate results (working storage).
4. The *procedure division* contains the instructions telling the computer what operations to perform.

All divisions except the identification division are further divided into *sections*. In our example, the environment division has two sections: 1) the configuration section, which describes the machine environment; and 2) the input-output section, which describes the file environment. The data division has two sections: 1) the file section, which describes the files to be processed; and 2) the working-storage section, which describes all variables containing intermediate results. The identification, environment, and data divisions are further divided into *paragraphs* containing *entries* and *clauses*, which are used to describe the various programming attributes discussed above.

```
    IDENTIFICATION DIVISION.
    PROGRAM-ID.
        PAYROLL.

    ENVIRONMENT DIVISION.
    CONFIGURATION SECTION.
    SPECIAL-NAMES.
        C01 IS TOP-OF-PAGE.
    INPUT-OUTPUT SECTION.
    FILE-CONTROL.
        SELECT CARD-IN-FILE ASSIGN TO UT-S-SYSIN.
        SELECT LINE-OUT-FILE ASSIGN TO UT-S-SYSOUT.

    DATA DIVISION.
    FILE SECTION.
    FD  CARD-IN-FILE
        LABEL RECORDS ARE OMITTED.
    01  CARD-IN-RECORD.
        05  I-OBCODE           PICTURE X(4).
        05  I-EMPNO            PICTURE X(9).
        05  I-HOURS            PICTURE 999V99.
        05  I-RATE             PICTURE 99V99.
        05  FILLER             PICTURE X(58).
    FD  LINE-OUT-FILE
        LABEL RECORDS ARE OMITTED.
    01  LINE-OUT-RECORD        PICTURE X(133).
    WORKING-STORAGE SECTION.
    77  WS-EXTRA               PICTURE 999V99.
    77  WS-OTIME               PICTURE 999V99.
1   77  WS-TOTAL               PICTURE 999V99 VALUE ZEROES.
    77  WS-FCRATE              PICTURE 9V999.
    77  WS-FTRATE              PICTURE 9V999.
    77  WS-STRATE              PICTURE 9V999.
    77  WS-RTRATE              PICTURE 9V999.
    77  WS-CURATE              PICTURE 9V999.
    77  WS-WHRS                PICTURE 999V99.
    77  WS-GROSS               PICTURE 9999V99.
    77  WS-FICA                PICTURE 999V99.
    77  WS-FIT                 PICTURE 999V99.
    77  WS-SIT                 PICTURE 999V99.
    77  WS-CUNION              PICTURE 999V99.
    77  WS-RETIRE              PICTURE 999V99.
    77  WS-NET                 PICTURE 9999V99.
2   01  OUT-OF-CARDS-FLAG      PICTURE X VALUE 'N'.
        88  OUT-OF-CARDS                 VALUE 'Y'.
3   01  FLAG                   PICTURE X VALUE 'N'.
    01  WS-DETAIL-LINE.
4       05  FILLER             PICTURE XXX VALUE SPACES.
        05  OBCODE             PICTURE X(4).
5       05  FILLER             PICTURE X(5) VALUE SPACES.
        05  EMPNO              PICTURE X(9).
6       05  FILLER             PICTURE X(4) VALUE SPACES.
        05  HOURS              PICTURE ZZ9.99.
7       05  FILLER             PICTURE X(4) VALUE SPACES.
        05  RATE               PICTURE ZZ9.99.
8       05  FILLER             PICTURE X(4) VALUE SPACES.
        05  GROSS              PICTURE ZZZ9.99.
9       05  FILLER             PICTURE X(5) VALUE SPACES.
        05  FICA               PICTURE ZZ9.99.
10      05  FILLER             PICTURE X(6) VALUE SPACES.
        05  FIT                PICTURE ZZ9.99.
11      05  FILLER             PICTURE X(4) VALUE SPACES.
        05  SIT                PICTURE ZZ9.99.
12      05  FILLER             PICTURE X(4) VALUE SPACES.
        05  CUNION             PICTURE ZZ9.99.
13      05  FILLER             PICTURE X(6) VALUE SPACES.
        05  RETIRE             PICTURE ZZ9.99.
14      05  FILLER             PICTURE X(6) VALUE SPACES.
        05  NET                PICTURE ZZZ9.99.
15      05  FILLER             PICTURE X(14) VALUE SPACES.
    01  WS-HEADER-LINE.
16      05  FILLER             PICTURE X(51) VALUE SPACES.
        05  FILLER             PICTURE X(16)
17          VALUE 'Payroll Register'.
18      05  FILLER             PICTURE X(66) VALUE SPACES.
    01  WS-COL-LINE-1.
19      05  FILLER             PICTURE X(57) VALUE SPACES.
        05  FILLER             PICTURE X(28)
20          VALUE 'Social     Federal      State'.
21      05  FILLER             PICTURE X(58) VALUE SPACES.
    01  WS-COL-LINE-2.
```

Figure 7-5 Payroll Program Written in COBOL

```
22              05  FILLER                PICTURE XX VALUE SPACES.
                05  FILLER                PICTURE X(118)
23                  VALUE 'Object      Employee     Hours     Hourly      Gross
     -                '     Security      Income      Income     Credit
     -                '                Net'.
24              05  FILLER                PICTURE X(16) VALUE SPACES.
            01  WS-COL-LINE-3.
25              05  FILLER                PICTURE XXX VALUE SPACES.
                05  FILLER                PICTURE X(117)
26                  VALUE 'Code        Number     Worked      Wage         Pay
     -                '        Tax          Tax          Tax        Union    Reti
     -                'rement      Pay'.
27              05  FILLER                PICTURE X(16) VALUE SPACES.
            01  WS-FOOTER-LINE.
28              05  FILLER                PICTURE X(96) VALUE SPACES.
                05  FILLER                PICTURE X(16)
29                  VALUE 'Total Earnings: '.
                05  TOTAL-EARNINGS        PICTURE ZZZZ9.99.
30              05  FILLER                PICTURE X(14) VALUE SPACES.
31          01  EMPTY-LINE                PICTURE X(133) VALUE SPACES.
            01  ERROR-MSG                 PICTURE X(21)
32              VALUE 'Invalid object code'.

33          PROCEDURE DIVISION.
            MAIN-LINE-ROUTINE.
34              OPEN INPUT CARD-IN-FILE
                     OUTPUT LINE-OUT-FILE.
35              PERFORM HEADER-PARAGRAPH.
36              READ CARD-IN-FILE
37                   AT END MOVE 'Y' TO OUT-OF-CARDS-FLAG.
38              PERFORM PROCESS-PAYROLL
                     UNTIL OUT-OF-CARDS.
39              PERFORM FOOTER-PARAGRAPH.

40              CLOSE CARD-IN-FILE
                      LINE-OUT-FILE.
            MAIN-LINE-ROUTINE-EXIT.
41              STOP RUN.

            HEADER-PARAGRAPH.
42              WRITE LINE-OUT-RECORD FROM WS-HEADER-LINE
                    AFTER ADVANCING TOP-OF-PAGE.
43              WRITE LINE-OUT-RECORD FROM WS-COL-LINE-1
                    AFTER ADVANCING 2 LINES.
44              WRITE LINE-OUT-RECORD FROM WS-COL-LINE-2
                    AFTER ADVANCING 1 LINES.
45              WRITE LINE-OUT-RECORD FROM WS-COL-LINE-3
                    AFTER ADVANCING 1 LINES.
46              WRITE LINE-OUT-RECORD FROM EMPTY-LINE
                    AFTER ADVANCING 1 LINES.
            PROCESS-PAYROLL.
47              MOVE 'Y' TO FLAG.
48              MOVE ZEROS TO WS-OTIME, WS-FCRATE, WS-FTRATE, WS-STRATE,
                              WS-RTRATE, WS-CURATE
49              MOVE I-HOURS TO WS-WHRS
50              IF I-OBCODE IS EQUAL 1111
                  THEN
51                   PERFORM OBCODE-1111-PARA
                  ELSE
52              IF I-OBCODE IS EQUAL 1120
                   THEN
53                    PERFORM OBCODE-1120-PARA
                   ELSE
54              IF I-OBCODE IS EQUAL 1122
                   THEN
55                    PERFORM OBCODE-1120-PARA
56                    PERFORM OBCODE-1122-PARA.
57              PERFORM COMPUTE-PAYROLL-PARAGRAPH.
58              PERFORM WRITE-LINE-PARAGRAPH.
59              READ CARD-IN-FILE
60                AT END MOVE 'Y' TO OUT-OF-CARDS-FLAG.

            OBCODE-1111-PARA.
61                  MOVE 0.007 TO WS-FTRATE.
62                  MOVE 0.008 TO WS-STRATE.
63                  MOVE 'N' TO FLAG.

            OBCODE-1120-PARA.
64              MOVE 0.067 TO WS-FCRATE.
65              MOVE 0.113 TO WS-FTRATE.
66              MOVE 0.03  TO WS-STRATE.
67              MOVE 0.05  TO WS-RTRATE.
```

Figure 7-5 *(continued)*

```
68          IF I-HOURS IS GREATER THAN 40.0
               THEN
69                SUBTRACT 40.0 FROM I-HOURS GIVING WS-EXTRA
70                COMPUTE WS-OTIME ROUNDED =
                           WS-EXTRA * I-RATE * 1.5
71                MOVE 40.0 TO WS-WHRS.
72          MOVE 'N' TO FLAG.

        OBCODE-1122-PARA.
73          MOVE 0.05 TO WS-CURATE.
74          MOVE 'N' TO FLAG.

        COMPUTE-PAYROLL-PARAGRAPH.
75          COMPUTE WS-GROSS ROUNDED = (WS-WHRS * I-RATE) + WS-OTIME.
76          MULTIPLY WS-GROSS BY WS-FCRATE GIVING WS-FICA ROUNDED.
77          MULTIPLY WS-GROSS BY WS-FTRATE GIVING WS-FIT  ROUNDED.
78          MULTIPLY WS-GROSS BY WS-STRATE GIVING WS-SIT  ROUNDED.
79          MULTIPLY WS-GROSS BY WS-RTRATE GIVING WS-RETIRE ROUNDED.
80          MULTIPLY WS-GROSS BY WS-CURATE GIVING WS-CUNION ROUNDED.
81          COMPUTE WS-NET = WS-GROSS -
                   (WS-FICA + WS-FIT + WS-SIT + WS-RETIRE + WS-CUNION)
82          ADD WS-NET TO WS-TOTAL.

        WRITE-LINE-PARAGRAPH.
83          IF FLAG = 'N'
               THEN
84                MOVE I-OBCODE TO OBCODE
85                MOVE I-EMPNO TO EMPNO
86                MOVE I-HOURS TO HOURS
87                MOVE I-RATE TO RATE
88                MOVE WS-GROSS TO GROSS
89                MOVE WS-FICA TO FICA
90                MOVE WS-FIT TO FIT
91                MOVE WS-SIT TO SIT
92                MOVE WS-CUNION TO CUNION
93                MOVE WS-RETIRE TO RETIRE
94                MOVE WS-NET TO NET
95                WRITE LINE-OUT-RECORD FROM WS-DETAIL-LINE
                      AFTER ADVANCING 1 LINES
               ELSE
96                WRITE LINE-OUT-RECORD FROM ERROR-MSG
                      AFTER ADVANCING 1 LINES.

        FOOTER-PARAGRAPH.
97          MOVE WS-TOTAL TO TOTAL-EARNINGS.
98          WRITE LINE-OUT-RECORD FROM WS-FOOTER-LINE
                AFTER ADVANCING 2 LINES.
99          WRITE LINE-OUT-RECORD FROM EMPTY-LINE
                AFTER ADVANCING TOP-OF-PAGE.
```

Figure 7-5 (*continued*)

The procedure division is structured differently than the other divisions. It consists only of *sentences*, which are combinations of *statements*. For example,

MOVE 0.067 TO WS-FCRATE.

is an imperative sentence telling the computer to assign the value 0.067 to the variable WS-FCRATE, and

```
IF I-OBCODE IS EQUAL 1122
   THEN
      PERFORM OBCODE-1120-PARA
      PERFORM OBCODE-1122-PARA.
```

is a conditional sentence where

PERFORM OBCODE-1120-PARA

is a statement beginning with the verb PERFORM.

A statement is a combination of words, symbols, and phrases beginning with a COBOL verb. COBOL words are of three types:

1. *Reserved words* have special meaning to the compiler. The COBOL verbs COMPUTE, ADD, and SUBTRACT are examples.
2. *User-defined words* are created by the programmer to be used in the program. Examples in Figure 7-5 are:
   a) CARD-IN-FILE b) LINE-OUT-FILE c) MAIN-LINE-ROUTINE
3. *System names* are supplied by the manufacturer of the hardware to allow certain elements in the program to correspond with various hardware devices. Examples are UT-S-SYSIN, specifying the card reader, and UT-S-SYSOUT specifying the line printer.

COBOL is a very standardized language and can therefore be moved between machines fairly easily. The advantage of COBOL for data processing is that the language itself was conceived with the objective of data processing in mind. COBOL is extremely readable and self-documenting. However, efficiency in terms of coding and actual execution is sacrificed. Also, because of the nature of its syntax, semantic errors can occur in COBOL that are very difficult to detect. For report generation, COBOL could be an extremely useful tool because of its report writer facility. COBOL has limited facilities for mathematical notation but does have excellent facilities for character data processing.

COBOL would be useful for a microcomputer because of its commercial applicability. However, COBOL is a "wordy" language and the compiler is fairly large in terms of memory allocation. COBOL translators have been developed for major microcomputers. Another disadvantage is that COBOL is a record-oriented, batch processing language and therefore may have limited use for a microcomputer because it lacks interactive facilities. However, some implementations of COBOL do provide support for screen layout and interactive processing.

PL/1

PL/1 (Programming Language/1) is a comprehensive language. Because PL/1 is so extensive, its richness has permitted a wide variety of applications. PL/1 can be used for scientific, business data processing, text processing, and systems applications. The language was conceived in the 1960s, when programmers were divided into three distinct groups: 1) scientific programmers; 2) business/commercial programmers; and 3) special-purpose programmers. IBM, along with SHARE and GUIDE, a scientific users group and a commercial users group respectively, developed PL/1 with the following objectives in mind:

1. machine independence
2. access to the machine's operating system
3. structured and modular programs
4. easy-to-learn language
5. readable and easy-to-write code
6. bridging the gap between commercial and scientific high level languages

In 1964, the specifications for the language were presented to GUIDE and SHARE. The specifications incorporated features from FORTRAN (scientific applications language), COBOL (business data processing language), and ALGOL (expressive algebraic language). PL/1 was successful in meeting the objectives established. The language was standardized by ANSI in 1976 after further development, but it is not as widely used as FORTRAN or COBOL.

The PL/1 program is a block structured program consisting of statements delimited by semicolons. Being a block structured language, PL/1 programs are headed by labeled statements and terminated by an END statement. The header statement in our example (Figure 7-6) is payroll:PROCEDURE OPTIONS (MAIN); where "payroll" is the program name. Another major block residing within the program must also be headed by a labeled statement (statement forty-two). This block of statements is called an *internal subroutine*.

The most widely used statements will be discussed by classification of statement type.

Data Definition Statement. Data elements are introduced into a PL/1 program through the use of the DECLARE statement. This statement specifies the data element, its data type, and its precision level. For example,

DECLARE total FIXED DECIMAL (6,2) INITIAL (0);

tells the PL/1 compiler that the variable "total" has a type of fixed decimal (for business applications) and a precision as shown below:

XXXXVXX

where the "V" is an implied decimal point. The value of zero is also placed in the variable at compilation time. Another variable type illustrated is the BIT (statement three), which is used in logical expressions, but not in arithmetic expressions. There are many other data types that can also be used, such as FILE, CHARACTER, and FIXED BINARY.

An interesting statement is the ON statement (statement five), which states that if the end of the input file is encountered, change the boolean (or logical) value in the condition flag to indicate the new condition. If this statement were not used, our program would abnormally terminate after the last record was read. This ON statement feature is known as exception handling.

Control statements. Statements controlling the flow of execution through the program in our example are 1) the IF-THEN-ELSE statement, and 2) the DO-WHILE statement. The IF-THEN-ELSE has already been introduced in the FORTRAN section. Statement twelve is the beginning of a DO-WHILE, which will perform the statements up to statement forty (the END statement) until the end of the input file is reached. In other words, the DO-WHILE is a repetitive loop in which no statements are executed until the condition in statement twelve is met.

Input/output Statements. Examples of input/output statements in our example are the GET EDIT and the PUT EDIT statements. Statement eleven is an *edit-directed* input statement, which means the programmer must tell the computer how the data is arranged when it is read into the program. Statements six through ten are edit-directed

```
payroll:PROCEDURE OPTIONS (MAIN);
   DECLARE empno                               FIXED DECIMAL (9),
          (fcrate,ftrate,strate,curate,
           rtrate)                             FIXED DECIMAL (4,3),
          (extra,otime,hours,whrs,fica,
           fit,sit,cunion,retire)              FIXED DECIMAL (5,2),
           rate                                FIXED DECIMAL (4,2),
          (gross,net)                          FIXED DECIMAL (6,2),
           total                               FIXED DECIMAL (6,2)
                                                  INITIAL (0),
           obcode                              FIXED DECIMAL (4);
   DECLARE(eof,no)                             BIT(1) INITIAL ('0'B),
           yes                                 BIT(1) INITIAL ('1'B);
   DECLARE sysin                               FILE STREAM INPUT,
           sysprint                            FILE STREAM OUTPUT;
   ON ENDFILE (sysin) eof = yes;
   PUT PAGE EDIT ('Payroll Register')(X(50),A);
   PUT SKIP(2) EDIT ('Social      Federal      State')(X(56),A);
   PUT SKIP EDIT ('Object','Employee','Hours','Hourly','Gross',
                  'Security','Income','Income','Credit','Net')
                 (X(1),A,X(5),A,X(5),A,X(4),A,X(5),A,X(5),A,X(5),A,
                  X(4),A,X(4),A,X(20),A);
   PUT SKIP EDIT ('Code','Number','Worked','Wage','Pay','Tax','Tax',
                  'Tax','Union','Retirement','Pay')
                 (X(2),A,X(7),A,X(5),A,X(5),A,X(7),A,X(8),A,X(9),A,
                  X(8),A,X(6),A,X(4),A,X(6),A);
   PUT SKIP;
   GET SKIP EDIT (obcode,empno,hours,rate)(f(4),f(9),f(5,2),f(4,2));
   DO WHILE (eof = no);
      otime = 0.0;
      whrs = hours;
      fcrate = 0.0;
      ftrate = 0.0;
      strate = 0.0;
      rtrate = 0.0;
      curate = 0.0;
      IF obcode = 1111
         THEN DO;
            ftrate = 0.007;
            strate = 0.008;
            CALL calc_payroll;
              END;
         ELSE
      IF obcode = 1120 | obcode = 1122
         THEN DO;
            fcrate=0.067;
            ftrate=0.113;
            strate=0.03;
            rtrate=0.05;
            IF obcode=1122
               THEN curate=0.05;
            IF hours > 40.0
               THEN DO;
                  extra = hours - 40.0;
                  otime = extra * rate * 1.5;
                  whrs = 40.0;
                     END;
            CALL calc_payroll;
              END;
         ELSE
            PUT SKIP EDIT ('Invalid Object Code.')(X(3),A);
         GET SKIP EDIT (obcode,empno,hours,rate)
                       (f(4),f(9),f(5,2),f(4,2));
   END;
   PUT SKIP(2) EDIT ('Total Earnings: ',TOTAL)(X(96),A,F(7,2));
calc_payroll:PROCEDURE;
   gross = (whrs * rate) + otime;
   fica = gross * fcrate;
   fit = gross * ftrate;
   sit = gross * strate;
   retire = gross * rtrate;
   cunion = gross * curate;
   net = gross - (fica + fit + sit + retire + cunion);
   total = total + net;
   PUT SKIP EDIT (obcode,empno,hours,rate,gross,fica,fit,sit,cunion,
                  retire,net)(X(2),F(4),X(5),F(9),X(4),F(6,2),X(4),
                  F(6,2),X(4),F(7,2),X(5),F(6,2),X(6),F(6,2),X(4),
                  F(6,2),X(4),F(6,2),X(6),F(6,2),X(6),F(7,2));
RETURN;
END;

END;
```

Figure 7-6 Payroll Program Written in PL/1

output statements. Again, the programmer specifies the layout of the data to be printed. PL/1 provides other I/O statements where the programmer need not specify the format of data. They are the PUT LIST and GET LIST statements. These are called *list-directed* I/O statements.

Assignment Statements. The assignment statement is in the following form: *variable = expression*—no punctuation follows the expression. The expression specifies that a particular computation takes place, and the results of the computation are assigned to the variable to the left of the equal sign.

For the novice programmer, PL/1 is a helpful language and is easy to learn because of its default features. If the programmer is vague in specifying any feature within the program, the compiler will assume (default to) the most frequently used specifications. PL/1 is also well-suited to the experienced programmer because it is designed to promote better utilization of computer resources. PL/1 allows the programmer access to the computer's operating system, providing versatility in coding.

PL/1 has substantial character handling facilities and is well-suited for business data processing. The language has very good file handling characteristics, as do COBOL and FORTRAN, without being limited to particular types of applications as those languages are. PL/1 is a powerful language, but efficiency in terms of compilation time, execution, and storage is sacrificed for this power.

PL/1 is not generally available on microprocessors due to the size of the compiler, although variations of PL/1 (PL/M and MPL) are available.

BASIC

BASIC (Basic All-purpose Symbolic Instruction Code) is a programming language that has been implemented on virtually every type of computer from the smallest micro to the largest mainframes. BASIC was conceived in 1963 and implemented in 1964 at Dartmouth College. The language was designed as an easy-to-learn, easy-to-use, interactive language with no particular applications area targeted. BASIC was created because of the trend away from batch processing toward interactive systems.

There are many versions of BASIC available having the essence of the Dartmouth version preserved within their design. An effort to standardize BASIC began in 1970, and an ANSI standard was established in 1978. However, many versions of BASIC still exist, either commercially or by some hobbyist's own invention. A standard does exist, but the term BASIC refers to a classification of the language and not to the particular, standard version of the language.

As previously stated, BASIC is an easy language to use, once the following core statements have been learned. These statements are used in almost every version of BASIC implemented.

Data Definition Statements. The data definition statement DIM is used to define arrays, and REF is used to define functions used within the program.

Control Statements. Control of the flow of execution is performed by the GO TO, IF THEN, FOR NEXT, and GOSUB RETURN statements. The GO TO statement causes an unconditional branching to a designated statement. The IF THEN statement (see statement 230 in Figure 7-7) causes a conditional two way branching. The FOR NEXT construct allows for repetitive looping. The statements will be executed at least once before the condition is tested. In other words, there is no pretest of the condition.

```
100    PRINT TAB(51),'Payroll Register'
101    PRINT ' '
110    PRINT TAB(57),'Social',TAB(68),'Federal',TAB(80),'State'
120    PRINT ' '
130    PRINT TAB(2),'Object',TAB(13),'Employee',TAB(26),'Hours',TAB(35),
140    PRINT 'Hourly',TAB(46),'Gross',TAB(56),'Security',TAB(69),'Income',
150    PRINT TAB(79),'Income',TAB(89),'Credit',TAB(115),'Net'
160    PRINT TAB(3),'Code',TAB(14),'Number',TAB(25),'Worked',TAB(36),
170    PRINT 'Wage',TAB(47),'Pay',TAB(58),'Tax',TAB(70),'Tax',TAB(81),
180    PRINT 'Tax',TAB(90),'Union',TAB(99),'Retirement',TAB(115),'Pay'
190    PRINT  ' '
200    LET T =  0.0
210    REM......read in object code, empno, hours, and hourly rate
220    READ O1,E1,H,R3
230    IF O1 = 0.0 THEN 580
240       LET W = H
250       LET O2 = 0.0
560       LET F1 = 0.0
270       LET F2 = 0.0
280       LET S1 = 0.0
290       LET R1 = 0.0
300       IF O1 = 1111 THEN 340
310       IF O1 = 1120 THEN 400
320       IF O1 = 1122 THEN 380
330       GO TO 610
340    REM....for object code 1111
350       LET F2 = 0.007
360       LET S1 = 0.008
370       GO TO 450
380    REM....for object code 1122
390       C1 = 0.05
400    REM....for object code 1120 and 1122
410       F1 = 0.067
420       F2 = 0.113
430       S1 = 0.03
440       R1 = 0.05
450    REM....calculate payroll and print line
460       LET G = (W * R3) + O2
470       LET F3 = G * F1
480       LET F4 = G * F2
490       LET S2 = G * S1
500       LET C2 = G * C1
510       LET R2 = G * R1
520       LET N = G - (F3 + F4 + S2 + C2 + R2)
530       LET T = T + N
540       PRINT TAB(3),O1,TAB(12),E1,TAB(25),H,TAB(35),R3,TAB(45),G,
550       PRINT TAB(57),F3,TAB(69),F4,TAB(79),S2,TAB(89),R2,TAB(101),C2,
560       PRINT TAB(113),N
570    GO TO 210
580    REM....write total net earnings
590    PRINT TAB(96),'Total Earnings: ',TAB(117),T
600    GO TO 690
610    REM....write error message
620    PRINT TAB(3),'Invalid object code.'
630    REM....data cards
640    DATA 1111, 400941648, 33.00, 4.51,
650    DATA 1122, 224949460, 40.00, 5.10,
660    DATA 1120, 900221792, 44.00, 4.51,
670    DATA 1122, 224885493, 45.00, 7.25,
680    DATA 1111, 900120001, 25.00, 3.25,
681    DATA 0, 0, 0, 0
690    END
```

Figure 7-7 Payroll Program Written in BASIC

The GOSUB, used in conjunction with a RETURN, allows modularity through the use of subroutines. The statements between the referenced statement in the GOSUB and the RETURN are executed and the flow of execution returns to the statement following the GOSUB.

Input/output Statements. Input of data is performed either by the INPUT statements for interactive mode, or the READ statement (see statement 220) for batch mode. The READ statement reads in the data contained in the DATA statements (see statements 640–681). Output is performed by the PRINT statement which sends output back to the terminal.

Assignment/arithmetic Statements. Assignment and arithmetic statements are similar to FORTRAN except that these statements must be prefixed with the key word LET (see statement 460). The syntax is as follows: *LET variable = expression*—no punctuation follows the expression.

Another statement illustrated in our example is the REMARK statement (abbreviated to REM). This statement is used when the programmer internally documents the program.

BASIC is not a "well-structured" programming language (even though more structured versions do exist, such as SBASIC). A structured programming language allows programs to be broken down into visible logical units that are easily read. Therefore, although BASIC is a simple language to learn, complex problems could make programming and readability difficult. Another factor leading to the lack of readability of BASIC is that variable names can only be one character long, with an optional digit or dollar sign ($) for character data.

BASIC is used, with much innovation, on most microcomputers. Even though BASIC is standardized, many versions are available. Consequently, the portability of the language (i.e., the transferability of programs from one machine to another) is low. In other words, one version of BASIC may not be compatible from one compiler to another. BASIC enjoys a great deal of popularity on the small computer even though it is an unstructured language and has very limited screen handling facilities. A major reason for this popularity is that the language is very easy to learn and has applicability to any area from a very simple arithmetic program to a very complicated file handling system.

MANAGEMENT CASE 7-2

Jim Shotts is a newly hired programmer analyst in the system development group of the Virginia Company. Jim has had training in several programming languages including COBOL, PASCAL, and BASIC. In a discussion with his supervisor, he has expressed concern about the company's policy of all business programs being written in COBOL. He feels there are better languages than COBOL. He argues that almost all business college graduates now know how to write programs in BASIC and that this will be even more true in the future. For this reason he feels that business programs should be written in BASIC since the language is familiar to a wide number of users. Evaluate Jim's position.

PASCAL

The programming language PASCAL (named for Blaise Pascal, a pioneer in computer science) was developed as an educational tool to encourage the writing of well-structured, readable programs. It is adaptable to business and scientific applications and is considered a simple yet versatile language. PASCAL was first implemented in 1970 in Zurich, Switzerland. The PASCAL language design is very similar to ALGOL-60 (as is PL/1). PASCAL was intended to be a low cost, student-oriented language. By low cost we mean in terms of storage and processing time.

PASCAL, like PL/1, is a block structured language consisting of groups of statements enclosed within the BEGIN statement (statement twenty-four), and the END statement (statement seventy-six). Header statements are needed for a major block of code. For the main program the statement PROGRAM payroll (INPUT,

OUTPUT); is needed in our example (Figure 7-8). As in PL/1, the internal procedure, located at the beginning of the PASCAL program, must also have a header statement (statement nine). Note that the procedure is also enclosed within BEGIN and END statements.

PASCAL is very similar to PL/1 in statement structure except for minor differences in the use of the BEGIN and END statements and the use of the semicolon as a statement separator. It also has certain core statements.

Data Definition Statements. Data within a PASCAL program may be introduced through the use of the VAR statement (statements two through seven). The programmer can specify the data type of the variables used within the program as REAL, INTEGER, CHARACTER, and BOOLEAN. The language has strong data structuring capabilities provided by the compiler, making less work for the programmer. In other words, the programmer does not include precision levels for the variables when declaring them, as is done in PL/1.

Control Statements. Statements controlling the flow of execution in a PASCAL program are 1) the IF-THEN-ELSE statement; 2) the WHILE-DO statement; 3) the REPEAT-UNTIL statement; and 4) the CASE statement. The IF-THEN-ELSE and WHILE-DO statements have already been illustrated in previous sections. The REPEAT-UNTIL statement is similar to the WHILE-DO in that it is a repetitive loop. However, the statements within the loop are executed before the condition is checked. Therefore, the statements are always executed at least once. The CASE statement is similar to a series of IF-THEN-ELSE statements. A certain path through the program will be taken, depending upon which of the multiple conditions is true.

Input/output Statements. Input into a PASCAL program is done by utilizing the READ or READLN statements. The READ statement reads until a blank character appears within the input file, while the READLN will read the input until the end of the line or card image. The READLN was used in the payroll illustration (statement thirty-nine). Data types are checked by the system, so the programmer need not specify the format of the input file, as with PL/1.

Output is performed by using the WRITE or WRITELN statements. The WRITE statement will write the data out to the output device, one data element at a time, without moving to the next output line. Therefore, the next output statement will place the data on the same line following the previous data element. The WRITELN will write the data out to the output device, and then move to a new line. Consequently, when the next output statement is encountered, its data will be written on the next line.

Assignment/arithmetic statements. The syntax of the assignment statement in PASCAL is *variable : = expression;*. The assignment statement is essentially the same as that used in PL/1, except the assignment operator is ":=" as illustrated in the example in statements eleven through eighteen.

PASCAL is an excellent language for a microcomputer because its compiler is of a manageable size, and is cost efficient in terms of memory allocation. Other favorable factors are the language's simplicity, versatility, and fast execution time. PASCAL is fairly standardized (de facto), largely due to the Jenkins and Wirth document "The PASCAL Report." The language is also extremely compact in that there are very few reserved words to learn. A disadvantage of PASCAL is its very poor character handling facilities. The language only processes one character at a time thus requiring the use of arrays which can be very cumbersome.

```
PROGRAM payroll (INPUT,OUTPUT);
   VAR
      empno,obcode : INTEGER;
      fcrate,ftrate,strate,curate,rtrate : REAL;
      extra,otime,hours,whrs,rate : REAL;
      fica,fit,sit,cunion,retire : REAL;
      gross,net,total : REAL;

PROCEDURE calculate_payroll;
   BEGIN
      gross := (whrs * rate) + otime;
      fica := gross * fcrate;
      fit := gross * ftrate;
      sit := gross * strate;
      retire := gross * rtrate;
      cunion := gross * curate;
      net := gross - (fica + fit + sit + retire + cunion);
      total := total + net;
      WRITELN (obcode:6,empno:14,hours:10:2,rate:10:2,gross:11:2,
               fica:11:2,fit:11:2,sit:11:2,cunion:10:2,retire:12:2,
               net:13:2)
   END;

   BEGIN
      total := 0.0;
      PAGE;
      WRITELN ('Payroll Register':66);
      WRITELN (' ');
      WRITELN ('Social      Federal      State':84);
      WRITELN ('Object':7,'Employee':13,'Hours':10,'Hourly':10,
                  'Gross':10,'Security':13,'Income':11,'Income':10,
                  'Credit':10,'Net':23);
      WRITELN ('Code':6,'Number':13,'Worked':11,'Wage':9,'Pay':10,
               'Tax':11,'Tax':12,'Tax':11,'Union':11,'Retirement':14,
               'Pay':9);
      WRITELN (' ');
      WHILE NOT EOF DO
         BEGIN
            READLN (obcode,empno,hours,rate);
            otime := 0.0;
            whrs := hours;
            fcrate := 0.0;
            ftrate := 0.0;
            strate := 0.0;
            rtrate := 0.0;
            curate := 0.0;
            IF obcode = 1111
               THEN BEGIN
                  ftrate := 0.007;
                  strate := 0.008;
                  calculate_payroll
                     END
               ELSE
            IF (obcode = 1120) OR (obcode = 1122)
               THEN BEGIN
                  fcrate := 0.067;
                  ftrate := 0.113;
                  strate := 0.03;
                  rtrate := 0.05;
                  IF obcode = 1122
                     THEN curate := 0.05;
                  IF hours > 40.0
                     THEN BEGIN
                        extra := hours - 40.0;
                        otime := extra * rate * 1.5;
                        whrs := 40.0
                           END;
                  calculate_payroll
                     END
            ELSE WRITELN ('Invalid Object Code.':24);
         END;
      WRITELN (' ');
      WRITELN ('Total Earnings: ':110,total:9:2);
      PAGE;
      WRITELN (' ')
   END.
```

Figure 7-8 Payroll Program Written in PASCAL

ADA

From 1975 to 1979, progressively comprehensive specifications were developed by the Department of Defense (DOD) for a new programming language. As a result of this effort, in 1979 ADA was designed (named for Augusta Ada Byron, the first programmer). The language is still in the development stage and is expected to be completed in 1984. ADA, based on PASCAL, was created for the DOD as a portable, well-structured language to be used primarily in a multiprocessor environment for scientific and systems programming. The language was developed because the DOD needed a common language to meet its programming needs. ADA is versatile enough to be used in a wide variety of applications.

ADA is a block structured language which provides for a *strict* form of modular programming. All major blocks of code are headed by declarative statements and are set off by BEGIN-END statements. Subroutines are located at the beginning of the program as seen in Figure 7–9. Modularity is enhanced in the language through the use of *modules* that can be written and compiled separately from the main procedure. Modules are collections of variables, constants, statements, subroutines, or other modules. Modules are of two types:

1. *Packages*—logical collections of entities (declarations, statements, procedures, etc.) that cover a certain logical aspect of the application.
2. *Tasks*—independent collections of statements executed in the order required by the system, without any dependency or order among the tasks. These tasks facilitate the multiprocessor environment.

In our example, the program uses the package TEXT IO for performing input and output of data.

ADA is very similar to PASCAL in syntax except for minor variations. The language uses *terminating keywords* (e.g., END IF, END LOOP, END CASE, etc.) in place of BEGIN-END statements, and semicolons are used as statement terminators (as PL/1) not as statement separators as in PASCAL.

Core statements include:

Data Definition Statements. The declaration statements for variables are in the form *variable : data type;*. Examples in the program are statements four through eight.

Control Statements. Statements controlling the flow of execution through the ADA program are as follows:

1. the IF-THEN-ELSIF-ELSE statement
2. the LOOP statement
3. the WHILE-LOOP statement
4. the FOR-LOOP statement
5. the CASE-OF statement

```
1 |   WITH TEXT_IO; USING TEXT_IO;
2 |   PROCEDURE payroll IS
3 |      PRAGMA MAIN;
4 |         empno,obcode : INTEGER;
5 |         fcrate,ftrate,strate,curate,rtrate : FIXED;
6 |         extra,otime,hours,whrs,rate : FIXED;
7 |         fica,fit,sit,cunion,retire : FIXED;
8 |         gross,net,total : FIXED;
9 |
```

Figure 7-9 Payroll Program Written in ADA

```
   PROCEDURE calculate_payroll IS
     BEGIN
       gross := (whrs * rate) + otime;
       fica := gross * fcrate;
       fit := gross * ftrate;
       sit := gross * strate;
       retire := gross * rtrate;
       cunion := gross * curate;
       net := gross - (fica + fit + sit + retire + cunion);
       total := total + net;
       PUT (obcode,6);
       PUT (empno,14);
       PUT (hours,10,2);
       PUT (rate,10,2);
       PUT (gross,11,2);
       PUT (fica,11,2);
       PUT (fit,11,2);
       PUT (sit,11,2);
       PUT (cunion,10,2);
       PUT (retire,12,2);
       PUT (net,13,2);
       PUT (NEWLINE);
     END;

     BEGIN
       total := 0.0;
       PUT ('Payroll Register',66);
       PUT (NEWLINE);
       PUT (' ');
       PUT (NEWLINE);
       PUT ('Social        Federal       State',84);
       PUT (NEWLINE);
       PUT (' Object       Employee      Hours       Hourly',40);
       PUT ('        Gross       Security       Income       Income',44);
       PUT ('      Credit                    Net',33);
       PUT (NEWLINE);
       PUT ('  Code          Number       Worked       Wage',39);
       PUT ('          Pay           Tax            Tax             Tax',43);
       PUT ('          Union       Retirement          Pay',34);
       PUT (NEWLINE);
       PUT (' ');
       PUT (NEWLINE);
       WHILE NOT END_OF_FILE LOOP
           GETLN (obcode,empno,hours,rate);
           otime := 0.0;
           whrs := hours;
           fcrate := 0.0;
           ftrate := 0.0;
           strate := 0.0;
           rtrate := 0.0;
           curate := 0.0;
           IF obcode = 1111 THEN
             ftrate := 0.007;
             strate := 0.008;
             calculate_payroll;
           ELSIF obcode = 1120 OR obcode = 1122 THEN
             fcrate := 0.067;
             ftrate := 0.113;
             strate := 0.03;
             rtrate := 0.05;
             IF obcode = 1122 THEN
               curate := 0.05;
             END_IF;
             IF hours > 40.0 THEN
               extra := hours - 40.0;
               otime := extra * rate * 1.5;
               whrs := 40.0;
             END_IF;
             calculate_payroll;
           ELSE
             PUT_LINE ('Invalid Object Code.',24);
           END_IF;
         END_LOOP;
       PUT (' ');
       PUT (NEWLINE);
       PUT ('Total Earnings: ',110);
       PUT (total,9,2);
       PUT (NEWLINE);
       PUT (' ');
       PUT (NEWLINE);
     END payroll;
```

Figure 7-9 *(continued)*

The IF-THEN-ELSE statement (statements sixty-one through eighty-one) is similar to other languages. However, a new keyword, ELSIF, is used that allows for nested conditional statements. The LOOP is an infinite repetitive loop terminated only by the EXIT statement, which flags an exception. This loop would be used in a program constantly monitoring an apparatus or device. The WHILE-LOOP statement (statement fifty-two) performs a pretest before executing the repetition, and the FOR-LOOP statement is an iterative repetition controlled by counting. The CASE-OF statement is similar to the CASE statement used in PASCAL.

Input/output Statements. ADA provides a package for input/output facilities. Subroutine calls are used for input/output functions. All text output in our example is performed by the procedure PUT (statements twenty through thirty-one), which is similar to WRITE in PASCAL. This procedure uses parameters specifying types of variables and their layout. Input of data is performed by the procedure GET, which is equivalent to READ in PASCAL. In our example, input is performed by the GETLN procedure (statement fifty-three), which is equivalent to READLN in PASCAL. These input/output procedures can be written by the applications programmer and contained within the package TEXT IO.

Assignment/arithmetic Statements. The syntax of the assignment statement in the ADA language is *«label» variable := expression;* where the statement label, enclosed in double angle brackets, is optional.

ADA is a very versatile language. However, unlike PASCAL, it is a very complex language intended for embedded programming environments. An advantage of ADA is that it is an up-to-date language incorporating new technology as well as experiences with other languages. Therefore, it is an efficient, modular language that is very amenable to change. A disadvantage of ADA is that it is a very complex language to learn and use. This disadvantage may possibly outweigh its substantial advantages. A version of ADA has been described for microcomputers, and a version for the DEC VAX computer also exists. ADA, however, is still in the developmental stage.

RPG

RPG (Report Program Generator) is a problem-oriented language. That is, the programmer or user describes the type of report desired, and the RPG system will create it. The basic objective of RPG is to simplify and facilitate the generation of reports from sequential files.

RPG was introduced in 1964, and an improved version, RPG II, followed in 1971. RPG is designed for only one application: to update and produce output from sequential files. RPG is a declarative or descriptive language. Input into the RPG system is specification forms on which the programmer describes the report to be generated.

A report is composed of three major parts: 1) the header; 2) detail lines; and 3) the footer. A programmer uses the specification forms to describe the input record layout and field definitions, indicators used in the program, intermediate calculations performed, and the formats of the header, detailed lines, and footer. The forms are described as follows:

1. The *input specifications form* is used to describe the layout of an individual input record. The type of records and which input records are to be read within the file are also defined. The input record is eighty characters long. The input form identifies

the input file for a particular record. A record is composed of *fields* (the basic unit of data in RPG). The input form also describes the format of each field within that record.

2. The *calculation specifications form* is used to describe what operation is to be performed. It also describes the conditions making it necessary to perform the operation as well as what tests should be performed on the results.
3. The *output specifications form* is used to describe the layout of the header, detail lines, and footer of the output files. Any file used for output must have an output format description. The output form specifies the exact layout of each report in the output file. The form also specifies the conditions under which each record should be generated. As with the input form, the output form has two parts: the file identification that identifies the output records and how they should be generated, and a file description that identifies the format of each field within the output record.
4. The *file description specifications form* identifies the I/O files as well as their attributes and characteristics. This form also designates the I/O device and medium to be used.
5. The *file extension specifications form* is used to provide descriptions for additional features such as table searching, merging multiple input files, and accessing nonsequential files.
6. The *line counter specification form* is used when reports are placed on an intermediate storage medium (tape or disk) from where they will ultimately be output. This form defines the carriage control during the process of creating the report.

RPG is a very machine dependent language, primarily supported by IBM. Other manufacturers also provide their own variations and so there is no standard for RPG. RPG is very limited in scope and is generally used for report generation in data processing applications. The language is not suited for complex problems requiring extensive programming logic. An advantage of RPG is that it can be implemented at small computer installations because it has minimal storage requirements.

LANGUAGE SELECTION

This section is not an attempt to make critical judgments concerning languages previously discussed. The choice of a particular language ultimately depends upon the individual programmer and the particular needs and objectives of the system. However, there are some objective factors influencing language selection.

The selection of a language for a particular programming application is a very important and sometimes difficult task. When evaluating the features of a given language, certain of its aspects should be considered. The first consideration should be the relevance of the language to the application for which it is to be used. Many languages have been designed for use in a particular programming application, and are therefore subordinate choices in others. For example, COBOL was designed for business data processing and does not have the facilities to support complex numerical computations characteristic of scientific applications.

Another consideration is whether or not a language can be efficiently implemented on an existing system. Efficiency is measured in terms of compilation time, execution time, and most importantly, primary storage requirements. For example, PASCAL and BASIC are excellent languages for microcomputers because these languages require very little primary storage for compilation and execution.

Organizational considerations must also be incorporated into language selection. Staff requirements should be determined, and the cost of training the staff should be weighed against the cost of acquiring new talent. A language can play a large role in determining the time and cost required for orientation. A language should also be versatile and flexible enough to meet the changing needs of the organization. For example, ADA is an extremely versatile, yet complex language compared to BASIC. However, ADA is a very flexible language, better suited to modification than BASIC. Therefore, a language selector must consider all the objectives and try to make an optimal decision. No language will satisfy all the objectives, and a selector must allow for trade-offs among desired objectives.

Keeping in mind these factors, we will now discuss the various features of a programming language. The following is a brief outline of essential features determining a language's effectiveness:

1. Readability/overall writing
   A. Modularity
   B. Structural clarity
   C. Compactness
   D. Simplicity
2. Applications-oriented features
   A. Functional support
   B. Flexibility
   C. Versatility
3. Software development aids
   A. Editing/debugging facilities
4. Efficiency
   A. Compilation
   B. Execution
   C. Primary storage requirements

These features have varying degrees of importance depending upon how a language will be used and in what environment it will be used. For example, in an interactive system execution time is critical. That is not necessarily the case in a batch processing environment where jobs can be run overnight.

When considering a new language, desirable qualities would be ease of readability and overall writing. These qualities can directly affect personnel costs associated with initially learning and acquiring proficiency in a language. Modularity and structural clarity are essential to enhancing readability and coding. That is, the program should be able to be broken down into more visible logical units. These features will also aid in the development and continual maintenance and modification of structured software throughout its life cycle. Examples of modular languages possessing structural clarity are ADA, PASCAL, and PL/1.

Other desirable features for ease of overall writing would be compactness and simplicity. Compactness refers to the ability to write a program with a minimum number of keywords and symbols. These features also aid in the maintenance of a language. Examples of compact languages are PASCAL and BASIC. COBOL is not a compact language because its goal of being "English-like" requires the use of words instead of symbols for coding.

Once again, relevance of a language to a given application is very important. When selecting a language, evaluate its functional support facilities. That is, does the language support facilities that enhance its performance within a given application thereby making less work for the programmer? For example, FORTRAN has several built-in functions for evaluating complex numerical equations. COBOL supports a built-in report writer and sorting routine; ADA supports multiprogramming operations. Flexibility is essential in meeting changing needs of an organization. Software that can be quickly and accurately altered to specification should be considered. Versatility is another feature that would also enhance a language's performance. ADA is a versatile and flexible language because of its modularity.

Software development aids are features that cannot be overlooked. A selector should evaluate the implementation's editing and debugging facilities. That is, are the compile-time and execution-time diagnostics adequate. The WATFIV version of FORTRAN is an example of an implementation with superior debugging facilities (i.e., descriptive diagnostics that aid debugging).

Finally, efficiency of a programming language is measured by compilation time, execution time, and primary storage requirements. Machine and assembly languages utilize these resources very efficiently at the expense of portability, flexibility, and programmer time. PL/1 has a large compiler and therefore uses more primary storage and takes longer to compile, whereas PASCAL is translated (not compiled), using very little primary storage.

SUMMARY

Software may be bought or be developed internally. If it is internally developed, a suitable programming language must be selected.

Machine language, written in binary representation, is the only language understood by the computer. Programs written in other languages must be translated into machine language, with the help of a compiler or translator.

Assembly language is similar to machine language in that every machine operation must be individually described. However, operations and variables are represented by mnemonics instead of binary numbers. This makes assembly language programs easier to read.

A high level language is much easier for humans to write and understand. The compiler automatically generates most of the routine machine instructions, making life easier for the programmer. High levels languages may be either procedure oriented, or problem oriented.

FORTRAN is one of the oldest high level languages. Although it was originally designed for scientific applications, it is sometimes used in business data processing.

COBOL is an English-like language, designed for business applications. A COBOL program contains paragraphs, sentences, and clauses. The major advantages of COBOL are high portability and self-documentation.

PL/1 is a comprehensive language suitable for both business and scientific programming. It is a powerful language because it may be used by the novice as well as the experienced programmer. Versatility in handling character data and strong file-management capabilities make PL/1 a good candidate for business applications.

BASIC is an all-purpose language, which is easy to learn. Although it is not a well-structured language, it is extremely popular among users of microcomputers. Many vendors and users have developed their own versions of BASIC, thereby reducing its portability.

Like PL/1, PASCAL is a well structured language suited to both business and scientific applications. it is suitable for use on microcomputers, because the compiler does not require an excessive amount of storage space.

One of the newest high level languages, ADA, is intended to be portable, well-structured, and versatile. ADA has been developed by the Department of Defense, primarily for use in a technical environment.

RPG is a popular problem-oriented language. Used widely on small computers, RPG operates only on sequential data files. Its basic function is to generate data files and reports. However, some limited data manipulation features are also available.

When selecting a computer language, it is necessary to consider its relevance to the application at hand. The availability of programming expertise is also an important factor in selecting a language.

When evaluating a computer language, the following characteristics should be considered:

1. Readability/overall writing
2. Applications-oriented features
3. Software development aids
4. Efficiency

KEY TERMS

Coding
Structured Design Specification
High Level Language
Machine Language
Semantic Gap
Object Code
Symbolic Language
Assembly Language
Mnemonics
Assembler
Compiler
Source Code
Pseudocode
Base Register
Relative Address
Macro Instructions
Problem Oriented Language
Procedure Oriented Language

Translation
Linking
Loading
WATFIV
Keywords
Executable Statements
Nonexecutable (specification) Statements
Data Type
Initialization
Assignment Statements
Control Statements
Input/Output Statements
Structured Programming
Documentation
Portability
Reserved Words
User-Defined Words
System Names
Semantic Errors
PL/1
Block Structured Language
Exception Handling
Edit Directed I/O
List Directed I/O
Data Definition Statements
BASIC
PASCAL
ALGOL
ADA
Subroutine
Syntax
Semantics
RPG
Specification Forms
Software Development Aids
Efficiency

REVIEW QUESTIONS

1. What is a machine language? How does it differ from an assembly language?
2. What is a macro-instruction?
3. In what ways do high-level languages aid the programming process?
4. Describe the three processes that a high level language program must go through before it is executed.
5. What are the two basic types of FORTRAN statements?
6. Describe the three different types of executable statements in FORTRAN.
7. What were the objectives in developing COBOL?
8. Discuss the functions of the four major divisions in a COBOL program.
9. List the objectives of developing PL/1.
10. Briefly explain the four different kinds of statements in a PL/1 program.
11. What was the motivation for creating the BASIC language?
12. Discuss the disadvantages of BASIC.
13. In what respects is PASCAL a better language than PL/1?
14. List the advantages and disadvantages of ADA.
15. What are the functions of the seven different specification forms used by RPG?
16. What essential features would you consider when determining the effectiveness of a language?

DISCUSSION QUESTIONS

1. Your firm, Hokies International, plans to install a new, computerized order processing system. Fast-Code Inc., a software firm, has offered to sell you its package FAST-SELL. It is a complete order processing program, written in COBOL, and Fast-Code agrees to maintain it for three years. The chief programmer at Hokies International believes that she can write a more efficient program in assembly language. Further, doing this will cost only two-thirds of what Fast-Code charges for its package. Which alternative would you choose, and why?

2. Some people believe that the existence of many different programming languages is undesirable. Some of the disadvantages of multiple languages are as follows:

1. It is difficult to transport programs between installations.
2. Training programmers in more than one language is costly and redundant.
3. It is difficult to integrate programs written in different languages.

In spite of these arguments, computer languages continue to proliferate. What are the possible reasons for this? Should the number of languages be controlled?

3. FORTRAN is a useful language for writing a quick, informal program. On the other hand, COBOL is suitable for writing formal, well-documented programs. For each of the following applications, decide which of these two languages is preferable.

1. A one-time, strategic report for top management.
2. A program, occasionally used by middle managers, to compare actual sales with budgeted sales.
3. A statistical computation used by the factory engineer to schedule machine maintenance checks.
4. An accounts receivable system, which will process about 800 transactions daily.

RESEARCH PROJECTS

1. The BASIC language has branched out into many different versions. Select any two versions and compare and contrast them.

2. The use of data base management systems is rapidly increasing. As a result, programming languages must now be extended to permit interaction with DBMS. Prepare a report on the data base interface facilities available for COBOL or PL/1. CODASYL publications, IBM manuals, and DBMS vendors' literature may be used as sources of information.

MIS AND MANAGEMENT

Adoption of Software Tools Allows Greater Opportunity for Writing, Testing and Developing Programs

(Reprinted with permission from MIS Week, Sept. 15, 1982, p. 25)

Some MIS directors boast of up to tenfold improvements in programmer productivity as a result of freeing up programmers' time through adopting software tools and more end-user contributions to programming simple applications.

These factors are helping to reduce programmers' maintenance loads, giving them more time to write programs; allowing them greater ease to make program changes and test programs as well as shortening the time it takes to develop programs, according to a sampling of MIS directors across the country.

The cost of getting a system up and running has been cut by about 20 percent, said one MIS manager, while another remarked that using programmer tools has led to a 20 percent increase in developing systems.

The value of one such software tool (Sperry Corp. Univac Div.'s "Mapper") is that it frees programmers to do systems development work, while cutting by about 20 percent the cost of getting a system up and running, said Steve Paris, manager of the information center for Bechtel Power Corp. in San Francisco.

"An added benefit is that once the system is completed a user can alter the system to suit his needs. User acceptance has been excellent, going from zero to 1,200 in two years," he said. "We now have 250 terminals dedicated to Mapper."

Bechtel has a staff of 300 programmers. With a 20 percent overall increase in getting systems developed, does that mean that Mapper has saved the company the expense of hiring an additional 60 programmers?

"No, it doesn't work that way. What it means is that we have been able to get to projects that wouldn't have been started otherwise," said Paris.

Bechtel has used Mapper for two-and-a-half years. It also has used a product called Foresight from United Computing Services for nine years.

"I would say we have a five- to tenfold improvement in programmer productivity with Mapper and maybe a threefold improvement using Foresight. But this improvement is not across the board. Mapper only works for certain applications," he said.

"If you have a real structured database, Mapper won't handle it and you have to go back to COBOL. Mapper is only good for report-writing types of applications."

So how much does Bechtel use Mapper? Only on about 20 percent of applications companywide. But if you don't count all the engineering applications at Bechtel, then Mapper is used on about half of all the business applications," Paris said.

With more programming being done more automatically through programming tools and by end-users themselves, the end result has been to free some programmers to act more as consultants.

Russell Omey, deputy director of systems and programming in data processing for the County of Los Angeles, said "We do use our programmers in a consulting vein. Some of our user departments have their own internal systems group and perform consulting themselves. But for other departments, senior people, who may have come up through the ranks of programming, do act as consultants."

"One of the reasons for acquiring Focus was so that we could provide it to end-user departments so that they can begin to develop simple applications themselves," Omey said, "It is in a pilot mode now. This will help reduce the backlog of applications that we have. Lower-priority items never seem to get done and now non-technical people can do these applications."

Omey continued, "We have 468 programmers. Three hundred ninety-six of them are in applications programming and 72 are in systems programming. The productivity tools we use include Time-Sharing Option (TSO) with Full-Screen Edit (FSE) by IBM. The license fee for that is $13,464 a year, with an annual maintenance fee of

$60. We also use Applications Development Facility (ADF), another IBM product, that licenses for $7,584 a year. On our IBM 8100s we use the Development Management System (DMS) for distributed processing which costs $5,892 a year. The Patient Care System (PCS) by IBM costs us $13,800 a year."

We have just installed Focus from Information Builders," Omey added. "That's an outright purchase for $112,000. Ten percent of that is maintenance and the first year of maintenance is free. We also use Mark IV and Inquiry IMS by Informatics. Mark IV licenses for $8,418 a year and Inquiry IMS for $4,500 a year. Another tool we use is the Statistical Analysis System (SAS) from SAS Institute Inc., which is $2,000 a year. The tool Demand, is the equivalent of TSO but for use with our Univac systems and the price of that tool is included within the system software from Univac. Query Language Processor is also used with our Univac and there's no extra cost for that either."

"Yes, we do find that our programmers have more time as a result of using these tools," Omey said. "It is much easier to make changes as well, such as ADF in a relationship to IMS applications. It is easy to handle changes requested by our customers. It also shortens the time for development in the programming stage."

Dave Amosson, vice president of data processing at National Investors Life in Little Rock, Ark., has employed a variety of methods to improve programmer productivity at the IBM "370–145" shop, ranging from simplifying clerical procedures, to reducing the overhead in documentation, to using a variety of programmer productivity tools.

Some of the software programming development/productivity tools include a text-editing and program development tool, "Roscoe," Cincom Systems Inc.'s Mantis applications development tool, and "Condor," another program development tool. "They give us quite a benefit," Amosson said, "The alternative is to go back to the old card decks and the batch submission jobs."

"I think the biggest tool that we have put in lately is the Mantis System (an on-line interactive development tool). It's much like using a personal computer, only we're on a large mainframe. For on-line development work, that package has probably increased our programmer productivity by at least 700 or 800 percent," Amosson said.

Amosson said the extra programmer time is used to accommodate a growth environment at National Life. The firm recorded revenues of $400 million in 1980 and that increased to $1.5 billion in 1982. He predicts that the firm will exceed $2 billion in revenues this year.

Amosson commented, "With that type of growth rate, you really don't have to worry what to do with programmer productivity; it's been gobbled up. But, correspondingly, my staff only had to increase about 20 percent."

With the increase in programmer productivity, Amosson said his department is looking good, handling the expansion in the workload and better satisfying his users. "We're able to get the work done much faster and we've reduced our applications backlog from in excess of three years down to about eight months," he said.

Amosson said the main factor contributing to programmer productivity increases is general improvements in software packages. "They enable you to get a quicker turnaround, the programming languages are simpler and there are less procedural statements," he said.

He continued, "These tools let you model an application and work it with a user before you really find the final product. If you don't like something, you get on the screen, change it and execute it, immediately.

He continued, "What that does is, we can do a better job on the front end (analysis, data gathering and testing), where we were crowding it before. We can do more work with the users, have them more involved and spend more time on the design. The end result is a better finished product."

"As a general rule, the users are a lot more satisfied. Our complaint level is going down. I think that's pretty complimentary, considering our growth," Amosson said.

At Hartford, Conn.-based Royal Business Machines, Jack George, director of MIS, said each programmer has his own office and his own terminal (an IBM "3278"). The cost of the terminal is a small percentage of the overall compensation, he said.

George said he has been in MIS for more than 22 years. "I would say that over the last 10 years, programmers must have doubled or tripled their productivity." Royal uses TSO, which runs under MVS (Multiple Virtual Systems). This allows for programmers to program right on their own terminals, rather than write things down then go to a terminal. "They can get and test programs right on the terminal," he said, adding that in many cases, "I'm getting back programs in the same day, when it used to take four or five days to complete."

George said when he first joined Royal Business two-and-one-half years ago, there were four terminals for 12 or 13 people. "People (programmers) were waiting in line for terminals," he said. By giving each programmer his/her terminal, he said, "we don't pay any more for the terminals than a company would pay for their social security."

Ron Waddell, director of data processing for Walter Pye's, a group of men's and women's apparel stores based in Houston, found that converting to a minicomputer system had increased productivity and freed programmers to spend more time on development functions.

The company, which includes four stores in Houston and one in Galveston, is in the process of converting from an NCR Corp. Criterion 8450 to a Prime Computer Inc. Information System 750.

The flexibility of the operating system and speed of writing programs has increased productivity "70 to 100 times over what we had with a COBOL shop," Waddell said.

"What took three people two-and-a-half months to do under the old system now takes one week in an interactive environment," he added. "We're tickled to death with the results."

With user-friendly software, the system also allows greater user participation, leaving more time for programmers to perform other functions. The system employs a processor, with 25 dumb terminals situated in various departments and tied to the processor, Waddell said.

"The conversion is really the thing that best helped us manage programmers' time," Waddell added. "In the past, we had the same problems other data processing shops had—getting programmers, being sure they were keeping up with documentation. Many, many of these problems have gone away."

James Jensen, assistant director of computing services and administrative DP, University of Washington, said the university has made a conscious effort over the past

18 months to reduce programmers' maintenance load and to concentrate more on development.

The Seattle University's information systems department has 40 analyst programmers. In years past, some 20 programmers found most of their time devoted to maintenance. The college simply decided to stop doing maintenance and set other priorities. The school is, of course, still fixing bugs and making sure the system is not becoming run down. But minor enhancements are not being stressed.

The college is using some new tools that "appear to be promising" in order to free up programmers' time. They are looking at software generators and several packages that will run on the school's Burroughs "6890" computer in order to come up with "more rapid and less costly implementation of applications systems."

Discussion

1. Are application generators likely to make any of the programming languages discussed in this chapter obsolete?
2. Given the fact that user-friendly application software tools are becoming increasingly available, is there still a need for business students to learn a language such as BASIC?

CHAPTER 8

DATA STORAGE AND PROCESSING MODES

INTRODUCTION

Earlier, in chapter 3, we covered basic data storage and processing modes. This chapter will cover these concepts in more depth. From chapter 3 you will remember the data hierarchy, listed below in ascending order of complexity:

1. Bit
2. Byte
3. Field or item
4. Record
5. File or data set
6. Data base

By this time you should feel fairly comfortable with these terms. If you don't, you should go back and review the section on basic data storage in chapter 3. This chapter will first look at how bits are used to represent data. We will also explore file organization in more depth than in chapter 3. Finally, the relationship of basic data processing modes and approaches to online direct access systems and realtime systems will be covered.

DATA REPRESENTATION

True Binary Representation

As you will recall from chapters 3 and 4, all data in digital computers are represented by a bit either being on or off. Recall that bit is short for binary digit. Since bits can only store two possible states, on or off, they are binary in nature. Data representation in a computer uses the binary number system. To illustrate the binary number system, let us first look at the decimal number system with which we are all familiar. The decimal number system uses the number 10 as a base.

Each place within a decimal number has a certain value. Refer to Figure 8-1. At the bottom of the figure is a table which indicates the value of each place within a decimal number. Starting with the right-most digit in the number, the first place has a value of 1 (10^0), the second a value of 10 (10^1), the third a value of 100 (10^2), and so on.

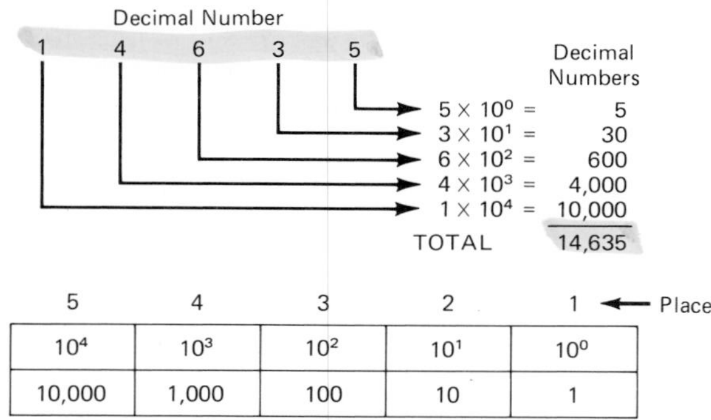

5	4	3	2	1
10^4	10^3	10^2	10^1	10^0
10,000	1,000	100	10	1

Figure 8-1 Decimal Place Values

Regardless of the number system, any number can be converted to a decimal number by multiplying each digit in the number by its respective place value. To illustrate, let's convert the decimal number 14,635 as shown at the top of Figure 8-1, to a decimal number. Of course, the conversion of a decimal number to a decimal number will result in the number you started with. But this will at least prove that our system works. First we multiply the digit 5 × its place value of 10^0 (or 1). Then we multiply 3 × 10^1 and so on. When we add up all of these products we find that the total is 14,635, the same as we started with.

Let's now look at the binary number system, a base 2 number system. At the bottom of Figure 8-2, we see the place values of a binary number system. The first place

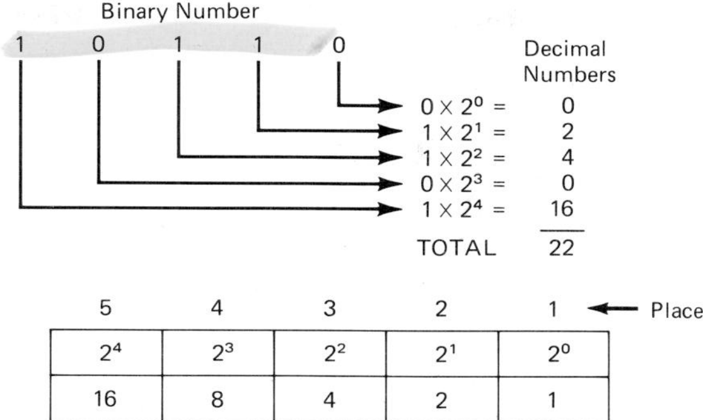

5	4	3	2	1 ← Place
2^4	2^3	2^2	2^1	2^0
16	8	4	2	1

Figure 8-2 Binary Place Values

from the right has a value of 1 (2^0), the second place a value of 2 (2^1), the third place a value of 4 (2^2), and so on. Note that these place values exactly double each time, since we are raising 2 to a power to derive the place values.

Conversion of a binary number to a decimal number proceeds in exactly the same manner as was done above with a decimal number. We multiply the digit in each place by its respective place value, as illustrated at the top of figure 8-2. 0×2^0 is equal to 0. 1×2^1 is equal to 2, and so on. We sum these products up and get a total of 22, so the binary number 10110 is equivalent to the decimal number 22.

True binary representation is used only to store numeric data. The primary advantage of true binary representation is that it requires fewer bits to store a given number. For example, the number 3985 can be stored in 12 bits using true binary representation. We know this because with 12 bits we can store a total of 4,096 (2^{12}) combinations. Using another binary coding scheme, EBCDIC, which was mentioned in chapter 3 and will be covered in more detail below, the computer would need 32 bits to represent the number 3985, since it would need 8 bits for each digit in the number.

EBCDIC Representation

The *Extended Binary Coded Decimal Interchange Code* or *EBCDIC* (pronounced ib-si-dick) is a binary code developed by IBM. It represents each numeric, alphabetic, or special character with 8 bits. For example, the decimal digit 9 is represented by the code 11111001. Table 8-1 illustrates the EBCDIC code for upper case alphabetic characters and the numeric characters 0–9.

As shown in Figure 8–3, the 8 bits in EBCDIC are divided into 4 numeric bits and 4 zone bits. You will notice in Table 8-1 that only the 4 right-most bits, the numeric bits, are necessary to code the numeric digits 0–9, since the 4 zone bits are always turned on and do not vary. The zone bits are used to code both upper and lower case alphabetic characters and special characters, such as commas and question marks. In fact, EBCDIC can code up to 256 different characters ($2^8 = 256$). This ability to code a wide range of characters is one of the primary advantages of EBCDIC.

Refer again to Figure 8-3. You will notice that the place values of the numeric bits and zone bits starting with the right most position are 1, 2, 4, and 8 for both zone and numeric bits. You will also recall that these were the place values of the first 4 places

Table 8-1 EBCDIC Coding Scheme

Character	EBCDIC Binary
A	1100 0001
B	1100 0010
C	1100 0011
D	1100 0100
E	1100 0101
F	1100 0110
G	1100 0111
H	1100 1000
I	1100 1001
J	1101 0001
K	1101 0010
L	1101 0011
M	1101 0100
N	1101 0101
O	1101 0110
P	1101 0111
Q	1101 1000
R	1101 1001
S	1110 0010
T	1110 0011
U	1110 0100
V	1110 0101
W	1110 0110
X	1110 0111
Y	1110 1000
Z	1110 1001
0	1111 0000
1	1111 0001
2	1111 0010
3	1111 0011
4	1111 0100
5	1111 0101
6	1111 0110
7	1111 0111
8	1111 1000
9	1111 1001

under true binary as illustrated in Figure 8-2. Notice that in Table 8-1, the decimal numeric value of any of the numeric digits 0–9 can be derived simply by adding together the place values of the on bits in the numeric bit portion of the EBCDIC code. For example, for the digit 9 the 1 bit and the 8 bit are on; therefore 1 + 8 = 9.

Another advantage of EBCDIC is that we can represent 2 numeric digits within

Place Values in EBCDIC							
Zone Bits				Numeric Bits			
8	4	2	1	8	4	2	1

Figure 8-3 EBCDIC Place Values

the 8 bits of the EBCDIC code. If the data we are representing is all numeric, the computer simply divides the 8 bit code into 2 separate 4 bit codes. In other words, the zone bits are used just as if they were numeric bits. This form of data representation is called *packed decimal.* It is possible because the maximum number of combinations we can represent with 4 bits is 16 (2^4). To represent all the numeric digits, we need only 10 combinations of bits.

ASCII-8 Representation

Another commonly used code for encoding bytes of data is the *American Standard Code for Information Interchange (ASCII)*—see Table 8-2. This code was developed

Table 8-2 ASCII-8 Coding Scheme

Character	ASCII-8 Binary
A	1010 0001
B	1010 0010
C	1010 0011
D	1010 0100
E	1010 0101
F	1010 0110
G	1010 0111
H	1010 1000
I	1010 1001
J	1010 1010
K	1010 1011
L	1010 1100
M	1010 1101
N	1010 1110
O	1010 1111
P	1011 0000
Q	1011 0001
R	1011 0010
S	1011 0011
T	1011 0100
U	1011 0101
V	1011 0110
W	1011 0111
X	1011 1000
Y	1011 1001
Z	1011 1010
0	0101 0000
1	0101 0001
2	0101 0001
3	0101 0011
4	0101 0100
5	0101 0101
6	0101 0110
7	0101 0111
8	0101 1000
9	0101 1001

by the American National Standards Institute (ANSI), with the objective of providing a standard code able to be used on many different manufacturers' computer hardware. Like EBCDIC, ASCII-8 is an 8 bit code, although there is a 7 bit version of ASCII (pronounced as-key). The advantages of ASCII are the same as those of EBCDIC. ASCII is used primarily in data transmission but is not as widely used as EBCDIC.

Hexadecimal Representation

Often programmers must examine the content of a storage location within the computer in order to debug a program. Of course, the internal storage is in binary form. To print out (or dump) the contents of memory in binary form would be of little use since the programmer would see on the printout only a string of ones and zeros. Conversion to decimal equivalents would be laborious and time consuming. Therefore, some computer systems perform memory dumps in a hexadecimal representation.

Hexadecimal has a base of 16. That is, there are 16 symbols in hexadecimal, 0 through 9 and A through F. Table 8-3 illustrates binary, hexadecimal, and decimal equivalent values. When hexadecimal is used, the contents of each four bits are converted to the corresponding hexadecimal symbol and printed out on the memory dump. For example, if the four bits are 0101, the hexadecimal symbol 5 would be printed out. Sixteen symbols are used since the maximum number of bit combinations of four bits is 16 (2^4).

Table 8-3 Binary, Hexadecimal and Decimal Equivalents

Binary System (Place Values)					
8	**4**	**2**	**1**	**Hexadecimal System**	**Decimal System**
0	0	0	0	0	0
0	0	0	1	1	1
0	0	1	0	2	2
0	0	1	1	3	3
0	1	0	0	4	4
0	1	0	1	5	5
0	1	1	0	6	6
0	1	1	1	7	7
1	0	0	0	8	8
1	0	0	1	9	9
1	0	1	0	A	10
1	0	1	1	B	11
1	1	0	0	C	12
1	1	0	1	D	13
1	1	1	0	E	14
1	1	1	1	F	15

The decimal equivalent of a hexadecimal number can be determined by multiplying each digit by its appropriate power of the base 16 and summing the products just as was done with decimal and binary number conversion to the decimal system. The primary advantages of a hexadecimal system are that conversion from the hexadecimal to decimal is much easier than from binary to decimal, and the volume of printout when using hexadecimal is much smaller than when using binary to print out a memory dump. Another system used by some computers for memory dumps is the octal system. The octal system uses the number 8 as a base.

Parity Bits

As indicated in chapter 3, the actual encoding of data using EBCDIC or any other coding scheme would also contain an extra parity or check bit added for checking purposes. For example, assuming an even parity machine, the computer expects the number of bits turned on in a byte always to be even (if the machine was designed as an odd parity machine, the number of bits turned on would always be odd). Refer to Table 8-4, which illustrates the use of parity bits. Notice that when the number of on bits is even in the regular 8 bits of the code, the parity bit is off. If the number of on bits in the regular 8 bits is odd, the parity bit is turned on to make the total number of on bits even. Bits can be erroneously changed from on to off, or vice versa when data is moved from one storage location or medium to another. Various environmental factors, such as specks of dust, can cause these types of errors to occur. Parity bits assist in detecting these errors. It is very important that computer hardware contains automatic parity checking.

Table 8-4 EBCDIC With Even Parity

Decimal Equivalent	EBCDIC Code with Parity									Place Values
	P*	8	4	2	1	8	4	2	1	
0	0	1	1	1	1	0	0	0	0	
1	1	1	1	1	1	0	0	0	1	
2	1	1	1	1	1	0	0	1	0	
3	0	1	1	1	1	0	0	1	1	
4	1	1	1	1	1	0	1	0	0	

*Parity Bit

FILE ORGANIZATION

There are basically two types of files: 1) those allowing sequential access to the data; and 2) those allowing direct access. The term *file organization* refers to various schemes allowing for sequential versus direct access to the data. Therefore, the terms access methods and file organization can be considered synonymous.

Sequential File Organization

In a sequential file, all the records are in ascending order by record key. The *record key* is the field that uniquely identifies each record. For example, in a sequential student records file, the records would be in ascending order by the students' social security numbers. To locate an individual record, a sequential search beginning at the first record on the file must be performed. Each individual record must be examined until the required record is located. Such a search can be time consuming. Therefore, sequential organization is impractical for an application that requires immediate access to individual records. On the other hand, sequential organization would be good for a payroll system run on a batch basis once a week with almost every record on the master file being accessed.

Certain storage media, like magnetic and paper tape, will allow only sequential file organization. To locate a record on a reel of magnetic tape, the tape must be read sequentially beginning with the first record. It is physically impossible for a tape drive to locate individual records directly because of the amount of winding and rewinding that must be performed. However, a direct access storage device (DASD), such as disk, allows sequential file organization and direct access, as will be discussed in the next section.

Direct File Organization

Direct file organization allows immediate direct access to individual records on the file. The four most widely used direct access techniques are 1) indexed sequential access

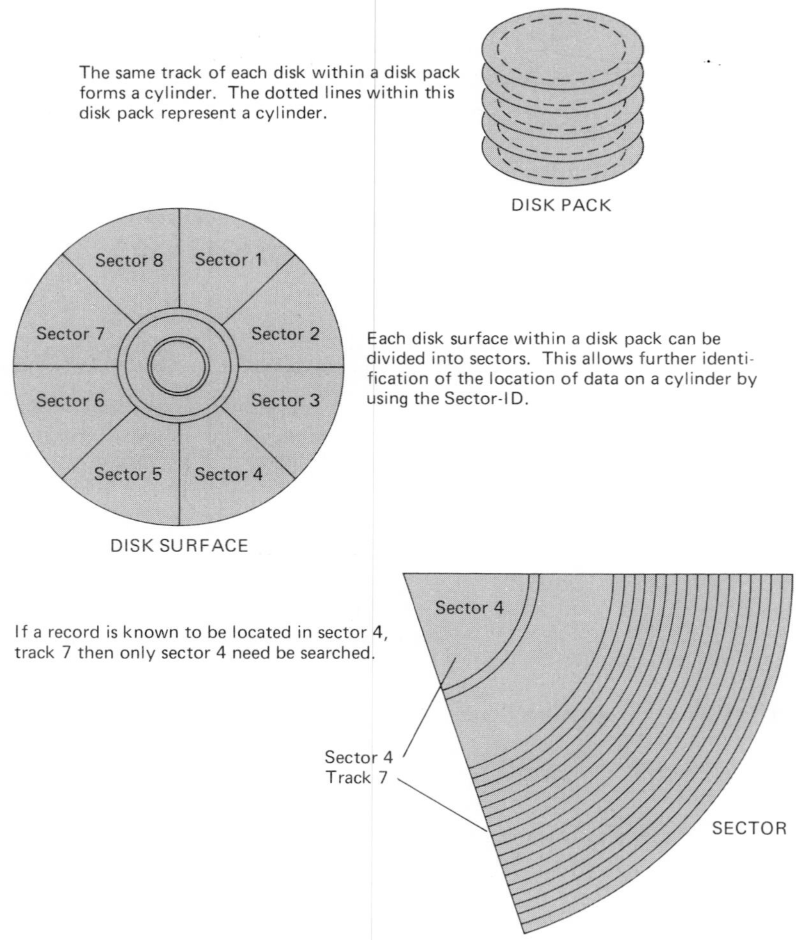

The same track of each disk within a disk pack forms a cylinder. The dotted lines within this disk pack represent a cylinder.
DISK PACK
Sector 8
Sector 1
Sector 7
Sector 2
Sector 6
Sector 3
Sector 5
Sector 4
DISK SURFACE
Each disk surface within a disk pack can be divided into sectors. This allows further identification of the location of data on a cylinder by using the Sector-ID.
Sector 4
If a record is known to be located in sector 4, track 7 then only sector 4 need be searched.
Sector 4
Track 7
SECTOR

Figure 8-4 Cylinder, Track, and Sector Addresses

method (ISAM); 2) simple direct; 3) random direct; and 4) virtual storage access method (VSAM). Although there are several types of direct storage devices, including disks, drums, and mass storage devices, disks are by far the most widely used. To understand direct file organization, it is necessary to understand the physical characteristics of a disk pack and the method by which data are written to and read from them. If these concepts are not clearly understood, the appropriate sections of chapter 4 should be reread.

To access an individual record on a disk file, its physical address must be known. The physical address is the cylinder and individual track (or surface) within the cylinder on which the record is stored. Once the proper track is located, the disk control unit can examine the records on that track to identify the proper record. However, if the time required to search through each record is excessive, the disk pack can be divided into pie-shaped sectors, as illustrated in Figure 8-4. When the sector containing the record is identified, a search of only that sector within the track is necessary. Therefore, the address of a specific record stored on a disk pack is composed of a cylinder address, a track address and, in some cases, a sector address. In the case of a floppy disk or other single disk media, the address is composed of a track and sector address. Since there is only one disk, the concept of a cylinder is not used. For illustrative purposes, we will assume a disk pack with multidisks in which only the cylinder and track addresses are used.

Indexed Sequential File Organization

The *indexed sequential* file organization, or indexed sequential access method (ISAM—pronounced i-sam), is a hybrid between sequential and direct file organizations. The records within the file are stored sequentially, but direct access to individual records is possible through an index. This index is analogous to a card catalog in a library. Figure 8-5 illustrates a cylinder and track index for an ISAM file. To locate a record, the cylinder index is searched to find the cylinder address, and the track index for the

Cylinder Index

Cylinder	Highest Record Key in the Cylinder
1	84
2	250
3	398
4	479
5	590

Cylinder 1 Track Index

Track	Highest Record Key in the Track
1	15
2	40
3	55
4	75
5	84

Cylinder 2 Track Index

Track	Highest Record Key in the Track
1	94
2	110
3	175
4	225
5	250

Cylinder 3 Track Index

Track	Highest Record Key in the Track
1	280
2	301
3	330
4	365
5	398

Figure 8-5 ISAM Cylinder and Track Index

cylinder is then searched to locate the track address of the record. Using Figure 8-5 to illustrate, we assume the desired record has a key value of 225. The cylinder address is 2, since 225 is greater than 84 but less than 250. We then search the track index for cylinder 2 and find that 225 is greater than 175 and equal to 225; therefore, the track address is 4. With the cylinder address and the track address known, the disk control unit can then search through the records on track 4 within cylinder 2 to retrieve the desired record.

The ISAM technique can be modified to accommodate differing file sizes. If the file is small enough to fit in one cylinder (for example, an IBM 3350 disk pack will hold 572,070 bytes per cylinder), then a cylinder index is not needed. The only index required in this case is a track index. On the other hand, if a file is very large and requires, for example, a complete disk pack (such as an IBM 3350), then the file will reside on 555 cylinders. In this case, it might be desirable to establish a master index that breaks the cylinder index into parts containing, for example, 25 cylinders per part. The master index would contain the highest key for each part of the cylinder index. In this scheme, a search would first be made of the master index to determine which cylinder index to search next.

An ISAM file is made up of three areas: 1) the index area; 2) the prime area; and 3) the overflow area. The *index area* stores the indexes discussed above. The *prime area* contains all the records of the file after it is initially created or reorganized. The *overflow area* contains any record additions to the file that cannot be inserted in the prime area. Additions are inserted in the prime area only when there is sufficient space in the proper sequence for the records. Existing records are not moved to provide space. If space is not available, the record addition is simply written to the overflow area. Reorganization of a direct access file consists of the merging of all records in the overflow area with those in the prime area so that all the records in the file reside in the prime area. Reorganization is done periodically to make access to individual records more efficient. Other forms of direct file organization have a prime and an overflow area and must also be periodically reorganized.

Simple Direct File Organization

Both simple direct and random direct addressing utilize the concept of relative record addresses—the address of an individual record relative to the address of the first record in the file. If we know the physical address of the first record, the amount of space each record occupies, and the relative address of the desired record, the physical address of any other record can be directly computed.

With *simple direct addressing,* a record's key is used as its relative address. Therefore, we can compute the record's address directly from the record key and the physical address of the first record in the file. The example in Figure 8-6 shows a sequential physical file containing 20 records with keys from 1 through 20. In order to retrieve the 12th record, we add the relative address of the record, 12 (which is also its key), to the absolute or physical address of the first record, 1376. Subtracting 1 from this total yields 1387, the physical address of the desired record. This computation assumes that there is only one record per track. However, we can devise simple direct file organization schemes in which multiple records per track exist, assuming each track contains the same number of records.

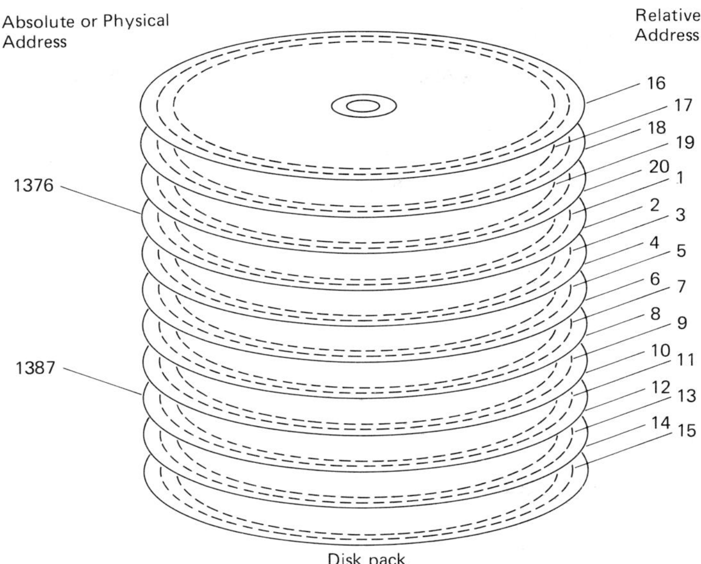

Figure 8-6 Simple Direct Addressing

The primary problem with simple direct file organization is that space must be set aside on the disk pack for each record over the entire range of possible record keys. If all the record keys are associated with active records, then no problem exists. However, in most business situations, many keys in a key sequence are not associated with active records. For example, consider the key sequence of employee number, which is usually the social security number. Even employees of the largest of firms have only a very small fraction of the total possible social security numbers. Therefore, it would be inadvisable to set up a file on a simple direct method when the record key is the social security number because the amount of wasted space would be unjustified.

Random Direct File Organization

Random addressing is sometimes called indirect addressing. This technique produces a series of relative addresses (one for each record key) randomly distributed over the available disk space. The most popular techniques for random addressing are listed below.

Digit Analysis. Digit analysis is a method for choosing certain digits in a record key to use for addressing purposes. Figure 8-7 illustrates digit analysis of 2,000 records having an eight-digit key field. The digits in digit positions 1, 2, and 5 tend to be clustered around relatively few values whereas in digit positions 3, 4, 6, 7, and 8, the digits tend to be evenly distributed among each of the digits 0 through 8. Therefore, we would choose digit positions 3, 4, 6, 7, and 8 to use for relative addressing purposes and ignore the other three digits, since they are not likely to produce even or random distributions over the available disk space.

Hashing. The *hashing* approach, which is sometimes called a division remainder scheme, divides the record key by a large prime number close to the total number of

Digit	Digit Position 1	2	3	4	5	6	7	8
0			155	327	981	210	165	109
1	345	1032	300	150		159	251	214
2		418	145	189		189	184	189
3			195	162		334	279	288
4	1000		200	215		206	216	257
5		450	207	197		181	331	175
6			193	100		178	179	168
7	655		400	228		213	143	301
8			105	200	100	151	105	125
9		100	100	232	919	179	147	174

Figure 8-7 Digit Analysis of 2,000 Records

records in the file. The remainder of this division is used as the record's relative address.

Folding. With *folding*, the record key is divided into two parts, and they are added together to form a relative record address.

Radix Transformation. The *radix transformation* approach converts the record key to a number in a nondecimal base and uses the number in that base as the relative record address.

A primary problem with random addressing involves synonyms. When two different record keys produce the same relative address through a random addressing technique, they are referred to as *synonyms*. Obviously both records cannot be stored in the same area on the disk. Therefore, one of the two will have to be placed in an overflow area. Figure 8-8 depicts such a situation. The records for James and White both have a relative address of 4. The greater the percentage of total records that are synonyms, the less efficient random addressing becomes. Generally, system designers attempt to keep the percentage of synonyms to 20 percent or less of the total records in the file. With a higher figure for synonyms, other file organization schemes, such as ISAM, may be more efficient.

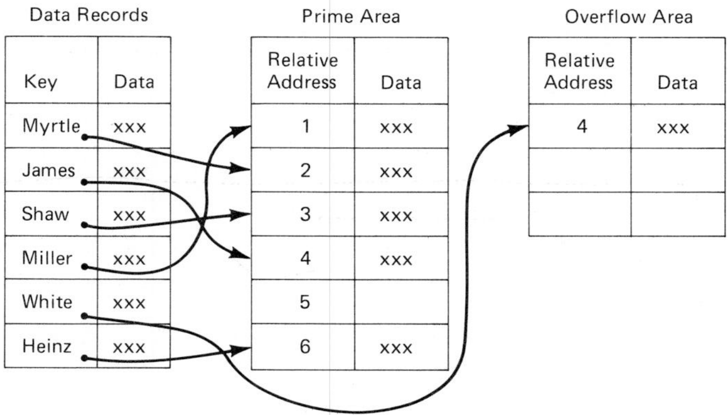

Figure 8-8 Overflow Storage of Synonyms

Virtual Storage Access Method

The *virtual storage access method* (VSAM) allows data to be stored in fixed-length blocks. As in the ISAM approach, indexes allow the block in which a particular record is stored to be determined. However, VSAM differs from ISAM in that the address of a record is the relative byte of the block in which the record is stored instead of a cylinder and track. This relative byte approach to addressing is similar to the way addressing is done in primary storage of the CPU. Therefore, each block of data resembles a page of a program (as discussed in chapter 6 under virtual storage as it applies to programs). As illustrated in Figure 8-9, the operating system moves blocks of data in and out of primary storage as they are required by the program.

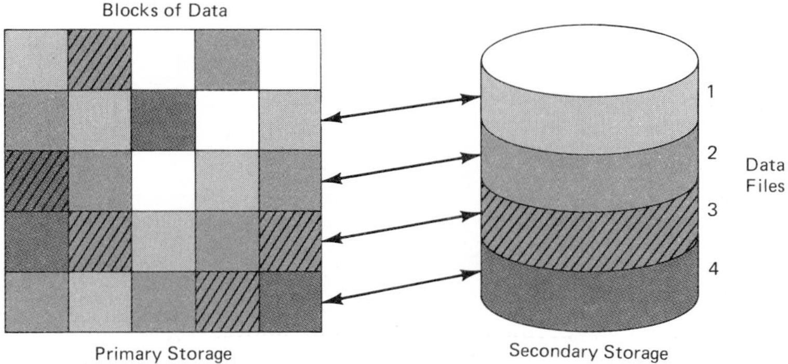

Figure 8-9 Movement of Data Between Primary and Secondary Storage

Benefits of VSAM

The benefits of VSAM are potentially very significant. The programmer does not need to devise complex cylinder and track addressing schemes since each individual record is addressed as if the entire file were stored in primary storage. In addition, the programmer has the illusion that unlimited primary storage is available and that even the largest of data files can be stored in primary storage. Of course, in actual fact, the data file is stored in secondary storage. The benefits of VSAM are making it an important file organization for new system development.

Chaining of Direct Files

Files organized using a direct access method must often also be processed in sequential fashion. To enable sequential processing, a chain and pointer system is used. Each individual record contains a pointer, a field that stores the key and (sometimes) the relative or physical address of the next record in the sequence. The first record identifies the second record and its address, the second identifies the third, and so on, forming a sequential record chain. Figure 8-10 illustrates the concept of chaining.

MANAGEMENT CASE 8-1

Brown, Inc. has stored 15 years of historical sales data on direct access file organization on disk. This data is used to analyze and project various sales trends. It is used very heavily for a one month period and then during the rest of the year it is rarely used. The manager of sales analysis, Randy Cunningham is concerned that a large amount of disk space is being taken up by data that is rarely used during an 11-month period. He has suggested to data processing that the data be stored in sequential files on tape. During the one month of active use the data would be transferred back to disk in sequential file organization. Data processing thinks this approach is impractical and they have suggested that the data be stored on tape in the same direct access format that it is stored on disk. During the one month of active use the data would be transferred to disk and would be in a direct access format. Is either of these two approaches practical? Which would you recommend?

Physical Address	Record Key	Data	Chain* Pointer
1	1	xxx	4
2			
3	7	xxx	
4	2	xxx	8
5	4	xxx	10
6	6	xxx	3
7			
8	3	xxx	5
9			
10	5	xxx	6

*The physical address of the next record in the sequence of the record key.

Figure 8-10 Chaining of Direct Files

Selecting a File Organization Method

The factors that must be considered when determining the best file organization for a particular application are file volatility, file activity, file size, and file query requirements. *File volatility* refers to the number of additions and deletions to the file in a given period of time. The payroll file for a construction company in which the employee roster is constantly changing is a highly volatile file. An ISAM file would not be a good choice in this situation, since additions would have to be placed in the overflow area, and frequent reorganization of the file would have to occur. Other direct access methods would be better. Perhaps even sequential file organization would be appropriate if there were no query requirements.

File activity is the proportion of file records actually used or accessed in a given processing run. At one extreme is the realtime file, where each transaction is processed immediately, and only one master file record is therefore accessed. This situation obviously requires a direct-access method. At the other extreme is a file, such as a payroll master file, where almost every record is accessed when the weekly payroll is processed. In this case, a sequentially ordered master file would be more efficient.

File query refers to the retrieval of information from a file. If the retrieval of individual records must be fast in order to support a realtime operation (such as an airline reservation system), some kind of direct organization is required. If, on the other hand, requirements for data can be delayed, then all the individual requests for information can be batched and run in a single processing run with a sequential file organization.

Large files requiring many individual references to records with immediate response must be organized under some type of direct access method. However, with small files, it may be more efficient to search the entire file sequentially to find an individual record than to maintain complex indexes or direct addressing schemes. A sequential file can be searched rapidly using a binary search. Binary searches split the file in half and then determine in which half the desired record is stored. That half is then split in half again to determine in which quarter of the file the record is stored, and so on, until the required record is found. A binary search is considerably more efficient than a sequential search of a sequential file. Figure 8-11 shows how a record is found using a binary search.

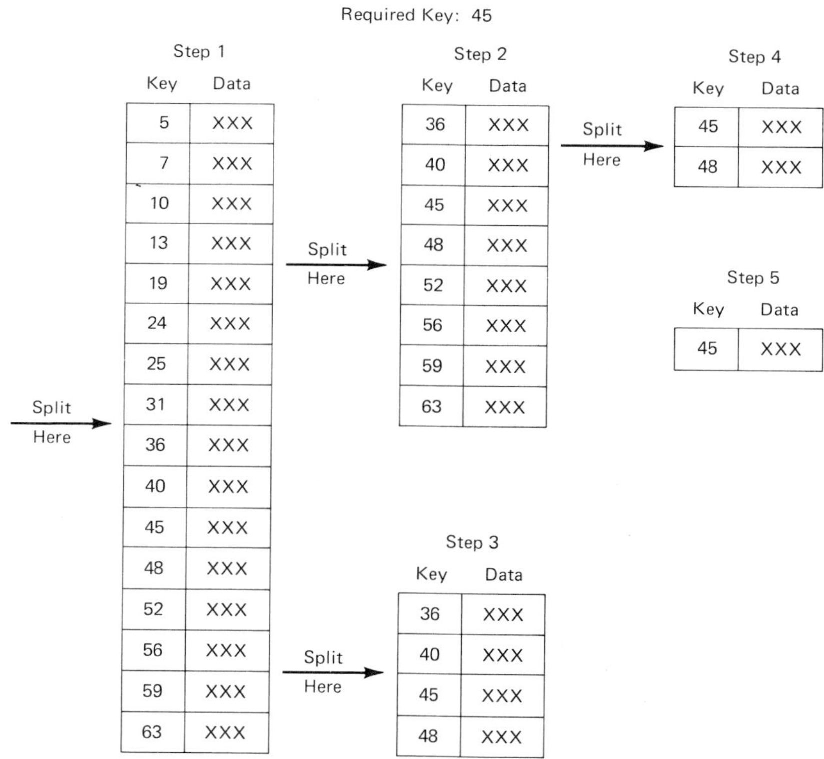

Figure 8-11 Binary Search

We have discussed only the important factors in determining the best file organization. "Best" is certainly a relative term, and the final answer depends on the individual application. Other factors most companies would consider are ease of implementing and maintaining a particular file organization, its cost, and whether software is readily available to implement the file organization.

DATA PROCESSING MODES AND APPROACHES

In the preceding sections we have discussed two basic types of file organization—sequential and direct. They are combined with two data processing modes—batch and immediate—to form three data processing approaches—batch-sequential, batch-direct and immediate-direct.

Batch Processing

With *batch processing*, changes and queries to the file are stored for a period of time. A processing run is then made periodically to update the file and to obtain information required by the queries and scheduled reports. Batch runs may be made on a scheduled periodic basis, such as daily, weekly or monthly, or they may be made on an *as required* basis.

Figure 8-12 illustrates batch processing with a sequential file stored on magnetic tape. As can be seen from the figure, a complete new master file is produced on a separate volume of tape whenever the file storage medium is magnetic tape. If the storage medium is direct access, the updating is called *in-place* updating and the new master file records reside physically in the same area of the DASD as the old records. With in-place updating, sometimes referred to as destructive updating, one simply writes the new data over the physical area that the old data occupied on the DASD. New

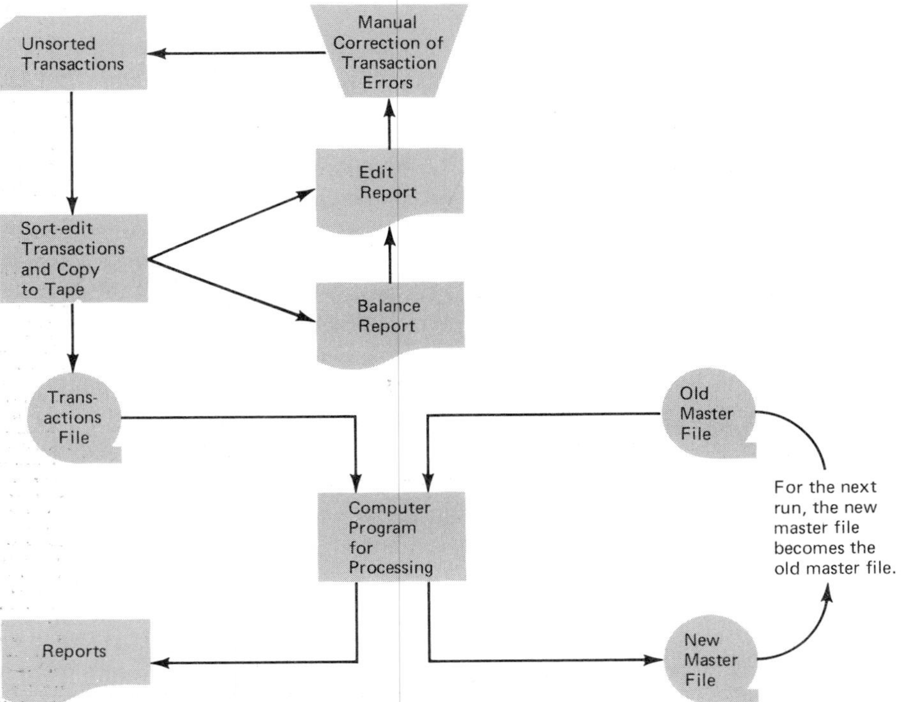

Figure 8-12 Overview of Batch Sequential Processing Using Tape Files

records are placed in the overflow area if there is not sufficient blank space in the prime area of the file. Records deleted from a DASD file are not physically removed until a reorganization of the file occurs. The record is simply marked with a flag that indicates deletion. These update concepts concerning DASD files apply to all the data processing approaches discussed in this section.

Immediate Processing

Using *immediate processing,* transactions are processed to update a file immediately or shortly after a real-world event occurs. Immediate processing is illustrated in Figure 8-13.

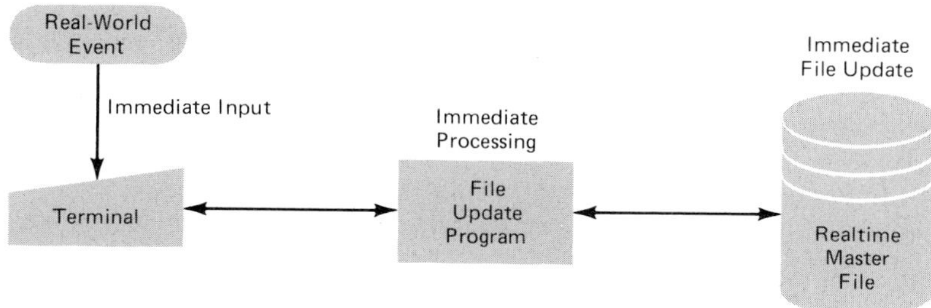

Figure 8-13 Immediate Processing

Data Processing Approaches

Batch-Sequential

Batch-sequential processing is illustrated in Figure 8-14. With batch-sequential processing, changes and queries to a file are batched and processed periodically on a sequential basis. In a practical sense, the only possible way to process a sequential master file is on a batch basis since there is no direct access to individual records. Earlier data processing applications were always batch-sequential, but the process is declining in popularity because of the decreasing costs of direct access storage devices.

Batch-Direct

Direct access files can be updated on a batch basis. For example, weekly payroll data are normally batched and processed on a batch basis even though the master file is often stored on a direct access storage device. Batch-direct processing is illustrated in Figure 8-15.

Immediate-Direct

Immediate processing of direct access files is the strategy toward which data processing is moving. It is essential for realtime systems, which are required in many information systems. For example, an airline reservations system could not function without realtime files. Other examples of information systems that require realtime files are

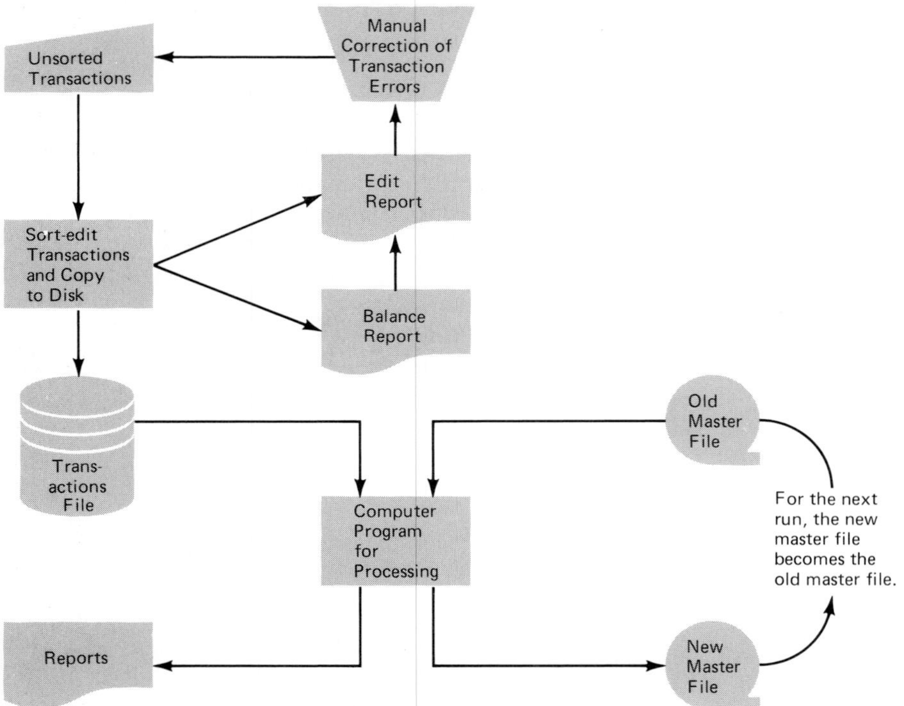

Figure 8-14 Batch Sequential Processing

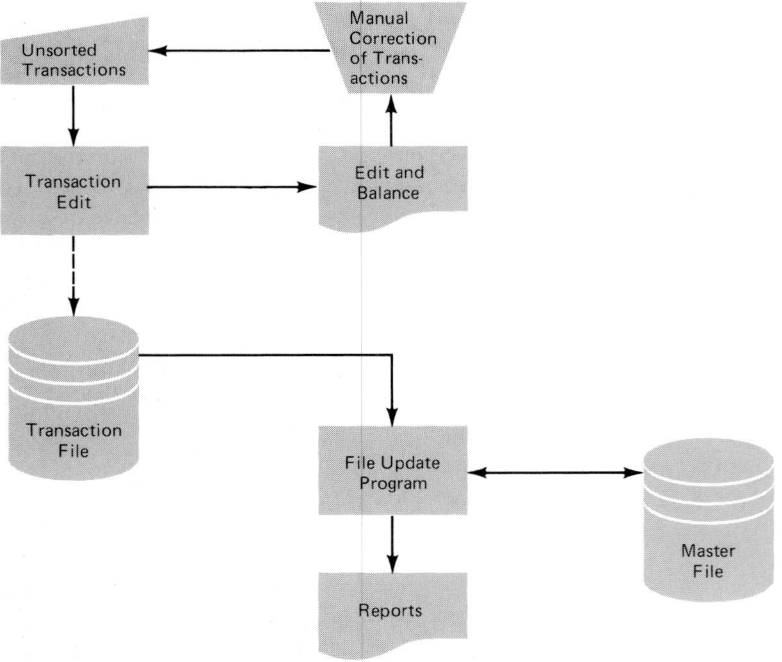

Figure 8-15 Batch-Direct Processing

finished goods inventory files in which order entry is computerized, and student record files for course registration systems.

Many other applications employ immediate-direct processing because transactions captured near the point of an event can usually be corrected for errors relatively easily. Contrary to popular belief, a properly designed immediate-direct processing system can potentially control input much better than a batch processing system. All of the edit checks performed on batch input can also be performed on immediate input. In addition, with an immediate-direct system, errors are communicated immediately to the data entry operator, who is thus better able to correct them. Furthermore, the computer can provide the data entry operator with instructions and aids through the terminal. Figure 8-16 shows an immediate-direct processing configuration.

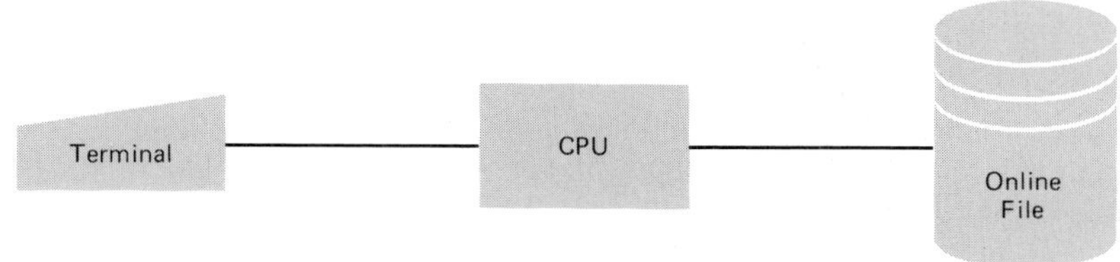

Figure 8-16 Immediate-Direct Processing

ONLINE DIRECT ACCESS SYSTEMS

The term *online direct access systems* is actually composed of two separate terms, *online* and *direct access*. *Online* refers to any computer system, peripheral device, or file, such as a terminal or disk pack, that the CPU can control without direct human intervention. For example, a reel of magnetic tape in the library cannot be processed by the CPU without human intervention and therefore is not online. In contrast, a disk pack mounted on a disk drive that is accessible to the CPU is online. Peripheral devices or files not in direct communication with the CPU are offline. *Direct access* refers to a file organization in which records can be retrieved by the CPU without a large amount of searching. File organizations allowing direct access are the indexed sequential, simple direct, random, and virtual storage file organizations.

Consequently, an online direct access system is one with several terminals in direct communication with the CPU, which in turn can retrieve data from one or more files directly for immediate processing without human intervention. Figure 8-17 provides an overview of the typical configuration of an online direct access system.

Online terminals without direct access capability would be impractical. The turnaround time and processing costs would be intolerable if an operator had to mount each file asked for and the record search was then performed sequentially.

In addition, direct access files are usually associated with online terminals. One of the primary reasons for direct access file organization is to allow for immediate processing of inquiries and updates to a file from online terminals scattered throughout the user organization. Otherwise, if the activity ratio were sufficiently high, it would be more economical to process inquiries and updates in a batch mode with a sequentially organized master file. Therefore, the terms online and direct access are normally used together when referring to a complete computer system.

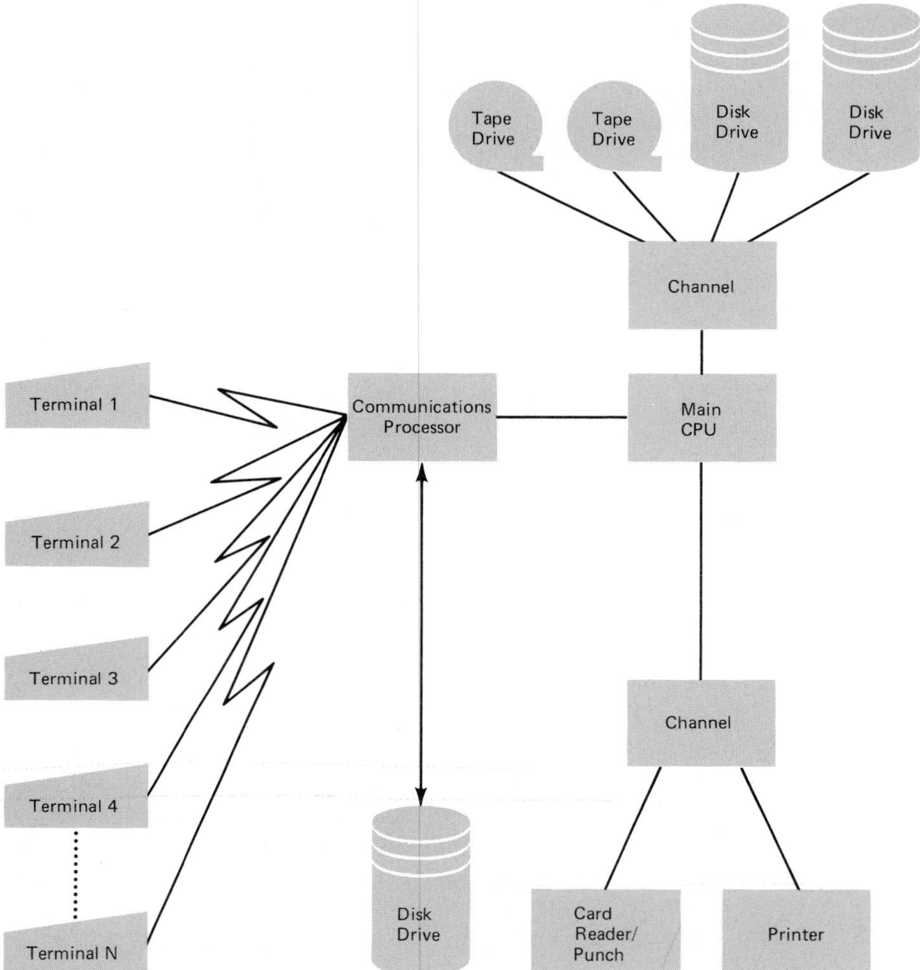

Figure 8-17 Typical Configuration of an Online Direct-Access System

Terminals directly wired to the computer are called *hardwired* terminals. Terminals not hardwired are connected to the computer through dial-up access. An advantage of dial-up access is that a communication line is used only when computer access is necessary. Its primary disadvantages are the time it takes to dial the computer, slower data transmission speeds, and the possibility that all dial-up ports to a computer may be busy when access is needed. Terminals physically close to the CPU are usually hardwired using company-installed lines rather than telephone lines. Remote, single terminal installations tend to be dial-up terminals. We will discuss other methods of terminal access in chapter 11 under data communications.

Online files do not have to be online at all times of the day. Some companies set aside certain times for particular files to be online. For example, the inventory file may be online from 8:00 A.M. until noon. At noon the disk pack containing the inventory file is removed from the disk drive, and the accounts receivable file is placed online from noon until 5:00 P.M. Rotating files saves the cost of additional hardware required to keep both files online at the same time. This procedure works well when access to files is necessary only during certain hours of the day.

Online direct access systems can serve three primary functions: 1) inquiry; 2) update, and 3) programming. Inquiry terminals retrieve information from files in response to inquiries. Update terminals access files, modify data, and provide information in response to inquiries. Programmers use online direct access systems widely when they write or change program code. Copies of production or new programs are stored in a programmer area in an online disk pack, and coding is done through a CRT terminal on the programmer's desk. However, for control purposes, these terminals should have access only to copies of production programs, not the actual programs. Control over program changes is discussed in chapter 19.

A final observation is that online direct access systems are not necessarily realtime systems. These two terms are often erroneously interchanged. The distinction between them will be discussed in the next section.

MANAGEMENT CASE 8-2

Basic Hardware is a medium sized chain of hardware stores located primarily in the southeastern states. They are considering some type of point-of-sale capture of sales data through cash registers for input to sales analysis and inventory reordering systems. The design of the system has been narrowed to a basic choice between a true realtime and a batch system that is updated daily. With a realtime system each cash register would be online to the central computer through regular telephone lines during business hours. Under the batch system each cash register would have the capability of storing one day's worth of sales data. At the end of the day the central computer would be dialed up and the data transmitted to the central computer. Although the realtime option has the advantage of providing realtime information it also is more expensive primarily because of the necessity of tying up telephone lines over long distances during the complete business hours. With the batch approach a line would be tied up for approximately 15 minutes at the end of each day. Do you think realtime information in this situation would justify the additional communication costs?

REALTIME SYSTEMS

A realtime computer system can immediately capture data about ongoing events or processes and provide the information necessary to manage them. Examples of realtime systems are manufacturing process control and airline reservation systems. An essential component of a realtime system is realtime master files, which are updated shortly after the transactions occur. Consequently, at any point in time, data in realtime master files should accurately reflect the status of the variables they represent. For example, when a customer reserves a seat on an airline flight, the reservations agent keys in that fact, and the inventory of nonreserved seats on that flight is immediately updated to reflect one less available seat. Obviously, a realtime system is necessary to respond to customer inquiries about available seats. A batch system would be inadequate because the data on the master file would not be current.

Many colleges and universities use realtime systems to register students for classes.

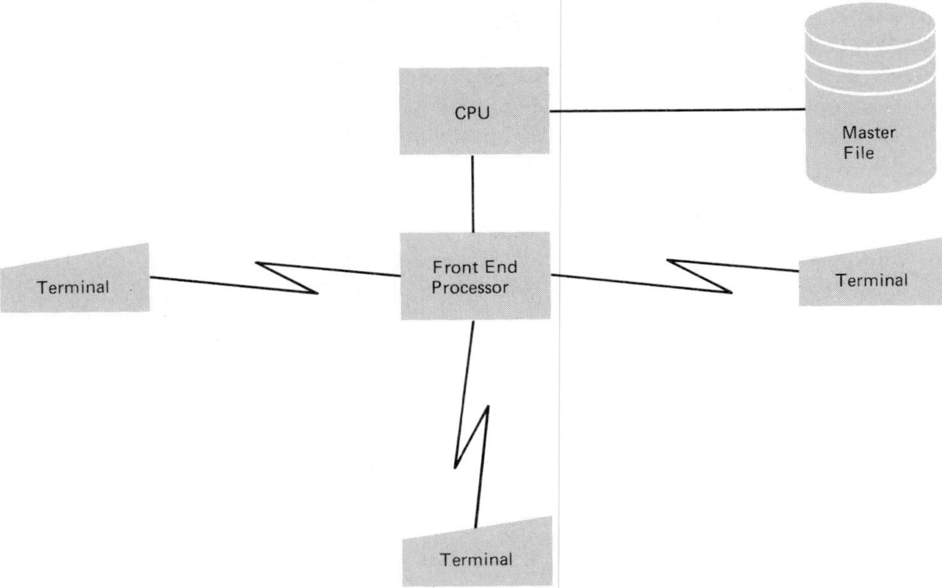

Figure 8-18 A Realtime System

In this process, students report to a terminal location and request classes. They can be notified immediately about whether their schedules are confirmed because the inventory of unfilled class seats is on a realtime file. Figure 8-18 shows the operation of a realtime system.

Realtime systems are most useful at the transaction processing and operational decision levels, such as in order-processing systems that depend on realtime inventory master files. Management decisions at the tactical and strategic levels generally do not require realtime information. Information that is a day, a week, or even a month old, such as profit and loss statements, can be just as valuable as realtime data for tactical or strategic decision making. However, as the cost of storage and processing declines, more realtime systems are being implemented for transaction processing. This trend makes more of the underlying data for tactical and strategic level information available on a realtime basis. For example, tactical sales analysis data can be retrieved from realtime point-of-sale systems, even though in most cases it is not necessary for such data to be realtime.

Certain types of applications do not require realtime updating even though they are transaction processing applications. For example, updating the payroll master file on a realtime basis for hours worked by each employee is unnecessary. If payroll checks are produced weekly, the information can be updated every week via the batch processing method.

The computer configuration needed to support a realtime system must allow online direct access. Files must also be structured to allow direct access, since fast response to inquiries is required, and update transactions are processed as they occur rather than on a delayed, batch basis.

Realtime systems have the primary advantage of providing timely information. Certain computer applications can function only on a realtime basis. Others are more cost-effective using a batch mode. The primary disadvantage of realtime systems is that hardware and communication costs are higher, and the operating system and applications software necessary to support them are more complex.

SUMMARY

Data is internally represented in the computer in the form of binary digits.

The Extended Binary Coded Decimal Interchange Code (EBCDIC) represents a character or a digit as a combination of eight bits, called a byte. This code is used extensively on IBM hardware.

The eight bit American Standard Code for Information Interchange (ASCII-8) is another popular coding scheme used by many hardware manufacturers.

If it is necessary to examine the contents of the computer's memory, the hexadecimal system may be used. Since this system represents numbers in base 16, it is much more compact and readable than binary representation.

Usually a byte of data has an extra bit, called a parity bit. The machine sets the value of the parity bit such that the total number of on bits in every byte is either always even or always odd. If a byte has an odd number of on bits in an even parity machine, it means the data has been damaged and must be corrected.

Data records stored in a sequential file are ordered by record key. Sequential files are normally used for batch type processes in which most of the records have to be accessed every time the program is run.

Direct file organization allows rapid access to any individual record regardless of the value of its key. Disk packs are commonly used to store direct access files. The division of a disk pack into cylinders, tracks, and sectors facilitates quick retrieval of data stored anywhere on the pack.

The indexed sequential access method (ISAM) uses an index to determine the approximate location of a record. That region is then searched sequentially for the desired record.

Under simple direct file organization, a key in the record is used as its address relative to the beginning of the file.

Random direct file organization also uses relative addressing. However, the relative addresses for records are chosen using some mathematical transformation of the record key.

Using the virtual storage access method (VSAM) frees the user from having to refer to any physical address at all. Any record may be accessed by specifying only its relative address.

To select the best file organization for an application, it is necessary to consider many factors, including file volatility, file activity, file size, and query requirements.

In a batch processing system, queries and updates to the system are accumulated for some time and are then executed all in one run. On the other hand, in immediate mode, transactions are individually entered into files soon after the actual real-world event occurs.

Three kinds of data processing approaches are used:

1. Batch-Sequential
2. Batch-Direct
3. Immediate-Direct

Most applications are now being designed in the immediate-direct mode.

An online direct access system consists of several terminals connected to the CPU, which is in turn connected to several direct access files.

A realtime system is a special kind of online direct access system. It captures data immediately after the occurrence of an event, processes it right away, and returns information to use in managing ongoing events.

KEY TERMS

Binary Representation
EBCDIC Representation
ASCII-8 Representation
Hexadecimal Representation
Memory Dump
Parity Bits
Field
Record
File
File Organization
Sequential File Organization
Direct File Organization
Indexed Sequential Access Method (ISAM)
Simple Direct Access Method
Random Direct Access Method
Virtual Storage Access Method (VSAM)
Disk Pack
Physical Address
Cylinder
Track
Sector
Index
Index Area
Prime Area
Overflow Area
Relative Address
Digit Analysis
Hashing (Division Remainder Method)
Folding
Radix Transformation
Synonyms
File Volatility
File Activity
File Query
Binary Search
Batch-Sequential Approach
Batch-Direct Approach
Immediate-Direct Approach
Updating
Online Direct Access System
Hardwired Terminals
Realtime System

REVIEW QUESTIONS

1. Explain the relationship among the elements in the data hierarchy.
2. What is the difference between a binary number and a decimal number?
3. Why is it necessary to use a coding scheme like EBCDIC or ASCII-8 to store data instead of pure binary representation?
4. Describe the advantages of the hexadecimal system.
5. How is a parity bit used to ensure data accuracy?

6. What are the two basic types of file organization?
7. Briefly explain the four direct access techniques of data retrieval.
8. What distinguishes VSAM from other access methods?
9. List the criteria used in selecting a file organization method.
10. Explain the difference between batch processing and immediate processing.
11. Is it possible to process direct access files in a batch mode?
12. List the benefits of the immediate-direct approach to data processing.
13. What makes a system online?
14. Why is direct access storage necessary for an online system?
15. What makes an online direct access system a realtime system?

DISCUSSION QUESTIONS

1. What type of file organization would be best suited for the following files:
    1. A payroll master file from which paychecks are issued biweekly.
    2. An accounts receivable master file in a large retail department store.
    3. A batch transaction file for a material inventory system in which the master file has an ISAM organization.
    4. The master file for a work-in-process, job order system used by management for operational control of production.
    5. An online class registration master file used by a university for student registration from online terminals.
2. Sequential file organization is conceptually simple and requires a minimum of storage space. Direct file organization, on the other hand, requires complex access methods and extra storage space for indexes. Discuss some business reasons for the increasing popularity of direct access systems despite their higher costs. What technological developments have aided in this process?
3. A large bank with branches in several different cities in a single state is reevaluating its demand deposit accounting (DDA) system. Essentially, it feels that there are three basic approaches to DDA:
    1. A centralized batch DDA system updated for changes on a daily basis. COM (microfiche) would be produced daily containing the beginning balance, the day's transactions, and the ending balance for each depositor. Each branch would receive COM (via courier service by 8:00 A.M.) containing the above information for all its depositors. The daily cutoff for the DAA system would be 2:00 P.M. each day. Therefore, the COM would reflect any transactions that have cleared by 2:00 P.M. the previous day. This COM would be used for depositors' inquiries concerning their accounts.
    2. A centralized batch DDA system similar to the system in 1 above, but no COM would be produced. Instead, CRT terminals (connected online via leased lines with the central CPU) would be used by each branch for processing depositors' inquiries concerning their accounts.

3. A realtime DDA system where both transactions and inquiries are processed immediately through branch CRT terminals via leased communication lines.

Required

1. What are the advantages and disadvantages of the three alternatives?
2. How would the necessity of using dial-up lines affect your choice of alternative 3?

RESEARCH PROJECTS

1. Investigate the application of realtime systems to process control in manufacturing companies. Identify and evaluate some systems used in typical industrial situations like quality control, manpower allocation, and inventory control.

2. Publications like *Computerworld* and *Infosystems* often carry articles that describe the information processing strategy of some business firm. Survey some recent issues of such publications and report on trends in the adoption of the immediate-direct approach to information processing.

APPLICATION CASE

Airlines Fight Over Systems for Bookings
(Wall Street Journal, Jan. 18, 1982, p. 25)

By John Curley, Staff Reporter of The Wall Street Journal

Computers are the latest battleground in the contest among airlines for passengers.

Carriers are competing to install automated reservations terminals at travel agencies, which account for 65% of all bookings. The airlines don't make money when they lease the terminals. But they hope that the systems will influence agents to choose their flights instead of competitors'.

"The automation war is fierce. Every agency is being pursued." says Richard E. Murray, in charge of American Airlines' Sabre reservation system. Adds Barry A. Kotar, director of United Airlines' Apollo network: "It's a distribution system that's vital to our health and will become more important in the future."

The reservation systems contain information on nearly all schedules and fares. But a carrier can bias a system in its favor by assuring that the computer lists its schedules first when asked for route information.

United, American Dominate

Some critics say the reservation systems can be used even more directly as weapons against competitors. The owner that owns the system can, for instance, decide to drop another airline's listings—and in one case, that has already happened. (Carriers that don't offer reservations systems usually pay to get their schedules on the computers.)

United and American have dominated the reservations business since the first commercial computer systems came to market in 1976. Together they have recruited nearly 10,000 agencies—85% of the automated agencies and 55% of all travel companies. Both claim market leadership.

Now they're going to get competition. Eastern Airlines and Northwest Airlines have announced new systems in recent months. Trans World Airlines, which already has 1,000 subscribers on its PARS network, is going after smaller agencies with PARS-2. And last year, Tymshare Inc. in Cupertino, Calif., entered the market with a system it bought from International Telephone & Telegraph Co.

With most systems, travel agents can store information about frequent customers, such as their telephone and credit card numbers and preferences for flights, seats, meals, hotels and cars. They can also save time by reissuing dozens of tickets automatically when fares or schedules change, and by providing tickets, seat assignments and boarding passes. And they can quote complicated international fares without testing their math skills.

A typical package which includes four terminals, two ticket printers, training and maintenance, costs an agency about $800 a month. TWA leases a PARS-2 terminal and printer for $159 monthly. Peter T. McHugh, staff vice president of passenger service planning, figures it will appeal to companies with as little as $500,000 in annual sales. "We've entered a whole new market no one else was touching," he says.

In the future, more systems will let agents connect with numerous airline computers from just one terminal, providing a firsthand look at the latest fare and schedule changes. The 700 agencies on Tymshare's MARS-Plus network have access to the computers of seven airlines. PARS-2 and Northwest's Polaris system are multiaccess; Eastern offers a variation of it, and American will introduce it this year.

In Waterville, Ohio, Travel Horizons Inc. uses MARS-Plus to save money for clients. Last month, the agency received a patent on a fare-scanning technique that produces four low-cost alternatives for any destination or schedule. The 20-minute scan costs $8.75. Owens-Illinois Inc., Toledo, tested the system last year and found potential savings of $1 million a year, or 10% of its travel budget.

American and United also compete in the growing market for travel accounting and management services. They lease computers and programs, that, when connected to automated systems, can produce invoices, sales reports, cash-flow projections, market analyses and other business services for agencies and their corporate clients. TWA plans to offer a business system this year.

Other automation features coming are word processing, budget planning, faster fare updates, improved international pricing and fare shopping techniques, and direct links with hotel and car rental agencies. American is bringing Deak-Perera Inc., the foreign currency exchange concern, into Sabre to update foreign conversion rates several times a day. The new program will allow Sabre agents to get foreign drafts, order international travelers checks and draw checks on international banks.

Along with such conveniences, automation brings problems. Agents complain of mechanical breakdowns, bias, inaccuracy and increasing complexity. It can take as long as a year for agents to become fully proficient with automated terminals. Some can't adapt. An agent in Philadelphia rarely uses the thousands of dollars of computer equipment he bought because it intimidates him.

The potential power of the systems against competitors has already been demonstrated.

Last month, United and American decided to charge for booking tickets on other carriers. The two giants say they are losing money on the service and want to recover costs. American wants to charge Muse Air in Texas $2 per booking.

"We feel it's an unjust charge. It can't be costing them that much to service us, grumbles Edward W. Lang, Muse's vice president, marketing. But Muse, a relatively new airline, will probably pay the fee rather than lose the ticketing arrangement, which is the primary benefit of being included in the computerized reservation system. "We don't have a choice," says Mr. Lang. "We'd lose business." People Express, however, refused to pay United's fee and has been dropped from the Apollo system.

That alarms Charles A. Moore, an official of the American Society of Travel Agents. "If they leave a Muse or People Express out now, how long would it be before American tries to drop United," he asks. "One of these days, we could have a real airline battle via computer."

Discussion

1. Why must an airline reservation system be a realtime system? Must all updates of an airline reservation system be realtime?
2. You are a salesperson for American Airlines. What arguments would you use to sell a travel agency on installing American's Sabre system?

CHAPTER 9

DATA BASE MANAGEMENT SYSTEMS

I. Introduction

II. The Traditional Approach to Information Processing
   A. Data Redundancy
   B. Lack of Data Integration
   C. Program/Data Dependence
   D. Lack of Flexibility

III. The Data Base Approach to Information Processing
   A. Logical Versus Physical Views of Data Storage
   B. The Users
   C. The Data Base Management System
   D. The Data Base Administrator
   E. The Data Base

IV. Logical Data Base Structures
   A. Tree Structures
   B. Network Structures
   C. Relational Structures
   D. Indexing

V. Advantages and Disadvantages of the Database Approach
   A. Advantages
   B. Disadvantages

INTRODUCTION

Perhaps the most important challenge facing information systems is to provide users with timely and versatile access to data stored in computer files. In a dynamic business environment there are many unanticipated needs for information. However, these information needs often go unsatisfied because appropriate data are contained in computer files that cannot be accessed and output in a suitable format on a timely basis. Data base management systems have the potential to meet this challenge. In this chapter we will first contrast the traditional with the data base approach to information processing. We will then look at some of the logical ways users view data stored in a data base. Finally, we will explore the advantages and disadvantages of data base management systems.

THE TRADITIONAL APPROACH TO INFORMATION PROCESSING

The traditional approach to information processing is file oriented. Prior to the advent of data base management systems (DBMS), each application maintained its own master file and generally had its own set of transaction files. Figure 9-1 illustrates the traditional approach to information processing. Files are custom designed for each application, and generally there is very little sharing of data among various applications. Programs are dependent on files and vice versa. That is, when the physical format of the file is changed, the program also has to be changed. The traditional approach to information processing is file oriented because the primary underlying purpose of many applications is to maintain data on the master file so that management information can be produced. Therefore, the master file for each application is the centerpiece of that application. Although the traditional, file-oriented approach to information processing

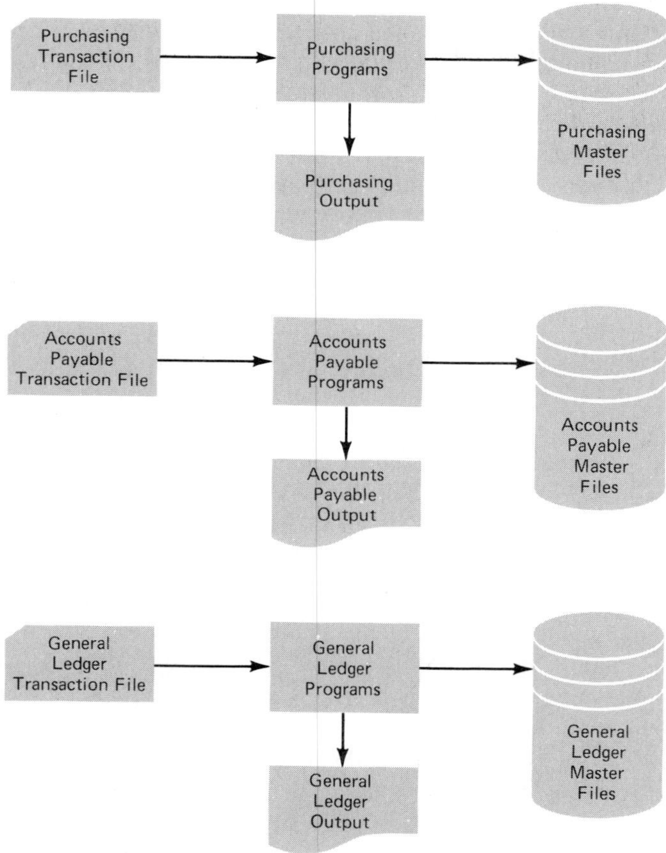

Figure 9-1 Traditional Approach To Information Processing

is still widely used, it does have some very important disadvantages. Among them are the following:

Data Redundancy

Identical data are often stored in two or more files. Obviously such redundancy increases data editing, maintenance, and storage costs. In addition, the same data stored on two different master files (which should in theory be identical) are often different with good reason; but such differences inevitably create confusion as to which set of data is correct.

Lack of Data Integration

Data on different master files may be related, as in the case of a personnel information master file and a payroll master file. However, the application approach does not have the mechanisms for associating such data in a logical way to make them useful for management's needs.

Program/Data Dependence

In the traditional file oriented approach, programs are tied to master files and vice versa. Changes in the physical format of the master file require changes in all programs that access the master file. Consequently, data management becomes the task of each applications programmer in each applications program that he or she writes and maintains. There is no centralized execution of the data management function. Data management is scattered among all the applications programmers.

Lack of Flexibility

The information retrieval capabilities of most traditional information processing systems are limited to predetermined information requests. Therefore, the information produced by these systems tends to be in the form of scheduled reports that the system has been previously programmed to produce. If management has a requirement for unanticipated types of information, the information can perhaps be provided if it is contained on the files of the system. However, providing this information often takes extensive programming. Consequently, by the time the programming is completed, the information may no longer be required or useful. This problem has long plagued information systems. Management knows that a particular piece of information could be produced through a management information system on a one-time basis. However, the time and expense required to produce this information are generally prohibitive. Ideally, information processing should be able to associate related data elements and produce information with a fast turnaround to service unanticipated requests for information.

THE DATA BASE APPROACH TO INFORMATION PROCESSING

Logical Versus Physical Views of Data Storage

A *data base management system* (DBMS) is a program serving as an interface between applications programs and a set of coordinated and integrated physical files called a data base. The physical files of the data base are analogous to the master files of the applications approach. However, with the DBMS approach, related data among the physical files are associated with various pointers, indexes, and keys. This association not only reduces data redundancy but also enables the retrieval of unanticipated related information. These chaining and pointer schemes will be discussed later in this section. Figure 9-2 illustrates the DBMS approach in a summary form.

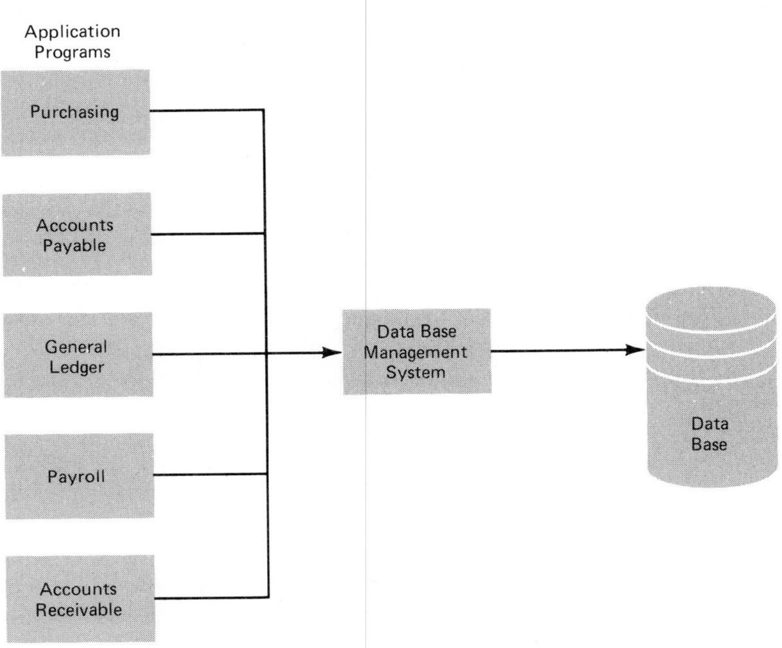

Figure 9-2 Summary of the DBMS Approach

In fact, the data might be physically disaggregated and stored on magnetic disk according to some complex addressing mechanism. But the data base management system assumes the responsibility of aggregating the data into a neat logical format whenever the application program needs it. (Table 9-1 illustrates a logical view of sales data.) This frees the applications programmer from having to worry about tracks and cylinders, and lets him or her concentrate on the business aspects of the problem to be solved.

Table 9-1 Logical View of Sales Data

Salesman			Year-to-date Sales		
I.D. #	**Name**	**Region**	**Product A**	**Product B**	**Product C**
223	Smith	S.W.	6,395	4,328	5,875
227	O'Neil	S.W.	4,326	898	1,587
241	Maxwell	S.W.	12,331	8,976	7,215
256	Ware	East	8,232	6,554	7,321
257	Charles	East	2,111	4,573	5,321
258	Scholar	Midwest	5,221	6,632	6,331
276	Williams	Midwest	11,213	10,709	9,318
283	Mufti	Midwest	2,124	5,335	6,326
285	Cadd	Midwest	7,224	5,019	2,020
300	Harris	N.E.	3,423	3,302	8,824
307	Bentley	N.E.	8,635	5,661	3,624
310	Curtis	N.E.	10,728	7,187	8,721
322	May	N.E.	7,853	5,354	6,332

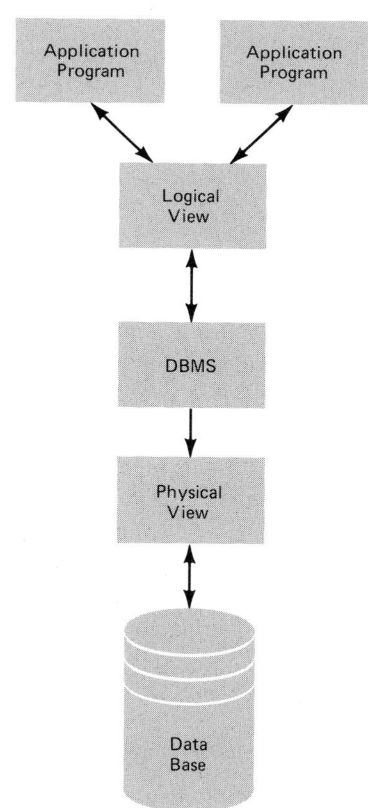

Figure 9-3 Logical versus Physical Views of Data

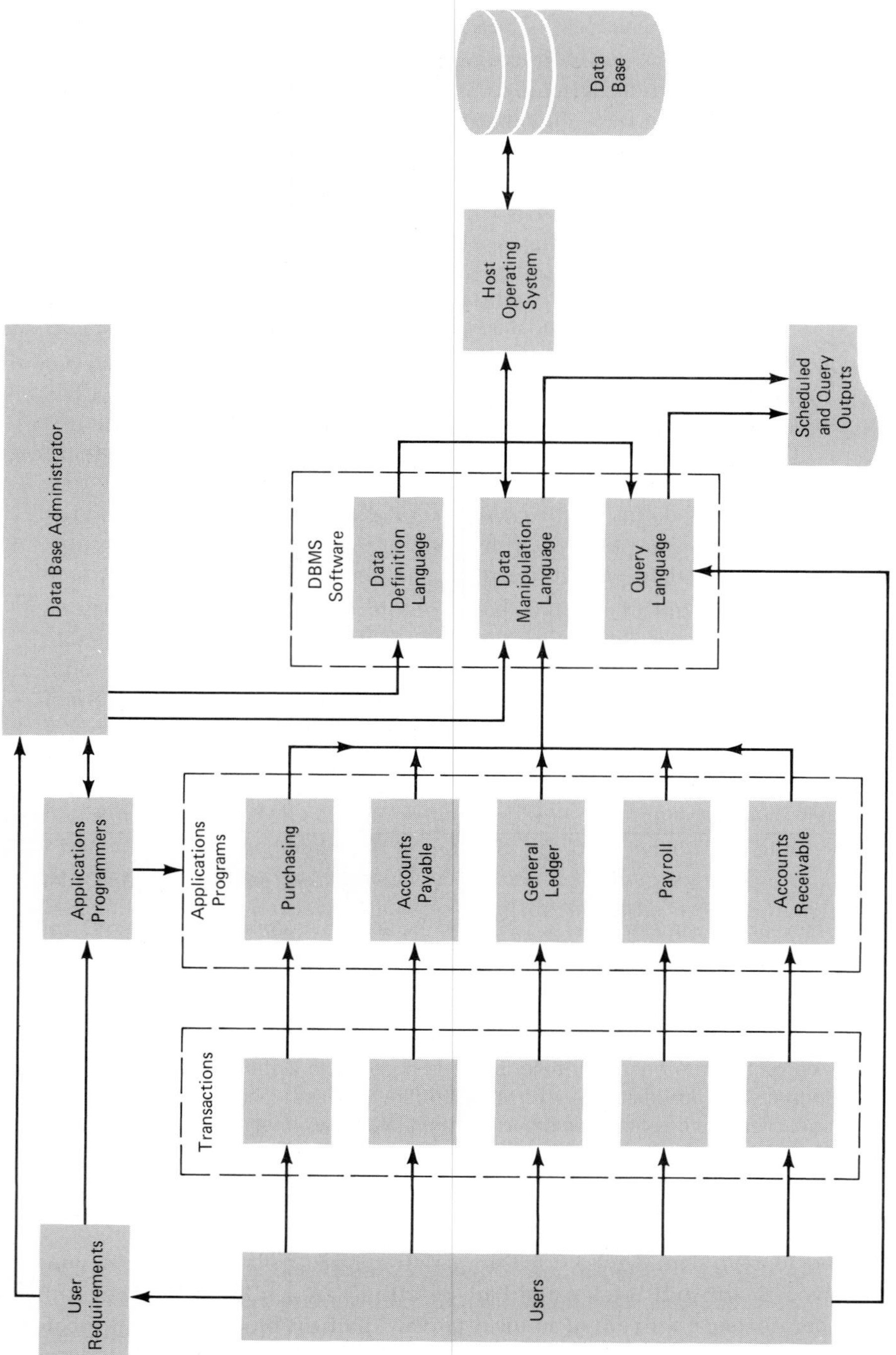

Figure 9-4 Interaction Among DBMS Components

Figure 9-3 shows how the DBMS insulates the user's logical view of data from physical storage details. The user or applications programmer can refer to data items using meaningful names like CUSTOMER-NAME and TOTAL-PURCHASE. He or she no longer has to worry about specifying things like the physical disk on which the data is stored.

The data base environment has four components: 1) the users; 2) the data base management system; 3) the data base; and 4) the data base administrator. Figure 9-4 illustrates the interaction among components of the data base environment.

The Users

Users consist of both traditional users (such as professional and clerical personnel) and applications programmers, who are not considered to be users in the traditional sense. Users interact with the data base management system indirectly via application programs or directly via a simple query language. This language enables the user to retrieve data on an ad hoc basis. Users' interactions with the data base management system include the definition of the logical relationships in the data base (i.e., the logical view), and the input, changing, deletion, and manipulation of data.

MANAGEMENT CASE 9-1

The Gilmer Company established a data base management system approximately four years ago. Since that time the firm has been gradually converting all of its applications to the data base management system. Recently the administrative vice president has been concerned about the security of data stored in the data base management system. She is particularly concerned that almost all the administrative and clerical personnel of the firm have access to the data base management system and yet there are substantial amounts of confidential data stored on the DBMS. She has stated, "with confidential wage and salary data stored on the DBMS, how can we be sure that this data remains confidential without everyone having access to the DBMS. It seems to me that a DBMS is sort of like putting all your eggs in one basket with no one guarding the basket." What would be your response to the administrative vice president's concerns?

The Data Base Management System

The data base management system is a complex software package enabling users to communicate with the data base. The data base management system interprets user commands so that the computer system can perform the task required. For example, the data base management system might translate a command such as GET CUSTNO, AMOUNT, INVNO into "retrieve record 458 from disk 09."

Conceptually, a data base management system uses two languages: 1) a *data definition language* (DDL); and 2) a *data manipulation language* (DML). The *DDL* is essentially the link between the logical and physical views of the data base. As was discussed earlier, logical refers to the way the user views data; physical refers to the way the data are physically stored. The logical structure of a data base is sometimes called a *schema*. A *subschema* is the way a particular application views the data from the data base that the application uses. There may be many users and application programs utilizing the same data base. Each user or application program utilizes a set of DDL

```
SCHEME NAME IS EDUCATION.
RECORD NAME IS STUDENT;
   SNO      ; TYPE IS FIXED DECIMAL 6.
   SNAME    ; TYPE IS CHARACTER 20.
   MAJOR    ; TYPE IS CHARACTER 10.
RECORD NAME IS TEACHER;
   TNO      ; TYPE IS FIXED DECIMAL 4.
   TNAME    ; TYPE IS CHARACTER 20.
   SUBJECT  ; TYPE IS CHARACTER 10.
```

Figure 9-5 Statements from a Data Definition Language

statements to construct a subschema that includes only those data elements that are of interest. Figure 9-5 shows statements from a data definition language.

The DDL is used to define the physical characteristics of each record, which consist of the fields within the record, each field's data type, and each field's length and logical name. This logical name, such as SNAME for the student name field, is used by both application programs and users to refer to a field for the purpose of retrieving or updating the data in it. The DDL is also used to specify relationships among records, such as tree or network structures where the records are chained together by means of pointers (these are discussed later in this section). The primary functions the DDL serves are to:

1. Describe the schema and subschemas.
2. Describe the fields in each record and the record's logical name.
3. Describe the data type and name of each field.
4. Indicate the keys of the record.
5. Provide for data security restrictions.
6. Provide for logical and physical data independence.
7. Provide means of associating related data structures such as trees, networks, and tables.

The *data manipulation language* (DML) provides the techniques for processing the data base, such as retrieval, sorting, display, and deletion of data or records. The DML should include a variety of manipulation verbs and operands for each verb. Table 9-2 contains some of these verbs and corresponding operands.

Table 9-2 Data Manipulation Language Verbs

Verbs	Operands
Delete	Record Key, Field Name, Record Name, or File Name
Sort	Field Name
Insert	Record Key, Field Name, Record Name, or File Name
Display	Record Key, Field Name, Record Name, or File Name
Add	Field Name

Most data manipulation languages interface with high level programming languages such as COBOL or PL/1, which are used in conjunction with the data manipulation language to provide sophisticated applications programs.

A key feature of a DML is that it refers to data using logical names, such as CUSTNO for customer number, instead of describing the actual physical storage of data in order to access and use it. This capability is made possible because the DDL provides linkage between the logical view of data and their physical storage. In summary, the functions of a DML are to:

1. Provide the techniques for data manipulation, such as deletion, replacement, retrieval, sorting, or insertion of data or records.
2. Enable users and application programs to process data using logically meaningful data names rather than physical storage locations.
3. Provide interfaces with programming languages. A DML should support several high level languages such as COBOL, PL/1, and FORTRAN.
4. Allow users and application programs to be independent of physical data storage and data base maintenance.
5. Provide for the use of logical relationships among data items.

Figure 9-6 gives examples of statements from three different data manipulation languages.

```
   Data Base Task Group (DBTG) DML defined for COBOL:

   PERFORM UNTIL FLAG = 'RED'
      FIND NEXT OVERDUE WITHIN ACCOUNTS
      IF EOF NOT = 'YES'
         IF OVERDUE = 'YES'
            MOVE 'RED' TO FLAG
         END-IF
      END-IF
   END-PERFORM

   Information Management System (IMS) DML (DL/1)

   GU ACCOUNTS (OVERDUE = 'YES')
VA GN ACCOUNTS (OVERDUE = 'RED')
   go to VA

   Structured English Query Language (SEQUEL)

   SELECT ACCTNO FROM ACCOUNTS
       WHERE OVERDUE = 'YES'
```

Figure 9-6 Statements from Three Different Data Manipulation Languages

The Data Base Administrator

The data base administrator's (DBA) department performs the following functions:

1. Maintains a data dictionary. The data dictionary defines the meaning of each data item stored in the data base, and describes interrelations between data items. Since the data base is shared among many users, it is necessary to have clear and commonly

agreed upon meanings for the stored items. Part of a data dictionary is shown in Figure 9-7.
2. Determines and maintains the physical structure of the data base.
3. Provides for updating and changing the data base, including deletion of inactive records.
4. Creates and maintains edit controls over changes and additions to the data base.
5. Develops retrieval methods to meet the needs of users.
6. Implements security and disaster recovery procedures.
7. Maintains configuration control of the data base. Configuration control means that changes to the data base requested by one user must be approved by other users of the data base. One user cannot indiscriminately change the data base to the detriment of other users.
8. Assigns user access codes in order to prevent unauthorized use of data.

```
                         LEDGER DED

                               *****SFNLACCT*****
          NAME:      ACCOUNT ATTRIBUTES
          NARRATIV:  THE RECORDING ACCOUNT NUMBER ALONG WITH IDENTIFIERS AND
                     ATTRIBUTES WHICH MAY CATEGORIZE, IDENTIFY, OR OTHER-
                     WISE DESCRIBE THE ACCOUNT
          COMMENTS:  THE ROOT SEGMENT OF THE FINANCIAL LEDGER DATA BASE
                     GENERALLY REFERRED TO SIMPLY AS THE ACCOUNT NUMBER
T E (P,C,SFNLACCT-RECORDING-ACCOUNT-NO,0)  +
          NAME:      RECORDING ACCOUNT NUMBER
          DEFINITN:  A NUMBER ASSIGNED BY THE UNIVERSITY FOR RECORDING AND
                     PROCESSING FINANCIAL ACTIVITY OF AN ACCOUNT
          COMMENTS:  A 9-CHARACTER IDENTIFIER
          SOURCE:    "FISCAL POLICY AND PROCEDURES STATEMENT NO. 3"
T E (P,C,SFNLACCT-ACCOUNT-TYPE,0)  +
          NAME:      ACCOUNT TYPE
          DEFINITN:  AN INDICATION OF WHETHER AN ACCOUNT IS INCOME,
                     EXPENDITURE, OR ASSET/LIABILITY/BALANCE
          COMMENTS:  A 1-CHARACTER CODE
          REFER NO:  168
T E (P,C,SFNLACCT-ACCOUNT-NAME,0)  +
          NAME:      ACCOUNT NAME
          DEFINITN:  THE NAME OF THE ACCOUNT ASSOCIATED WITH A RECORDING
                     ACCOUNT NUMBER
          COMMENTS:  MAXIMUM 30 CHARACTERS
T E (P,C,SFNLACCT-ACCOUNT-NAME-SORT,0)  +
          NAME:      ACCOUNT NAME SORT KEY
          DEFINITN:  ANY 6 SIGNIFICANT CHARACTERS OF THE ACCOUNT NAME WHICH
                     WILL PLACE AN ACCOUNT IN THE DESIRED POSITION OF
                     ALPHABETICAL ORDER
          COMMENTS:  MAY BE THE FIRST 6 CHARACTERS OF THE NAME, OR INITIALS,
                     OR SOMETHING ELSE.
```

Figure 9-7 A Data Dictionary

A data base administrator is extremely important, working very closely with users in order to create, maintain, and safeguard the data base. In effect, the data base administrator is the coordinator between the data base and its users and therefore must be familiar with their information requirements. The administrator must also be technically competent in the areas of DBMS and data storage and processing. Although the function of the data base administrator is relatively new, it is quickly evolving into an important management position. Data base administration is becoming an attractive career option for individuals with programming, systems, and business backgrounds. Figure 9-8 indicates the position of the DBA in a business organization.

The Data Base

The data base is the actual physical repository of data. For most practical applications data must be stored on direct access devices like magnetic disks. However, well-managed installations normally create backup copies of the data base on offline storage

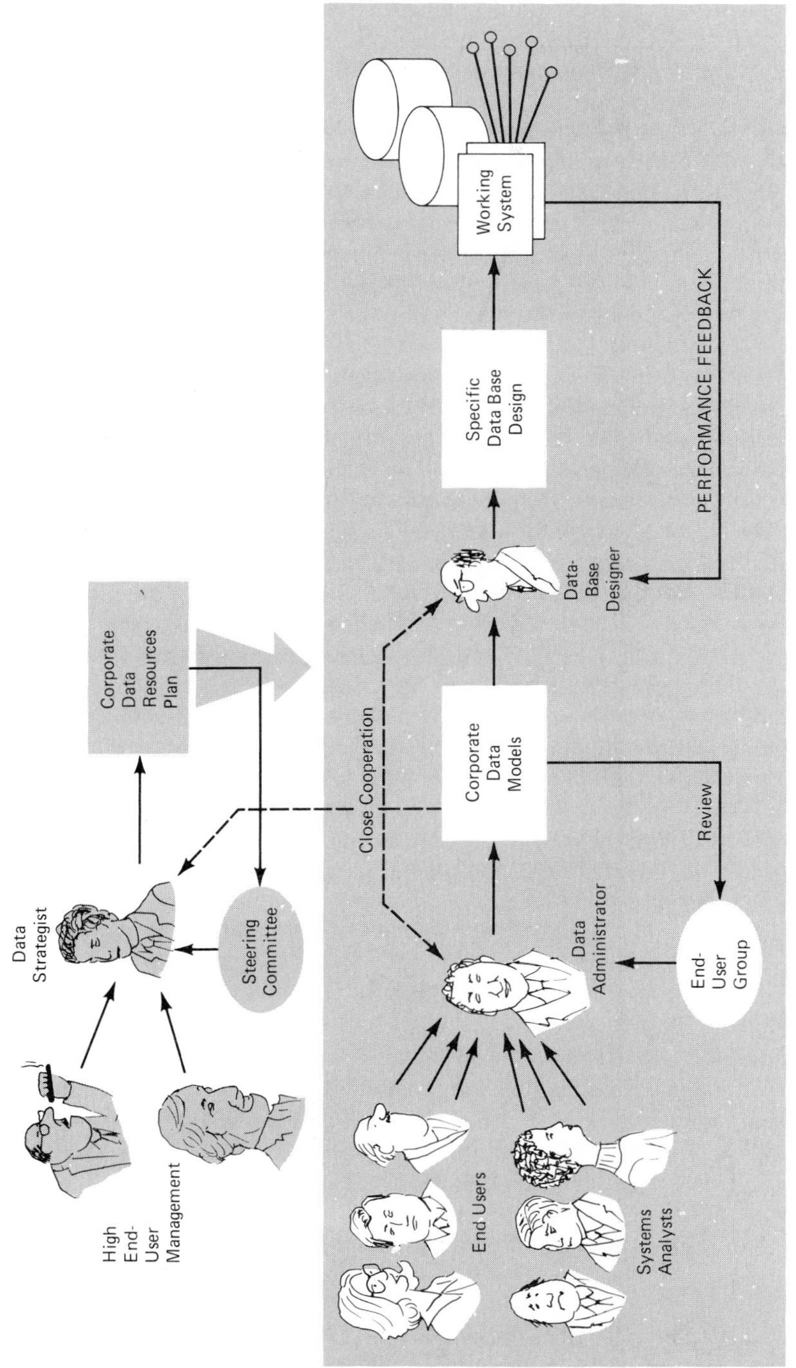

Figure 9-8 The Data Base Administrator (James Martin, An End-User's Guide to Data Base, © 1981, p. 33. Reprinted by permission of Prentice-Hall Inc., Englewood Cliffs, N.J.)

media like magnetic tape. Such security measures are extremely important in a data base environment, since many departments and application programs may be dependent on a single centralized data base.

Data base management systems are designed with a view toward optimizing the use of physical storage and CPU processing time. The logical view may contain redundant data items to make them more understandable for humans, but the DBMS makes sure that physical storage is nonredundant. This not only saves space, but also precludes the possibility of different values existing for the same data item at one time. DBMS also use other techniques to optimize resource utilization. For instance, data records that are seldom used may be placed on inexpensive, slow memory devices, while frequently used data may reside on the faster but more expensive media.

Data base systems are rapidly gaining popularity among business users. Since data base operations tend to be high volume processes, they often consume a large portion of the time and memory resources of a computer. Some vendors have now developed computers dedicated entirely to data base operations. These computers, frequently referred to as data base machines, are special purpose units. They have certain capabilities built into their hardware that make operations like retrieval, sorting, and updating much more efficient than with software programs.

LOGICAL DATA BASE STRUCTURES

Two key features of a DBMS are the ability to reduce data redundancy and the ability to associate related data elements. DBMS implement these two objectives through the use of keys, embedded pointers, and chains. An *embedded pointer* is simply a field within a record containing the physical or relative address of a related record in another part of the data base. The record referred to may also contain an embedded pointer that points to a third record, and so on. The series of records tied together by embedded pointers is a *chain*. There are three basic types of logical data structures that are used by DBMS: 1) tree; 2) network; and 3) relational structures.

Tree Structures

Figure 9-9 illustrates customer and invoice data in a tree (hierarchical) structure. A *tree structure* consists of nodes or records that are linked to related records through branches. The top node is called the root. The distinguishing feature of a tree structure is that nodes have a one-to-many relationship. That is, each node may have only one parent but an unlimited number of children. As shown in Figure 9-9 each customer can have one or more invoices, and each invoice can have one or more line items. However, each invoice is tied to a single customer, and the line items are in turn tied to a single invoice.

An important point to understand concerning tree structures (as well as network and relational structures) is that the structure is a logical representation of the data. The physical storage of the data in Figure 9-9 might simply be three separate files—a customer file, an invoice file, and a line item file—with the related records linked together by keys or embedded pointers within each record. With a tree structure, each

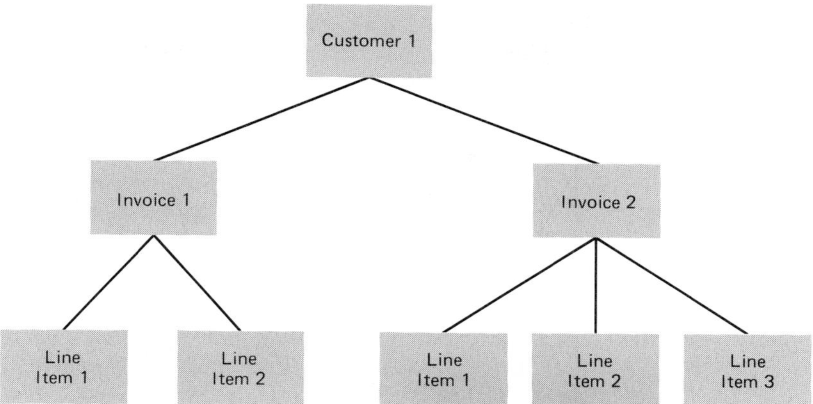

Figure 9-9 A Tree Data Structure

record must have a minimum of two embedded pointer fields. One field contains the address of the child or the first child of the node; the other contains the address of the twin of the node. For example, using Figure 9-9, the node invoice 1 contains the address of line item 1 (the first child) and also contains the address of invoice 2 (the twin of invoice 1). Tree structures can represent many different types of data. For example, the faculty-class-student relationship is a one-to-many relationship that could be structured on a tree basis.

Network Structures

many - to - many

A *network structure* is a data structure that allows a many-to-many relationship among the nodes in the structure. Figure 9-10 illustrates a network structure between classes and students. Each student can enroll in several classes; each class has many students.

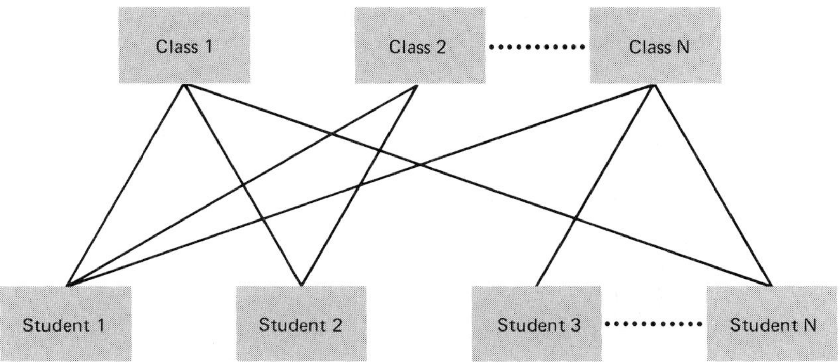

Figure 9-10 A Network Data Structure

The actual physical storage and linking of data in a network structure can be similar to that of a tree structure in that embedded pointers are included in each node. There are several different schemes for using pointers with network structures. One is similar to the scheme discussed under tree structures in which each node (for example, class 1) contains the address of the first student in the class. Student node 1, in turn, contains the address of the second student in the class, and so on, thereby forming a chain. The second student in the class is a twin of the first student in the class. In another scheme, each node (for example, a class) contains addresses of all the student nodes in that particular class. In turn, each student node contains the addresses of all classes for which the student is enrolled.

Data represented by a network structure can also be represented by a tree structure by the introduction of redundancy, as illustrated in Figure 9-11. As can be seen, the tree structure requires that student information be stored two or more times, depending on the number of classes in which a student is enrolled. The use of tree structures can become inefficient if the amount of such redundancy is substantial. The avoidance of redundancy is an advantage of network structures when many-to-many relationships exist in the data.

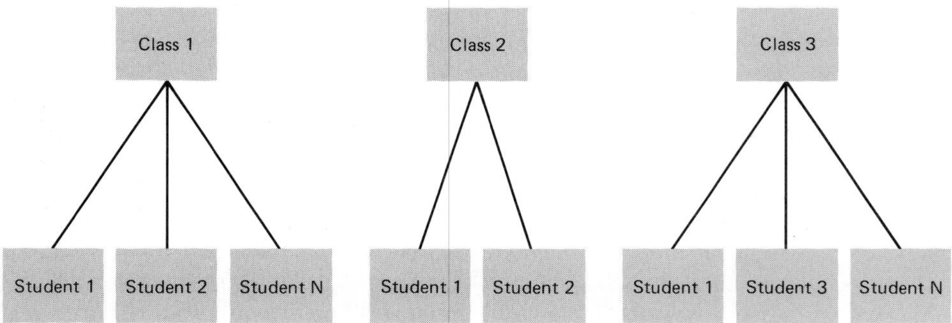

Figure 9-11 Tree Representation of Network Data Given in Figure 9-10

Relational Structures

Most business data has traditionally been organized in the form of simple two dimensional tables. In a relational DBMS these tables are called relations. This data model is known as the *relational model*, since it is based on the mathematical theory of relations. The relational or tabular model of data is used in a large variety of applications, ranging from a weekly shopping list to the annual report of the world's largest corporation. Nondata base files are normally organized as two dimensional flat files (that is, in tabular format). In recent years, data base management systems have also been developed that allow users to view data in a tabular format. Table 9-3 shows how a warehouse manager may perceive some of his or her data to be stored when using this kind of DBMS. In fact, the data may be physically stored using some complex addressing scheme. But the user is not aware of this fact. Whenever he or she accesses the data, the DBMS converts it to the logical format shown in Table 9-3.

Table 9-3 Flat Files or Relations

Daily Shipping Orders Record				
Order Date	**Shipping Order No.**	**Customer No.**	**Sales Order No.**	**Description**
07/18/8X	37501	4832	XP300	Tables
07/18/8X	37502	6991	XP355	Tables
07/18/8X	37503	3715	PD503	Shades
07/18/8X	37504	8200	XP751	Tables
07/19/8X	37505	0103	GP372	Chairs
07/19/8X	37507	6228	XP232	Tables
07/19/8X	37508	4373	PD655	Shades

Daily Shipment Record				
Shipment Date	**Shipping Order No.**	**Shipping Order Date**	**Carrier**	**Weight**
07/17/8X	37496	07/17/83	N. American	60
07/17/8X	37498	07/17/83	Hot Wheel	85
07/18/8X	37499	07/17/83	N. American	73
07/18/8X	37500	07/17/83	Smith Transfer	82
07/18/8X	37502	07/18/83	Smith Transfer	66
07/18/8X	37504	07/18/83	Hot Wheel	82
07/19/8X	37501	07/18/83	Georgia Freight	90
07/19/8X	37503	07/18/83	N. American	83

A relational DBMS allows a conceptually simple view of data, but also provides a set of powerful data manipulation capabilities. For example, if the warehouse manager wants a report listing all those shipping orders that were issued yesterday (07/18/8X), but were not shipped yesterday, it could easily be derived from the files shown in Table 9-3. Using a simple DML statement like the one shown below, the report in Table 9-4 may be produced.

```
SELECT  Shipping Order No., Customer No.
FROM    Daily Shipping Orders Record
WHERE   Order Date = 07/18/8X AND Shipping Order No. NOT IN
        SELECT  Shipping Order No.
        FROM    Daily Shipment Record
        WHERE   Shipment Date = 07/18/8X
```

Table 9-4 Data Manipulation with a Relational DBMS

Unfilled Orders	
Shipping Order No.	**Customer No.**
37501	4832
37503	3715

With a traditional, nondata base system it would have been necessary to write a complex computer program to perform this kind of data manipulation. A tree or network structured data base would have permitted this manipulation, but only if it had been anticipated at design time and the necessary pointers had been embedded in the records. Since the relational approach does not suffer from either of these restrictions, it is an effective tool for quickly generating unanticipated reports for management. Relational data bases are being implemented now and they are likely to be the dominant data base of the future.

MANAGEMENT CASE 9-2

Bohlin Inc. has been converting existing and developing new applications on IBM's Information Management System over the past five years. Initial expectations were that the data base management system software would assist in producing highly integrated application systems. This would allow managers to easily associate related data within the data base management system. Currently, it is evident that this expectation has not been fulfilled. For example, the manager of personnel, Chuck Bloss is very upset that when he retrieves data from the personnel system and attempts to retrieve related data from the payroll system that the link between the two systems does not exist. In addition, there are other numerous examples of lack of integration of the systems on the DBMS. How do you think this situation occurred? After all, aren't data base management systems designed to produce integrated systems that can associate related data automatically?

Indexing

No matter which logical structure is used, the data base will contain information relating to a number of distinct entities. An entity may be an employee, an order, a customer, or anything else for which we need to store a record of data. Each entity may have certain attributes like name, number, color, and size. These attributes correspond to the fields within each record. We normally access individual records in a file through the entity's primary key, such as a social security number. However, we need information from the files about the attributes of entities within the file. For example, assume a university with employees consisting of faculty, clerks, administrative personnel, and students who are working for the university under a work-study program. Assume further an employee data base for the university in which records contain typical information, such as social security number, age, sex, occupation, and so on. The contents of this data base would appear as shown in Table 9-5.

Table 9-5 Contents of a Data Base

Primary Key I.D. Number	Name	Occupation	Sex	Year Born
1	Johnson	Clerical	Female	1930
2	Jones	Professor	Male	1931
3	Jackson	Professor	Male	1930
4	Henry	Student	Male	1935
5	Houston	Student	Female	1934
6	Miller	Administrator	Female	1931

It may be necessary to retrieve data records pertaining to employees within a certain occupational group only. The DBMS would have to access each record and check the occupation field to determine whether the employee belongs to that group or not. In a large data base, with thousands of records, this can be a time consuming process. A large proportion of data base operations involves this kind of selective retrieval of data. In order to speed up these operations, a technique called indexing is used. One or more indexes may be maintained to access data through attributes instead of the primary key. Table 9-6 illustrates an index that may be used to access records in the data base shown in Table 9-5.

Table 9-6 A Data Base Index

Attribute (Occupation)	I.D. No. of Records Containing the Attribute
Professor	2, 3, 44
Student	4, 5, 90, 95
Clerical	1, 88, 89
Administrator	6, 87, 91, 92
Male	2, 3, 4, 7, 90, 94
Female	1, 5, 6, 88, 89
Born 1930	1, 3
Born 1931	2, 6, 84, 86
Etc.	

The index simply groups together the primary keys of all the records belonging to each occupational category. This is analogous to a subject catalog in a library, which groups together the call numbers of all books under convenient subject headings. To find the data records for, say, all clerical employees, the DBMS looks at the index and finds the ID numbers of all clerical employees. It then goes and retrieves records with just those ID numbers, instead of checking every record in the data base. Indexing is a powerful data retrieval technique, used by almost all data base management systems. It can help to find any desired record from among millions, just by consulting a few indexes and checking a few dozen records. The tradeoff in using indexing is the extra storage space and processing time required to maintain the indexes. But if the attributes to be indexed are chosen carefully, the benefits should easily outweigh the costs.

An index may also be used with a traditional, nondata base system. In such cases the index is often called an *inverted file* because it reverses the normal access procedure. Normally we retrieve the attributes of a record by specifying its primary key. With an inverted file we retrieve the primary keys of desired records by specifying an attribute value.

ADVANTAGES AND DISADVANTAGES OF THE DATABASE APPROACH

Advantages

The advantages of DBMS include the following:

Eliminates Data Redundancy. With a DBMS, data normally stored at two or more places are stored only once. This obviously reduces both storage costs and the confusion that can occur when data are stored at two or more places and are different (when they should be identical).

Ability to Associate Related Data. The ability to associate related data not only allows data redundancy to be reduced but also provides the ability to process unanticipated requests for data.

Program Data Independence. With a DBMS, programs can be changed without changing the data, and data storage can be changed without changing the programs. The DBMS serves as an interface between programs and data so that programs are concerned only with the logical symbolic names of the data, not physical storage. This advantage frees a programmer from the detailed and complex task of keeping up with the physical structure of the data.

Improvement of the Interface between the User and the System. DBMS provide simple query languages with which a user, or a user assisted by an applications programmer, can retrieve information quickly to fill unanticipated needs for information. In addition, these languages enable users to write their own programs to retrieve information on an ad hoc basis.

Increased Security and Integration of Data. Data contained in a data base are likely to be more secure and better integrated than data stored using the traditional file approach because the data base administrator's primary function is to provide for the integration, physical storage, and security of the data. With the traditional approach, this function is scattered among several different individuals.

When you consider the advantages of DBMS you should be able to see the importance of DBMS to MIS applications. In particular, the ability to associate related data in processing unanticipated requests for information and the improvement of the interface between users and the system are both fundamental tools indispensable to an MIS. A caveat, though—some would lead you to believe that a DBMS is an MIS, which is certainly not the case. A DBMS is simply a powerful tool that can be used in implementing an MIS. In addition, you will learn in chapter 17 that a DBMS is central to a decision support system.

Disadvantages

The disadvantages of DBMS are relatively few, and in the long run will certainly be outweighed by the advantages. One disadvantage is that data base management systems software is complex. The concepts used in DBMS are also new and equally complex. Therefore, DBMS requires sophisticated data processing personnel and a reeducation of users.

In addition, DBMS software places additional overhead on a computer system because it requires computer time to execute, disk space for storage of the software, and so on. However, as we saw in chapter 6, this is a disadvantage of all systems software. It is also not likely to be a major disadvantage in the future, as the cost of computer hardware declines.

SUMMARY

Traditional information processing is file oriented—each application has its own separate data storage. This approach has several disadvantages:

1. Redundant data may be stored.
2. It is difficult to integrate data from various sources.
3. Data storage is tied up with specific application programs.
4. It is difficult to respond to unanticipated information requests.

The data base approach integrates data into one large storage structure that may be used by many different users and application programs.

The physical view of data defines the layout of data records on actual physical devices like disk packs.

The logical view represents the data in a way that is meaningful to the applications programmer and user.

The data base may be accessed by users either directly or through an application program.

A data base management system is a complex program that manages a firm's data resources. It uses a data definition language to link the logical view with actual physical storage.

A data manipulation language allows the user to input, access, modify, and retrieve data in a data base. Data manipulation languages are often used in conjunction with a regular programming language to process data in complex ways.

The data base administrator is a key person in a data base environment.

The DBA function has the following major responsibilities:

1. Maintain a data dictionary
2. Ensure physical security of the data
3. Control changes in the logical and physical structures of the data base

The data base is typically stored on direct-access devices. The DBMS tries to arrange data storage in a way that minimizes storage and processing costs.

DBMS use keys and embedded pointers to reduce data redundancy and to establish logical relationships among data elements.

A tree structure is a logical data model that arranges data according to some natural hierarchy.

A network structure allows logical relationships among entities on a many-to-many basis.

A relational structure organizes data in the form of two dimensional tables. The data in these tables may be manipulated in many different ways. Due to its conceptual simplicity and powerful data manipulation capabilities, the use of this data model is increasing rapidly.

The indexing technique is used to access those data base records having certain specified attributes. This is a very efficient data retrieval technique since it eliminates a great deal of sequential searching.

The data base approach offers the following major advantages:

1. Eliminates data redundancy
2. Integrates related data items
3. Provides data independence
4. Provides an interface between users and the data through query languages

The disadvantages of DBMS are that they are complex and require substantial computer resources to execute.

KEY TERMS

Data Base Management System (DBMS)
Data Redundancy
Data Integration
Data Independence
Data Base
Pointers
Keys
Chaining
Logical View
Physical View
Data Base Administrator (DBA)
Query Language
Ad hoc Data Retrieval
Data Definition Language (DDL)
Data Manipulation Language (DML)
Schema
Subschema
Data Structures
Retrieval
Sorting
Data Dictionary
Data Base Machines
Tree Structures
Network Structures
Relational Structures
Nodes
Branches
Relational Model
Indexing
Entity
Attribute
Primary Key
Inverted File

REVIEW QUESTIONS

1. What is the relationship between a traditional file and an application program?
2. Explain the concept of data redundancy.
3. Why is program/data dependence undesirable?
4. Distinguish between a data file and a data base.
5. What is the difference between a logical and a physical view of data? Which view is more relevant for the applications programmer?

6. What are the four components of a data base environment?
7. How does a data base management system use its data definition language? Its data manipulation language?
8. Describe the major tasks performed by a data base administrator.
9. What is the difference between a data base and a data base management system?
10. What kind of logical relationship may be expressed with a tree structure?
11. Describe the major characteristics of a network structure.
12. What is the conceptual advantage in using a tabular structure? What other advantages does the relational model offer?
13. Why are indexes used by DBMS?
14. Why is an index also called an inverted file?
15. How does a DBMS improve data independence?

DISCUSSION QUESTIONS

1. Clemento Corporation has a large data processing facility that uses separate tape and disk files for different applications like production, sales, distribution, and payroll. You have been appointed to the newly created post of data base administrator. It is your job to design a data base for the corporation. You are also expected to convince the line and staff managers that it is to their advantage to switch from files to data base usage. Outline the plan of action you will use to achieve these goals.
2. Many data base users prefer one logical model over others. Proponents of the tree structure present a number of strong arguments in favor of that model. These include:

   1) The tree structure is an excellent way to represent many hierarchical relationships that exist in the business world.
   2) Hierarchical data structures are efficient from the point of view of optimizing storage space and CPU time.
   3) IBM's Information Management System (IMS), one of the most widely used DBMS, is based on the tree concept.

   Enthusiasts of the more recent relational model hold that:

   1) The tabular format seems more natural to business users since they have used it for centuries.
   2) It provides much easier data manipulation since one does not need to bother with pointers and chains.
   3) With decreasing hardware costs, machine efficiency is not as important a consideration as it once used to be.

   Evaluate the merits and demerits of each model. Which model would you select for your firm?
3. If you are designing an inventory data base for a grocery store, for which attributes would you provide indexes? Remember, an index is a tool for quick retrieval of data. It

is useful to set up indexes only for those attributes frequently used as a basis for retrieving records.

RESEARCH PROJECTS

1. Publications like *Data Management* and *Datamation* often carry articles describing new data base management systems. Select any two systems and compare such characteristics as data model, DDL, DML, and hardware requirements.
2. Select a firm that has adopted the data base approach to data processing. Critically evaluate their strategy in implementing the new system. Determine how successful they have been in their effort. You may find case material either from a firm you know or from the numerous articles that appear in the business and data processing press.

PANEL DISCUSSION

Is New Era Just Around Corner?
Forecasts Kick Up Controversy
(Reprinted with permission from MIS Week, Jan. 9, 1983, p. 34)

By Mike Egan

CHICAGO, Ill.—If there is one statement that the leading proponents of today's database management systems (DBMS) software enjoy arguing about, it just may be a statement made by Thomas M. Nies, president of Cincom Systems Inc.: "We're at the end of one era, but we're not yet really starting the new era."

Major changes are haunting the DBMS field, say the industry pundits. Distributed data processing has won acceptance as an overall corporate systems approach, and a new style of DBMS technology, "relational," is being described as the potential DBMS of the future. Yet, both technologies are far from arriving. The threat of costly and timely conversion efforts keeps both solutions off in the 5- to 10-year future.

Thus, the argument begins among the experts. Has an era ended? Has another era begun? And, what will be the effect of promised new technologies such as bubble-memory, database machines and fourth generation languages when they become commercially available? Some, including the languages, are here now, while other, such as non-rotating disk memory, are not expected for another decade.

It is Nies's contention that the next generation of DBMS technology is necessary because of the complex requirements that distributed data processing (DDP) places on a DBMS. Nies said that traditional first-generation DBMS, launched in the early '70's (including Cincom's "Total"), are very weak in supporting "ad hoc" and "end-user" requests.

"The key performance problems of the first-generation technology is a very heavy dependence upon pointers, indexes and tables as the primary means to maintain data relationships, along with limited data structuring power," he said. Nies also criticized the additional time and cost factors because of the increased programming required with first-generation DBMS.

"Completely Inappropriate"

It is not surprising that these "old-style DBMS's are becoming completely inappropriate for ad hoc, end-user and information-center-type usage," Nies said.

James Martin, an internationally known consultant, author and lecturer, agreed. "Many of the databases that had hot sales in the 1970s are inappropriate for the needs of the 1980s. You really can't build the type of decision support or management support systems that management needs today, with the older types of databases."

"Five years from now, these systems will be the most important section of computing to corporations. You'll want end-users to be able to get at the data they need and to have the tools with which they can manipulate that data, without much more difficulty than using their pocket calculators."

He continued, "What I'm describing is something very different from IBM's IMS or the CODASYL systems which we have today."

Gerry Ryan, product manager for IBM's IMS database management system, sees it differently. Users are not ready to leap into a new era, they are most interested in seeing their first-generation technology evolve, he said. "I believe that when a customer puts in a DBMS with an impact on his application spectrum, it takes him a period of time before he is fully utilizing that DBMS."

What may appear to be a slowdown is more of a "digestion process," he added. As an example, IBM recently released a multiple systems coupling capability for IMS, tying IMS DBMS on two different CPUs, in different locations, to provide a single system image to the application program running from either system's terminals. Customers are just now starting to implement that kind of system in a full production environment, he said.

"An Evolutionary Thing"

"Do we need to change the technology in order to move ahead with DBMS? In the operational environment, I don't think so. I believe it's an evolutionary thing; we are providing additional functions on a continuing basis. Heavy usage of the functions will probably lag the delivery to the marketplace by approximately three-to-five years," said Ryan.

He objected to the characterization of first-generation technology as being inappropriate. "I don't believe there is a higher-performance, full-function DB/DC system on the market than IMS Fastpath. And yet, that is a system that relies on pointers, indexes and tables."

Martin and Nies agree on the value of the next generation of DBMS systems, and all three agree that it will be years before it is available. Nies argues that "relational database" will not provide the solution for the high-volume IBM users for many years.

"Not A Panacea"

Nies commented, "I'm not sure relational is the wonderful answer that it's cracked up to be. It has a lot of substantial advantages, but it's not a panacea. Also, the conversion to a new database technology is a problem, not because it is so difficult to implement, but because the conversion away from the old technology is so difficult."

Martin agreed on the cost and conversion problems. "We can't scrap the current databases, because there's been a gigantic investment. I suspect that IMS will still be around, maybe ten years from now, because of the high cost of reprogramming everything done, in past years."

Ryan agreed with the analysis that relational will not be a widely-implemented DBMS for many years. "A customer not only has the databases, he has a whole set of application systems. In many cases, and particularly in the IMS case, they're really running his business. Some of the manufacturing companies that I'm familiar with couldn't deliver parts without IMS."

"Because they have a whole set of interrelated systems that are growing up around that and because of applications investment they have, it's not simply a matter of migrating to a relational database. It's a matter of changing the way we do business and, if we start down the path of changing that, it will take years," Ryan said.

Therefore, Martin concludes, what's going to happen is that most organizations will go to two (or more) different—fundamentally different types of databases: one for high-volume production systems and another for supporting ad hoc, decision-support systems.

Five-Year Pattern

"I think that the pattern we're going to see for the next five years, and probably longer than that, is installations keeping IMS, Total, IDMS, and, at the same time, installing much more flexible systems with much more powerful languages. We're getting SQL from IBM, from other vendors we're getting Focus, Nomad, Ramis and a variety of other tools with applications generation and management support systems," Martin said.

"In the long-term history of computing, we're seeing a short-term solution," he said. Martin notes that not all users need the dual-DBMS set-up, the problem exists more for the high-volume user who already heavily uses an IBM-type DBMS.

Martin concluded, "If IMS is your main corporate database facility, the best way to pull resources for end-users is probably to extract subsets from IMS and to rebuild them with other data management facilities, like Sequel (IBM's SQL-DS) for some applications, Stairs for building information retrieval, Focus, where you want to do fourth-generation language manipulation, or Sasgraph."

Duality: A Natural Division

At IBM, the dual path is more of a "natural division," said Ryan. "SQL-DS has some particular characteristics that make it very well-tuned to a data structure that will change frequently from time to time."

"I think the two products evolved separately and differently. Our current products (IMS) evolved in the operational area and SQL-DS evolved in the ad hoc, query-oriented area," he said.

Thus, IBM is looking towards the multiple database environment to last at least throughout the 1980s.

Further, IBM is giving the multiple database issue significant attention, Ryan said. "I think the really key item is going to be the tie between operational and user-oriented systems.

Calls It "Horrible" Idea

However, Nies believes the dual DBMS approach is a "horrible" idea. He said, "That decision means a complete abandonment of the common database idea, which was recognized as a major problem almost 20 years ago. So, we're reverting back 20 years in the thinking process by having separate databases for separate applications."

He continued, "Users should realize that the approach of multiple database systems and redundant storage of similar data, just because of the limits of the database technology, is a long-term strategic error."

Still, Nies conceded, "Until technology is made available which will support both types of requirements, users feel like there is no other choice but to do that. They have a need for ad hoc requests, which their conventional IMS and IDMS or Total databases do not satisfy too well, and yet, they have to do something."

The solution that Nies sees arriving between 1984 and 1986, lies in normalized data structures, often called the "third normal form."

"Normalized structures are the only ones which can satisfy both the performance needs of mainline data processing requirements, and still have the flexibility to satisfy ad hoc end-user requirements. No other data structure will support this," he said.

Nies described normalization as a process of developing simplified, stable, and also flexible database structures that can support different application processing and usage requirements. Complex data record structures are "broken down" or "decomposed" into their "lowest common denominator," and then recombined into new groupings which eliminate predefined relationships and repeating groups, thus enabling the data to be considered in its "purest," most usable and flexible form, he said.

James Martin supports the theory, "Third normal form is very much one of the basic principles of design of better systems." "In the long run, organizations are going to have to pay a high price for not having normalized their data. You'll get all sorts of problems, such as much more expensive maintenance later on."

Discussion

1. Why would you say that DBMS are at the end of an era?
2. Does it make sense for a firm to install two DBMS, with one being a traditional tree structured DBMS such as IMS and the other being a relational DBMS?

CHAPTER 10
PERSONAL COMPUTERS

- I. Introduction
- II. The Structure of a Personal Computer
  - A. The CPU
  - B. Input/Output Devices
  - C. Data Communications
- III. The Personal Computer Industry
  - A. The Hardware Market
  - B. The Packaged Software Business
  - C. Retail Outlets
  - D. The Information and Consulting Market
- IV. Personal Computers in Business
  - A. General Business Software
  - B. Special Interest Software Packages
- V. Personal Computers in the Home
- VI. Personal Computers in Education
- VII. Future Directions

INTRODUCTION

Much of our discussion in this book is oriented toward medium and large sized computer systems, which reflects the fact that most information processing is presently done on such systems. It appears, however, that this situation will be changing in the future. Currently, the fastest growing segment of the computer market is that of personal computers. *Personal computers* are small systems, designed to be operated by a single user possessing very little programming expertise.

Just as the industrial revolution of the nineteenth century opened up large markets for inexpensive mass produced goods, the personal computer industry today is broadening the information processing market by offering cheap and easy-to-use systems. Personal computers make enormous computing power available to people from all walks of life. Consequently, both the number of users and the variety of applications are growing rapidly. Whether the application is mundane, as in the case of balancing a checkbook, or novel, such as composing a symphony, the personal computer effectively serves the needs of the nonprogrammer type of user. It is this versatility and user-friendliness that promises to help the small personal computer prevail in its struggle against today's mainframe giants.

In this chapter we will briefly study the structure of a typical personal computer. This will be followed by a more detailed discussion of different vendors, software systems, and application areas for personal computers. The purpose of this chapter is to make you aware of the vast potential for applications of the personal computer. It is beyond the scope of this book to study any specific application in depth. If you have access to a personal computer, you will enhance your knowledge of both personal computers and programming by developing an application of your own using BASIC or one of the easy-to-use electronic spreadsheets, such as Supercalc or Lotus 1-2-3.

THE STRUCTURE OF A PERSONAL COMPUTER

The major components of a simple microcomputer system are shown in Figure 10-1. Most of these devices should be familiar from our discussion of mainframe systems in earlier chapters. Despite the similarity, there are significant differences between microcomputers and their mainframe cousins, especially with respect to speed and capacity. We will first consider the CPU of a personal computer. You might have noticed that the term microcomputer is being used interchangeably with personal computer. Technically, a personal computer is only one member of the family of machines known as microcomputers. For our purposes, this distinction is not very important and we will continue to use the two terms interchangeably.

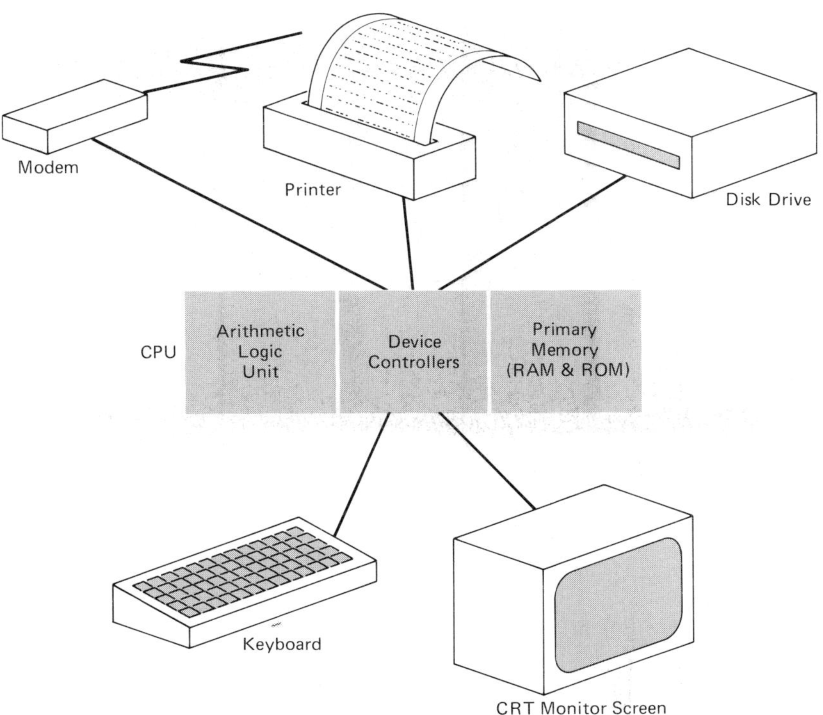

Figure 10-1 Typical Hardware Configuration for a Personal Computer

The CPU

The CPU consists of three basic components: 1) device controllers; 2) arithmetic-logic unit; and 3) primary memory. Device controllers are mechanisms that manage communication with external components like secondary memory and I/O units. These communications go through a link called a *bus*. The arithmetic-logic unit or microprocessor is the central part the computer, since all computations are performed here. The arithmetic logic unit of a microcomputer may be evaluated in terms of two characteristics, speed and word size.

Speed refers to the number of machine operations performed in a second. Within the past few years CPU speeds have increased tenfold to about ten million cycles per second. While such speeds may seem incredibly high, users are demanding even faster turnaround, since they dislike wasting time sitting at the keyboard while the CPU performs lengthy computations.

Another way to speed up computations is to increase the word size of the machine. The word size of a CPU determines the amount of information processed in one

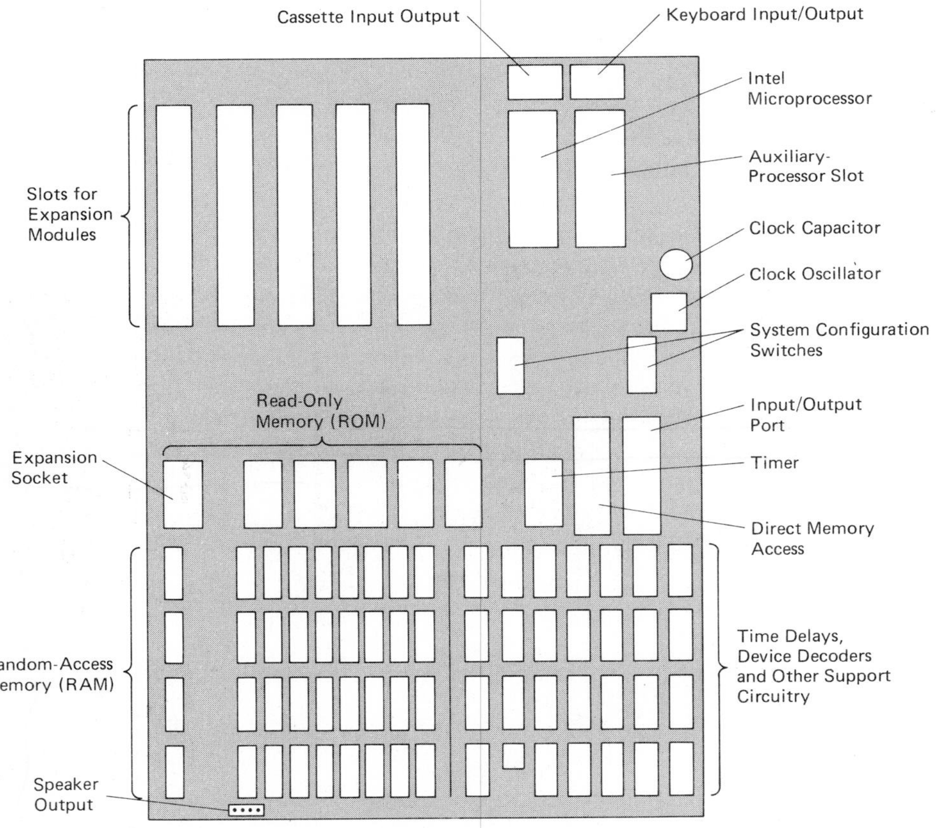

Figure 10-2 Main Circuit Board of the IBM Personal Computer (Copyright © 1982 by Scientific American, Inc. All rights reserved)

machine cycle. The larger the word size, the fewer the machine cycles required to do a job. The first microcomputers had 8-bit words. Today, however, 16-bit and 32-bit machines are more popular.

The third component of a CPU is primary memory. This consists of some read-only memory (ROM) and some random-access memory (RAM). These are illustrated in Figure 10-2. The ROM contains programs that were built into the computer at the factory, and may not be changed by a user. It is used primarily for systems programs, such as those needed to bring the system up when power is turned on. As the cost of ROM decreases, more and more programs are being placed in ROM, including BASIC language compilers and word processors.

Application programs are normally stored in random-access memory. A typical personal computer has between 16 and 64 kilobytes of RAM, although 128K, 256K and larger systems are also available. The advantage of having a larger memory is that larger and more powerful programs may be executed. Most personal computers are constructed so that their primary storage may be expanded later by adding *memory modules* if a user's needs increase. Before buying a personal computer it is a good idea to determine the memory requirements for the programs you intend to run on it. The literature for software packages normally indicates their minimum storage requirements.

Input/Output Devices

A user normally interacts with a personal computer through a keyboard and a monitor screen (see Figure 10-3). Commands, program instructions, and data are typed in and the computer echoes them (i.e., displays them on the screen) so that a check may be

Figure 10-3 Keyboard and Monitor (Courtesy of Apple Computer, Inc.)

made for errors. During execution of a program the computer may display instructions or informative messages on the screen, or prompt the user to key in data items. In most cases the program is written so that the final result of the run is also displayed on the screen.

Most systems like the IBM Personal Computer and the Apple Lisa support color monitors. Color monitors may be used in a wide variety of applications, such as engineering design and business data graphics. Some programmers use bright colors to highlight important information, making it easier for the user to sift through the screenfuls of information often generated by a computer. While color output has its advantages, it also has costs. The hardware is more expensive, color programming is complicated, and a great deal of memory is required to store all the information for a multicolor image.

Most business applications require output from a computer to be stored permanently on a machine-readable medium. The most popular secondary storage medium for personal computers is magnetic disk. Generally a flexible disk known as a diskette or floppy disk is used. A diskette may be either $5\frac{1}{4}$ inches or 8 inches in diameter. Figure 10-4 shows how a diskette is inserted into a disk drive before the computer may read the information on it. The diskette rotates inside the square jacket and a magnetic head reads off or writes data through the aperture. A diskette normally stores between 80 and 500 kilobytes of data, depending on the diameter and the number of bits stored per inch. Some systems use a hard disk called a Winchester disk (see Figure 10-5). A hard disk stores up to 50 times more data than a floppy disk, and rotates much faster providing quicker access to data. The main disadvantage of a Winchester disk is that it is sealed inside the disk drive and may not be removed.

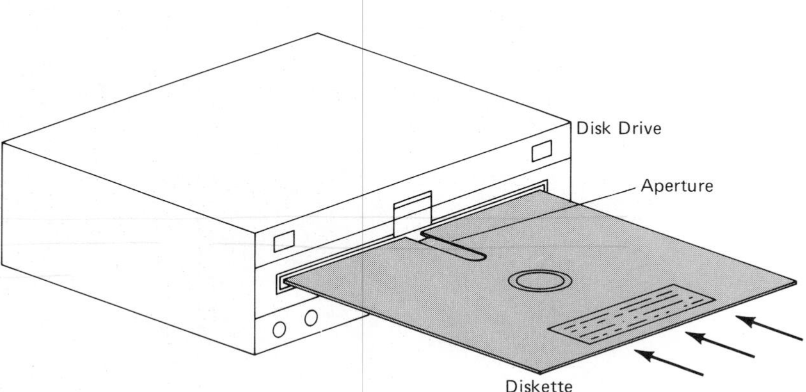

Figure 10-4 A Diskette and Disk Drive

Audio cassettes are also used for data storage, especially in the earliest microcomputer systems. A cassette is an inexpensive, nonvolatile storage medium. But it does suffer from the drawback that data may not be accessed at random. The computer has to read every bit of information sequentially until it reaches the desired data. Further, a cassette drive is much slower than a disk drive, making it less desirable even for sequential storage of data.

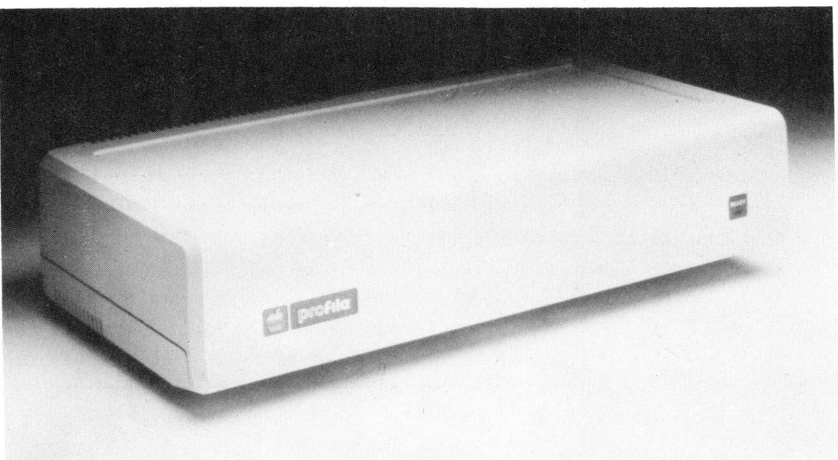

Figure 10-5 Winchester Disk Unit (Courtesy of Apple Computer, Inc.)

A large variety of printers are available for microcomputers. Figure 10-6 shows a dot matrix printer often used with personal computers. Many users prefer better quality machines like daisy-wheel printers, which produce "correspondence quality" output. Such output is especially suitable for word processing and mailing applications. Of course, the better quality printers cost more, sometimes more than the computer itself.

Many specialized input devices are now available like mouses, joysticks, light pens, and optical scanners. On the other side of the coin, output devices are also available for audio output and graphics plotting (see Figure 10-7), among other things. A few years ago these devices would have seemed very exotic and may have required complex programming, possibly in assembler language. With today's easy-to-use software, even a novice can create an application using a complex configuration of input and output devices.

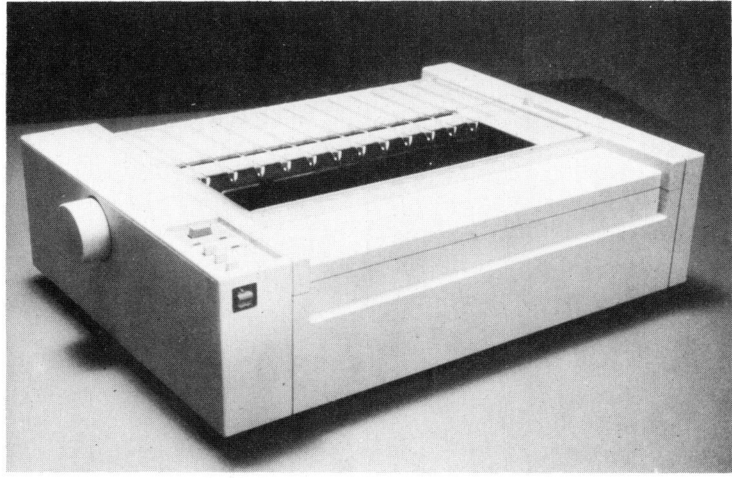

Figure 10-6 Dot Matrix Printer (Courtesy of NCR Corporation)

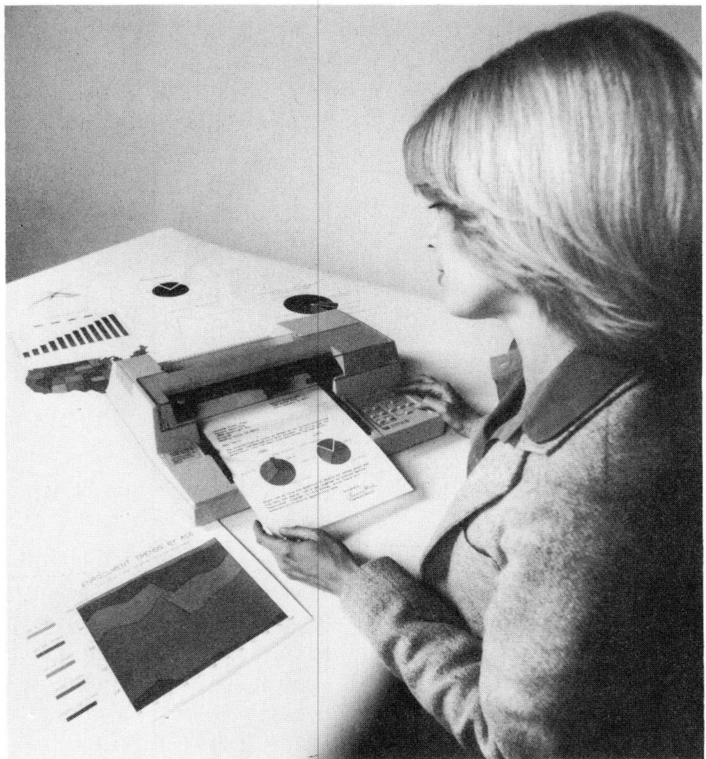

Figure 10-7 Microcomputer Plotter (Courtesy of Hewlett-Packard)

Data Communications

Data communication is an important aspect of many personal computer systems. It allows users to share data bases, programs, printers, and other resources with each other. Typically, a personal computer has a communications processor that converts data to a standard protocol. The converted data is then transmitted through a modem over private or public lines. Figure 10-8 shows a modem that may be used for the transmission of data over telephone lines. We will discuss communication networks for computers more fully in chapter 11.

Figure 10-8 Modem (Courtesy of Hayes Microcomputer Products, Inc.)

MANAGEMENT CASE 10-1

The typical advice given to purchasers of personal computers is to first choose the major software which will perform the primary task that the purchaser requires and then to choose the hardware which will execute the software. The rationale behind this advice is that it is the software that is really important in the computer system. Buying hardware first could leave a company with a rather restricted choice of software. The Davis Company however, has been advised to buy hardware first, specifically their consultant strongly advised them to buy the IBM PC without regard to looking at available software to perform their required tasks. The consultant's rationale was that IBM will dominate the personal computer market, they are a reliable computer manufacturer, and the widest range of business software will be available for the IBM PC. Evaluate the consultant's advice.

THE PERSONAL COMPUTER INDUSTRY

The advent of the personal computer has created a whole new industry. Interestingly, the initiative for developing this industry was taken by small, entrepreneurial firms, rather than large, established vendors of mainframe computers. In this section we will present an overview of the personal computer industry, including not only the markets for hardware and software but also the very important market for information and consulting.

The Hardware Market

Apple Computer Company started the personal computer industry in 1977 when its founders, two young college students, built the first personal computer in a garage. Despite fierce competition from subsequent entrants to the market, Apple has managed to keep a leading position. Figure 10-9 shows the estimated market shares for various

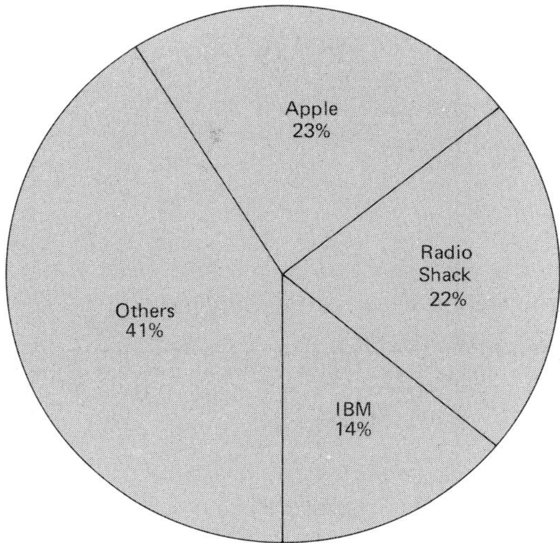

Figure 10-9 Estimated Shares of the U.S. Market for Personal Computers in 1982 (Copyright © 1982 by Scientific American, Inc. All rights reserved)

hardware manufacturers in 1982. Radio Shack, a manufacturer and seller of electronic products has used its extensive network of retail outlets to gain a strong position in the personal computer industry. Radio Shack's TRS-80 series computers are very popular with users. IBM, a latecomer to the personal computer business, has already gained an impressive share of the market. IBM's established reputation as the world's largest manufacturer of computers has certainly helped it achieve this market share. A survey done in late 1983, showed that 35 percent of all personal computers in use by 3000 large companies were IBM PCs. In addition, of those that were on order 93 percent were IBM PCs. Most observers feel that IBM will dominate the business market for personal computers.

Stiff competition in the personal computer business has generally been beneficial for consumers. Prices have steadily decreased while equipment quality and capabilities have continued to improve. Moreover, manufacturers have been forced to standardize many features, like communication protocols and diskette characteristics, in order to appeal to a wider customer base. As with any competitive market, there have been a number of casualties. Some of the small vendors have gone under, leaving their customers without maintenance support. A buyer of microcomputer equipment should carefully consider the track record of the supplier before making a major purchase. Purchasing from an unreliable supplier could cause not only a loss on investment in equipment, but also other business losses, such as customer dissatisfaction over poor service. It is also important to determine whether a particular component is plug-compatible with the rest of the equipment the buyer has or is likely to acquire.

The Packaged Software Business

A great deal of microcomputer software is bought "off the shelf" rather than developed by users. Literally thousands of software houses have sprung up, creating a large and diverse market for computer programs. Given the variety of uses a personal computer can be put to, this is not a surprising development. But the vast array of programs available on the market can be confusing, even intimidating, for the first-time user who has little knowledge about computers.

In the rest of this chapter we will mainly discuss the various categories of personal computer software and their application. In the limited space available it will not be possible to consider specific systems. Instead, we will attempt to gain a broad perspective of the software market, so that you can properly classify and evaluate any software packages you may happen to encounter. The following paragraphs describe the major operating systems software packages in use. Figure 10-10 illustrates the position of the operating system in a personal computer system. Application software is described in later sections of this chapter.

Control Program for Microcomputers (CP/M) is a widely used operating system for personal computers. It has been in use for a long time, and is continuously being updated. A more recent version, CP/M-86, supports several high level languages including COBOL and FORTRAN. This improvement makes it very attractive for business users who want to run existing COBOL programs on their new personal computer. CP/M-86 also provides strong file protection facilities like read-only (R/O) protection. Another advantage of CP/M is its powerful memory management facility, which allows optimal use of limited primary storage space.

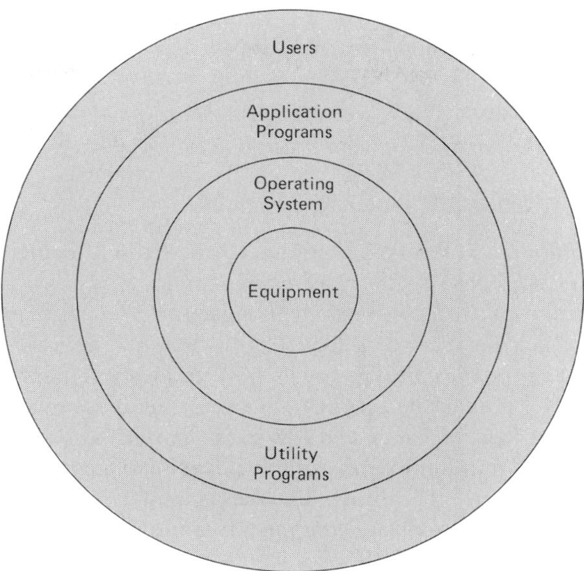

Figure 10-10 The Position of the Operating System in a Personal Computer System

For years the CP/M operating system was considered to be the *de facto* standard for the microcomputer industry. But IBM, with the introduction of its personal computer, has decided to support another system, the Disk Operating System by Microsoft (MS-DOS). MS-DOS possesses a number of strengths, including high speed disk I/O, efficient use of disk space, and easy recovery from errors. This last quality can be very important for the nontechnical user who is likely to make many errors. While CP/M-86 does not have comparable error recovery procedures, it does provide an extensive online help facility to guide the user in times of trouble.

Most operating systems not only manage system resources but also support utility programs that assist users in general tasks like editing files, copying diskettes, and system configuration. Recently some sophisticated operating systems have been introduced that manage the resources of a network of microcomputers. These systems are likely to become very important as the use of data communications increases.

Retail Outlets

There are several sources of supply for computer equipment. Franchised retail chains such as Computerland are a major outlet for equipment. Due to their large sales volume they are able to support a staff of technical advisors and maintenance personnel. Since these chain stores specialize in the computer business, they can carry a full line of products, allowing customers a large variety to choose from. Many dealers in office equipment also offer business oriented hardware and software. Even some electronics stores have entered the personal computer business, although they sometimes do not have much expertise to back up their computer sales.

There are also many mail order suppliers of personal computer equipment. Mail order equipment tends to be less expensive than equipment bought from a store, but buyers assume the extra risk of purchasing a product without testing it. Furthermore, one is likely to get less personal support from a mail order house than a local dealer. Given the complexity of most computer equipment it is very important that you test it thoroughly before buying, and ask questions about anything that seems unclear.

The Information and Consulting Market

The computer business is sometimes called the information business, and with good reason. Computers not only perform computations, they help us manage large volumes of information. It is interesting, though, that the machine assisting us in coping with information has caused a flood of information itself. Books, articles, and magazines related to personal computers have proliferated in recent years.

Byte is one of the most widely circulated computer magazines dealing with small computers. *Interface Age* and *Personal Computing* are also quite popular among users of personal computers. All these magazines carry articles of general interest for business and home users. There are flowcharts and program listings for applications like portfolio management and computer games. Advertisements for software and hardware are an important source of information about products and prices. There are also magazines devoted to a single widely used microcomputer. For example *PC Magazine* covers only the IBM Personal Computer. In addition to computer magazines, articles related to personal computers often appear in various professional periodicals. Journals serving professional groups often publish articles describing microcomputer applications in various areas of expertise.

Finally, to help users in selecting equipment and designing a system, microcomputer consultants are also available. Consultants come from a variety of backgrounds, including computer programming, systems analysis, marketing, accounting, and engineering. Before selecting a consultant you should make sure that he or she has a thorough understanding of your application area. One way of checking out the credentials of a consultant is to talk to previous customers and ask their opinions of the service received. You can also find out about microcomputer consultants either through referrals by professional colleagues or by looking in the yellow pages. Some consultants also give courses in programming and the use of various software packages.

MANAGEMENT CASE 10-2

Montgomery Electric Steel is a local specialized steel foundry. Currently the company's central management information system is implemented on a Digital Equipment Corporation (DEC) computer. The company is currently evaluating which personal computer to standardize upon. Those involved in the decision have split into two groups. One group believes that Montgomery should buy DEC personal computers since the central computer is a DEC machine. They feel that down loading of information, relations with computer vendors, and staff training problems will go much smoother if both the PC's and the central computer are from the same manufacturer. The second group feels that the IBM PC will dominate the business market. Therefore, they recommend purchase of the IBM PC. Their primary rationale is that a much wider variety of business oriented software would be available for the dominant machine in the market. Which personal computer would you recommend buying?

PERSONAL COMPUTERS IN BUSINESS

Businesses, especially small, entrepreneurial ones, are rapidly converting their record keeping to computerized systems. The primary reason for this change is the availability of powerful, yet inexpensive software packages for microcomputers. Let us now survey the different kinds of business software that is on the market.

General Business Software

Probably one of the first applications that a business computerizes is accounting. Excellent packages are available for general purpose accounting including the following:

1. Accounts Receivable
2. Accounts Payable
3. General Ledger
4. Payroll
5. Depreciation Schedules
6. Financial Statements

These packages are advertised in professional accounting journals. Figure 10-11 shows the output from an accounting software package. Before purchasing an accounting software package it is necessary to ask the following questions:

1. Are there sufficient accounting controls in the system?
2. Are the various programs integrated so that data input once need not be input again for another program?
3. What are the limitations on the number of accounts and transactions the system can process?
4. What level of technical expertise is required to operate the system, and is this expertise available to the business?
5. Will the programs produce flexible management reports that may be easily modified to suit changing business needs?

Another important application of personal computers is in financial management. Financial planning packages may be used to project the financial results of alternative management decisions. Based on projected financial statements produced for various alternatives, management can make an informed judgment. Other financial programs focus on problems like portfolio management, securities analysis, capital project analysis, budgeting, tax planning, and cash management.

One powerful tool available to the finance manager is the spreadsheet. Most personal computers support some kind of spreadsheet program (such as VISICALC or SUPERCALC), allowing users to build a matrix on the screen. The elements of the matrix may be constants, variables, or simply titles and labels. To illustrate the use of a spreadsheet package, a finance manager could produce a cash budget on the screen, allowing revenue to be a variable. Then, different values may be input for revenue to

ACCOUNTS RECEIVABLE
SUMMARY AGED TRIAL BALANCE
D & G ENTERPRISES INC

REPORT NO RR6315
RUN DATE 10/31/8X
COMPANY AA

ACCOUNT	NAME	FUTURE DUE	CURRENT DUE	1–30	31–60	PAST DUE 61–90	91–120	OVER 120	OUTSTANDING RECEIVABLES
784612	WYGANT DISTRIBUTORS, INC.	HARTWELL ROAD		JUPITER HILLS	DE	19702-2614			
	MR. W. RAMSDEN								
	AVG. DAYS–36 CR/LMT–3500								
ACCOUNT TOTAL:		652.19	1,125.64	294.81	108.45				2,181.09
		30%	52%	13%	5%				
799426	ZELLER COMPANY	124 MILLBROOK RD		EAST GALLANT	AL	36902-1157			
	MR. P. GORHAM								
	AVG. DAYS–63 CR/LMT–1000								
ACCOUNT TOTAL:				456.24	178.26	312.49			946.99
				48%	19%	33%			
GRAND TOTAL****									
	SALES TERRITORY: 01A	1,576.72	16,459.32	9,621.14	1,164.91	447.56	78.60	120.41	29,468.66
		5%	56%	32%	3%	2%	1%	1%	
	DISTRICT CR MGR: BB	6,482.19	39,412.80	24,562.44	2,051.23	2,114.86	594.60	403.19	75,621.31
		8%	52%	31%	3%	4%	1%	1%	
	REGIONAL CR MGR: WF	10,398.65	98,714.37	52,114.71	5,662.17	3,729.29	1,700.68	1,288.74	173,608.61
		6%	57%	30%	3%	2%	1%	1%	
	COMPANY TOTAL:	26,042.03	256,622.13	107,781.58	12,715.25	7,520.12	3,918.45	2,542.60	417,142.16
		6%	62%	25%	3%	2%	1%	1%	

Figure 10-11 Sample Printout of an Accounting Package

	A	B	C	D	E	F
1	THIS IS A SAMPLE SUPERCALC WORKSHEET					
2						
3		JAN	FEB	MAR	APR	MAY
4	NET SALES	1000	1100	1210	1331	1464
5						
6	COST OF GOODS SOLD	300	330	363	399	439
7	------------------------------	------	------	------	------	------
8	GROSS PROFIT	700	770	847	932	1025
9						
10	RESEARCH & DEVELOPMENT	160	176	194	213	234
11	MARKETING	200	224	251	281	315
12	ADMINISTRATIVE	140	151	163	176	190
13	------------------------------	------	------	------	------	------
14	TOTAL OPERATING EXPENSES	500	551	608	670	789
15						
16	INCOME BEFORE TAXES	200	219	239	261	285
17						
18	INCOME TAXES	80	88	96	105	114
19	------------------------------	------	------	------	------	------
20	Net Income	120	131	144	157	171

> D3 P Text = ' ' MAR
Width: 9 Memory: 25 Last Col/Row: N20 ? for HELP
1>

Figure 10-12 A Spreadsheet Program (Courtesy of Sorcim Corp.)

determine the effect of different sales levels on cash flow. The spreadsheet program automatically recomputes the values of all items when the value of a variable is changed. Figure 10-12 shows how a spreadsheet appears on the screen. Second generation spreadsheet packages are now available that combine spreadsheet, graphics, and data base capabilities. An example of such a package is Lotus 1-2-3.

Marketing personnel can use programs that generate sales projections. Some packages have powerful graphic capabilities, generating pie charts, bar graphs, and trend lines. These devices can substantially reduce the paperwork a marketing manager has to do to prepare for a sales meeting. Software packages written for salespeople remove most of the tedium of booking orders. A well-designed order processing system will price the order, prepare an invoice, update perpetual inventory records, and produce the shipping authorization document. Similarly, there are families of microcomputer programs that assist in warehousing and production management functions. These range from inventory management routines to production scheduling to manpower planning.

One of the most important uses of microcomputers in business is in the area of word processing. When linked to a high quality printer, a personal computer can produce excellent written documents. In addition, a word processing program allows users to store, edit, and neatly format all these documents with a few keystrokes. Business people suffering under an overload of paperwork have welcomed this opportunity to reduce clerical costs. Many good word processing programs are now on the market. Some even provide abilities to check the text for spelling and grammatical errors. If your word processing application involves a lot of correspondence, be sure to buy a package that includes mailing facilities like the printing of address labels. A sample printout for a microcomputer based word processor using a letter quality printer is shown in Figure 10-13.

Personal computers are also playing a central role in the implementation of decision support systems. Data can be transferred from large central data bases to personal computer storage and subsequently analyzed using tools such as spreadsheets and graphics. The combination of all the tools available in a personal computer is often referred to as a personal workstation.

```
                         459 North Main Street
                         Staunton, WV  28013
                         November 28, 1983



John W. Bray
RDM Products Inc.
3301 West Hampton Avenue
Blacksburg, VA  24060

Dear Mr. Bray:

Thank you for your prompt shipment of the truck parts I
recently ordered.  I have found your service and parts to be
of exceptional quality.

However, in this most recent shipment (Shipping Order No.
A435-7894) one of the wheel bearings was not the correct
size.  Since we could not afford to have a truck out of
service for the time it takes to return the bearing and
receive a replacement we purchased the bearing from a local
supplier.  Therefore, I am returning the incorrectly sized
bearing to you for credit to my account.  If you have any
questions please contact me at 304-938-2600.

                         Sincerely,

                         Ray N. Shea

                         Ray N. Shea
                         Shea Trucking Co.
```

Figure 10-13 Word Processing Printout

Special Interest Software Packages

Some small businesses, especially professional practices, have very special information processing requirements. To serve the needs of these businesses, special purpose software packages have been developed. These packages are normally advertised in professional journals and at conventions and conferences.

A major market for specialized software is the medical profession. Faced with increasing government regulation and rapidly changing medical technology, doctors and pharmacists are being forced to use computers for their record keeping. Applications vary from patient billing to data bases for medical history records. Similarly, lawyers now have their own packages to assist with routine chores such as preparation of lengthy legal documents and searching data bases for legal precedents. Accountants and auditors are now able to better manage their practices with the aid of time keeping and billing programs.

PERSONAL COMPUTERS IN THE HOME

The personal computer is not only changing the way we do business but is even affecting the way we live at home. The first domestic use of a computer that comes to mind involves personal finances. Programs are available that will balance your checkbook, keep track of tax deductible items, and help manage your investments. Many people use word processors to handle personal correspondence and address lists.

When linked to other electromechanical devices, a personal computer can control room temperature, lighting, burglar alarm systems, and even minimize energy costs. It can also remind you about such things as when to send in payments on bills and when it is time to plant geraniums. A personal computer with communication capabilities may be used by professionals who like to work at home and need to communicate with the mainframe computer at their place of work. It may also be used for shopping at home and accessing commercial data bases.

Personal computers are often used for entertainment purposes. The best known use in this area is video games, which let you do things like shoot down enemy space ships. A more serious game played by the computer is chess. But entertainment and games are not synonymous for the personal computer. For instance, a system with a sound synthesizer and an interface to acoustic equipment can assist you in composing music. A color monitor and knowledge of BASIC could have you on your way to creating your own cartoon movies. The possibilities of using the computer at home are limited only by your imagination.

PERSONAL COMPUTERS IN EDUCATION

Schoolchildren are probably the least "computer-phobic" part of our population. It is no wonder then that many children have learned more about computers than their parents. Computers enter into the educational system by many routes. For example, many students take data processing and programming courses in high school. In addition, personal computers are used as instructional tools for self-paced courses. In these courses the computer interacts with the student, explaining a concept in different ways and testing the student's knowledge until he or she understands it and is ready to go on. An important benefit of using personal computers in schools is that children learn to accept them as a normal part of life, and are in a better position to adapt to new applications than their parents.

The rising level of computer literacy among young people is not an unmixed blessing. Sometimes it can place more power in their hands than is necessary. In one instance, some American high school students used a microcomputer in their school laboratory to connect to the computer of a Canadian corporation. Using data communication facilities they were able to damage some important business records. Such actions point to the necessity of better control of personal computers in an educational environment.

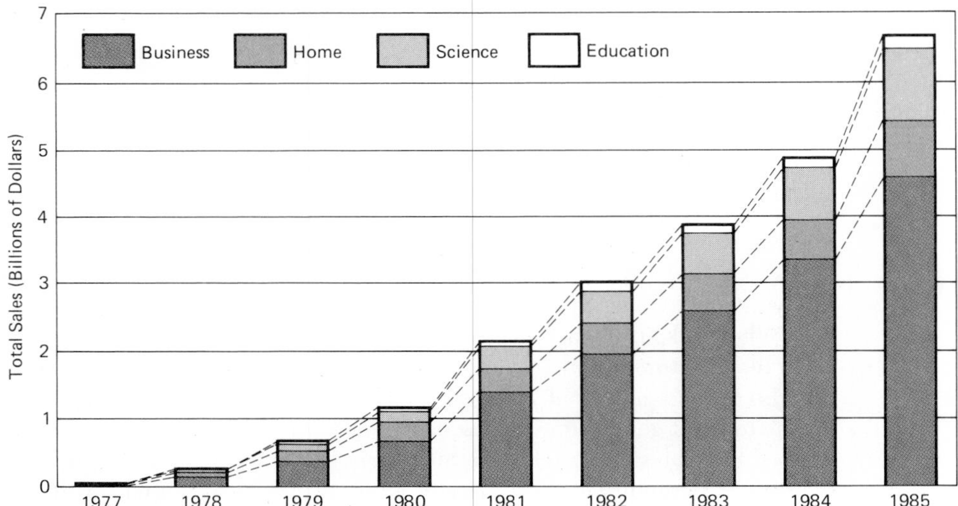

Figure 10-14 Personal Computer Sales (Copyright © 1982 by Scientific American, Inc. All rights reserved)

FUTURE DIRECTIONS

As Figure 10-14 shows, sales of personal computers are expected to keep growing in coming years. Increased business use is expected to provide the major impetus for this growth. However, the use of personal computers at home and in the school is likely to make a qualitative difference in our lifestyles. As more routine chores are performed by computers, humans will have greater freedom to indulge in interesting and creative activities.

Business people will be relieved of much of the dull paperwork they have to do to satisfy accounting, legal, and governmental requirements. This freedom will leave them with more time and energy to devote to productive work and decision making. In short, the personal computer places all the power of the digital computer in the hands of the ordinary individual, allowing him or her a better chance to compete in a computerized world.

SUMMARY

Personal computers are the most rapidly growing type of computer system. They are versatile machines that may be used by a person possessing very little computer expertise.

The CPU of a personal computer is basically evaluated in terms of its speed and word size. The major components of a CPU are the device controllers, arithmetic-logic unit, and primary memory.

A personal computer may support a number of I/O devices including the following.

1. Keyboard
2. Monitor Screen

3. Color Monitor
4. Floppy Disk Drive
5. Rigid Disk Drive
6. Audio Cassette Drive
7. Dot Matrix Printer
8. Daisy Wheel Printer
9. Joysticks
10. Light Pens
11. Sound Output Devices

The market for personal computer hardware is very competitive. Apple, Radio Shack, and IBM are the leading suppliers. But there are also a large number of other manufacturers selling high quality equipment.

A large variety of packaged software is available for personal computers. The most popular systems software packages are CP/M and MS-DOS.

Personal computer equipment may be purchased from a variety of sources, including chain computer stores and office supply dealers. Numerous periodicals are published providing users with information and ideas for the use of personal computers.

Sophisticated software packages are available for major business functions like accounting, finance, marketing, and production. Special purpose software is also available for many businesses, such as professional practices.

Personal computers may be used in the home for a large number of applications, including personal finances, energy conservation, and entertainment. They are being used in schools not only for instruction in computer usage but also as teaching devices for other subjects.

KEY TERMS

Personal Computer
Microcomputer
Device Controller
Bus
Speed
Word Size
Machine Operation
Machine Cycle
Read-Only Memory (ROM)
Random-Access Memory (RAM)
Memory Modules
Keyboard
Monitor Screen
Echo
Color Monitor
Diskette (Floppy Disk)
Rigid Disk (Winchester Disk)
Disk Drive
Cassette Drive
Dot Matrix Printer
Daisy-Wheel Printer
Communications Processor
Modem
Plug-compatible
Package Software
CP/M
MS-DOS
Error Recovery
Consultants
Accounting Controls
Spreadsheet
Graphics
Word Processing
Sound Synthesizer

REVIEW QUESTIONS

1. How much programming expertise is required to operate a personal computer?
2. Describe the three major parts of a microcomputer CPU.
3. Explain the concepts of speed and word size.
4. Distinguish between RAM and ROM.
5. What are the major I/O devices used by a personal computer?
6. What are the advantages and disadvantages of using a Winchester disk?
7. What is the function of a communications processor?
8. Describe the price and quality trends in the market for personal computer hardware.
9. List the important characteristics of the two major operating systems.
10. Where can you buy supplies for your microcomputer?
11. What functions are served by the microcomputer magazines?
12. List the different categories of general business software.
13. What points would you consider before buying an accounting software package?
14. How does a microcomputer help a professional in managing his or her practice?
15. Describe some of the uses of a personal computer in the home.
16. What are the advantages of having personal computers in schools?

DISCUSSION QUESTIONS

1. Why is it that small, unknown firms assumed the leadership in exploiting the personal computer market, while the large, established manufacturers of computers stayed out for years and then decided to follow suit?
2. Will the introduction of small computers create fundamental changes in the way small businesses operate? Will it make them more competitive? Discuss your expectations regarding the role of the personal computer in small business management.
3. Personal computers are not an unmixed blessing. Their introduction into the home and the office makes many people feel insecure and foolish. What problems do you see with personal computers? What remedies would you suggest?

RESEARCH PROJECTS

1. Investigate the hardware characteristics and software available for any two personal computers. Perform a comparative analysis of the two and recommend one for use in a small retail business.
2. Study the use of personal computers at a local school. Talk to teachers and students to find out how the computer is being used in the classroom. Prepare a report on the

effectiveness of computer assisted instruction (CAI). Would CAI be useful for industrial training? How?

ESSAY

Personal Computer Revolution: How To Manage It

(Reprinted with permission from MIS Week, Sept. 8, 1982, p. 23)

By Dean L. Hiller, President, D.L. Hiller & Associates, Sterling Heights, Mich.

Three dominant and apparently separate trends are facing MIS management in the 1980s. One of these is the personal computer revolution. Another is the information center and the third is office automation.

It seems appropriate to call the personal computer trend a revolution, because many of these systems are being bought directly by users.

Historically, the MIS function has had approval authority over computer-related purchases. Now, in many cases, users are forsaking the consultation and advice of the data processing professional. They are buying personal computer systems and software on an individually justified basis.

In some cases, no purchase justification is needed. The cost is too "small" to consider costs and benefits.

As several different types of personal computer hardware, application software and operating systems emerge in large companies, a support problem arises.

The technical and applicational support expertise required becomes several times greater. Each manufacturer provides his own operating system and basic interpreter with the personal computer. There are even differences in the operating systems between the manufacturer's various models of personal computers.

The support problem becomes more difficult when the user wants to hook up his personal computer to the mainframe computer.

As the user gains "literacy" with his personal computer, he wants more capability. He will be asking for data from the big machines to be accessible from his personal computer. He will want to use his personal computer directly interfaced to the mainframe.

Interfacing several different personal computer operating systems and software can be a nightmare. Letting purchases of personal computers continue uncontrolled will contribute to a future credibility gap between systems professional and user.

The MIS organization will run the risk of being replaced in its consultative role by other technical people. A definitive approach to managing the procurement and utilization of personal computers early-on is a must.

Another major and closely related trend is that of the information center. Conceptually, the information center is a place the user goes to develop his own computer uses.

The information center is staffed by a few MIS consultants to assist the computer users. Computer equipment and selected general purpose software are provided to those using the information center. It is the computer user, however, who develops his own applications using these tools.

At first glance, the information center seems to be in conflict with the widespread use of personal computers, but, in fact, it can actually support "personal computing."

The information center can tap the wealth of the large computer databases and provide the ease of personal computing. The products exist now for the individual to get at either through a personal computer.

The strategy for the '80s must integrate the personal computer success story with any information center plans.

A last, major related trend is that being pushed by the computer industry. Office automation is coming. The hardware and software for interconnection of office and computer equipment will be more and more a practical reality. When it gets here, its real story will be personal computing.

The concepts are analogous. The capability of interconnection enhances the resources and capabilities that the personal computer user has now. The major-vehicle office automators will target for their systems personal computers. The resources brought to the personal computer user will include the demanded mainframe access that the user wants.

Office automation will be accomplished through local-area networking.

With local area networking to personal computers and improved operating systems, the user should be able to easily switch back and forth between direct-connect and stand-alone computing. He should also be able to request data "downloaded" from the mainframe. In other words, he should be able to get files of data passed to his applications for him to work with.

With more advanced operating systems, this can and will be accomplished simultaneously while the user does other work on the personal computer—i.e., the system will be capable of multi-processing or doing the task of downloading and running an application at the same time.

Getting these capabilities to the computer user won't be easy. His demands will none the less be simple.

He wants "data portability," and he wants to be able to run on other personal computers as he travels or works at home at night. He also wants "application portability." He doesn't want to relearn the new commands that come with other software packages. He wants to work with his familiar "electronic spread-sheet" system or his usual "textwriter" software.

His demands of data portability, software availability on varying equipment and access to mainframe data will be tough to meet. Technical planning and a corporate strategy to advise personal computer users on software and hardware purchase is needed now.

Personal computers are the next credibility challenge.

Slowly, many data processing organizations are supporting the information center approach. Local-area networking is experiencing similar, gradual acceptance, but information centers and local-area nets are seen as costly programs.

Managing the future of the personal computer in light of its aggregate costs and its potential should be a key focus of MIS management. A strategy will emerge to guide deployment of personal computers.

MIS organizations must begin to recognize their technical support role. They do not currently see the flexibility they have to control the individual buying of personal computers within their company. They are not using their powers of persuasion through involvement and consultation. They are not exploiting the economics of personal computer buying.

Personal computers can easily replace purchases of direct-connect terminals to mainframes. In most cases, the costs will be comparable. The added capability of stand-alone usage and direct mainframe connection will benefit the user.

Emulator software and hardware is available in the marketplace to accomplish this, yet most companies are letting this opportunity get away.

The personal computer revolution brings new threats to traditional MIS organization security. The tons of floppy diskettes it requires represents a backup and security problem of new dimensions. It now becomes much easier for theft of programs and company data than ever before.

Recognizing the problems with floppy disks and the growth of personal computers, an experimental office automation program should be attempted. The project could use Winchester disk and two personal computers.

Backup to the mainframe from the Winchester disk could be planned. Electronic mail can be tested for benefit. Terminal emulators can be reviewed. Interfacing plans can be developed. The economics make sense. Software emulators can provide the needed direct connect capability to make it happen. The strategy that is emerging is to learn, to advise the users, and to plan ahead of their demands. Experience is the best teacher. A pilot or experimental program is needed to accomplish this.

If MIS professionals do not meet the demand for managing personal computing, then it will not be met effectively. The absence of an approach now to allow for the future demands of data portability, software standardization and mainframe access will raise future costs substantially.

Large amounts of new hardware will have to be bought and significant custom software programming accomplished. The aggregate investment we are making now will have to be repurchased in large part.

We are also seeing a new trend occurring in the systems profession. The best people are those who never stop learning and thinking. These are the same people who are embracing the personal computer revolution. They have bought personal computers themselves.

Many corporate data processing organizations are losing some of these best people to a new breed of information companies. These high potential young people are going to work for computer retailers.

Jobs for salesmen and for technical support people are growing rapidly. The retailers with foresight are beginning to service MIS organization directly. They are getting the best young people. MIS management must cultivate, educate, and retain their own people now for the support tasks ahead.

Those who embrace the problems with the emerging trends of computing will profit. Those who tackle the diverse technologies of computing with forward planning will benefit the most. The consultants, the users, the retailers and the longer-range MIS thinkers will lead that effort.

Discussion

1. Should the personal computer revolution be managed or will they be used most productively if management takes a laissez-faire attitude toward their purchase and use?
2. How are information centers, office automation, and personal computers interrelated?

CHAPTER 11

DISTRIBUTED DATA PROCESSING AND OFFICE AUTOMATION

I. Introduction

II. Data Communications
   A. Types of Data Communication
   B. The Data Transmission Process
   C. Communication Hardware
   D. Network Systems

III. Distributed Data Processing
   A. The Need for Decentralized Processing
   B. Hardware Distribution
   C. Software Distribution
   D. Data Decentralization

IV. Word Processing and Office Automation
   A. Word Processing
   B. Electronic Mail
   C. Office Automation
   D. Integrated Word Processing/Data Processing
   E. Office Decentralization and Productivity
   F. Human Factors

INTRODUCTION

In the early days of electronic data processing the computer was a centralized company resource. Equipment costs were high and software systems were difficult to operate. The spread of EDP resources to user departments was thus not feasible. During the past decade, however, this situation has changed dramatically. The cost of hardware has decreased sharply, and software is becoming easier and easier to use. As a result, a much larger number of people can now use the computer directly, without the help of EDP specialists. By carefully dispersing computer resources, a business can significantly reduce paperwork costs and improve turnaround time on applications. The management of dispersed EDP facilities is generally known as distributed data processing (DDP). In this chapter we will discuss the major issues in designing and operating a DDP system.

The entry of data processing equipment into user departments has far-reaching effects on office procedure. While managers are delighted to see the productivity of their offices grow rapidly, they also have to ensure that office personnel willingly adopt the new procedures. Nothing could be more disastrous for a distributed data processing system than a hostile attitude among users. The last section of this chapter will discuss the automation of some major office procedures, and issues arising from the man-machine interface.

Distributed data processing facilities depend heavily on the communication of data between computers and peripheral equipment. Designing a communication system is a complex engineering task, generally beyond the competence of a business manager. It is nevertheless important for the manager to understand the fundamentals of data communications. This can help him or her recognize communication problems, and formulate policies regarding the efficient use of alternative communication methods. Therefore, we will start this chapter with a discussion of basic data communications concepts.

DATA COMMUNICATIONS

The communication of data from one point to another is a crucial business function. Methods of communication range from using existing telephone lines to utilizing satellite transmission. In a DDP environment the communication function can become very complex as a result of growth and integration of previously independent systems. Every DDP system has a unique communication system to link its devices together. This system typically evolves as a response to the company's growth and the information processing strategy employed by management.

Types of Data Communication

No matter how complicated a particular system may be, it can be considered a combination of the three basic configurations described below.

Computer-Peripheral Device Configuration: This kind of configuration involves the transfer of data between a CPU and a peripheral device, such as a terminal or storage device. The storage or terminal device is completely controlled by the CPU. It is customary to call this kind of setup a *master-slave* relationship. The master (i.e., the CPU) determines when and how data is to be transferred to and from the slave (i.e., the peripheral device).

As illustrated in Figure 11-1, it is possible to place a number of terminals on a single line from the computer. The computer addresses each terminal in turn for input or output (I/O). Such terminals are considered *intelligent* since they know when the computer is talking to them. There are also *dumb* terminals, which need to be connected to the computer through separate lines, since they are not able to tell when they are being addressed. Dumb terminals assume that any signal coming down the line is meant for them. Figure 11-2 shows a number of dumb terminals linked to a CPU.

Computer to Computer Communication: Often it is necessary to transfer data from one computer to another. For instance, some large grocery stores have linked their computers to those of their major suppliers through communication lines (refer to

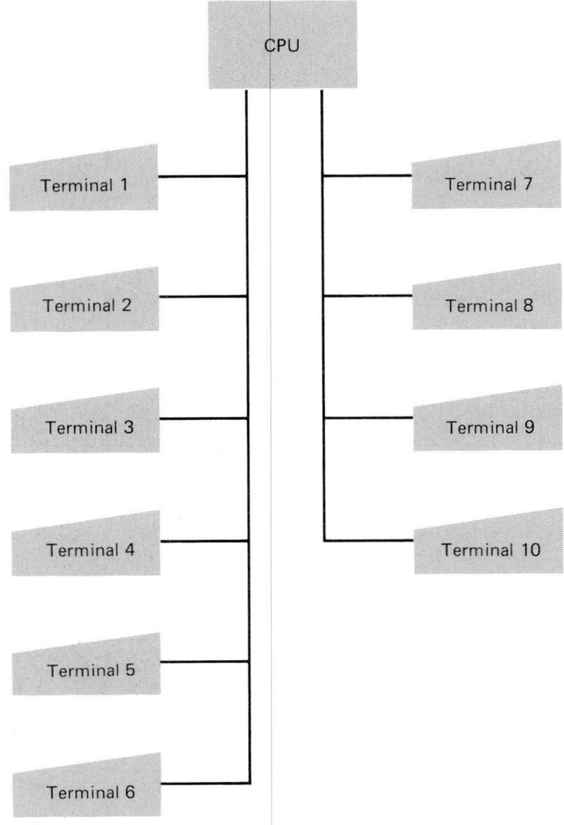

Figure 11-1 Intelligent Terminals Connected to a CPU

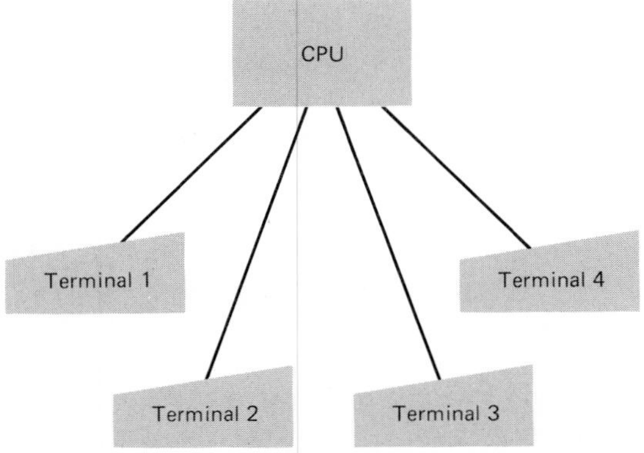

Figure 11-2 Dumb Terminals Connected to a CPU

Figure 11-3). Whenever the inventory of an item is reduced to the reorder level, the computer automatically places an order over the communication link. The supplier's computer can then process the order immediately. This procedure not only eliminates the possibility of human error, but also permits better inventory management by speeding up the reordering process.

Figure 11-3 CPU to CPU Communication

Communication between two computers may be a master-slave connection. An example of this is the relationship between a mainframe computer and a special purpose minicomputer (see Figure 11-4). The minicomputer typically performs an auxiliary function for the mainframe, such as editing input data. However, since the minicomputer is in the position of a slave, it cannot initiate any communication with the mainframe unless the mainframe allows it to do so. On the other hand, a communication link may be a connection between equals. As in the grocery store example above, two mainframe CPUs may be interacting. In this kind of situation each computer has to have the consent of the other machine's operating system before it can initiate a data transfer.

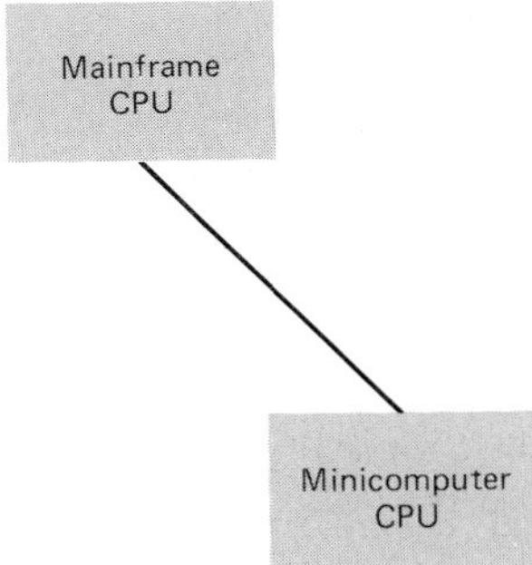

Figure 11-4 Mainframe-Minicomputer Link

Communication Through a Data Switch: A data switch is a device similar to a telephone exchange. The switch links a number of CPUs and peripheral devices, and can connect any two of them together on demand. This kind of arrangement has several advantages. For instance, a user may access many different computers from the same terminal or a CPU may exchange data with any one of the other CPUs on the network.

A data switch can be used not only to link communication lines but also to provide various translation services. As we will see in the next section, hardware devices differ in the way they organize data flows. The data switch, which is actually a minicomputer, can change the format of data in transit so that it conforms with the hardware requirements of the receiving device. Figure 11-5 depicts a data switch configuration.

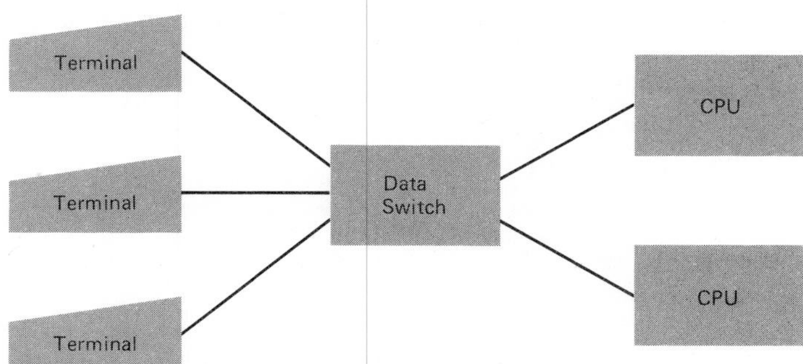

Figure 11-5 A Data Switch

The Data Transmission Process

The flow of data between devices is basically a stream of bits represented by "on" or "off" line conditions. Unfortunately, it is not enough merely to send raw data from place to place. It is also necessary to package the data into blocks or "messages." The intervening communication hardware can then check for transmission errors and route the message to its correct destination.

A *communication protocol* is a set of rules governing information flow in a communication system. These rules define the *block format*, or *message envelope*, which packages each message to be transmitted. This envelope usually contains control characters to mark its beginning and end, along with an address, so that data can be directed to particular terminals. It may also contain some characters that are used for error detection. Figure 11-6 shows a typical message envelope. A terminal conforming to an error checking protocol operates error free since it automatically retransmits erroneous data. Communication protocols enable terminals to be clustered together on a single line because they can be selectively addressed or *polled* by the CPU. The computer polls the terminals by addressing each one in succession. If a terminal does not respond, the computer moves on to the next one.

Data is normally sent along a single line, with successive intervals of time defined as consecutive bits in a byte. Two possible conditions, "on" and "off," representing binary 1 and 0 respectively, are imposed on the line by the transmitter. The receiver monitors this train of signals and reconstructs the incoming byte. Transmission is accomplished in one of two ways.

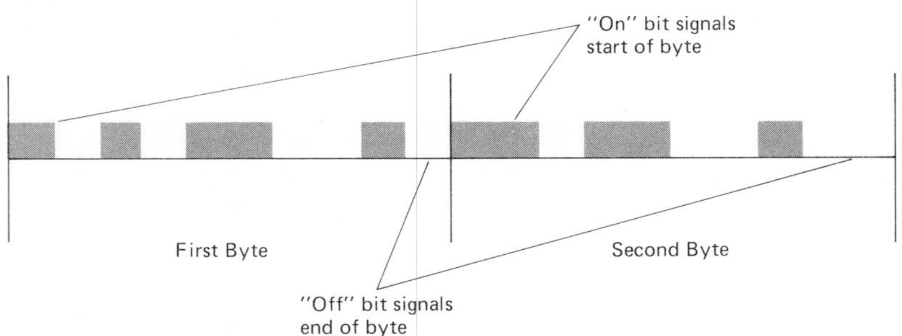

Figure 11-6 A Message Envelope

The simpler method, typically employed by microcomputers, is *asynchronous transmission*. In this type of transmission the condition always reverts to "off" for at least one interval at the end of each byte, and always goes to "on" for one interval before starting to send the next byte. This allows the receiver to synchronize with the transmitter at the beginning of each byte and start reading at the correct time. The two extra bits per byte increase the number of bits transmitted from eight to ten, but the real information content of the package is only eight bits. Since 20 percent of the data transmitted is merely control information, this method is considered inefficient in terms of line usage. It is, however, easy to implement.

A more economical method, used by complex, high speed terminals, is *synchronous transmission*. With this method, the receiver's clock is not synchronized with the sender for each individual byte. It is synchronized at the beginning of the transmission session and is allowed to run continuously. Therefore, it is not necessary to send signals at the beginning and end of each byte. However, if there are gaps in the data stream, they must be filled with "idle" bytes to maintain synchronization. At the beginning of the data stream there is a predetermined pattern of bits that causes the receiver to synchronize its clock and start receiving the data. Figure 11-7 shows the synchronous and asynchronous transmission processes.

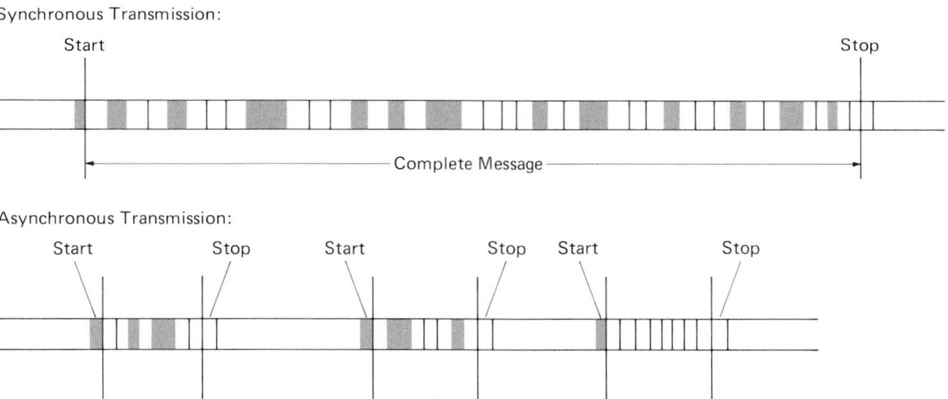

Figure 11-7 Synchronous and Asynchronous Transmission

Data transmission speed is measured in bits per second (bps). Sometimes the term "baud" is used interchangeably with bits per second. This is not exactly correct, since baud rate is a telegraphic concept not necessarily applicable to computer data communications. Some devices employ a technique called *serial transmission* (see Figure 11-7). A byte is transmitted one bit at a time in a serial fashion over a single communication channel. Other devices employ a technique known as *parallel transmission*. This involves the simultaneous transmission of eight bits across an eight-channel line (refer to Figure 11-8). Since these eight bits constitute a byte or character, the speed of such systems is quoted in characters per second. I think you can see that parallel transmission is faster than serial. Most microcomputers communicate with their peripheral devices, such as printers, in parallel mode, and with other computers in serial mode.

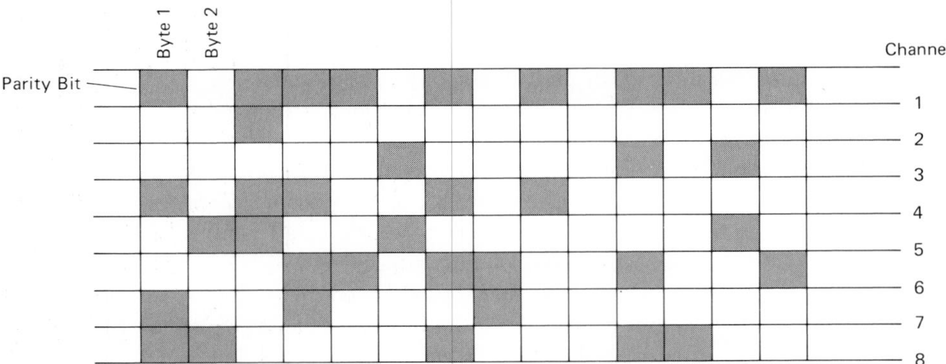

Figure 11-8 Parallel Transmission

The transmission of data is also affected by the mode in which the terminal is operating. A terminal may work in one of three different modes, as shown in Figure 11-9. In half-duplex mode it can send and receive data, but only in one direction at a time. In full-duplex mode, it can both send and receive data at the same time. The simplex mode allows data to be transmitted only in one direction. This mode is rarely used, since data must normally flow in both directions between a terminal and the CPU.

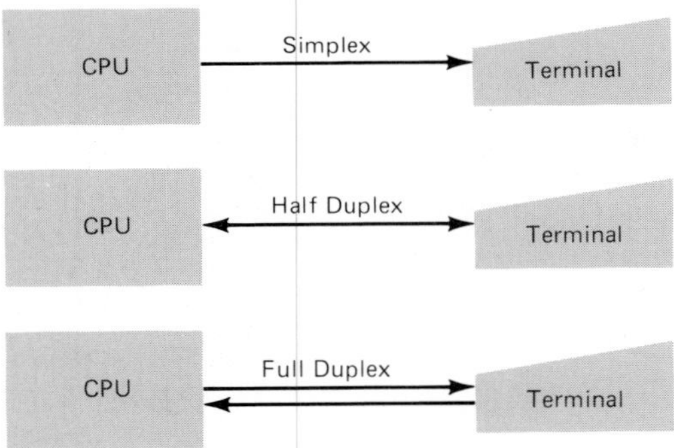

Figure 11-9 Simplex, Half-Duplex, and Full-Duplex Modes

Communication Hardware

Many different media are used to convey data. Satellite communication is increasingly being utilized for long distance transmission. Short and medium distance communication is done primarily through telephone line microwave transmission. Although telephone systems are being designed to carry digital signals, most lines now used for data transmission are traditional telephone lines in that they carry voice data. The shapes of electrical pulses that are suitable for human voice transmission are not compatible with the needs of digital data transmission. Figure 11-10 illustrates the difference between voice and digital signals. Before transmission, it is necessary to convert the digital signals into sound-like waves. This conversion process is called

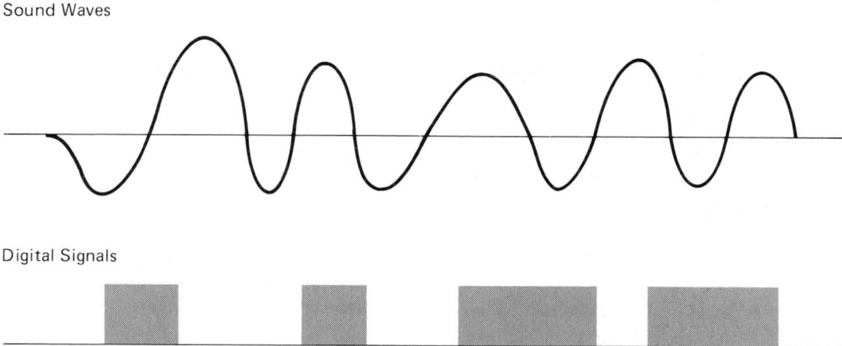

Figure 11-10 Comparison of Sound Waves and Digital Signals

modulation. At the receiving end, the sound signals are converted back to digital form through a *demodulation* process. A device called a *modem* (short for modulator-demodulator) is employed for this purpose. Figure 11-11 shows a typical modem.

Data communications is rapidly moving away from analog transmission with modems. Many of the networks discussed later in this chapter use digital transmission. Furthermore, most voice messages will probably be transmitted and stored by digital means in the future.

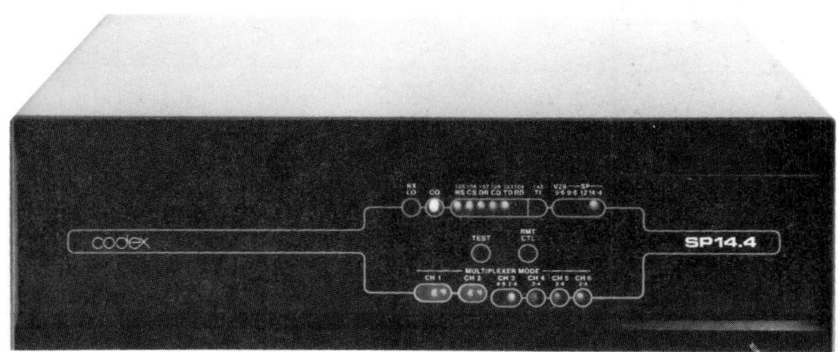

Figure 11-11 A Modem (Courtesy of Codex)

While data is keyed into a buffer at a terminal or is processed by the CPU, the communication line remains idle. If a number of terminals are installed at one location, line idle time can be reduced by sharing the line among them. This is done by using a sophisticated modem known as a *multiplexor*. Some multiplexors divide the telephone line into different frequency bands. Each band is then allocated to a separate terminal. Others divide their transmission into small "time slices." Each terminal is allowed one time slice in turn. Figure 11-12 illustrates both kinds of multiplexing. A *statistical multiplexor* is similar to a time division multiplexor but is a more intelligent device that allocates more transmission time to terminals sending and receiving a larger volume of data than other terminals (see Figure 11-13).

One of the most complex hardware configurations is a data switching network. As was discussed earlier in the chapter, this kind of setup allows communication among

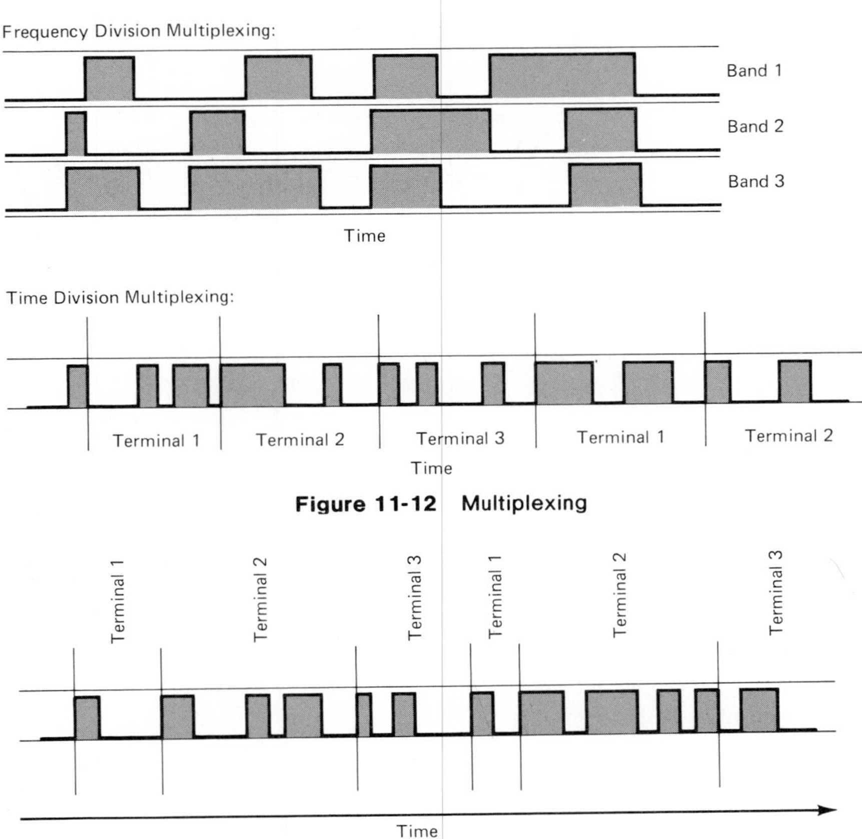

Figure 11-12 Multiplexing

Figure 11-13 Statistical Multiplexing

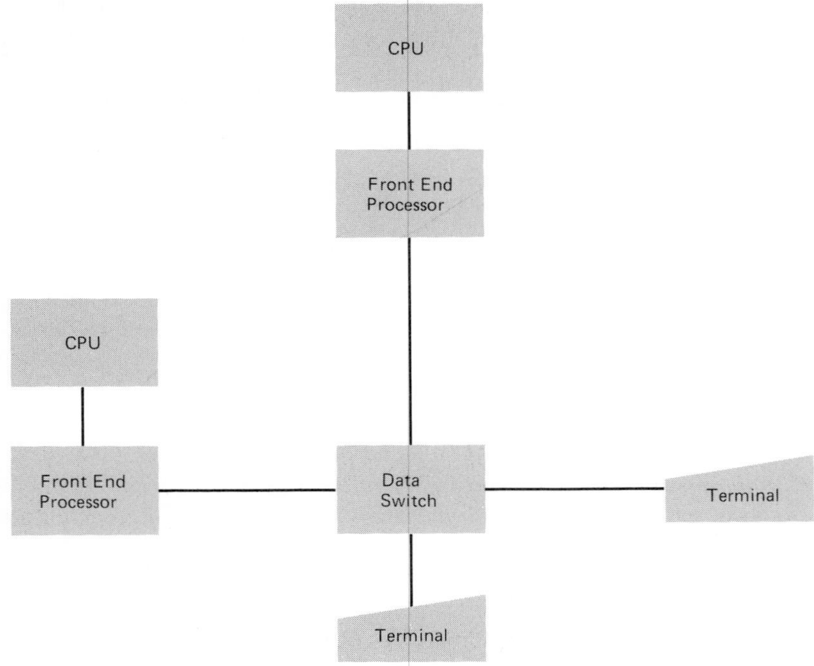

Figure 11-14 Front End Processors in a Communication Network

many terminals and CPUs. Using statistical multiplexors, the network converts many low speed data streams into a few high speed streams. These are then transmitted in digital form over long distance lines. Some of these networks transmit data at over 50 million bps.

In most hardware configurations, a CPU has to communicate with several terminals concurrently. Routine communication tasks like polling, synchronization, and error checking can absorb a large proportion of the CPU's processing time. This often leads to degraded performance on more important jobs. To avoid this waste of precious mainframe CPU time, many systems install a small computer which is dedicated solely to the communication function. Known as a *front-end processor*, this computer manages all routine communications with peripheral devices. Figure 11-14 depicts a network that uses front-end processors to manage communications.

Network Systems

The rapid growth of the data communications industry has given birth to literally hundreds of types of networks. Many of these systems are designed to work primarily with one vendor's products. Others try to establish communication between different vendors' equipment. We will briefly consider two major systems that represent both these categories.

System Network Architecture (SNA): Developed and promoted by IBM, this system fulfills all the communication needs for a distributed data processing system built with IBM equipment. The basic structure of SNA comprises a large CPU, which controls a number of terminals through a front-end processor (see Figure 11-15). An enhanced version of SNA allows several CPUs to access a population of terminals through a network of front-end processors. In case one of the CPUs fails, its work may be transferred to another processor.

Advanced Information System/Net 1: A project of AT&T, this system is still in the development stage. When it is fully operational, the AIS is expected to provide comprehensive data switching facilities. Working similar to a telephone exchange, this

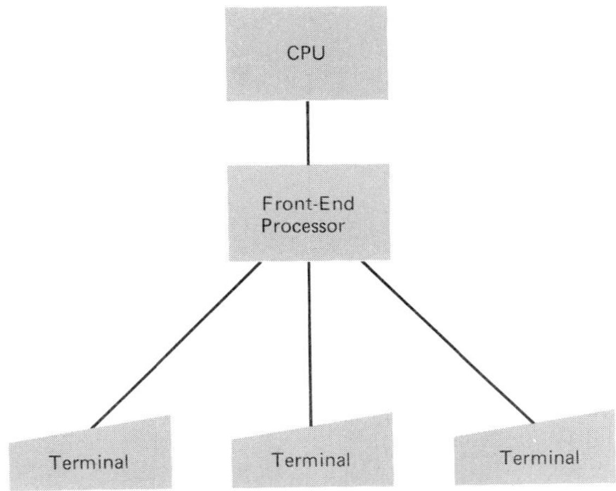

Figure 11-15 Basic Structure of SNA

network can put through "calls" between terminals and computers connected to them. Each terminal or CPU is referred to as a *node*. Unlike the hierarchical structure of SNA, AIS treats all nodes as equals. It is expected that AIS will ultimately be able to link up with the equipment of most computer vendors, and thereby provide a truly public data switching network. While AIS will be a public network, many larger firms have established their own wide area private networks.

An even more widespread phenomenon is the establishment of local area networks. Firms are installing these networks to provide for local communication needs, such as in an individual plant. These networks will probably be PBX (Private Board Exchange) based so that they can handle both voice and data communications. They transmit information in a digital format on a single-channel cable system at very high speeds.

MANAGEMENT CASE 11-1

Dublin Furniture is a medium sized furniture manufacturing operation in Virginia with a total of 5 manufacturing plants scattered over 5 counties in Southwest Virginia. Currently the company has one central computer, an IBM 4341. Each of the plants have access to the central computer through a variety of online terminals. For the last few months manufacturing management at the various plants have been building a case for distributed data processing. They argue that manufacturing resources planning (MRP) systems are becoming essential to effective manufacturing management. Under the plan they advocate, a minicomputer would be purchased for each of the five plants and each would run their own MRP system. In addition, they argue other applications could be distributed from the central computer to these minicomputers. For example, each plant could maintain its own personnel system. If you were chief executive officer of Dublin Furniture, would you approve the distributed data processing proposal?

DISTRIBUTED DATA PROCESSING

Spreading the data processing function throughout an organization entails more than merely dispersing physical equipment. It requires creative programming and systems design so that maximum benefits may be derived from the distributed data processing system. The following section considers some of the major reasons for adopting DDP, and the types of problems to be expected when implementing it. A discussion will follow on how to distribute hardware, software, and data resources. While reading this section it is useful to remember that the distributed computers can be mainframe, mini, or micro computers.

The Need for Decentralized Processing

DDP has several advantages over centralized processing. First, it is often cheaper to dedicate a micro or minicomputer to performing certain tasks instead of using a mainframe. This strategy may also reduce data communication costs because more processing is done at branch locations. Second, system reliability may be improved in the event of a CPU failure, as its workload may be distributed to others. Third, and probably most important, DDP allows end users to interact directly with the computer. While this does create some control problems, it has a very favorable effect on employee productivity.

DDP also offers many advantages to the system designer. Since system components may be added as demand grows, DDP is extremely modular. This is in contrast to a traditional system in which a large computer had to be installed in anticipation of future workload increases, even though current needs did not justify it. Moreover, the system designer can tailor the DDP system to the firm's organizational structure. A centralized firm may want its central computer to closely supervise branch office computers. A decentralized firm might require only a loose connection between home office and branch office processors.

Distributed data processing also suffers from a number of disadvantages that must be kept in mind when switching to this kind of system:

1. Communication costs can easily run over budget unless line usage is carefully controlled.
2. It may be difficult to link together incompatible hardware at various locations.
3. Software at different locations may have to be rewritten to make it consistent.

Some of the most difficult problems arise when selling the DDP system to employees. DP managers often resent their loss of control. Employees might resist working directly with a computer. Some opposition is expected to any kind of change but, because of its very nature, a distributed data processing system requires widespread acceptance and support from users. The list of DDP systems that have failed due to user indifference is long.

Hardware Distribution

A primary requirement for a DDP system is the presence of more than one CPU on the network. The CPUs may be arranged in many different configurations. Here we present some of the more common configurations in use.

Star Configuration: In this arrangement, remote computers are connected radially to a central processor as depicted in Figure 11-16. The remote computers perform I/O

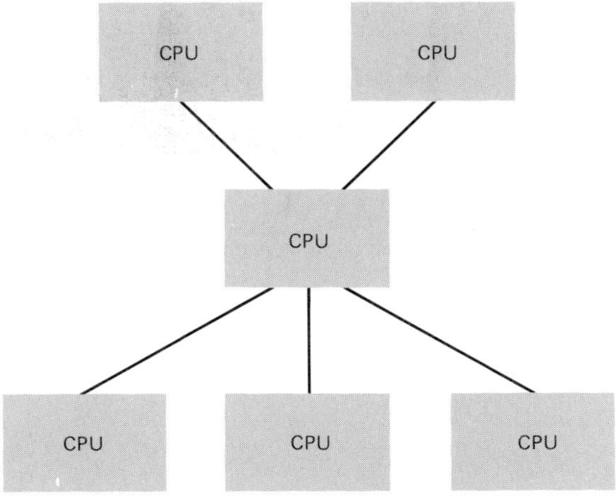

Figure 11-16 Star Configuration

operations as well as data processing. For example, minicomputers at branch offices of a bank may process deposits and withdrawals, and then transmit summary data to the head office.

Ring Configuration: This setup joins a number of CPUs in a circular pattern. As can be seen in Figure 11-17, each computer can communicate with its neighbors. Actually, a CPU can communicate with any other CPU on the ring. It just has to ask the intervening computers to relay the message on towards its destination.

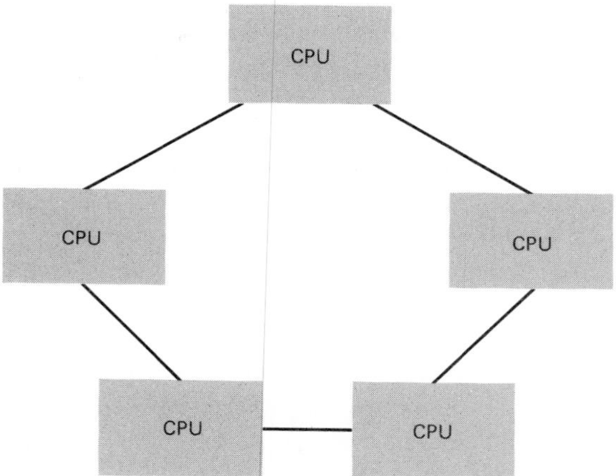

Figure 11-17 Ring Configuration

Hybrid Configuration: This is a ring structured network in which every node is the center of a star network. Such an arrangement is often used in a data switching environment. The nodes on the ring (see Figure 11-18) perform only data communication functions. The actual processing is done by computers on the tips of the stars.

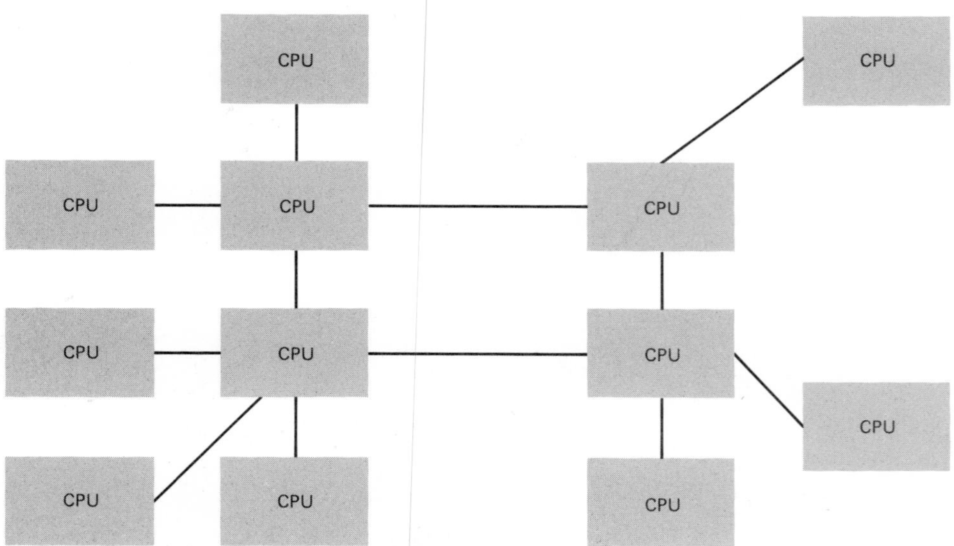

Figure 11-18 Hybrid Configuration

Fully Connected Configuration: This is an extension of the ring configuration. All computers can directly communicate with each other (see Figure 11-19). While this speeds up communication between CPUs the additional hardware cost may be substantial.

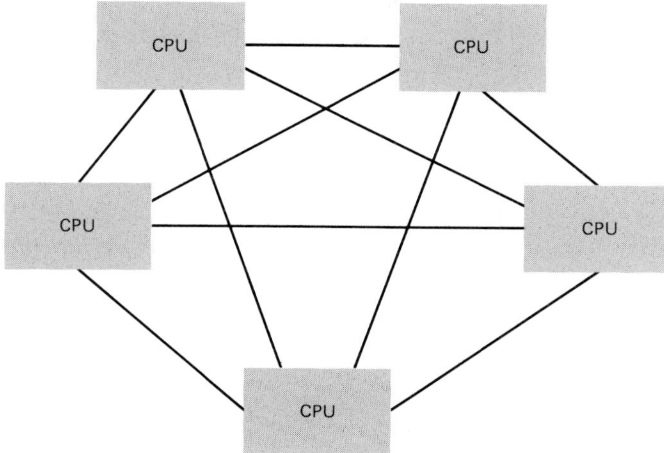

Figure 11-19 Fully Connected Configuration

Tree Configuration: As Figure 11-20 shows, a tree structure links a number of computers in a hierarchy. This arrangement might be suitable for a large, centralized firm. A central mainframe would control the operations of several computers in regional offices. Each regional office computer would, in turn, be responsible for supervising a number of minicomputers at branch locations.

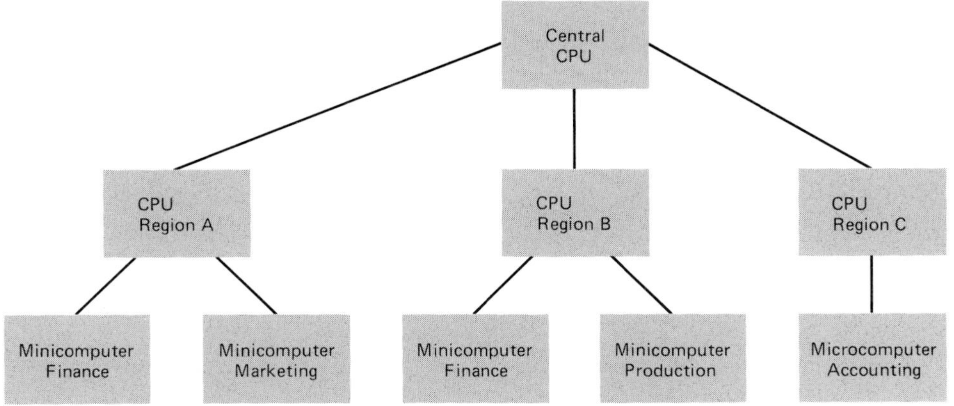

Figure 11-20 Tree Configuration

Software Distribution

A distributed system provides communication between several CPUs. However, it is not necessary that these CPUs spend most of their time communicating with each other. In most cases, a CPU uses the bulk of its time for local processing, devoting only a small fraction to communicating with other computers.

Many application programs executed by a computer are specific to that location. For example, different divisions of a large firm may run specialized applications on their computers (Figure 11-21). Under these circumstances, it is possible to decentralize the tasks of application development and maintenance. Each functional area (manufacturing, marketing, etc.), develops its own application software and assumes the responsibility of maintaining it.

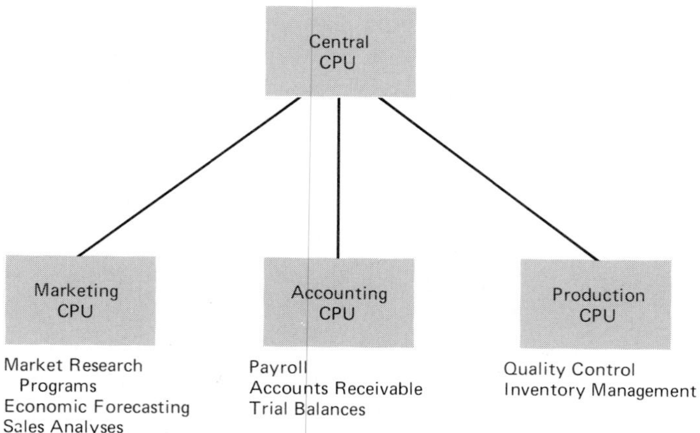

Figure 11-21 Applications Specific to Each Application

In effect, such decentralization requires application development know-how to be dispersed throughout the organization. This notion is sometimes unappealing to DP managers, who may feel that their authority would be undermined. But with the demand for application software increasing rapidly, it is necessary to decentralize application development. User departments should be able to create their own application programs either by training non-DP staff or by setting up their own specialized application development departments.

While some applications programming may be distributed, some of it has to be done centrally. For instance, a large holding company may allow its subsidiaries to develop their own manufacturing and marketing software, but develop most of the financial software at headquarters. In general, most applications software used across the communication network must be centrally developed. Moreover, the central DP department should ensure that uniform documentation standards and security controls are used by local DP departments.

A major concern in DDP systems is system software. The complexity of the hardware configuration places a great burden on the operating system. In a DDP environment, a computer also has access to the memory and I/O devices of other computers. Its operating system must have the ability to recognize and address these foreign devices as well as do the same with its own peripheral equipment.

As we will discuss in the following section, a DDP system might involve the maintenance of a distributed data base. In this case, the DBMS must be capable of accessing memory devices on different machines. Again, this involves interaction among the operating systems of various computers. Obviously, centralized programming is required in this situation.

Data Decentralization

When data processing is distributed, the problem of data storage tends to get very complex. A decision has to be made as to where the data should be stored. Some of it is shared among various nodes and must be made accessible to them all, but a large amount is only used locally. No useful purpose would be served by making all data available to the whole network. Whether data is stored in files or in a data base, it is necessary to keep track of what is stored and where. The data base administrator must maintain an up-to-date data dictionary for all shared items.

DDP is often used for realtime applications, such as inventory control, hotel reservations, and law enforcement. Since realtime applications are best supported by a data base management system, it is not surprising that distributed data bases have become a major concern in the distributed data processing field. Every DDP system tends to develop a unique distributed data base depending on its hardware configuration and user demands. The part of the data base required locally presents no special problems. The DBMS treats it in the regular manner, as we discussed in chapter 9 (see Figure 11-22). However, there are two different approaches to maintaining that part of the data base shared among nodes: partitioning and replication.

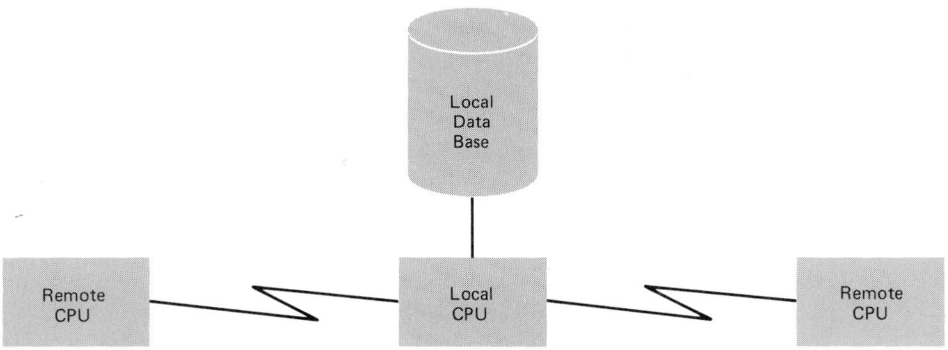

Figure 11-22 Local Data Base

Partitioning: In this approach a particular kind of record is stored at the location using it the most (see Figure 11-23). When another node requests that record, the DBMS consults the data dictionary to determine its location, and retrieves it from there. For instance, a bank may store a customer's account balance at the branch where the customer normally does business. On rare occasions the customer might execute a transaction at another branch. The DBMS would then have to retrieve the data via communication lines. Since most data retrievals are done locally, communication costs are thus minimized.

Replication: With this method, duplicate copies of the data base are stored at all locations. Changes to the data base are promptly propagated to all locations. This approach is useful with small data bases because it is cheaper to store multiple copies of data rather than use communication lines to retrieve individual records from distant

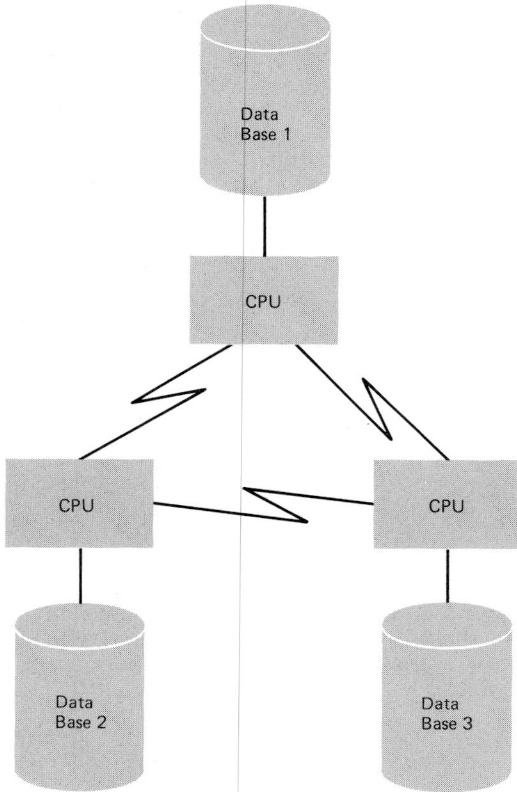

Figure 11-23 Partitioned Data Base

locations. For example, a large east coast textile manufacturer uses replication in its distributed data base. The data base, containing orders, customer data, production data, and warehouse information, is periodically updated at all locations. Another example of replication of data bases is the case of a local decision support system on a micro. The user may periodically replicate from the central data base those portions of the data underlying his or her decision support system.

WORD PROCESSING AND OFFICE AUTOMATION

As data processing equipment continues to move out of the EDP department and into users' offices, office workers depend more and more on the computer to do their daily jobs. The remainder of this chapter describes the changes occurring in today's computerized office, and how they affect the lives of office personnel.

Word Processing

Computers can process words as well as numerical data. Textual material, such as letters, reports, and books can be stored on the same storage media as numerical data. A

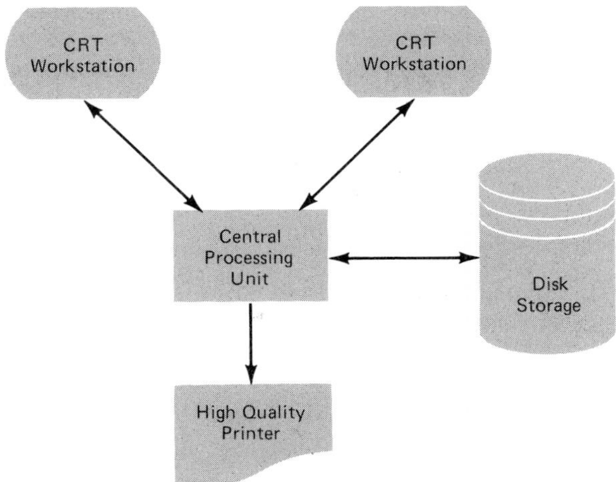

Figure 11-24 Typical Word Processing Configuration

word processing system is essentially a small computer with one or more CRT input stations, a high quality printer, and disk storage as shown in Figure 11-24. As can be seen, this is a typical computer configuration. In fact, word processors are small computer systems that range in cost from $5,000 to $25,000.

From a computer hardware technology standpoint, perhaps the most sophisticated part of a typical word processing configuration is the high quality printer. Word processing printers are typically based on either ink jet or daisy wheel technology. The CRT work stations are standard CRTs that enable the typist to see the words being processed. The CPUs in word processors are relatively low power and are usually microprocessors. Processing of words requires comparatively little processing capacity. The disk storage may be either floppy or hard disk. Some word processing systems have only one CRT work station while others have many work stations—as many as one hundred or more.

The advantages of word processing are based on the fact that the system will store textual data on a disk and retrieve, modify, or print it on command. A report, for example, can be initially typed through a CRT work station, stored on disk, and printed. Corrections to the report can be made directly through the CRT. Words, sentences, paragraphs, or even whole pages can be inserted, deleted, or moved. The report can be corrected and polished before a final copy is printed. Among the capabilities of word processing are the following:

1. Detection and correction of spelling errors.
2. Changing the width of margins automatically. This is done without retyping the material. The operator simply tells the system the new margins and the CPU automatically processes the text to achieve the new margins.
3. Deletion, insertion, or modification of any text material.
4. Automatic centering of titles.
5. Automatic underlining.
6. Automatic hyphenation of words.
7. Automatic page numbering.

The advantages of word processing are many. Some of them include:

1. Reduction of typing time (some say up to 50 percent of the typing and retyping time is saved with a word processor).
2. Reduction of proofreading time.
3. Cleaner, more professional looking final copies.
4. In some cases, typists can be eliminated altogether since the original preparer can type the material directly into the word processor.

Most individuals who are not skilled typists find that typing on a word processor is easier than on a typewriter because corrections can be made so readily. The fear of making an error and having to correct it with an eraser or correction fluid is totally eliminated. If the material is dictated, the typist can enter the original material on a word processor. The originator of the text then calls it up on his or her CRT work station, reviews it, makes final corrections, and prints the final copy.

Electronic Mail

Many companies with multiple word processing systems are now expanding these systems into an *electronic mail* network as illustrated in Figure 11-25. Since the textual material is stored in electronic form in the word processing system, it can be easily transmitted over long distances through regular commercial channels such as microwave or telephone lines. This electronic mail approach is rapidly being implemented. Some companies, such as Amoco Oil and Citicorp, have extensive electronic mail capabilities. The advantages are delivery speed and elimination of mail costs. These promise to make electronic mail widespread in the future. In fact, the postal services in Great Britain, Canada, and the United States are becoming involved in the electronic mail area so that the service can be provided between companies as well as within companies.

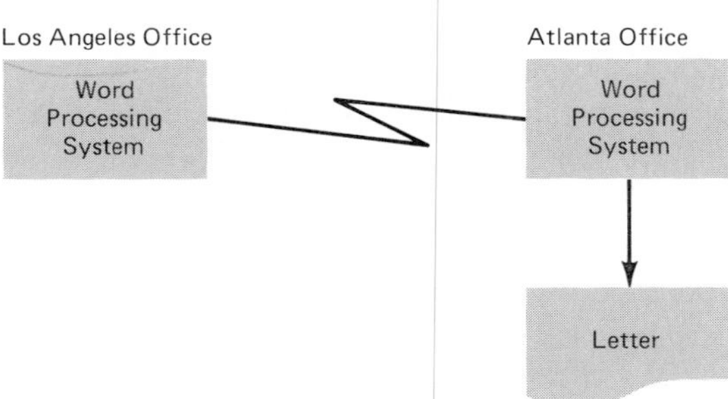

Figure 11-25 Electronic Mail

When an executive receives electronic mail on the local word processing system, he or she can read it on the CRT screen and perhaps never print a copy of the letter. However, a printed copy is readily available if it is needed. These systems have several advantages which include the following:

1. The time between creation of information, and its receipt by interested parties is minimized.

2. Managers waste less time on dialing the telephone, only to hear a busy signal.
3. Messages and documents may be routed to as many people as necessary, without physically copying them.
4. Electronic mail may be filed by the recipient, or dispatched to an "electronic wastebasket." The wastebasket retains messages for a week before destroying them.

Office Automation

A step further in the word processing evolution is office automation. Under the *office automation* concept most, if not all, printed documents would be stored electronically rather than in printed form. These could be retrieved from disk files, used, or printed whenever necessary. Advanced data base oriented systems even have the capability of storing textual data in data bases. Using the system's data manipulation language, managers can easily retrieve required information without physically searching through thick volumes of reports. Lawyers often make use of this technique. By specifying a few keywords, a lawyer can get the computer to search through a large data base of court cases and print out relevant citations. Another use of text searching is in strategic planning. Top managers frequently need descriptive data on various subjects, but don't know where to look. Using a DBMS, they can search different data bases and quickly pinpoint the required information sources. In general, this approach is called the paperless office. However, considerable advances will have to be made in the ease with which human beings can use office automation systems before paperless offices are feasible.

MANAGEMENT CASE 11-2

Norfolk Shipbuilding is one of the largest shipyards in the country. Their central computing facility contains several large mainframe computers. These mainframe computers are used for a wide variety of purposes, including the typical management information system applications, engineering and scientific applications, and word processing. Norfolk has a computer steering committee made up of middle level executives from all of the computer user areas. As is typical with most computer installations the central facility becomes overloaded at times and response time on the terminals deteriorate. When this happens there is always a group within the steering committee which advocates prohibiting the use of the central computer facility for word processing. They argue that the highest and best use of the computer is for scientific and engineering number crunching and management information systems. They feel that word processing should be given a low priority. Evaluate this position.

Integrated Word Processing/Data Processing

Very often, businesses need to combine the output of their data processing system with textual material to create a final document. If data processing and word processing are performed on separate systems, it is necessary to retype some of the information in order to obtain the final printout. Integrated WP/DP systems can save this extra labor by processing the data and then using the results as input to a text processing operation. The following illustrations should help in understanding integrated WP/DP systems.

Customer Mailing Lists: Data from accounting or marketing records may be combined with text to create high quality correspondence material. For instance, a hospital computer can check patient records to find patients who have not been in for a

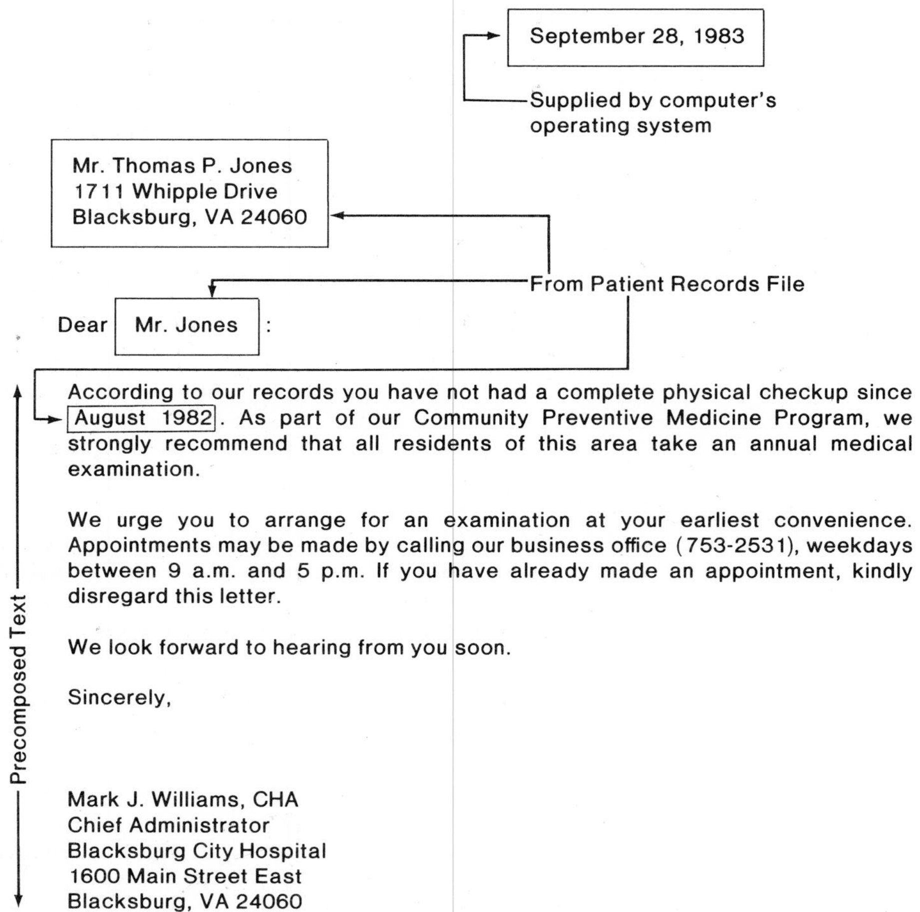

September 28, 1983
Supplied by computer's operating system
Mr. Thomas P. Jones
1711 Whipple Drive
Blacksburg, VA 24060
From Patient Records File
Dear Mr. Jones :
According to our records you have not had a complete physical checkup since August 1982. As part of our Community Preventive Medicine Program, we strongly recommend that all residents of this area take an annual medical examination.
We urge you to arrange for an examination at your earliest convenience. Appointments may be made by calling our business office (753-2531), weekdays between 9 a.m. and 5 p.m. If you have already made an appointment, kindly disregard this letter.
We look forward to hearing from you soon.
Sincerely,
Mark J. Williams, CHA
Chief Administrator
Blacksburg City Hospital
1600 Main Street East
Blacksburg, VA 24060
Precomposed Text

Figure 11-26 Personalized Letter Produced by WP/DP

physical checkup in over a year. After checking the current appointments file, the system can automatically produce letters reminding the patient to come in for an annual checkup. Figure 11-26 shows how the system would print a high quality letter by merging data files with precomposed text.

Report Generation: Managers frequently prepare reports on operations that include both data and descriptive text. For example, a report from a regional sales manager may include detailed sales data as well as a subjective evaluation of the future market. Figure 11-27 illustrates how an integrated WP/DP system would produce a tabular report combined with the regional manager's remarks. In addition, systems are now available that can insert graphics output on a report along with data and text.

Office Decentralization and Productivity

A major incentive for office automation is improved productivity. Information processing technology serves the cause of productivity in two ways. First, computers

Data

Green Forest Products, Inc.
Quarterly Sales Summary ($'000)
Southwest Region
2nd Quarter 1983

Product	% Change	April	% Change	May	% Change	June
White Paper	+1.4%	162	+ 0.62%	163	− 7.98%	150
Hard board	+0.85%	85	+ 2.35%	87	+ 5.75%	92
Plywood	+1.43%	123	+ 4.88%	129	+ 6.20%	137
Wallpaper	+3.15%	55	−23.64%	42	+21.43%	51

Text

Comments

1) White paper sales dropped in June, mainly due to school and office vacations.
2) Hardboard and plywood sales were up sharply because of a seasonal rise in construction activity.
3) Wallpaper sales fell drastically during May. The major reason was the low introductory prices of a new competitor, Frisco Paper Company. However, we were able to regain our market share in June, because of aggressive marketing and an increase in Frisco's prices.

Figure 11-27 Sales Report Including Both Data and Text

perform many of the routine tasks that humans used to perform manually. This not only speeds up work but also reduces errors in results. Second, information processing equipment lets people produce better quality output in greater quantity.

Using distributed data processing, many firms are now decentralizing office operations. Marketing professionals use portable terminals to enter data from remote places. Executives save on travel time by employing "teleconferencing." Technical experts improve their productivity by staying at home and working through remote terminals. This not only saves commuting time but also helps them avoid the distractions of the office. In short, office automation reduces the need for direct person-to-person contact and accelerates the throughput of work.

Unfortunately, this increased productivity is not an unmixed blessing. Many workers do not like to work in isolation. The opportunity to socialize in the work environment is of significant value to them. To take it away would have a negative impact on their morale. In addition, the business itself may suffer if employees do not interact on a personal basis. Many new ideas and strategies develop during informal communications between employees. Excessive decentralization of the office would be detrimental to such brainstorming. The following section considers some other human aspects of office automation.

Human Factors

Just as the "scientific management" techniques of the early twentieth century caused concern among factory workers, "office automation" is a disturbing phenomenon for many office personnel today. Since office technology is still evolving, there is great uncertainty about its ultimate impact on office life.

Many white collar workers fear losing their jobs to a machine. These fears are not entirely justified. While computers do automate many manual functions, they also tend to create new jobs that are more interesting and challenging. What is really needed is a retraining of existing personnel to take over the newly created jobs. Most data processing installations arrange seminars and hands-on training courses for the benefit of user department personnel. Many private firms and software vendors provide similar services on a commercial basis.

As more experience is gained with office machines, the design of computer equipment is being more closely tailored to human needs and comfort. Design engineers are making keyboards and CRT screens more compatible with the human physique. These improvements greatly affect the work environment of clerical personnel, who have to use computer terminals for hours at a stretch.

Some executives are reluctant to use computer terminals because they dislike typing. Devices like light pens and touch-sensitive screens can help them overcome this "terminal phobia." High quality printing and graphic output are other means of winning over skeptical top managers.

One major obstacle to users' acceptance of a system is poorly designed software. Very often, application programs are written without much regard for the end user's requirements. A good system designer must always keep in mind the technical competence and knowledge level of the end user. While actual system design depends on the unique requirements of the business, the following guidelines should generally be kept in mind in order to make the software "user-friendly."

1. Screen messages should be clear and concise, so that a nonprogrammer can understand them. Unnecessary abbreviations must be avoided.
2. Whenever possible, provide complete error messages online instead of listing error numbers. The user probably has more important things to do than to search through heavy manuals to find out what error number "X953-E22$G" stands for.
3. Provide online help facilities. If a user does not know what to do at any point in the program, the system should display the available options to him or her.
4. Design input and output formats to coincide with the user's conceptual view of documents.
5. Supply easy-to-use but comprehensive user manuals, manuals should be written in plain language, not programmer jargon. For instance, a record may simply be called a line, and an attribute, a column. The purpose is to aid the user in operating the system, and not to write a formal technical document. A friendly, easy-to-use system is much more likely to be accepted by office personnel than an exacting and intolerant program that does not permit any human error at all.

SUMMARY

In recent years there has been a tendency to disperse data processing facilities throughout the user organization. As a result, office procedures and work habits are rapidly changing.

A DDP system is critically dependent on the data communication system used to connect various devices.

Three basic configurations are used in a data communication network:

1. Computer-peripheral device configuration
2. Computer-to-computer communication
3. Communication through a data switch

The flow of information is governed by a set of rules known as the communication protocol. The protocol also determines whether transmission will be asynchronous or synchronous.

Depending on the characteristics of the communication line, data may be transmitted either one bit at a time or one character at a time. The mode of the terminal determines whether data flows in one direction or both.

A large number of devices exist to facilitate data communication and use either telephone lines or special digital cables. The most important devices are:

1. Modems
2. Multiplexors
3. Statistical Multiplexors
4. Front-End Processors

Two of the most important data communication systems are IBM's SNA, and ATT's AIS/Net 1.

DDP offers several advantages, such as more efficient CPU time utilization, lower data communication costs, and direct interaction between users and the computer. Further, the system designer is better able to tailor the system to the company's need.

The disadvantages of DDP include high communication costs and equipment incompatibility problems. The most difficult part of implementing a DDP system is to obtain the active support of user personnel.

There are many different ways of arranging computers in a distributed system. The most important configurations are listed below.

1. Star Configuration
2. Ring Configuration
3. Hybrid Configuration
4. Fully Connected Configuration
5. Tree Configuration

In a DDP system, software development and maintenance is distributed among user departments. However, it is necessary to centralize system software and those application programs shared among nodes.

In a distributed data base environment, some data is shared among nodes, while some is only used locally. Local data is stored at the appropriate node. Shared data is stored either at the node that uses it most or is replicated and stored at all locations.

Word processing facilities can enhance office productivity in many ways:

1. Electronic filing systems speed up document storage and retrieval.

2. Text searches may be executed using DBMS.
3. Interoffice communications are improved through the use of electronic mail.

Word processing may be combined with the company's data processing facilities. This combination leads to the efficient generation of high quality output for such items as mailing lists and management reports.

Distributing the data processing function allows decentralization of office facilities in some cases. This may improve productivity by reducing travel time and preventing the distractions of a large office.

The reaction of human beings to office automation critically affects the success of a DDP system. Automation of the office can raise questions about job security and the quality of the work environment.

The design of friendly software systems is an important element in selling DDP to user departments. Programs must be written with the user's convenience in mind.

KEY TERMS

Distributed Data Processing (DDP)
Data Communications
Data Transmission
Master-Slave Relationship
Data Switch
Communication Protocol
Block Format
Polling
Asynchronous Transmission
Synchronous Transmission
Bits per Second (bps)
Baud
Serial Transmission
Parallel Transmission
Full-Duplex Mode
Half-Duplex Mode
Simplex Mode
Modem (Modulator-Demodulator)
Multiplexor
Statistical Multiplexor
Front End Processor
System Network Architecture (SNA)
Advanced Information System/Net 1 (AIS/Net 1)
Node
Modularity
Star Configuration
Ring Configuration
Hybrid Configuration
Fully Connected Configuration
Tree Configuration
Distributed Data Base
Shared Data
Local Data
Partitioning
Replication
Office Automation
Text Handling
Electronic Filing
Memory Management
Electronic Mail
Integrated Word Processing/Data Processing (WP/DP)
Report Generation
Human Factors
User Friendly Software

REVIEW QUESTIONS

1. Explain the three basic types of data communication.
2. Why are communication protocols necessary?

3. Describe the three communication modes used by terminals.
4. What is the function of a modem in data communication?
5. Explain the advantage of using a front-end processor.
6. What do you consider to be the major difference between SNA and AIS/Net 1?
7. List the advantages of decentralized data processing.
8. How does the star configuration differ from the tree configuration?
9. Explain the concept of software distribution.
10. Explain the terms shared data, local data, partitioning, and replication.
11. What is electronic filing?
12. How can a DBMS be used to manage large volumes of text data?
13. What is WP/DP?
14. How does DDP improve office productivity?
15. Why are human factors important in the design of a computer system?
16. List some techniques that can be used to make software more friendly.

DISCUSSION QUESTIONS

1. Spreadout Inc. has decided to connect its computers in twelve different states with a data communication network. Elmer Ware, the president, is not sure how a communication network functions. Explain to him the important functions of a communication system, and how they relate to Spreadout's data processing operations.
2. Describe the job of a data base administrator in a DDP environment. Would the DBA maintain one data dictionary for the whole system, or would there be a separate dictionary for each location? How would he or she convince user departments to make their data available to departments at distant locations? If software development is highly decentralized, does that pose special problems for data base design?
3. What kind of personnel grievances can be expected to arise when automating an office? What can an office manager do if data entry operators complain of excessive eye strain from looking at CRTs? How does he or she pacify disgruntled executives complaining about slow turnaround during peak hours?

RESEARCH PROJECTS

1. *Mini-Micro Systems* often carries articles on developments in the data communication field. Using this periodical, or other sources, write an essay on the role of minicomputers in data communications.
2. Find out whether your company or educational institution uses distributed data processing. If it does, interview a senior DP staff member. Based on your interview, prepare a report on the approach adopted in introducing DDP, the major difficulties faced, and how these difficulties were overcome.

ESSAY

Office MIS An Unmixed Blessing?

(Reprinted with permission from MIS Week, January 19, 1983, p. 33)

By Charles H. Nobs, Senior Vice President, General Staff Services, Bankers Trust Co., New York

One of the most difficult decisions managers face in the implementation of office technology is the choice of when to say "stop."

The notion of office machines as worksavers and cost displacement tools is a traditional belief, yet one which shows signs of breaking down under the onslaught of hundreds of new products being offered for such functions as word processing, personal computing, electronic mail and document reproduction.

Vendor offerings in search of a business need, rather than the other way around, are proving to be a real problem for firms concerned with the double-digit growth rate of office expense.

Take word processing, for example. No one would question the fact that basic WP increases typing throughput, offers a chance for clerical-advancement/job enrichment, and gives professionals the chance to fine-tune text to a degree previously not feasible.

But it also magically results in more corporate reports of greater length, which then need to be distributed, read and often responded to, thus beginning the cycle all over again. Hence, a new variation on Parkinson's Law has been created: "Information today expands beyond the time available for its digestion."

Technology, though, has only been the enabler in the process. The growth in staff functions and related service industries is proving to be the expanding market incentive which all office equipment vendors dreamed of. Advanced text processing capabilities seem now to be increasing staff output as did robotics and CAM (computer-assisted manufacturing) for line operations in heavy industry.

Document reproduction is another case in point.

The advent of inexpensive, uncomplicated and relatively trouble-free photocopiers has eased what used to be the single biggest office bottleneck—i.e. information dissemination. It has also, however, resulted in enormous increases in paper consumption for most large corporations and has placed consequent expense burdens on mail and courier budgets.

The advertising jingle, "when it absolutely, positively has to be there overnight . . ." would not have had much meaning in the pre-electronic office.

But copier manufacturers have still more new ideas on the way. The so-called "intelligent copier" will soon be available which not only reproduces at one location, but also can trigger reproduction at multiple sites for a broadcast type of effect.

Another new market to be tapped is the "personal copier" idea which promises a cheap and space-efficient unit designed to serve the needs of a small work space.

The prospect of these new developments evokes memories of the classic scene found in the Jane Fonda-Dolly Parton-Lily Tomlin movie "9 To 5" where a behemoth copier is uncontrollably spewing forth pages despite all best efforts to stop it.

So, are we really better off today than in the office of the past? Well, yes and no.

Everyone would agree that the office of yesterday was clumsy, inflexible to any changes in business requirements and certainly labor-intensive. But it did have a built-in cap on production levels—a sometimes useful constraint when dealing with non-revenue-generating entities. It didn't stifle ideas, though it did clearly limit their mobility.

Finally, the office of the past did force managers to present concepts in straightforward fashion with a minimum of verbiage. Somehow, sales—both internal and external—were still made in spite of the absense of sophisticated graphics and color exhibits.

All this is somewhat moot, since the office of the future is upon us and no one would seriously propose that the clock should or could be turned back in a large corporation. What's important is that we not lose sight of the goals which workplace automation should support—improved effectiveness and profitability.

"Effectiveness" is the key word, for all too often we substitute the term "productivity" in its place.

Productivity, as expressed by output divided by input, makes eminent sense in an industrial context where true value is added at each successive step in the production process. An automotive assembly line would be a good example.

The office is a far different matter, and the concept of value-added is much more subjective. Management here must decide where they want output maximized and also where they want it minimized. Automation resources should be allocated accordingly.

Hence, a paradigm shift in the importance accorded to office management will be required if technology implementation is to serve business needs.

The historical approach to controlling office segment expense was to ration workers—both clerical and professional—in relation to organizational strategy and need. The theory held that direct people-related costs would drive the requirements for indirect items such as real estate, communications, stationary and supplies, etc.

New electronic offerings promise or threaten—depending on your point of view—to change this simple linkage to the extent that workers armed with the latest gadgetry can incur several multiples of expense more than their pre-electronic cohorts. Putting aside the capital costs associated with operational burden is a serious concern.

Personal computers have a tremendous potential for good, but they do occupy space, use energy, voraciously consume paper and supplies, and necessitate considerable training time in order to be constructive.

Electronic mail systems and other forms of open-ended communications are very, very expensive to operate at this point in time and rarely would receive corporate approval if viewed on a cost-per-message basis.

Teleconferencing absolutely must become vividly available in the future, but today it is technically complex and prohibitively expensive for all but the largest firms.

Terminals displaying MIS accessed from remote databases may well displace paper costs, but are subject to usage-sensitive data communications charges in many areas of the country which more than offset other savings.

Therefore, it's easy to understand why capping staff levels won't contain office costs in an electronic age.

The leveraged output factor arising from the marriage between office workers and electronic tools is increasing rapidly as new vendor offerings and technologies come into use. Employee power in the 1980s will truly be measured by the ability to collect, analyze, compose, store and distribute both words and numbers.

This leverage can enhance functionally or cause dysfunction, can be economic or decidedly diseconomic, and can bolster competitive position or detract from the job at hand.

The difference needed to achieve effectiveness in office automation is a direct result of senior management attention. Knowing where and how to automate one's office are key issues worthy of debate and organizational reflection.

Giving every employee the tools he/she desires in quest of timesaving and work quality improvement is a sub-optimal approach which can produce unexpected results. Knowing when to say "enough" is important.

Discussion

1. Do you agree or disagree with Mr. Nobs argument in this essay? Support your position.
2. As an executive in a large organization, how would you control the potential explosion in verbiage that office automation makes possible?

PART THREE

CONCEPTUAL FOUNDATIONS OF INFORMATION SYSTEMS

CHAPTER 12
BEHAVIORAL AND ORGANIZATIONAL CONCEPTS

INTRODUCTION

An information system supports human beings when decisions need to be made. Behavioral research has shown that people share certain characteristics when processing information for decision making. However, at the same time differences exist in individual approaches to gathering information and making decisions. Computer-based systems can complement some of the weaknesses humans have as information processors. In designing information systems it is crucial that we be aware of these characteristics of human beings as information processors.

Information systems also operate within organizations. They are in effect a subsystem of the organization. The design of an information system must fit the organization structure which it serves. Different types of organizational forms necessitate different information system designs.

In this chapter we will first explore the process of decision making. We will then look at the characteristics of human beings as information processors and decision makers. Next, individual differences in decision making will be explored. Finally, we will cover organization theory and its relationship to information systems.

DECISION MAKING

Types of Decisions

Decisions may be categorized as being either programmed or nonprogrammed. In a *programmed decision* the rules for making the decision are explicit. That is, given a certain set of conditions, a certain set of actions will be taken. Programmed decisions are often incorporated into transaction processing systems, and thus computer systems can make the decision without human intervention. An example of such a decision is the inventory reorder decision. Based on economic order quantity and safety stock rules, a computer automatically reorders inventory items. In designing an information system it is very important to isolate those decisions that can be programmed, thereby relieving human beings of the necessity of making these routine day-to-day decisions.

Nonprogrammed decisions deal with nonrepetitive and ill-defined problems, and require human decision making. Nonprogrammed decisions are made at all levels within an organization, including operational, technical, and strategic levels. However, as one moves to higher levels of decision making, a greater percentage of decisions made are nonprogrammed. Examples of nonprogrammed decisions include plant location, product line expansion, merger, and employee hiring decisions.

Programmed decisions tend to require timely, accurate, and reliable information whereas nonprogrammed decisions require a great deal of flexibility on the part of the information system. The decision maker must interact with the information system to gain information to make a nonprogrammed decision. In chapter 17, *Decision Support Systems*, we will see how information systems can be designed very flexibly. The type of decision making dealt with in the rest of this chapter is nonprogrammed decisions. We will find that in the decision making process a decision maker goes through certain stages. Computer-based information systems can greatly assist the decision maker in this process. We will also find that individual differences exist in approaches to decision making.

Stages in Decision Making

Simon has identified three stages in decision making: 1) intelligence; 2) design, and 3) choice.[1] In the *intelligence stage*, a decision maker becomes aware that a problem exists. In this stage the decision maker also gathers information concerning the problem. In the *design stage*, the decision maker attempts to develop alternative solutions to the problem. Of course, this stage may require additional information concerning alternative solutions. The final stage, *choice of a solution*, relies heavily upon the quality of the design stage, including the alternative solutions and the information concerning these alternative solutions. In fact, if stage two, design, is done properly, stage three, choice, is rather straightforward.

[1]Herbert A. Simon, *The New Science of Management Decision* (New York: Harper & Row Publishers, 1960) 2.

I think you can see that information permeates the decision making process. Information is necessary for the identification of problems. It is also the basis of considering possible alternative solutions. Finally, information is used to evaluate alternative solutions. Much of this information can come from a firm's information system. However, you will note that in nonprogrammed decision making we are relying very heavily upon human beings as information processors. In the next section of this chapter we will discuss characteristics of human beings as information processors in a decision making context.

HUMAN INFORMATION PROCESSING AND INFORMATION SYSTEMS

The primary advantages that human beings have over machines in decision making are the ability to use a complex associative long-term memory to focus on likely problem solutions and a facility for guiding the information search for problem solutions. Computer-based information systems can of course store large amounts of data for long periods of time, but computers lack the ability to associate related data in a quick way like human beings can. Of course, computers, if instructed to, can associate related data but humans must provide the instructions.

There is no question that human beings are efficient information processors and decision makers. However, research shows that people have certain biases in the decision making process. In the remainder of this section we will discuss these biases and suggest some aids in counteracting them, which information systems designers should keep in mind.

Generally human beings fail to consider a sufficient number of alternative solutions to problems. They tend to rely on a relatively small subset of the available information concerning solutions to the problem. Such behavior, of course, makes for an efficient information search. After all, large amounts of information may produce an overload, leading to confusion on the part of the decision maker. Research though has shown that almost every decision maker who at any time considered the correct solution to a problem selected this solution as his or her final choice.[2] These findings illustrate the critical nature of the search for possible solutions to a problem. If the correct solution is identified it is highly likely to be chosen. Narrowing the search for alternative solutions may produce an efficient information search but it may also result in overlooking the correct solution.

In designing information systems we should keep in mind the need to augment a human being's short term memory. As indicated by the name, *short term memory* is a capacity to store items for a short period—perhaps minutes, or at the most a few days. We cannot expect human beings to remember all possible solutions to problems even though they have been aware of these solutions in the past. Interactive menu-driven information systems are an example of systems that compensate for human beings' failures to consider a sufficient number of alternative solutions to a problem. On the screen these systems provide a checklist of possible actions, thereby guiding a decision

[2] A. S. Elstein, L. Schulman, and S. A. Sprafka, *Medical Problem Solving: An Analysis of Clinical Reasoning* (Cambridge, Massachusetts: Harvard University Press, 1978).

maker in the information search process and assuring that possible solutions are not overlooked.

A second bias that human beings have in the decision making process is a failure to search for evidence that contradicts an apparent solution to a problem or neglecting such information once it has been gathered. Once a decision maker has used a particular solution in the past or is leaning toward a particular solution currently, he or she tends to narrow the information search rather quickly. People tend to anchor on a particular solution and do not like contradictory evidence about that solution even though an alternative may be better. This bias commonly manifests itself when an information system designer is told by a manager that a particular piece of information is important in making a decision. The system designer knows that other types of information are more important and in fact would lead to a different decision than what the manager makes. A system designer must realize that the manager is not likely to change his or her opinion quickly about what information is needed. A long and skillful educational process may be needed before the manager will use different information.

The final human information processing bias that we will discuss is the limited ability to integrate information from multiple sources into global judgments. This bias is related to the previous two. As human beings, we tend to use a rather narrow range of information in making decisions. We have difficulty in assessing information from multiple sources and then integrating it into a decision. We are much better at selecting and gathering information than we are at integrating it. Solutions to this bias fall into two categories. First, we could replace the decision maker with a model in at least a portion of the decision process, and second, we could change the format in which the information is presented to human beings.

Decision aiding models, such as multiple regression and linear programming have been used successfully in a number of business areas. However, the introduction of such models has often been met with defensive reactions from decision makers. Their objections are usually along the lines of: 1) there are technical problems with a model; 2) models dehumanize the decision process; and 3) models are an attack on the decision makers prized judgement abilities. However, as managers see the additional profits to be had through the use of some models, they are gradually being adopted. System designers should realize though that adoption of models is not a straightforward and easy task.

Changing the way information is presented can have a large impact on the ability of human beings to integrate multiple pieces of information. Ehrenberg suggests that a good report should make patterns and exceptions obvious when the probable exceptions and patterns are known beforehand.[3] He provides four basic guidelines for a good report:

1. Round to two significant digits.
2. Use row and column averages.
3. Present the main pattern of data in the columns.
4. Order the rows and columns by some measure of their size.

Rounding to two significant digits may seem severe, but it is necessary for mental arithmetic. Averages help one keep important relations, such as above or below average

[3]A.S.C. Ehrenberg, "Some Rules of Data Presenatation," *Statistical Reporter*, 7 (1977), 305–310.

in mind. Columnar presentation allows one to compare individual digits by running the eye up and down the column, and an ordering by size aids in interpreting the figure because one can see the general pattern of the surrounding ones.

Another way of changing information format is through the use of graphics. Currently available hardware and software make graphics presentation relatively inexpensive. Graphics combining several variables in a multidimensional format can be particularly effective. One such technique is Chernoff schematic faces.[4] *Chernoff faces* are constructed by assigning each variable of interest to a different feature on a schematic face. Figure 12-1 illustrates Chernoff faces for the W. T. Grant Company from 1965 to 1974.[5] W. T. Grant declared bankruptcy in 1974. In Figure 12-1, thirteen key financial ratios are represented by different features on the face. Even though one may know little about key financial ratios, I think you can see in Figure 12-1 that something was seriously wrong with W. T. Grant in 1974. In fact, you can easily see the trend starting in 1967 and progressively getting worse. This provides an excellent example of the possibilities for using multidimensional graphics in presenting informa-

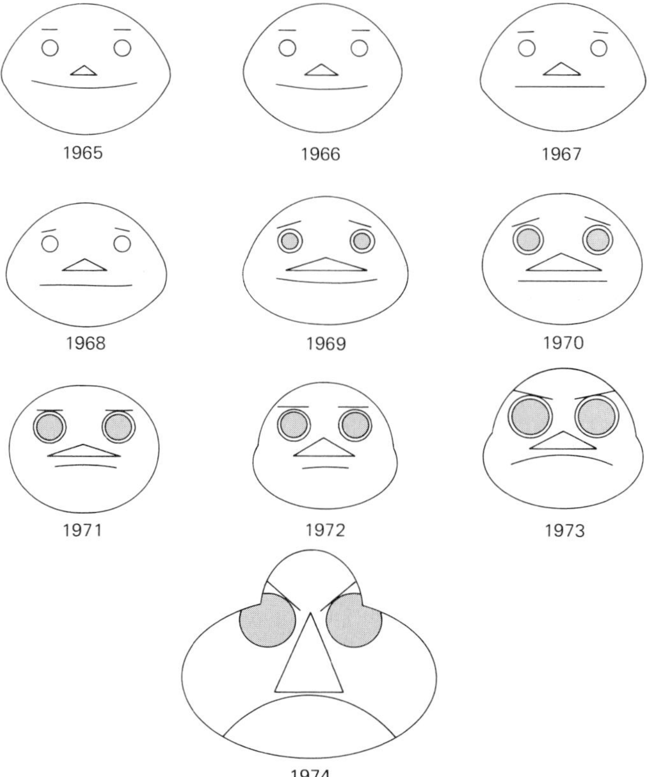

Figure 12-1 Chernoff Faces Representing W. T. Grant Data (Courtesy of S. Moriarity and W. Roach)

[4]H. Chernoff, "The Use of Faces to Represent Points in k-Dimensional Space Graphically," *Journal of the American Statistical Association* 68 (June 1973), 361–368.

[5]S. Moriarity and W. Roach, *Chernoff Faces As an Aid to Analytic Review*, Unpublished paper presented to the committee on statistics in accounting, American Statistical Association annual meeting (August 1977).

tion for decision making. Such approaches can be particularly useful for integrating several different pieces of information into one composite, thereby compensating for human beings' inability to integrate information from different sources.

Thus far we have talked about biases that all human beings tend to exhibit in decision making and information processing. The next section will look at individual differences in decision making.

MANAGEMENT CASE 12-1

Bob Olds has been assigned as the senior systems analyst on a project by the McGregor Company to analyze and design a new budgetary control and reporting system. In the initial stages of the project, he and his staff have interviewed many different management personnel who make use of budgetary reports. The primary purpose for the interviews was to determine a consensus of reporting for the new system. However, the most striking feature concerning the interviews as a whole is the lack of consensus as to the type of reporting the managers want. For example, some managers like to see a great deal of detailed reporting on a very frequent basis. At the other extreme there are managers who would rarely use reports produced by the existing system or the proposed system. Bob is in a quandary as to how the new system will meet this wide variety of needs. Are there any behavioral characteristics of humans that would explain this lack of consensus? How would you advise Bob to proceed?

INDIVIDUAL DIFFERENCES IN DECISION MAKING[6]

Often the study of information systems is based on the assumption that human components in the system can be viewed as deterministic black boxes; that is, all humans act the same. However, an extremely large set of outcomes is possible in decision making due to individual differences.

Individuals often conclude that their personal view of the world is correct and shared by most other people. In a decision making situation, human beings often assume that if everyone saw the facts as they see them, a similar decision would result. This position fails to consider the role of the personality in decision making. In this section a decision making model will be developed that includes the variable of personality.

Basic Personality Theory

Carl Jung is responsible for the theoretical and empirical research that supports the problem-solving model adopted in this section.[7] He employs an open system view of personality that results in two important concepts. One is that subsystems within the personality can interact with each other, and the second is that subsystems can change as a result of interactions with each other or with the environment. Jung identifies four basic psychological functions that serve as a basis for the model: 1) thinking; 2) feeling; 3) sensing; and 4) intuition.

[6]This section is based on Hellriegel and Slocum, *Organizational Behavior* (St. Paul, MN: West Publishing, 1979), 221–236.

[7]C. G. Jung, *Collected Works* (especially Vols. 7, 8, and 9 of Part I), edited by H. Read, M. Fordham, and G. Adler (N.J.: Princeton University Press, 1953), 110.

Thinking and feeling are at extreme ends of a continuum. They are each a basis for dealing with external facts when making decisions. Sensation and intuition are paired opposites along another continuum that represents extremes in individual perception preferences. This perception or information search process is the means by which an individual becomes aware of events in the environment.

According to Jung's theory, only one of these four psychological functions is dominant in an individual, and it is backed up by only one of the other functions. In describing the model, each of the four psychological functions will be considered. The combinations of the two perceptual orientations (sensation and intuition) will then be considered in combination with the two decision-making orientations (thinking and feeling).

Feeling-Thinking Orientations in Decision Making

Feeling types tend to be "aware of other people and their feelings, like harmony, need occasional praise, dislike telling people unpleasant things, tend to be sympathetic, and relate well to most people."[8] These people are very aware of the feelings of other people and enjoy pleasing them. They tend to avoid conflict and are very likely to alter their position on an issue if they perceive that a new position will be more acceptable to other group members. Establishing and maintaining friendly relationships is of primary importance to a feeling type. In summary, an individual with a feeling decision-making orientation is likely to emphasize affection and personal processes in decision-making for the purpose of obtaining approval from others.

At the other end of the continuum are the thinking types, who tend to be "unemotional and uninterested in peoples' feelings, like analysis and putting things into logical order, are able to reprimand people or fire them when necessary, may seem hardhearted, and tend to relate well only to other thinking types."[9] Thinking types tend to be impersonal, and they employ stereotyped procedures in decision making. They tend to base decisions on external data and are frequently accused of neglecting humanistic considerations. Frequently, they neglect personal health, family, and finances for the sake of achieving some goal.

The intellectual processes of thinking types are often modeled on the scientific method. This rational, problem-solving approach is probably a result of contemporary educational practices. Thinking types tend to be productive because their style leads to the discovery of new concepts based on seemingly unrelated empirical data.

Sensation-Intuition Perceptual Orientations

Individuals with sensation perceptual orientations tend to "dislike new problems unless there are standard ways to solve them, like an established routine, must usually work all the way through to reach a conclusion, show patience with routine details, and tend to be good at precise work."[10] Sensation types find the uncertainty of unstructured problems and environments distasteful. They also dislike situations in which a great deal of discretion must be exercised. They prefer positions in well-structured bureaucracies

---

[8] *Ibid*, 114.
[9] *Ibid*, 110.
[10] *Ibid*, 115.

where the environment is dominated by rules and standard operating procedures. Because sensation types are oriented toward realism and external facts, they are not inclined toward personal reflection and avoid making personal decisions in unstructured areas.

On the other hand, a person whose perceptual orientation is intuitive "likes solving new problems, dislikes doing the same things over and over again, jumps to conclusions, is impatient with routine details, and dislikes taking time for precision."[11] Sensation types tend to view the external environment in terms of details and parts; intuitive types tend to view the whole environment and look for relationships. When engaged in problem solving, they tend to identify and evaluate alternatives rapidly. They also keep the overall problem in mind while considering means of redefining it at the same time. Intuitive types dislike stable conditions and seek new situations in which they are intellectually challenged. When they are oriented toward people, they are capable of identifying the potential abilities of others.

A Composite Model

A model of individual decision making styles based on the decision-making and perceptual orientations of individuals is presented in Figure 12-2. Although this model is simplified, it is a convenient means of demonstrating the impact of personality on individual decision making. Like communication, decision making can produce a variety of outcomes.

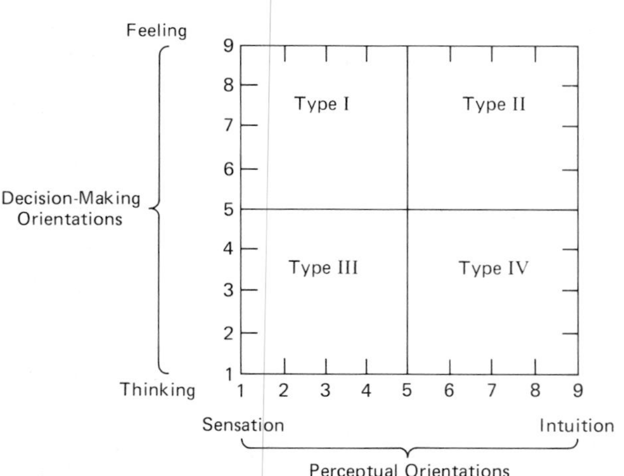

Figure 12-2 A Model of Individual Problem Solving Styles

Sensation-feeling individuals (type I) are primarily concerned with facts about people that they can collect and verify directly by their senses. Because of their feeling orientation in decision making, these people evaluate facts with a personal and human concern. They tend to be very organized and give great attention to detail.

For a sensation-feeling type, an ideal organization consists of a well-defined hierarchy with a well-defined set of rules to specify relationships. Such types believe

[11] *Ibid*, 116.

that an organization should satisfy the members' needs and should allow for open communication.

Intuition-feeling individuals (type II) rely primarily on intuition in their perception and feelings when making decisions. They generally avoid specific details. They like to be involved with new projects, ideas, and concepts, and they prefer to focus on broad themes, like serving humanity and satisfying human needs. In their view, the ideal organization is decentralized, has few rules and standard operating procedures, no strong leaders, and loosely defined lines of authority.

Sensation-thinking types (type III) tend to focus on external facts and analyze problems logically. They focus on the specific details of a problem and are very practical in their problem solving. Their ideal organization is a classic bureaucracy. They prefer well-defined positions and extensive use of rules. They believe that an organization should contain a well-defined hierarchy and that people should be evaluated on the basis of their technical ability.

Intuition-thinking (type IV) individuals emphasize a theoretical or technical approach to problem solving, and favor situations that lack structure and require abstract skills. They prefer impersonal organizations that emphasize conceptual skills. Goals of the organization should be consistent with the environment and the needs of the members of the organization. Intuition-thinking types tend to handle issues from an impersonal, abstract frame of reference.

Model Application

This model of individual styles of decision making has many implications for information systems. First of all, in a problem situation, different personalities seek different types of information. Second, people interpret the same information differently because of variations in their perceptions. Third, personality influences an individual's perception of an ideal organization. Therefore, a policy that seems quite reasonable to one individual might elicit a hostile reaction from another.

It is important to keep in mind throughout the study of information systems that no amount of data processing equipment and standard operating procedures will ensure consistent communication, perception, and problem solving by individuals within the organization. We are all different, and even with some understanding of information systems, we are not capable of controlling human behavior.

On the other hand, we recognize that the human component in an information system is the only component capable of adapting the system to meet the ever-changing demands from the environment. Throughout the life cycle of any information system, it will be necesssary to alter the goals of the system. Of all the components of the system, human beings alone possess the ability to adapt. Therefore, they make the most significant contribution to the successful functioning of an information system.

The next section will consider some general organizational concepts as they relate to an information system. Keep in mind how the different personality types view an ideal organization.

MANAGEMENT CASE 12-2

The Champion Corporation is experiencing severe space shortage in its administrative offices. One proposal to alleviate this space shortage is to encourage those employees whose jobs are closely tied to working through CRT terminals, with a computer, to work at home. An example of such an employee would be a programmer. Those that advocate the work at home plan have argued that individuals like programmers would be much more productive at home and perhaps would enjoy their work more since they would not have to commute every day of the week. In addition, employees with small children could be with their children while they are working. Some of the stronger supporters of this idea feel that there will be basic changes in organizations in the future as more and more administrative tasks are performed through the computer. Would you advocate a company adopting this approach? What are its advantages and disadvantages?

ORGANIZATIONAL THEORY AND INFORMATION SYSTEMS

Information systems operate within organizations and information systems must be tailored to fit the form of organization. In this section we will explore the four most common organizational forms and relate them to information systems.

Functional Form

In the functional form of organization, an organization's structure is aligned with basic managerial functions, such as marketing, personnel, manufacturing, engineering, finance, and accounting. Figure 12-3 illustrates the functional form of organization. The functional form of organization allows clear assignment of responsibilities. It also increases the opportunity for mutual support of employees doing similar kinds of work. The primary disadvantage of the functional form of organization is that it may narrow an individual's viewpoint. He or she may concentrate on optimizing the function's performance and ignore the well-being of the organization as a whole.

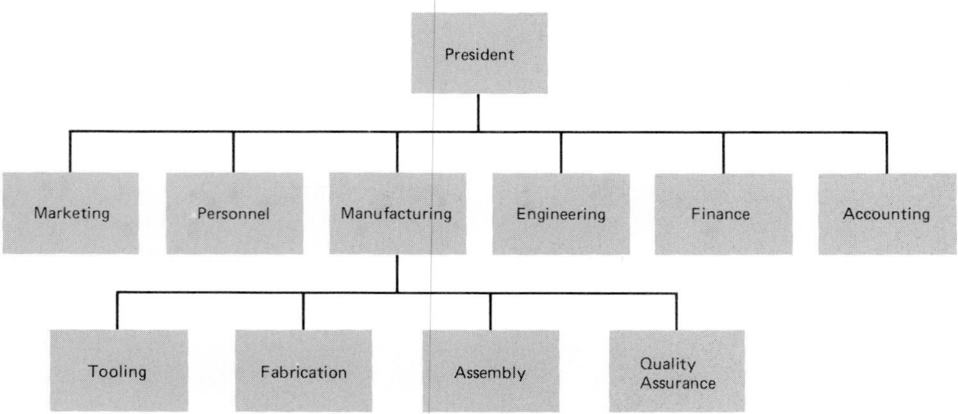

Figure 12-3 Functional Form of Organization

Information systems for functional forms of organizations tend to be very hierarchical in nature. The reporting is subdivided by function, and data that is reported in a lower level of functions is hierarchically summed up to provide reporting at the high level functions.

A problem that often occurs with information systems in a functional organization concerns the difficulty of producing summary information by product. This is due to the fact that information systems are generally set up to report by managerial function. Of course, if information systems designers recognize this possible shortcoming in the analysis and design of the system, they can usually provide for product reporting capabilities also.

Product Form

Figure 12-4 illustrates the product form of organization. With the product form of organization, activities are grouped together by outputs of the firm or by products. For example, in Figure 12-4, the organization of a large chemical firm is illustrated. The organization is subdivided by major product groups, such as paints and pigments, fibers, and fertilizers. Each one of these product divisions is organized internally by managerial function, such as engineering, marketing, and manufacturing. The primary advantage of the product form of organization is that individuals can build expertise and knowledge of particular product lines rather than spreading their abilities over too many different types of products.

However, the product form of organization can be more expensive in personnel costs than the functional form since individuals with primary managerial function expertise such as engineering, manufacturing, and marketing are usually present in each of the product divisions. Duplication of activities can easily occur. For example, the paints and pigments division may develop a sales information system while at the same time the fibers division may be also developing such a system. Lack of coordination between the divisions may result in two separate sales information systems instead of one set of software that could be used by both.

In a product form of organization it is particularly important that information systems personnel in the various product divisions communicate freely with one another in order to avoid duplication of activities. This is often accomplished through a formal information steering committee that has representatives from all product divisions. As

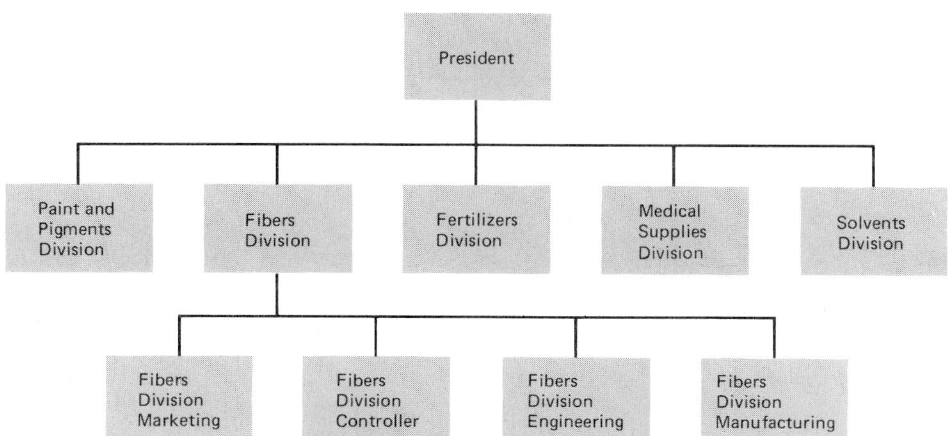

Figure 12-4 Product Form of Organization

would be expected, reporting within a product form of organization tends to follow product lines. Consequently there is a danger of overlooking the ability to report in summary form by managerial function, such as engineering.

Bureaucratic Form

Max Weber, a German scholar of the early 1900s, described the bureaucratic form of organization. Quite often when we hear the term "bureaucracy," we envision an organization with unreasonable and complex rules that is also incompetent and full of red tape. Therefore, the term bureaucracy has developed a negative connotation. In reality the bureaucratic form of organization can be very efficient. Basically the bureaucratic form of organization assumes that an individual employee cannot be trusted to perform his or her job satisfactorily without specific rules and procedural specifications.

A bureaucratic organization has six basic characteristics:

1. There is a definite hierarchy of authority.
2. There is a division of labor based on functional specialization.
3. There is a set of rules governing the actions and responsibilities of individuals holding specific positions.
4. Procedural specifications provide a sequence of steps an employee must follow in performing tasks and dealing with problems.
5. Employees as well as outsiders are treated in an impersonal manner. The primary rationale for this characteristic is to prevent excessive personal favortism on the part of those in power.
6. Technical competence is the primary measure used in selection, retention, or advancement of employees.

From the above, you can see that a bureaucratic organization is often mechanistic and impersonal. You can also see that the type III (sensation-thinking) types of people would prefer a bureaucratic form of organization.

Information systems in bureaucracies tend to reflect the bureaucratic approach. That is, they are often very formal, have predetermined rules for actions, and may be inflexible. Due to these characteristics, bureaucratic information systems can easily become outdated. In fact this has happened with several of the systems at the Federal government level in the United States. For example, both the Internal Revenue tax processing system and the Social Security system have at times been on the verge of collapse due to outdated equipment and software.

Matrix Form

Figure 12-5 illustrates a matrix form of organization for a large aerospace firm. The primary feature of a matrix organization is duality of authority, information reporting relationships, and systems (refer to Figure 12-5). The organization is subdivided into functional departments. At the same time, each major program or product is assigned to a different program department. Usually these programs are headed by an individual at the vice presidential level. As you can see, a matrix form of organization is, in effect, a

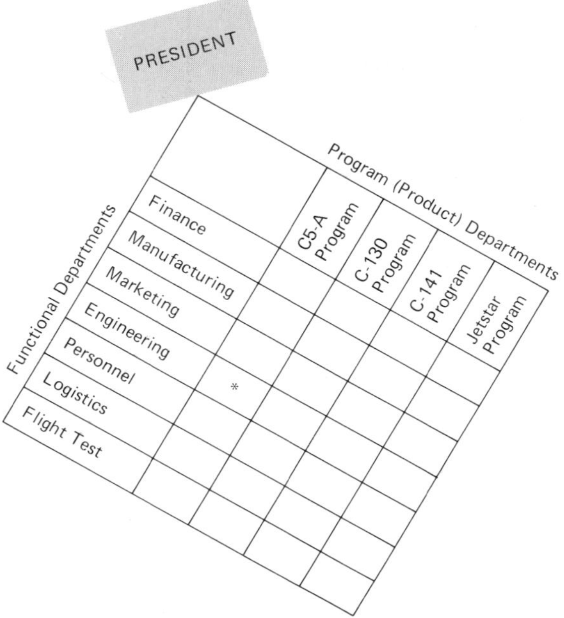

Figure 12-5 Matrix Form of Organization

hybrid of the functional and product forms of organization. For example, individuals within the engineering department, denoted by an asterisk in the figure, would report both to functional executives and to program executives.

The matrix form of organization allows firms to adapt quickly to new products. Team members assigned to individual programs usually come from diverse functional backgrounds, therefore bringing a broad and rich level of expertise to an individual program. The primary disadvantage of the matrix form of organization is the ambiguous nature of authority. Individuals who expect a hierarchical, one-superior, approach to management are often frustrated in a matrix organization. They do not like reporting to two different command hierarchies, both functional and program. The problem of split loyalties is very difficult for some individuals.

The information system for a matrix form of organization is necessarily more complex than for the other types of organizations. It is imperative that such a system be able to report from both the functional and the program viewpoint.

SUMMARY

Decisions may be categorized as either programmed or nonprogrammed.

In a programmed decision the rules for making the decision are well known and straightforward.

Nonprogrammed decisions deal with nonrepetitive and ill-defined problems.

There are three stages in decision making: intelligence, design, and choice.

The primary advantages that human beings have over machines in decision making are the abilty to use a complex associative long-term memory to focus on likely problem solutions and a facility for guiding the information search for problem solutions.

Human beings fail to consider a sufficient number of alternative solutions to problems.

In designing information systems we should keep in mind the need to augment a human being's short-term memory.

Human beings often fail to search for evidence that contradicts the likely solution to a problem or neglect such information once it has been gathered.

Human beings have a limited ability to integrate information from multiple sources into global judgments.

Changing the way information is presented can have a large impact on the ability of human beings to integrate multiple pieces of information.

Individuals differ in their approach to decision making and gathering information.

Decision making approaches may be categorized along a feeling-thinking continuum.

Perceptual (information gathering) orientations may be categorized along a sensation-intuition continuum.

Individual decision making among individuals includes sensation-feeling, intuition-feeling, sensation-thinking, and intuition-thinking types of styles.

In a problem situation, different personalities seek different types of information, people interpret the same information differently because of variations in perception, and personality influences individuals' perception of an ideal organization.

A functional form of organization is constituted on the basis of major managerial functions, such as engineering, marketing, and finance.

A product form of organization organizes a firm by major product or product groups.

A bureaucratic form of organization assumes that employees need specific rules and procedural specifications to perform their jobs satisfactorily.

A matrix form of organization is, in effect, a hybrid between the product and functional forms. Its major characteristic is a duality of reporting to both functional executives and program or product executives.

KEY TERMS

Programmed Decision
Nonprogrammed Decisions
Intelligence Stage
Design Stage
Choice Stage
Human Information Processing
Short-term Memory
Decision Aiding Models
Chernoff Faces
Feeling
Thinking
Decision Making Orientation
Sensation
Intuition

Perceptual Orientation
Sensation-Feeling Individuals
Intuition-Feeling Individuals
Sensation-Thinking Individuals
Intuition-Thinking Individuals
Functional Organizational Form
Product Organizational Form
Bureaucratic Organizational Form
Matrix Organizational Form

REVIEW QUESTIONS

1. What are the two basic types of decisions?
2. Which type of decision is a computer most adaptable to? Why?
3. What type of computerized information system is necessary for nonprogrammed decisions?
4. What are the three stages in decision making?
5. How can information help in each stage of decision making?
6. In which stage is information most important?
7. Outline the basic weaknesses human beings have as information processors.
8. Research has shown that human beings have limited ability to integrate information from multiple sources into global judgments. What are some potential solutions to this bias?
9. Define the two basic orientations in decision making.
10. Define the two basic orientations in perceptions.
11. Describe type I sensation-feeling individuals.
12. Describe type II intuition-feeling individuals.
13. Describe type III sensation-thinking individuals.
14. Describe type IV intuition-thinking individuals.
15. What is the functional form of organization?
16. What is the product form of organization?
17. Certain aspects of information systems may be overlooked in functional and product forms of organizations. What are these aspects?
18. Describe the bureaucratic form of organization.
19. How does a matrix form of organization differ from the functional and product forms?

DISCUSSION QUESTIONS

1. Listed below are several different decision situations. Which of them are programmed and which are nonprogrammed? Explain your rationale.

   1. Selection of a new plant site.

2. Ordering parts for an aircraft assembly line.
3. The daily assignment of production personnel to individual jobs in a machine shop.
4. Selecting stocks for an investment portfolio.
5. Selecting the best location for a warehouse from which deliveries are to be made to customers.
6. Deciding whether to discontinue a product line.

2. Think for a few minutes about the following questions:

1. Do you like solving new problems or do you prefer having a structured job situation that is more routine?
2. Would you have any difficulty in firing an employee who works for you?
3. Do you show patience with routine details and tend to be good at precise work?
4. Do you like an organization that contains a well-defined hierarchy?
5. Do you evaluate facts with a personal and human concern or do you tend to handle issues from an impersonal, abstract frame of reference? Based on these questions, which of the four types of decision making styles and perceptual orientations do you fall into?

3. How would the information systems department fit within the different forms of organizational structure? Would a matrix form of organization be useful in any information systems development efforts? Explain your answer.

RESEARCH PROJECTS

1. Select a real world organization in your geographic area. Determine its organizational form. What effects has its organizational form had on the structure of its information system?

2. Select an organization that is highly decentralized or one that has a very definite hierarchical structure or a bureaucracy. Administer the Myers-Briggs type indicator test to several individuals within the selected organization. This test indicates whether a person has a sensation or intuition perceptual orientation and whether they have a thinking or feeling decision making orientation. The test may be obtained from your instructor or from the Educational Testing Service in Princeton, New Jersey. Do the type of individuals employed by the organization fit its organizational structure?

ESSAY

Catching the World Off Guard

(Reprinted with permission from PC World, Vol. 1, No. 5, p. 13)

By David Bunnell

A recent headline in *Computerworld* declared that the data processing (DP) departments in many corporations had been caught off guard by personal computers. Although DP departments in many corporations had been planning to introduce "micros," as they call them, on a very controlled basis within the next year or two, personal computers started to show up in just about every corporate department before these plans could be realized, without any input from company DP departments.

The PC is such a useful tool for the management of information that people have adapted to it at an amazing pace considering its complexity. When a PC shows up on an assistant manager's desk, it not only gets the attention of other assistant managers but is noticed by the manager and director as well.

For many reasons, some of which are nearly logical, DP departments have found this situation a real nightmare. Of course, they find it frightening that so many PCs are already in place, but the real nightmare is that they come in so many brands and models—Apple IIs, IBM PCs, TRS-80s, North Star Advantages, Apple IIIs, Fortune 32:16s.

"How are we ever going to hook these little beasties together so we can start controlling them" seems to be one of the most urgent concerns.

This situation is nothing new because personal computers have been catching people and institutions off guard since their birth in 1975. I expect that they will continue to do so until the entire fabric of all our organizations is restructured into patterns far more diversified and interchangeable.

Implementing a corporate PC policy when PCs seem to multiply like rabbits has given DP departments and their comrades in corporate planning enough challenges to keep them in a tizzy through the remainder of the decade.

The reason for the PC's rapid acceptance is that increasingly more business and professional jobs revolve around managing quantities of information. Workers who use personal computers have an advantage over their colleagues and competitors. The PC's ability to rapidly create and shape documents and reports enables workers to be fast on their feet as they scramble up the corporate ladder or launch enterprises of their own.

The real danger comes when the acceptance of information is based more on form than on content. You can do more than access, manage, and format information with a PC—you can create it.

The DP nightmare is not without foundation. If everyone had a computer and the multitude of computers were not interfaced with each other, how would we know that we were all working from the same assumptions?

However, tying all computers together wouldn't necessarily return control to DP departments. Corporate data would actually become increasingly decentralized. DP departments would try hard to control this trend with access codes and security schemes, but over time this strategy would break down. Thus, one of the ultimate effects of personal computers in corporations will be to disseminate power.

Not only will DP departments be caught off guard, but so will the people who think they run the show. Corporations, governments, and all other institutions will become assemblages of autonomous groups.

By bringing sophisticated information management skills to the work place, the personal computer will ultimately lead to more democratic institutions.

DISCUSSION

1. Do you agree with Bunnell's premise that personal computers will lead to major changes in organizational forms and lines of authority?

CHAPTER 13

SYSTEMS FUNDAMENTALS

INTRODUCTION

This chapter contains a general introduction to the concepts of systems. Material of this type is very abstract and has broad potential application. The initial section of the chapter offers a rationale for studying this material. The remainder describes such systems concepts as feedback, variety and control, black box, boundary, input, and output. After each of these concepts is described, familiar examples are used to reinforce the understanding of the concept.

WHY STUDY SYSTEMS?

In education, economic savings can be realized if students master abstract material that has broad potential application. For example, mathematics is studied throughout primary and secondary schools and in the early years of college. Indeed, most students at one time or another are frustrated in the study of mathematics because of the abstract concepts they are required to master. Math teachers are very familiar with the cry, "Where am I ever going to use this?" However, these skills serve as a basis for study in engineering, agriculture, science, and business.

Most colleges of business are organized along the functional lines of finance, marketing, management, management science, information systems, and accounting. Such organizational structures result in specialization, and also condition student expectations. For example, business students often expect material in a business course to increase their ability to address specific business problems in one of these specialties. Therefore, knowledge that is highly transferable and consequently abstract is sometimes viewed unfavorably by students because they fail to see its immediate application in their area of specialization. Such reservations are addressed in this section before the material concerning systems is presented.

Systems and *systems analysis* are, respectively, a philosophy and methodology for viewing complex wholes at a manageable level of abstraction. It should certainly not be hard to convince someone that the information system of a multinational corporation is

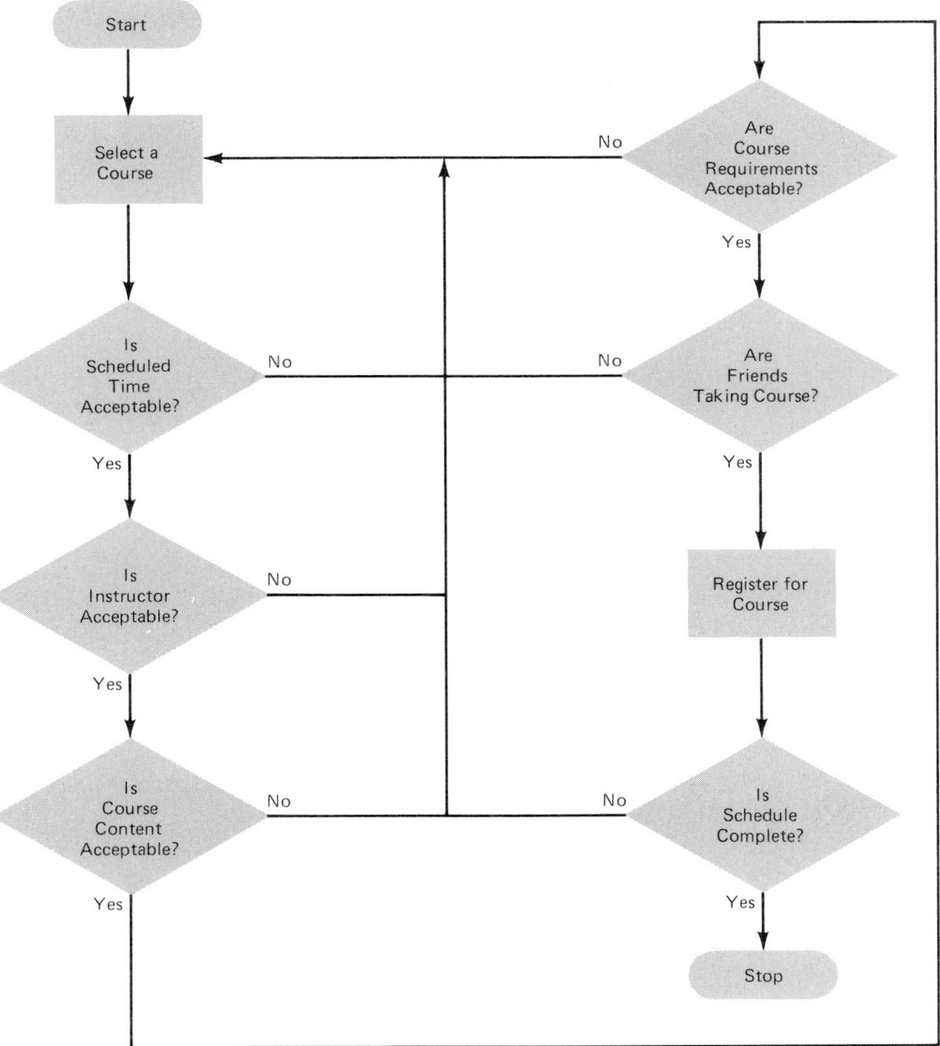

Figure 13-1 Course Registration Decision

a complex entity. Where does one begin to analyze such a system? One can be so overwhelmed with detail that such a system may be viewed as too complex to analyze.

Systems analysis is a method for dealing with complex systems. By moving to a level of abstraction that contains manageable detail, it is possible to identify and specify alternatives for the design and modification of a system. Movement to a manageable level of abstraction is demonstrated in the following example. Assume that a flow diagram is required to illustrate the decision process of a student electing to take a course in information systems. Figure 13-1 is a possible representation of the process.

However, note that the diagram includes nothing about cognitive processes the student employs in making the decision. Even if it were possible to incorporate all that detail, it might require a diagram as large as this book. By identifying a reasonable level of abstraction, the diagram is a workable representation of the decision process. This approach is the basis of systems analysis. In addition, educational economy can be realized because the same method can be used to represent and analyze all types of systems.

Another reason for studying systems is that many of their characteristics are similar, and the strategies for analyzing and improving them are therefore similar. For instance, the systems approach is used to determine why an automobile is not operating properly. It can also be employed on an information system. In addition, when one begins to view complex phenomena as systems, analogies can be drawn between systems that initially might seem unrelated. For example, consider the common characteristics of airline reservation and university course registration systems.

For the above reasons and others that will become evident as the material is mastered, this chapter contains a discussion of systems in an abstract form. Examples are used throughout the presentation so that you will be able to maintain the connection with business.

SYSTEMS

What is a System?

In the abstract, a *system* is defined as a set of interacting components that operate within a boundary for some purpose. The boundary filters the types and rates of flow of inputs and outputs between the system and its environment. The specification of the boundary defines both the system and the environment of the system.

Figure 13-2 provides an overview of a system. The essential concept you should learn here is that a system accepts inputs from its environment and transforms them into outputs, which are discharged back into the environment. Each of the items on this figure will be discussed in more depth later in this chapter.

Within the confines of this definition it is possible to conceive of a system within a system. For example, a company can be viewed as a system and its particular industry as a suprasystem. Alternatively, the industry can be defined as a system and the company as a subsystem. To carry the example an additional step, the industry can be viewed as a subsystem within a national economy. Finally, the national economy can be viewed as a subsystem within the world economy.

An accounting information system also can be viewed in this manner. Payroll,

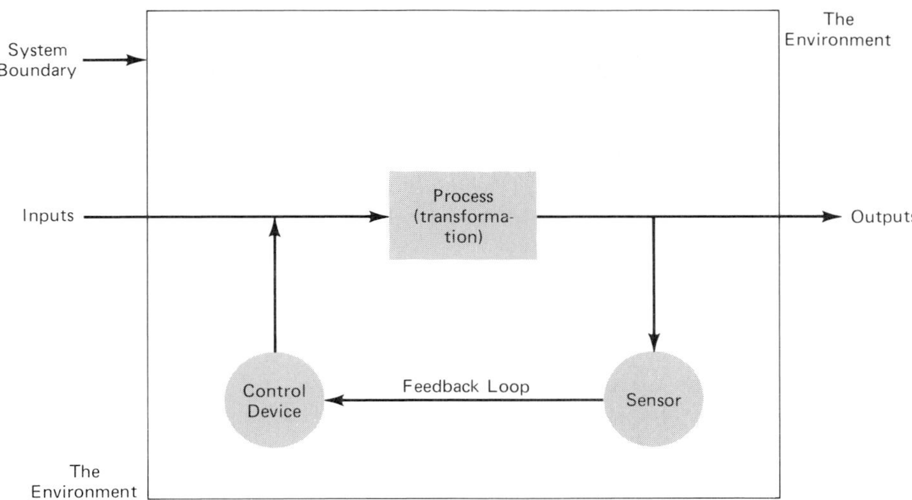

Figure 13-2 Overview of a System

accounts receivable, accounts payable, and inventory can be viewed as subsystems. This relationship is shown in Figure 13-3. Each of these subsystems can be considered systems, and the accounting system can be viewed as the suprasystem or it can be viewed as a subsystem of the management information system. The ability to adjust the level of abstraction by altering the boundary is one of the major advantages of the systems approach.

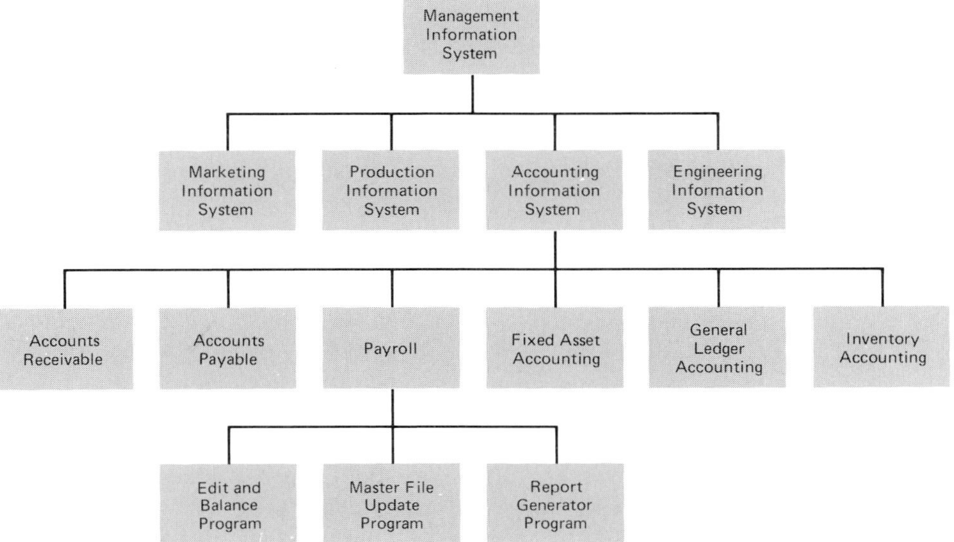

Figure 13-3 Relationship within the Management Information System

Components

Components of a system are units (subsystems) acting in combination with other units to modify inputs in order to produce outputs. Components within a system do not have to be homogeneous. For example, a police officer directing traffic at a congested intersection can be viewed as a component of a complex traffic control system. In this system, signals, signs, lines in the street, and the officer are all components of the system. Systems controlling air traffic and inventory control systems have many nonhomogeneous components.

Boundary

The *boundary* is the area separating one system from another. In information systems, the boundary should not be conceived of as physical in nature. It is a region through which inputs and outputs must pass during exchanges with the system's environment. Definition of the boundary of a system is one of the most important steps in system analysis. C. West Churchman, a leading systems analyst, has suggested posing two questions in order to determine whether an object is within the boundary of a system.[1] First, can the systems analyst do anything about the object in question? Second, is the object important to the objectives of the system? If the answer to both questions is yes, then the object is within the boundary of the system.

The use of these questions is demonstrated in the following example. Assume that a university with a nationally ranked women's basketball team is located in a state with an extensive women's high school basketball program. The basketball coach is considering whether the university should actively recruit and offer scholarships to female basketball players. The other alternative would be to allow the reputation of the team and the location of the university to be the main factors in attracting outstanding players.

If the objective is to maintain the national ranking of the team, then the answer to Churchman's second question is yes. Quality high school players (the object) are important to the objectives of the system (the university maintaining national ranking). If the basketball coach decides not to recruit, the answer to the first question is no, and the state high school basketball program is part of the environment. The boundary of the university women's basketball program lies somewhere between the university and the high school program. If, on the other hand, the coach decides to recruit, then the high school program becomes part of the system to maintain an outstanding women's basketball program at the university. The boundary is then outside the high school program within the state.

In an accounts receivable system, if the customer is defined as part of the environment, the firm has concluded that it cannot influence the time in which the receivable will be paid. However, if the customer is defined as part of the system, the firm has determined that it can influence the timing of payment. Cash discounts, credit limits, interest charges, and other collection policies are actions that can be taken to influence the payment of receivables. A similar situation exists in an inventory control system. If the supplier is considered part of the system, then delivery dates, quantities,

[1] C. West Churchman, *The Systems Approach* (New York: Dell Publishing, 1968), 36.

and modes of transportation can be influenced by the firm. If the supplier is defined as part of the environment, then the firm cannot influence actions by the supplier.

Environment

The *environment* of a system is defined as anything outside the boundary of the system that influences the operation of the system and cannot be controlled by the analyst. Weather is certainly part of the environment of a vegetable garden. If a greenhouse with a climate control system is built over the garden, the boundary of the system has been changed. The environment of the system now includes those systems that supply gas, water, and electricity to the greenhouse.

Inputs

Inputs are the energies taken into the system, and are classified as either maintenance or signal. Maintenance inputs energize the system and make it ready to operate. Signal inputs are the energies to be processed to produce the outputs. Consider a coal-fired electrical generating plant. Maintenance inputs include the electricity necessary to energize the control systems, lubricants for the machinery, and the human input necessary to maintain the system. Signal inputs are the coal used to fire the system and the water that is transformed into steam to power the generators. Electricity and computer programs are the maintenance inputs into a computerized information system. Data are the raw material or signal input processed to produce output from the system.

Outputs

Outputs are the energies discharged from the system into the suprasystem. They are generally classified as products useful to the suprasystem or as waste. The product from the generating station is electric power. Waste includes the steam, smoke, heat, and ash that are discharged into the environment. Modifying some of the waste output so that it goes into making a useful product is one means of improving systems performance. For example, if a greenhouse is built next to the power plant, some of the discharged steam can be used to heat the greenhouse. Industry has used this approach to systems improvement extensively because of the recent emphasis on pollution control. Heat generated by computers and lights is now captured and used for heating some office buildings. CRT screens and reports are examples of the products of an information system. Heat generated by a computer is one of the waste outputs of the system.

Black-Box Concept

It is often impossible to describe the way a system effects a transformation. In addition, it may not be economical to describe a complex system. In some cases, the structure of the transformation may be unknown. If the description of a complex system is too detailed, human beings may not be able to comprehend and manage it.

Under such circumstances, the analyst invokes the *black-box concept*. Rather than describing in detail how the system effects a transformation, the system is defined in terms of inputs and outputs. The black-box concept is based on two assumptions. First, the analyst assumes that the relationship between inputs and outputs will remain stable. In other words, it is assumed that the internal operations of the black box will not change through time. Second, black boxes are assumed to be independent. For example, if a subsystem is described as a black box and is linked to another black box, it should be possible to predict the output from the combination, given the input. The black-box concept makes it possible to enter a hierarchy of systems at any level. The black-box assumption is employed rather than developing a detailed description of each subsystem.

The medical profession makes wide use of the black-box concept in diagnosis. Assume you visit a doctor complaining of stomach pain. First the doctor evaluates other outputs from the system by taking your temperature, blood pressure, pulse, and respiratory count. He or she then might evaluate the appearance of the system by examining your eyes, ears, mouth, and skin color. Then the doctor would begin questioning you about your past medical history and the inputs you have been placing in the system.

After completing the evaluation, the doctor will probably suggest some changes in the inputs. A change in diet and perhaps some medication may be prescribed. Outputs are then evaluated, especially pain. If the pain continues, the doctor will alter the inputs again. When the combination of inputs that eliminates the output of pain is found, you are pronounced cured. If it takes an extended period of time and a number of changes in the inputs before you are cured, you may begin to understand why the doctor is licensed to practice medicine.

In this situation, the doctor has assumed that your body is a black box. Only the inputs and outputs have been considered in your treatment. The situation would have to be very serious before the doctor would consider entering the black box to observe its internal condition. There is considerable risk in opening the black box because infection or other problems might result. There is also a considerable economic advantage realized in treating the system as a black box.

Now consider the information system of a large corporation. The system could be analyzed at a very macro level by considering such subsystems as marketing, inventory control, and manufacturing to be black boxes. Another approach might be to consider the inventory control system. Raw materials, work in process, finished goods, and supplies subsystems could then be viewed as black boxes. At a more micro level, the supplies inventory control system could be considered, and the subsystems for various types of supplies could be seen as black boxes. In this way, the analyst can move back and forth between a macro and micro description of the system. In moving from macro to micro subsystems, a point is eventually reached where the black-box concept is invoked. Certainly, when considering an information system, one is not concerned with the molecular structure of the paper used in the system.

MANAGEMENT CASE 13-1

Sharon Smith is a new internal auditor for General Motors. During her recruitment she was told that General Motors has one of the most complex and effective cost accounting systems in the world. She knows that in her new job she will be expected to perform audits on this cost accounting system. Currently she is very concerned about her capability to understand the cost accounting system. She feels that it is so large and complex that it will take years for her to master it. Do you think the black box concept would be of any use to Sharon?

Interface

Interface is a term frequently used in systems analysis. The *interface* is the region between the boundaries of systems and is also the medium for transporting the output from one system to the input of another system. It does not alter the output of one system that is input to another system.

For example, assume that an individual taxpayer and the Internal Revenue Service are systems. The United States Postal Service is then the interface between the two systems. When two people are engaged in a conversation, air is the interface that transports the sound between them. The interface between two computer systems can be a telephone line or a microwave transmission system.

Open and Closed Systems

Open systems accept inputs from the environment; *closed systems* are assumed not to interact with the environment. All systems are open to some degree, but it is often convenient to assume that a system is closed for purposes of analysis.

When considering open and closed systems, the concept of entropy is important. *Entropy* is a measure of disorder within a system. It was noted when inputs were discussed that maintenance inputs are required by open systems. One of the functions of maintenance inputs is to maintain order within a system. In open systems, depending on the quantity of the maintenance inputs, entropy can decrease, remain constant, or increase. In a closed system, entropy never decreases.

Several examples should help clarify the concept of entropy. Consider a body in a sealed casket. It can be viewed as a closed system. The body will slowly decompose, and the matter that made up the body will move from a state of order to increasing disorder. Entropy within the system will therefore increase.

A watch can be viewed as a closed system, but some watches must be wound periodically. Winding is an energy input necessary to keep the watch operating. Some might believe that a self-winding watch is an example of a closed system. However, it is necessary to move the watch to keep it operating. This is an energy input, and therefore the watch is an open system. Battery-run watches can operate for several years before a new battery is necessary. However, at some point an input from the environment will become necessary. This type of analysis leads to the conclusion that no system operates in isolation from its environment.

Now consider entropy in terms of a human organization viewed as a system. The Shakers were a religious group that did not believe in engaging in sexual relations. Therefore, new membership was limited to those born outside the church who elected to join. New members could not join the church as a result of being born into Shaker families since birth was precluded by the beliefs of the church. This is an example of a system that is open, but only to a limited degree. Members die off, and the church moves toward a state of disorder. Eventually it will cease to exist unless new members from outside the church can be found.

On the other hand, a bureaucracy is an example of a human organization that moves toward increasing order. The bureaucratic solution to any variation within the organization is to create rules and procedures for dealing with any new situation. This may explain in part why the bureaucratic form of organization is frequently considered inefficient. If the system is moving toward more order, part of the input is being utilized to make the increasing order possible. As order increases further, more of the input must be employed to maintain the existing order within the system.

Assuming that a system is closed greatly simplifies the definition and analysis of that system. However, this assumption also limits analysis. Since all systems exist within a suprasystem, the outputs from a system must be acceptable inputs for some component of the suprasystem. Also, the inputs required by the system must be supplied by some component of the suprasystem. Therefore, when a system is viewed as being closed, there is a danger that the life support relationship between the system and its suprasystem will not be considered.

FEEDBACK

To comprehend how systems survive and adapt to their environment, it is necessary to understand the concept of feedback. *Feedback* is a process by which the output of a system is measured against a standard. Any difference between the two is corrected by altering the input. A system with and without a feedback loop is shown in Figure 13-4.

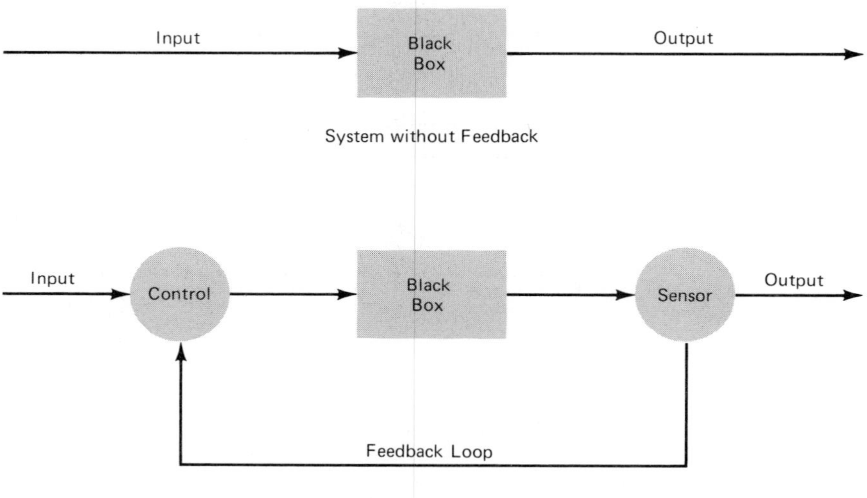

Figure 13-4 A System with and without a Feedback Loop

Consider a traffic light that is operated by a timer. Every ninety seconds the light changes, and the direction of traffic through the intersection is altered. Signals of this type often cause traffic jams because they stop traffic on a heavily traveled street when there are no vehicles on the cross street. This is an example of a system without feedback. The performance of such a system could be improved by installing sensors in the surface of the street. The sensors would indicate when a vehicle was waiting at the intersection. This feedback loop would eliminate the problem of the signal cycling when no vehicles are in the cross street.

Incorporating a memory into the feedback loop also improves system performance. For example, the traffic light's feedback loop could contain a memory that would operate the light at different sequences at various times of the day.

The concept of feedback is very important in an information system. Output from this system is used in decision making. If the output is not relevant to the decisions, then the system is of little use to management. Therefore, it is important that a feedback loop be incorporated into the system to determine the relevance of output to the decision environment.

An example of a feedback loop in an information system is the inclusion of standard costs in a purchasing subsystem. Signal inputs into the system are the quantities purchased, specifications, identification codes, and actual purchase prices. Outputs from the system that serve as input to the inventory control system are the quantities purchased at the standard unit cost. In the feedback loop, the standard and actual costs for the purchased items are compared. This information can then be forwarded to the purchasing manager, who can take the necessary steps to ensure that future purchase costs do not deviate significantly from standard costs.

In this example, if the standard costs are out of date, the feedback information will be irrelevant to identifying inefficiencies in the purchasing operation. Therefore, one of the necessary maintenance inputs of the system is adjustment of standard costs in order to keep them current.

VARIETY AND CONTROL

Consider a basketball team of such skill that its members never miss a shot, make a bad pass, or commit a foul. Given these attributes, it is impossible for this team to lose a game. It might be interesting to play against this team or watch it play once or twice. But interest would quickly decrease for spectators and opponents alike. Why watch or play against a team that never loses or makes any mistakes during the game? Because of this team's overall efficiency, there is no variety in the winner of any contest.

If all activities were similar to those of this hypothetical basketball team, life would be very boring. Indeed, we enjoy basketball and other contests because of the potential variety in their outcomes. Even the greatest basketball players miss shots, commit fouls, and throw bad passes.

Basketball can be viewed as a game with a generally accepted set of rules that are enforced by officials. The rules state that for a player to advance the ball, it must be passed or dribbled. Body contact is limited, and a defensive player must follow certain rules when guarding an offensive player. For each violation of the rules there is a penalty. When a player walks with the ball, his or her team loses possession. If one player blocks another, that player is charged with a foul. Under certain conditions, the fouled player can shoot a foul shot. Other circumstances may allow his or her team to gain possession of the ball. There is a limit to the number of fouls a player can be charged with before disqualification from the game.

For every variety of infraction of the basketball rules, the referees have a countermeasure. In this way they can control the game, ensuring that, in their judgment, it is played according to the rules. This is an example of a law developed by Ross Ashby that relates to the control of systems. *Ashby's law of requisite variety* states that to control a system there must be available a number of countermeasures equal to the variety displayed by the output of the system.[2]

[2]H. R. Ashby, *Introduction to Cybernetics* (New York: John Wiley, 1963).

For example, if a basketball player commits a foul in getting the ball, and there is no countermeasure (penalty) available to the referee to enforce the rule, the game is out of control. The player can continue to violate the rule indefinitely. With a countermeasure, the referee can penalize the offending player and control the game. In general, then, to control a system, it is necessary for the control mechanism to possess the same amount of variety displayed by the system.

In the real world, we often develop countermeasures only for those events that have a high probability of occurring. While reading this material, you probably do not have a countermeasure for the sudden collapse of the roof of your building. By the same token, you will not count the words in this chapter because you assign an extremely low probability to your instructor asking how many it contains. Indeed, this is how individuals learn to control their environment. Without this filtering process, we could not cope with the variety in our environment.

There are several consequences of the law of requisite variety in dealing with systems. To gain control of a system, two basic strategies are available: 1) decreasing the variety of outputs from the system; or 2) increasing the number of countermeasures. When dealing with large systems that exhibit a great variety of outputs, Ashby's law gives the analyst a sense of proportion. For instance, it may not be feasible for the analyst to obtain the necessary number of countermeasures to gain control over a system. In this situation, the analyst seeks countermeasures for events that only have a high probability of occurring or that will produce a large expected loss.

In the business world, there are many examples of how the variety of system output is controlled by various countermeasures. For instance, in an inventory control system, procedures accounting for gold used in a production process are different from those accounting for metal fasteners with a unit cost of one cent. In a credit card system, different procedures are employed in evaluating available credit depending on the amount of purchase. Consider your experience when purchasing an appliance or piece of jewelry compared to the purchase of a candy bar.

MANAGEMENT CASE 13-2

Ruth Kowalski is enrolled in an MBA program and she is also working as a manager of the product development department of the Southern Corporation. Currently she is enrolled in an MIS course and has covered the concepts of variety and control. She was particularly interested in these concepts and thought they made a lot of sense. In fact, she feels she can apply them immediately to her job. She plans to look upon her job as the management of a system. In fact, she feels that she can anticipate most of the variety that will occur within her department. With predesigned controls she feels that she will be able to guide the department toward her objectives. Ruth is convinced that this will be her basic philosophical approach to management. Do you think that the concepts of variety and control can be the basic underlying theory upon which a manager builds his or her approach to management?

SYSTEMS AND INFORMATION PROCESSING

General systems theory, which we have covered thus far in this chapter, is the theory underlying information systems. It is a very good fit. When we cover systems analysis in chapter 14 you will see that we use many of the concepts that have been introduced in this chapter. To deal with complex systems we must use a methodology for hierarchically decomposing these systems into manageable subsystems. This is the basic approach of general systems theory and systems analysis.

An information system itself is a subsystem of a firm. It is the subsystem providing formal information for managing the firm from the highest to the lowest levels of decision making.

In analyzing and designing an information system, an analyst directly applies many of the concepts introduced in this chapter. Drawing the boundary around a proposed information system helps an analyst isolate the problem with which he or she is dealing. The black-box concept is useful in areas where it is not necessary for the analyst to understand the transformation process that is going on. Many information systems, especially accounting-type information systems, are essentially feedback systems for management. These systems produce reports summarizing results of the firm's operations and allow management to take corrective actions in the firm's inputs to change future outputs. In designing an information system, an analyst must constantly keep in mind the concept of variety and control. There are many ways that information systems can get out of control and not function properly. An analyst must anticipate these problems, and design countermeasures in the system to bring it back under control. For example, an erroneous material item number in a manufacturing resources planning system could cause the wrong material to be ordered for manufacturing. The manufacturing assembly line would then be shut down for a period of time. The system should be designed to detect erroneous material item numbers and correct them prior to ordering material.

In summary, it would be a mistake to conclude that general systems theory concepts are too abstract and therefore not important to an information systems practitioner. These concepts are the theoretical basis for many day-to-day actions taken by information systems professionals. The usefulness of general systems theory is also not limited to information systems. As stated earlier in this chapter, systems and systems analysis are a philosophy and methodology of dealing with many different kinds of complex problems.

SUMMARY

In education, economic savings can be realized as students master abstract material that has broad potential application.

Systems and systems analysis are a philosophy and methodology for viewing complex wholes at a manageable level of abstraction.

A system is defined as a set of interacting components that operate within a boundary for some purpose.

The boundary is the area separating one system from another.

The environment of a system is defined as anything outside the boundary of the system that influences the operation of the system and cannot be controlled by the analyst.

Inputs are energies taken into the system.

Outputs are energies discharged from the system into the suprasystem.

Using the black-box concept, a system is defined in terms of inputs and outputs rather than in terms of the transformation that occurs.

An interface is the region between the boundaries of systems and is also the medium for transporting the output from one system to the input of another.

Open systems accept inputs from the environment.

Closed systems are assumed not to interact with the environment.

Entropy is a measure of disorder within a system.

Feedback is a process by which the output of a system is measured against a standard. Any difference between the two is corrected by altering the input.

Ashby's law of requisite variety states that to control a system there must be available a number of countermeasures equal to the variety displayed by the output of the system.

General systems theory is the theoretical basis for many day-to-day actions taken by information systems professionals.

KEY TERMS

System
Systems Analysis
Components
Subsystem
Suprasystem
Boundary
Environment
Inputs
Outputs
Black Box Concept
Interface
Open System
Closed System
Entropy
Feedback
Variety and Control
Ashby's Law of Requisite Variety
Process Transformation

REVIEW QUESTIONS

1. In the study of systems, what might a biologist, an economist, a psychologist, and an industrial engineer have in common?

2. Explain why marketing majors study finance and economics. Relate your answer to the study of systems.

3. A system consists of a set of interacting components (subsystems). For each of the following systems identify some appropriate subsystems.
a. Blood cell
b. Human body
c. County school system
d. University
e. Management information system
f. Industrial firm
g. Legal system
h. Basketball team

4. Identify the objectives, inputs, outputs, and performance measures of your college or university. Make some recommendations for improving the performance of the system by analyzing the inputs and outputs.

5. Explain why the identification of a system's boundary is very important in system analysis.
6. Identify some of the maintenance and signal inputs received by a college student majoring in a business area.
7. Identify and classify the inputs and outputs of a gasoline engine.
8. Identify and classify the inputs and outputs of the United States income tax system.
9. Is it possible to describe a system without invoking the black-box concept? Explain.
10. Identify some examples in which an information systems analyst would employ the black-box concept.
11. Conceptually, what are the advantages realized from viewing a system as open rather than closed? Can you identify circumstances under which it might be advantageous to view a system as closed?
12. Describe the feedback mechanism in a budgeting control system.
13. Describe some of the typical feedback mechanisms used in a collegiate educational system.
14. Employing the concepts in Ashby's law of requisite variety, discuss your professor's guidance and control of your class.
15. Assume you are watching five children, all of whom are under the age of four. Describe how you would use the two basic strategies from Ashby's law of requisite variety to control the situation.
16. Arrange the following in a hierarchy from micro to macro systems:
    a. Electron
    b. Biological system
    c. Organism
    d. Tissue
    e. Molecule
    f. Universal system
    g. Organ
    h. Atom
    i. Cell
17. Indicate some of the countermeasures (requisite variety) that might be useful in the following systems that are considered out of control:
    a. Murder in a social system
    b. Overpopulation in a biological system
    c. Shortage of cash in a cash receipts system
    d. Theft of inventory in an inventory system

DISCUSSION QUESTIONS

1. Discuss the pros and cons of the following statement: General systems theory is abstract and rarely applicable in the real world.

2. Most students using this text are pursuing a college degree. Discuss how the concepts of general systems theory would be useful to you in evaluating your pursuit of this degree.

3. Although we will be covering this subject in depth in the next two chapters, anticipate how general systems theory could be used in the analysis and design of information systems.

RESEARCH PROJECTS

1. Interview faculty from several different departments within your university or college and determine if general systems theory is taught within these departments. Suggested departments for interviewing are: Industrial Engineering, Management Science, Management, Accounting, Economics, Computer Science, Electrical Engineering, and Education. If you find that general systems theory is taught within several different disciplines, what does this indicate about the usefulness of general systems theory?

2. Identify a real world business system. Employing the concepts of Ashby's law of requisite variety, outline countermeasures used to keep the system in control.

APPLICATION CASE

DP/Management Gap Seen Getting Wider

(Reprinted with permission from MIS Week, July 28, 1982, p. 19)

By Linda Stein

CAMBRIDGE, Mass.—Index Systems Inc., an information systems consulting and software development firm here, stresses the need to bridge the gap between information systems technology and management needs.

"The culture gap between management and DP is still widening as the second wave of the computer revolution breaks full force on both business and society," said John Thompson, Index vice president.

"As a result, an operational swamp of old application software systems which need to be replaced by new technology, and of mounting demands from top management due to changing business requirements, has ensnared DP managers of small and large companies alike in what looks like a no-win situation," he added.

In its efforts to tie technological innovation to bottom-line business results, Index uses a variety of techniques and methodologies, among them the Critical Success Factor (CSF) technique, created by John F. Rockart, director of the Center for Information Systems Management at MIT's Sloan School.

The CSF technique, introduced by Rockart in 1979, is a procedure for developing plans and setting priorities on the use of information technology in support of business decisions.

The technique, said Gary K. Gulden, Index vice president, "is an interviewing technique to help a manager separate out in his or her mind the end results that he or she wants to achieve, as opposed to the things that must go right for the result to be achieved." Gulden added, "People's thinking is primarily oriented to the end result, and not to day-to-day activities."

Gulden pointed out that technological proliferation has made many firms "data-rich and information-poor," with managers in possession of information that is not as useful as it could be in the business context.

"The reason Index worries about this is that we feel the only reason a firm should have information systems at all is to provide them with a competitive advantage," Gulden said.

Thompson added, "We want to provide a way of looking at the use of information systems technology so it can accomplish a business gain for our client. An information system has no value in and of itself. And if you're in the information systems business it's easy to get carried away with technology."

He continued, "The value of the CSF technique is to back off from this, to make information systems more relevant, so that information systems activities are clearly linked to strategic objectives."

To illustrate the use of the CSF technique, Gulden said, "A company may wish for an end result of 'sales growth' or 'market share,' but you can't 'do' market share." Instead, he said, the firm can use the technique to isolate the critical success factors necessary for achieving those end results, for example, "getting new products to market first" and "penetrating the Southeast."

Jacque Huber, vice president of sales at Ohio Steel Inc., Hamilton, Ohio, said, "We were introduced to CSF by Gary (Gulden) and the Index team. We had engaged them to do an analysis and forward look to our second phase of computerization."

Before Index could analyze the firm's computer science needs, they "needed an idea of what our needs, goal and critical success factors are," Huber said.

The CSF analysis, done from the point of view of Ohio Steel's information systems needs, "boiled down to three major areas," said Huber. These were "the ability to merchandise steel which is the matching of buyers with sellers; management of the inventory, and customer happiness in relation to service," Huber said.

"Having identified those as the three things important to our success, we used those three to design our information systems," he said. "The CSF technique not only kept us on the right track—it created the track. All of us were entering into a new MIS arena, and none of us had a great deal of knowledge about what to expect. We felt skeptical because we had grown successful with our old manual systems and seat-of-the-pants development."

Huber continued, "To say you're going to expose these things (previous successful development) to MIS made us fear loss of control, and fear that we would lose touch with reality. But CSF enabled us to have information systems which dealt with our critical success factors in a reasonable and logical fashion, with a great deal of control and clarity."

Robert Benjamin, manager of information management strategic planning, Xerox Corp. corporate staff, Rochester, N.Y., called CSF "a nice friendly interviewing technique to try to deal with the dialogue between the systems crowd and senior management to identify what management thinks is important. It's nice to keep the technique in your bag of tricks to fall back on."

Discussion

There is no doubt that application software is the most important aspect of computers for business users. It is often too easy to get carried away with technology. In systems analysis, the first step is determining the critical success factors. The information requirements for the system must be based on these critical success factors.

1. How are critical success factors related to objectives?
2. Do you feel that managers have difficulty in identifying their critical success factors? Do you feel that interview techniques as discussed in the application case are necessary?

PART FOUR

DEVELOPMENT OF USER APPLICATIONS

CHAPTER 14
SYSTEMS ANALYSIS

INTRODUCTION

As a user, all of the hardware, operating systems, data storage approaches, etc., that we have discussed thus far are useless to you unless you have the application software for the job you wish the computer to perform. Application software, acquired through purchasing or self-development is fast becoming the most expensive aspect of information systems. The price of hardware has continued to decline due to technological advances. Unfortunately, advances in software development have not kept up with those in hardware. In fact, the cost of software continues to increase primarily because software development is a labor intensive process.

However, there have been significant advances in approaches to the development of application software. Chapters 14, 15, and 16 will introduce you to the latest approaches to application software development. These approaches have resulted in significant time and cost savings for the many firms that have applied them. Such firms have avoided some of the perennial problems of application development, which are being over budget, and being sometimes years behind schedule. There have been some real disasters in the application development process. These include systems that did not produce desired output, systems that did not work at all, and systems that were out of date as soon as they became operational.

If you, as a user, are to avoid these pitfalls, you should be thoroughly familiar with the latest approaches to application software development or purchase. For the application development process to be successful, you must be able to communicate with the systems analyst who is responsible for designing and implementing the system. Ultimately, if a system fails, you as a user will lose because, after all, it is your system that is being developed and you are ultimately responsible for it. This chapter explores the first major step in systems development, which is systems analysis. First, we will briefly discuss partitioning of systems, upon which systems analysis is based. We will then consider classical systems development. This section is followed by a more detailed discussion of structured analysis, an approach that has become quite popular in recent years.

PARTITIONING OF SYSTEMS

As discussed in chapter 13, *systems analysis* is a method for dealing with complex systems. Perhaps the most important concept in systems theory for the development of computer applications is the idea that any system can be partitioned into subsystems (refer to Figure 14-1). This figure illustrates a hierarchical partitioning of a management information system into leveled sets of subsystems. Notice that we have partitioned the accounting information system into its various subsystem, and the payroll system into three subsystems. If the objective of our systems development project is to modify reports produced by the payroll system, then we have drawn a boundary around a subsystem. The report generator program will be our primary interest in the development process.

Figure 14-1 is an oversimplification since the inputs and outputs of each system and their interfaces with other systems are not depicted. An *interface* is the movement of inputs or outputs from one system to another. Certainly, in a systems development project we must be concerned about these interfaces. We will see later in this chapter, and in the next chapter, how these interfaces are handled. However, the crucial point to understand here is that this hierarchical partitioning is the key to structured analysis, design, and programming of computer applications. We will use this concept in one form or another throughout the systems development process.

In fact, the term "structured" is closely related to hierarchical partitioning. The American Heritage Dictionary defines structure as the interrelation of parts, or the principal organization in a complex entity. Our use of the term in this book simply means a system is hierarchically partitioned into subsystems, and these subsystems' interfaces with one another are rigorously defined.

CLASSICAL SYSTEMS DEVELOPMENT

Feasibility Study

Classical systems development is illustrated in Figure 14-2. The feasibility study is equivalent to a minianalysis phase. In fact, in the feasibility study the analyst performs

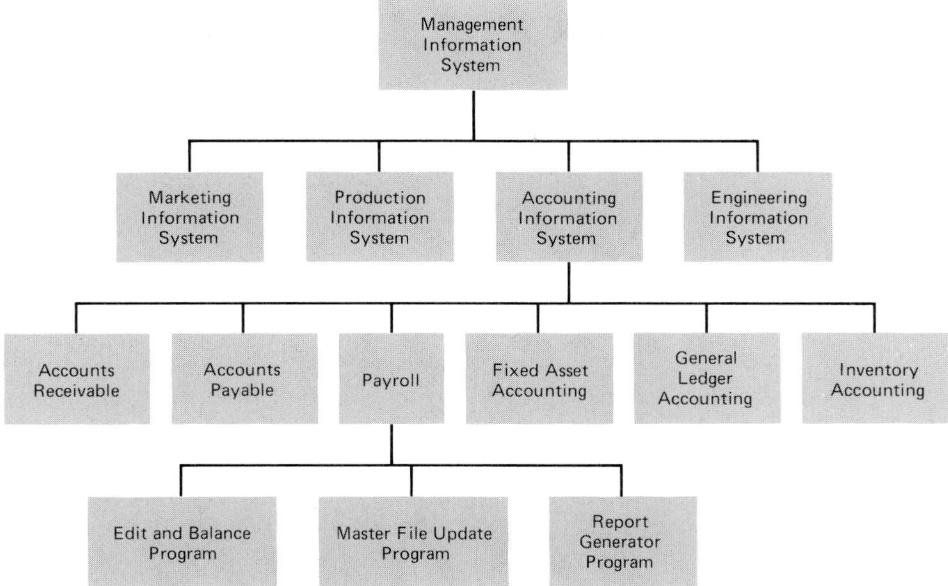

Figure 14-1 Partitioning of a System

many of the same steps that will be performed in the analysis phase, but much less thoroughly. The primary purpose of a feasibility study is to identify the objectives of a user system, and to determine whether or not the benefits of a new system justify the expense of a systems development project. The major inputs to the feasibility study are interviews and collection of source and working documents from users. The feasibility study produces a feasibility document, which should contain the following:

1. project name
2. description of the problem
3. statement of the critical assumptions on which the feasibility document is based
4. statement of the performance requirements of the system
5. general description of the proposed system solution (this can be a new, modified or existing system)
6. evaluation of the feasibility of the proposed system
7. feasible alternative solutions

Analysis

The analysis phase has as its major input the feasibility document and additional interviews with users. This phase produces a budget and schedule for the development effort, the physical requirements (which are the major input to the hardware study), and a functional specification document. The functional specification contains much the same types of information as the feasibility document, but in much greater depth. In classical systems development, functional specification documents tended to be

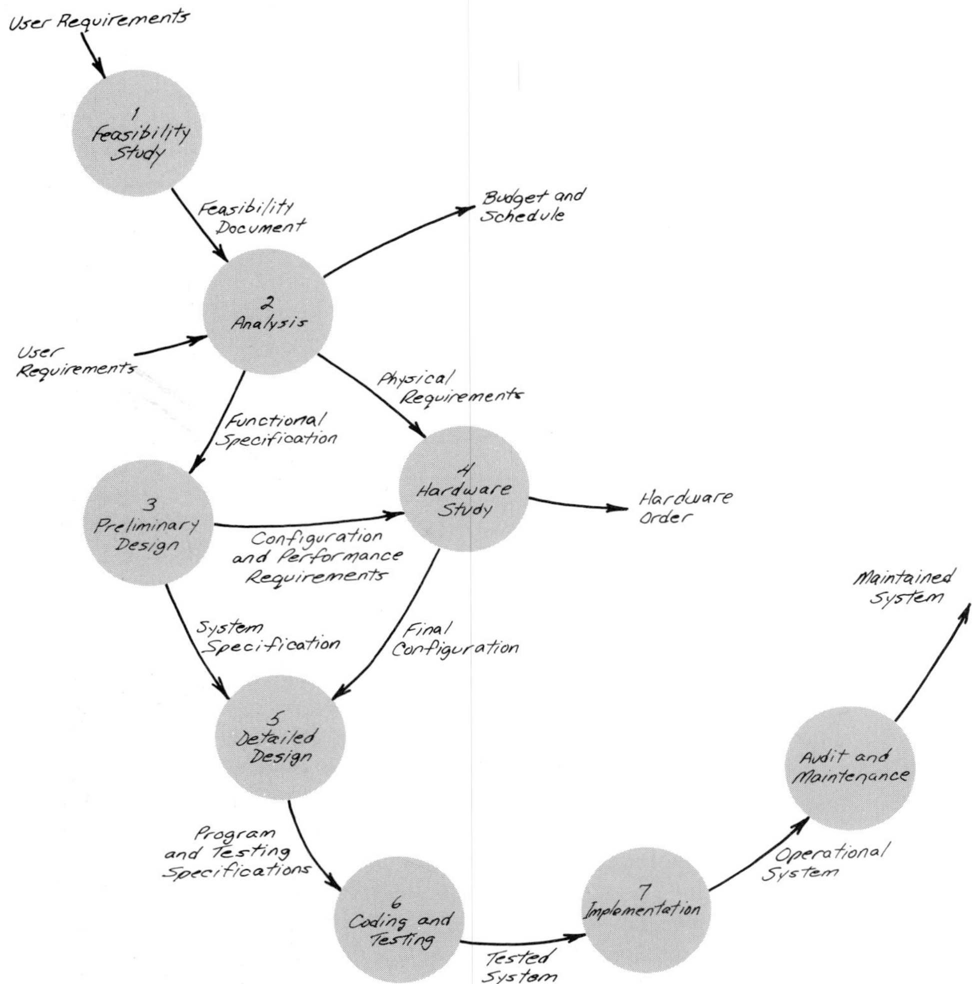

Figure 14-2 Classical Systems Development Life Cycle. Adapted with permission from Tom DeMarco, *Structured Analysis and System Specification* (New York, Yourdon, Inc., 1979), 20.

primarily narrative in nature. This is a major drawback since a narrative is often difficult to read, interpret, and update whenever changes are necessary.

One of the graphic tools often used in classical systems development, which is sometimes used in structured system development, is the system flowchart. Figure 14-3 illustrates a system flowchart for an accounts receivable system. *System flowcharts* represent the flow of data or information through a system. Figure 14-4 defines the symbols used in these flowcharts. System flowcharts do not give detailed characteristics of each program within the system. For example, in Figure 14-3, the master file update program is depicted without indicating the detailed steps within this program. These

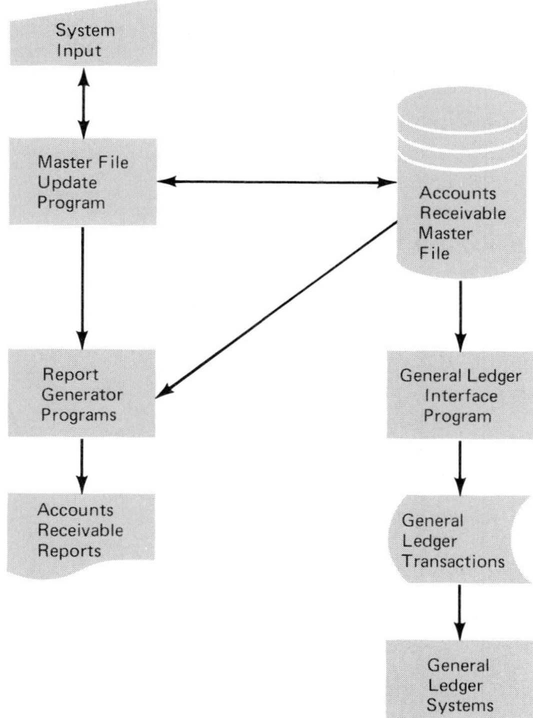

Figure 14-3 Accounts Receivable System Flowchart

detailed steps are depicted by program flowcharts, which we will discuss later in this chapter.

The major focus of the system flowchart is on inputs, processes, and outputs resulting from sequences employed on computer programs. System flowcharts are often drawn in much greater detail than in Figure 14-3. For example, see Figure 14-5, which depicts a payroll system. Note also that system flowcharts tend to be physical in nature. That is, they identify the ways that data are physically stored, input and output. For example, the accounts receivable master file in Figure 14-3 is depicted as being physically stored on a disk file. Later on, when we discuss structured analysis, we will see that the data flow diagrams used there tend to deemphasize physical aspects of the system.

Design and Implementation

The hardware study and preliminary design phases can go on concurrently. The hardware study should result in at least a tentative selection of hardware (evaluation of computer hardware will be covered in more depth in chapter 18). The preliminary design phase involves decisions concerning the primary modules or programs that the proposed system will contain, drawing system flowcharts, and defining major files and output reports. Essentially, these two phases provide enough overall design to the

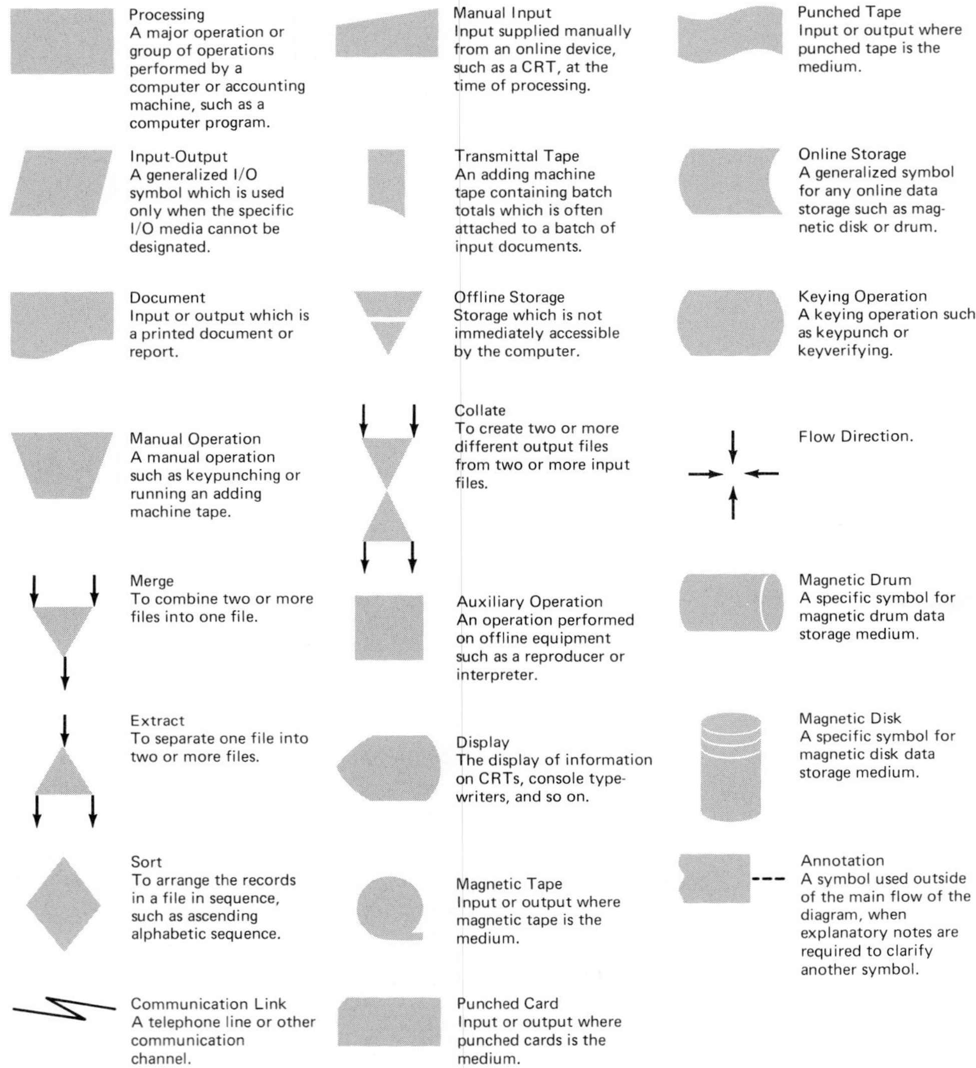

Processing
A major operation or group of operations performed by a computer or accounting machine, such as a computer program.
Manual Input
Input supplied manually from an online device, such as a CRT, at the time of processing.
Punched Tape
Input or output where punched tape is the medium.
Input-Output
A generalized I/O symbol which is used only when the specific I/O media cannot be designated.
Transmittal Tape
An adding machine tape containing batch totals which is often attached to a batch of input documents.
Online Storage
A generalized symbol for any online data storage such as magnetic disk or drum.
Document
Input or output which is a printed document or report.
Offline Storage
Storage which is not immediately accessible by the computer.
Keying Operation
A keying operation such as keypunch or keyverifying.
Manual Operation
A manual operation such as keypunching or running an adding machine tape.
Collate
To create two or more different output files from two or more input files.
Flow Direction.
Merge
To combine two or more files into one file.
Auxiliary Operation
An operation performed on offline equipment such as a reproducer or interpreter.
Magnetic Drum
A specific symbol for magnetic drum data storage medium.
Extract
To separate one file into two or more files.
Display
The display of information on CRTs, console typewriters, and so on.
Magnetic Disk
A specific symbol for magnetic disk data storage medium.
Sort
To arrange the records in a file in sequence, such as ascending alphabetic sequence.
Magnetic Tape
Input or output where magnetic tape is the medium.
Annotation
A symbol used outside of the main flow of the diagram, when explanatory notes are required to clarify another symbol.
Communication Link
A telephone line or other communication channel.
Punched Card
Input or output where punched cards is the medium.

Figure 14-4 System Flowchart Symbols

system so that a decision can be made whether to go ahead with the more expensive, detailed design of the proposed system.

In the detailed design phase the nitty-gritty of the system is designed. This includes completion of the modularization of individual programs within the system, file layouts and data definitions (see Figure 14-6), report layouts (see Figure 14-7), interfaces between program modules, and testing specifications. The detailed design phase provides programmers with a blueprint of the system, which can be used for coding and testing programs.

A primary tool used in classical detailed design is the program flowchart. Figure

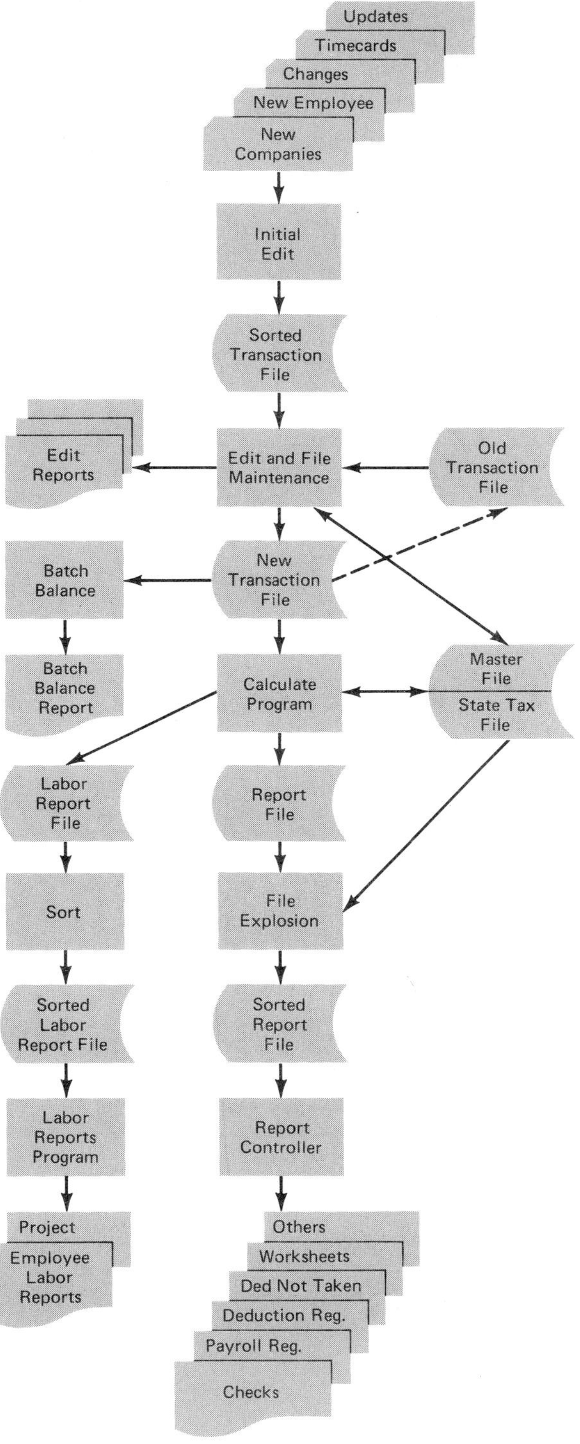

Figure 14-5 Payroll System Flowchart. Used by permission of General Computer Services, Inc.

IBM RECORD FORMAT

APPLICATION . . Accounts Receivable . . . . RECORD NAME . . . Master File . . . .

Field Name	Parent Segment	Customer Number CUST-NO	Customer Name CUST-NAME	Customer Address CUST-ADDR	Customer City and State CUST-CITY-STATE	Cus C
Characteristics*		9(6)	X(35)	X(35)	X(35)	
Position**		1-9	10-44	45-79	80-114	11

Number of Invoice Segments NO-INVOICES	Number of Payment Segments NO-PAYMENTS	
9(3)	9(3)	
176-178	179-181	

Payment Segment	Date PMT-DATE	Payment Number PMT-NO	Payment Amount PMT-AMT	Unapplied Balance UNAPPLIED	
	9(6)	9(9)	9(6)V99	9(6)V99	
	1-6	7-15	16-23	24-31	

Invoice Segment	Date INV-DATE	Invoice Number INV-NO	Payment Terms TERMS	Customer P O Number PO-NUM	Number of Item Segments NO-ITEMS	
	9(6)	9(9)	X(9)	9(9)	9(3)	
	1-6	7-15	16-24	25-33	34-36	

Item Segment	Item Number ITEM	Item Description DESC	Quantity QTY	Price Each PRICE	Payment Number Reference PMT-NO-REF	
	9(8)	X(35)	9(4)	9(6)V99	9(9)	
	1-8	9-43	44-47	48-55	56-54	

**POSITION
Hexadecimal / Decimal
Numbering
from
00 to FF / 0 to 255

HEXADECIMAL	00	01	02	03	04	05	06	07	08	09	0A	0B	0C	0D	0E	0F	10	11	12	13	14	15	16	17	18	19	1A	1B
DECIMAL	0	1	2	3	4	5	6	7	8	9	10	11	12	13	14	15	16	17	18	19	20	21	22	23	24	25	26	27
HEX	40	41	42	43	44	45	46	47	48	49	4A	4B	4C	4D	4E	4F	50	51	52	53	54	55	56	57	58	59	5A	5B
DEC	64	65	66	67	68	69	70	71	72	73	74	75	76	77	78	79	80	81	82	83	84	85	86	87	88	89	90	91
HEX	80	81	82	83	84	85	86	87	88	89	8A	8B	8C	8D	8E	8F	90	91	92	93	94	95	96	97	98	99	9A	9B
DEC	128	129	130	131	132	133	134	135	136	137	138	139	140	141	142	143	144	145	146	147	148	149	150	151	152	153	154	155
HEX	C0	C1	C2	C3	C4	C5	C6	C7	C8	C9	CA	CB	CC	CD	CE	CF	D0	D1	D2	D3	D4	D5	D6	D7	D8	D9	DA	DB
DEC	192	193	194	195	196	197	198	199	200	201	202	203	204	205	206	207	208	209	210	211	212	213	214	215	216	217	218	219

File Description Accounts Receivable Master File

Recording Mode Variable

Records per Block

Record Size

Label Records are Standard

File Identification AR. MASTER

File Serial Number ZBL 594

Retention Cycle 2 years

Organization Type Indexed Sequential

- - fold to here

*CHARACTERISTICS

Check the box that corresponds to the characteristics used:

☐ System/360 Characteristic Codes

A - address value, full word
B - binary
C - character, 8-bit code
D - floating-point, double word
E - floating-point, full word
F - fixed-point, full word
H - fixed-point, halfword
P - packed decimal
S - address, base displacement
V - address, external symbol
X - hexadecimal, 4-bit code
Y - address value, halfword
Z - zoned decimal

☑ General Characteristics

A - alphabetic or blank
X - alphanumeric
9 - numeric
V - assumed decimal point

Examples of Signed Fields:
X9999 999X
X999V99 9999V9X

Figure 14-6 A File Layout

.... BY .. John Smith......... DATE .. 9-25-8X .... PAGE . 1 . OF .. 1 .....

tomer Zip Code UST-ZIP	Salesperson Code SALESPERSON	Telephone No. PHONE-NO.	Contact Name CONTACT	Credit Limit CREDIT-LIMIT	Credit Rating CREDIT-RATING
9(5)	99	9(10)	X(35)	9(6)	X(3)
5-119	120-121	122-131	132-166	167-172	173-175

1C	1D	1E	1F	20	21	22	23	24	25	26	27	28	29	2A	2B	2C	2D	2E	2F	30	31	32	33	34	35	36	37	38	39	3A	3B	3C	3D	3E	3F
28	29	30	31	32	33	34	35	36	37	38	39	40	41	42	43	44	45	46	47	48	49	50	51	52	53	54	55	56	57	58	59	60	61	62	63

5C	5D	5E	5F	60	61	62	63	64	65	66	67	68	69	6A	6B	6C	6D	6E	6F	70	71	72	73	74	75	76	77	78	79	7A	7B	7C	7D	7E	7F
92	93	94	95	96	97	98	99	100	101	102	103	104	105	106	107	108	109	110	111	112	113	114	115	116	117	118	119	120	121	122	123	124	125	126	127

9C	9D	9E	9F	A0	A1	A2	A3	A4	A5	A6	A7	A8	A9	AA	AB	AC	AD	AE	AF	B0	B1	B2	B3	B4	B5	B6	B7	B8	B9	BA	BB	BC	BD	BE	BF
156	157	158	159	160	161	162	163	164	165	166	167	168	169	170	171	172	173	174	175	176	177	178	179	180	181	182	183	184	185	186	187	188	189	190	191

DC	DD	DE	DF	E0	E1	E2	E3	E4	E5	E6	E7	E8	E9	EA	EB	EC	ED	EE	EF	F0	F1	F2	F3	F4	F5	F6	F7	F8	F9	FA	FB	FC	FD	FE	FF
220	221	222	223	224	225	226	227	228	229	230	231	232	233	234	235	236	237	238	239	240	241	242	243	244	245	246	247	248	249	250	251	252	253	254	255

SORTING FIELDS (Major to Minor)	
1 Customer Number	7
2	8
3	9
4	10
5	11
6	12

WHERE USED	
Input From	Output To
A.R. Update	A.R. Update
	A.R. Reports
	A.R. Query

Date	Revisions By

REMARKS

† The number of forms per pad may vary slightly.

144/10/6 PRINT CHART PROG. ID. PREDIT PAGE 1 of 1
(SPACING: 144 POSITION SPAN, AT 10 CHARACTERS PER INCH, 6 LINES PER VERTICAL INCH) DATE 3-15-81
PROGRAM TITLE Payroll Edit
PROGRAMMER OR DOCUMENTALIST: Ray M. Hart
CHART TITLE Time Card Proof List

Fold back at dotted line — Fold in at dotted line

Sort Sequence: Last Name within Department Number

IBM Form X20-1776-0 U/M 025 Printed in U.S.A.

NOTE: Dimensions on this sheet vary with humidity. Exact measurements should be calculated or scaled with a ruler rather than with the lines on this chart.

CARRIAGE CONTROL

```
 2  REPORT ID: PREDIT-02                                    TIME CARD PROOF LIST                                   PAGE 999
 3                                                                                                             DATE 99-99-99
 5          SOCIAL                                                PERIOD
 6   DEPT   SECURITY                                          M    END      REG     OT    SICK    VAC
 7  NUMBER  NUMBER             LAST NAME         FIRST NAME   I    DATE     HRS    HRS    HRS    HRS              ERROR MESSAGE
 9   9999   999999999   AAAAAAAAAAAAAAAAAAAA   AAAAAAAAAA   A   999999    ZZ.9   ZZ.9   ZZ.9   ZZ.9XXXXXXXXXXXXXXXXXXXXXXXXXXXXXXXXXXXXXXXXX
10   9999   999999999   AAAAAAAAAAAAAAAAAAAA   AAAAAAAAAA   A   999999    ZZ.9   ZZ.9   ZZ.9   ZZ.9XXXXXXXXXXXXXXXXXXXXXXXXXXXXXXXXXXXXXXXXX
11   9999   999999999   AAAAAAAAAAAAAAAAAAAA   AAAAAAAAAA   A   999999    ZZ.9   ZZ.9   ZZ.9   ZZ.9XXXXXXXXXXXXXXXXXXXXXXXXXXXXXXXXXXXXXXXXX
12   9999   999999999   AAAAAAAAAAAAAAAAAAAA   AAAAAAAAAA   A   999999    ZZ.9   ZZ.9   ZZ.9   ZZ.9XXXXXXXXXXXXXXXXXXXXXXXXXXXXXXXXXXXXXXXXX
13   9999   999999999   AAAAAAAAAAAAAAAAAAAA   AAAAAAAAAA   A   999999    ZZ.9   ZZ.9   ZZ.9   ZZ.9XXXXXXXXXXXXXXXXXXXXXXXXXXXXXXXXXXXXXXXXX
14   9999   999999999   AAAAAAAAAAAAAAAAAAAA   AAAAAAAAAA   A   999999    ZZ.9   ZZ.9   ZZ.9   ZZ.9XXXXXXXXXXXXXXXXXXXXXXXXXXXXXXXXXXXXXXXXX
15   9999   999999999   AAAAAAAAAAAAAAAAAAAA   AAAAAAAAAA   A   999999    ZZ.9   ZZ.9   ZZ.9   ZZ.9XXXXXXXXXXXXXXXXXXXXXXXXXXXXXXXXXXXXXXXXX
16   9999   999999999   AAAAAAAAAAAAAAAAAAAA   AAAAAAAAAA   A   999999    ZZ.9   ZZ.9   ZZ.9   ZZ.9XXXXXXXXXXXXXXXXXXXXXXXXXXXXXXXXXXXXXXXXX
18   9999 DEPARTMENT TOTALS
```

NOTE: Symbols used to Format Information Fields

A = Alphabetic
B = Embedded blank in an alphanumeric field
X = Alphanumeric (characters or numbers
Z = Replace leading zeroes with blanks
9 = Numeric
$ = Floating dollar sign when substituted for Z
* = Replace leading zeroes with asterisk for dollar protection
. = Decimal point

Figure 14-7 A Report Layout

14-8 illustrates a program flowchart. Program flowchart symbols are defined in Figure 14-9. *Program flowcharts* are used to document the logic within an individual program or module. They serve as a blueprint for the programmer, showing in detail the steps within a program and the sequence in which they will be executed. Frequently, an overall or macro program flow chart specifying the general logic of the program will be developed first. More detailed or micro program flow charts will then be developed, showing each individual program step.

Program flowcharts are not used in structured design, as we will see in the next chapter. Structured design uses structure charts, structured English, decision tables, and decision trees to document the logic of programs and their modules. The final two phases of classical systems development, coding of programs, and testing and system implementation are similar to phases in structured systems development. They will be covered in more detail in the next chapter.

STRUCTURED SYSTEMS DEVELOPMENT[1]

Figure 14-10 illustrates the structured systems development life cycle. Very little difference exists between this diagram and Figure 14-2. In Figure 14-10 the analysis and preliminary design phases have been combined into a structured analysis phase, and detailed design has become structured design. Coding and testing have been renamed implementation, and implementation has been renamed conversion. However, there are vast differences in the two approaches as we shall see in the remainder of this chapter and in the next chapter, when structured design is covered.

The essence of the structured approach is threefold: 1) we partition the system into manageable levels of detail or modules; 2) we rigorously specify the interfaces that exist between modules; and 3) we rigorously specify the processes or transformations that go on within the modules. In the remainder of this chapter we will explore structured analysis, and consider the advantages and disadvantages of structured analysis compared with those of classical analysis.

MANAGEMENT CASE 14-1

Sam Jones is vice president for marketing for Giles Development Corporation, a large developer of condominiums, apartments, and single family homes. Sam has requested systems development to commence work on a new marketing analysis system. This system will have the capability of tracking historical sales, following demographic trends, and projecting sales trends into the future. The primary objective of the system is to provide Giles Development with information that will help them decide what type of housing unit to develop in the future and where are the best locations for the various types of housing units. Systems development has estimated that 40% of the effort in developing the system will be spent in the analysis phase. Mr. Jones is upset with this estimate. He feels that much less time should be spent on analysis and that system development should quickly get into the design and implementation of the system. Do you agree or disagree with Mr. Jones position?

---

[1]Much of the conceptual basis for the remainder of this chapter is adapted with permission from Tom DeMarco, *Structured Analysis and System Specification* (New York: Yourdon Inc., 1979), 3–44.

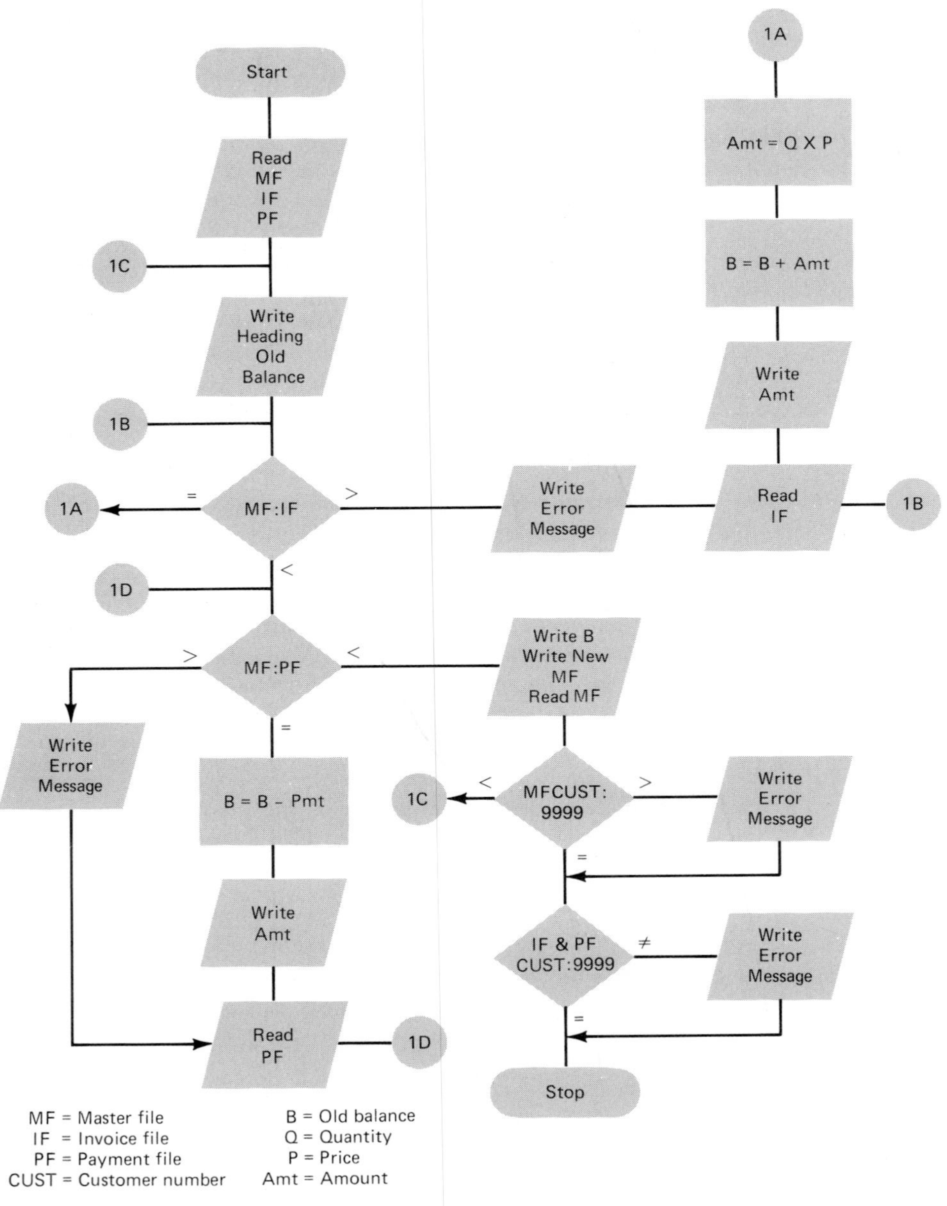

Figure 14-8 Flowchart for Accounts Receivable Statement Program. (The flow is assumed to be top to bottom and left to right unless otherwise indicated.)

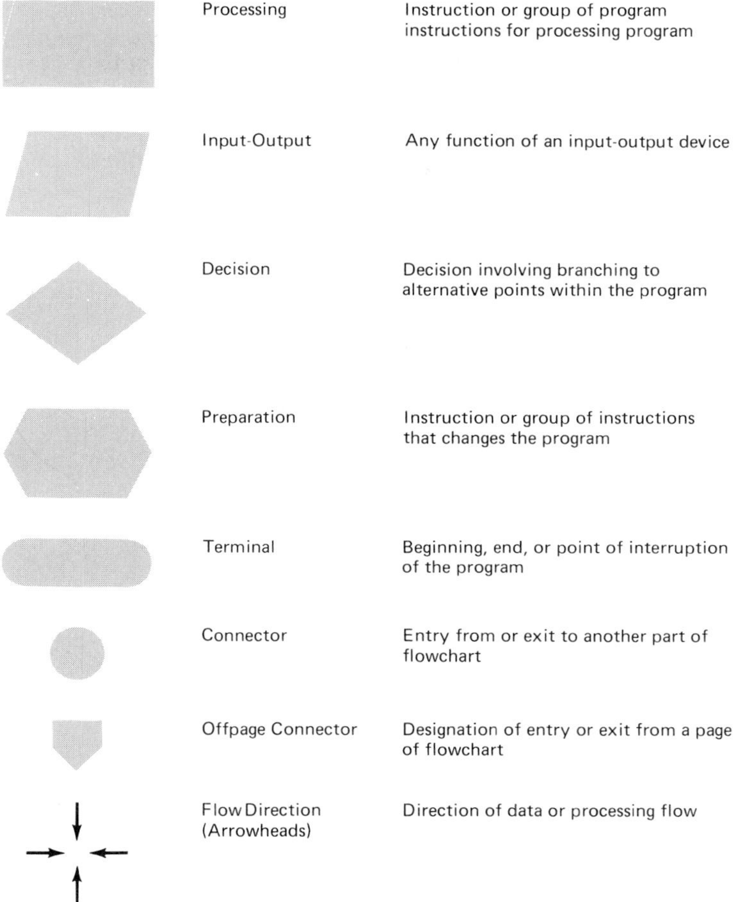

Processing
Instruction or group of program instructions for processing program
Input-Output
Any function of an input-output device
Decision
Decision involving branching to alternative points within the program
Preparation
Instruction or group of instructions that changes the program
Terminal
Beginning, end, or point of interruption of the program
Connector
Entry from or exit to another part of flowchart
Offpage Connector
Designation of entry or exit from a page of flowchart
Flow Direction (Arrowheads)
Direction of data or processing flow

Figure 14-9 Program Flowchart Symbols

STRUCTURED ANALYSIS

Figure 14-11 illustrates the phases within structured analysis. You will note that this figure is a partitioning of process two, which is structured analysis in Figure 14-10. In fact, Figures 14-2, 10, and 11 in this chapter are all *data flow diagrams* (DFD). Data flow diagrams are the primary tool used in structured systems development to graphically depict systems. You probably found that you could understand these figures without an explanation of the data flow diagram. This is one of the distinct advantages of data flow diagrams. They are easy for users to understand since they are not cluttered up with many different technical symbols as system and program flowcharts are.

Note the numbering system used in a data flow diagram. The fact that the first digit of the numbers of the processes in Figure 14-11 is a two indicates that Figure 14-11 is a partitioning of the second process in Figure 14-10. We can carry this partitioning to as many levels as necessary. This partitioning is called *leveled data flow diagrams*. In

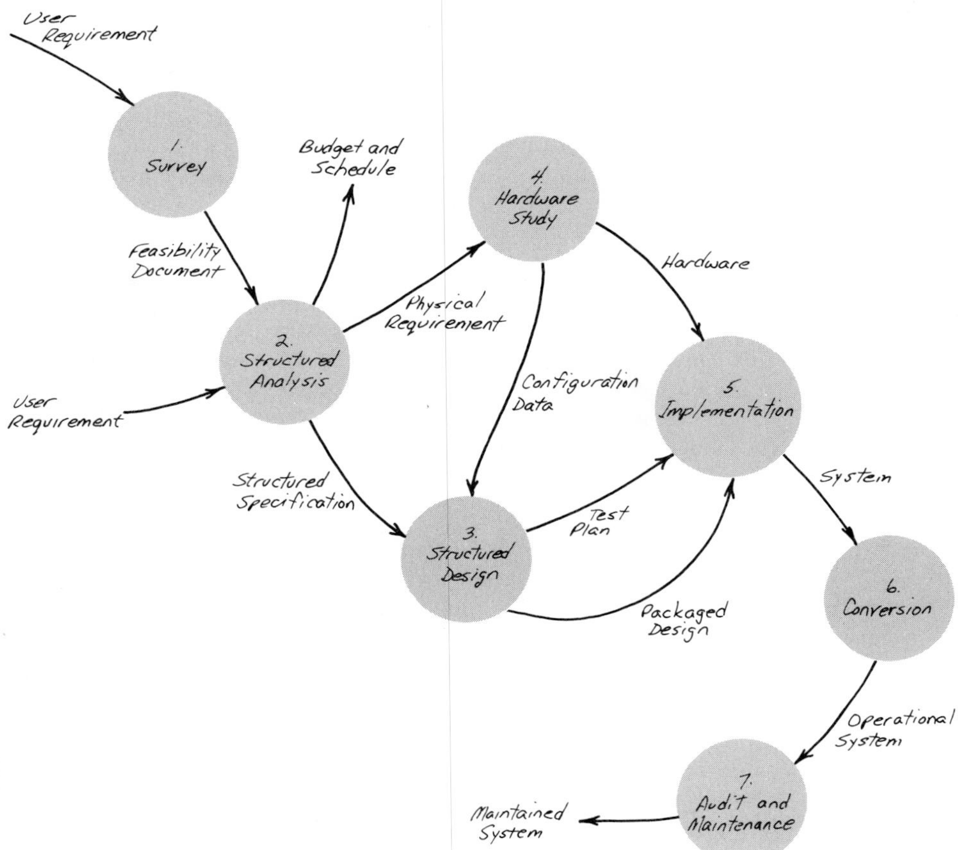

Figure 14-10 Structured Systems Development Life Cycle. Adapted with permission from Tom DeMarco, *Structured Analysis and System Specification* (New York, Yourdon Inc., 1979), 26.

practice it is rarely necessary to exceed five or six levels to provide enough detail to understand what occurs even within a complex system. We will discuss data flow diagrams in greater depth in the next section.

Study of the Current Environment

The first phase of structured analysis is a thorough study of affected user areas. This process relies on extensive interviewing of user personnel and frequent reviews with users of the systems analysis documentation that the analyst is creating. These reviews are often called walkthroughs. The purpose of this study is to thoroughly understand and document the current physical system. The primary documentation tool used is a leveled set of data flow diagrams. These data flow diagrams will be physical in nature as shown in Figure 14-12. You will notice that specific reports (Report 21B) and people who do the processing are identified in this data flow diagram. These references to documents, people, and departments are necessary so that users will understand the data flow diagram. You will note, however, that the emphasis of the data flow diagram

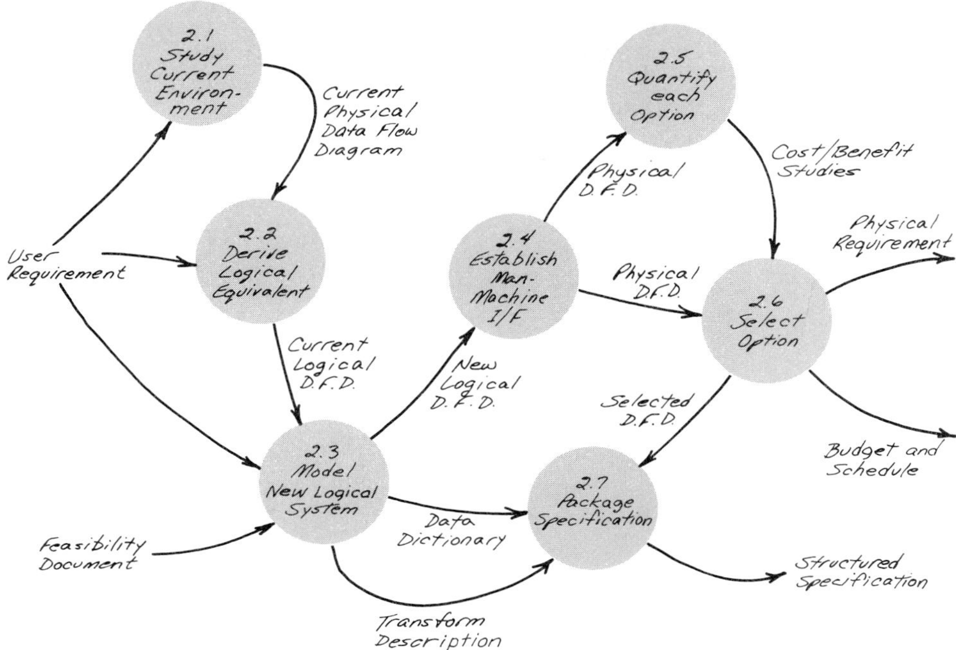

Figure 14-11 Structured Analysis. Adapted with permission from Tom DeMarco, *Structured Analysis and System Specification,* (New York, Yourdon Inc., 1979), 26.

is on the flow of data. We draw these diagrams from the viewpoint of data, not people. After all, the basic reason for an information system is the processing of data.

By leveled set of data flow diagrams we mean that each process in Figure 14-12 signified by a circle will be partitioned into levels of detail similar to those of Figures 14-10 and 14-11. We will partition down to a level of understandable detail that documents the process which, for example, Marie performs on Report 21B.

Figure 14-13 provides another example of leveled data flow diagrams. The highest

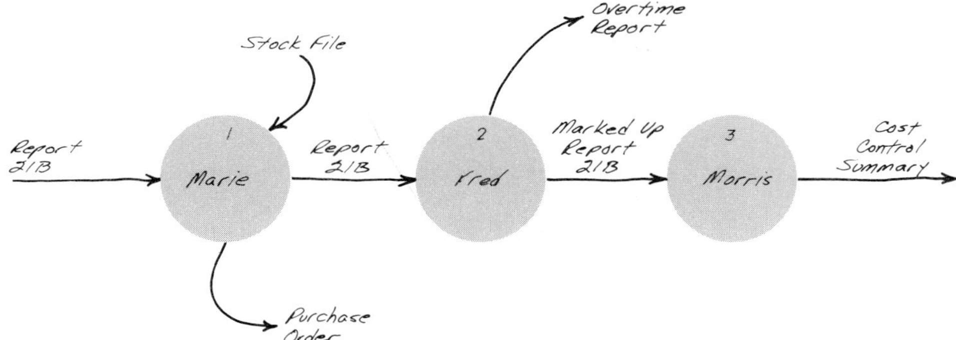

Figure 14-12 Physical Data Flow Diagram. Adapted with permission from Tom DeMarco, *Structured Analysis and System Specification,* (New York, Yourdon Inc., 1979), p. 29.

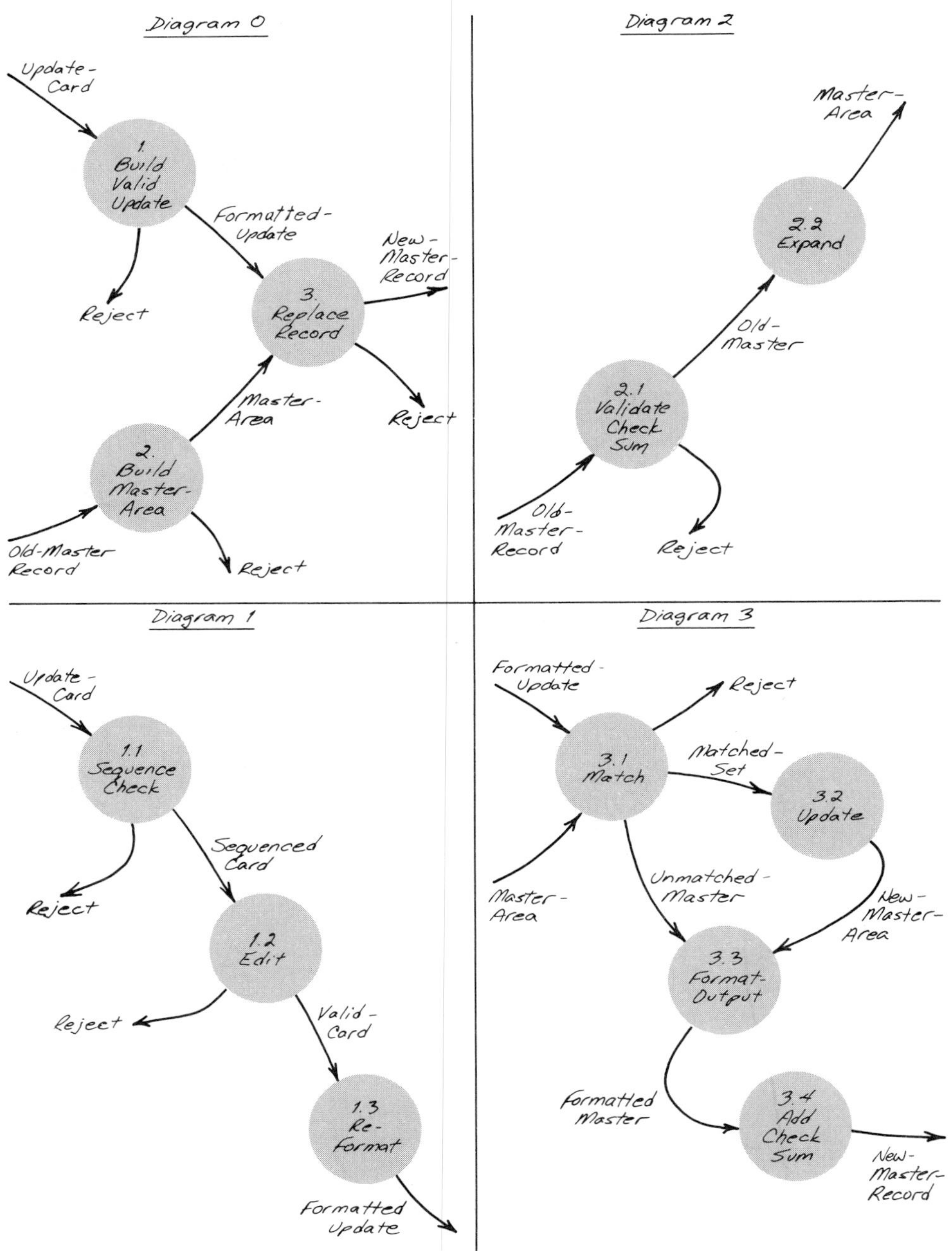

Figure 14-13 Leveled Data Flow Diagrams. Adapted with permission from Tom DeMarco, *Structured Analysis and System Specification* (New York: Yourdon Inc., 1979), 73.

level diagram is labeled diagram 0. The second level of diagrams (diagrams 1, 2, and 3) documents the processes that occur, respectively, within each of the three processes in diagram 0. If we had a third level of diagrams to explain what goes on within process 1.2 edit, this third level diagram would be labeled diagram 1.2.

Notice that the primary interfaces shown in diagram 0 (the inputs and outputs of processes) are also shown in the second level of diagrams. For example, in process 1 the input is an update card and the output is a formatted update. If we look at diagram 1, we see the same input and output.

Data flow diagrams are so easy to understand, I am sure that you have already figured out most of the notation used on these diagrams. Just in case, however, let's review them. First, the arrow, called a *data flow*, portrays a data path. The circle or bubble, called a *process*, portrays a transformation of data. A straight line underneath the name portrays a *file* or *data base*. For example, in Figure 14-14 the stock file is depicted by a straight line. Finally, we can use a square box to portray a *net originator* or *receiver of data*, which is typically a person or an organization outside the domain of our study. For example, if an invoice is sent to a customer, we would depict the customer with a square box.

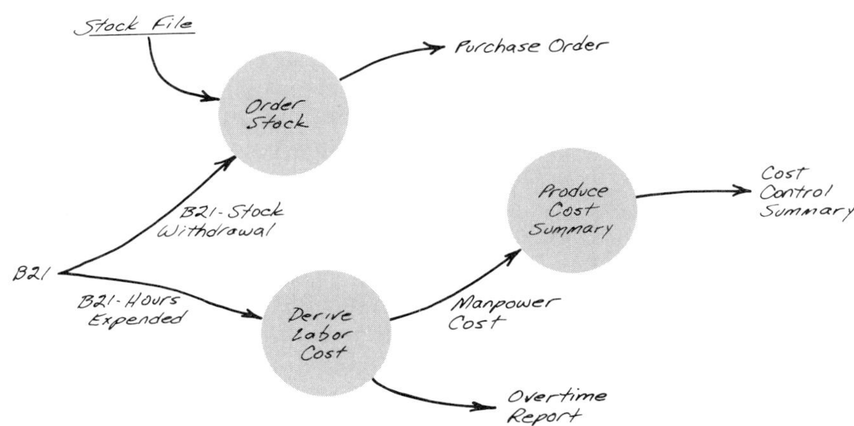

Figure 14-14 Logical Data Flow Diagram. Adapted with permission from Tom DeMarco, *Structured Analysis and System Specification* (New York: Yourdon Inc., 1979), 29.

The results of our study of the current environment are a leveled set of data flow diagrams and other supporting documentation. These include sample input/output documents, processing volumes, file descriptions, and a description of the organizational structure of the area we are studying.

Deriving Logical Equivalents

In the previous process we developed a physical data flow model of the current system. In this process we convert this physical model to a logical model (refer to Figure 14-14, which is the logical equivalent of Figure 14-12). We have simply removed the physical aspects of the physical model. In the logical model, we emphasize what is done rather than the how and who, which is emphasized in the physical model. Notice that the logical model does not indicate at all how the data transformations are done, or who or what performs them. For all we know, Figure 14-14 might depict either a manual or a computerized system. We have simply depicted data flows and processes that transform this data.

Focusing on the logical data flows helps us immensely in the design of a new system. Regardless of whether the system is manual or computerized, certain data flows will have to occur. Physical considerations of how things are done are an unnecessary complication when deciding what data are logically necessary in the new system.

Modeling the New Logical System

Thus far we have focused on the current system. At this stage the analyst should be thoroughly familiar with both the physical and logical aspects of the current environment. Furthermore, we are still working in a logical mode in that we are trying to describe what has to be done, not how it will be done.

The tools we use in this subphase are the data flow diagrams, *data dictionary* (to document files and data flows), and *transform descriptions* (to document the insides of data flow processes). Even though we partition processes through the leveled data flow diagram approach, at some point we cease to partition the data flow diagrams. At this lowest level of the data flow diagrams, processes are called *functional primitives*. However, to be rigorous we still have to specify transformations that occur within these functional primitives. Such specifications are called transform descriptions. We will discuss transform descriptions in greater detail later, and will first cover data dictionaries.

Data Dictionary

A *data dictionary* consolidates information and definitions about data used in a system in a convenient form. It contains definitions of data flows, components of data flows, files, and sometimes processes. In addition, it may contain many other types of information and definitions depending upon the wishes of the analyst. For example, concerning a particular data flow, such information as frequency, volume, affected users, security considerations, and implementation schedule may be included.

To illustrate, a data flow on a DFD might be called payment-data. An entry in the data dictionary might look like this:

payment-data = customer-name + customer-address
+ invoice-number + amount-of-payment

In other words, the data flow called payment-data consists of the items customer-name, customer-address, invoice-number, and amount-of-payment. They must all be present and appear in that order.

Just as we have partitioned data flow diagrams, we can also partition data flows. For example, invoice-number may be defined in the data dictionary as:

invoice-number = city code + customer-account-number
+ salesman-id + sequential-invoice-count.

For our structured specification to be complete, every data flow indicated on our leveled set of data flow diagrams must have a definition entry in the data dictionary. Data dictionaries are also used to define files by specifying the data contained within each individual record.

Transform Descriptions

There are three ways we can describe transformations that occur within functional primitives on the data flow diagrams. These are structured English, decision tables, and decision trees. Structured English is colloquial English with a few restrictions. It is often also called pseudocode, because of its similarity to program code. In fact, the syntax of structured English is limited to the same basic patterns as structured programming. Figure 14-15 illustrates allowable structured English patterns. You will note that when we discuss structured programming in chapter 15, we will use these same control patterns. Therefore, it is very easy to write a structured program based on structured English.

Figure 14-16 illustrates structured English for an invoice processing functional primitive from a data flow diagram.

Decision Tables

Decision tables offer a means of standardizing documentation of decision rules, and allow large numbers of conditions to be documented. Figure 14-17 illustrates a decision table for the same invoice processing example we described in structured English in Figure 14-16. Decision tables are read from top to bottom. In the example, there are four different sets of conditions that can occur. Looking at rule 1, if the invoice is greater than 500 and the account is overdue by 60+ days, then we do not issue a confirmation, an invoice, or a message to the credit action report. The primary advantage of a decision table is that many different combinations of conditions and their appropriate actions can be documented in a compact form.

Decision Tree

As another alternative, the invoice processing policy can be documented with a decision tree as shown in Figure 14-18. As you can see, the decision tree is not as compact as a decision table, but many people find a decision tree easier to understand than a decision table.

Generally, analysts use structured English for transform descriptions because it is much easier to write program code based on structured English rather than from decision tables or decision trees. Decision tables and decision trees are used when there are large numbers of conditions and, consequently, several possible different actions that could occur based on condition combinations. However, they are used in relatively few situations.

Data Structure Diagram

In some cases, a user will be operating in a data base environment. If so, it is necessary to create another document, the data structure diagram. A data structure diagram (DSD)

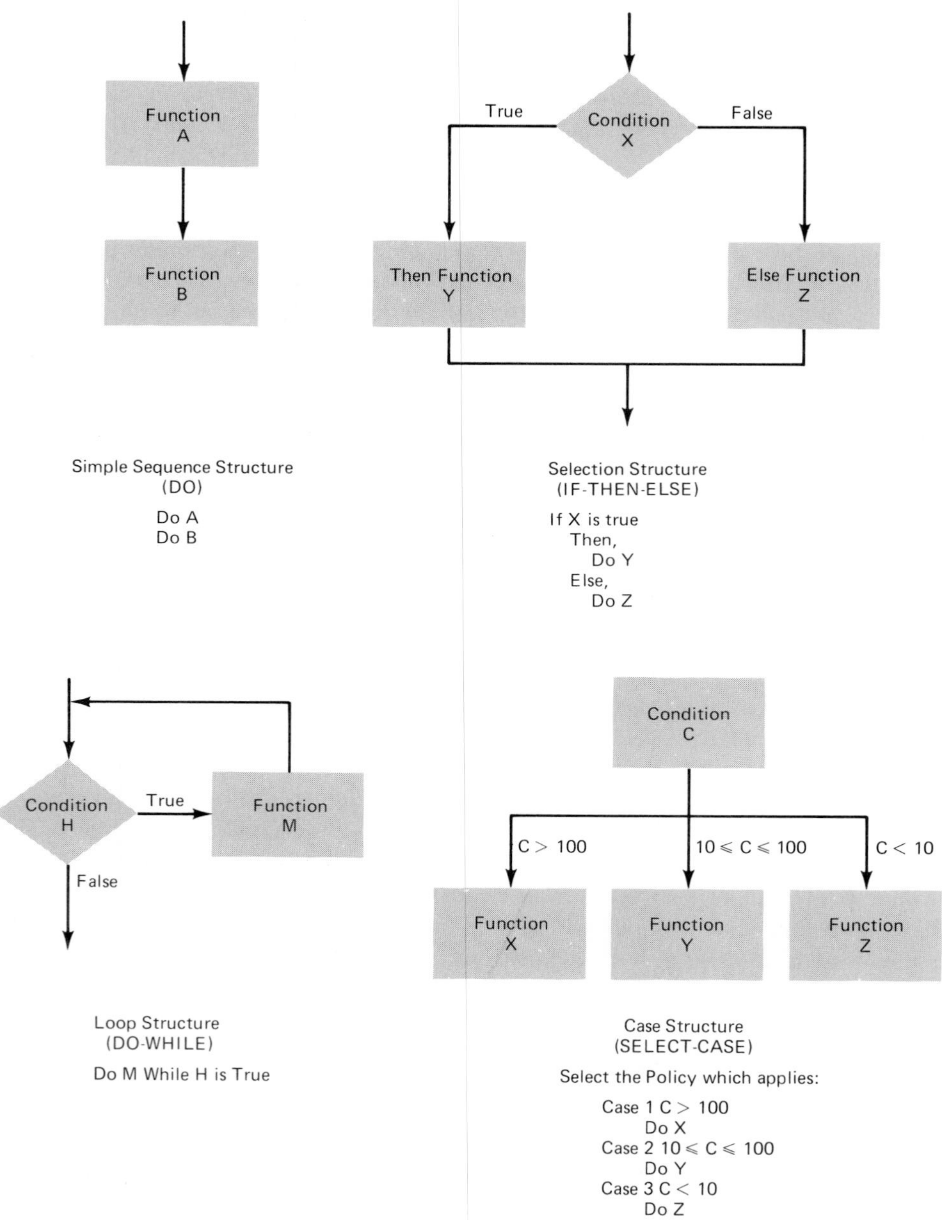

Figure 14-15 Allowable Structured English Control Patterns

represents the logical relationships between various data items. It also shows the "key" data items that may be used to access data. Figure 14-19 shows a DSD for a physician's office. Each box represents a file, and the data item in the left part of the box is the key to the file. The arrows represent logical connections between files. We can see that if the prescription number is known, it is possible to determine the details about all drugs in

Policy For Invoice Processing

If the amount of the invoice exceeds $500.
If the account has any invoice more than 60 days overdue, hold the confirmation pending resolution of the debt.
Else (account is in good standing), issue confirmation and invoice.
Else (invoice $500 or less),
If the account has any invoice more than 60 days overdue, issue confirmation, invoice and write message on the credit action report.
Else (account is in good standing), issue confirmation and invoice.

Figure 14-16 Structured English for Invoice Processing. Adapted with permission from Tom DeMarco, *Structured Analysis and System Specification* (New York: Yourdon Inc., 1979), 43.

	RULES			
CONDITIONS	**1**	**2**	**3**	**4**
1. Invoice >$500	Y	N	Y	N
2. Account overdue by 60+ days	Y	Y	N	N
ACTIONS				
1. Issue Confirmation	N	Y	Y	Y
2. Issue Invoice	N	Y	Y	Y
3. Msg to C.A.R.	N	Y	N	N

Figure 14-17 Decision Table. Adapted with permission from Tom DeMarco, *Structured Analysis and System Specification* (New York: Yourdon Inc., 1979), 44.

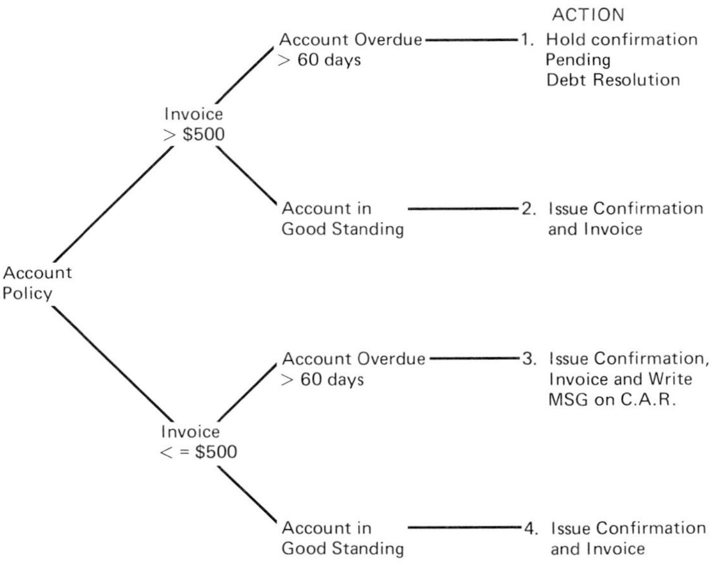

Figure 14-18 Decision Tree. Adapted with permission from Tom DeMarco, *Structured Analysis and System Specification* (New York: Yourdon Inc., 1979), 44.

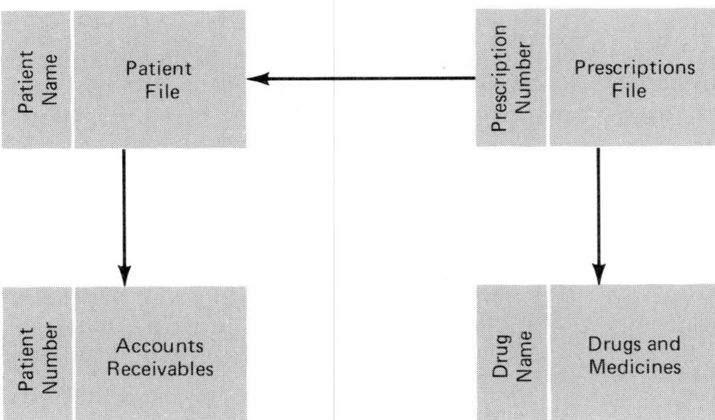

Figure 14-19 Data Structure Diagram

the prescription. However, knowing the name of a drug does not permit us to find the prescriptions in which it is prescribed. The direction of the arrow determines the access path in a DSD.

In this phase of the analysis (modeling the new logical system), the analyst must have a complete understanding of users' essential information needs. Essentially, what the analyst does here is develop a logical model of a system that will take data inputs and transform them into essential information that users need. In doing this the analyst will rely heavily upon the original feasibility study and user interviews to determine the essential new information requirements. The output of this phase is a leveled set of data flow diagrams, transformation descriptions of functional primitives on the data flow diagrams, a data dictionary, and possibly a data structure diagram. These all serve to document the new logical system.

Establishing the Man-Machine Boundary

In this phase of structured analysis, we are essentially developing a physical data flow diagram of the proposed new system or systems. Note that we emphasize systems because at this point there may be several different system configurations that will produce the required information. In fact, people in management generally expect systems analysts to propose several different options from which they can choose.

In establishing the man-machine boundary, we are dealing with the how and what of the system—that is, its physical aspects. Essentially, we are deciding which part of the system will be manual and which will be automated. The output of this phase will be several alternative physical data flow diagrams. When we say "physical" at this point, we do not mean that we will select such things as hardware or programming languages. We are simply delineating the manual from the automated portion of the proposed new systems.

Figure 14-20 summarizes what we have done thus far in the analysis phase. In studying the current environment and deriving its logical equivalent we are concerned with the current system. In fact, we are documenting the current physical system and converting that system into its logical equivalent. Remember that in a physical system

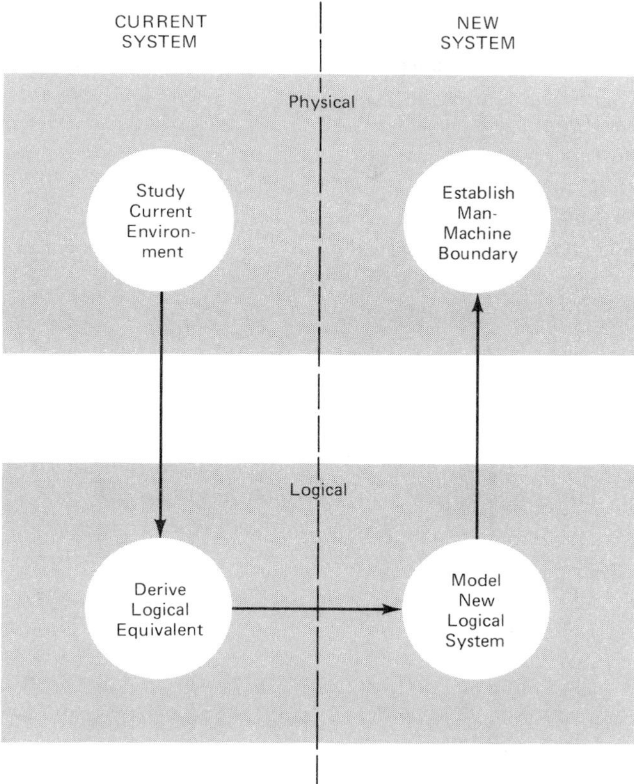

Figure 14-20 Overview of Structured Analysis Process

we are concerned not only with what is done but also with how it is done and who or what does it. In a logical system we are concerned only with what is done (what data flows and transformations occur). When we are modeling the new logical system and establishing the man-machine boundary, we are concerned with the new system.

We are developing a new logical system based on the data or information flows necessary to support users' decision needs. That logical system is then packaged into several alternative physical systems by establishing the man-machine boundary.

Quantifying Options

Each of the tentative new systems we develop in the previous subphase will have certain costs and benefits associated with it. To determine these costs and benefits, we must make a tentative selection of hardware. Initially this is only a very general selection. For example, we might decide that the automated system would be executed on a mini computer or a mainframe, or it might be an online system rather than a batch system. We do not want to lock ourselves into a certain set of hardware or software at this point.

Both costs and benefits can be classified as tangible or intangible. Tangible costs include:

1. Maintenance and operating costs.
2. Personnel costs.
3. Training and orientation.
4. Lease or purchase of new hardware or software.
5. Site preparation.
6. Design costs.

Intangible costs include:

1. Negative effects on employee morale resulting in decreased productivity.
2. Negative effects on customers resulting in decreased business.
3. Decrease in control of the information system by operating management.
4. Increased centralized control of the information system.
5. Increased specialization in information processing.
6. Increased potential cost for breakdowns or disaster when the information system becomes more centralized.

Tangible benefits include:

1. Reduced maintenance and operating costs.
2. Reduced personnel costs.
3. Reduced investment in hardware and software.
4. Reduced rental costs.
5. Reduced space requirements.
6. Reduced age of accounts receivable.
7. Increased inventory turnover.
8. Reduced investment in inventory.

Intangible benefits include:

1. Freeing operating management from information processing activities.
2. Improved control over information processing activities.
3. Improved decision making.
4. Increased emphasis on long-range planning.
5. Improved employee morale.

Selecting an Option

Based on the alternative options the analyst has developed, and costs and benefits associated with each, management will make a decision on which option to implement. The logical and physical data flow diagrams of the new system are very important tools in this phase. Since data flow diagrams are easy to understand, the analyst can readily employ them in presenting proposed options to management.

Packaging the Specification

The final outcome of the structured analysis phase is a structured specification consisting of an integrated set of the following:

1. an introduction containing the system's goals, objectives, and any background information that might be useful.
2. data flow diagrams depicting the major partitioning of functions, and all interfaces among the parts.
3. data dictionary documenting each of the interface data flows and data stores (that is, files).
4. transform descriptions documenting the transformations occurring within each of the DFD processes in a rigorous fashion through the use of structured English, decision tables, and/or decision trees.
5. input and output documents.
6. security, control, and performance requirements.

De Marco has suggested several qualities that a structured specification should have:

1. It should be *graphic*. The data flow diagrams should present a meaningful picture of what is being specified, a conceptually easy-to-understand presentation of the subject matter.
2. It should be *partitioned*. The processes on the data flow diagrams are the basic elements into which the system is decomposed. As we shall see, this partitioning can be done in a top-down fashion so that there is a smooth progression from the most abstract to the most detailed.
3. It should be *rigorous*. The data dictionary will provide a rigorous documentation of the interfaces and the transform descriptions, and also a rigorous specification of process.
4. It should be *maintainable*. Redundancy is minimized and used in a controlled manner. The process of changing the structured specification can be tightly controlled.
5. It should be *iterative*. Portions of the structured specification have the characteristic of being able to be dealt with separately. We can move them back and forth across the user's desk with a short author-reader cycle until they are right. The working documents that the user deals with are actual components of the structured specification. When he or she approves them, they will appear unchanged in the resultant structured specification.
6. It should be *logical, not physical*. By eliminating elements that depend upon hardware, vendor, and operating procedure from the structured specification, we protect ourselves against changes to the specification caused by changes in physical thinking.
7. It should be *precise, concise, and highly readable*.[2]

---

[2]Tom DeMarco, *Structured Analysis and System Specification* (New York: Yourdon Inc., 1979), 32. Used with permission.

MANAGEMENT CASE 14-2

Jane Montgomery is manager of systems development for White Motor Corporation, a large manufacturer of trucks. In the previous five years as manager of systems development she has maintained a policy whereby newly hired individuals for the system development group must have an educational background in either computer science, math, or industrial engineering. These newly hired employees are filling either programming or systems analysts positions. Jane's primary justification for her policy is that she believes that computer professionals must first understand computer hardware and system software to perform their jobs properly. Furthermore, she believes that the development of application software requires high logical reasoning and design skills. Therefore, she believes in addition to those with a computer science background, industrial engineers and mathematicians produce good computer professionals. Several management level individuals in user organizations have suggested that systems development should hire more individuals with backgrounds in user areas such as marketing, finance, personnel, and accounting. Jane's reply to these suggestions has been that it is the user's responsibility to convey to the systems analyst's and programmer's what the user needs in an information system. It is the systems analyst's and programmer's job to design, code and implement the systems. She argues that these are two separate disciplines and that the advantages of specialization support her current hiring policy. Evaluate Jane's position.

CLASSICAL VERSUS STRUCTURED SYSTEMS DEVELOPMENT

In this chapter we have presented both classical and structured systems analysis. Although the classical approach was used for many years, and is still being used, most systems analysts are beginning to see that the structured approach has significant advantages over the classical approach. Among these are:

1. Structured analysis requires a rigorous study of the user area, a study frequently skipped in the classical approach.
2. Structured analysis requires the analyst to partition what he or she has specified. The tools of the classical approach, system and program flowcharts, were not well suited for partitioning. As we have emphasized, partitioning is the key to many of the advantages of the structured approach.
3. The structured systems specification is very graphic and, therefore, easy to understand compared to the classical systems specification, which tended to be heavy on narrative and, therefore, more difficult to understand.
4. The classical approach tended to focus on physical aspects of the system hardware, vendor, and operating procedures. By focusing on the logical aspects of data flows and data transformations, the analyst can readily see essential information flows and processes required in the new system.
5. The structured approach produces highly maintainable systems not only from the standpoint of the analysis phase but, as we will see in the next chapter, also for design and programming purposes.
6. Structured development documentation is cumulative. The documentation developed in any phase builds on the preceding documentation and serves as the basis for work in subsequent phases. For example, as we will see in the next chapter, the

DFDs, transform descriptions, etc., developed in the analysis phase will be used heavily in design and coding.

A system's *maintainability* is simply the ease with which it can be changed as required by new conditions. In the real world, requirements change often. Maintainability problems are perhaps the primary reason for the demise of most systems. Therefore, maintainability is a very important consideration. The structured approach produces maintainable systems primarily because of its partitioned or modular approach to systems design.

SUMMARY

Software development is the most expensive part of implementing a computerized system. A rational approach to systems analysis can help to minimize this expense.

Systems analysis enables us to partition a complex system and focus on the interaction among its parts.

The study of a large system is made possible by partitioning it into smaller, manageable parts.

In classical systems analysis, the feasibility study is the first step in the process of determining the necessity of a new system.

The feasibility study is followed by an analysis of the existing system. Interviews, narrative descriptions, and system flowcharts are some of the tools used at this stage.

Finally, the new system is designed, coded, implemented, and maintained.

Structured analysis begins with a detailed analysis of the current system. Data flow diagrams are developed to depict the existing system.

DFDs are stripped of their physical characteristics, leaving a simpler logical model.

A new logical system is then designed. The major tools used in this process are data dictionaries, transform descriptions, decision tables, decision trees, and data structure diagrams.

The division of duties between human beings and machines is then determined. Since many different combinations may exist, it is necessary to compare the costs and benefits of various options.

Once an option is selected, various system specifications are integrated into a complete package.

Structured analysis is superior to classical analysis in many respects. Its primary advantage is that it leads to the creation of systems that are easier to maintain.

KEY TERMS

Systems Analysis
Systems Development Life Cycle
Classical Systems Development
Structured Systems Development

Hierarchical Partitioning
Interface
Structured Analysis
Feasibility Study
Functional Specification Document
System Flowchart
Data Flow Diagrams (DFD)
Modules
Preliminary Design
Detailed Design
Structure Charts
Structured English
Decision Tables
Decision Trees
Leveled Data Flow Diagrams
Logical Model
Functional Primitives
Data Dictionary
Transform Descriptions
Data Structure Diagram (DSD)
The Man-Machine Boundary
Packaged Design
Maintainability

REVIEW QUESTIONS

1. Why does the user need to be familiar with application software development?

2. How does systems analysis make software development a more manageable task?

3. Explain the concept of partitioning.

4. List the elements of a feasibility document.

5. Discuss the use of system flowcharts.

6. What is the essence of the structured systems development approach?

7. Describe the importance of data flow diagrams in structured analysis.

8. Differentiate between physical and logical data flow diagrams.

9. Explain the following terms:

1. Data Dictionary
2. Transform Descriptions
3. Functional Primitives
4. Decision Table
5. Decision Tree
6. Data Structure Diagram

10. What is a man-machine boundary?

11. List the tangible costs and benefits that should be considered in hardware selection.

12. Describe the components of a structured specification.

13. What qualities should a good structured specification possess?

14. Discuss the advantages of the structured approach over the classical approach.

DISCUSSION QUESTIONS

1. Often, managers are reluctant to allow a systems analyst to "interfere" with their work. Some common objections are:

1. An outsider cannot understand the nature of the work within a short time period.
2. We have been working like this for years. Why can't we go on indefinitely?
3. Interviews and questionnaires take a lot of time, and our personnel are already overburdened with production work.

How would you respond to these objections?

2. Draw a set of data flow diagrams to describe the data flows of some part of your business or some business firm you are familiar with. Does this help you better understand the operations of the organization? Can you suggest any improvements to the system, based on this analysis?

3. Structured analysis and structured design are superior in many respects to classical analysis and design. They do, however, suffer from certain drawbacks. Critically review structured techniques, and identify their weaknesses.

RESEARCH PROJECTS

1. Select some recently developed systems analysis technique like structured English and evaluate its usefulness in a business environment. Also, pinpoint potential drawbacks of the technique you have selected. *The Journal of Systems Management* is an excellent source of information on this subject.

2. Evaluate the costs/benefits of buying a personal computer for your own use. Using the list of criteria given in this chapter, prepare a formal cost/benefit analysis.

APPLICATION CASE

In-House Effort Proves Fertile for Farm Eqpt. Firm

(Reprinted with permission from MIS Week, March 24, 1982, p. 50)

By Mike Egan

CRYSTAL LAKE, Ill.—In 1979, the Mathews Co. here found itself in a traditional data processing cul-de-sac—there was no existing software that would allow the firm to utilize a $50,000 Texas Instruments Inc. "TI 990/10" minicomputer system for on-line production control and inventory control of 15,000 different manufacturing parts.

Then 63-year-old B.C. "Matt" Mathews, president of the firm, found a simple answer.

He hired a consulting firm to move inside the seven-acre agricultural equipment manufacturing plant and paid it to build the system he wanted.

Now, on a 10-acre site surrounded by forest in the rolling countryside northwest of Chicago, Mathews Co.'s "M-C Manufacturing System" is helping the firm increase productivity, speed-up production, save millions annually through reduced inventory investments and reduce work force size.

"It's an inventory control and production control system that goes beyond traditional manufacturing resource planning systems (MRPs). It controls all production activity, every movement, every time-frame, from the raw materials stage to the finished product stage," said John Heisler, manager at M-C Data Services.

"It suggests what we need before we need it," he added.

Perhaps the most important benefit Mathews Co. has received through its manufacturing software system is the end to a particular nightmare unique to the manufacturing world, Heisler said.

That's when a worker discovers that he can't find one of the necessary parts, such as sprockets." The worker has to rush to inventory with a shopping list of missing parts, necessary for production.

However, the time lost can be disastrous for a manufacturer, costing $1,000 a minute as every worker on the 700-foot line is idle and production stops. Occasionally, a firm will have to shut down production until the new parts can be flown in by airplane.

"It's a very serious problem. But, it doesn't happen anymore," Heisler said. The system eliminates the problem by preprogramming and mapping out all assembly line parts needed for each of the 35 different products manufactured by Mathews, and by providing automatic warnings when supplies are low." Each time there's a production explosion, the computer coughs up what we need to know," Heisler said.

A second major benefit that Mathews Co. has experienced with its year-old system has been automated inventory control, a particularly difficult process because the firm manufactures its own parts and subcomponents.

"All the way through, from sheet stock purchase to the shipping docks, rail cars and trucks, we can follow each piece on the system," Heisler said. "At any time of day, we can get a statistical report on what has happened to the sheet metal and where it is in the production run."

"The system has reduced inventory by one-third. That has saved us several million dollars a year, just from the tremendous costs of carrying that inventory, and so we've been able to reduce margins and pass them on to customers," said Dave Mathews, president at Mathews Equipment Co.

Mathews also noted that the M-C Manufacturing System gives the company a greater continuity in the manufacturing product line, guaranteeing continuous parts similarity, resulting in an improved finished product.

Even warehousing operations have been significantly improved with the manufacturing system. In the past, warehouse workers often needed up to an hour to locate parts upon sales office request. Now that time is down to a minute.

"That's significantly improved customer relations," Heisler noted.

The Mathews Company's M-C Manufacturing System is based upon a Texas Instruments Inc. "TI 990/10" CPU with 240 kilobytes memory and three additional 50 megabyte disk drives.

Some 17 different TI dumb terminals, all with on-line immediate access and retrieval capabilities, are located in seven separate locations inside the manufacturing facility.

The star of the system is the M-C Manufacturing System for inventory and purchase control, with 65 software applications rolled into one large, Cobol system.

Inventory control runs with three standard manufacturing categories each containing several applications. They are: raw materials, work in progress (assembly) and finished goods.

Also, there are two additional inventory control subsystems, a raw materials file and a purchased parts history file.

"The raw materials file contains complete information on all purchased materials, such as steel sheets or coils, and it includes material description, vendors, cost unit, quantity on hand, etc.," Heisler said.

Some additional sub-inventory applications perform routines such as purchase order status report, inventory integrity, location of parts, etc.

The other half of the M-C Manufacturing System is Production Control, Heisler said, "an integrated series of programs and records that interface with engineering, production, purchasing and the sales department.

The link between the two halves of the system is the Bill of Materials (BOM).

The production control software oversees production explosion, raw material requirements, purchased parts requirements, machine and parts costing (tracks material cost changes), employee shop cards, and several parts tickets (picked, moved, purchased, etc.)

Sales, accounting, purchasing, parts warehouse, engineering, production and inventory departments are all connected via computer. Each department has from one to five terminals, with at least one dual-quality speed printer.

The interface between sales and inventory has perhaps benefitted the most from the new system.

"We do a pretty headstrong parts business," Dave Mathews said. Sales personnel can instantly track and log sales of all spare parts, including the 4,500 different pieces used just to build Mathews Co.'s 32-foot-high "1195 EM" continuous flow grain dryer.

The engineering department uses two CRTs to create the BOM, tying inventory and production control together. With complete data on all parts, parts history and manufacturing phases, engineers have all the tools they need to run statistical parts analysis to test possibilities of using new and different raw materials.

"It allows engineering to do the job it's supposed to do," Heisler said. "They can add new product lines onto our operations, without any concerns of whether the lines will be able to slip into our operating environment. They will. We can also change product lines without major difficulties."

MIS operations have also been eased through overnight job control capacity. Heisler said, "Some jobs, depending on the volume or magnitude of the data files, take too long to operate during the day. We increase our work performance by running more at night."

Discussion

1. What are the advantages of a computer-based manufacturing resource planning system (MRP)?
2. How would structured analysis contribute to the inhouse development of a system such as that developed by Mathews Co.

CHAPTER 15

SYSTEMS DESIGN AND IMPLEMENTATION

INTRODUCTION

In the previous chapter we learned techniques applicable to structured analysis of a proposed system. The structured analysis specifications (data flow diagrams, transform descriptions, data dictionary, and data structure diagrams) that were developed will be the primary inputs for the structured design phase. In fact, we will find that designing a new system with these structured specifications is a relatively easy process. In Figure 15-1 we have repeated the overview of the systems development cycle so that you can readily see where structured design fits within the overall systems development cycle. This chapter will cover structured design, coding and testing of the system, and its implementation.

STRUCTURED DESIGN[1]

Figure 15-2 is an overview of the structured design phase. *Structured design* is the process of designing computer programs that will be used in the system. The output of

[1]Much of the conceptual basis for the Structured Design section of this chapter is adapted with permission from Tom DeMarco, *Structured Analysis and System Specification* (New York: Yourdon Inc., 1979), 283–331.

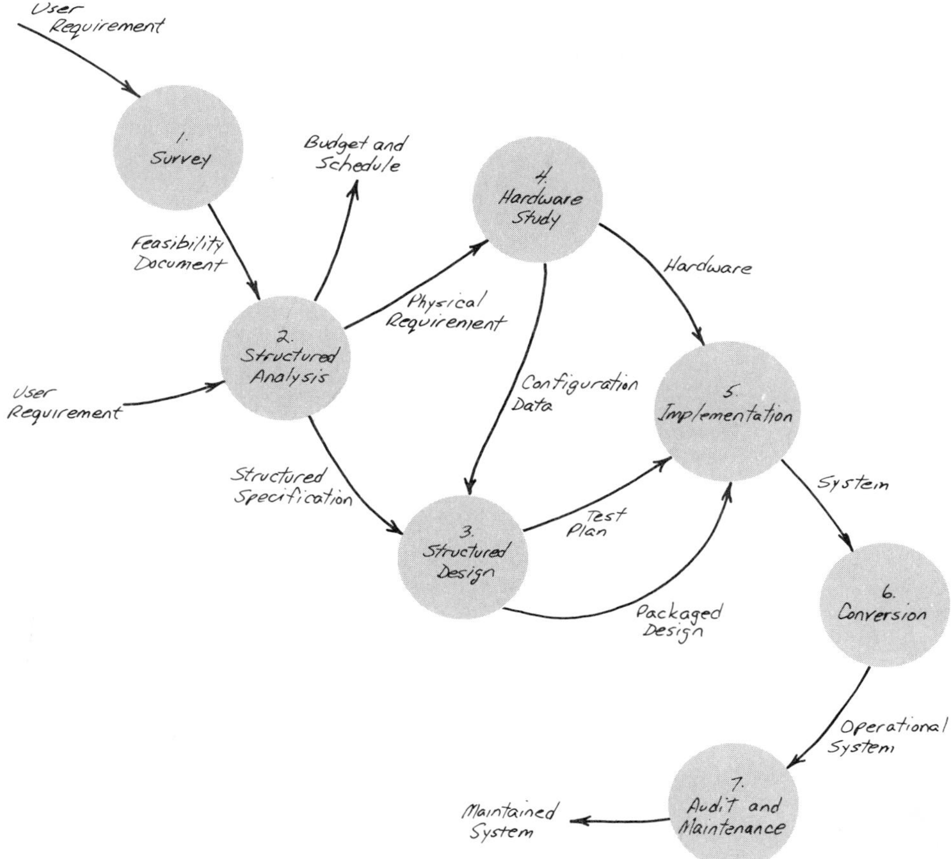

Figure 15-1 Structured Development Life Cycle. Adapted with permission from Tom DeMarco, *Structured Analysis and System Specification* (New York: Yourdon Inc., 1979), 26.

the structured design process is, in effect, a "blueprint" that the programmer can follow in coding and testing the programs. You will note that there are only three subphases within structured design. When we use structured analysis, there is relatively less work to be done in the structured design phase. In fact, a characteristic of structured analysis is that, compared to classical analysis, more work is done in planning the system and in the analysis phase; less work is done in the later phases of the systems development cycle.

As the chapter progresses, we shall see that the primary advantage of structured design are its production of programs 1) that are more easily maintained; 2) that can be tested module by module in a top-down fashion; and 3) that can be more easily understood. All of these advantages occur primarily because the program is broken down into logical modules during the structured design phase. The design phase is normally performed by the systems analyst, although in some cases a person called a systems designer will perform the design phase. Systems designers are sometimes called

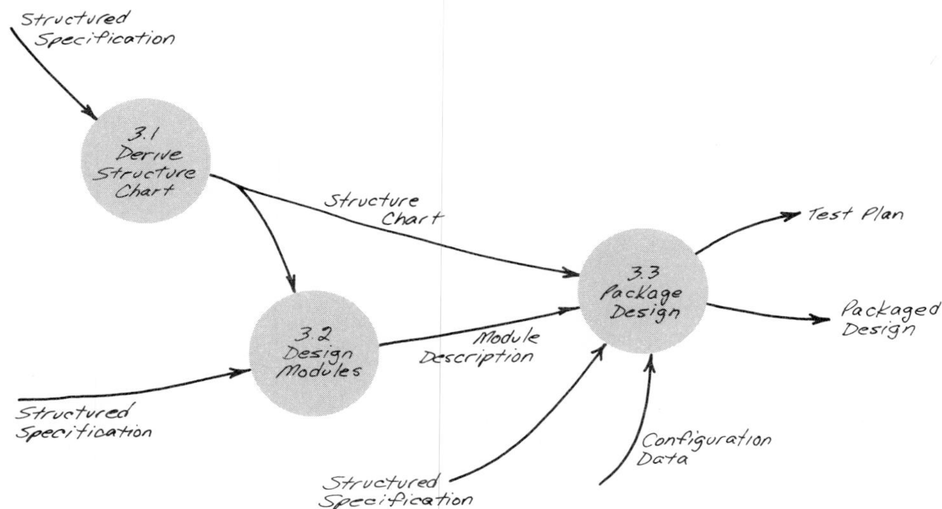

Figure 15-2 Overview of the Structured Design Phase. Adapted with permission from Tom DeMarco, *Structured Analysis and System Specification* (New York: Yourdon Inc., 1979), 23.

programmer analysts since the process of designing the system requires both analyst and programmer skills.

Derive Structure Chart

The primary tool used in structured design is the structure chart. An example of the structure chart is illustrated in Figure 15-3. When a program is designed in a structured way, the design approach is often called top-down design. As you can see in Figure 15-3, we break the program into independent modules or subroutines. The module at the top is called a control module. In our example, it is the accounts receivable system. At appropriate times, this module will call the three modules underneath to get imputs from files, perform the processing, and write outputs. We can continue subdividing modules into smaller parts to simplify the program structure. Ideally, each module should perform a single function.

By now, you probably have noticed that this structure chart resembles a data flow diagram in concept. Of course, they do not look alike physically, but a structure chart is certainly an exercise in hierarchical partitioning, just as a data flow diagram is. In fact, all the advantages we talked about in relation to data flow diagrams also apply to structure charts. There is a very strong correlation between structure charts and data flow diagrams.

A data flow diagram documents what has to be accomplished. It is a statement of information processing requirements, whereas a structure chart documents how the requirements will be met. The structure chart is the hierarchical partitioning of the programs we will write for the system.

Since there is a close relationship between DFDs and structure charts, we should be able to derive the structure chart directly from the DFD. In the next few paragraphs we

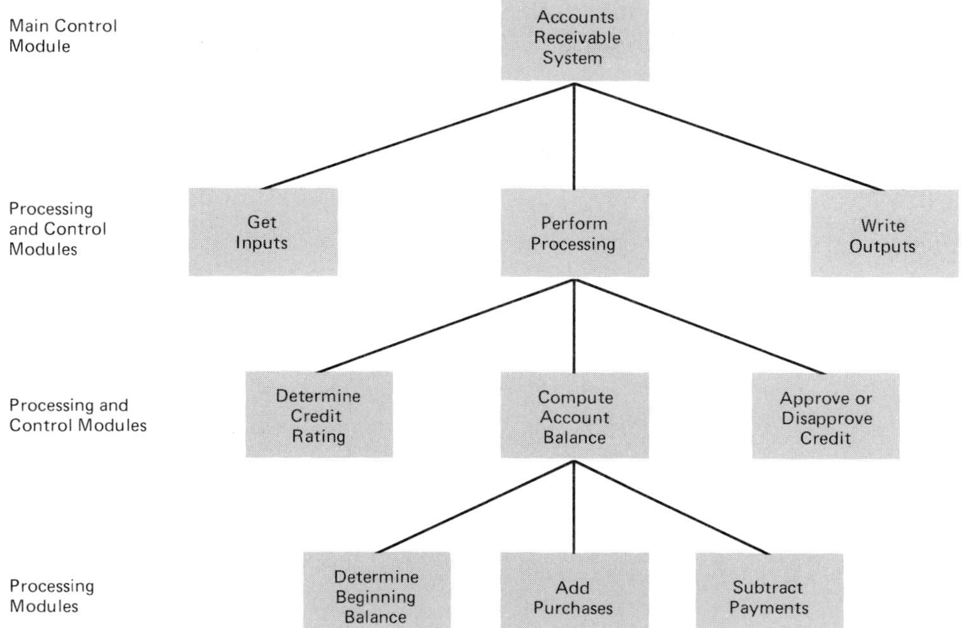

Figure 15-3 Structure Chart of an Accounts Receivable System

will show how this is done. First, however, a refinement of our knowledge of structured design is needed.

As we have stated, a design is structured if it is made up of a hierarchy of modules. However, a second structured design requirement is that each of these modules or subroutines must have a single entry and a single exit back to its parent module. Except for its parent, each module should be as independent of all other modules as possible. For example, there should be no exit directly from the Determine Beginning Balance module to the Add Purchases module. Once the Determine Beginning Balance module has completed its processing, control is passed back to the parent Compute Account Balance module. From there, control can go back up to Perform Processing, or back down to any of the fourth level modules. Control passes along the connecting lines.

A third structured design requirement is that within each module the code should be executed in a top to bottom fashion. There must not be any GO TO statements that cause the program statements to be executed in other than a top-to-bottom fashion. This design feature is often called GO TO-less programming. GO TO-less programming makes programs much easier to read. Having too many GO TO statements in a program would be like reading a book that told you to go and reread previous paragraphs; then said to go forward three pages and read something on that page; then said to go back two paragraphs; and finally told you to transfer again to another page. I am sure you can see the problem with reading and understanding a program module that indiscriminately uses GO TO statements.

There are also certain notational conventions used in structured design. These are illustrated in Figure 15-4. By now you probably already recognize that the rectangular

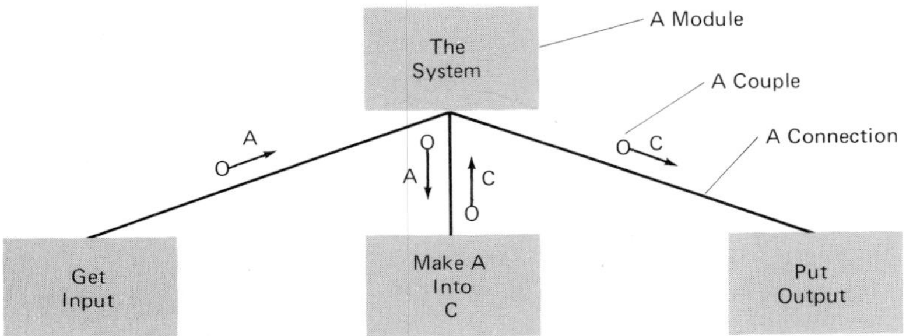

Figure 15-4 Notational Conventions Used in Structured Design

box is a *module*. A module is a bounded, named, and contiguous set of program statements often referred to as a *subroutine*. The line joining two modules is called a *connection*. This connection means that the upper module has the capability of calling the lower module. Finally, a *couple* is represented by a short arrow with a circular tail. A *couple* is a data item that moves from one module to another. For example, in the illustration the system sends data item A to the module labeled "Make A Into C"; this module then sends C back to the system.

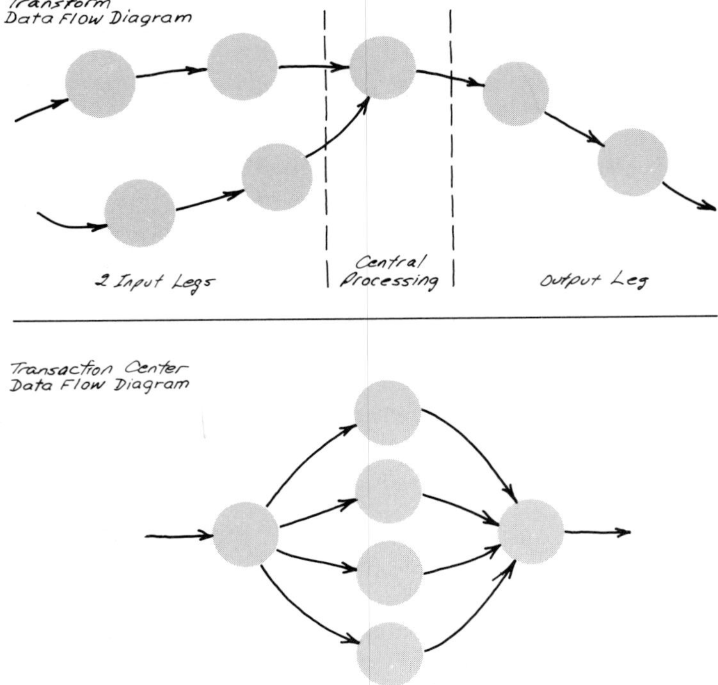

Figure 15-5 Two Basic Types of Data Flow Diagrams. Adapted with permission from Tom DeMarco, *Structured Analysis and System Specification* (New York: Yourdon Inc., 1979), 316.

Deriving structure charts from data flow diagrams is rather straightforward. There are two basic types of data flow diagrams as illustrated in Figure 15-5. The first type is the transform data flow diagram, which is linear in nature. A *transform data flow diagram* has clearly identifiable input and output streams. The second type of data flow diagram is a transaction center. A *transaction center* DFD is characterized by parallelism of data flow as illustrated in Figure 15-5.

The derivation of a structure chart from the transform data flow diagram is appropriately called *transform analysis*. Figure 15-6 illustrates transform analysis. First, we will identify the central process in the DFD. The *central process* is in the center of the linear DFD, and therefore it is not concerned with getting input or generating output. In this case the central process is No. 3. We will put this process at the top of the structure chart, where the system is represented.

At the second level of the structure chart, we will design one module for each input stream, one module for each output stream, and one for the central transform. We use a similar approach for each of the succeeding lower levels. For example, taking the second level module, Get C, there is one input stream, which is Get B, and the transform of making B into C. Similarly, to get B we move to the fourth level and get A, and then

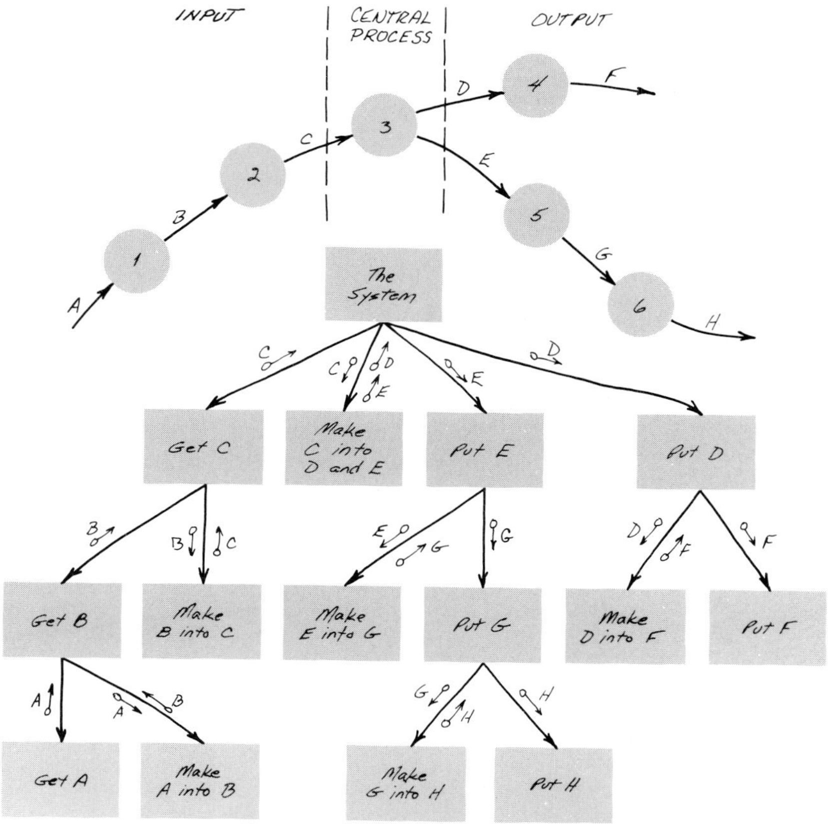

Figure 15-6 Transform Analysis. Adapted with permission from Tom DeMarco, *Structured Analysis and System Specification* (New York: Yourdon Inc., 1979), 317.

make A into B. Note that the couples represent the flow of data to and from the various modules.

Another pattern you should notice in Figure 15-6 is that for each input process on the DFD, there is one two-part substructure (or get module and a transform module) on the structure chart. For each output process on the data flow diagram, there is also one two-part substructure (a transform module and a put module) on the structure chart.

You may be thinking by now that Figure 15-6 represents a simple level 0 data flow diagram and is, therefore, relatively simple to convert to a structure chart. What happens when we consider a more complex leveled set of data flow diagrams that may consist of as many as four to six levels? Figure 15-7 illustrates the derivation of the structure chart from leveled DFDs. In the figure, we have depicted the level 1 diagram for process 2 within the process 2 circle. On the structure chart below, the system module and the three modules immediately below it would be a complete structure chart for the level 0 DFD. However, we can depict the level 1 DFD on the structure chart by simply dropping down to another level under the module Make B into C. You should review this third level of the structure chart in Figure 15-7 to verify that the structure chart represents the same processes and data flows as shown in the level 1 DFD above.

Before leaving transform analysis, consider one of the major advantages of the

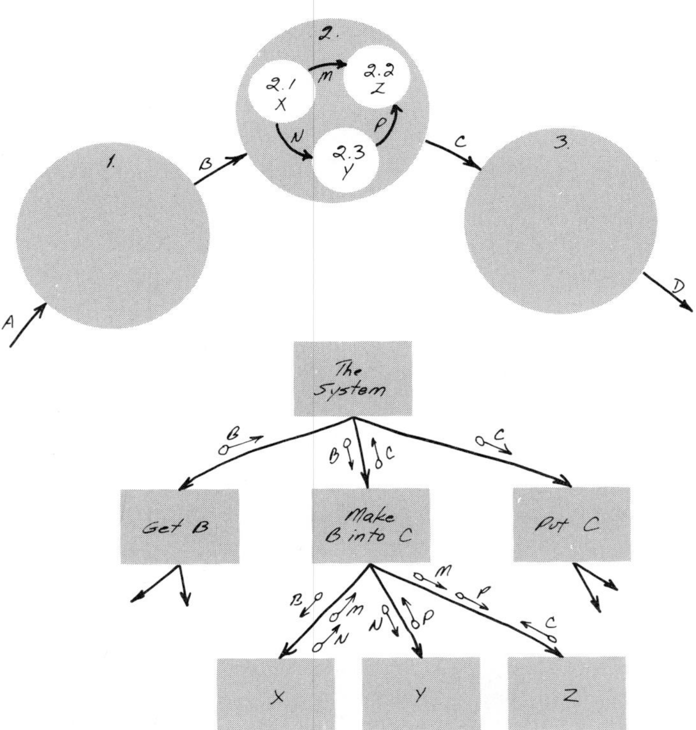

Figure 15-7 Derivation of Structure Chart from Leveled DFDs. Adapted with permission from Tom DeMarco, *Structured Analysis and System Specification* (New York: Yordon Inc., 1979), 318.

procedure. Referring to Figure 15-6, note that we have isolated the central part of the system from physical aspects of the input of A and the output of F and H. In fact, the input of A is down at the fourth level of the structure chart; the output of F is at the third; and the output of H is at the fourth level. When changes occur in systems, they will probably affect inputs and outputs. We have hierarchically partitioned the system in such a way that these inputs and outputs are isolated. Therefore, it is very possible that we could make a change in this system by merely adjusting one of these three isolated input or output modules. Remember that one of the primary advantages of the structured approach is the ease with which maintenance can be performed on the system. Many companies are now finding that they spend more money on maintaining existing systems than in designing and implementing new ones. Therefore, ease of maintenance is an extremely important consideration when designing a new system.

Figure 15-8 depicts the use of transaction analysis to derive a structure chart from a DFD of the transaction center type. Note that at the second level of the structure chart

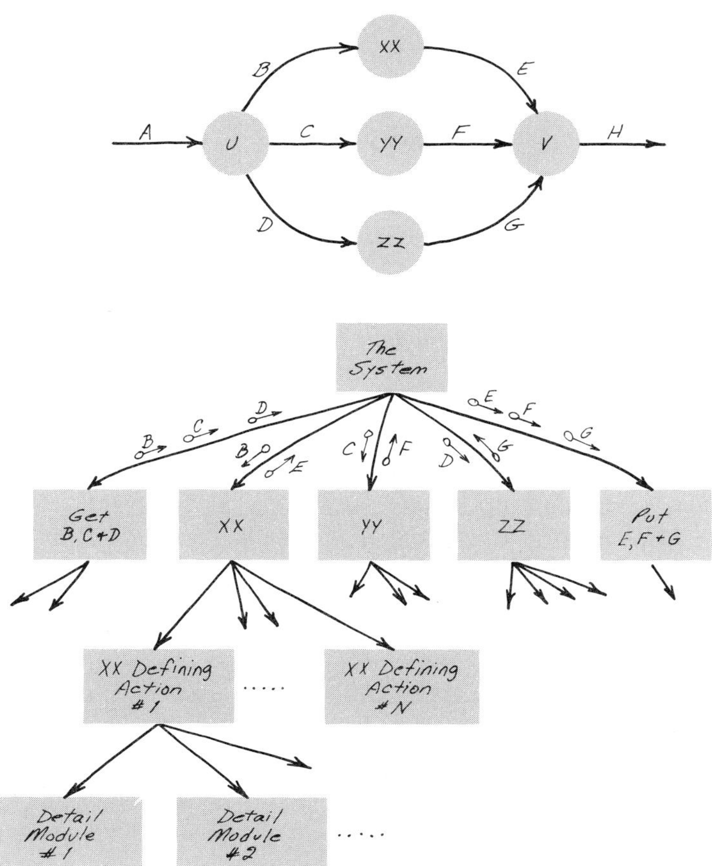

Figure 15-8 Derivation of Structure Chart from Transaction Center type DFD. Adapted with permission from Tom DeMarco, *Structured Analysis and System Specification* (New York: Yourdon Inc., 1979), 320.

we have one module for each input and output stream and one module for each of the parallel data flows. We can, of course, add additional modules below the second level (as we did in Figure 15-7) to further partition any of the second level modules.

Of course, it is highly unlikely in the real world that any system would be totally of the transform type or totally of the transaction center type. A system will probably be a mixture of the two. Figure 15-9 illustrates a more complex DFD and the derivation of a structure chart using both transform analysis and transaction center analysis. Note that when both transaction analysis and transform analysis are used, the latter should be used first to determine the primary structure of the structure chart.

The structured design documented on the structure chart is based on our statement of information processing requirements, the data flow diagram. One might think that our structure chart at this point is complete. However, we need to add a few other

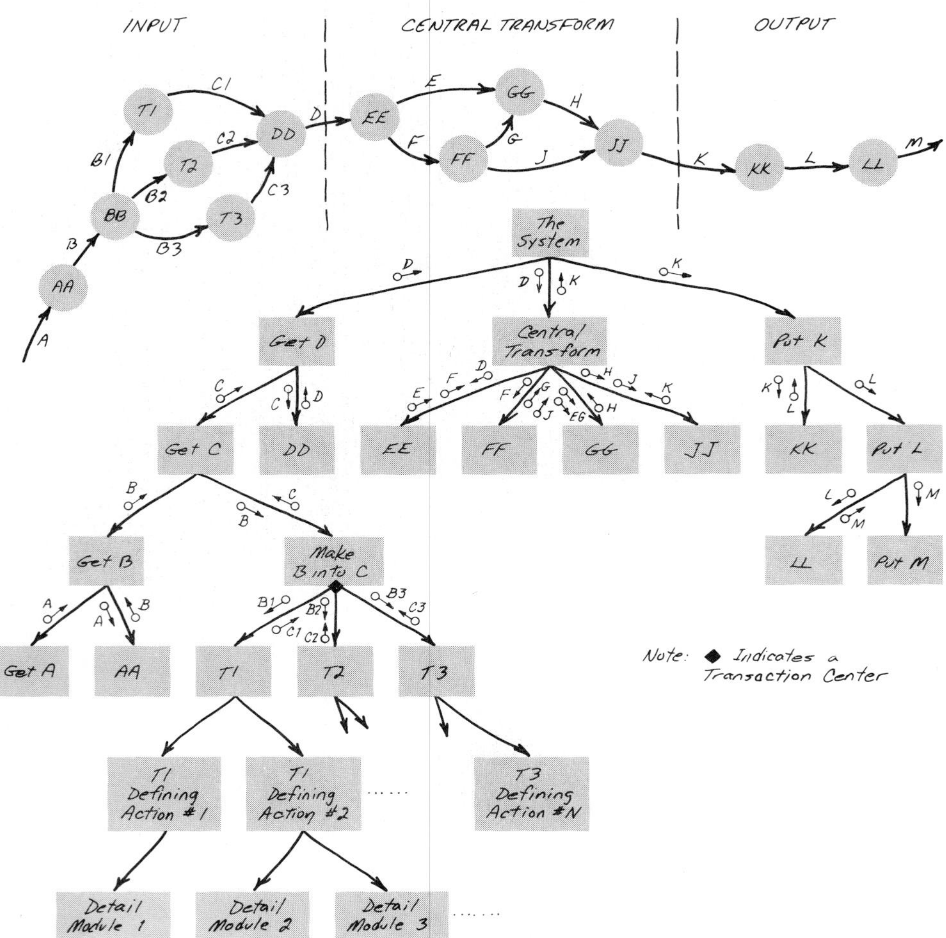

Figure 15-9 Derivation of a Structure Chart from a Complex DFD. Adapted with permission from Tom DeMarco, *Structured Analysis and System Specification* (New York: Yourdon Inc., 1979), 322.

things. We have not indicated the flow of data between modules when errors occur. In fact, up to this point we have ignored error conditions altogether. In addition, programs process items other than computational items and character information, which are necessary for producing the ultimate output. The other primary type of data a program processes is *control data*. Control data are data the program uses solely for making processing decisions. For example, in any system that processes multiple file records, control data tells the program whether or not the last record on the file has been processed. Once the control data (sometimes called a switch) indicates that the last record has been processed, then end of job processing, such as totals, can commence.

Furthermore, there are two major considerations that might cause us to change our module structure from that derived directly from DFDs. These considerations are coupling and cohesion. *Coupling* is a measure of the interdependence of modules. Obviously, coupling is central to the structured design approach. At the beginning of our discussion of structured design, we indicated we would like to create modules that are as independent of each other as possible. Naturally, there will be some coupling between modules, especially between parent and child modules. But the higher the coupling, the more likely it is that changes to the inside of one module will effect the correct functioning of another module. Our goal should be to design modules in such a way that one module can be easily modified without disrupting others. To do this, we must minimize coupling. If coupling is minimized, a module can be read through without having to look inside any other module, and the module being read can be completely understood. A module should not branch into the interior of other modules. In summary, a module's interfaces to the rest of the world should be minimized and stated explicitly.

Cohesion is a measure of the strength of association between the internal functions of a given module. A highly cohesive module will have statements and data that are very closely related. For example, a payroll system program module that calculates weekly gross pay and also prints the payroll check is not cohesive. These are two separate functions and therefore should be partitioned into separate program modules. However, taken separately, each would probably be highly cohesive.

Cohesion and coupling are related concepts. If a module has high cohesion, then an attempt to break it into two or more modules would result in very high coupling between the resulting modules. In fact, one can use this criterion to decide whether or not a module has high cohesion. If simply attempting to break the module into two or more modules produces high coupling, then the original module should be left as it is since it has high cohesion. In other words, the statements or functions within the module are highly related.

Modules having acceptable cohesion perform only one allocated task or perform several strongly related tasks because they use the same data. Another clue to the cohesion of a module is its name. If the name involves multiple verbs and multiple objects (for example, calculate gross pay and federal tax withholding) then it probably will have unacceptable cohesion. A module with a strong name, having one verb and one object is likely to be strongly cohesive.

MANAGEMENT CASE 15-1

Many of the Cobb Company's data processing systems were developed in the early to mid-1970s prior to widespread acceptance of the structured design and structured programming approaches.

Although the systems are working properly at this time and they meet management's needs for information, an increasing percentage of systems development's time is spent in the maintenance of existing programs. Currently about 65% of the effort in systems development is on maintenance of these existing programs. In addition, in the past two years the internal audit department has hired two EDP auditors. In the performance of their duties they must often review the code in these programs. However, they have found that it is almost impossible to follow the logic of the code. Therefore, they have essentially abandoned direct review of program code as an audit technique. Do you think that Cobb has a problem here? If so, what is the nature and cause of the problem and what do you recommend to correct it?

Design Modules

In this subphase of the structured design phase, we design the internal processing within each module. If we did a good job with our structured English transform description back in the analysis phase, and if the structure chart closely resembles the data flow diagrams, then this subphase will be relatively simple to accomplish. We can convert structured English to pseudocode by adding input and output statements and control type statements, such as those that process error conditions. Decision tables and decision trees, which we developed in the analysis phase, will also be useful in documenting the internal design of the modules.

Some designers still prefer to use program flowcharts, which we discussed in the previous chapter. If program flowcharts are used to document internal module design, they should be of a structured nature. In the previous chapter we introduced the allowable control patterns of structured English. The same control patterns are allowed when doing pseudocode or structured program flowcharts. These control patterns are reproduced in Figure 15-10 to refresh your memory. When drawing a structured program flowchart, only these patterns should be used. Note again, as mentioned previously, that there is no reason to ever use a GO TO type of control pattern in structured programming.

Long and complex program flowcharts are often difficult to follow even when drawn in a structured manner. Therefore, many designers are adopting the structured English or pseudocode approach to documenting the processing that goes on within a module. Figure 15-11 provides an example of a structured program flowchart, and shows the same procedure documented in pseudocode.

Package the Design

In packaging the design, we consider modifications appropriate to the physical hardware and software configurations on which the system will be implemented. This physical environment can include such things as the coding language, the operating system, limitations of disk drives, or time restrictions. Thus far in the structured design process we have attempted to produce a design independent of the physical environment that maximizes cohesion and minimizes coupling. Therefore, in packaging the design, we will modify it to fit the physical environment in such a way as to minimize deviation from the ideal design. For instance, we may have to combine modules to

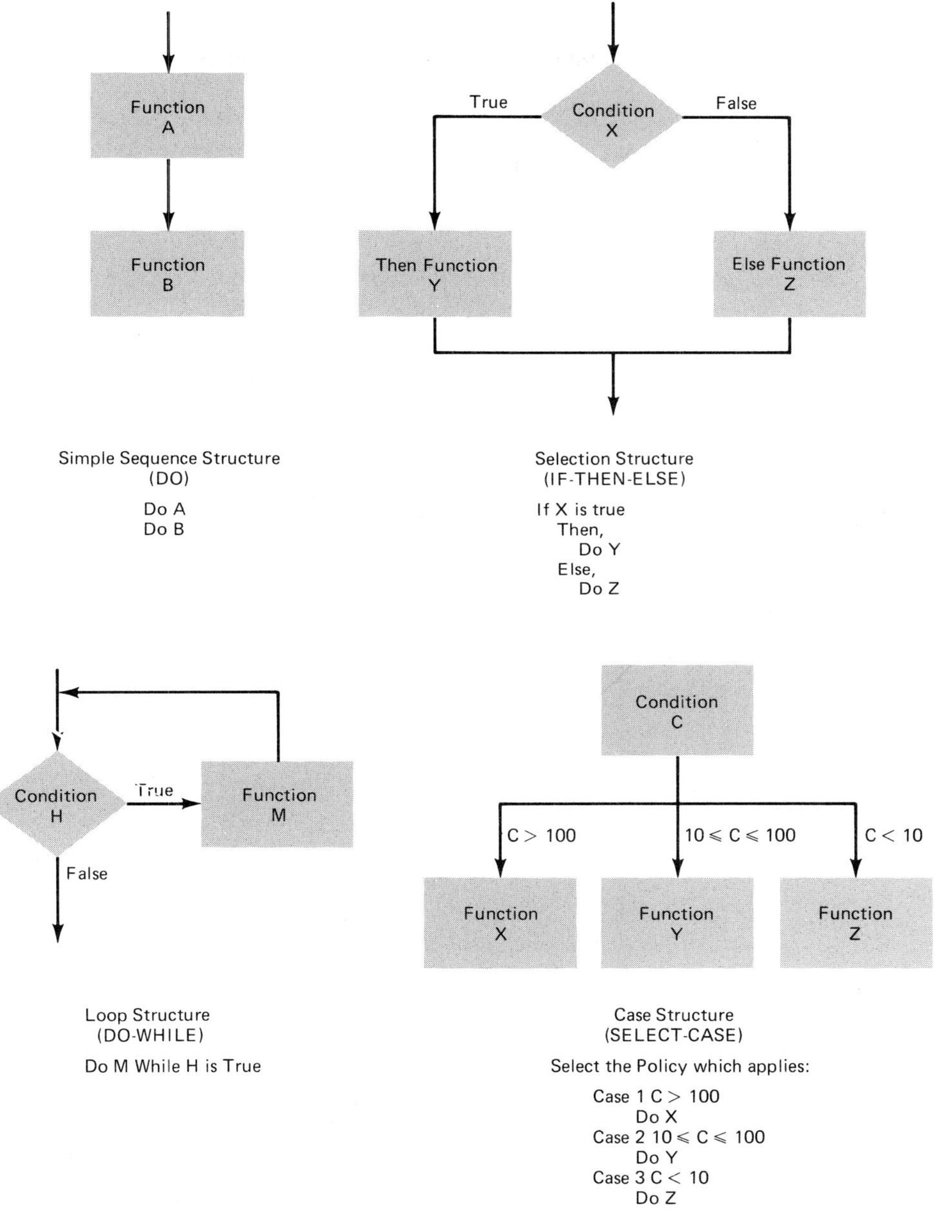

Figure 15-10 Allowable Structured English Control Patterns

produce an efficient system. However, in our pursuit of efficiency we do not want to go so far as to produce a system that compromises our modularity. Such a system would be difficult or even impossible to modify.

Some analysts go as far as saying that regardless of the physical environment, we

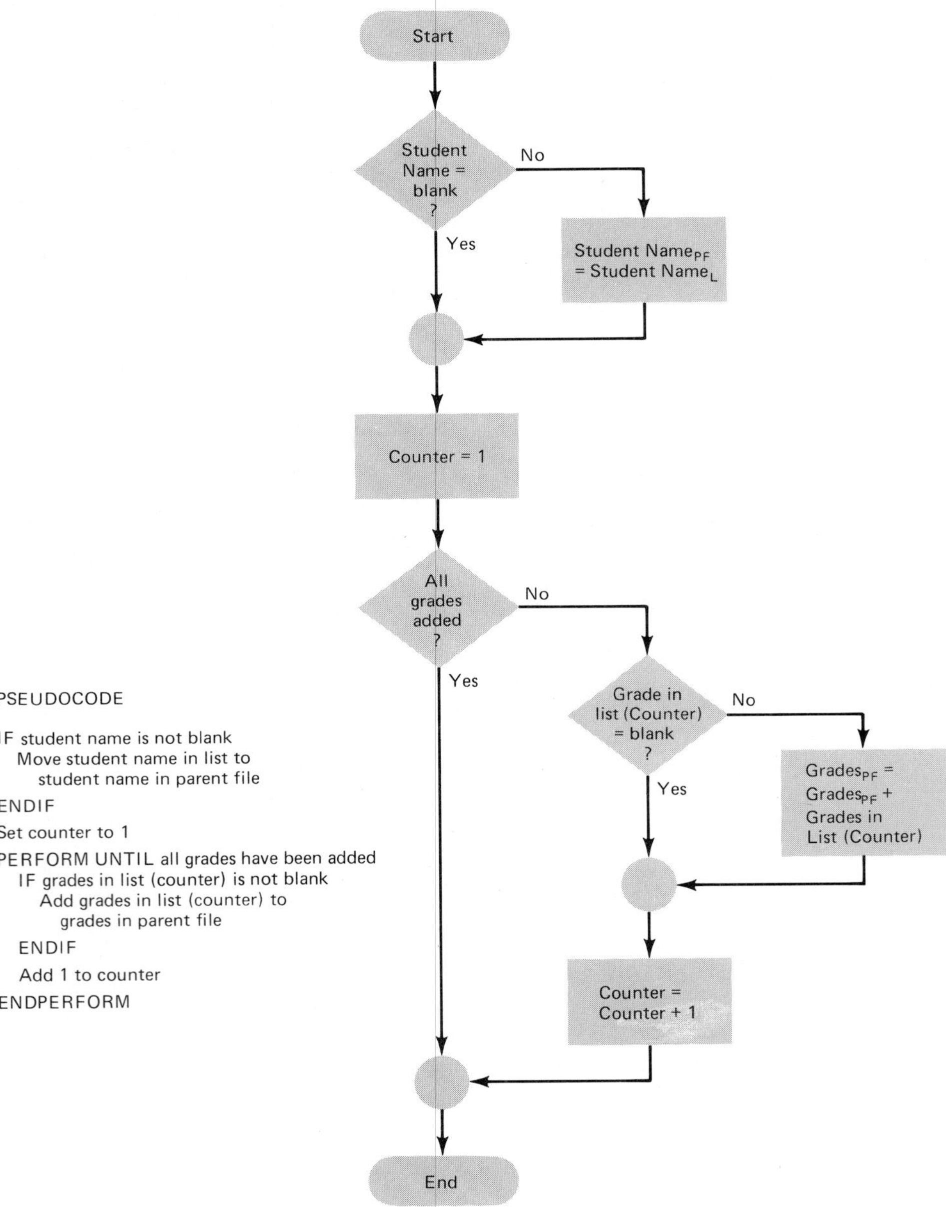
STRUCTURED FLOWCHART
Start
Student Name = blank ?
No
Yes
Student Name$_{PF}$ = Student Name$_{L}$
Counter = 1
All grades added ?
No
Yes
Grade in list (Counter) = blank ?
No
Yes
Grades$_{PF}$ = Grades$_{PF}$ + Grades in List (Counter)
Counter = Counter + 1
End
PSEUDOCODE
IF student name is not blank
Move student name in list to student name in parent file
ENDIF
Set counter to 1
PERFORM UNTIL all grades have been added
IF grades in list (counter) is not blank
Add grades in list (counter) to grades in parent file
ENDIF
Add 1 to counter
ENDPERFORM

Figure 15-11 A Structured Program Flowchart and Pseudocode

should first implement the system based on the ideal design developed back in the design modules phase. After the system is working, we can then worry about efficiency and modify the system to improve it.

The above approach of implementing the ideal structured system, with maximum cohesion and minimum coupling, is likely to become more widespread in the future. As hardware prices continue to decline, the efficiency at which a system executes is becoming less and less important. The human labor required to maintain and modify complex, nonstructured systems is a much more important consideration than how efficiently the system executes in a particular physical hardware environment.

The package design phase produces two primary outputs: 1) the test plan, which documents a plan for testing the system prior to implementation; and 2) the packaged design itself. The packaged design includes the structured specifications of data flow diagrams, data dictionary, and module descriptions including pseudocode, structured English, decision tables, decision charts, and sometimes program flowcharts. In addition, the packaged design would include input form designs, report layouts, and system configuration, including specification of hardware requirements.

IMPLEMENTATION

The primary activities occurring within the implementation phase are: 1) coding; 2) testing; and 3) manual procedure development. However, two other activities, structured walkthroughs and chief programmer teams, are also often used to support these primary activities. We will explore all five of these in this section.

Structured Walkthroughs

Prior to coding, many companies are now performing a *structured walkthrough* of the design. In a formal, structured walkthrough the design documentation is made available to a walkthrough review team of two to four people. These individuals review the design, and in a formal meeting the designer presents the system design to the review team. As the designer "walks" the review team through the design, questions that the review team have about the design are clarified. Quite often, this walkthrough process yields significant improvements in system design.

Structured walkthroughs are often also performed on program code after a module is coded. This process is called a *code inspection*, and like the structured design walkthrough, the programmer will walk members of a review team through the module's program code. During this process, the program code is checked for compliance with module specifications and for other types of errors in coding.

Top-Down Coding

Coding is the process of writing a program (or module) in a computer language based on the packaged design generated in the structured design phase. The task of coding the modules is often divided among several different programmers to decrease the elapsed time necessary for coding. A well-structured and well-specified system will help ensure that each module is compatible with other modules even though they are written by different programmers.

Many firms using structured programming advocate top-down coding. With top-down coding, modules are coded starting with the top module on the structure chart; then lower levels are coded from higher to lower levels. For example, the first thing that must be done is to write job control language statements for the top modules. The top module will then be coded and tested. Successively lower levels of modules will then be coded and tested, going from top to bottom of the chart. Realistically, many modules will be coded concurrently. In fact, in some firms the coding phase will overlap the systems design phase. However, the emphasis will be on starting and completing the coding of the top modules first. Certainly, coding of higher level modules can commence before the design of lower level modules is complete.

Top-Down Testing

After a module is coded, the first test performed on it is a *desk check*, which is the manual review of a module's logic. Both the programmer and supervisor review the module. Desk checking also includes manual tracing of hypothetical data (both valid and invalid) through the module's logic to verify that it will process data correctly. For example, an account number with incorrect check digits, a payroll check for $1 million, or a requisition from inventory in excess of $10,000 can be evaluated in terms of the logic and controls incorporated in the system.

As discussed above, a structured walkthrough of the program module code can be very useful at this point. Either formal or informal inspections of the code by other programmers will often identify improvements that can be made in the program code.

After desk checking, modules are compiled without execution. The compilation step (compiler diagnostics) almost always detects deviations from the rules and syntax of the particular computer language being used. After these errors are corrected, the module is compiled and executed with test input.

When programs are structured, this testing can be performed in a top-down fashion. Figure 15-12 illustrates this type of testing. Top-down testing is performed with

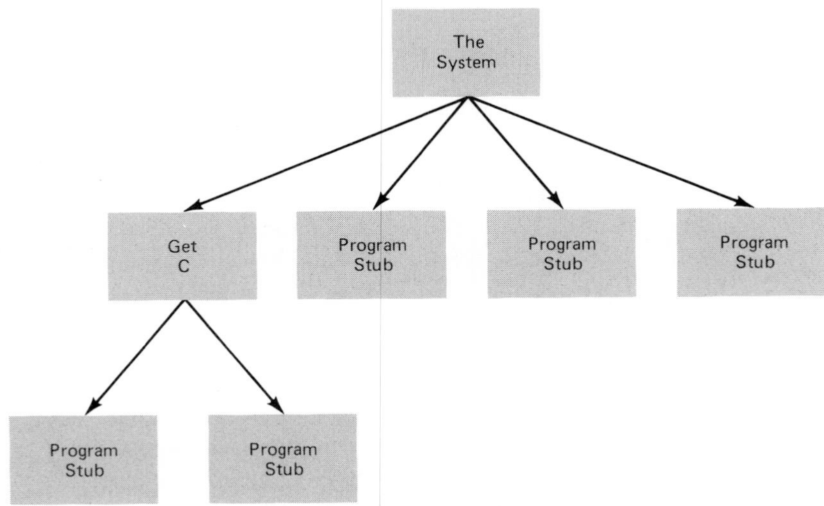

Figure 15-12 Top-Down Testing

program stubs when enough modules have been coded so that the testing will not be trivial. Effective testing can be done when the top level module and some of the second level modules have been coded.

Program stubs, which are dummy modules called by the parent routine, can be used to test modules. These program stubs have input/output behavior sufficiently similar to the yet to be coded real module so that the parent module can be executed. Figure 15-12 illustrates testing with program stubs of a system (depicted previously in Figure 15-6). The top module has been coded and one second level module, the GET C module, has also been coded. All of the program stub modules would perform input and output functions simulating the modules that are yet to be coded.

In addition, the program stubs would write out a message such as "GET B has been called" each time the particular module is called. This would provide a trace so that the programmer could identify when each program stub was called by the parent routine. Traces thus make the debugging task easier. As modules are coded they can be substituted for program stubs. In turn, if these modules call other modules that are yet to be coded, new program stubs can be inserted.

Top-down testing has very significant advantages. For example, testing of the system can proceed in a top-down fashion as each module is coded. Testing is then spread over a longer period of time, which prevents a crash testing approach in a restricted period of time after all modules have been coded. In addition, errors are much easier to isolate because, when detected, they are likely to be related to the most recently inserted module. Since all other modules would have been previously tested and corrected, detected errors would probably not be related to them.

Preparation of test data is a very important step in the testing process. Inadequate test data at this stage can be very costly later on because of undetected errors (bugs). Test data should be comprehensive, covering every possible type of valid and invalid input that could occur when the module is operational. Development of adequate test data generally requires users to participate since they are most familiar with the various combinations of input that can occur. Test data should cause every statement in the module to be executed, including logic that is seldom used. Otherwise, the test will not be thorough. Software tools are also available to identify executed or unexecuted module statements. Given a set of test data, the expected output from the module's execution of this data should be determined manually, so that the programmer can ascertain whether the module's processing is valid.

After each coded module has been tested in a top-down fashion and corrected, they are tested collectively as a system using similarly comprehensive test data. Once the system has been tested with hypothetical test data, the final test prior to implementation should be the processing of actual live data at volume levels expected when the system is operational.

Procedure Development

Systems analysis and user personnel normally develop procedures as module coding and testing progresses. A complete written set of manual procedures must be developed that documents all manual processes to be performed by both user and data processing operations personnel in the actual operation of the system. The procedures should cover such items as input preparation, control and balancing, error correction, batch run setups, and computer operator instructions. Collectively, these procedures form a critical part of the system's documentation.

Documentation is sometimes the most neglected aspect of the systems development life cycle. Firms frequently depend on a key individual or group of individuals to design and operate an information system. If these people rely on their memories for programming, systems, and operating information, and then find other employment, the firm has to study and document the existing system before work can begin on modifying it or designing a new one. Rarely can anyone remember all the detailed design information of a complex, computer-based system.

Adequate documentation includes: 1) all the specifications in the systems development lifecycle; 2) data flow diagrams and structure charts; 3) data dictionaries; 4) hardware specifications; 5) performance specifications; 6) job descriptions; and 7) procedure manuals.

Chief Programmer Teams

Many firms organize their programming efforts into chief programmer teams. A chief programmer team consists of a chief programmer who acts as supervisor of the programming team, one or more programmers, a librarian, and a backup programmer. The backup programmer acts as an assistant to the chief programmer. The chief programmer, with the assistance of the backup programmer, will code the more important modules of a system while the other modules will be coded by the other programmers in the team.

The librarian is one of the key people on the chief programmer team. The primary responsibility of the librarian is to maintain up-to-date documentation for the systems on which the team is working. Often, programmers do not enjoy doing the clerical filing tasks that are necessary to maintain this up-to-date documentation. The documentation is centralized, rather than being under the control of individual programmers, and is available to anyone on the team. The librarian's functions include maintaining copies of source and object listings, updating test data, picking up computer output, and maintaining up-to-date documentation in a secure file.

CONVERSION

In the conversion phase of the development life cycle, user and systems personnel must work closely together. Selling the new system to user personnel is a very important factor in its future success. Any new system, especially one involving a computer, can be viewed as a threat to the security of user personnel. This opposition to change must be overcome. In some instances, user personnel have sabotaged new systems because the former's conversion was not well conceived and executed. Some resistance to change can be overcome if user personnel are meaningfully involved in the development life cycle. Most phases of the development life cycle do not preclude such involvement.

A substantial training program may be required if the change is significant. Employees sometimes view training programs as a threat because they believe that any evaluation that might come at the end of such a program will be used against them. These people sometimes lack the self-confidence to return to school after many years of absence. The analyst must take these reservations into account when planning a training program. An orientation program should be prepared for all personnel who will in any way have contact with the system.

Two potentially difficult personnel problems are the relocation of displaced personnel and adjustments to the organizational structure. If relocation is necessary, individuals from the personnel department should be involved in the process as soon as possible. Relocation can require a significant adjustment on the part of an employee, and professional staff from the personnel department are equipped to handle such problems. Also, employees should be kept fully informed of changes so that rumors are reduced to a minimum.

Adjustments to the organizational structure will also cause problems in human relations. Changes in supervisory positions or in line and staff relationships should be handled in a professional manner. New positions should be meaningful and not created simply to postpone the retirement of an older employee. Job enrichment and other personnel programs are appropriate in these circumstances.

The analyst must realize that a major emphasis of the conversion phase is on the nonmachine components of the system. Care must be taken to ensure that the new system receives good input. Many new systems have failed because of quality control problems with input.

The major physical changes involved in the conversion phase are site preparation and file conversion. Changes in hardware or work flow will require changes in the physical location of the system or personnel, or both. These must be well planned and coordinated. Inadequate preparation of the site will impair the performance of the system when it begins to operate.

Prior to conversion, master files and databases must be created for the system either through manual inputs (if the old system was manual), or a combination of manual inputs and conversion of data from old files. Conversion of master files and data bases is often time consuming and costly. It requires special conversion programs. A critical control point in this phase is the control of conversion of files. File conversion programs must be thoroughly tested, listings of the new master files must be manually reviewed for errors, and control totals must be balanced. Until file conversion has taken place, it is not possible to operate the new system. The actual conversion of the complete system can be performed using four basic approaches: 1) parallel conversion; 2) direct conversion; 3) phased conversion; and 4) pilot conversion.

Parallel Conversion

Parallel conversion (Figure 15-13), a widely used approach, consists of operating both the old and new systems simultaneously until management is confident that the latter will perform satisfactorily. At this point, the old system is discontinued.

Parallel operation is often necessary but it is very demanding on employees. They must operate two systems and then compare results. Because of this apparent problem, it might be viewed as desirable to minimize the time of parallel operation. However, the successful implementation of any new system requires sufficient testing to eliminate most major problems. In many situations, a parallel operation of several weeks or months is desirable.

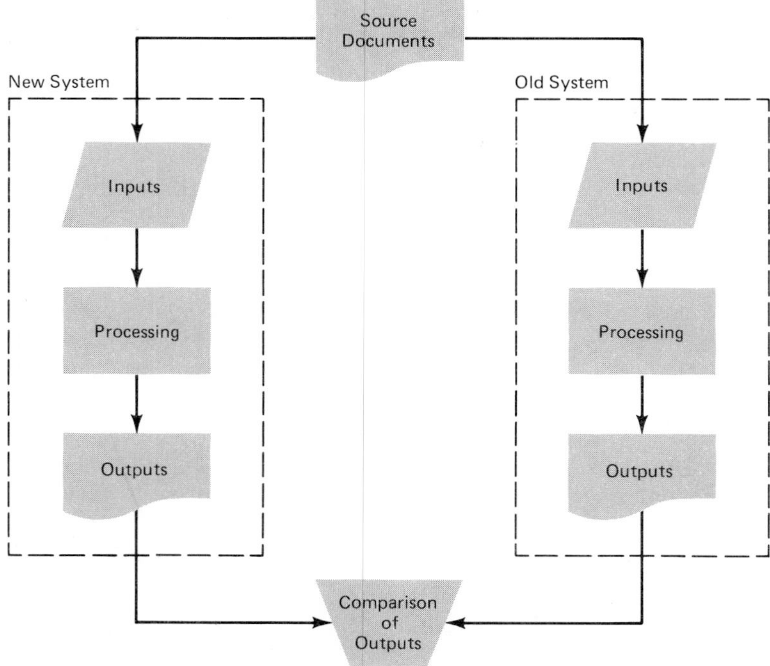

Figure 15-13 Parallel Conversion

Direct Conversion

When parallel conversion is not appropriate, the direct approach (Figure 15-14) may be used. *Direct conversion* (sometimes referred to as cold turkey, or crash conversion) consists of terminating the old system at the end of one workday and starting up the new system the next. This can be extremely risky, but it is gaining in popularity for the following reasons:

1. With the parallel approach, demands of operating two systems may not allow enough resources to be allocated to the new system to make it successful. Furthermore, employees may keep using the old, familiar system and not make a genuine effort to support and use the new system. The direct approach avoids both problems.
2. With thorough testing of the system and training of personnel, the new system may operate at acceptable levels from its inception.
3. In many cases, the risk of failure of the new system may be acceptable. For example, in most situations reversion to the old system may be possible if failure occurs.

Phased Conversion

The third conversion approach is *phased conversion* (Figure 15-15), in which the old system is gradually phased out, and the new one gradually phased in at the same time. There are a number of ways this phase-in can be accomplished. For example, with a

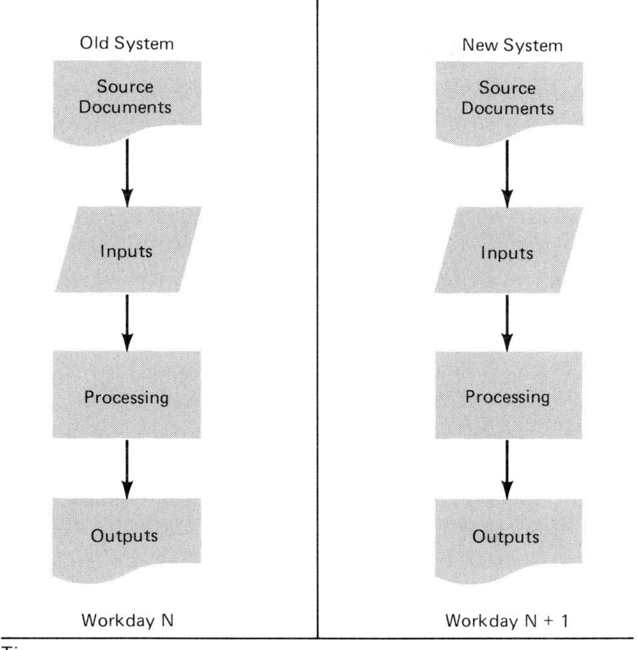

Figure 15-14 Direct Conversion

new accounts receivable system, all newly opened accounts can be processed by the new system while existing accounts continue to be processed by the old system. As accounts gradually turn over, the new system will replace the old. When the new system is operating satisfactorily, the accounts remaining on the old system can be transferred to the new, and the old system can be terminated. This approach has many of the same problems as the parallel approach, the primary one being the necessity of operating two

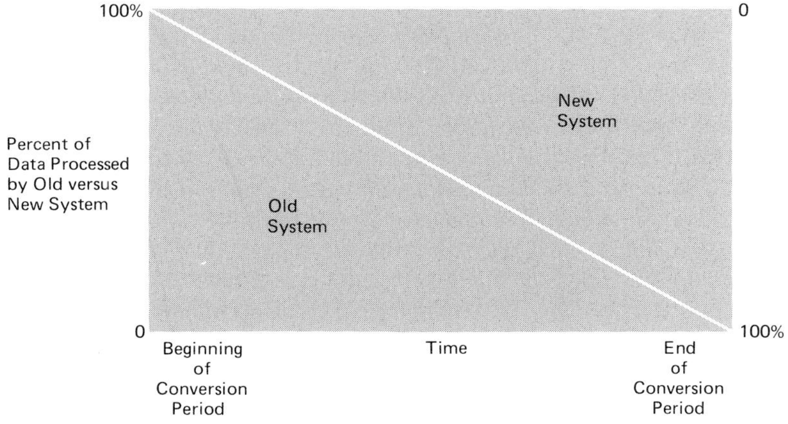

Figure 15-15 Phased Conversion

systems simultaneously. In addition, two other significant drawbacks of phased conversion are:

1. The outputs of the two systems must be combined to gain a total picture.
2. A false sense of security may be created since backup by the old system does not in fact exist for data being processed by the new system, except in the case of a total reversion to the old system.

Pilot Conversion

The pilot approach to conversion is often an excellent alternative (Figure 15-16). *Pilot conversion* consists of implementing the new system in only a selected portion of its ultimate implementation area (for example, in an organizational unit like a plant, branch, or division). If the system operates satisfactorily in the pilot implementation, it is then fully implemented. Within the pilot area, the system can be implemented by parallel, direct, or phased methods. The pilot method avoids many problems of the other three methods but does not test whether the system will operate satisfactorily under the increased volume of full implementation. Furthermore, in many cases it may not be possible to segregate an appropriate area for the pilot conversion.

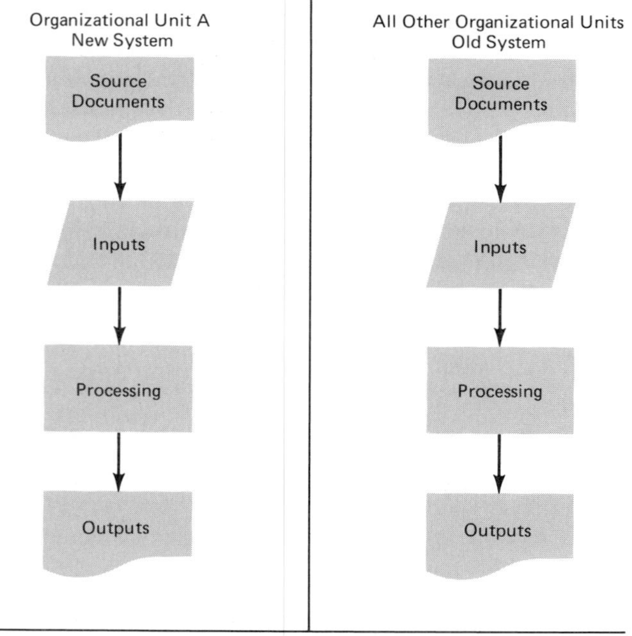

Figure 15-16 Pilot Conversion

After personnel and physical changes have been taken care of in the implementation stage, steps must be taken to phase out the old system. Although this may seem obvious, there are numerous examples of new systems being brought online without the old systems (especially manual systems) being terminated.

MANAGEMENT CASE 15-2

Smith's is a regional department store chain located in the middle atlantic states. Smith's extends credit to all of its creditworthy customers and has a large number of outstanding accounts receivable. About 60% of Smith's sales are on credit. They have had an online accounts receivable system for the past 8 years. Recently this accounts receivable system has been converted to a data base management system. In the process most of the input screens, output screens, and much of the program logic was modified to better meet user and customer needs. The new system has been thoroughly tested and is now ready for conversion. The manager of systems development has advocated using a direct conversion approach while others in the organization prefer a pilot approach whereby two or three stores would be converted initially. The manager of systems development feels that direct conversion is the most appropriate since the new system has been thoroughly tested, employees can be trained in the use of the new system prior to conversion and furthermore, the current employees are familiar with the use of an online accounts receivable system. Would you support either a direct or pilot conversion or some other method? Support your position.

POST-IMPLEMENTATION AUDIT AND MAINTENANCE

A frequently overlooked but necessary step in the systems development life cycle is the post-implementation audit. Two general areas are reviewed at this point: 1) the performance of the new system is evaluated in terms of objectives stated in the survey and analysis phases; and 2) the systems development life cycle is reviewed. Budgets and schedules developed in the survey and analysis phases can be used to evaluate the performance of the systems development team.

For example, error rates and processing times can be compared with rates in the design specifications of the system. User complaints can also be considered. Failure of the system to achieve design specifications might mean that expected benefits from the new system will never be realized. It also may mean that the system is not being operated according to specifications. Another aspect of evaluating the performance of the new system involves comparing actual operating costs of the new system with estimated costs. Significant deviations from estimated costs will have a negative impact on cost-benefit ratios of the new system.

Performance of the design group can be reviewed in several areas during the post-implementation audit. Besides comparing actual time with estimated time, and actual costs with budgets, users can be interviewed to evaluate their acceptance of the new system. Frequently, results of the post-implementation audit will serve as the basis for beginning the systems development cycle again.

Who should conduct the audit is an important question. For small projects, the supervisor in charge of systems analysts is generally an appropriate choice. When a large project is reviewed, a team of systems personnel and managers who were not involved in the project is appropriate. Internal auditors are frequently involved in the post-implementation audit of a large system. Occasionally, it is proper to bring in outside people to conduct the audits. Lack of personal connections, broader experience, and a different view of the organization all contribute to their conducting an objective review. Many companies also perform periodic audits of systems in addition to the post-implementation audit.

The life span of an application system can be significantly extended through proper maintenance. Maintenance consists of promptly correcting any additional errors discovered in modules, updating program modules to meet changed requirements, and maintaining documentation to reflect system and module program changes.

SUMMARY

The documents produced during structured analysis are used extensively during systems design and implementation.

A structure chart is a hierarchical diagram showing the relationship between various program modules. It is derived from DFDs. Important objectives here are to minimize coupling between modules and to maximize cohesion within modules.

Using the structure chart as a guideline, we now design individual modules. The structured English statements written earlier may be used for documentation at this stage.

The design is then packaged and modified to suit the hardware and software environment. In addition to the packaged design, a test plan is produced at this time.

Structured walkthroughs are often used to review the packaged design as well as the program code.

Coding and testing are done in a top-down manner. This means that the upper level control modules are coded and tested before the detailed, lower-level modules are even written.

Procedure manuals are generally written concurrently with coding and testing. These form a critical part of the final system.

Programming personnel are often organized as chief programmer teams. Many firms have found this to be an efficient organization structure.

The conversion phase may involve many problems, such as user resistance, personnel relocation, and changes in the organizational structure. Careful planning is a must at this stage.

Four different approaches may be used when converting from the old system to the new:

1. Parallel Conversion
2. Direct Conversion
3. Phased Conversion
4. Pilot Conversion

After the system is converted, an audit is done to judge its performance against the original system objectives.

Maintenance of a system consists of removing any additional program errors and changing the system to meet new information processing requirements.

KEY TERMS

Structure Chart
Top-down Design
Module
Subroutine
Connection
Couple
Transform Data Flow Diagram
Transaction Center Data Flow Diagram
Transform Analysis
Transaction Analysis
Control Data
Coupling
Cohesion
Pseudocode
Packaged Design
Test Plan
Coding
Structured Walkthrough
Code Inspection
Top-down Coding
Program Stubs
Debugging
Test Data
Documentation
Chief Programmer Team
Parallel Conversion
Direct Conversion
Phased Conversion
Pilot Conversion
Post-Implementation Audit

REVIEW QUESTIONS

1. What is the difference between a structure chart and a data flow diagram?
2. Explain the following terms:
   a. Module
   b. Subroutine
   c. Connection
   d. Couple
   e. Transform DFD
   f. Transaction Center DFD
3. What makes a module cohesive?
4. How can you determine if a module is cohesive?
5. What is module coupling?
6. What is the relationship between coupling and cohesion?
7. Why are coupling and cohesion important to the user of information systems?
8. What are the outputs of the design packaging subphase?
9. Explain the concept of a structured walkthrough.
10. What is top-down coding?
11. How are program stubs used in testing?
12. What is test data? What qualities should it possess?
13. Why is documentation important to the users?
14. Describe the composition of a chief programmer team.
15. List the major problems that may be encountered during system conversion.

16. Discuss the four approaches to system conversion.
17. What is the significance of the post-implementation audit?

DISCUSSION QUESTIONS

1. Omega Systems, a management consulting firm, is designing a new inventory control system for Nordener & Mufti Inc., a distributor of petroleum products. The President of Nordener and Mufti feels that costs can be minimized by designing the new system such that it uses most of the existing hardware and software. The project manager at Omega does not agree. She believes that this would unduly restrict the design options, and probably lead to the development of an inefficient system. Discuss the merits and demerits of both viewpoints, and give your own opinion on the matter.
2. Despite the popularity of the top-down approach, some programmers are skeptical about its usefulness. One common complaint is that the top level control modules cannot be coded unless the programmer knows exactly what takes place in the lower level modules. Another problem is the difficulty of creating a simple hierarchy. Since some lower level modules are called by more than one upper level routines, the neat, inverted tree structure sometimes cannot exist. Maintenance is not as easy as the proponents of top-down design claim it to be. Most modifications made to a system were never anticipated at the time of original design. The top-down structure is therefore unable to accommodate these changes. Comment on the validity of these objections. If they are valid, does it mean we should abandon the top-down approach?
3. For each case listed below, decide which of the four conversion methods you would use when switching to a new system. Justify your choice.
   a. An inventory reordering system at a fertilizer plant.
   b. A military strategic surveillance system.
   c. The book checkout system in your library.

RESEARCH PROJECTS

1. Obtain users' manuals and other documentation related to any software system being used at your institution. Critically review the documents, and point out their strengths and weaknesses. Suggest some changes to improve the documentation from a user's point of view.
2. Write a brief paper on the personnel problems encountered during the implementation of a new system, and how to deal with them. An excellent source of information on this subject would be interviews with systems designers. There are also many good articles in journals like *Computer Decisions* and *Personnel Journal.*

ESSAY

Qualities of Good Software

(Reprinted with permission from MIS Week, Oct. 13, 1982, p. 38)

By Rikki L. Welsh, Operations Research Analyst, GFP Management Branch, Army Corps of Engineers, Summit Point, W. Va.

Good software is a thing of beauty—both to use and to look at and to comprehend. It is as easily recognizable to be good as bad software is to be bad. But what are the qualities that make it good? Can they be quantified?

Regardless of the machine or language selected, superior software exhibits the same set of attributes. The National Bureau of Standards in special publication No. 500-11 has given us a list of these attributes.

I have separated these into two areas—human engineering and software engineering. Although rankings in these areas may be somewhat subjective, a set of factors can be used which gives a reasonable profile of a piece of software.

Human engineering simply refers to how easy a program is to use. This area is of great significance to the user in an interactive environment. The aggregate rating of these factors will indicate whether a user feels that the computer is helpful or is a burden and willfully tries to mislead him.

The qualities to be considered are:

(1) Reliability. Programs perform all functions as documented without detectable errors. Note that this implies there is adequate user documentation and that incorrect documentation is as serious as incorrect software.

(2) Robustness. Programs are "forgiving." Unacceptable input or inconsistent commands should not cause detrimental results.

(3) Usability. Programs have functions and usage techniques that are natural and convenient for people rather than machines. Too often programs are developed which are easy to write rather than easy to use. Aspects of this include:

- No arbitrary codes for data. Although a "code" can sometimes be a convenient means of identifying data, it should be an alternative. The use of actual data names or screen-formatted input should have preference.
- Understandable and logical commands. Command syntax should make sense and do the obvious thing. That is, commands should be "intuitive."
- Terms and conventions used consistently in all modes of operation. An example to avoid would be having some commands use the "break" key to interrupt output to the screen, while others use "break" to kill the program; and another using "D" to delete a record in one phase of processing and "D" for "done" in another phase—will inevitably lead to problems.
- Good diagnostic messages for errors or violations. Understandable diagnostics can make the computer seem helpful rather than mysterious or reluctant.
- Adequate "help" routine. Help should be available for any requested input.
- Response-time well within a user's attention span.

(4) User clarity. The purpose of the program and how it generally goes about its tasks should not remain a mystery.

The factors under software engineering relate to how well the program meets its requirements and will continue to do so. These are considerations of the programmer who must implement or modify the software:

(1) Correctness. Programs perform all the functions from the specifications. Although related to reliability, correctness is more a measure of how well the programs address the specifications, rather than how error-free the programs are, which is reliability.

(2) Validity. This is a question of the quality of specifications as well as the computer programs. Assessing validity requires a judgment of what the user really requires and how well the software provides that requirement.

(3) Clarity. The program design and structure should be readily apparent from the program listing. Components of this attribute are: well written documentation with examples if needed to explain complex operations; meaningful variable names with structures used to group-related variables, and naming conventions explicitly giv-

ing the family for each variable; frequent and meaningful comments; modular structure isolating separate small, well-named functions with logical, concise calling sequences; modules which modify parameters or global variables are clearly marked; known and clearly stated algorithms; consistent naming conventions (e.g., for global vs. local variables) used throughout; and carefully designed and logical program flow.

(4) Maintainability. Programs with a low score in "clarity" will never get a good one in maintainability. Clarity is essential to maintainability.

(5) Extensibility. Closely allied to maintainability, extensibility also means that a concerted effort is made to anticipate major changes.

(6) Generality. Programs are not limited to a small range of input values when they can reasonably be extended to a more general case.

(7) Testability. Programs are structured in such a fashion to facilitate step-by-step testing of capabilities. The various functions may be isolated and independently tested.

(8) Efficiency. Cost of program operations should be kept as low as possible through high-performance algorithms and conservative use of computer resources, such as main storage, CPU, disk.

(9) Portability. In general, portability implies use of a standard programming language or at least a language which is available on a number of different processors. Any hardware specific features should be isolated for easy change.

The accompanying checklist can be used to determine an overall rating. Have a user score the human engineering attributes. Obviously, if the software is not for use by human beings, e.g., a process control program which drives machinery, the affinity index does not apply (unless you can get the machine to fill it out). The software engineering attributes need to be rated by a programmer.

Score two points for excellent, one for good, zero for passable, and minus two for poor. A total score of zero for affinity means you can probably use the program without tearing out your hair, but it won't be fun!

Discussion

1. How does the use of structured analysis and design contribute to qualities of good software?
2. As a computer user why are the qualities of good software important to you? Which qualities are most important to you?

CHECKLIST FOR COMPUTER SOFTWARE

		Excellent (2)	Good (1)	Passable (0)	Poor (−2)	
Human Engineering	Reliability Robustness Usability No arbitrary codes Intuitive commands Consistency Good diagnostics Help Response time Clarity					Affinity index (User measurements)
Software Engineering	Correctness Validity Clarity Documentation Meaningful variable names Comments Modular structure Algorithms Consistency Design Maintainability Extensibility Generality Testability Efficiency Portability*					Operability index (Programmer measurements)

*(Not always relevant)

CHAPTER 16

APPLICATION DEVELOPMENT BY USERS

INTRODUCTION

Many data processing experts are beginning to argue that a large percentage of business applications can be developed by users. Such application development means that users develop software directly without the assistance of programmers, and quite often without systems or information analysts. Individuals who hold this maintain that conventional development cycles, whether classical or structured, are not useful in many business situations.

There are essentially three ways users can create or obtain application software without using programmers. One is that users can be given powerful but easy-to-use computer tools to create their own application software. These tools are often called application generators. *Application generators* allow the user to specify what needs to be done and then generates program code based on user requirements. A second way is for consultants or system analysts to work directly with users. Application software can then be generated through the use of application generators and other types of powerful software tools. The third way involves purchase of preprogrammed application software packages from outside vendors. Since we will cover purchase of application software in chapter 18, alternatives one and two will be dealt with in this chapter. We will look at some problems associated with the conventional development approach. The various methods users can employ to develop application software will then be covered, followed by a discussion of the blending of user development with conventional development. Finally, the impact of user-developed software on the conventional data processing organization will be discussed. In this area, we will cover the concept of an information center and the changing role of systems analysts and programmers.

PROBLEMS WITH CONVENTIONAL DEVELOPMENT

Conventional application program development is the process we have studied in the two previous chapters. Conventional development may follow either the classical or the structured approach. Figure 16-1 illustrates the conventional application development cycle using the structured approach.

Increasing Labor Cost

The conventional development cycle is a labor intensive, time-consuming process. Creating both physical and logical data flow diagrams, for the old and new systems, drawing structure charts, and writing the programs is essentially a manual process. While labor costs associated with programming and systems analysis continue to increase, the price of computer hardware continues to decline. This relationship is shown in Figure 16-2. In the late 70s the cost of hardware dipped below labor costs for computer organizations. This relationship between labor and computer hardware costs makes it economical to substitute hardware for labor.

In the case of user applications software development we can develop software directly through the use of computers and application generators. The labor cost of programming is thus eliminated, and the cost of systems analysis is reduced significantly. Obviously, this practice increases hardware costs because we have to use a computer to execute application generator packages. Also, the application generator packages usually do not produce program code that executes as efficiently as program code written by programmers. However, this is of little concern because of the dramatic decline in hardware costs.

Time Required for Applications Development

A major disadvantage of the conventional development approach is the usually very long time span, sometimes months or years, required for development of application software. Due to the dynamic nature of most businesses, software needs originally defined in the feasibility stage may have changed substantially by the time the system is operational. Therefore, the system is sometimes obsolete by the time it is implemented.

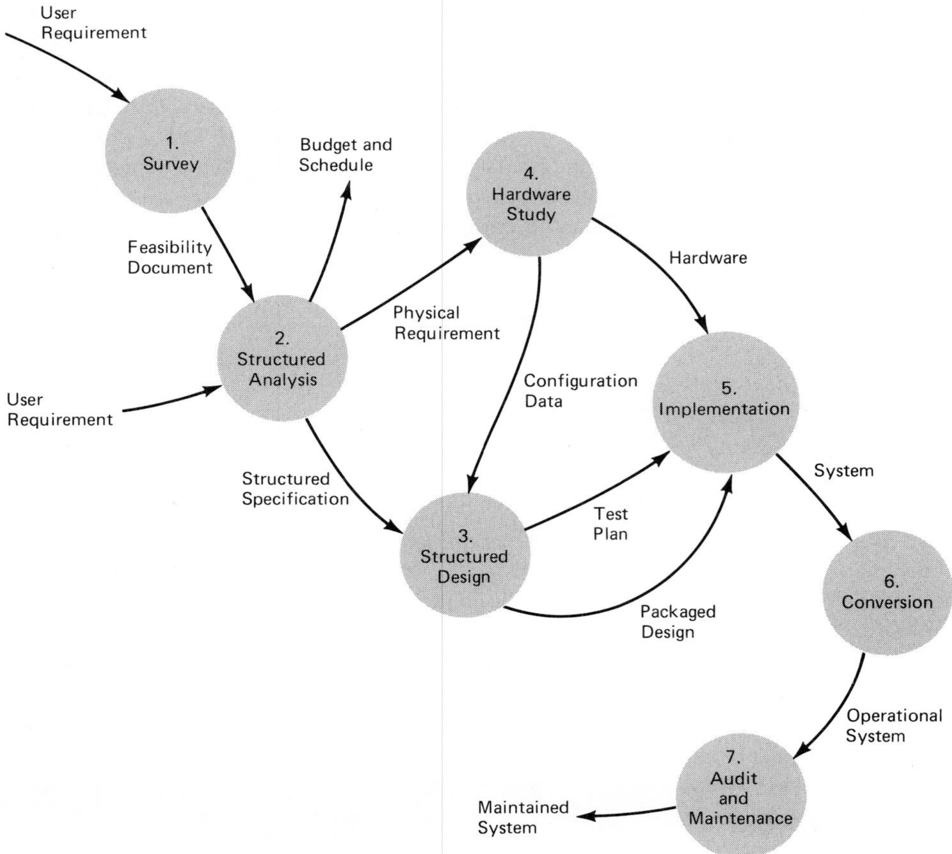

Figure 16-1 Structured Development Life Cycle. Adapted with permission from Tom Demarco, *Structured Analysis and System Specification* (New York: Yourdon Inc., 1979), 26.

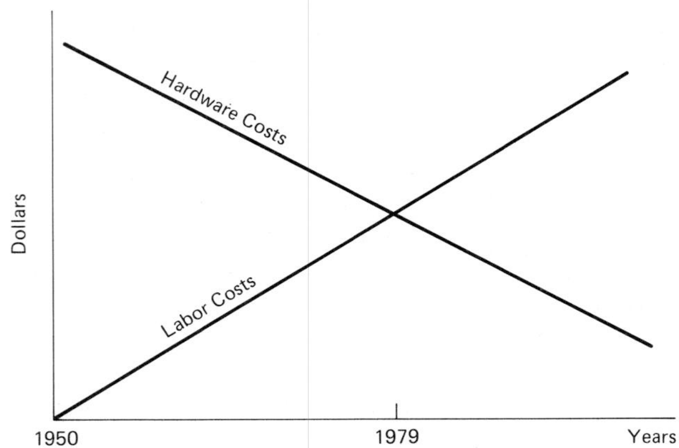

Figure 16-2 Software Costs versus Hardware Costs

Slow Implementation of Changes

Closely related to the long time span required for application development is the typically slow implementation of changes to the system. James Martin has stated that the mere act of implementing a system changes the requirements for that system.[1] In other words, after a system is implemented it will affect the user department in unforeseen ways. Martin maintains that it is impossible to foresee all the effects of a new system on a department's information needs. There will be requests for changes to the system as soon as it is implemented, since the user really cannot experience the new system until it is implemented. If systems are going to be successful we must be able to implement changes rapidly. This is often difficult to do using the conventional development cycle.

Work Overload

As discussed previously, maintenance of application software is a major concern. In fact, most mature data processing organizations find that over half (up to 60 percent) of their programming effort is directed toward maintenance of existing systems as opposed to programming new systems. If this trend continues, we may find situations in which almost all of the programming effort of data processing departments is spent on maintenance of existing systems.

Due to the declining price of hardware, many new users have purchased computers. If we depend upon programmers to write software for these new users, there simply will not be enough programmers to go around. In fact, for several years now there has been an acute shortage of business application programmers. If all new users of computers are going to get even minimal use of their computer hardware, we simply must find new ways of creating application software other than utilization of the conventional development cycle.

Prespecified Versus User-Driven Computing

Martin has classified computing into two categories, prespecified versus user-driven computing.[2] In *prespecified computing,* processing requirements can generally be determined ahead of time. Therefore, formal requirement specifications can be created and we can use the conventional development cycle. By contrast, in *user driven computing,* users do not have a detailed knowledge of what they want until they use a version of it. Thus, they may modify the system frequently and quickly. Figure 16-3 summarizes the distinctions between prespecified and user-driven computing.

Today, it is not entirely clear what percentage of business computing should be developed using the prespecified approach and what percentage should be developed with user-driven techniques. However, as users gain experience with new tools that allow them to develop their own applications, the percentage developed through user-driven techniques is certain to increase and become the predominant development

---

[1]James Martin, Application Development Without Programmers (Englewood Cliffs, NJ: Prentice-Hall, 1982) 61–62.

[2]*Ibid.*, 54

PRESPECIFIED COMPUTING

- Formal requirements specifications are created.
- A development cycle such as that in Fig. 16-1 is employed.
- Programs are formally documented.
- The application development time is many months or years.
- Maintenance is formal, slow, and expensive.

Examples: Compiler writing, airline reservations, air traffic control, missile guidance, software development.

USER-DRIVEN COMPUTING

- Users do not know in detail what they want until they use a version of it, and then they modify it quickly and often frequently. Consequently, formal requirement specification linked to slow application programming is doomed to failure.
- Users may create their own applications, but more often with an analyst who does this in cooperation with them. A separate programming department is not used.
- Applications are created with a generator or other software in Table 16-1 more quickly than the time to write specifications.
- The application development time is days or at most weeks.
- Maintenance is continuous. Incremental changes are made constantly to the applications by the users or the analyst who assists them.
- The system is self-documenting, or interactive documentation is created when the application is created.
- A centrally administered data-base facility is often employed. Data administration is generally needed to prevent chaos of incompatible data spreading.
  Examples: Administrative procedures, shop floor control, information systems, decision support, paperwork avoidance.

Figure 16-3 Prespecified versus User-Driven Computing. James Martin, *Application Development Without Programmers,* © 1982 p. 55. Reprinted by permission of Prentice-Hall Inc. Englewood Cliffs, N.J.

approach. Quoting Martin:

> The requirements for management information systems cannot be specified beforehand and almost every attempt to do so has failed. The requirements change as soon as an executive starts to use his terminal. The point . . . is *not* that conventional application development . . . should be abandoned, but rather *it only works for certain types of systems.*[3]

[3] *Ibid.*, 52

MANAGEMENT CASE 16-1

The systems development department of Floyd Incorporated is in what many might say is an enviable position. The department has been growing at a very rapid pace due to the demands placed upon it by users of computers in the company. In the past 2 years the number of employees in the department have increased by 40% each year. Even with this increase in staff the backlog of user requests for new systems and modifications to existing systems is continuing to grow. A normal priority request for change to a system currently takes about 8–9 months to implement. If you were the president of Floyd Incorporated would you continue to approve increases in the staffing level of the system development department? If not, how would you propose to handle the demand for new computer application software and changes to the existing software?

METHODS FOR USER DEVELOPMENT OF APPLICATION SOFTWARE

Application development by users became practical in the late 1970s and early 1980s. The availability of very powerful software for the development of applications made application development by users possible. This kind of software can be classified into six categories: 1) query languages; 2) report generators; 3) graphics languages; 4) application generators; 5) very high level programming languages; and 6) parameterized application packages.

Query Languages

We briefly discussed query languages in the chapter on data base management systems. These languages are normally associated with data base management systems, and allow a user to search a data base or file using simple or complex selection criteria. The results of the search can be displayed in detail or in summary format. For example, the query might state "List of customer accounts which are 30 to 60 days overdue, and which have a balance in excess of $1,000." This type of software is widely available today. Many of the packages also allow update of the data base as well as data retrieval.

Report Generators

Report generators are similar to query languages except that they can perform more sophisticated data processing tasks and produce reports in almost any format. Generally, query languages are designed to be used by users without assistance from data processing professionals. However, use of report generators often requires help from DP professionals, such as systems analysts. One popular report generator, RPG, is discussed in Chapter 7.

Graphics Languages

Graphic output, usually through terminals, is becoming increasingly important to today's business management. Graphics languages allow users to retrieve data from files or data bases and display it graphically. Users can specify data they wish to graph as well as the basic format, such as pie graph, line graph, or bar graph.

Application Generators

Application generators can create an entire data processing application, including input validation, file update, processing, and report generation. Most application generators allow the user to specify what needs to be done, and the application generator then decides how it will be done. In other words, the application generator generates program code based on the user's requirements.

Many data processing operations are routine and tend to be performed in the same manner regardless of the application. For example, most applications have to communicate with terminals, update files, and produce reports. These types of operations are preprogrammed in generalized modules included in the application generator. When these operations are required in an application, the application generator invokes the preprogrammed modules and modifies them slightly for particular application needs.

It is unlikely that everything a particular application requires can be generated by an application generator. Each application is likely to have certain unique requirements. Therefore, most application generators contain what are known as user exits. *User exits* allow a user or programmer to insert program code in the generated application that performs these unique requirements of the application. User exit routines can be programmed in a variety of languages, including COBOL and PL/1.

Interactive application generators are available. Sitting at a terminal, a user and a systems analyst respond to questions from the application generator. Their responses define application inputs, files, processes, and reports. In addition, the application generator generates code to execute the application. In a matter of hours, a prototype of the application may be up and running. This allows a user to experiment with the new application and make modifications if necessary.

Very High Level Programming Languages

Languages such as NOMAD and APL (A Programming Language) allow coding to be performed in a much shorter version than languages such as COBOL and FORTRAN. Therefore, users familiar with these languages can write their own programs in a very short period of time. These languages make heavy use of default options. *Default options* perform a standard operation whenever the user fails to specify how the operation is to be done. For example, if the command to LIST certain data is used, the language would default to a standard format for a report. Therefore, the user does not have to write several lines of code describing the format of the report.

Although most data processing professionals would not consider BASIC a very high level programming language, it certainly has some of the characteristics of such languages. It has an abbreviated syntax and is very easy to learn. BASIC has quickly become the most widely used language by computer users.

Parameterized Application Packages

Parameterized application packages are prewritten application software packages widely available on the market. There are packages for all major business applications.

When these application packages are parameterized they are designed for flexibility. They may be tailored through the input of parameters to fit the needs of a particular application. Data that are input, stored, and reported can be greatly modified. For example, a payroll package would allow users to specify what types of data are to be stored and how it is to be reported. Purchase of application packages will be explored in more detail in chapter 18.

Personal Computers

One of the most promising approaches to application development by users is the use of integrated packages on personal computers. These integrated packages such as LOTUS 1-2-3 and VisiOn perform, in an integrated fashion, several information processing tasks such as data base management, electronic spreadsheet and graphics. Data can be maintained either on the personal computer or on a mainframe system. When maintained on a mainframe system the data can be down loaded to the personal computer. These packages are designed to be user friendly. With a relatively small amount of training users can perform complex data modeling, data manipulation, and graphics on these personal computers independently of the mainframe and programmer assistance.

Examples of Application Development Tools

Table 16-1 provides examples of the different types of application development tools we have just discussed. Note that the figure classifies these packages into those suitable for end users and those requiring DP professional help. A package is classified as suitable for end users without DP assistance if a typical end user can learn how to use it in a two-day course and if he or she can return to the package and use it after being away from it for several weeks. Those packages suitable for end users should be easy to start to use. This allows the user to gain confidence quickly in his or her ability to use the

Table 16-1 Different Types of Application Development Packages*

	Suitable for End Users*		Suitable for DP Professionals	
		Vendor		Vendor
Data-Base Query Languages	QUERY-BY-EXAMPLE	IBM	SQL	IBM
	SQL	IBM	QWICK QWERY	CACI
	ON-LINE ENGLISH	Cullinane	EASYTRIEVE	Pansophic
	QWICK QWERY	CACI	GIS	IBM
	EASYTRIEVE	Pansophic	MARK IV	Informatics
	ASI/INQUIRY	ASI	DATATRIEVE	DEC
	DATATRIEVE	DEC		
Information Retrieval Systems	STAIRS	IBM		
	CAFS	ICL		
Report Generators	NOMAD	NCSS	NOMAD	NCSS
	QWICK QWERY	CACI	QWICK QWERY	CACI
			GIS	IBM
			IBM SYSTEM 34 UTILITIES	IBM
			RPG II	Various
			RPG III	IBM
			ADRS	IBM
			MARK IV/REPORTERS	Informatics

Table 16-1 (*continued*)

		Vendor		Vendor
Application Generators	MAPPER	Univac	ADF	IBM
	RAMIS II	Mathematica, Inc.	RAMIS II	Mathematica, Inc.
	FOCUS	Information Builders	DMS	IBM
			ADMINS 11	ADMINS
			USER 11	Northcounty Comp., Inc.
			OADS	Cullinane
Very High-Level Programming Languages	APL (simple functions)	Various	APL	Various
	BASIC	Various	APL-PLUS	STSC
	NOMAD (simple functions)	NCSS	ADRS	IBM
			NOMAD	NCSS
			MANTIS	CINCOM

*James Martin, *Application Development Without Programmers,* © 1982 p. 19. Reprinted by permission of Prentice-Hall Inc. Englewood Cliffs, N.J.

package. As more experience is gained with the package, he or she will then learn to use it for more sophisticated applications.

To illustrate how easy some application development tools are to use, consider an example from MARK IV. Figure 16-4 shows the use of MARK IV in generating the report in Figure 16-5. As you refer to Figure 16-4, note that only a minimum amount of information must be entered on the basic request form to produce a report. In the first line of the request we enter a request name and the word TODAY. This causes today's date to print at the top of the report. Next, the title that appears at the top of the report is entered. The next section of the request, record selection, allows the user to specify which records from the file will be printed on the report. In this case we want only those records whose item number equals D77 or M89. In addition, we want to multiply the item price (ITMPRICE) by .9 and assign the product the name NEWPRICE. Finally, we tell MARK IV what record fields are to appear in each column of the report. Notice that by entering a G on the QTYBKORD line we cause MARK IV to provide a grand total for Quantity Back Ordered.

MARK IV can easily produce much more sophisticated reports than the one illustrated in Figure 16-5. With approximately two hours of lecture time and some self-study, students can prepare their own forms and produce reports more sophisticated than that in Figure 16-5. Students experienced in writing programs in COBOL, BASIC, and FORTRAN are pleasantly surprised at how easy it is to produce meaningful reports with a software package such as MARK IV.

BLENDING USER DEVELOPMENT WITH CONVENTIONAL DEVELOPMENT

Types of Application Development

When a firm attempts to implement application development by users, three types of application development usually evolve:

1. Traditional development using the conventional development cycle as illustrated in Figure 16-1. This type of development is often used for those applications whose

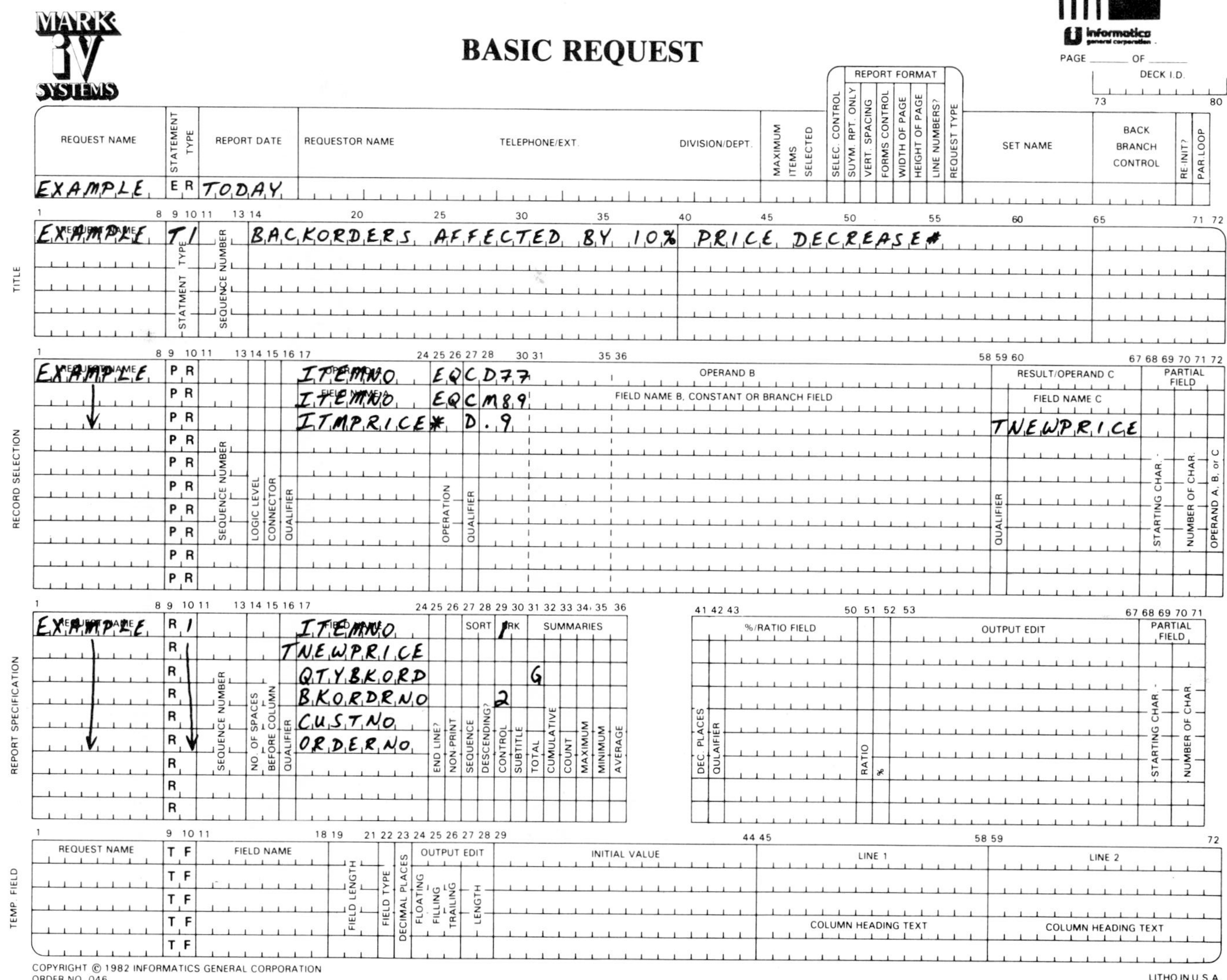

MARK IV SYSTEMS

BASIC REQUEST

informatics general corporation

PAGE ____ OF ____

DECK I.D.

REQUEST NAME	STATEMENT TYPE	REPORT DATE	REQUESTOR NAME	TELEPHONE/EXT.	DIVISION/DEPT.	MAXIMUM ITEMS SELECTED	REPORT FORMAT: SELEC. CONTROL, SUYM. RPT. ONLY, VERT. SPACING, FORMS CONTROL, WIDTH OF PAGE, HEIGHT OF PAGE, LINE NUMBERS?, REQUEST TYPE	SET NAME	BACK BRANCH CONTROL	RE-INIT?	PAR.LOOP
EXAMPLE	E R	TODAY									

TITLE

REQUEST NAME	STATMENT TYPE	SEQUENCE NUMBER	TITLE
EXAMPLE	T 1		BACKORDERS AFFECTED BY 10% PRICE DECREASE#

RECORD SELECTION

REQUEST NAME		SEQUENCE NUMBER	LOGIC LEVEL	CONNECTOR	QUALIFIER	FIELD NAME A	OPERATION	QUALIFIER	OPERAND B (FIELD NAME B, CONSTANT OR BRANCH FIELD)	RESULT/OPERAND C (FIELD NAME C)	PARTIAL FIELD
EXAMPLE	P R					ITEMNO	EQ	C	D77		
↓	P R					ITEMNO	EQ	C	M89		
	P R					ITMPRICE*	D		.9	TNEWPRICE	
	P R										

REPORT SPECIFICATION

REQUEST NAME		SEQUENCE NUMBER	NO. OF SPACES BEFORE COLUMN	QUALIFIER	FIELD NAME	END LINE?	NON-PRINT	SORT: SEQUENCE	DESCENDING?	CONTROL BRK	SUMMARIES
EXAMPLE	R 1				ITEMNO					1	
↓	R ↓				TNEWPRICE						
	R				QTYBKORD						G (TOTAL)
	R				BKORDRNO					2	
	R				CUSTNO						
	R				ORDERNO						

%/RATIO FIELD (DEC. PLACES, QUALIFIER, RATIO %) — OUTPUT EDIT — PARTIAL FIELD (STARTING CHAR., NUMBER OF CHAR.)

TEMP. FIELD

REQUEST NAME		FIELD NAME	FIELD LENGTH	FIELD TYPE	DECIMAL PLACES	OUTPUT EDIT (FLOATING, FILLING, TRAILING, LENGTH)	INITIAL VALUE	LINE 1 (COLUMN HEADING TEXT)	LINE 2 (COLUMN HEADING TEXT)
	T F								

LITHO IN U.S.A.

Figure 16-4 Mark IV Basic Request Form. Courtesy of Informatics Inc., Canoga Park, Calif.

11/02/83 BACKORDERS AFFECTED BY 10% PRICE DECREASE PAGE 1

	ITEM NUMBER	NEWPRICE	QUANTITY BACK ORDERED	BACK ORDER NUMBER	CUSTOMER NUMBER	ORDER NUMBER
	D77	$1.35	3	01	00013	3215
		$1.35	3	02	00115	2613
	M89	$23.40	3	12	00013	3216
		$23.40	3	13	00115	2632
		$23.40	3	14	09999	3205
GRAND	TOTAL		15			

Figure 16-5 Report Generated by Mark IV. Courtesy of Informatics Inc., Canoga Park, Calif.

requirements can be prespecified, and are likely to remain stable over a reasonable period of time.

2. An application generator is used as a prototyping tool. In effect, the systems analyst and the user quickly generate a skeleton application program serving as a model for the application. The end user can interact and experiment with this prototype and thereby refine his or her requirements. After the final requirements are defined, the application may be coded in a conventional fashion. Quite often parts of the prototype code can be used directly in the conventional application coding process.
3. An application generator or other software development tool is used to develop the entire application. With this approach no programmers are used. The prototype itself becomes the application software.

The second approach is more likely to be successful in applications that process high volumes of data because of efficiency considerations. The basic model of the application can be developed using an application generator. However, the final application program is written in a traditional programming language so that code produced is more efficient in terms of processing time and storage space. There are many business data processing applications, though, in which the processing volume is not very high, and the number of times the program is run is very low. For example, some programs are of a one-time nature. Such applications are likely to use the third type of application development. Also, the third type of application development is more likely to be used whenever the application must be operational in a very short period of time and when requirements are very dynamic and likely to change frequently.

We should also point out that the efficiency at which a particular program runs (that is, machine efficiency), is becoming less and less of a consideration because hardware costs are declining. Therefore, one of the primary reasons for using type two application development is declining in importance. Some would even argue that for most business data processing applications, machine efficiency is not a significant consideration. Table 16-2 illustrates the effects of these three types of application development on various steps of the application development cycle. Note that when application development is done without professional programmers, the development cycle is radically modified and compressed in time. The development process becomes a quick, informal, and interactive process. A user directly, or with the aid of a systems analyst, creates and modifies his or her own applications.

Table 16-2 Effects of Types of Application Development on the Application Development Cycle*

	Conventional Application Development	**Application Generator Used as a Prototyping Aid Followed by Programming**	**Application Development Without Professional Programmers**
Requirements Analysis	A time-consuming formal operation, often delayed by long application backlog.	The user's imagination is stimulated. He may work at a screen with an analyst to develop requirements.	The user's imagination is stimulated. He may develop his own requirements, or work with an analyst.
System Specification Document	Lengthy document. Boring. Often inadequate.	Produced by prototyping aid. Precise and tested.	Disappears.
User sign-off	User is often not sure what he is signing off on. He cannot perceive all subtleties.	User sees the results and may modify them many times before signing off.	No formal sign-off. Adjustment and modification is an ongoing process.
Coding and Testing	Slow. Expensive. Often delayed because of backlog.	The prototype is converted to more efficient code. Relatively quick and error-free.	Quick. Inexpensive. Disappears to a large extent.
Documentation	Tedious. Time consuming.	May be partly automated. Interactive training and HELP response may be created on-line.	Largely automatic. Interactive training and HELP responses are created on-line.
Maintenance	Slow. Expensive. Often late.	Often slow. Often expensive. Often late.	A continuing process with user and analyst making adjustments. Most of these adjustments can be made very quickly—in hours rather than months.

*James Martin, *Application Development Without Programmers,* © 1982 pp. 66-67. Reprinted by permission or Prentice-Hall Inc. Englewood Cliffs, N.J.

Data Base Administration

By now you may be thinking that application development by users will result in isolated users creating redundant data files, which could result in chaos. After all, wasn't one of the primary advantages of the data base approach (discussed in chapter 9) to reduce data redundancy? How can we have users from various departments going off and creating their own files containing redundant and uncoordinated data that cannot be accessed by other legitimate users? For example, data in a payroll system is often used by both the payroll department and the personnel department.

The solution to this potential problem is effective *data base administration*. Data bases are essential for the effective use of application development by users. As a result, the role of the data base administrator becomes very important. It is his or her role to be sure that data contained in the data base is sufficient to meet the needs of various users, and to be certain that one or more users cannot modify data in such a way so as to destroy its usefulness to other users. Does this mean that each user is constrained in the ways that he or she can use data because of the needs of other users in the firm? Certainly not. A user can extract portions of the data base and set this data up in his or her own files. This extracted data base can then be modified or massaged in any way without harming the underlying data stored in the data base.

INFORMATION CENTERS

If application development by users is to succeed, it must be coordinated and managed. The purpose of an *information center* is to manage the support for application development by users. The primary objective of an information center is to encourage and accelerate the use of new software tools for application development by users. There are several reasons why application development by users should be managed:

1. To encourage the rapid adoption of application development by users
2. To assist users in their application development efforts
3. To prevent redundancy in application creation
4. To ensure that data used in the various applications is coordinated and not redundant
5. To ensure that data is not simply created and stored in isolated personal files
6. To ensure that the systems created are controlled and auditable.

Figure 16-6 illustrates a typical organization for a data processing department containing an information center. Technical specialists in the information center are

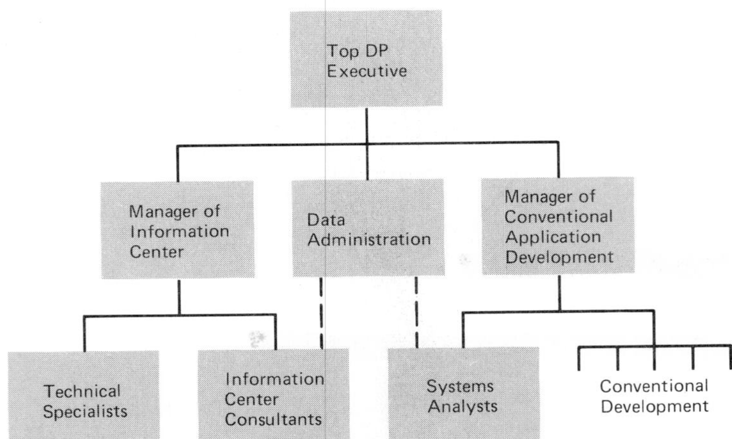

Figure 16-6 Organization of a Data Processing Department with an Information Center. James Martin, *Application Development Without Programmers*, © 1982 p. 302. Reprinted by permission of Prentice-Hall Inc. Englewood Cliffs, N.J.

experts on various software tools, and can assist in training end users to utilize these tools. In a smaller organization, the information center would usually rely on technical specialists from the software vendor rather than employing their own. For example, if a firm were using MARK IV and a technical problem occurred, the firm would get in touch with a technical specialist at Informatics, Inc., the MARK IV vendor.

The information center consultants work directly with users in creating applications. Note that information center consultants also work closely with the data base administrator. This is necessary to ensure that data used in both conventionally developed applications and user-generated applications is coordinated and not redundant. Figure 16-7 lists the functions typically performed by an information center.

By the Consultants:

- Training the users to employ the tools and create applications
- User encouragement, education, and selling
- Generation of applications (without programmers) in conjunction with users
- Generation and modification of prototypes
- Specification of changes to prototypes that may be needed to make them into working systems
- Consulting on user problems
- Determining whether a proposed application is suitable for Information Center development, and selecting the software and methods
- Demonstrations of Information Center capabilities to users, including senior management
- General communication with senior management
- Communication with traditional DP development
- Linking to the data administrator(s) in defining and representing data
- Maintaining a catalog of available applications and data bases
- Coordination to prevent duplicate or redundant application development

By the Technical Specialists:

- System set-up and support
- Dealing with technical and software problems
- Selection of languages and software and the versions of those which are used
- Assistance in choosing techniques or software for a given application (the job of the Techniques Analyst)
- Communication with vendors
- Monitoring systems usage and planning future resources
- Charge-back to users
- Tuning or reorganizing an application for better machine performance
- Auditing system usage and application quality

Figure 16-7 Functions of an Information Center. James Martin, *Application Development Without Programmers,* © 1982 p. 306. Reprinted by permission of Prentice-Hall Inc. Englewood Cliffs, N.J.

MANAGEMENT CASE 16-2

Approximately two years ago, the JDF Corporation established an information center. Since then the corporation has strongly supported application development by users. Consequently, many users are actively engaged in developing their own applications both for personal computers and for the mainframe. Recently the internal audit department has performed an audit of the application development by users approach as it is implemented at JDF. The audit report contains some rather disturbing findings. The auditors found numerous instances of the same data being stored several different times, both on the mainframe and on personal computers. In addition, they found that essentially the same application software had been created several times. For example, the home appliances division and the home electronics division had both created marketing analysis systems using a mainframe program generator. Although these two systems are not identical they are very similar. Based on their findings, the internal auditors have recommended that the corporation reassess its commitment to application development by users. Do you agree with the auditors that their findings are a serious problem? What recommendations would you have for the JDF Corporation?

CHANGING ROLES OF SYSTEMS ANALYSTS AND PROGRAMMERS

The advent of software enabling application development by users produces a change in the role of systems analysts. If the new software is to be used effectively, systems analysts must recognize that there are many ways to create a new application. In the requirements analysis or feasibility study phase, the systems analyst must realize that he or she has a bag of tools, any of which may be appropriate to solve the user's problem. The tools for obtaining new applications are:

1. Conventional systems development cycle
2. Purchase of an application software package
3. End users generating their own applications without outside help
4. End users working with systems analysts or information center consultants to generate the application
5. Systems analysts and end users generating a prototype experimenting with the prototype, and then coding the application in a conventional manner

Many systems analysts trained in conventional application development find it difficult to change their roles. Perhaps the best mind set for a systems analyst who wants to encourage the use of these new software tools is to:

1. Search constantly for more effective and efficient ways of creating applications
2. Avoid the use of programmers whenever possible
3. Take on a consultant role that encourages user independence in employing software.

Those of you planning for a career in programming may be quite disturbed by the material we have covered in this chapter. It would be easy to imply that the demand for programmers would decrease drastically, or perhaps disappear, as users increase the generation of application software without programmers, as they will most certainly do. However, there will continue to be a large demand for programmers. There are several reasons for this:

1. The explosion in the use of computers has created a very large demand for application software—both application software developed through conventional programming, and through user development.
2. There will continue to be a significant proportion of all applications that are of a prespecified nature and therefore are well-suited to the conventional development cycle.
3. Systems software (such as operating systems and data base management systems) and application software created for sale by vendors are likely to continue to be developed using conventional programming because of efficiency considerations. There is a large demand for programmers in this area. In fact, the most highly skilled programmers work for software vendors.

SUMMARY

The conventional application program development process suffers from several disadvantages:

1. The high cost of programming expertise makes it very expensive
2. The time span for program development is usually very long
3. Program maintenance absorbs a great deal of programmer time to the detriment of new systems development.

Computing may be classified into two categories: 1. Prespecified; and 2. User driven.

User-driven systems may be created through the use of six different techniques:

1. Query Languages
2. Report Generators
3. Graphic Languages
4. Application Generators
5. Very High Level Programming Languages
6. Parameterized Application Packages

Where application development by users is employed, three different types of application development usually evolve:

1. Conventional application development cycle
2. Prototyping with an application generator and subsequent coding with a conventional language
3. Total system development with an application generator.

The data base administration function is crucially important when users develop their own applications. The DBA has to ensure that data redundancy is minimized and that shared data resources are properly used by all.

The application development efforts of users may be coordinated by an information center. This center assists users in developing their own applications.

With more and more users creating their own applications, the role of systems analysts and programmers is changing.

KEY TERMS

Application Development by Users
Application Generators
Information Center
Prespecified Computing
User-Driven Computing
Query Languages
Report Generators
Graphics Languages
Generalized Modules
User Exits
Prototype
Very High Level Programming Languages
Default Options
Parameterized Application Packages
End User
Skeleton Application Program
Consultant

REVIEW QUESTIONS

1. What is application development by users?
2. Which is more important for an EDP organization, labor costs or equipment costs?
3. How does the time span of conventional application development affect a system's utility?
4. Discuss the work overload on programmers and its implications.
5. Distinguish between prespecified and user-driven computing.
6. What is a query language?
7. Describe the basic purpose of a report generator package.
8. Why are graphics languages becoming important for business people?
9. Explain the concept of an application generator.
10. What is the difference between a high level language and a very high level language?
11. How does a parameterized application package differ from an application generator?
12. Briefly describe three basic types of application development.
13. Discuss the role of the DBA in a user-driven data processing environment.
14. Why is it important to have an information center to manage application development by users?
15. Discuss the changing roles of programmers and systems analysts.

DISCUSSION QUESTIONS

1. Many large computer installations prescribe standard languages, like COBOL and PL/1, for all programs to be executed on their equipment. While this practice results in consistent documentation, it can lead to certain problems. Based on the material discussed in this chapter, what problems would arise in this kind of environment?

2. Which of the six application development methods would you use for each of the following applications? Explain the reasons for your choice.

1. Sales forecast by territory
2. Manufacturing process control
3. Customer billing and accounts receivable
4. Mailing list
5. Course registration at a university
6. Portfolio management

RESEARCH PROJECTS

1. Interview some professional programmers and determine what proportion of their time is spent on maintenance as opposed to new systems development. Also, find out whether they assist users in developing their own programs. If so, what kind of attitudes do they have toward user-driven information systems?

2. Write an essay on the role of information centers in application development by users. What kind of interfaces are necessary among information center consultants, data base consultants, and data base administration? What specific techniques can the information center employ to educate users about application generators and other user-friendly software?

ESSAY

An Economical Approach To End-User Programming

(Reprinted with permission from MIS Week, Sept. 16, 1981, p. 32)

By John Gochenouer, Manager Information Systems Development, Harris Corp., Melbourne, Fla.

This essay describes the implementation of end-user programming for financial applications at the corporate headquarters of Harris Corp. By writing an interface to the higher-level language, the process of putting that language into the hands of the user was made simple. Examples of how interactive text editor programs were used to bring end-user programming into user departments quickly and inexpensively are described below.

End-user programming does not come cheaply. The software is expensive and for some systems, minicomputer hardware must be purchased as well. In addition, training the user is time-consuming and could meet resistance if the effort involved appears to exceed the eventual benefit.

We have found that it is not necessary to wait for the perfect end-user software. Several packages available to us had user-friendly features or features that could be made user-friendly through an interface which was written in a text-editing language. Once the user begins to use the language with the interface, a desire to do more will frequently lead to further training and the migration to true end-user programming.

This linkage with text editors goes a step further than merely purchasing a non-procedural language and handing the user a manual. From these experiences, other MIS shops may find they can develop applications quickly, without purchasing additional software or hardware. This presents a cost savings of thousands of dollars, not only in the purchase price but also in retraining data processing staff.

An end-user is defined as a non-programmer who is the recipient of information from data arranged on automated files. Because of the varied backgrounds of these users, a variety of languages and methods for using the languages will have to be developed.

An end-user language should be non-procedural, that is, geared toward "what you want," not "how to get it." A user should be able to use major features after a couple of days of formal training and the language documented in such a way that an average person could build a higher level of skill without further formal training. It should be friendly (HELP) and forgiving (RESTORE).

All end-user languages have weak spots in their capabilities. Those we have worked with include languages which have an extremely slow editor, an awkward report writer, poor file manipulation, etc. If a heavily used function of a language requires considerable effort, then you will have trouble migrating that language into the user environment. But coupled with a text editor, a weak spot may be overcome which might otherwise result in the purchase of additional software.

Finally, for a user to learn all the facets of any language will result in wasted learning. This is frequently the reason for resistance to do-it-yourself programming. Most users have such narrow areas of interest that only limited features of the language have to be learned in order to successfully program the requirements.

Most users want to control every aspect of information processing in their departments. We have begun the process of shifting control into the user environment. This has been done, as mentioned before, through the use of high-level languages coupled with a powerful text-editing language. We feel the methods used have minimized resistance and cost. What follows are two examples of how this is being accomplished.

The first example is from the development of an automated retirement plan. The Harris Corp. retirement plan has over 16,000 participants and a fund of over $200 million. Until July 1979, this plan was being administered by a system which was primarily manual. At that time, a highly automated system was implemented which included both retirement plan and human resources administration. The information resided in a complicated database with several hierarchical record types.

Nearly 100 Cobol programs were written to perform the routine monthly administration functions and to produce standard personnel reports. However, there was considerable dissatisfaction over the inability to produce ad hoc reports quickly. Questions that top corporate management had about the composition of their personnel often went unanswered or took weeks to answer.

To resolve the problem, a report writer was purchased which could interface with the database and a non-programmer on the professional staff was trained in its use. This project failed primarily due to the complexity of the report writer and the hierarchical nature of the database. While more convenient than Cobol, it was still difficult for a non-programmer to use.

A second solution was developed which involved the use of an interactive text editor and a statistical language (SAS). Since the database only changed on a monthly basis, it was possible to produce an extract file of all employees (one record per employee). This file contained demographic information and other variables that related to the questions asked by top management. The information in this file would be valid for a month and then another file produced as part of the monthly processing.

The way the system currently works, the editor will automatically bring in the extract when the user signs on. He then reduces the file to the population of interest by deleting records with variable values outside the range of interest.

If the bottom line is a single number, such as "How many hourly workers do we have at our Rochester Plant?," then the session is concluded after counting the number of remaining records. If the bottom line is more complicated, such as "What is the age-by-sex breakdown of these workers?," then the editor brings in a file containing JCL (job-control-language) and SAS code. The code is automatically modified by the editor and submitted as a batch job to produce the desired report.

This inquiry system took two weeks to implement which includes the time required to write the database extract routine. The reports produced by this system have received a more favorable response and a wider distribution than the 100-program parent which took several man-years to develop. The cost of a normal request is less than $10 and the elapsed time around five minutes.

The second example of our end-user systems is a general accounting system. The corporate headquarters accounting staff consolidates the balance sheet and income statement accounts of all the operating divisions and subsidiaries of Harris Corp. The roll-up of accounts and corporate entities resulted in over 75 pages of financial information.

The financial reports were being produced using the report writer sold as part of a general ledger package. The report writer was touted as a user-oriented system; however, the MIS department became the author of most of the code after a few frustrating trials by the accounting department.

Harris Corp. is a rapidly growing company with frequent organizational refinements due to growth or acquisitions. These changes resulted in near-disasters as the programming staff worked around the clock to rewrite the 75 reports before reporting deadlines became due. The final corporate reorganization that was made under this system required three man-months to include the new division in the reports. The report writer we were using was obviously not the right tool.

A non-procedural modeling language (IFPS) was available in our shop which was capable of producing financial spreadsheets. This end-user language had the additional advantage of running on a minicomputer.

The language itself proved to be so easy to use that virtually all financial departments at the corporate headquarters have at least one professional using or learning the language without the need for an interface.

The problem of recoding the financial reports to allow for corporate organizational refinement was solved by using an interface to IFPS and not by recoding IFPS directly. The user signs onto the super-mini and uses the Vulcan text editor to modify tables which represent the corporate structure easily and quickly.

Before the reports are run, a procedure accesses the tables and rebuilds the non-procedural code to fit the new organization. The IFPS code is then also available to members of the accounting staff who modify it to produce ad hoc reports.

Using the interface the corporate reorganization (report), which previously took three months, now takes less than a day and is accomplished by the accounting staff. In fact, the process has become so simple, it is possible to model several contemplated reorganizations in a single day.

Both examples demonstrate the following points. First, the software and hardware used was already available in our shop. Second, these applications required the use of a text editor to generate code in higher-level languages. This has many advantages over program generators which produce Cobol or Fortran code and over the use of user languages as a stand-alone tool.

One significant advantage of this method is the speed at which the product can be delivered to the user. The code generator itself is written in a high-level text-editing language, the code it generates is also in a high-level language, and the application is limited to an area of specific interest.

Discussion

1. Harris Corp. has used a combination of multiple software tools, such as a text editor, a statistical language, and a nonprocedural modeling language, to implement application development by users. What are some advantages and disadvantages of this approach?
2. How large an impact does the ability to produce ad hoc reports quickly have on end-user satisfaction with a computer application? Why?

CHAPTER 17

DECISION SUPPORT SYSTEMS

INTRODUCTION

In the first two chapters of this book we followed the natural evolution of computer systems in organizations. Most organizations start with data processing systems that support transaction processing and evolve to management information systems, which support tactical and strategic level decision making. In the past few years a new type of system, called a decision support system, has gained a great deal of popularity in the information systems field. In this text we view decision support systems as an extension of management information systems.

In this chapter we will define a decision support system, identify its functions, and explore the need for decision support systems. Finally, we will explore some characteristics of organizations in which decision support systems are likely to be successful, and cover the steps in building a decision support system.

WHAT IS A DECISION SUPPORT SYSTEM?

In chapter 2 we covered the relationship between objectives, decisions, and information. We stressed that the purpose of management information systems was to provide information for decision making. If a management information system supports decision making with information, why then is a decision support system an extension of an MIS? Management information systems in the past have been most successful in providing information for routine, structured and preanticipated types of decisions. In addition, they have been successful in acquiring and storing large quantities of detailed data concerning transaction processing. They have been less successful in providing information for semistructured or unstructured decisions, particularly unanticipated ones. The basic idea underlying decisions support systems is to provide a set of computer-based tools so that management information systems can produce information to support semistructured and unanticipated decisions.

Based on the above, we will define a *decision support system* as an integrated set of computer tools that allow a decision maker to interact directly with computers to retrieve information useful in making semistructured and unstructured decisions. Examples of these decisions include such things as merger and acquisition decisions, plant expansion, new product decisions, portfolio management, and marketing decisions. It is important that a distinction be made between a decision support system and software and hardware computer tools that make the decision support system possible. A particular decision support system is an application of these computer tools.

The software components for decision support systems are illustrated in Figure 17-1. Major components include: 1) a *language system* enabling the user to interact with the decision support system; 2) a *problem processing system* made up of several components that perform various processing tasks; and 3) a *knowledge system* providing data and artificial intelligence capabilities to the decision support system.

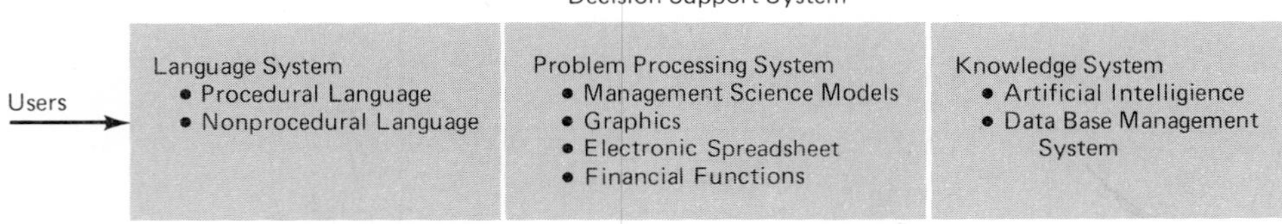

Figure 17-1 Components of a Decision Support System

The language system may have both procedural and nonprocedural language capabilities. A *procedural language* requires the user to provide the logical steps or procedures to be used in solving a particular problem. Examples of procedural languages are FORTRAN, COBOL, and BASIC. Most decision makers would not use procedural languages; they are normally used only by professional programmers. However, in the case of a decision support system there may be specific problems that the nonprocedural language cannot address, and therefore a procedural language would be employed.

With a *nonprocedural language* the user simply specifies the characteristics of a problem or information query. Determination of the logical steps necessary to provide information is left to the decision support system. An example of a nonprocedural command is the following: "Retrieve sales for last year for all stores in the state of New York." This nonprocedural query is very English-like. Nonprocedural languages can be English-like or take other forms that are user-friendly.

The problem processing system is the heart of the decision support system. It should have several capabilities, including the ability to collect information from data bases through data base management systems. It should make available a wide variety of management science models, such as regression, time-series analysis, and goal programming. It should also have a graphics capability, and an electronic spreadsheet feature similar to those afforded by packages such as LOTUS 1-2-3 and Supercalc. In fact, many decision support systems are primarily built around the concept of an *electronic spreadsheet*. These spreadsheets allow users to store data in a two or more dimensional matrix form. Users can make any cell within the matrix a function of one or more other cells of the matrix. Finally, most decision support systems include standard financial functions, including return on investment and net present value.

The knowledge system is made up of the data base management system and associated files stored and managed by the data base management system. These two components contain basic, detailed data collected mainly through transaction processing. Another source of knowledge beginning to be useful in decision support systems is *artificial intelligence*. These systems are sometimes called expert systems. They act much in the same manner as a human consultant would, providing advice and explaining that advice under certain conditions. Artificial intelligence is beginning to be applied successfully in several areas, including medicine and prospecting for minerals.

MANAGEMENT CASE 17-1

Bob Lexington is the chief executive officer of Phillips Products Incorporated. In a recent meeting with his vice presidential level staff, he expressed the opinion that computer-based systems are very valuable for transaction processing and for support of operational level decision making. However, he feels that computer-based systems are a long way from providing significant support for tactical and strategic level decision making especially for unstructured and unanticipated decisions. He states that, "for the type of decisions I make most of the data and information come from informal and often outside sources. Of course, our computer based systems may provide me with some background information. But, this is a relatively small percentage of the information I need to make most decisions. The idea of a decision support system for tactical and strategic level decisions is just too new. I think we should wait several years before investing our resources in this untried concept." Do you agree with Mr. Lexington?

FUNCTIONS OF A DECISION SUPPORT SYSTEM[1]

Model Building

The building of a descriptive model is a central purpose of most decision support systems. This model is often in the form of a two-or-more dimensional table, such as the electronic spreadsheet mentioned above. For example, the first two dimensions on the

[1]Based on Warren G. Briggs, "An Evaluation of DSS Packages," *Computer World* XVI, No. 9 (1982), 31.

table might contain an income statement; the third dimension would represent various products; and the fourth dimension could represent multiple retail outlets. Model development involves specifying relationships among various cells, rows, or columns within these electronic spreadsheets.

Procedural and/or Nonprocedural Language

As discussed above, these languages allow the user to communicate with the DSS. Most users will find a nonprocedural language more convenient to use than a procedural one.

What-If and Incremental Assumptions

The ability to show the impact of changes in data and assumptions is perhaps the most useful feature of a DSS. For example, a DSS could show the impact on profit if sales grew at a rate of 7 to 10 percent instead of 5 percent. Most DSS applications can instantaneously show the impact of such changes and assumptions on the CRT.

Backward Iteration

A DSS should be capable of showing what value a particular independent variable, such as sales, would have to have in order to produce a certain target value for a particular dependent variable, such as profit. An example of a question making use of this ability might be "What level of growth must we have in sales in order to double our profit every three years?"

Risk Analysis

A very useful piece of information for a decision maker is a probability distribution. It provides projections about whether a particular critical measure, such as profit, that will reach a certain level. For example, it would be useful to know that the probability of the profit growth rate being 0 would be 2 or 4 percent. Such information can be generated using simulation, providing we have certain data. The necessary data is the probability distributions of the underlying independent variables used to calculate the profit, such as sales and various expenses.

Statistical Analysis and Management Science Models

A good DSS will be capable of providing several useful management science models, such as regression and time-series analysis. These models may be used in conjunction with historical data to make projections about future trends in various areas, such as sales and profits.

Financial Functions

Preprogrammed functions for commonly used financial calculations are normally included in DSS packages. They may include corporate tax rates, depreciation methods, net present value, and return on investment.

Graphics

An extremely important feature in a decision support system is graphics capability. The system should be able to depict any data contained in the system in various forms, such as line or pie graphs.

Hardware Capabilities

Decision support systems in one form or another can be implemented on machines as small as micros or as large as mainframes. When installed on micros, a large amount of data storage is required. Mainframes normally have large data storage and processing capacity, and therefore more complex models can be implemented on them. A current trend expected to continue in the future is the use of micros in combination with mainframes for decision support systems. In such a linkage, the micro is linked to the mainframe to retrieve data for subsequent processing on the micro if data and processing volume are relatively small. On the other hand, if large amounts of data and processing are required, some parts of the DSS may be performed on the mainframe.

Databases and External Files

It is crucial that a DSS be able to access data stored in organization files. This can be done either through the data base management system's interfaces or through the DSS's own capability to access files external to the DSS. In addition, a DSS generally is capable of maintaining its internal files once data is retrieved from other sources.

WHY DO MANAGERS NEED DECISION SUPPORT SYSTEMS?

The need for types of information produced by decision support systems has always been present. Decision support systems have become popular primarily because of their capability to fill this need. Declining cost of computer hardware has made computer processing and storage relatively inexpensive. In addition, the microcomputer is becoming ubiquitous in business. Secondly, the advent of data base management systems in the 1970s provided means for storage and management of large amounts of detailed data. Such data are now relatively easy to retrieve for use in a decision support system. Third, there has been a large increase in the number of software packages incorporating the functions of a decision support system. These packages can be used directly to implement DSS applications. Finally, many MBAs who were trained in analytic techniques are now reaching the middle and upper levels of corporations. These individuals know how to use the tools that decision support systems provide.

MANAGEMENT CASE 17-2

Wythe Industries is a fast growing clothing manufacturer located in the southeast. Most of Wythe's data processing applications are computer based. However, none of them are installed on a data base management system. Each application stands alone although there are some links constructed between the applications. Central data processing and its systems development staff have traditionally performed all of the application development within the company. Most of the systems development staff have a computer background with very little background in user areas.

The management of Wythe is considering developing a decision support system. Would you advise Wythe to invest resources in a decision support system at this time? Support your answer.

ORGANIZATION ENVIRONMENT FOR SUCCESSFUL DSS

Organizations that have been the most successful in implementing DSS have much in common. First, they have established a base of well-controlled and well-structured data processing systems, which provide transaction processing data necessary for DSS. Second, such organizations have the extra dollars and personnel necessary to maintain a research and development focus. These organizations are willing to commit resources to a DSS development effort in which tangible benefits may be elusive. Third, the line departments of these organizations have established open communication with central computer groups. Fourth, the line departments have sufficient confidence to initiate and manage systems projects. They are continually looking for new ways to use computer-based systems. Fifth, the central computer groups act primarily as consultants to assist line departments in implementing systems. Sixth, the central computer groups have several people on its staff who either came from line departments or have substantial background in disciplines such as manufacturing, finance, accounting, or marketing. Finally, education and training are used by such organizations to build mutual understanding between line departments and the computer group.

Many characteristics we have listed above are similar to those of organizations that have adopted an application development by users approach. The subject of application development by users is closely related to DSS. You should note the potential application of the techniques discussed in chapter 16 to decisions support systems.

BUILDING A DECISION SUPPORT SYSTEM

In chapter 14 we presented the structured system development life cycle. In it are the major processes involved in developing either a data processing or management information system. Building a decision support system is quite different from the structured system development life cycle. Specifically, design, implementation, and evaluation of decision support systems tends to go on concurrently. These processes are evolutionary in that when a decision support system is initially implemented, it is likely to be incomplete. Due to the semistructured and unstructured nature of problems addressed by decision support systems, managers will change their perceived needs for information and so the DSS must change also. There may be no precise end point for implementation. Since decision support systems are likely to be in a constant state of change, it is extremely important that users be directly involved in initiating and managing this change.

Predesign

Keen and Morton have stated the major processes involved in building a decision support system.[2] Figure 17-2 is a summarized view of these major processes. The first

[2]Peter G. W. Keen and Michael S. Scott Morton, *Decision Support Systems: An Organizational Perspective* (Reading, Mass.: Addison-Wesley, 1978), 167–225.

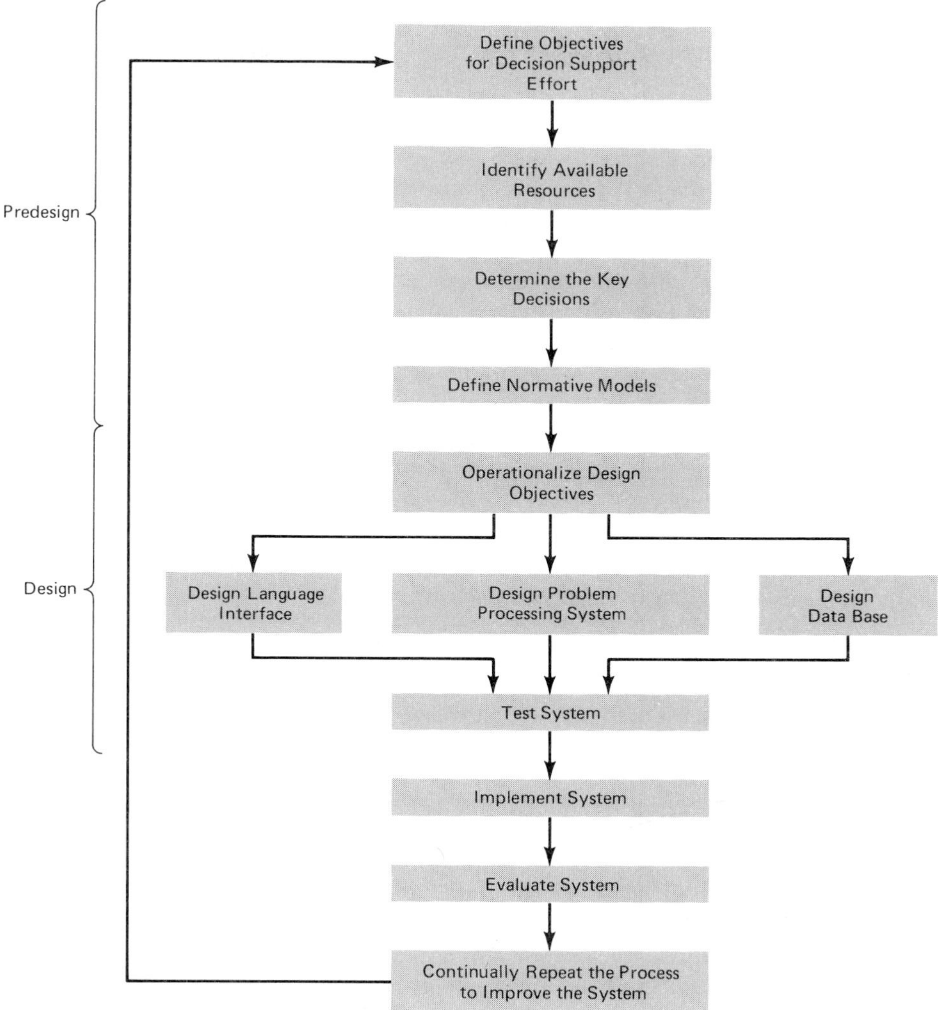

Figure 17-2 Steps in Building a Decision Support System

step in the predesign process is to define the objectives for the decision support effort. This involves a laying out of the overall goals of the decision support project and is crucial in orienting the project to working on the right problems.

The second step is to identify available resources that can be used in the project. Quite often a firm will already have hardware and software, such as the data base management system, that can be used in a DSS.

Perhaps the most crucial step in the project is to determine key decisions in the problem area. For example, in a portfolio management system the key decision might be selecting the correct stocks for a particular customer's needs. One might conclude that it would be difficult to provide information that would tell a portfolio manager which stock to select because of the many factors involved. For instance, some customers might be very conservative and would therefore want their money invested in safe stocks. Others might prefer high risk situations because of potential high gains. Two points should be made relating to this concern. First, the decision support system is only a tool providing information to the portfolio manager. The portfolio manager makes the final decision on which stock to select. Secondly, even though we may find it difficult to provide relevant information for a decision, it is still very crucial to identify what the key decision is. Providing very relevant information for the wrong decision will get us nowhere. However, providing marginally useful information for the key decision is a useful contribution.

The next step is to define normative models that can provide information for key decisions. A *normative model* is a highly rational approach to providing the information that a manager should have in making key decisions. The word *normative* refers to a standard or what should be. These normative models are likely to be highly idealistic and theoretical. In the actual implementation of the DSS it is unlikely that we will attain the level of the normative model. It is a goal we must try to operationalize in a real world situation. Even though it may not be practicable or advisable to implement the normative model, we must keep it in mind when designing the actual DSS. Such normative models are a major part of our design objectives.

Design

The first step in the design process is to operationalize the design objectives. In this step we decide what can be done practically in a real world implementation of the DSS. The next step is to design the language interface. Ideally, this language interface should be a nonprocedural language. Most users find it easier to communicate a problem to a decision support system rather than telling the decision support system procedural steps necessary to solve the problem. Designing the problem solving system is largely a matter of selecting particular management science models (such as regression) and choosing the computer software (such as graphics and electronic spreadsheet) that can be applied to the decision support system application. These models and software must be combined in such a way that users can readily select and implement them in operating the DSS.

Portions of the knowledge system may already be in place. Most companies implementing DSS already have a great deal of basic data stored in data base management systems. The final step in design is to thoroughly test the system prior to its implementation.

Implementation

Implementation is a crucial process in building a DSS. Essentially, in an implementation effort the user is being asked to change from something he or she is doing now and accept a new system. Many theories of individual and social change are applicable to the implementation process. Basically, though, the organization or individual must have a felt need for the new DSS. There are several different ways in which this need can be created. Obviously if one's boss says that you *will* use the new DSS, a need can be created. However, in the long run this may be counterproductive. Developing user confidence and creating need for a system really begins early in the building process. Perhaps one of the most effective ways to promote these conditions among users is to have them be heavily involved in the development process. As we have mentioned previously, users should initiate and manage this process with a computer systems specialist acting as consultant. If the process occurs as it should, users will see a system as their own and be much more likely to support and use the DSS.

Evaluation

If one is to evaluate the contributions of a DSS there must be some criteria for evaluation. Evaluation is particularly difficult with a DSS since the system is evolutionary in nature and therefore does not have a neatly defined completion date. It is unlikely that a DSS will be justified through such factors as reductions in clerical costs. Normally, the justification is the provision of more timely and better information, but this is a very general benefit that is difficult to evaluate. However, it should be possible to measure the impact of this information on decision making and the kinds of results that follow. For example, in a portfolio management system used by an investment firm, the ultimate result should be more satisfied customers and greater numbers of customers providing more revenue for the firm.

Essentially, there are three components in the evaluation process. First, there should be prior definitions of "improvement." Such definitions, or criteria for evaluation, should be established very early in the building process. Second, a means of monitoring the progress towards these improvements must be defined. Finally, a formal review process that periodically measures performance against stated definitions of improvement should be established.

SUMMARY

A decision support system is an integrated set of computer tools allowing a decision maker to interact directly with computers to retrieve information useful in making semistructured and unstructured decisions.

Major components of a decision support system include the language system, problem processing system, and knowledge system. A decision support system should have the following functions and features:

1. Model Building
2. Procedural and/or Nonprocedural Language
3. What-If and Incremental Assumptions
4. Backward Iteration
5. Risk Analysis
6. Statistical Analysis and Management Science Models
7. Financial Functions
8. Graphics
9. Hardware Capabilities
10. Data Bases and External Files

Organizations that have been successful in implementing DSS have the following characteristics:

1. A well-controlled and well-structured data processing system

2. Willingness to commit dollars and personnel to the project
3. Good communications between line departments and central computer groups
4. Line departments with sufficient confidence to initiate manage system projects
5. The central computer groups act primarily as consultants
6. The central computer groups have several people on their staff with expertise in user disciplines
7. Education and training are used to build mutual understanding between line departments and computer groups

There is usually no precise end to the development and implementation of a DSS. The major steps in building a DSS are predesign, design, implementation, and evaluation.

KEY TERMS

Decision Support System
Language System
Problem Processing System
Knowledge System
Procedural Language
Nonprocedural Language
Artificial Intelligence
What-If and Incremental Assumptions
Backward Iteration
Risk Analysis
Management Science Models
Financial Functions
Electronic Spreadsheet
Key Decisions
Normative Model

REVIEW QUESTIONS

1. What is a decision support system?
2. What are the major components of a decision support system?
3. Distinguish a procedural language from a nonprocedural language.
4. What is an electronic spreadsheet?
5. What are the components of a knowledge system in a decision support system?
6. What are the major functions of a decision support system?
7. What type of hardware capabilities should a decision support system have?
8. Why is a data base management system important to a decision support system?
9. What are the characteristics of organizations that have had success in implementing DSS?
10. How does building a decision support system differ from the structured system development life cycle used in developing other data processing or management information systems?
11. What activities occur in the predesign step of building a DSS?

12. What is meant by the term "operationalize the design objectives?"
13. What is the essence of the implementation process?
14. Define the key components of the evaluation process.

DISCUSSION QUESTIONS

1. Some people have argued that a decision support system is no different than a good management information system. They would argue that conceptually there is nothing new in the decision support system idea. Take one side of this argument and support your position.
2. Discuss how the functions of what-if and incremental analysis are related to risk analysis. Why are these areas so important to decision support systems?
3. Some people would argue that decision support systems, especially those having artificial intelligence components, will evolve to the point where they supplant human decision makers. Others argue that machines will never have the ability to think (when thinking is defined as the process of understanding why a particular decision is made). Take one side of this argument and support your position.

RESEARCH QUESTIONS

1. Research the area of decision support systems and find an example of a real world decision support system. Outline what its objectives are, how it accomplishes them, and evaluate its effectiveness.
2. Research the area of artificial intelligence, particularly its application to business problems. There have been several articles written in this area in recent years. How successful are the applications currently being used? Do you expect this area to become more important to business decision makers in the future? How would the widespread use of artificial intelligence affect the things you should be learning in your college career?

ESSAY

Decision Systems: Working Smarter, Or Not At All?

(Reprinted with permission from MIS Week, Feb. 17, 1982, p. 24)

By Richard Sneider, Product Manager, Information Systems Division, Data General Corp., Westboro, Mass.

It's the year 1987, a prominent manufacturing firm has to solve the problem of whether its sales, financial position, and market forecasts justify increasing the size of one of its plants to accommodate a new product line.

Harvey Thomson, a 26-year-old administrative assistant, sits in front of his work-station and describes the problem to the computer in abbreviated English. He states his problem directly, without the aid of programming languages or programmers.

Within 10 seconds, the computer processes the problem and suggests eight formidable reasons why the company should not expand its production facilities. Thomson and the financial analysts use this information to convince upper management not to expand the facilities.

Such a scenario is rapidly becoming possible. But, as computers are utilized more and more in the decision-making process, it is also possible that they could become—by default—the actual decision-makers? Such a radical step is highly unlikely, because of the very nature of the decision-making process. Rather, computers will be most effectively used as powerful support tools in service of the human decision-makers.

A widely held notion is that modern decison-making is a highly structured process. According to this view, management makes decisions by gathering and analyzing all the relevant information, reviewing all possible alternatives and then calmly and rationally choosing the course of action that provides maximum benefits at minimal risk.

But we all know that, in the vast majority of cases, business decisions just are not made that way—particularly not complex decisions such as whether to diversify operations or when to expand facilities.

The highly disorganized, intuitive nature of the decision-making process is often a double-edged sword. In some cases it can be quite effective, in others, disastrous. Already, the high failure rate of the typical experience/intuition-based method has opened the door for computers to enter the decision-making process.

Within the past several years, computers have been used increasingly in areas of financial management, production analysis, short-term planning and geographical analysis. And this has been happening in spite of the fact that few people would really want to surrender the skill, judgment and creativity involved in making such decisions to the highly formulated, programmed methods in which computers excel.

We believe, however, that while instinct alone won't adequately support a corporation's bottom line, neither will computerized systems that don't maximize the human capabilities of managers and other office professionals.

What, then, is the way to avoid the extremes characterized by each approach to decision-making?

The answer lies in using the computer to help support the so-called "knowledge workers" in quickly gathering, manipulating and presenting accurate, updated information in the ways that will enhance the ultimately intuitive decision-making process.

Users must carefully consider several important aspects of any decision support system (DSS) if they are to reap its benefits as a support tool, rather than as a substitute decision-maker.

The first, and most important consideration is the DSS's ease of use—its ability to allow non-technical people to deal with it directly. The single greatest and most enduring problem with computers has been their inflexibility, their inability to let the person who actually needs the data to deal directly with the computer.

An unfortunate and long-standing DP tradition has had skilled technicians—programmers—intimately involved in designing systems for office professionals. Too often, these programmers did not really understand how, why and by whom these systems would be used.

Particularly because of the intuitive nature of the decision-making process, it is essential to have the knowledge workers interfacing directly with the computer—using the DSS to develop the type of resource that best supports their unique approach. In this way, these professionals can draw on the technical expertise of DP or operations research personnel when needed.

Second, the ability to access information should not be restricted to only one part of an organization, or to only certain managerial or professional groups. Instead, the resource should be distributed to all of the people and parts of an organization needing it. Without widespread access, the power of advanced, distributed processing systems will go untapped, as they typically have in the past.

Assume, for the moment, that the decision-maker now has access to a powerful computing resource that can be used without the need for technical intermediaries. The focus of the DSS now shifts to the resource itself.

Third, the ideal decision support system—in sharp contrast to previous methods of designing applications—should not be a "system" at all, in the strict sense of the term. Rather, it should be a highly adaptive decision support generator that can easily be used by professionals to quickly design data support prototypes suited to each specific decision-making task. This adaptive tool must allow quick design changes if the original design does not closely match a person's information-gathering style or needs.

Fourth, to adequately support the human element, this highly adaptive support capability must be able to provide access to operational data, as well as to summary data that already has been processed by applications programs designed for other specific operational tasks. Equally important, this tool must provide the professional with access to an organization's raw data, and it must allow the access to be accomplished in one step, using a single uncomplicated procedure or command, and without having to re-key non-summary data.

The need to access original data, however, creates a fifth need. Because efficiency is related to how well the original data is organized in the system, the decision support generator should be able to interface with a true database management system. It should also be able to access standard "flat" files indirectly, using the power of the host computer to facilitate both the user interface and data access without changing existing files.

It should now be obvious that such a support tool has great power. But, unless it lets decision-makers narrow their information search, it will innundate them with unnecessary information. The way to avoid scaring professionals away is to design the support tool with the ability to handle interactive queries and ad hoc information requests.

Next, the decision support generator should let the user decide whether information should be displayed on the CRT screen for immediate use (and what the screen format should look like), or whether it should be printed for later use. The best way to accomplish such flexible data presentation is through a workstation. The management or professional information workstation would incorporate a keyboard, display screen and an interface to a printer which could print everything from straight text to graphics like pie charts, bar charts and line charts.

To facilitate formatting and manipulating displayed data, the decision support generator should ideally be able to interface with word processing software. With this capability, the DSS becomes the critical link between data processing and office automation, integrating both functions in an easily-used, straightforward, extremely powerful system.

Finally, because this support tool must interface with several different systems and capabilities, it must be compatible with all of them. The tool must provide users with a single, easily-used language to access, manipulate and present data in a way that will best support the end-user.

Properly designed and integrated, the DSS becomes a very powerful support tool that enhances the capabilities and effectiveness of today's decision-makers. Such a tool can increase the productivity of professionals at all organizational levels in all departments. It can effectively extend the organization's present DP staff by reducing its workload, thereby increasing its productivity. And, with today's technology and state of the art software tools, it can bring us even closer to bridging the chasms still separating the traditional data processing world from the office automation and operations research worlds.

Taken together, these features can offer today's organizations—pressed more than ever before to maximize efficiency while reducing costs—unprecedented benefits in the utilization and management of both their human and computer resources.

Discussion

1. How are decision support systems and management information systems interrelated? Which must be more flexible?
2. You are likely to be a knowledge worker in your planned career. What is a knowledge worker? How will your college studies prepare you to interface directly with the computer—using the DSS to develop the type of information that best supports your unique requirements?

CHAPTER 18

COMPUTER SYSTEM EVALUATION AND ACQUISITION

INTRODUCTION

Users have become increasingly involved with the evaluation and acquisition of computer hardware and software. Often, managers have to serve on user committees responsible for selecting a computer system. Even when the data processing function is not a routine responsibility of the manager, he or she will sometimes become involved with selecting a computer system because of the computer's impact on his or her department.

The techniques and concepts covered in this chapter are primarily applicable to a firm purchasing its first computer, replacing an existing computer, purchasing a software package, or making significant changes in its hardware and software.

CONDUCTING A COMPUTER SYSTEM EVALUATION

The approach to acquiring computer hardware and software has changed over the years. Available hardware and software used to be much more limited. Purchasing a particular manufacturer's hardware usually locked a buyer into that manufacturer's system software and utility programs since they were sold as a package. This selling practice was known as bundling. At this time hardware components of different manufacturers were usually incompatible. *Plug-compatible* hardware unit (units produced by manufacturers that directly replace hardware units produced by major manufacturers such as IBM) did not exist. Therefore, acquiring a computer tended to be very informal. Decisions were based on a review of the manufacturer's specifications, what competitors were doing, other computer users' recommendations, or the desire to buy from a favorite manufacturer. Today, sophisticated computer users employ a more structured approach. The range of alternative systems and costs within the computer industry is simply too broad for an unstructured evaluation to be successful.

The evaluation process has five primary phases: 1) feasibility study; 2) analysis; 3) development of a request for proposal; 4) proposal evaluation; and 5) vendor selection. Although we will discuss the evaluation steps sequentially, the actual process can be highly iterative, and phases can overlap. Phases 1 and 2 were discussed in chapter 14; therefore, this chapter will begin with phase 3, which is the first task to be completed when purchasing hardware or software.

Development of a Request for Proposal

The *request for proposal (RFP) document* specifies requirements for the equipment and software to be purchased. It serves as a communication tool between the potential buyer and the computer vendor. It is sent to each vendor, and each is asked to propose hardware and software for the system. Among areas the proposal should cover are:

1. A description of present and proposed applications, including for each application: processing mode (batch or realtime), input/output volumes, data flow diagrams, file descriptions (including size), data base characteristics, and how often the application will be run.
2. Reliability requirements.
3. Backup requirements.
4. Vendor service requirements.
5. Outline of any specific hardware or software features required, such as printer speed or disk capacity.
6. Criteria for evaluating proposals.
7. Plans for vendor demonstration of hardware and software.
8. Implementation schedule.
9. Price constraints.
10. List of any specific questions about characteristics of the vendor's hardware and software.

11. Procedures for clarifying and submitting the RFP, including the person to contact for RFP clarification and the scheduled date for submitting the proposal.

The RFP is sent to each prospective vendor along with an invitation to bid. The buyer should expect a notification from each vendor as to whether it will bid or not.

Proposal Evaluation

Hardware and Software Demonstration

In the first phase of the proposal evaluation stage, vendors demonstrate their proposed systems to potential users. Normally, only a select few are invited to demonstrate. Vendors usually present the major features of their proposals orally. They may have the complete system on hand at the potential buyer's location for demonstration purposes if the system is easily portable. The vendors' presentations enable several of the buyer's employees to gain an understanding of features of the various proposals. However, most buyers employ more substantial techniques to evaluate vendor proposals than merely listening to oral presentations and reading vendor proposals.

Evaluation Techniques

Performance evaluation of computer hardware and software is a major tool used in selecting new equipment. Ideally, the buyer would like to know performance characteristics (job run time, throughput, idle time, response time, and so on) for each proposal when executing current and planned applications. Obtaining such information is obviously impossible. Planned applications have not yet been programmed, and current applications may not execute on the different equipment involved without program modification. However, there are techniques available to assist the buyer in obtaining approximate performance data. Performance evaluation techniques fall into two categories. Traditional techniques provide a very gross measure of a system's performance characteristics. Current techniques provide the buyer with much more reliable and extensive measures of a system's performance.

Traditional Techniques

Traditional techniques of performance evaluation compare performance characteristics such as word size, core cycle time, add time, instruction time, and an average time for mix of instructions. All are very gross measures of computer performance with only limited usefulness—and then only when alternative computers have similar internal organization. All of these techniques totally ignore the effects of software on system performance.

Another traditional technique is the *kernel program*, which is a sample program of small size executed on each alternative computer. In some cases the kernel program is not actually executed, but the run time is derived on the basis of instruction execution time. This approach may be useful for standard mathematical applications, but it is not very useful for business systems since software and input/output effects are ignored.

Current Techniques

Several more reliable techniques are benchmark programs, workload models, simulation, and monitors.

Benchmark programs are sample programs representing at least a part of the buyer's primary computer workload. They include software considerations and can be current application programs or new programs that have been designed to represent planned processing needs. The buyer can design these programs to test any characteristic of the system. For example, the benchmark might test the average response time for inquiries from terminals when the system is also executing a compute-bound batch job. Terminal inquiries during the test can be handled manually, or with a tape or disk unit set up to simulate them.

Workload models are computer programs that accurately represent the buyer's planned computer workload. Model programs require the same mix of demand for computer resources that the buyer's application programs would require. For example, if the buyer's total workload is expected to contain 15 percent high CPU demand work, 10 percent compilation, 30 percent terminal input/output, and 45 percent batch input/output, the workload model programs should contain the same mix. Workload models differ from benchmark programs in that the latter usually do not accurately represent the buyer's complete planned workload.

Simulation techniques have been used extensively to evaluate complex alternative systems when it is not possible to derive an analytical solution that will indicate which alternative is preferable. For example, a computer simulation can be used to determine which aircraft would be the best purchase for an airline given its present fleet, its expected route structures, and its passenger demand. Simulation is equally applicable in the evaluation of alternative computer systems.

Simulation packages can simulate almost any computer system. Input to these packages includes descriptions of expected workloads, files, input/output volumes, and the vendor's equipment. The simulation program then simulates the running of users' described workload on the described equipment. Simulating the equipment of different vendors is accomplished by changing the equipment description input. Validity of the simulation depends greatly on how accurately the simulation models the equipment and the buyer's anticipated workload. Since a valid simulation can be difficult to achieve and perhaps more difficult to recognize by those inexperienced in simulation, it should be used only by more sophisticated computer buyers.

Monitors are either hardware or software devices that monitor the operation of a computer and provide operating statistics, such as idle time of the CPU and average job execution time. *Software monitors* are programs that periodically interrupt processing to collect operating statistics. They are part of the operating system and therefore have access to all operating system data. *Hardware monitors* are devices attached to the component being monitored, and collect data on whatever characteristic is being measured.

Monitors are used primarily in the evaluation and fine tuning of existing computer systems rather than in selection of new systems. Employed as a fine tuning tool, they can indicate where bottlenecks occur within the system. For example, the CPU may not be fully utilized while jobs are waiting in queue because input-output channels are operating at capacity.

We have discussed several traditional and current techniques for evaluating computer systems. For most firms, benchmarking with some simulated programs, which represent a partial workload model, is the best technique for evaluating performance. Since many of today's computers operate in a multiprogramming mode, a user should run the benchmark or workload programs several times in differing sequences so that average statistics can be obtained. The sequence in which jobs are submitted can affect turnaround time in a multiprogramming environment.

Other Evaluation Criteria

Equipment Criteria. Many technical criteria should be considered in selecting computer equipment. Some examples are:

1. Memory size
2. Storage device characteristics:
   a) Disk drives (including average access time, capacity, and whether removable or fixed)
   b) Tape drives (including speed, number of tracks, transfer rate, and recording density)
3. Data channels:
   a) Transfer rate
   b) Type (multiplexor or burst)
   c) Number
   d) Effect on CPU

Software Criteria. In software, the primary areas of concern are operating systems, compilers, and application programs. Operating systems have a major impact on the efficiency of computer processing. Some of their features that should be evaluated are:

1. Multiprogramming capabilities.
2. Job management features.
3. Job control languages.
4. Availability of utility programs.
5. CPU time and primary storage space overhead required by the operating system.
6. Extent of the operating system's documentation.

In the compiler area, users should determine whether the major compiler to be used is available and if it is well supported by the vendor. In business information systems, COBOL is the primary compiler; PL/1 is also used quite often on IBM equipment. On minicomputers and microcomputers, BASIC is often used.

The primary concern in the area of application programs is the availability, capabilities, and reliability of necessary application programs. Users may want to purchase applications software and make minor modifications to adapt programs to their particular needs. In such cases, the extent of documentation and the ability of programs to be modified are important considerations. The reliability and capabilities of applications software can usually be best determined by consulting current users. The evaluation of purchased software is covered in more detail later in this chapter.

General Criteria. Other, more general criteria to be evaluated when selecting equipment include vendor support, compatibility, and modularity. *Vendor support* is crucial to the success of a computer system in a variety of areas, including:

1. personnel training
2. repair and maintenance

3. installation
4. preinstallation testing
5. hardware backup arrangements.

Vendor support is generally adequate among the larger, more established computer vendors. However, there are many new firms in the mini and microcomputer industry, and in some cases their support is minimal. In addition, even with larger computer vendors, repair and maintenance services may be slow and expensive when the user is located in rural or remote areas. Repair persons may have to travel many miles from a major city at the expense of the user. For a user located in a remote area, the speed of repair service can be a major factor in hardware selection.

Compatibility can be divided into two parts: hardware and software compatibility. Users should know how compatible a potential vendor's hardware is with the hardware of other vendors. Compatibility enables a buyer to consider other vendors for certain components of the system. For example, since there are many vendors of remote terminals, substantial savings can result by purchasing them from vendors other than large mainframe vendors. In addition, some computer manufacturers specialize in less expensive, plug-compatible units that will replace major components (the CPU, for example) of large vendors' systems. However, the use of mixed systems (plug-compatible units) can increase management problems because it is difficult to assign responsibility for hardware failures when two or more vendors' units are involved.

The primary concern about software compatibility is whether users' existing software will execute on the proposed system. In addition, users should determine whether new software executed on the proposed system is compatible with other computer systems, both from other vendors and from the proposed vendor. If the compatibility of proposed new software is limited, a potential buyer can be severely restricted if a change of systems is desired. Vendors frequently offer families of computers (such as the IBM 370, 303X, and 308X series). Transition from one member to another of these families is very easy since peripheral equipment and operating systems are compatible throughout the line.

A final general criterion that a user should evaluate is *modularity*. The modularity of a computer system is its ability to add capacity or components. This ability allows for growth without changing systems. For example, additional main memory or disk units can be added when processing requirements dictate such expansion.

EVALUATION OF PURCHASED SOFTWARE

Systems software has almost always been purchased from a vendor or supplied as a package along with hardware. Now, there is also a definite trend toward purchasing applications software instead of developing it in-house. In this section we will discuss the evaluation of purchased software. In-house development was covered in chapters 14, 15 and 16.

Purchasing applications software packages has several advantages:

1. Software development is basically labor intensive. Therefore, it is becoming increasingly expensive. Cost per user can be cut by spreading development and maintenance costs over many users.

2. Purchased software is often better documented.
3. Purchased packages are often very flexible, and can be modified to fit specific user needs.
4. Applications can be implemented faster since the long lead time involved in software development is eliminated.
5. The risk of large cost and time overruns of in-house development is reduced.

Among the disadvantages of purchased software are:

1. Purchased software is not likely to meet the needs of users as closely as software developed in-house.
2. Certain uncontrollable risks are assumed when software is purchased. For example, the vendor may go out of business, or fail to maintain and update the package.
3. The expertise in the application program is outside the user company, whereas with in-house development that expertise is also in-house.

There are many sources of applications software. To find out what packages are on the market, a potential buyer should consult software directories such as those published by International Computer Programs Inc., Auerbach, or Datapro.

The overall approach to evaluating software packages is very similar to evaluating hardware. The primary factors are:

1. Does the package meet the user's needs or can it be modified at a reasonable cost?
2. What are the initial and yearly costs of the package?
3. How efficient is the package? That is, how much computer resources (run-time, primary storage, and secondary storage) does the package require?
4. Will additional hardware be required?
5. What are the operating system requirements of the package?
6. How satisfied with the package are other, similar users?
7. Is the package well-documented?
8. Does the vendor provide extensive training in the use of the package to the user's employees?
9. Is the vendor viable? What is the vendor's financial status? How long has it been in business?
10. Does the package appear to be viable over the long run? Can it accommodate changes in hardware and operating systems as well as changes in the user company's needs?
11. Are performance claims of the vendor specifically guaranteed by terms of the contract?
12. Does the vendor provide a free trial period? Is this period sufficiently long, given normal implementation timespan?
13. Does the package provide adequate data editing, audit trail, and other control features?

MANAGEMENT CASE 18-1

American Chemical is a large chemical company headquartered on the West Coast. Approximately two years ago American decided that it needed a new computer-based accounts payable system.

After doing a feasibility study and developing a requirements document they decided to purchase an accounts payable package from a large and reputable software house. Based on demonstrations of the system and subsequent evaluations it was decided that the package should be modified to fit American's specific needs. A contract was developed with the software house to make the necessary modifications. Approximately 8 months after the software house began to make the modifications it became apparent that they were not going to be successful in making these modifications. Even though, by this time American had invested several hundred thousand dollars in the package. The software house couldn't even get the package to execute after the modifications. In an attempt to salvage its investment, American hired another outside software development firm to attempt to straighten out the mess. This attempt was unsuccessful also. Primarily because of this disastrous experience, the director of MIS for American Chemical instituted a policy which stated that before purchasing an outside software package, the package must meet American's needs close enough that no modification will be required or alternatively, it must be a situation where American Chemical can change their way of doing business to fit the way the package operates without modification. Evaluate this policy.

VENDOR SELECTION

In most cases, more than one computer system or software package will be able to meet a user's needs. A method of ranking competing systems is to assign points based on the degree to which each system meets various important system characteristics. The points are then totaled to obtain a point ranking. See Table 18-1 for an illustration of this approach. Of course, the difference among vendors on one or two factors can override the total score. For example, vendor support could be so poor that it precludes the purchase of an otherwise outstanding system. Communicating with vendors about the point ranking system can be an effective tool for helping them respond more effectively to the RFP.

Table 18-1 Outline of Point Ranking System

		Points Assigned			
		System			
System Characteristics	**Maximum Points**	**A**	**B**	**C**	**D**
Hardware					
Memory size	20	10	15	20	10
Data channels	10	10	8	5	10
Disk capacity	20	20	5	15	10
Modularity	30	30	20	25	15
Compatibility	30	30	10	15	20
Software					
Operating System	30	20	15	25	30
Compilers	20	15	10	15	20
Application programs	40	30	40	20	25
Compatibility	30	30	30	25	25
Vendor support	40	20	30	35	40
Cost	50	30	40	40	50
Benchmarking results	50	50	40	45	30
Total	370	305	263	285	285

COST-BENEFIT ANALYSIS

The cost-benefit analysis of a proposed computer system is not a trivial task. This is particularly true when a company is considering its first computer installation since no internal data exist on which projected costs and benefits can be based. Historically, many companies have tended to overestimate benefits and underestimate costs of computer installations. This tendency has been fostered by computer salespeople, who quite naturally tend to emphasize benefits and deemphasize costs. It is easy for company management to become euphoric about push-button answers to information problems, especially when competitors or business associates have installed computers. To avoid this tendency, a realistic cost-benefit analysis should be completed regardless of the difficulty involved. Potential costs and benefits can at least be identified even if they cannot be estimated with acceptable accuracy.

Costs are usually separated into two categories—nonrecurring and recurring. *Nonrecurring costs* are initial costs not expected to arise again after installation of the system. Examples include hardware and installation costs. *Recurring costs*, on the other hand, are expected to occur continually throughout the life of the installation. Examples include operator salaries, forms, data entry, and the like. The terms costs and benefits refer here to cash flows, not to an accrual concept. A capital budgeting model, which discounts cost-benefit cash flows back to their present values, should be used to compare costs to benefits.

Nonrecurring Costs

Perhaps one of the most difficult aspects of estimating the costs of a computer system is identifying all potential costs. To aid the process, nonrecurring costs can be classified in five categories. First is the cost of computer hardware. We classify this as nonrecurring, but if the hardware is rented or leased, the cost is recurring. However, due to decreasing costs of hardware, many companies are now purchasing it. Aside from the cost of the basic computer configuration, there are costs of installing terminal communication lines, office equipment for the computer staff, form decollators, form bursters, and so on.

The second area of nonrecurring costs is software costs. Systems software, the operating system, compilers, and the like, are usually purchased. Applications software can be purchased or developed in-house. Often, software costs are also recurring due to annual lease payments required by the software vendor or periodic additions of application programs. Software costs are likely to be the largest of nonrecurring costs, regardless of whether software is purchased or developed in-house. The costs of in-house software development are easy to underestimate. For this reason, most companies prefer to purchase most, if not all, of their software.

A third category of nonrecurring costs includes personnel and organizational costs. New personnel may have to be hired and trained, and almost certainly there will be costs associated with relocating personnel. The cost most often overlooked in this area is the temporary decline in organizational efficiency. Change is often not readily accepted, and morale and efficiency are sure to decline during the implementation period. Considerable resources are often spent to minimize the disruptive effects of the change to new computer-based systems.

A fourth category of nonrecurring costs includes all aspects of preparing the site for computer equipment and personnel. These are space, air conditioning, power requirements, fixtures, fire protection, backup sites, and so on.

Conversion costs are the fifth category of nonrecurring costs. They include such things as the creation of new master files and the cost of parallel operations. Normally, extensive overtime costs are incurred during the conversion phase because it is necessary to operate the old and new systems simultaneously and to iron out problems in the new system. In addition, temporary personnel may be necessary to handle the increased workload.

Recurring Costs

Recurring costs include such things as hardware rental payments, maintenance, personnel costs, insurance, electricity, and space occupancy costs. Maintenance is often included in the hardware rental payment but can usually be identified separately. The option of performing one's own maintenance or buying vendor maintenance is, of course, always available when equipment is purchased.

Personnel costs are the largest portion of recurring costs. In addition to computer operator personnel, a system and programming staff is usually necessary to maintain and update software. The latter positions usually are those of systems analysts, systems programmers, and applications programmers. Personnel costs also include salaries of EDP supervisory and management personnel, data input and control personnel, and any additional user staff necessary under the new system.

Conversion to a computer-based system tends to concentrate a firm's information resources. Destruction of all or part of the EDP operation can represent a substantial—even fatal—loss to a company. Therefore, insurance, including business interruption insurance, is a necessary recurring EDP cost.

Finally, space occupancy costs should not be ignored even if the space is owned. Normally, an opportunity cost is associated with the space since alternative uses for it may be available.

Benefits

Benefits of a proposed computer installation are usually more difficult to estimate than costs. Some benefits, such as elimination of the cost of certain operations, are tangible and therefore relatively easy to estimate. However, others are highly intangible, such as the increased customer goodwill resulting from prompt shipment of orders.

Many companies have installed computer-based systems even though cost projections exceed benefit projections. These companies are willing to invest the excess costs. They want to gain expertise with computers because they feel that computerization is inevitable, and as a result this benefit of a computer installation is very difficult to quantify. However, the inevitability of computerization appears to be borne out in the decreasing cost of hardware.

A major benefit often cited for computer installation is the resultant savings in clerical costs. However, these savings usually occur slowly over a period of time, and the increase in computer-related staff usually offsets the savings in clerical costs. It is usually difficult, if not impossible, to justify a computer installation solely on the basis of such savings.

Perhaps the most important and most difficult benefit to quantify is the increase in the timeliness and reliability of management information that a computer system produces. The system can often provide information that simply was not available at an acceptable cost using a manual system.

Computer-based systems can reduce working capital requirements for a given level of sales through better accounts receivable and inventory control. Better monitoring of accounts receivable and faster billing can accelerate cash flows and reduce bad debts. One of the more successful areas in which computers have been applied is inventory control. Sales forecasting and economic order quantity techniques can significantly reduce inventory levels.

Computers can substantially increase labor productivity. An example in this area is computer-based labor and job scheduling. Many manufacturing firms now use computers for their day-to-day scheduling of both machines and labor.

For most companies, customer service improves when a computer-based system is installed. Orders can be processed quicker, customer inquiries can be handled more expeditiously, and customer records, such as accounts receivable, tend to be more accurate.

An often overlooked but important benefit of installing computer systems is that they allow for expansion. Growth of a business will often overwhelm a manual system whereas most computer systems have sufficient processing and storage slack to permit substantial expansion. Furthermore, additional processing and storage hardware can normally be added at a reasonable cost. However, this is not always the case. The capacity of a computer system to expand is a critical variable that should be evaluated during the selection process. Expansion can be provided for through a modular system design, as discussed in the section on general criteria earlier in the chapter.

Making Estimates

In all cases, cost and benefit quantities are estimates. Since we are dealing with future costs and benefits, they cannot be measured directly. Some estimates will be highly reliable; others may be off the mark considerably. There are at least three techniques for coping with the inexactness of computer system cost-benefit analysis.

One such technique is to quantify only those costs and benefits that can be quantified reliably. Those difficult to quantify can simply be identified as potential costs or benefits that cannot be quantified.

A second technique is to attempt to quantify almost all costs and benefits and develop three estimates for each one—a most likely, a pessimistic, and an optimistic estimate. This technique at least suggests the potential divergence of actual from estimated costs and benefits.

The final technique, the expected value approach, is in theory the preferred approach for dealing with estimated variability. With this technique, one develops a probability distribution for each cost-benefit estimate. This distribution is an estimate of the probability that costs and benefits will actually attain a certain magnitude. Based on these distributions, one can derive the expected value of costs and benefits as well as the estimated probability that benefits less costs will attain a certain magnitude.

FINANCING ALTERNATIVES

Essentially, there are three financing alternatives: purchase; rental; and lease. Normally, these alternatives are available from all manufacturers, although rental and lease can be arranged through a third party.

Purchase

The primary advantage of purchasing equipment is the potential cost savings if the equipment is kept for its useful life, which is normally five to ten years. Furthermore, the purchaser can take an investment tax credit and depreciate the computer (as an asset) for tax purposes. Of course, a rental or lease payment is also tax deductible.

Although the purchase approach generally results in lower overall costs, the purchaser assumes the risk of obsolescence, and does not have the flexibility of canceling the arrangement. Furthermore, purchasing requires capital that may be better utilized elsewhere.

Another consideration when purchasing computer equipment is maintenance. With the rental option, a manufacturer will normally provide maintenance services. If the equipment is purchased, the company has three maintenance alternatives:

1. Purchase a maintenance agreement that provides for all maintenance, parts, and labor.
2. Pay for maintenance on a per call basis, as required.
3. Use the company's own employees for maintenance.

Rental

Using the rental alternative, a company rents the equipment on a monthly basis directly from the manufacturer or a third party. Most agreements have a minimum rental period, such as ninety days. After the minimum period, the user is free to cancel the agreement with short notice, usually one to two months. This flexibility is perhaps the major advantage of the rental alternative. If users are dissatisfied, they can simply cancel the agreement. However, the value of this flexibility is often overestimated since the user may have a large investment in training, preparation, and implementation.

Rental agreements typically provide for 176 hours of use of the equipment per month (8 hours per day × 22 average workdays per month = 176 hours). Using the equipment for more than eight hours daily usually requires an additional rental payment, although at a reduced rate.

Renting is the most costly approach in terms of overall cash flow. However, a user does not need the large capital outlay required in purchasing. In addition, the risk of obsolescence and the responsibility for maintenance are borne by the manufacturer. In some cases, renting equipment may produce greater continuing contact with, and support from, the manufacturer than purchasing would.

Leasing

Leasing is a compromise between purchasing and renting. Typically, leasing costs less than renting but more than purchasing. The risk of obsolescence can be effectively transferred to the lessor through an option to purchase the equipment at the end of the lease. Moreover, leasing is not as flexible as renting because the lessee is locked in until the lease expires—typically after five years. However, the lease may allow early termination through payment of a termination charge.

Lessors are often third party, independent leasing companies. The lease agreement may provide a maintenance contract and does not usually charge for operation beyond 176 hours per month. Leasing offers substantial cost savings over renting for the user who is willing to forego the additional flexibility that renting offers.

The ultimate choice of financing involves a basic tradeoff between flexibility and costs that should be measured using a present value approach. The flexibility variable has become less important because computer systems themselves are now designed to be much more flexible. They can be upgraded through additional primary storage, secondary storage, or attached processors.

MANAGEMENT CASE 18-2

Carolina Manufacturing is considering installing a manufacturing resources planning (MRP) system. Carolina has had extensive experience in the use of computers having installed its first computer-based system in the late 1950s. In addition, Carolina has a great deal of manufacturing expertise on its staff. However, no one working for the company has had a substantial amount of experience with MRP systems. The director of manufacturing and the director of MIS currently disagree on the approach to gain the necessary MRP experience to implement this system. Angela Battle, the director of MIS advocates hiring an outside consulting firm to guide the company in the implementation of the MRP system. Consulting rates in the area are $125 per hour and it is expected that the total consulting fee would be approximately $100,000. Jim Johnson, the director of manufacturing feels that it would be much better for Angela to hire a senior individual for the MIS staff who has MRP experience. Such an individual could be hired for approximately $50,000 per year which includes fringe benefits. Which approach do you think Carolina should take?

SOURCES OF EDP EQUIPMENT AND SERVICES

EDP equipment and services are widely available. The computer industry is intensely competitive, and this has been a major factor in the rapid technological advancement of the industry. Suppliers are lean, innovative, and continually looking for unfilled customer needs. This competitive atmosphere can result in substantial cost savings for the buyer. In this section, we will discuss the major equipment and service alternatives that are available.

Mainframe Manufacturers

Mainframe manufacturers produce complete, large computer systems, including the CPU. IBM dominates with over 50 percent of the data processing market. Interestingly, IBM was late entering the computer market. When it introduced its 650 computer in the mid-1950s, Sperry Univac was already established. However, IBM quickly became dominant and successfully defended its market against strong competitors such as RCA, General Electric, and Xerox, all of which have dropped out of the mainframe business.

Other producers of large computers include Burroughs, Sperry Univac, Amdahl,

Cray Research, Honeywell, National Cash Register (NCR), Digital Equipment Corporation (DEC), and Control Data Corporation (CDC). These manufacturers tend to specialize in areas that IBM historically has not covered well. Amdahl and Cray Research specialize in very large computers that usually have scientific, military, or space applications. Control Data Corporation also tends to specialize in scientific computers. Banking applications have traditionally been Burroughs' area of expertise, although it does have small business computers. Hewlett-Packard, DEC, and Honeywell have tended to specialize in engineering/scientific, minicomputer/microcomputer, and interactive computer areas. This specialization has placed them in a strategic location to exploit the distributed data processing market. Honeywell and DEC computers are also often used in scientific applications. In the area of small business computers, the primary manufacturers are IBM, NCR, and Burroughs.

Microcomputers are now used extensively in both large and small businesses. IBM also dominates this market with the IBM-PC. There are, however, a host of other microcomputer manufacturers including Apple, Radio Shack, and almost all mainframe and microcomputer manufacturers.

All these manufacturers sell software for their computers. Prior to 1969, computer hardware and software were sold as one inseparable package (bundle). When IBM unbundled in 1969, most other manufacturers followed suit. The most extensive business-oriented software is available from IBM, Burroughs, NCR, and UNIVAC. Minicomputer manufacturers and companies specializing in scientific computers naturally offer less business software.

Software Vendors

Unbundling in the early 1970s produced a new market for companies that did not manufacture computers but did produce software. Since hardware and software no longer come together automatically, users are now free to purchase software separately.

In addition, the advent of microcomputers has spawned a large number of software vendors for these machines. Purchasing software from software vendors often affords significant price and performance advantages. The complete range of software, including application programs, application generators, data base management systems, utility programs and operating systems, is available from these vendors. In the application programs area, a software vendor will often have specialized programs, such as a package for preparing tax returns, that are not available from computer manufacturers.

Service Bureaus

Service bureaus are companies that provide batch computer processing services as needed, and charge at an hourly rate. They are a primary source of computer services for small businesses, and routinely handle standard applications, such as payroll and accounts receivable. Either the service bureau or the customer provides the program.

Using a service bureau can reduce costs and provide an opportunity to test programs prior to installing a new computer. Another advantage is the potential for arranging backup services for a company that owns its own computer. Service bureaus also handle temporary data entry and processing overloads.

The main disadvantage of service bureaus is that a company may lose control over data, which could result in serious security problems. Related to the question of data security is the problem of data file ownership. Users of service bureaus or timesharing services (discussed in the next section) should be sure that they retain all rights of file ownership, including access and use. Another potential problem with service bureaus is lengthy processing turnaround since the user does not have control over the processing schedule.

Timesharing Services

Timesharing services provide access to a computer through a remote terminal located at the user's place of business. The CPU and secondary storage are physically located at the timesharing service. Execution of user programs is initiated through commands issued at the terminal. Turnaround is very fast because programs are executed using a multiprogramming operating system that rotates among programs, allowing each program a CPU time slice. Thus, many independent users can gain access to a single computer system concurrently. Each user has his or her own programs, can expect fast response time, and appears to have a computer system's undivided attention. Characteristics of a typical timesharing system include the following:

1. Each user has access to the computer system through one or more terminals, typically a hardcopy typewriter or a CRT device with hardcopy print capability.
2. Data and instructions arrive at the CPU simultaneously from many users, but all users are serviced concurrently by giving each small time slices of CPU time on a rotating basis.
3. Each user feels that he is the sole user of the system.
4. Each user's data file is stored by online, direct access storage devices at the central computer site, and is protected by password access systems. This arrangement allows a user immediate access to data.
5. Users can have their own private application programs or can use public programs provided by the timesharing service.

Timesharing in commercial firms tends to be limited to jobs with small amounts of input and output, such as statistical programs and financial planning models. However, timesharing is ideally suited to scientific jobs since they normally have less input/output than computation.

Advantages of timesharing include the following:

1. The user has immediate and continuous access to the computer, and the response is immediate.
2. Small jobs unable to be handled by service bureaus because of excessive processing and transport time are often quite feasible as timesharing jobs since the access is immediate.
3. Timesharing for the casual user of computers is often less expensive than alternative modes of access to computer services.

Disadvantages of timesharing include the following:

1. The potential for loss of data or unauthorized access to a user's data is increased since data are stored at a central computer site. A timesharing user should closely evaluate the installation's data control procedures.
2. Timesharing is typically more expensive than service bureau processing.
3. Input-output capabilities of most timesharing services are limited. Therefore, jobs requiring large I/O are impractical to process using timesharing.

Remote Batch Job Entry

To avoid the input-output problems of timesharing, some services offer *remote batch job entry* (RJE) capabilities. Under RJE, the user has a high speed card reader, card punch (or key-to-floppy-disk device and reader), and printer installed. Jobs are input through the reader to the CPU and are accepted and processed by the CPU as a normal batch job. Therefore, turnaround is not immediate, although some systems allow the user to designate a higher priority for processing at an additional cost. Output is printed on the user's printer, which typically prints at a much higher speed than a hard copy terminal.

Computer Lessors

A potential computer user can lease hardware rather than purchase it. Many companies specialize in the leasing of computers. Typically, the user can lease a computer for substantially less than it would cost to rent one. However, the lessee gives up flexibility since leasing is a long-term commitment.

Facilities Management Vendor

A facilities management vendor specializes in managing, staffing, and operating computer installations for users. Typically, users own or lease the hardware installed at their sites. Of course, users establish guidelines under which the facilities management vendor operates the computer.

The facilities management approach is advantageous primarily for a company installing its first computer. A facilities management vendor can offer expert advice and competent personnel to the new user. The primary disadvantage of facilities management is that outsiders manage an extremely important segment of a company's operations.

Peripheral Hardware Manufacturers

Much of the peripheral hardware in a computer system can be acquired from vendors other than CPU manufacturers. Components such as tape drives, disk drives, and printers are plug-compatible with hardware produced by large mainframe manufacturers. In fact, some companies produce CPUs capable of replacing widely used CPUs, such as those in IBM computers. Such peripheral equipment can be significantly less expensive. However, users can encounter service and maintenance problems when dealing with more than one vendor. When equipment failures occur, it may be difficult to pinpoint which vendor's equipment is responsible for the failure.

EDP Consultants

Large CPA and management consulting firms both provide EDP consulting services. Typically, almost all management advisory service (MAS) work that CPA firms provide is in the area of EDP consulting. Consultants can be invaluable to new and experienced users who are making major changes in their systems. Since equipment salespeople are not always accurate in their performance claims, consultants can help users evaluate them and choose a satisfactory system.

SUMMARY

Normally, users are heavily involved with the evaluation and acquisition of computer hardware and software.

A system evaluation consists of the following phases:

1. feasibility study,
2. analysis,
3. development of a request for proposal,
4. proposal evaluation, and
5. vendor selection.

Even though many costs and benefits of a computer-based system are difficult to quantify, a cost-benefit analysis should be completed. At a very minimum, potential costs and benefits can be identified even if they cannot be estimated with acceptable accuracy.

Essentially, three financing alternatives are available:

1. purchasing,
2. renting, and
3. leasing.

The tradeoffs among the three alternatives primarily involve considerations of cost, capital availability, risk of obsolescence, and flexibility.

The buyer or user of computer-based systems has a wide choice of available sources for EDP equipment and services. Among them are:

1. mainframe manufacturers,
2. software vendors,
3. service bureaus,
4. timesharing services,
5. remote batch job entry,
6. computer lessors,
7. facilities management vendors,
8. peripheral hardware manufacturers, and
9. EDP consultants.

KEY TERMS

Bundling	Modularity
Plug-Compatibility	Software Directory
Request for Proposal (RFP)	Recurring Costs
Monitoring	Nonrecurring Costs
Kernel Program	Leasing
Benchmark Program	Service Bureaus
Workload Model	Timesharing Services
Simulation	Remote Batch Job Entry
Fine Tuning	Facilities Management Vendor
Vendor Support	EDP Consultant

REVIEW QUESTIONS

1. What are the five primary phases of the computer system evaluation process?
2. What areas should be covered in a request for proposal?
3. What are some current techniques a buyer can use to evaluate a computer system's performance?
4. Distinguish between a benchmark program and a workload model.
5. How can simulation be employed to evaluate computer systems?
6. Describe and evaluate the usefulness of monitors.
7. What are the primary criteria with which a computer system should be evaluated?
8. Discuss the importance of compatibility as a criterion for evaluating a computer system.
9. What are the major kinds of nonrecurring costs of a computer system?
10. What are the financing alternatives available to the computer user?
11. What are the available sources of EDP equipment and services?
12. Are monitors used more in the selection of new systems or in the evaluation of existing systems? Why?
13. What is modularity and why is it important in selecting a computer system?
14. List four criteria for equipment that should be considered in vendor selection.
15. What is meant by compatibility in computer systems? Why is it an important consideration?
16. List six software criteria in the selection of a computer system.

DISCUSSION QUESTIONS

1. Janet Smith, owner and manager of a small business that produces delicate instruments for engineering purposes, has decided to acquire a computer system. She plans to use it for accounts receivable, accounts payable, payroll, and work-in-process control. The

company deals with relatively few customers and suppliers. Most orders are large and designed to customer specifications. Smith, who is also an engineer, has managed operations firsthand, usually relying on her own observations for control. Her management philosophy is that no reports are as beneficial as "seeing it for herself." She has always been fascinated with gadgets and computer technology. Based on the information presented, should she acquire a computer system? Why?

2. The Cascade Company has completed a review of five different proposed computer configurations. Based on the review, the five different configurations have been rated below on a scale of one to ten (ten being the highest):

Characteristic	Weighting Factor	Configuration Rating				
		A	B	C	D	E
Hardware						
Memory size	0.9	10	9	8	7	5
Data channel	0.5	10	10	6	9	8
Disk capacity	0.8	9	8	10	7	9
Modularity	1.0	8	7	10	9	8
Compatibility	1.0	10	9	10	10	10
Software						
Operating system	0.9	6	10	8	7	10
Compilers	0.6	10	10	9	10	10
Application programs	0.4	10	5	5	9	8
Compatibility	0.9	6	9	8	5	10
Vendor support	1.0	2	9	6	9	8
Cost	1.2	7	10	8	7	9
Benchmarking Results	1.1	10	8	10	7	10

Determine which configuration should be selected. Fully justify your choice.

3. Curtis Company operates in a five-county industrial area. The company employs a manual system for all its record keeping except payroll, which is processed by a local service bureau. Other applications have not been computerized because they could not be cost-justified previously. The company's sales have grown at an increasing rate over the past five years. With this substantial growth rate, a computer-based system seemed more practical. Consequently, Curtis Company engaged a management consulting firm to conduct a feasibility study for converting their record keeping system to a computer-based system. The consulting firm reported that a computer-based system would improve the company's record keeping system and still provide material cost savings. Therefore, Curtis Company decided to develop a computer-based system for their records. Curtis hired a person with experience in systems development as manager of systems and data processing. His responsibilities are to oversee the entire systems operation with special emphasis on the development of the new system.

   Describe the major steps that will be undertaken to develop and implement Curtis Company's new computer-based system. (Adapted from CMA Examination, June 1976, Part 5, No. 4.)

RESEARCH PROJECTS

1. Contact some computer vendors in your area and obtain detailed information about three different software packages related to the same application area (e.g., accounts

receivable). Determine some selection criteria, evaluate the packages based on these criteria, and come up with a comparative ranking.

2. Select a computer application familiar to you (e.g., course registration at your institution, mailing lists, payroll at your place of employment, etc.). If you were to implement the system from scratch, what source of equipment and/or services would you choose? Support your answer with a cost benefit analysis, and show that your choice is the most economical alternative available.

MIS AND MANAGEMENT

Buying Software—High Cost, Long Delays, Personnel Lack Cited In Move From In-House Creation To Outside Purchase

(Reprinted with permission from MIS Week, March 17, 1982, p. 27)

By Linda Stein

Factors such as cost, development time, availability of maintenance personnel and service to users are leading some MIS installations to buy software rather than develop it in-house, MIS managers told MIS Week last week.

At the same time, other MIS executives said they are enhancing purchased software packages, in order to fill their users' business needs more effectively.

"Our inclination these days is to adapt to what's available," Jeffry A. Alperin, assistant vice president, information systems support, corporate administration, said of operating systems software at Aetna Life & Casualty, Hartford, Conn.

Alperin said that 10 years ago, the situation was "precisely the opposite. We had an inclination to modify and develop software, believing that we'd do a better job, and get exactly what we wanted."

Alperin said that the main reasons for the change in emphasis from 10 years ago were "ongoing maintenance costs, the cost and availability of trained technical personnel, and the fact that the frequency of having to revise and maintain old software has increased."

Aetna is leaning toward packages for operating systems software, Alperin said, because packages "are up and running faster, and the responsibility for continued availability of the package becomes the vendor's. When a new generation of computer becomes available, the vendor develops the new software."

The key to successful implementation of packaged software is the definition of requirements, Alperin said. "If you're serious about taking advantage of packaged software, you must realize it's general," he said. "You must structure your requirements in a general sense—in other words, state your needs, but not how they will be met. Then you do research into the available products."

Alperin said, "You must be honest, and not structure requirements that can't be satisfied." If requirements can't be met as stated by packaged software, he added, "You can redefine your requirements, which I strongly suggest, or you can do a detailed analysis of the whole cost of meeting your need through development."

Software development, Alperin said, "should be viewed as a financial decision and an investment. Those making the decision should apply the same kinds of techniques as they would to a property or business acquisition decision. There should be a cash-flow analysis, vis-a-vis cash in-flow. It shouldn't be automatic that you will develop software if you can't acquire it."

Alperin noted that the trend to use of packaged software indicates "a substantial change in DP's understanding of its role in a company. In the past, we in data processing weren't as aware of the customer's business as we are now, and we didn't have sufficient sensitivity to business needs. DP was automating the operational aspects of business."

"Now it is trying to support a broader range of activities—the business as a whole. DP now definitely wants to advance its company's business objectives through effective application of technology," Alperin said.

Frank Smith, director of computing services, corporate information management, Honeywell Inc., Minneapolis, said, "We do a little of everything—we share software among different Honeywell units; we use internally what the information systems side develops for sale; we develop, and we purchase. But, all things being equal, we buy."

Smith noted, "There is a trend away from doing your own thing, because that is expensive, and it delays the time for results. The reason that you buy is that you need the capability in a hurry. Also, there is the non-recurring cost element—it's cheaper to go buy software than to build it. Also, by buying, you avoid the recurring maintenance costs."

In deciding whether to develop or buy software, one must "sort out the options of timing and cost, and also ask how critical the applications are," Smith said.

A decision would probably be made to develop software in-house, Smith said, if "you didn't have an immediate need for an application, and also if you couldn't find packaged software to satisfy the requirements." These would include "the raw requirements of the application and/or the interface needs between that application and some other application."

In developing the Banco Trust System, a total trust system, for use by all the trust entities in Northwest Bancorporation (Banco), the decision was made to "use some software as is, modify some, and add-on a significant portion of our own to the base," said John T. Carroll, assistant vice president and manager, affiliate conversion, Northwestern National Bank Trust Systems, Minneapolis. (Banco is a multi-bank holding company of which Northwestern National is the largest bank.)

Carroll said of the software for the Banco Trust System, "We reviewed the wares of a number of software vendors, and decided we'd be better off purchasing the foundation software and adding what we needed. No vendor had everything we needed now and for the future."

He added, "There are a lot of trust accounting packages out there, but we developed a total trust system, including management information and financial information, as well as accounting. Most of the trust packages deal mostly with the accounting aspects—getting the numbers in, and then out to customers."

Carroll explained, "To service the customer, we needed more sophistication. We wanted a flexible system tailored to our needs that we could modify down the road—a system designed for and geared to the future."

Discussing the advantages and disadvantages inherent in the different routes to obtaining software, Carroll said that creating software in-house gives the staff "more sense of ownership. You're always going to see something you don't like among the vendors' products.

"If you develop your own, you're not reliant on outside sources. This pride of authorship and control over the final result would be two intangibles that are big factors in the make-or-buy decision. These are subtleties and intangibles that won't show up on a cost-benefit analysis," Carroll said.

He continued, "The make-or-buy decision should also take into account what data processing capability you have. In developing your own software, you may get in over your head and 'under-systemize' yourself.

"Or, if you have a lot of capability, you tend to want to utilize this expertise and can 'over-systematize' yourself, and build a system that's almost too complex to run," he said.

Carroll advocated maintaining good user relations, since that will "yield a prior track record for the MIS department" that decides to develop its own software for some applications. If software development becomes "a drain on user time and leads to animosities," users could say to the MIS department, "There are packages out there—why don't you just get them?" Carroll pointed out.

A good understanding between MIS and users can prevent users saying to MIS, "You don't understand my business. How can you develop a system for me?" Carroll said.

Peter H. Fischer, vice president, Information Services Group (ISG), Chemical Bank, New York, said that it was "rare to just buy a package" for use in ISG.

"We buy and develop," Fischer said. "We buy software and then do enhancement. The vendor does it under our direction, or we do it ourselves."

Chemical Bank has operated for the past two years under Chemnet, an integrated communications environment, in which systems can communicate with each other, and there is no duplication of databases, Fischer said. "Every system we build has to be under that environment. It has to fit into Chemnet and conform to that environment."

Also, each system must fit into the bank's business requirements, he said. "You rarely find a package that conforms to the requirements of big banks," he added.

Fischer said that the type and the extent of software enhancement done for each new application "depends on the criticality of the hookup to our environment." He added that cost payback is determined on every project "to make sure it is cost-effective."

Discussion

1. What are the advantages and disadvantages of purchasing software?
2. For what types of applications is software most likely to be purchased? What types are most unlikely to be purchased?
3. Do you think the trend towards purchasing software will increase in the future?

CHAPTER 19

CONTROL OF COMPUTER-BASED SYSTEMS

INTRODUCTION

Without doubt, effective controls have been ignored in many information systems. Furthermore, many attempts to implement good control have been thwarted by unforeseen accidents or intentional multimillion dollar frauds. In the area of computer fraud alone, the U.S. Department of Commerce estimates that only one out of every hundred cases is ever exposed. Unfortunately, a large number of cases exposed are uncovered purely by accident. In one survey, the average take in computer fraud was

$1.09 million. During a recent year, people perpetrating computer fraud in the banking industry took about twenty-four times as many dollars per crime as their counterparts in other types of white collar bank crime. Events of this nature have made information systems control and security one of the most popular topics in the computer field.

CHARACTERISTICS OF COMPUTER SYSTEM CONTROLS

The underlying concept of control does not change when a firm starts using electronic data processing. Many controls utilized in manual information systems are also used in computer-based systems. However, the methods of application and the appearance of these basic controls are often very different in the latter. Computer system controls have the following characteristics:

1. They are more formal and extensive than in a manual system. This is because most processing is performed in a mode invisible to humans, and it is not possible for personnel to detect unexpected errors during processing, as often occurs in manual systems.
2. Documentary evidence is lacking in computer processing. Input can be combined with other input and transformed to such an extent that the trail between input and output is lost. Audit trails must be specifically designed into a computer system or they will not exist.
3. Controls must be incorporated early in the design process. It is expensive and often very difficult to install controls after a system has been implemented.
4. Because processing steps and information stored in computer files are invisible, system documentation is critical. The backup procedure of examining documents and interviewing clerical personnel to determine processing steps and to gather information is not available in computer systems.
5. Information files are centralized. Thus physical control is easier, but good control is more important. Loss of computer files would force many of today's firms out of business temporarily, or even permanently.
6. The computer provides an opportunity for greatly enhanced control compared to manual systems. Once a control is implemented in a computer program, it will be performed with nearly 100 percent reliability. No manual control can be that reliable. The key to control is to utilize the power of the computer creatively.
7. As in manual systems, the internal controls in a computer system can overlap. Thus, strong control in one area can compensate for weak control in another.

The American Institute of Certified Public Accountants, in its audit and accounting guide titled *The Auditor's Study and Evaluation of Internal Control in EDP Systems* (1977), provides a taxonomy of computer controls. It is adapted here, providing the overall structure of this chapter. The primary categories of controls are general and application controls. *General controls* are overall managerial controls applied to all software, hardware, and personnel involved in the information system. They include 1) management controls; 2) system development controls; 3) hardware and system software controls; 4) access controls; and 5) miscellaneous controls. *Application controls* relate to specific applications in the installation, such as accounts receivable. They can be subdivided into input, processing, and output controls.

GENERAL CONTROLS

Management Controls

The information system is a complex, valuable resource. It should be subject to the same kinds of management controls devoted to other important company resources. Management controls include 1) an information system master plan, 2) the segregation of functions; 3) the selection and training of personnel; 4) written systems and procedures; and 5) a budget and user billing system.

Information System Master Plan

The information system master plan should outline overall strategy for implementing the system. This plan should include major components of the system and interfaces among them. A good plan lists the order in which each component should be implemented as well as implementation dates. Such a plan clarifies objectives and provides a sense of ordered progress to the development of the information system. Without a master plan the information system is likely to become a hodgepodge of incompatible computer programs. Of course, the master plan should be a flexible tool that is updated periodically as circumstances change. Technological changes in hardware can have a large impact on a master plan. For example, a decrease in online storage and communication costs has caused a shift from batch to realtime processing.

Segregation of Functions

A cardinal principle of good internal control is the segregation of functions. Those responsible for operations and custody of assets should be separate from those who record transactions relating to those assets. This principle is even more critical in computer systems because if the environment is left uncontrolled (unsegregated) it is easy to change data or program files and conceal the changes.

The EDP department should be segregated from users and should have control over the data and program files. However, it should never have the authority to originate inputs or correct errors in them, unless the errors themselves originate in EDP.

Functions within the EDP department should also be segregated. The structure of a small, medium, and large EDP organization are shown in Figures 19-1, 19-2, and 19-3, respectively. It is most important to segregate the duties of systems and programming personnel from the duties of equipment operators. The former know the details of program logic, record layouts, and file structures. This knowledge gives them the ability to enter a program in the job stream or to operate equipment. The programmer or analyst thus has an ideal avenue to surreptitiously modify production programs or data files.

Programmers, analysts, and equipment operators should not have direct access to production programs or data files. A librarian should be responsible for cataloging, custody, and security of program and data files. These files should be issued only to authorized personnel when they are needed for approved tasks. The programmer should use copies of production source programs and data files to make changes, but never the actual production file. A log should be maintained either manually or on the

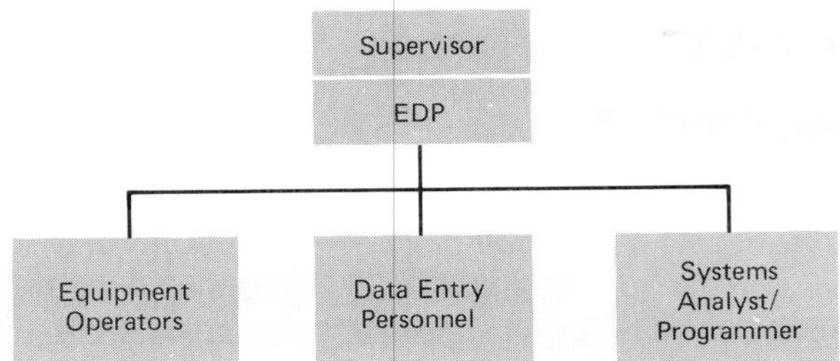

Figure 19-1 Small EDP Organization

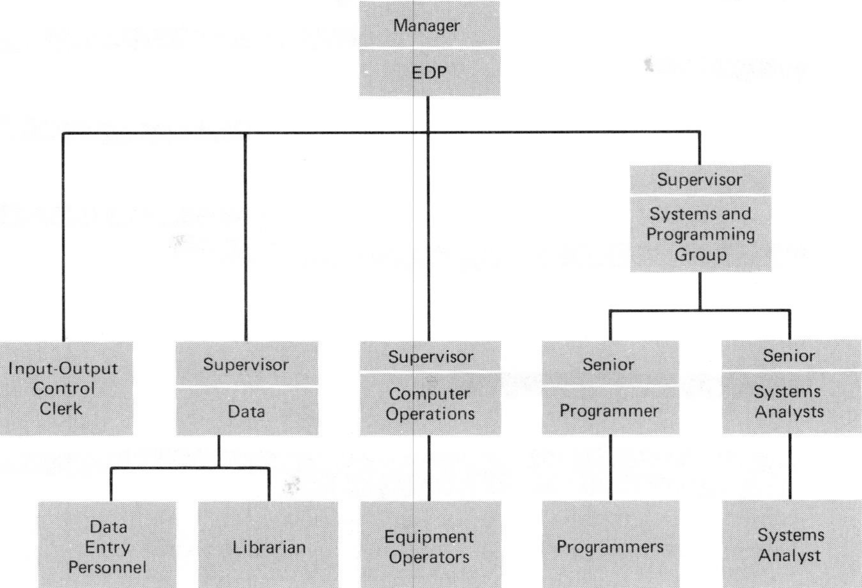

Figure 19-2 Medium EDP Organization

computer to indicate time of issuance, to whom issued, time returned, and the person returning each file removed from the library.

Programmers, analysts, and equipment operators should also not have access to input/output controls, such as batch control totals or master file field totals. Otherwise, fraudulent modifications could be concealed by changing an application's input/output controls. Often, in small and medium-sized firms, these input/output controls are maintained in the user organization. However, there is a trend, especially in larger firms, toward establishing a control group within the EDP organization in addition to controls maintained in user organizations. The latter approach allows more uniform control to be exercised over all EDP applications.

Equipment operators should not have access to application documentation, except that which is necessary to perform their duties. Otherwise, they may be able to modify programs and data files, especially if they have some knowledge of programming. Information about specific applications should be provided to equipment operators only

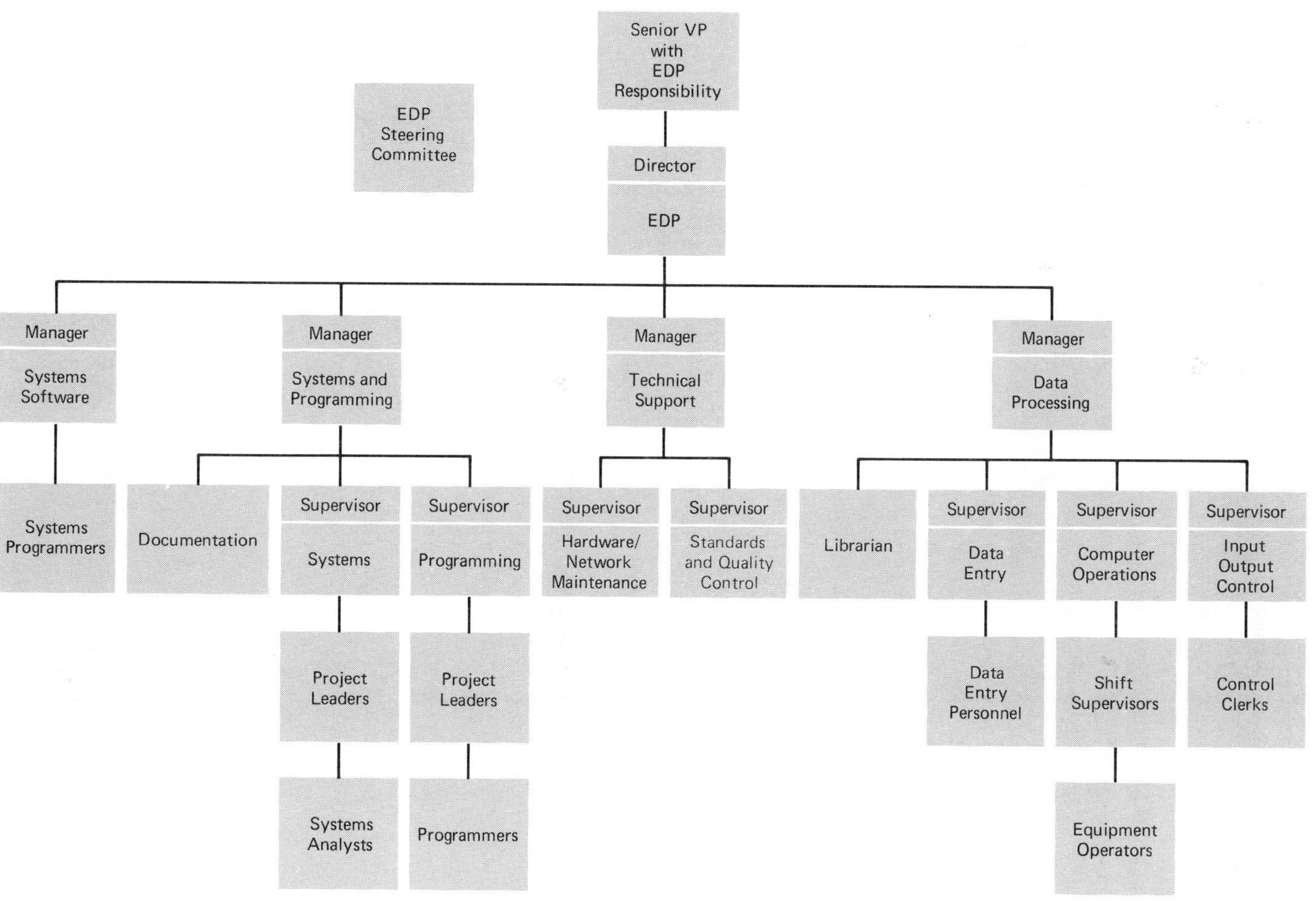

Figure 19-3 Large EDP Organization

if they need to know it to run the job. The operating system gives instructions to the operator via the operator's CRT console each time the job is run. There is no reason for operators to know program logic, record layouts, or file structures. Furthermore, operators should not attempt to correct errors in application programs. This is the responsibility of systems and programming staff. With the control features described above, those best able to modify program and data files—system analysts and programmers—are isolated from equipment, production programs, data files, and input/output controls. Although operators have access to equipment, they are isolated from program documentation, input/output controls, and program and data files, except when jobs use a particular program or data file. Such controls substantially decrease the risk of fraud and make for easier detection if and when it occurs.

A final control involves rotated duties and mandatory vacations. Rotating duties is accomplished by rotating personnel among shifts or by rotating the scheduled run time of applications among shifts. Rotation of duties is obviously easier to accomplish among lower-level personnel like operators and control clerks. At a minimum, higher-level personnel should be required to take vacations.

Much of what we have discussed in this section applies to mainframe and minicomputer installations. But how do we handle segregation of functions in microcomputer installations, where one person may be the user, operator, and programmer? First, quite often microcomputer programs are purchased and thus the user does not program. Therefore, unauthorized changes to programs are unlikely. However, beyond this there is very little that can be done to provide segregation of functions for micros. Consequently, the other controls discussed in this chapter must be relied on more heavily to compensate for the lack of segregation of functions.

Selection and Training of Personnel

Ultimately, the success of any information system depends on the skills of the people who operate it. The basic skills required for different EDP functions vary widely. For example, programming demands exactness, abstract reasoning, and an ability to work with minute details. A programmer does not need advanced interpersonal skills within the organization since successful programming does not require a large amount of interaction with other people. On the other hand, a systems analyst must be able to interact with managers to determine their information needs and sometimes to tactfully convince them that their needs are different from what they seem. Such interactions require very advanced interpersonal skills. Analysts must also work often with abstract concepts, and must be generalists who work well with uncertainties. A working knowledge of computer capabilities, quantitative methods, accounting, information theory, organization theory, and other disciplines is necessary for successful systems analysis. Therefore, matching basic human characteristics and skills with particular job requirements is essential.

The careful selection of personnel is important, especially in positions that lend themselves to fraud. One of the best examples of such a position is that of the systems programmer. Systems programmers are usually the most highly qualified of programmers. Since they maintain the operating system programs, they have indirect access to all application programs and data of the installation. In addition, they have access to security programs, such as password systems. Therefore, in selecting systems programmers, integrity and trustworthiness as well as skill are of critical importance. Employee bonding and security investigations are excellent practices when hiring a systems programmer. Security investigations should continue to be conducted, with employee permission, on a periodic basis.

Training EDP personnel differs from training in most other areas of an organization. Since EDP knowledge is rapidly changing and highly technical, many companies rely heavily on outside sources for training. Among these sources are hardware vendors, software houses, universities, and organizations that specialize in technical EDP training. EDP personnel tend to spend more time in training than other personnel because of the rapid technological changes in their field.

Written Systems and Procedures

To maintain effective control over EDP operations, standard procedures must be established. In effect, many of the controls discussed in this chapter are procedures, or depend on regular execution of procedures to be effective. Once established, procedures must be written and maintained in a manual or they are unlikely to be followed. When specified procedures are not followed, there is a tendency to regress to practices that process data with the least inconvenience to personnel. Such regression, in turn, produces a lapse of control.

EDP operations should be reviewed periodically to confirm that written procedures are up-to-date and that actual operations conform to them. This review function is usually performed by a group from outside EDP, such as internal auditing. Of course, EDP management continually reviews procedures on an informal basis in its day-to-day supervision of operations.

Budget and User Billing System

The EDP organization is an important and valuable economic resource, representing a large investment. In the early stages of a company's conversion to a computer system, EDP is often treated as a free resource. This encourages otherwise reluctant users to develop computer applications and to employ idle computer capacity. Although this approach can be defended for new installations with excess capacity, in the long run users must be charged for EDP services in order to produce a cost-effective installation.

The EDP department should be an integral part of a firm's budgetary control process In this approach, the EDP organization is established as a service center, and users are charged for the service. However, choosing among proposed new applications on a cost-benefit basis may be difficult because of the inability to quantify cost-benefit variables. This topic is covered in more detail in chapter 18.

System Development Controls

System development controls can be divided into three areas: 1) controls related to the system development cycle; 2) system documentation controls; and 3) controls over program changes.

System Development Cycle Controls

As mentioned above, there should be a formal procedure for conducting cost-benefit feasibility studies for each proposed application. Senior management should be involved in the planning of major applications and should approve all but minor applications. User departments should be involved in the early phases of a new application and throughout the complete development cycle. Furthermore, accounting personnel, internal auditors, and external auditors should be a part of most system design projects, even though they are not direct users. Internal and external auditor input can ensure that the system is auditable.

Throughout the system development cycle, review points should be established that allow users and management the opportunity to approve, disapprove, or modify the system design. This is often accomplished through weekly review meetings.

The system design phase should produce a set of detailed specifications. They should be reviewed and approved at the appropriate management level and by user departments before proceeding to the next phase.

The system should be thoroughly tested prior to implementation. Testing is a joint effort of EDP and application users. Initial tests are run by the programmer on individual program modules using test data usually prepared by the programmer. However, as the programs are integrated into a system, users should be heavily involved in preparing test data and evaluating system output. System testing is covered in more detail in chapter 15. Prior to conversion, the final system should be reviewed and approved by users and an appropriate level of management.

The conversion process is itself a critical point of control in the development cycle. During conversion, records or data can be altered or lost. Data file conversion programs must be thoroughly tested to assure that file modifications occur as planned. Control totals are required to assure that critical data are properly converted. Appropriate control totals include record counts and grand totals of numeric fields. These totals should balance after conversion. Samples of individual records should also be reviewed after conversion.

The conversion and implementation process is often accompanied by a sense of urgency and apprehension. Undiscovered program bugs crop up and must usually be fixed under pressure of a deadline. In such an atmosphere, more errors can be expected to occur. It is important that these possibilities be foreseen, planned for, and controlled. Otherwise, errors and fraud can escape totally undetected.

A final development cycle control is the post-implementation audit. Each application should be audited regularly to ascertain that its objectives are being met and that system controls are functioning. The first audit should occur within one year after implementation.

System Documentation Controls

Documentation is the primary vehicle of communication about the system among systems analysts, programmers, users, management, and auditors. Much documentation is initiated during the system development cycle. In fact, development would be almost impossible without it.

There is a tendency among analysts and programmers to get their jobs done without developing minimum, permanent documentation. This lack of documentation inevitably becomes very expensive to the company when program modifications are necessary or when the systems analyst or programmer, who knows the system, leaves the firm. There is no doubt that tight implementation schedules contribute to documentation deficiencies. Often, however, programmers consider it a boring chore to go back and document an elegantly designed program after coding. The programmer is more interested in testing and implementing than documenting.

Many EDP organizations have found that assigning the responsibility of documentation to a documentation specialist or librarian of a chief programmer team is the best solution to the documentation problem. Such a specialist does not originate documentation—this is the responsibility of systems analysts, programmers, users, and others. However, the specialist does ensure that documentation meets firm standards, that it is updated when the system is modified, and that he or she maintains custody over all documentation. Such custody is itself an important control feature. It prevents access to documentation by those who have no need to know about the system. Documentation standards should be established, published, and enforced. They include flowcharting conventions, coding conventions, and methods of revising documentation. System documentation provides an overview of the system and includes:

1. A system description.
2. Data flow diagrams and/or system flowcharts showing the flow of information through the system and the interrelationships among the processing steps, inputs, programs, and outputs.
3. System specification documentation that governed design and implementation of the system.
4. Input forms and descriptions.
5. Output layouts and descriptions.
6. File and record layouts and descriptions.
7. Descriptions of controls.
8. Program change authorizations and their implementation dates.
9. Descriptions of audit trails.
10. System backup procedures.
11. A data dictionary.
12. Structure charts.

Program documentation relates to individual programs and normally includes:

1. A narrative description of the program.
2. Structured English, program flowcharts, decision tables, and/or decision trees that document details of program logic.
3. Source statement listings.
4. Program test data listings.
5. A testing log.
6. Card images of Job Control Language (JCL) and other control input.
7. Input/output formats and distribution.
8. A detailed description of file structures and record layouts.
9. Copies of program change request forms, the authorization for changes, and their implementation dates.

10. Instructions for the console operator.
11. File retention procedures.
12. A description of error detection and control features.

Operations documentation provides EDP operations with the necessary instructions to run a computer-based application efficiently. It includes for each program:

1. A brief description.
2. Setup instructions.
3. Input keying procedures.
4. Procedures for balancing input and output, and control and distribution procedures.
5. Operating notes explaining program console messages and actions required of the operator.
6. Recovery and checkpoint restart procedures.
7. Emergency instructions.
8. Normal and maximum run time.
9. Hardware and operating system requirements.

User documentation includes the following:

1. A narrative description of the system.
2. Data flow diagrams and/or system flowcharts.
3. Instructions for interacting with the system through a CRT to make input and produce response to queries.
4. Instructions covering the proper completion of input forms, if any.
5. Description of control procedures and indication of personnel or position responsible for each procedure.
6. Procedures for error correction.
7. Computer output balancing and checking procedures.
8. Input cutoff procedures.

Library documentation includes the following:

1. Backup procedures.
2. Retention procedures.
3. Restrictions on file access and file checkout procedures.
4. File labeling procedures.
5. Procedures for maintaining a log or inventory of each logical and physical file.

MANAGEMENT CASE 19-1

Joe Hagen was the lead programmer for the demand deposit accounting system in the Southeastern Banking Corporation. Joe devised a scheme whereby he could defraud the bank of $1,000,000. The basic element of the scheme was that Joe inserted code in the demand deposit accounting system to cause his account to be increased by one million dollars whenever a check for $20 was processed through Joe's account. In other words, the $20 check would trigger the program to increase Joe's account by $1,000,000. Joe had also been involved in programming applications for wire transfers of money. Therefore, he knew how wire transfers from one bank to another were initiated. However, he wanted to be out of the country whenever the scheme was executed, so he scheduled his annual vacation in a foreign country. Just prior to leaving for the airport he stopped at the local drug store and cashed a check written for cash for the amount of $20. Joe knew that it would take approximately 24 hours for the check to clear the bank and to trigger the transfer of money to his account. By that time he would certainly be out of the country. Upon arriving at his destination he waited for a day and initiated the wire transfer from his account to a foreign bank account. A few days later Joe called from the foreign country to say that he liked his vacation so well that he had decided to resign from his job and take an extended vacation. The bank never heard from Joe again. But they did discover the fraud approximately six months later. What could have been done to prevent this computer crime?

Control Over Program Changes

The uncontrolled ability to make changes in production application programs can be the equivalent of having direct, uncontrolled access to a company's cash. For example, a programmer could change the order entry program to send regular shipments of inventory to friends and prevent accounts from being invoiced and updated. When checks are produced by computer, the possibilities for fraud are nearly endless.

In one payroll application, a programmer was caught stealing from his fellow employees rather than from the company. He changed the program module that produced annual W-2 forms so that his W-2 withholdings were overstated, and the withholdings of other employees were understated by the same amount. Therefore, the total W-2 withholdings reported to the IRS balanced with the actual withholding amount. To prevent other employees from becoming suspicious because too little was being reported withheld on the W-2, the programmer had each employee's withholding amount understated by only one dollar. The company, however had approximately two thousand employees. Upon filing his federal tax return, the programmer was thus able to claim a refund for excess withholdings that were fraudulently overstated. However, each of the other employees were paying balances due on their federal income tax, which was overstated by one dollar. The fraud was discovered several years after it was put into operation when an employee found that the withholdings reported on his W-2 form did not balance (by one dollar) with the withholdings reported on his weekly paycheck stubs.

Prevention of fraud is not the only rationale for good control of program changes. Control makes it more likely that authorized program changes will be made promptly, that they will be tested thoroughly prior to implementation, and that production programs will not be disrupted by haphazard changes.

Changes to both application and system programs should be based on written authorizations as illustrated in Figure 19-4. Authorizations should be approved by the user and an appropriate level of management.

Programmers should not be able to change production programs directly. To make the change, a programmer should obtain a copy of the production source program from the librarian, and program documentation from the documentation specialist. Program changes are made to the copy, and this, of course, has no effect on the original. After

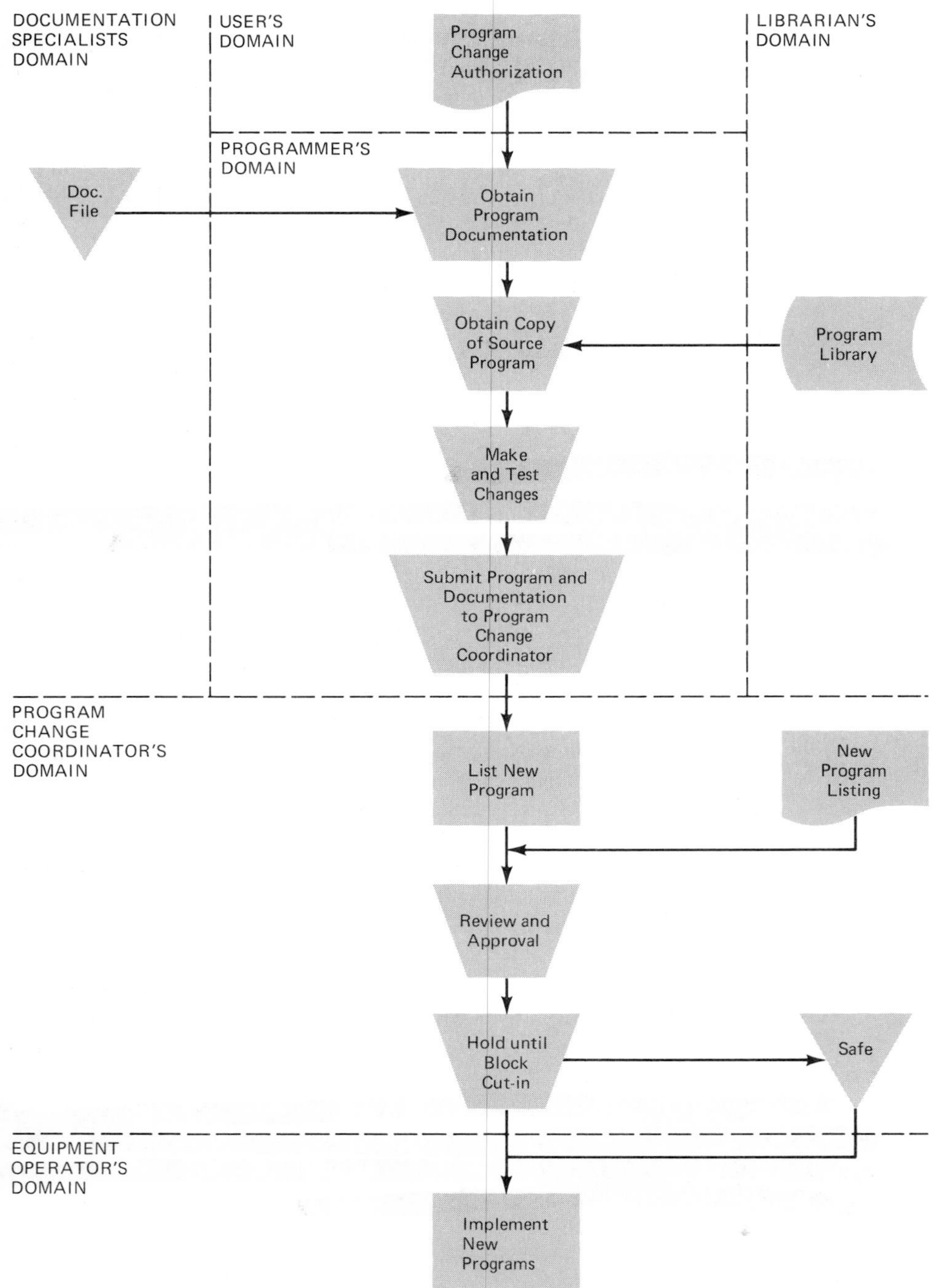
DOCUMENTATION SPECIALISTS DOMAIN
USER'S DOMAIN
Program Change Authorization
LIBRARIAN'S DOMAIN
PROGRAMMER'S DOMAIN
Doc. File
Obtain Program Documentation
Obtain Copy of Source Program
Program Library
Make and Test Changes
Submit Program and Documentation to Program Change Coordinator
PROGRAM CHANGE COORDINATOR'S DOMAIN
List New Program
New Program Listing
Review and Approval
Hold until Block Cut-in
Safe
EQUIPMENT OPERATOR'S DOMAIN
Implement New Programs

Figure 19-4 Program Change Control

testing, the changed program is submitted to a program change coordinator along with authorization and evidence of the testing performed. The program change coordinator can be the manager of systems and programming, a committee, or another responsible individual from systems and programming.

The program change coordinator reviews the new program and supporting documentation submitted, and approves or disapproves implementation of the new program. As a basis for this review, the coordinator should directly list the new program. A program listing submitted by the programmer may not accurately represent the program submitted, since changes could be made to the program after the listing was made. Another useful tool for the coordinator is to run a source code comparison between the current production source program and the new source program. The output of the source code comparison is a complete listing of all changes from the current to the new source program.

After the new program is approved, the program change coordinator holds it in custody until a block cut-in date. *Block cut-in* is a procedure in which all program changes are collected (batched) and implemented in the production program library at a predetermined time (e.g., once a week). Block cut-in improves control over program changes since changes can be made only at a specified time. All changes should thus be traceable to specific block cut-ins. Operations implements the new programs at a block cut-in when it receives them from the program change coordinator.

An additional program change control is the implementation of software that monitors and records read and write accesses to the production program library. This software can record and report such statistics as time of access, the device from which the access was made, and the user identification of the individual accessing the library. Of course, write accesses should occur only at block cut-in. However, emergency program changes are sometimes necessary before a block cut-in. Such changes should be implemented only by the operations staff. Operations should make copies of the old and new source programs and deliver them directly to the program change coordinator. This procedure allows the coordinator to review the change after implementation.

Hardware and System Software Controls

Vendors build control features into computer hardware and systems software. These controls are separate from those exercised by application programs or people. Although the controls discussed in this section are not necessarily incorporated into all hardware and software, one of the criteria for selecting new hardware or software should be the control features that the vendor has incorporated.

Hardware Controls

Parity checks are a basic hardware control. Data are represented in the computer on the basis of a scheme of binary digits. When a character is moved or stored internally, either in the CPU or in secondary storage, a redundant bit (parity bit) is added to the bits necessary to represent the character. Parity bits detect equipment malfunctions that cause the alternation of a bit within a byte during processing. Figure 19-5 illustrates parity bits. The parity bit causes the number of on bits within a byte to be either even or odd, depending on whether the computer is an even or odd parity machine. For

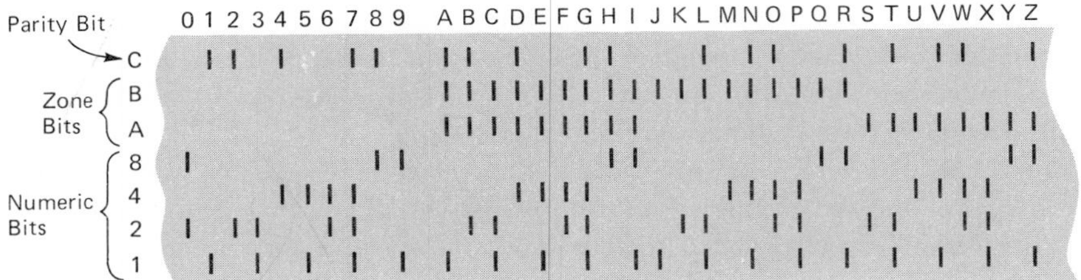

Figure 19-5 Even Parity Check. (Courtesy of IBM Corporation). Note that the C row bit is on when it is necessary to make the number of on bits in a byte (column) even.

example, if a computer is designed with even parity, the occurrence of a byte with an odd number of on bits would indicate a parity error.

In a *redundancy check*, two hardware units perform a task independently of each other. The results of the two operations are then compared to make sure they are the same. If they are not identical, an error has occurred. For example, in a card reader, two independent read stations read each card, and the reader compares the results for read errors.

Write-read checks are similar to redundancy checks. As data are written on magnetic tape, the tape passes through the write head, and then immediately through a read head. The data are read and compared to the characters that should have been written. A difference indicates that an error has occurred. Write-read checks are available on a variety of data storage devices.

Validity checks monitor the bit structure of bytes to determine whether the combination of the on and off bits represents a valid structure within the character set of the computer.

Two types of tape protection rings are used—write and no-write rings. A *write ring* is a plastic ring that must be inserted on a reel of magnetic tape before data can be written on the tape. Absence of the ring physically prevents a tape drive from writing on the tape. If a *no-write ring* is inserted on a reel of tape, it physically prevents the write ring from being inserted. This affords an extra measure of protection since the no-write ring has to be removed and the write ring has to be inserted in order to write on a tape. These rings protect against accidental destruction of data when an operator mounts a tape in error or a hardware malfunction occurs. *Read-write* suppress on disk drive units prevents a disk from having data read from or written on it. This control feature can be used to prevent writes on a disk containing production programs. The only time that writes to this disk are required is at block cut-ins of changed programs. Similarly, the write notch on a floppy disk can be covered with tape to prevent writing to that disk.

Echo checks verify that a device has been activated to carry out an operation that it was instructed to perform. For example, when the data channel is ready to transmit data to the printer, it transmits a signal activating the printer. If the printer is ready, it sends an echo signal back to the data channel. If an echo signal is not sent, the data channel postpones transmission and signals the operator that the printer needs attention.

Preventive maintenance checks help avert hardware failures. Components are periodically examined to check if adjustment or repair is necessary. Vendors offer customers preventive maintenance service, which attempts to repair components before they actually fail. At the same time, components are cleaned and adjusted. A good preventive maintenance program can significantly reduce hardware failure.

Today's computer hardware is substantially more reliable than earlier hardware. If other elements in a computerized information system were as reliable as the hardware, we would indeed have highly reliable systems.

System Software Controls

System software consists of the operating system, which is designed to control and manage computer resources during execution of application programs. The operating system functions basically as a manager, and has several built-in control features. For example, it provides password protection for access to files. In addition, it processes file header and trailer labels. The first record on a file is a *header label*. The header record contains information about the file, such as data set name, logical record length, and block size. The data set name is read by the computer to verify that the correct file has been mounted. The last record of a file is a *trailer label*. It contains control information, such as a count of the number of records in the file. Operating systems automatically execute the control features inherent in header and trailer labels.

Access Controls

Access controls give limited numbers of authorized individuals access to program documentation, program and data files, and computer hardware. Furthermore, authorization is given only to individuals whose jobs require it. Many controls already discussed are related to access controls. For example, augmentation of access controls is accomplished through segregation of functions within the EDP organization and between users and the EDP organization.

Program Documentation

Access to program documentation should be restricted to individuals whose jobs require it such as the programmer assigned to a particular application and his or her supervisors. The assigned programmer needs access to documentation only when working on the application. At all other times, documentation should be in the custody of the documentation specialist, if there is one, or the systems and programming manager.

Program documentation is a valuable resource. Fraudulent changes to programs are difficult without access to program documentation, even for experienced programmers.

Program and Data Files

The librarian exercises primary control over access to program and data files. There are two kinds of libraries. One is the manual library, which consists of a separate room or fireproof vault in which magnetic tapes, disk packs, and any other removable storage media are stored. The library should be accessible only to authorized library personnel, which specifically excludes programmers, system analysts, or equipment operators. The librarian maintains physical control over all removable files when they are not being processed. Accountability records are maintained for each file. They include:

1. The date the file was created.
2. The serial number of the magnetic tape reel or disk on which the data are stored.
3. The names of logical files stored on the physical volumes (reels or disks).
4. The date the file is to be scratched (reused).
5. The person currently holding the file and its location.
6. The backup file's remote storage location.

Authorization for release of files to operations is based on each shift's schedule of jobs to be processed. However, an individual file is not released until it is called for by the operating system. Individual files should be returned to the library when processing is complete. The librarian should issue all files to be processed overnight before leaving work, and the library should be locked.

The second method of setting up a library is through system software. In more advanced EDP systems, most program and data files are stored online. Access to these files is through remote terminals or batch programs. Control is maintained by password schemes, device authorization tables, and encoding of data.

The three-level password scheme is the most common. First, the user logs on to the system by entering a unique user ID. The system then asks the user to enter a password in order to gain access to the system. Finally, to access an individual file, the file name or data set name must be entered. Password systems can also require separate passwords to read from or write to a file. This feature allows individuals to read a file with the read password but prevents them from changing the file without a write password.

Passwords should be changed regularly for sensitive files because their secrecy may not be maintained. Readable recordings of passwords should be minimized. For example, hardcopy terminals should either not print passwords or print them over a mask, which makes reading the password impossible. Otherwise, discarded output can be used to obtain passwords. The system should keep a record of each invalid password that is input. The record should include not only the invalid password but the terminal from which it originated, the user ID, and the time it was used. Monitoring invalid passwords can isolate attempts to gain unauthorized access to files through trial and error.

A federal government system containing sensitive information records erroneous passwords and then goes one step further. The user is allowed three opportunities to enter the correct password within thirty seconds. If the user fails, the system assumes that an unauthorized attempt to access the system is occurring and therefore cancels the ID under which the user logged on. The user is thus completely excluded from the system until he or she gets a new ID.

A *device authorization table* lists the files to which each device (terminal) can gain access for reading and writing, and when access can be gained during the day. When used with a password system, a device authorization table provides additional file security. For example, a terminal in manufacturing could not gain access to the accounts receivable file since manufacturing personnel do not need such access, even though they may have the password of the accounts receivable file.

For particularly sensitive data, an encoding approach can be used. Data are stored on the file in coded form. If unauthorized access occurs, the data cannot be used unless the code is broken. Authorized access to data or data modification must go through an encoding or decoding step, which is performed by encoding software modules.

Dial-up terminals have vastly increased the need to control access to online data files. Technically, it is possible to access a file via regular telephone lines from anywhere in the world if one knows the valid telephone number, user ID, and password. Smart, programmable terminals have compounded the security problem. It is now possible to write a program instructing a smart terminal to follow a trial and error or other scheme to gain access to a computer system and its files. Therefore, sensitive data should be accessible only from hardwired terminals, over leased telecommunication lines, or through a dial-back procedure for terminal connections. With a dial-back procedure, the individual attempting to connect a terminal gives the phone number from which he or she is dialing. A computer operator (or computer) establishes the connection by dialing back after verifying that the phone number is a valid location from which to connect to the system.

Computer Hardware

Access to computer hardware should be limited to those who are authorized to operate it. Users, analysts, and programmers should not be allowed to operate the equipment. Otherwise, the risk of unauthorized changes is too great. Limiting hardware operation to equipment operators is often called a closed shop approach. Access can be limited through the simple expedient of a locked door. Work can be passed to and from the equipment room through a window. Terminals remote from the central computer room must normally be used with a key and are often kept in locked rooms.

Miscellaneous Controls

Control Group

The control group is separate from computer operations and maintains input-output controls. It logs all batches of input, records batch control totals, and reconciles them to intermediate and final output control totals. After the control group verified that processing has been completed successfully, it is responsible for distributing the output to authorized users. The control group can also provide quality control by maintaining logs of various types of errors and their sources.

Internal Audit Review

EDP should be subject to periodic review by internal auditing or some other external group. Also, during the system development process, periodic external reviews should be conducted for work completed to date and plans for completing the project.

The professional association of internal auditing, the Institute of Internal Auditing (IIA), has moved strongly into EDP auditing. It has published several books about EDP control and auditing. In addition, the Association of EDP Auditors has been formed. One of its activities is the Certified Information Systems Auditor program, which certifies individuals as auditors. Certification is based on an examination, experience, and continuing education requirements.

Physical Security

Physical security begins with the physical location of data processing equipment. It should be away from potential threats such as floods, fire, and explosions. Basements are subject to floods, manufacturing areas are subject to fire, explosions, and dust, and aircraft are more likely to crash on the take-off or approach paths to runways than anywhere else. These types of increased risk areas should be avoided. The location and its design should make it more difficult for an individual planning destruction to gain access to equipment or files. Large glass windows showing off the computer room to visitors are definitely a security weakness.

If practical, the computer room should be enclosed in a fire and bombproof room. Safe fire-suppression equipment that does not use water (halon gas is effective) should be installed. Environmental control equipment should regulate temperature and humidity and remove dust particles from the air. There should be protection against damaging electrical power surges caused by lightning or other factors. Some installations have uninterruptible power sources in the form of backup batteries or generators. Others monitor all access routes to the computer area by closed circuit television.

Obviously, it is not possible or cost-effective to remove all risk. One must assume that computer operations will be interrupted at times. Accidental destruction of a portion of a file may occur relatively frequently. Destruction of the complete installation, however, is unlikely. In either event, the installation should be protected by an interruption recovery plan with the following components:

1. Offsite backup storage of program and data files, documentation, and supplies. Local banks will often provide storage services in their vaults.
2. Backup hardware sites. A backup site can be another company with similar equipment that has agreed to provide backup on a reciprocal basis. Other possibilities include service bureaus and the equipment vendor.
3. A set of documentation outlining procedures to be followed during an interruption.
4. Business interruption insurance.

Backup data files can be a natural by-product of normal processing. Updated files stored on magnetic tape are backed up by retaining the old (parent) master file and transaction file used in creating the new, updated (child) master file. If the new file is destroyed, it can be recreated by simply rerunning the file updating run that originally created it. This procedure is called grandparent-parent-child backup (see Figure 19-6).

Files and data bases stored on a direct access storage device and updated in place are more difficult to back up. The contents of such files and data bases should be periodically written (dumped) onto magnetic tape or another removable disk and then stored. Between backup dumps, all transactions (changes) to the file or data base should be captured in a transaction log stored on magnetic tape or disk.

Backup data files have other values. They can provide audit trails, be used to construct test data, and can be processed to derive data useful in managing online

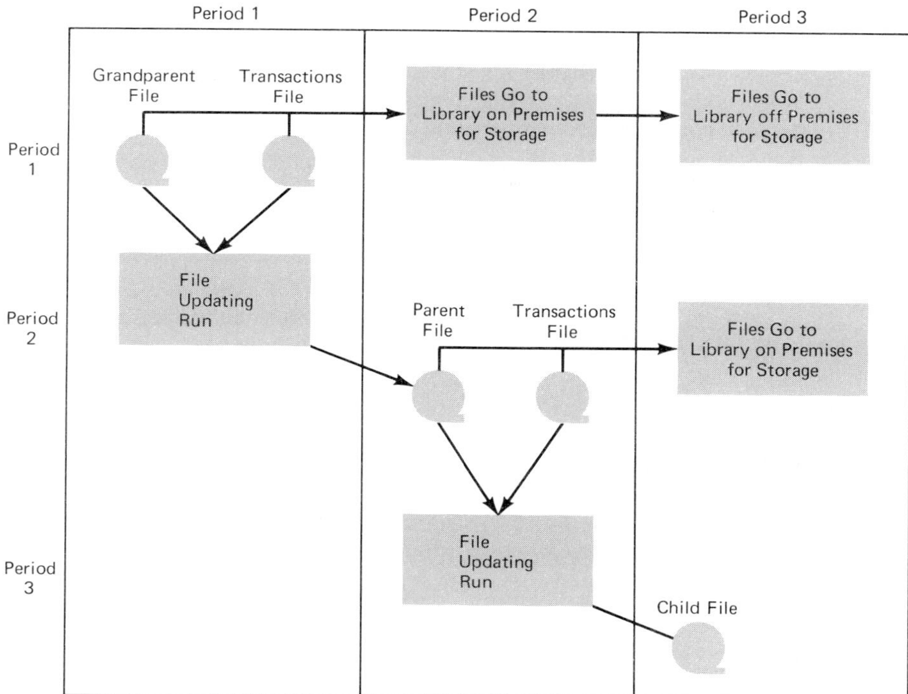

Figure 19-6 Flow of Files in Grandparent-Parent-Child Backup. Vertical dimension illustrates the flow of Grandparent-Parent-Child master files in processing, and horizontal dimension illustrates the flow of these files for backup storage.

systems. If time data are also captured, some examples of useful management data that can be derived from backup files are:

1. Which terminals make the most use of the system.
2. Which types of transactions are most numerous.
3. What the turnaround time is for transaction processing.
4. What the distribution of transactions is on the basis of time of day.

The degree of backup should be related to the potential loss involved. In a very critical application—for example, an airline reservation system—it may be necessary to back the system up completely with an additional independent system. Each of the two systems has its own hardware, software, and personnel. In this case, both systems are updated with each customer reservation transaction. Either system could carry on the reservation processing if the other system went down.

MANAGEMENT CASE 19-2

Winchester and Company is a large international management consulting firm specializing primarily in computer-based systems. Recently a large bank in a southeastern city has become concerned over the security of its automated teller machines. The bank has a total of 20 of these machines scattered over the city. The bank has hired Winchester and Company to determine if there are any security weaknesses in these automated teller machines. As a part of its review of the automated teller machine system, Winchester has decided to assign two of its staff to the task of breaking into the system by nonphysical means and stealing as much money as they can. After discussing the plan with the bank management, they approved the operation. Over a period of two days the two Winchester staff members managed to steal $8,000 from the bank's automated teller machines. If you were on Winchester's staff and was assigned this task, how would you attempt to break into the system? How do you think the Winchester staff employees managed to steal the $8,000?

APPLICATION CONTROLS

Input Controls

Input controls provide reasonable assurance that inputs are authorized, converted to machine-readable form correctly, processed as intended, and free from errors. These controls include 1) input authorization; 2) data conversion; 3) data editing; 4) error handling; and 5) data communications.

There are four basic types of inputs to computer-based systems, and each should be subjected to appropriate input controls. The four types of input are listed below:

1. Information retrieval inputs request the computer system to display, either on hard copy or CRT screens, the information it has stored or can produce.
2. Transaction inputs result directly from the firm's transactions and are normally the largest volume of input. For example, transaction inputs can be computer-generated purchase orders based on inventory stock levels.
3. File maintenance inputs are all changes to files other than transactions. They are made less frequently than transaction inputs but can have more permanent and far-reaching effects. For example, a change in the price of a widely sold product could affect many individual invoices and accounts receivable.
4. Error correction inputs correct errors resulting from the three previous inputs. Perhaps the primary control problem in this area is making sure that errors are corrected promptly and that the corrections are authorized properly.

Input Authorization

Most transaction inputs are based on some type of source document. For example, credits to accounts receivable can be based on cash receipts. The flow of source documents to data conversion should be strictly controlled. Whenever possible, documents should be batched. The user or the originating department and the EDP input/output control group should compute batch control totals and maintain them. Authorization signatures are appropriate in many cases, such as on an accounts payable voucher approval for payment. Other control devices, such as prenumbering source documents, restricting their storage, and logging their transmittal between organizations, increase control of input authorization. Finally, those who are authorized to make each of the different types of input should be identified, and procedures for identifying and validating the source of all inputs should be installed.

Data Conversion

Data conversion often requires two steps. The data is first transcribed to a source document and is then keyed onto a machine-readable medium. Transcription should be eliminated if possible because one of the best ways to reduce errors in data conversion is to eliminate manual conversion of this type. For example, the system could include a cash register that handles by-product recording of sales and inventory transaction inputs. Similarly, point-of-sale equipment could capture bar-coded data.

Transcription can also be eliminated if transaction documents are designed on forms that can be keyed in directly. These forms should guide the initial recording of transactions into a uniform format. Such forms should have repetitive information preprinted, should contain authorization blocks, and should have room for control totals.

The primary data conversion control is batch control totals. Figure 19-7 illustrates batch control. The originating department should batch source documents in limited numbers. Batches can consist of natural logical groupings of documents, such as a day's transactions or the source documents from an organizational unit. However, they do not have to be based on any logical grouping.

Batch control normally consists of a total of a quantity field, such as the total hours worked by employees in a given batch of time cards. If there is no quantity field, hash totals can serve for batch control. *Hash totals* are a summation of a nonquantity field—for example, the sum of the first three digits of the social security numbers on the payroll file maintenance inputs that update employee names. Hash totals have no meaning except for control purposes.

Each batch must have an identification number, which normally is keyed into the input record. If batches are based on logical groupings, such as departments or days, the department number or date can serve as the identification number.

Batch control totals are keyed in a separate batch control record for each batch. A balancing and edit program verifies whether each batch balances prior to further processing. Alternatively, the batch control record can be omitted, and the balance and edit program can be designed to output a total of each batch. The control group then balances totals manually.

Batch control is equally important for realtime input, which is often based on some hardcopy document. After-the-fact batch control totals based on natural input groupings, such as department number, can be constructed periodically. These totals can be balanced with totals produced by the computer system. Alternatively, realtime systems can be designed to artificially assign each input to a batch number and produce control totals by batch. In this approach, the system must notify the originating input station to assign an input to a particular batch.

Data Editing

Many errors that occur while data are being collected and converted can be detected before processing through creative use of the computer to edit input. For batch input, these edits are often performed by a separate edit and balancing program.

Key-to-disk input systems are usually controlled by a minicomputer. Such systems can detect errors with edit programs and immediately notify the keying personnel that

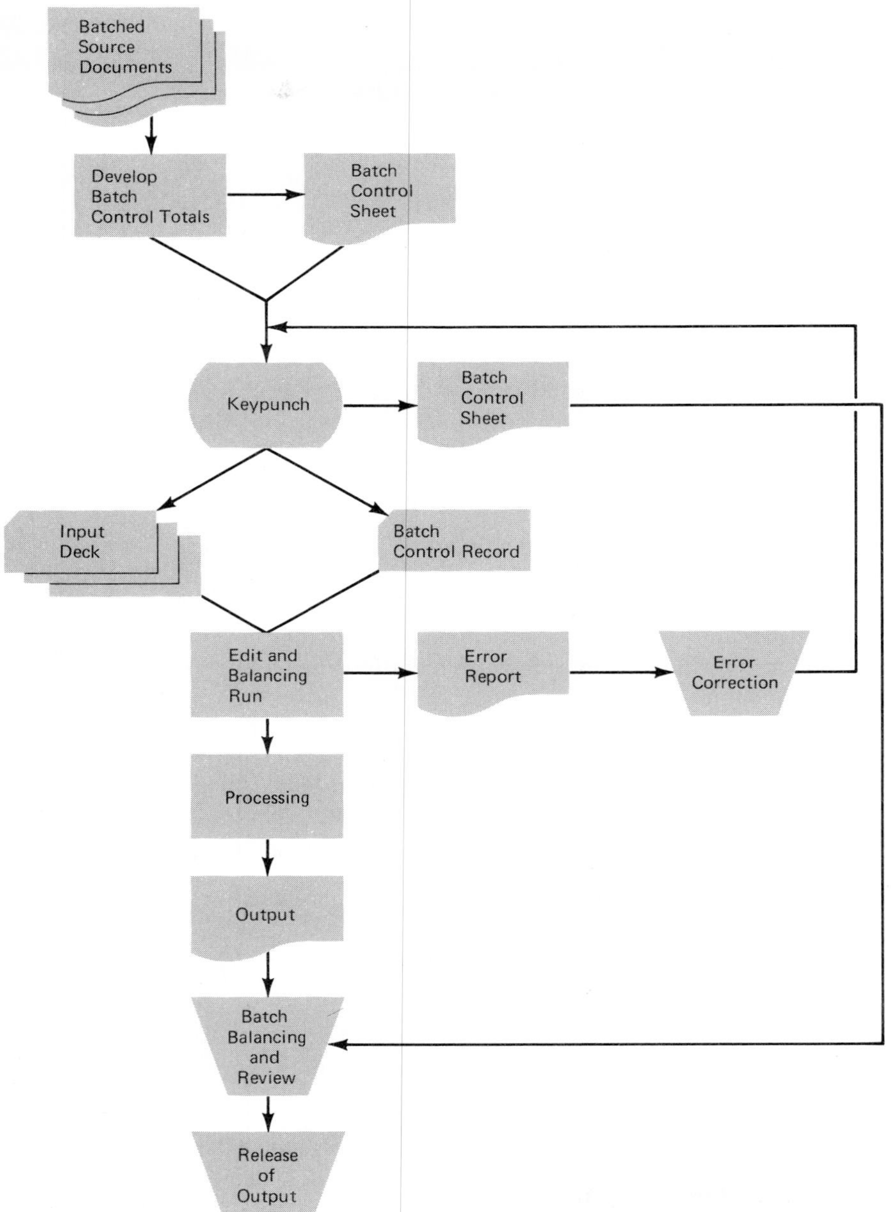

Figure 19-7 Batch Control

an error has occurred. The keying personnel then correct the error if possible. If not, the computer enters it on a list of errors to be corrected later.

Realtime or batched input entered through online terminals located where data originate provide an important advantage in the editing and correction of input. As each input record is entered it can be edited, and the terminal operator can be notified immediately if an error occurs. The advantage of this procedure, called *up-front editing*, is that the input originator has either made the error or has the information to correct it. Therefore, errors can be corrected immediately. Up-front editing is more reliable than an error list created by the EDP department that is sent to the user department for correction.

The types of edit techniques normally found in well designed edit routines and programs are:

1. *Anticipation checks*, which are based on the fact that certain fields in an input record should always be nonblank or that an input record is expected for each master file record. For example, we can always expect the hours worked to be nonblank on employee time card records. If no hours were worked, we would expect a zero in the field. Furthermore, we can expect that each employee in the master file would have a time card input record for each payroll processing period.
2. *Limit* or *reasonableness checks*, which verify that data items are within reasonable limits. For example, we can expect that hours worked per week will never be negative and never exceed seventy-two. An accounts payable system for a milling company might check invoice input by computing a price per pound for grain invoices and verifying that the price is within established limits. There are many possibilities for reasonableness checks. This technique is limited only by the systems analyst's imagination.
3. *Arithmetic proof checks*, which verify the results of other computations. An obvious example of this check is that the total of debits should equal the total of credits for accounting system inputs. Batch control total verifications are an example of arithmetic proof checks.
4. *Numeric and alphabetic checks*, which ascertain that numeric input record fields contain only numeric characters, and that alphabetic fields contain only alphabetic characters.
5. *Invalid code checks*, which verify codes contained in input records to assure that they are valid. Examples are department or sales territory codes. Each type of input record usually has a unique record code that enables the system to identify the type of input. For example, an accounts receivable payment record can have a record code of 5. Verification of these codes is a necessary preliminary step since most of the other edit checks depend on the type of input record received.
6. *Sequence checks*, which should be made on all input to sequential processing programs to verify that the input records are in ascending sequential order by the record key field. In another form of sequence checking, the input records are expected to be in a certain sequence. For example, an airline reservation system can require that the reservation agent's identification be input prior to the customer reservation data.
7. *Check digits*, which are an extra digit in identification codes, such as part numbers. With check digits the validity of codes can be determined by performing an

arithmetic operation on them. An example of check digit generation by the arithmetic progression method follows:

Part number:	7	8	4	5	3
	×	×	×	×	×
Multiply by	6	5	4	3	2

$$42 + 40 + 16 + 15 + 6 = 119$$

Subtract 119 from the next highest multiple of 11:
$121 - 119 = 2$.

Therefore, the check digit is equal to 2, and the complete part number is 78453-2. The check digit becomes an integral part of the part number. If a transcription or transposition error occurs, it will be discovered when the arithmetic progression is performed on the part number.

Error Handling

Once errors are detected, it is necessary to ensure that they will actually be corrected. Simply printing errors on an error list and sending them to the user department to be corrected is insufficient. In the rush of day-to-day operations, the department may ignore the lists or give them a low priority. Another tendency is to correct only errors that are easy to correct, and leave those that require more intensive investigation until later. The most elegant and creative error detection system will fail if errors are not actually corrected.

Several techniques can be used to control the error handling process:

1. A cumulative error list can be used. It contains not only the error detected in the current processing run, but all errors detected in previous runs that have not been corrected. Cumulative error lists are produced from an error file of uncorrected errors. The error record on the file should contain at least the following:
   a. A unique error number that identifies and serves to tag each error.
   b. The date and time the error was detected.
   c. A description of the error. Sometimes an error type code is assigned. It can be looked up in the system documentation to obtain a more detailed explanation of the error.
   d. All the data contained in the record on which the error was detected.

A simple listing of the application's error file produces a cumulative error list. An error record is removed from the file only when the error has been corrected. In some applications, the error file is known as the suspense file because the error is held in suspense or abeyance until corrected. A copy of the cumulative error list should be routed to user management. This enables management to monitor levels of input errors as well as the status of uncorrected input.

2. Correcting errors is often the responsibility of a senior individual in the user department. In such a case, errors are likely to be corrected more carefully because

users have a greater direct interest in the system's integrity than data originators, who can be in nonuser departments. The individual responsible for error correction should be thoroughly familiar with the application system since proper interpretation and correction of errors often requires considerable skill. To correct most errors, it is usually necessary to communicate with data originators because they have the original supporting documentation for the input. Data processing personnel should not correct input errors. Furthermore, all error corrections should be subject to the same authorizations as the original input. Otherwise, fraudulent inputs could be introduced along with valid error corrections.

3. As discussed previously, realtime input allows up-front editing. However, realtime input can present some error handling disadvantages. For example, how do we control a situation in which an operator deliberately or inadvertently fails to correct an error displayed on the CRT screen? At least two control approaches are possible. First, the input system can be designed to refuse additional input until the error is corrected. Second, a hardcopy record of all errors and their corrective entries can be made. This list can then be reviewed periodically to assure that errors are being properly corrected.
4. All error corrections should flow through the same edit procedures that control original input.

Data Communications

Whether communication of data is accomplished by documents, input transmittals, magnetic tape, or telecommunications, its movement between departments and from one processing step to another must be controlled. In the case of documents or input transmittals, batch control totals are the primary instrument of data communication control. For tape or telecommunication record counts, hash or field totals effect the control. Each time data are processed, totals are taken and compared with control totals to assure that data have not been altered or lost.

In addition, some companies are implementing data encoding devices for the transmission of sensitive data over telecommunication channels. It is relatively easy to intercept transmitted data, especially when they are transmitted over microwave channels. Encoding gives some protection, but some codes are easily broken.

Processing Controls

Even though a system has well-designed input controls, some errors can slip by or additional errors can be created during the processing phase of a system. Therefore, controls that increase the integrity of processing are essential. Most processing controls are very similar to input controls, and we will therefore describe them only briefly:

1. Run-to-run control totals, such as record counts and critical quantity totals, should be verified at appropriate points in the processing cycle. This control can detect such operator errors as mounting the wrong version of the master file because control totals will not balance.
2. Reasonableness checks should be incorporated into all processing programs. Although most errors of this type should be detected and corrected during input,

errors (or intentional unauthorized changes) can be created during processing. Furthermore, incorporating these checks into programs provides additional assurance that errors detected by input editing are actually corrected.

3. Controls should detect operator errors such as processing the wrong file. External file labels or, more importantly, an internal file labeling system that allows the computer to verify file identifications automatically can prevent this type of error.

Output Controls

Output controls are executed by the EDP control group. They help assure the accuracy of computer results, and control the distribution of output. They include the following:

1. Output control totals should be reconciled with input and processing totals before EDP releases reports.
2. The computer console log or job execution stream on the computer output should be reviewed to determine whether any unusual interrupts or patterns of processing occurred that would affect the validity of output.
3. Job control language (JCL) listings should be checked to assure that no unauthorized programs have been executed during processing.
4. Output reports should be visually scanned to make sure they look correct. Critical input transactions should be compared individually with output reports to assure that the changes were made correctly. Other techniques, such as statistical sampling, are sometimes used to review output.
5. Copies of output reports should be delivered only to authorized recipients. An integral part of a system's documentation is a list of all system output and recipients of each copy.
6. The use of accountable documents (e.g., blank check stock) should be verified by comparing computer-generated counts to actual usage recorded from preprinted sequence numbers on the documents.

SUMMARY

Users can make significant contributions to the application of controls in computer-based systems. Although computer controls have sometimes failed to detect fraud and errors, they are potentially far more reliable than manual control systems if their power is used creatively.

This chapter divided computer controls into general and application controls.

General controls are the overall managerial controls applied to all software, hardware, and personnel involved with the information system.

Management controls include activities like planning the information system development process, segregating functions, personnel selection, procedure writing, and cost controls.

System development controls ensure that application systems are developed and documented in accordance with prescribed standards.

Control over equipment and systems software is a crucial area of general controls.

It is necessary to restrict access to various documents and data files related to production programs.

Internal audit groups and control groups can play a useful part in ensuring proper use of EDP resources.

Application controls relate to individual system applications, such as the payroll and manufacturing resources planning application. These controls can be divided into those applying to input, processing, and output.

Input controls help assure that inputs to the system are authorized and free from errors. Processing controls control the integrity of computer processing. Output controls help assure the accuracy of computer results, and control the distribution of output.

KEY TERMS

Fraud
Audit Trail
Backup Procedures
General Controls
Management Controls
System Development Controls
Access Controls
Application Controls
Input Controls
Processing Controls
Output Controls
Segregation of Functions
Control Group
Internal Audit Group
Control Totals
Record Counts
Hash Totals
Documentation Standards
Control Over Program Changes
Code Comparison
Tape Protection Rings
Preventive Maintenance Checks
Password Schemes
Data Encoding
Physical Security
Grandparent-Parent-Child Backup
Error Handling
Reasonableness Checks
Arithmetic Proof Checks
Invalid Code Checks
Sequence Checks
Check Digits

REVIEW QUESTIONS

1. Outline and discuss the characteristics of controls in a computer-based system.
2. What are the general controls of computer-based systems?
3. Many computer frauds are executed through unauthorized changes to computer programs. How should program changes be controlled? Do program change controls differ for small and large EDP organizations?
4. Why should the systems analysis and programming functions be segregated from the equipment operating function?
5. In regard to billing users for computer services, what is the normal evolutionary process through which most firms go?
6. What are the elements of good systems documentation?

7. How do hardware and system software controls differ?

8. Identify two different ways to set up a file library.

9. How do companies protect themselves from unexpected interruption of computer services? Explain this in terms of hardware, software, and computer-based files.

10. Indicate what type of general control each of the following represents:
    a. Construction of hash totals
    b. Parity checks
    c. Documentation
    d. Rotation of duties
    e. Passwords
    f. Segregation of functions
    g. Trailer labels

11. What are the application controls of a computer-based system? How do they differ from general controls?

12. What are the four basic types of inputs to computer-based systems?

13. How is the data conversion process controlled?

14. Discuss the types of edit techniques that can be incorporated into computer programs.

15. Once detected, how should errors be processed and handled?

16. Why are controls over computer output necessary?

DISCUSSION QUESTIONS

1. The Smith Company is in the process of computerizing several of its accounting applications. It has three programmers and wants you to allocate the programming among them to maximize internal control and minimize fraud. The programs will perform the following functions:
    a. Maintain general ledger
    b. Maintain accounts payable ledger
    c. Maintain accounts receivable ledger
    d. Print checks for signature
    e. Maintain cash disbursements journal
    f. Issue credits on returns and allowances
    g. Reconcile bank account

    Allocate programs to the programmers in the best way. Justify your allocation. How does your answer relate to segregation of duties?

2. The documentation of information systems applications is an important step in the design and implementation of any computer-based system. Documentation provides a complete record of information processing applications. However, documentation is a phase of systems development that is often neglected. While documentation can be tedious and time-consuming, the lack of proper documentation can be very costly for an organization.
    a. Briefly identify and explain the purposes proper documentation can serve.

b. Briefly discuss the basic types of information that should be included in the documentation of a data processing application.
c. What policies should be established to regulate access to documentation data for the following four groups of company employees?
   1. Computer operators.
   2. Internal auditors.
   3. Production planning analysts.
   4. Systems analysts.

(Adapted from CMA Examination, December 1977, Part 5, No. 2)

3. The North Face Company is considering the implementation of an accounts payable EDP system. Top management has instructed the EDP department to design the system in such a way that efficiency is maximized and potential fraud is minimized. The tentative proposal for the system has been delivered to you for your evaluation. The proposal follows:

All purchase orders are sent directly to the EDP department biweekly from the purchasing department. After their "batch" delivery, the price, quantity, and other pertinent information are processed directly to the accounts payable disk file. When the receiving department notifies purchasing that the order has been received, EDP pays the vendor on the basis of data input from the purchase order. Because of the expertise of the EDP staff, no editing run is implemented. It is considered too costly. Additionally, purchase orders for orders received are used to update the inventory file biweekly. The staff analyst who constructed the system feels that it is efficient and could potentially save the company quite a few dollars due to the reduction of historical master files.

a. List the areas of weakness in this system.
b. Present a data flow diagram of a revised accounts payable system that will maximize internal control and minimize the potential for fraud. Utilize the concepts presented in this chapter of grandparent-parent-child files. transaction files, error files, edit runs, and input hash and batch totals.
c. Does the revised flowchart utilize the concept of an audit trail?
d. What other source documents should be utilized in this system?

RESEARCH PROJECTS

1. Most of the techniques discussed in this chapter are applicable to large computer installations. It might not be possible to apply the same techniques to the control of mini- and microcomputer systems. Identify the major differences between large and small computer systems in the area of general controls. Recommend some techniques to control the operations of a small installation. You might find relevant articles in *EDP Auditor* and *Mini Micro Systems*.

2. While stories of multimillion dollar computer fraud are often in the headlines, experts hold that routine errors in data input and processing cause much greater losses than intentional fraud. Study the data input, processing, and output procedures for some application system. Determine the probability of error at various steps and the corresponding monetary risk. Are additional controls necessary? Would they be cost-effective?

APPLICATION CASE

Disaster Plan Worked, Despite Unforeseen Loopholes

(Reprinted with permission from MIS Week, July 28, 1982, p. 22)

By Tom Keown General Manager, McCormick & Dodge Corp., Huntsville, Ala.

On Feb. 19, 1980, General Computer Services, Inc., an applications software company in Huntsville, Ala.—now a part of McCormack & Dodge Corp.—experienced a disastrous fire which completely destroyed its facility.

The fire occurred in the early morning hours, and the facility was completely destroyed by 7 a.m.

This situation was a classic one in which a disaster plan was needed. The plan had to be well thought out and well communicated to the management team in order for effective recovery actions to begin immediately.

Most medium to large companies have made contingency plans and have a well-thought-out disaster procedure. Many small companies, however, are so involved in day-to-day activities, that, even though they recognize this to be a valid process, plans just have not been put into place.

Fortunately, General Computer Services had a disaster plan. The plan was actually put together following a "near miss" in 1973 when a number of severe tornados struck the city. Although the facility was unharmed, much of the city was without power and many businesses and homes were destroyed.

The plan made provision for back-up computer processing facilities. Reciprocal processing agreements were worked out with two companies within a radius of 30 miles, so that, in the event of a power outage or other work disruption at the facility, processing could be carried out at the other sites on a "time available" basis until operations could be restored.

Although no firm arrangement for adequate time had been arranged, considerable thought and planning went into the back-up/restore procedures so that job control, operating system, tape, disk configurations, etc., were all thought through and adequate provision was made to bring up the operating programs and proceed with a minimum of delay.

Off-site vault storage for backup tapes, documentation, etc., was also secured and procedures were established for weekly backup of source and object programs, job control procedure libraries, etc.

In addition, provision was made to store documentation off-site on a periodic basis as new versions or additions to documentation were printed.

This plan, we felt, was reasonably well thought out and should serve as a good basis for reacting to almost any catastrophe, and, in fact, it did serve us well. However, there were a number of deficiencies within the plan. These point out some areas of significant problems which possibly are overlooked in the overall planning process by many companies.

One of the principal deficiencies in our plan had to do with our lack of follow-through in updating the disaster-and-recovery plan documents as circumstances changed.

For example, in September 1979 (about six months prior to the fire), we elected to discontinue the operation of our own data center and had opted to remote processing services. The remote site was 100 miles from our facility, thus the requirement for alternate computer processing sites no longer existed.

The requirement for backup/restore procedures for tape libraries and so forth was pertinent for the remote center but not for our main facility. However, the requirement for continued backup of documentation and procedural instructions remained a real requirement. When the remote processing site was activated, we de-activated our backup procedures, and thus did not have current documentation in the vault at the time of the disaster.

We, in fact, were placed in a situation where we had to call on customers to provide copies of documentation which they received from us in order to build a starting point from which to construct up-to-date documentation. Since we launched a major rewrite of a new release of our software, this constituted a serious problem which required almost six months to correct.

Another area of real deficiency was in the area of corporate records. We had protected, or attempted to protect, the principal revenue-producing activities of the company through the backup procedures, but had not considered the implications of poor backup of our business records. For example, the contract files, the fixed asset ledgers, the correspondence and all normal business records such as accounts receivable, were not backed up at all and, therefore, all were lost.

We did have our general ledger computerized and therefore computer records were in existence to allow us to restore our accounting records, but the source documents and much of the backup material was completely lost. Perhaps it is impractical to backup much of this information, but certainly key records could be backed up, such as contract commitments and fixed asset records.

In addition to the principal business records listed above, we also neglected to have any backup of basic materials—brochures, presentations, prospect lists and standard proposal responses. All of these items required significant time to rebuild. Had we maintained the master copies of sales brochures, etc., we could have saved ourselves many weeks of intense effort as we reworked all of this material and, in addition, we lost a good deal of prospective new business in the process.

One of the most significant problems related to establishing a basis for collection of insurance on the facility. We obviously needed to collect as quickly as possible and we did not even have a copy of the insurance policy in the backup location.

In order to establish a basis for collection at replacement cost, we manually reconstructed a record of all the property involved. We drew a layout of the destroyed facility and then gathered the key managers into a conference room and created, from memory, a list of the contents of each room.

We thus, delivered a well-documented inventory list with our insurance claim and since there was no doubt about the total destruction of our facility, the insurance company paid the face value of the policy with no questions asked.

The well-documented and well-researched statement of assets lost was undoubtedly essential to the collection of this insurance money. However, we wasted valuable time in the documentation process and, therefore, the suggestion here is that fixed asset records and insurance policies are two items which definitely must be stored off-site.

One of the more difficult items to recover after the fire consisted of the many day-to-day operating procedures and instructions which were developed over time and were kept within each work group and in the offices of many employees. These daily procedures and processes included standard test procedures, test data, operating procedures on many production systems, and other normal work-activities documentation.

These items were considered mundane and also too voluminous to back up, and that is probably the case in most instances. However, thought should be given to the key procedures and key operating instructions and then this smaller set of procedures can and should be backed up.

Much of our loss was in-process work. It is obviously impractical in most cases to back this up, but in situations where remote processing sites are in use and where backup computer procedures are in place, these items of work should be entered into the computer in the course of day-to-day activities and then under the normal computer backup procedures, the in-process computer programming work will be automatically backed up. Major system design documents should be backed up within the standard documentation backup procedure.

Another important item of loss—and one for which no backup was provided—consisted of preprinted computer forms, payroll checks, etc.

As all data processing people know, it takes time to obtain preprinted forms. Since we were in the service business, we ran into several difficulties in producing payrolls, since all checks were destroyed in the fire as well as payroll registers and other preprinted forms.

We were able to borrow these from customers, but there were many special arrangements which had to be worked out to allow this to suffice during the emergency period.

In summary, the principal deficiencies in our plan consisted of the lack of periodic updating of our disaster plan to accommodate changes in our circumstances and a lack of adequate backup for documentation, customer contracts and standard business records.

We failed to backup our fixed asset records and did not have a copy of our insurance policy in the vault.

So the net effect was that, in spite of the deficiencies listed above, the company did survive. No customers were lost as a result of the catastrophe and the employees themselves were encouraged since there was a plan of action.

We had a plan. It did work, but it could have worked much better if the items listed above were appropriately taken into account.

Discussion

1. Many individuals have stated that without backup capabilities, the destruction of a company's primary computer facility could literally force the company out of business. Do you agree or disagree with this statement? Why?
2. Of the several areas in which General Computer Services, Inc. did not have adequate backup, which was potentially most serious?

PART FIVE

INFORMATION SYSTEMS, MANAGEMENT, SOCIETY, AND YOU

CHAPTER 20

MANAGING INFORMATION SYSTEMS RESOURCES

INTRODUCTION

Management of information systems resources has seen significant changes in recent years. In the 60s and 70s, information systems managers gradually increased their power and influence within most organizations. Typically, they moved from managerial positions within another function, such as accounting, to full-fledged vice presidents of information systems. These managers were looked upon as experts in information processing and in effect held the keys to the computer resource. However, in recent years a potential challenge to the power of the information systems manager has developed because of distributed data processing and application development by users. With users directly purchasing hardware, and either purchasing or creating software, many see the role of the information systems manager changing to that of a consultant, advisor, and coordinator. Of course, we will continue to have centralized computer facilities, especially for large batch runs and large data bases. The challenge of administering centralized data bases and communication networks with distributed computing will certainly mean that information systems managers will continue to play a crucial role in the management of business organizations. In this chapter we will first discuss the structure of the management information systems (MIS) function. We will then look at managing system development, system maintenance, and DP operations. Finally, we will cover physical security of computer operations.

STRUCTURE OF THE MIS FUNCTION

Typically, the MIS function is located in one of two areas in an organization. The chief MIS executive may be reporting to the vice president and controller as depicted in Figure 20-1. He or she may be reporting directly to the president as vice president of

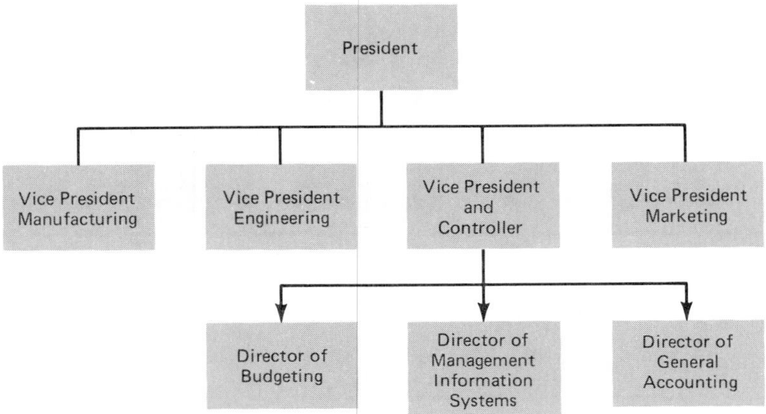

Figure 20-1 Chief MIS Executive Reporting to the VP / Controller

management information systems as depicted in Figure 20-2. There are advantages and disadvantages to both organizational locations for the MIS function.

Being the chief accounting officer in a corporation, the controller was looked upon as the primary provider of quantitative management information. In addition, functions in the controller's area, such as payroll, accounts payable, and accounts receivable, were often the first applications to be computerized. Therefore, the information systems function often originated and matured within the controller's organization. The primary disadvantage of the chief MIS executive reporting to the controller is that the computer resource may be dominated and used primarily to solve problems within the controller's area, leaving other functions neglected. Marketing, engineering, and production applications of the computer are of equal or greater importance than many applications in the accounting area. The primary advantage of the chief MIS executive reporting to the controller is that accounting is an information oriented discipline, and accountants are well-trained in the area of control. The skills of accountants may produce a computer-based system that is adequately controlled and auditable.

Many of the larger, more mature MIS organizations are separate from any one function, and have a chief MIS executive who is a vice president reporting directly to the president as illustrated in Figure 20-2. This location for the MIS function helps to ensure that each of the functional areas will receive unbiased attention from the MIS department. Today, with computers penetrating many aspects of all functions, it is

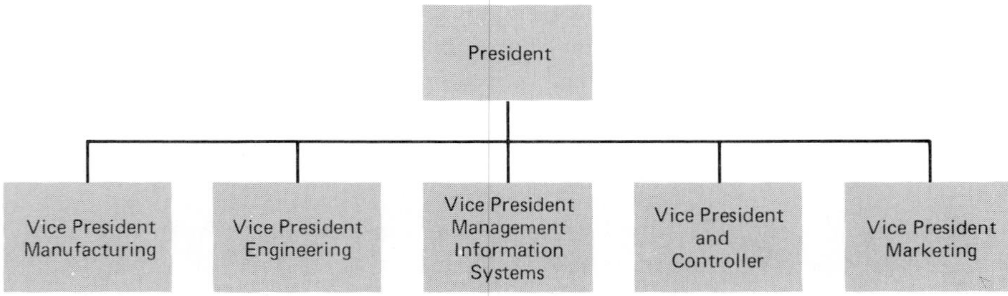

Figure 20-2 Chief MIS Executive Reporting to the President

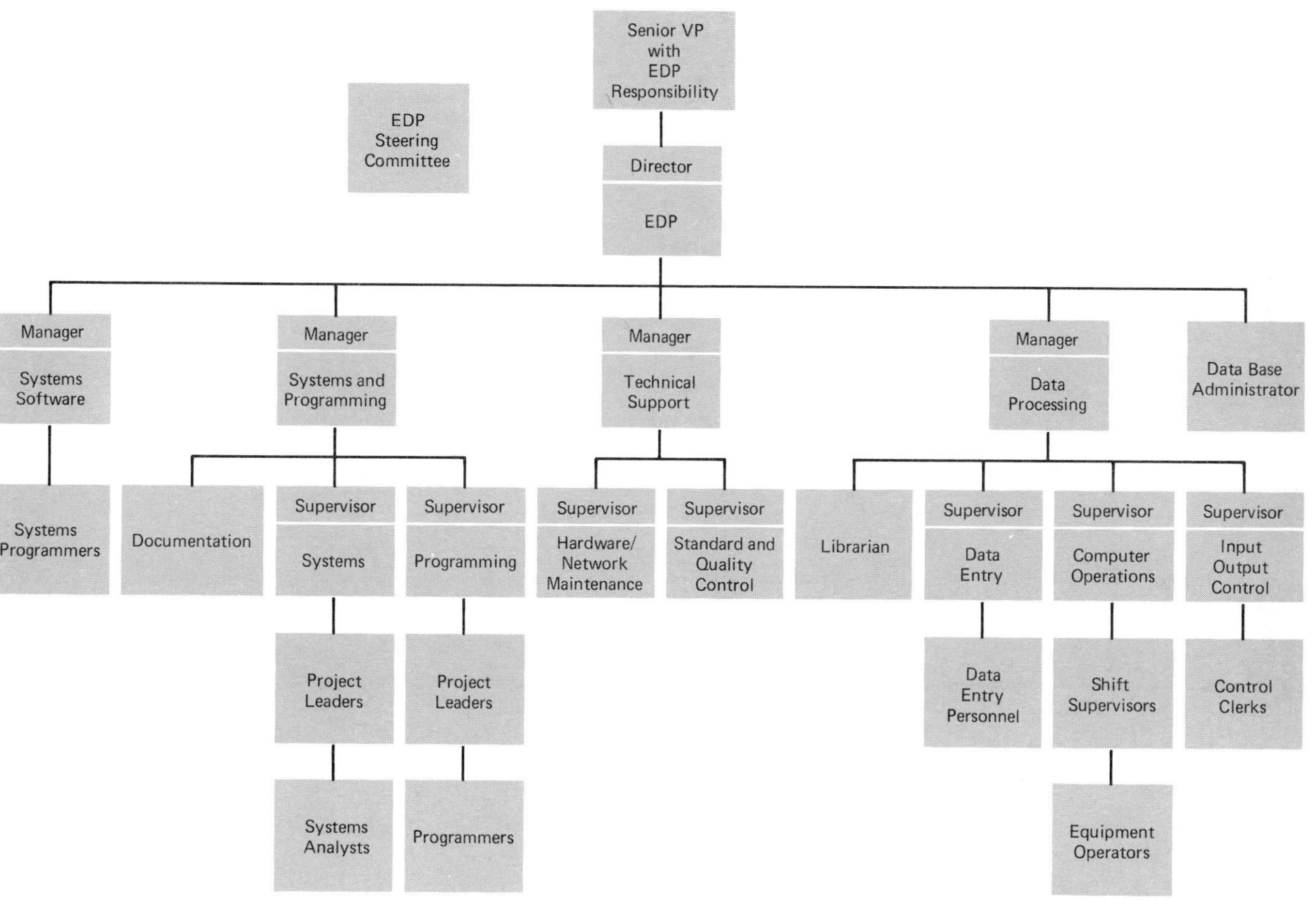

Figure 20-3 Large EDP Organization

particularly important that the chief MIS executive be a member of the unbiased vice presidential level of management.

Organization of the MIS function varies from firm to firm, particularly between small and large firms. Figure 20-3 depicts a typical MIS organization in a large firm. In smaller organizations many of these functions would be consolidated or would not exist. For example, in a small firm all software may be purchased so that no need exists for the systems and programming and systems software functions.

There are five distinct functions that must be carried out within MIS or arranged through outside sources. First, the systems software group installs and maintains systems software such as operating systems and data base management systems. These are technical and very highly skilled programmers. Second, application software is developed, or selected and purchased, by systems and programming. Third, the technical support staff is in charge of hardware maintenance and establishing data processing standards. Standards are very much like procedures for the data processing function. They include such things as program, data, application-naming conventions, procedures for maintaining the integrity of communication systems, and standards governing the content of user procedure manuals. Fourth, the data processing operations department manages day-to-day operations of the computer hardware and the processing of computer jobs. Fifth, a function that is relatively new in most larger MIS organizations is that of the data base administrator (DBA). The DBA is responsible for coordinating the data base including provisions for data security.

MANAGEMENT CASE 20-1

The Mitchell Company has decided to support and encourage as much as possible the application development by users concept. However, instead of establishing a central information center containing systems analysts who would support users in the application development efforts, Mitchell has decided to place systems analysts in each of the functional organizations such as manufacturing, finance, accounting, and engineering. They feel that these systems analysts reporting directly to functional management rather than central MIS will be a better approach. Do you agree with Mitchell's decision? Why or why not?

MANAGING SYSTEM DEVELOPMENT

Perhaps the most important aspect of managing the system development effort is the methodology used. In previous chapters we discussed the structured approach to systems analysis and design. It is important that this or some other structured methodology be used to develop new systems.

Another aspect of managing system development is the process by which development efforts are actually controlled. Most system development organizations use a project management approach. In the project management approach, each application development of significant size is assigned to a project development team. This team is usually headed by a senior systems analyst or sometimes a user department manager who has system development experience. Sufficient resources in the form of programmers, systems analysts, computer hardware, etc., are assigned to the team to complete the project.

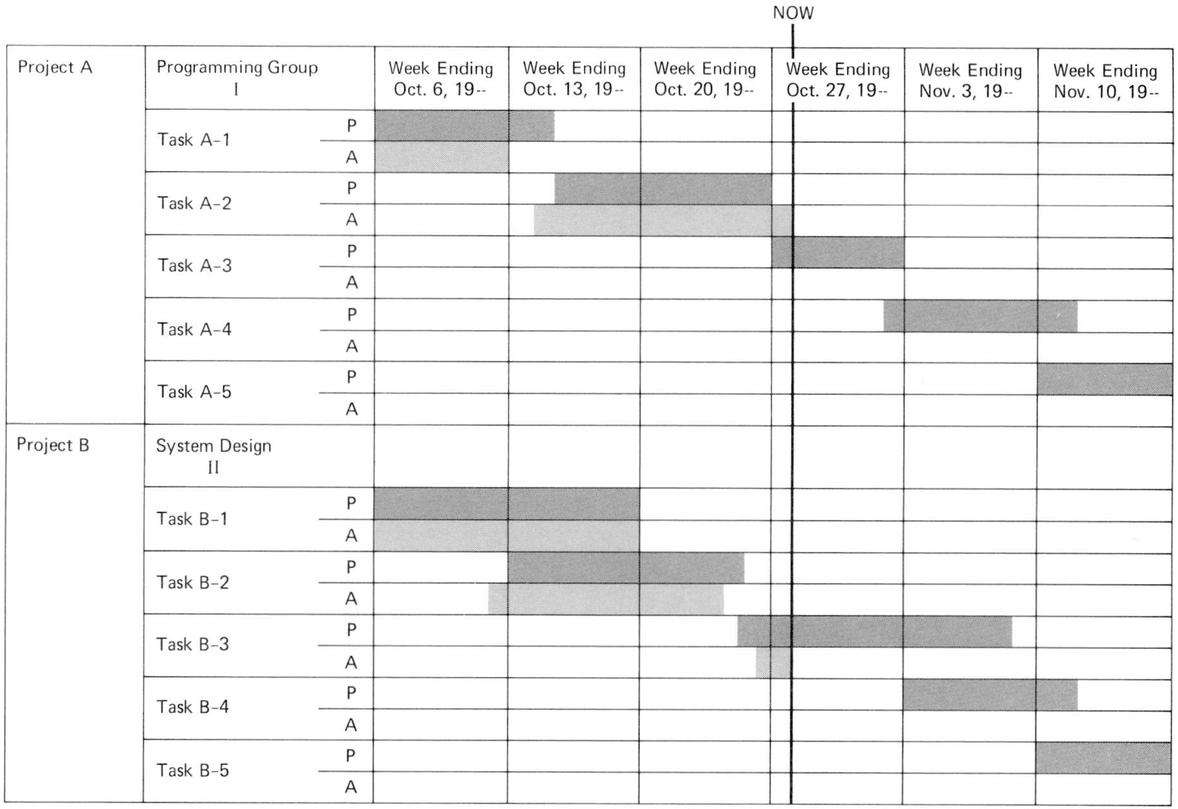

NOW

Project A	Programming Group I		Week Ending Oct. 6, 19--	Week Ending Oct. 13, 19--	Week Ending Oct. 20, 19--	Week Ending Oct. 27, 19--	Week Ending Nov. 3, 19--	Week Ending Nov. 10, 19--
	Task A-1	P						
		A						
	Task A-2	P						
		A						
	Task A-3	P						
		A						
	Task A-4	P						
		A						
	Task A-5	P						
		A						
Project B	System Design II							
	Task B-1	P						
		A						
	Task B-2	P						
		A						
	Task B-3	P						
		A						
	Task B-4	P						
		A						
	Task B-5	P						
		A						

Figure 20-4 Gantt Chart

Each project is assigned its own budget and time schedule. Budget performance is tracked by periodic reports, which compare expenditures to budgeted amounts. Schedule performance is managed and controlled through one of several project schedule performance tools, such as program evaluation and review technique (PERT), critical path management (CPM), or Gantt charts.

Gantt charts are the most conceptually simple of these techniques. Figure 20-4 illustrates a typical Gantt chart. Planned times for various tasks are shown with solid bars; actual times are shown with cross-hatched bars. The chart shows that for project A, task A-1 was started on time and completed ahead of schedule. Task A-2 was started ahead of schedule and has not yet been completed, although more than the planned time has elapsed. A Gantt chart can be a valuable measurement tool in a complex project. It aids in scheduling and coordinating and provides a visual means of evaluating progress. Since preparing a Gantt chart does not require extensive effort or data, potential benefits of its use generally exceed the cost of preparation.

MANAGING SYSTEM OPERATIONS

System Maintenance

As with managing system development, the adoption of a structured system development methodology will greatly enhance the ability to manage system maintenance. Efficacious system maintenance requires understanding the program to be modified. Programming personnel must be able to effect modifications by changing program statements in a confined and isolated area of the program. If a change requires modification in many different areas of the program or system, system maintenance becomes an almost impossible task. As discussed in previous chapters, structured methodologies produce modular programs. Each of these modules is as independent and self-contained as is practical. Therefore, changes are likely to affect only a restricted area of one module.

Requests for changes in programs originate with users. A formalized change authorization or request form should be used. On this form users identify the program and/or system to be changed, and outline the changes desired. An important part of this form is the authorization signatures that must be obtained prior to changing programs. Authorizing signatures typically include user management, the systems and programming manager, and sometimes the data processing steering committee. Figure 20-5 shows a simple request form.

Actual changes to programs must be well managed and controlled (control of program changes was covered in detail in chapter 19). After changes have been made, the system must be thoroughly tested prior to implementation. In fact the same set of tests used when the system was developed should be run before implementing the changed system.

Data Processing Operations

Managing data processing operations is much like the management of any production shop within an organization. Management must be concerned with maintaining

REQUEST FOR SYSTEM MODIFICATION

User Name:

Department:

Telephone No.:

System Name:

Module(s) to be changed (if known):

Please describe the change(s) desired and explain the reasons thereof:

Signature	Approved	Rejected	Comments
Requestor			
Dept. Manager	☐	☐	
EDP Liaison Officer	☐	☐	
Manager, Systems and Programming	☐	☐	

Figure 20-5 Change Request and Authorization Form

sufficient capacity to process computer jobs. Users of the resource should be billed for resources they use. Personnel must be hired, managed, and sometimes dismissed, and machines must be maintained in operable condition.

Processing capacity may be limited by any number of factors, including primary storage size, secondary storage size, CPU power, and number of terminals. Any of these factors can become the bottleneck that limits the capacity of the computer system. Data processing management must monitor these resources and determine if one is likely to become a bottleneck in the future. Additional resources can usually be obtained at a reasonable price if the potential bottleneck is identified promptly. Software monitors such as IBM's systems management facility (SMF) are very valuable in determining the levels of use of various system resources. For example, we could determine the percentage of time various terminals are being used and the time of day they are being used. We could also determine if the CPU is running close to its maximum capacity at any given point during the day. Trends of system resource utilization enable us to project when expansion should be planned for various resources. Hardware monitors are sometines used to detect bottlenecks and determine utilization levels for various devices. Figure 20-6 shows the output of a hardware monitor used to control resource usage.

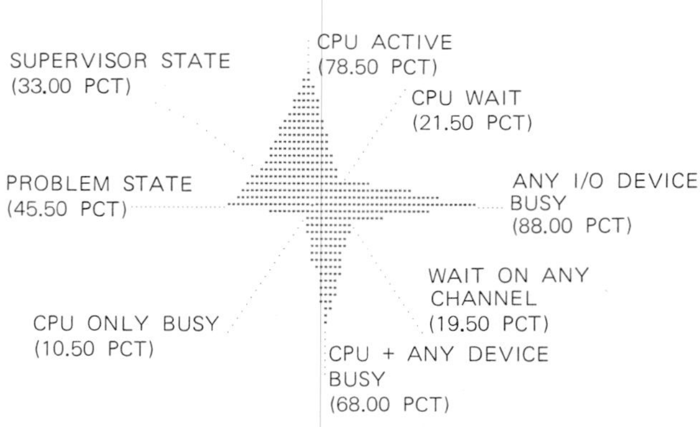

Figure 20-6 Sample Hardware Monitoring Report

One of the best ways to assure that the computer resource is used efficiently is to bill users for use of various computer resources, including CPU time, disk space, tapes, and printing. With a user billing system, DP operations are set up as a service center to the rest of the firm. Its services are available to anyone in the firm willing to pay for those services. Rates for services should be similar to rates that would be charged if the user contracted for data processing services outside the firm with, for example, a service bureau.

Many jobs within data processing operations are filled by personnel with a high school or vocational technical education as opposed to college training. For example, the job of computer operator is not significantly more demanding than a job running any production machine, and certainly does not require a college education.

MANAGEMENT CASE 20-2

Thomas Incorporated has a large centralized computer operations facility. The computers are operated on a seven-day per week, twenty-four hour basis. Jim Harper is a computer operator in the facility. Jim is considered by operations management to be their most valuable computer operator. He is highly experienced and very loyal to the company. Whenever a problem arises, he can be counted on to diligently work towards its solution. In fact, he is so dedicated that during the past five years he has not taken a vacation. From the standpoint of the company, do you see any problem with the fact that Jim has declined a vacation in the past five years?

Physical Security

In the chapter on control of computer based systems (ch. 19), we discussed access controls. That discussion dealt primarily with access to data through terminals and other means. It was pointed out that passwords and encryption could be used as safeguards to prevent unauthorized access to data and programs. In this chapter we will discuss physical security in more depth. Security may be broken down into five areas: 1) entry controls; 2) sabotage controls, 3) fire controls; 4) natural and environmental disaster controls; and 5) power controls.

A well designed computer control facility will control entry to the computer room. This is usually done by having doors to the computer room locked to all except those having plastic cards with magnetic identification strips. The cards are inserted into a reader, which then automatically opens the door.

TV cameras are often used to monitor all entrances to the building in which the computer is installed. Only operations personnel are allowed to enter the computer room itself. Programs and data manually delivered to the computer room are passed through a window. Today, of course, many programs and data are transmitted electronically to and from the computer.

Physical sabotage of hardware, programs, and data is controlled to a large extent through passwords and by physical entry controls over the computer room itself. In addition, firms that have designed a computer facility with security in mind usually construct the computer room to bombproof specifications. It is interesting to note that when computers were first used in business in the 50s and 60s, it was common to have large glass windows in the walls of the computer center so that a firm could show off its computer facilities. A saboteur could have easily tossed a bomb through these windows.

The most likely physical threat to a computer facility is fire. The best security procedure for coping with the threat of fire is to store backup copies of data, procedures, and programs offsite and to arrange for emergency use of alternative computer hardware. In addition, many computer centers use a fire suppression gas known as halon. Halon is released by fire and smoke detection systems and is effective in suppressing fires. The primary disadvantage of halon is its expense. An accidental release of the gas may cost a firm several thousand dollars in replacement costs. There are less expensive gases, but they are impractical because they would be poisonous to operations personnel. Halon is a nonpoisonous gas.

There are many natural and environmental disasters that should be considered when choosing the site for a computer room. These include floods, hurricanes, and bursting pipes, among others. Water can easily destroy sensitive electronic equipment in a computer room. One potential environmental disaster that is sometimes overlooked is water-based fire control sprinklers on floors above the computer room. Water leaking down through pipe holes and other crevices onto computer equipment, tapes, and disks can be very damaging. For this reason the floor above the computer room should be thoroughly sealed to prevent water leakage.

Large computer systems must have uninterruptable and controlled power supplies. Plugging such computer systems directly into electrical lines is not a good idea. Remember that if the power goes off, even momentarily, data and programs stored in semiconductor primary storage are lost because such storage is volatile. Furthermore, power spikes (increases in current voltage), can heavily damage a computer system.

Such power spikes are quite often caused by electrical thunderstorms. Some computer centers guard against this type of power spike by simply shutting down computer operations during electrical thunderstorms. However, in many situations, shutting down the computer during electrical thunderstorms is not a viable alternative.

Many firms use power supply systems, which consist of batteries and backup generators. The batteries are continuously being charged by incoming electrical service, and the computer draws its power from the batteries. The computer is thereby insulated from electrical service lines, preventing power spikes. In the case of a power outage, batteries would be sufficient for a short duration. Longer power outages are covered by the backup generator system.

SUMMARY

In recent years the role of information systems manager has changed as users have become more actively involved in data processing.

The MIS function may be located within the controller's organization where the controller is considered to be the primary provider of information. On the other hand, most businesses treat information systems as a separate function, having a vice president who reports directly to the president.

It is important that a structured system development methodology be used. Normally, system development is carried out using the project management approach for project control.

If a structured methodology is used for system development, program maintenance becomes a much easier task. However, all changes must be authorized and properly documented in order to prevent confusion and chaos.

Operations should be constantly monitored to detect bottlenecks and inefficiencies. User billing should be used to ensure efficient use of resources.

Physical security of the EDP system is a major responsibility of systems management. Procedures should be implemented for both the prevention of disasters and recovery from disasters like fire and flooding.

KEY TERMS

Information Systems Resource
Controller's Organization
Auditable System
Systems Software Group
Systems and Programming Group
Technical Support Staff
DP Operations Department
Data Base Administrator
System Development Methodology
Project Management Approach
Program Evaluation and Review Technique (PERT)
Critical Path Management (CPM)
Gantt Charts
Change Authorization Form
User Billing System
Bottlenecks
Hardware Monitors
Software Monitors
Entry Control
Sabotage Control
Fire Control
Disaster Control
Power Control

REVIEW QUESTIONS

1. What developments are causing a change in the role of the information systems manager?
2. What are two possible locations for an MIS department within a firm? How do they differ?
3. Identify the five major functions within an MIS department.
4. Explain the project management approach. List some of the tools that may be used to control a project.
5. Why is it important to have formal change authorization procedures?
6. List some factors that could limit processing capacity.
7. What is user billing? What is its advantage?
8. Briefly describe the idea of entry controls.
9. What controls would you use to cope with the threat of fire?
10. List some of the major natural disasters that may threaten a computer installation.
11. How can we prevent damage due to irregularities in the power supply?

DISCUSSION QUESTIONS

1. As president of Hi-Tek Inc., you have to decide whether the manager of the MIS department should report to the controller or directly to you. Which alternative would you choose? Why? If you think that neither of these arrangements is suitable, what would you suggest instead?
2. Assume that you are redesigning the EDP facilities of a company located on the eleventh floor of a downtown office building. What are the physical security features that must be built into the new design? Give reasons to justify the cost of these security features.

RESEARCH PROJECTS

1. Collect ten want ads for information systems managers from various newspapers or magazines. Using the characteristics listed in these advertisements, develop a profile of the ideal systems manager.
2. Interview the operations manager at any EDP installation and prepare a report on the major current bottlenecks at that installation. Make recommendations to remove these bottlenecks.
3. Interview the operations manager at any EDP installation and prepare a report on major bottlenecks that have occurred in the recent past. How were these bottlenecks detected? How were they corrected?

MIS AND MANAGEMENT

Emerging Roles—New-Technology Implementation Draws Information Execs Deeper Into General Management Involvement

(Reprinted with permission from MIS Week, July 21, 1982, p. 20)

By Linda Stein

Increased responsibility for implementing new information systems technology, often including coordination across departmental lines, is helping MIS executives evolve into full-fledged corporate managers instead of isolated technicians, according to an MIS Week survey of such executives last week.

Most of these queried said that coordinating technology needs for disparate user communities, sometimes in far-flung locations, often serves to draw the MIS executive into general management. Also, sources noted that balancing users' requests for state-of-the-art technology with overall corporate goals is a major factor in sharpening the managerial expertise of MIS executives.

"The burgeoning technology changes the role of the MIS manager to . . . a much broader, corporate-wide viewpoint than was necessary in the past," said Paul Case, vice president of MIS for Mr. Steak Inc., Denver, Colo. "The manager's decisions have a corporate-wide impact for a much longer period of time," Case said.

"With distributive data processing, for instance, you are buying a network architecture that you will be stuck with for a long period of time. The job (of MIS director) has become more difficult, and demands a much wider scope of vision and the making of longer-range decisions," Case said.

Michael Dille, managing director of data processing for Fingerhut Corp., a direct mail marketing concern based in Minnetonka, Minn. said of planning for his firm's new Four Phase Inc. word processing system: "First of all, it is new for us in data processing to suddenly become involved in something that is not traditional data processing."

Dille explained, "Generally in the industry for some time, the office has not been addressed in terms of automation. It is new to most data processing people, and suddenly you find yourself in an unfamiliar realm of work. You not only have to worry about your own secretary, but everybody else's secretary, too."

Dille, who was directly involved in choosing the new system, said that "most importantly we looked for standardization. Automating the office should be done in an organized manner. We took a view that was more far-ranging than what would have been taken by any of the individual departments involved, either clerical/office or data processing."

Because the company went with standardized terminals for the whole firm, the system makes extensive use of electronic mail for transferring memos and documents.

Dille said of user pressure for state-of-the-art equipment: "I don't see it as a specific problem at Fingerhut, but lots of users do come asking us about some new equipment they have read about or seen advertised. There is a lot of curiosity about what technology can do for individual jobs."

He said the MIS director "has to resist the pressure to procure that equipment fast, and has to take the global view, even though the user may get impatient waiting for his particular piece of equipment."

He said of his own experience, "If we hadn't taken the long view at Fingerhut, we might easily have ended up with a lot of different word processing and text editing systems, but we'd have gotten no electronic mail capability. It turns out that the electronic mail is one of the most time-saving features of the system, even though it wasn't the top item on the checklist."

Woody Hanson, vice president of MIS at Days Inns of America, Atlanta, sees the role of the MIS director becoming less that of a provider of computer services to users and more a provider for guidance for users from the business point of view. This is because users new to data processing see only their particular applications, and not the horizontal impact across the corporation, Hanson said.

The motel chain has in the past 18 months begun using Kachina I microcomputers at its motel sites. The micros offer interactive communications with the reservation systems at headquarters. Also, the MIS department can use them to send administrative messages throughout the system.

Hanson said of the MIS department: "We play more of a role in reviewing the users' design or applications. We have become more of a guardian, or watchdog, of all the computer resources throughout the company."

Company policy requires any users considering the purchase of stand-alone computers to have their choices reviewed by the corporate MIS department, to make sure that their choice is compatible with the overall plans, Hanson said, adding, "we also assist users in their contact with vendors, to make sure they're getting the necessary service and maintenance."

Hanson also said end-user education is very important. His department has embarked on a program of videotape presentations and short seminars, to teach users the risks involved down the road, he said, after the first easy and successful applications.

He said of the impact of sophisticated technology: "I think it makes the position of the MIS director less and less of a technical data processing, and more of a managerial position. . . . The new technology gives you a much wider range of choices, of potential solutions to problems, but this is a double-edged sword, because there is also more to choose from and this makes choices difficult."

With new products constantly becoming available, Hanson said, "the manager of today has to be more of a strong-willed person, willing to take a chance, rather than waiting to be 100 percent positive of his selection."

He said that a business perspective can help an MIS executive choose the correct equipment for his own firm. "A technical person is much more concerned with the state of the art, whereas a business person is more concerned with providing the company with information needed to run the business efficiently. The business person doesn't care if the equipment that does this is state-of-the-art or not."

Jerrold L. Patz, manager of information systems planning, City of Boston, said the following about pressure for up-to-date equipment: "Number one, I don't want state-of-the-art technology. I want to be one step behind because I don't want to have to debug and become a beta test-site for somebody. I want something field-tested and proven. We run the police, fire and hospitals. We can't run the risk of state-of-the-art failing."

While Patz said in general he believes there is competition for state-of-the-art technology in the MIS field, he pointed to another advantage of not purchasing the latest equipment: "Every time there is a new product in a family, there is a price breakthrough for the product below it. Generally, in cost/performance, the next lower item is greater than the state-of-the-art item."

Patz explained how his department plans overall for coordination of all the city's systems: "We designed the RFPs (requests for proposals) or commissioned the design of the RFPs for acquisition of all new technologies. In terms of actual black boxes, we looked for devices that would interconnect/communicate with current systems."

The importance of education was stressed by Gary Anderson, supervisor of design and analysis for the Texas Department of Human Resources in Austin, and Robert Kilgore, systems analyst II and project coordinator for the human resources departmental efforts to automate the legislative appropriations request. Both Anderson and Kilgore said their operation found it easy to adjust to new technology, since extensive education of users before new equipment was brought in allowed its implementation with no period of lesser productivity.

Anderson and Kilgore said that new technology is expanding the control of the MIS executive, bringing the DP shop out into more areas of operation, and extending the DP department's area of influence.

Bill Paul, vice president of information systems, Santa Fe Industries Inc., headquartered in Chicago, has expanded his management expertise in setting up procedures for controlling his end-users' use of Sperry Univac's "Mapper" (Maintaining, Preparing and Producing Executive Reports) system. The newly installed Mapper system is a real-time, on-line general purpose applications development system that gives users the ability to develop their own applications and information files.

Paul said that controlling the users' use of Mapper was the main priority he had in planning for the system as a manager.

He said, "We didn't want to take (away) their incentive for discovering the system's capabilities for improving management resources, yet on the other hand, we can't let them go completely uncontrolled and over-use the capacity of the hardware."

He noted, "With trained programmers together in one spot, it's easier to control, but we have users scattered all over the United States." Paul said the solution was to set up a type of traffic-signal operation that controlled user access.

Paul added, "I like the idea of users being able to develop the kinds of programs they would use to manage their areas as a business. It's a little tougher management job for use in data processing, but overall, the users are happier because they are getting more of what they want."

(Contributing to this article were Juli Cortino in San Francisco, Anne Dukes in Atlanta, Mike Egan in Chicago, Velina Houston in Los Angeles, Gail Kauranen in Boston and David Stamps in Minneapolis. It was written by Linda Stein in New York.)

Discussion

1. Do you see the new technology expanding or contracting the role and power of the MIS executive?
2. Should users considering the purchase of stand-alone computers be required to have their choices reviewed and approved by the MIS department? Why or why not?

CHAPTER 21

INFORMATION SYSTEMS AND SOCIETY

INTRODUCTION

Our assumption throughout this book has been that computers will certainly enhance both our work and personal lives. Most would agree with this assessment, although some would say that these enhancements have been slow in coming and that the computer has not yet produced the revolution it has promised. However, assuming that this revolution is in progress, we must be aware that any change has both positive and negative impact. Personal dislocations occur and the change must be adjusted to. In this chapter we will look at what kind of impact computer-based information systems may have on society, and some of the challenges that these systems pose. We will first look at the potential impact of information processing. The areas of automation and artificial intelligence will then be explored. Next we will consider privacy questions associated with computerized information and the very significant effects that personal computers are having upon our lives. Finally, we will explore the problems of international data transfers and the very interesting area of computer crime.

THE POTENTIAL IMPACT OF INFORMATION PROCESSING

The Information Revolution

Information is wealth. Although some would say that the computer has caused information to be wealth, information has always been wealth. For example, if one knew where an interstate highway was planned to be built before most others knew the location, purchase of land in that area was almost certain to produce wealth. The only difference the computer has produced in this area is that it is obviously a new source of significant amounts of information. Those who can afford to buy computer technology and have the skills to use it are likely to have significant advantages in acquiring information over those who cannot use such technology. Will the computer produce two new classes in our society, the information rich and the information poor?

Presently, there are capabilities to produce electronic newspapers. An individual simply connects his or her personal computer to the newspaper's large computer through regular telephone lines, thus giving him or her the ability to retrieve any news item that would be in a regular newspaper. In addition, one can retrieve articles from past newspapers up to several years old through use of key words. One could select only those news articles that are of interest. For example, you could simply enter the name of your favorite sports team and retrieve any articles about that team.

There are already information services to which one can connect, such as THE SOURCE, which allows retrieval of a wide variety of information. Figure 21-1 shows the DIALOG data base being accessed with a remote terminal. It contains information

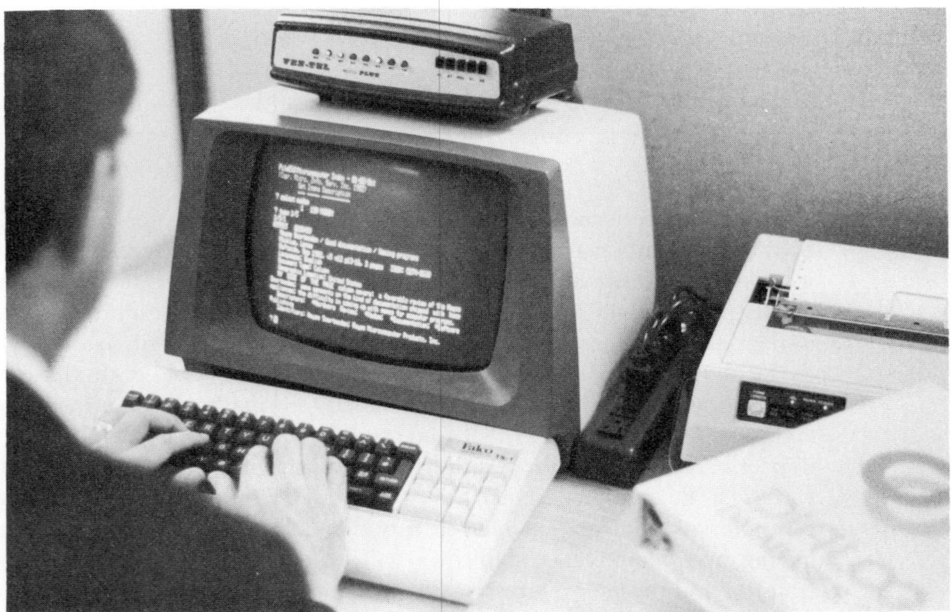

Figure 21-1 Using the Dialog Data Base (Courtesy of DIALOG Information Services, Inc.)

on a large number of subjects ranging from anthropology to zoology. These types of services allow retrieval of stock market quotes, and ordering of airline tickets and various merchandise. A specific example how one could save money with such a service would be allowing the computer to search for the least expensive airline tickets between two cities on a particular date on which travel is planned.

Some have even gone as far as saying that an information assistance program will have to be established that is similar to current fuel assistance programs for the disadvantaged in our society. Without it, the information poor will become further disadvantaged because of their lack of access to data that personal and business computers can provide. To implement such a plan, of course, is a political decision. However, this perception illustrates the degree of impact that some feel the computer revolution may have on society.

If we get to the point where a significant amount of shopping is done through electronic means, work is performed at home on our personal computer or terminal hooked up to the office computer, and most of our entertainment and religious programs are received through cable TV, some very significant questions arise. Can we all retreat into our electronic cottages and still function as a society? Possibly not. Many would argue that a democratic society requires frequent face-to-face interaction among its citizens. Further, an electronic society provides very grave threats to privacy, as we will discuss later in this chapter. These threats decrease our personal freedom and increase the ability of others to manipulate and monitor our personal lives. The potential for abuse is a reality, as we will see in this chapter.

Working at Home

Would you really want to work for a company in your home using electronic means? Off the top of your head you might answer that question with a yes. No doubt there would be some advantages to such an arrangement. You could live almost anywhere you wanted to and spend more time with your family. But working where you have direct contact with coworkers also has significant advantages. The social interaction, exchange of ideas, and sharing of triumphs with one's coworkers is a significant contributor to the mental well-being of most individuals. To illustrate the significance of this face-to-face contact with coworkers, consider the fact that most surveys have shown that the number one way we meet our marriage partners is at work.

In any case, in the very near future you may have the opportunity to decide to work at home instead of in a traditional workplace environment. If significant numbers of our population decide to work at home there will be a noticeable impact on society. However, it is a good guess that most individuals will quickly become bored with working at home and prefer to perform at least a portion of their work in a traditional workplace environment.

Control Problems

To illustrate another potential problem that computers and emerging communication technology can cause, consider electronic shopping systems such as QUBE. QUBE is a system that has been tested in Columbus, Ohio. It is essentially a combination of a cable TV system with computer technology, which allows viewers of any TV program to respond electronically to such things as surveys and orders for merchandise. Some have said such a system could produce instant responses to surveys, allow shopping by electronic mail, and even allow instant electronic democracy in which voters could respond to an issue through their QUBE terminal systems. However, such proposals are questionable. For example, how do we know who is pushing those buttons out there in a survey? Is it an adult or a three-year-old child who just happens to be watching the program and likes to push buttons?

We can picture our presidential candidates appearing on TV in a debate, stating their positions and after the debate is over, we push our buttons and elect the president! This, of course, is absurd. The control problems for such a scenario would be horrendous. To illustrate the problem, consider the case of a very religious and proper housewife on the QUBE system who began receiving sexually explicit materials through the mail. To her amazement she found that her four year old child had actually ordered the materials by pushing the appropriate button while watching a cable TV program. Since she was the cable TV subscriber, the materials were shipped in her name and she, of course, ended up on many mailing lists as an individual who was likely to purchase such materials. What if your five year old turned on your personal computer and started transferring your bank account funds around? Certainly many of the problems can be worked out, but as yet the problems still exist.

DISPLACEMENT OF HUMAN BEINGS

In the 50s, when computers were first introduced, many individuals were concerned that computers were going to displace them from their jobs, particularly in the clerical occupations. As clerical functions were automated, they feared there would be no need for clerical skills. This did not happen. In general, more jobs were created than were lost, although the created jobs called for different skills, such as programming and systems analysis.

Automation

In general, management uses newly-installed computers to generate more information than was previously available rather than generating the same amount of information and reducing the labor force. However, things are beginning to change. Computers are being used to control robots that are quickly replacing human workers on assembly lines in industry (see Figure 21-2). There are now factories in Japan in which the whole production line is automated on certain shifts. The only human beings at the factory are security guards. These robots even have the capability of repairing themselves whenever they breakdown. For example, when a drill bit breaks, the machine simply replaces it from a bin of replacement bits. However, such factories require maintenance personnel during the day shift. In offices, automation is likely to reduce the need for typists, clerical, and other office personnel. Prior to personal computers, computers were only used in business for larger jobs while many day-to-day tasks were still performed manually. Personal computers are changing all of this.

If automation through computers does displace significant numbers of workers from jobs, society will have to support their retraining. Will there be enough alternative

Figure 21-2 A Robot in an Industrial Plant (Courtesy of SRI International)

jobs? It seems there will. There is always something to be done, regardless of how many tasks are performed by computers and machines. Usually, these remaining jobs and new jobs are more interesting. The computer often does dull and routine jobs, such as assembly line and clerical work. The bottom line, though, is that anytime we can replace a human being with a machine at a cheaper cost, society as a whole benefits because the standard of living rises. Of course, we have to be concerned with those who lose their jobs and are (hopefully) temporarily inconvenienced. If we want to progress as a society we certainly cannot allow the threat of joblessness through automation to slow down our application of computer technology to the problems of life.

Artificial Intelligence

Artificial intelligence is an application of the computer in which it makes decisions or judgments that appear to require human intuition, reasoning, and intelligence. Such computer systems are often called expert systems. In the very limited areas in which they have been successful, these systems can equal and often surpass the best judgments made by human beings. For example, they have been used in the diagnosis of illness.

Given the symptoms of the patient, the expert system may ask additional questions. Once these are answered, the system may request laboratory tests and eventually arrive at a diagnosis that is as good as or better than that of the best doctors in very limited areas of medicine. One approach to developing these expert systems is to model the thought processes that a physician goes through when he or she makes a diagnosis. Such an approach not only results in an artificial intelligence system, but also provides very interesting insights into how human beings reason and make judgments.

Will these systems ever replace such experts in our society as doctors, lawyers, engineers, and accountants? Certainly, some expert systems may make better judgments than the least competent of professionals in these areas, but most professionals will probably only use the systems as tools. A medical diagnosis expert system could assist doctors greatly in narrowing down the possibilities in the diagnosis of a particular patient. Will professionals accept these expert systems that appear to diminish the former's importance to society? I think they will. Most true professionals are always looking for ways to improve their productivity and quality of service provided to clients.

One other danger of expert systems is that people may think they are infallible since they are computer-based. Nothing could be further from the truth because ultimately these systems are models of the human judgment process, and consequently many imperfections of the human judgment process will also be a part of them. Human professionals, such as doctors, must continue to know enough about the field they are involved in to recognize when the computer-based expert system is providing answers or diagnoses that are unreasonable.

MANAGEMENT CASE 21-1

The Fairfax Company is in the process of developing a new computer-based accounting system. This new system will result in the loss of ten clerical positions in the accounting department. Overall though, the company will not experience a reduction in personnel due to the new system. New positions will be created both in system development and accounting. However, these new positions require different and a higher level of skills than the current clerical personnel have. In the case of three of the current clerical personnel, retraining for the new positions is feasible. The other seven are long-time employees of the company and most will reach retirement age in approximately ten years. Management has decided that retraining these employees would not be feasible. Furthermore, even if it were feasible it is doubtful that any of them would want to go through the retraining. If you were the manager in the company making the decision concerning the future of these seven employees, what would you do?

COMPUTERS AND INDIVIDUAL PRIVACY

Potential Problems

If I were asked by a totalitarian regime to suggest the best way to provide almost total surveillance over the country's population, I would say that the best way would be to establish a pervasive electronic funds transfer system (EFTS) and do away with paper money, coins, and checks as much as possible. I would also recommend installing two-way cable TV systems with centrally located computers as a part of the cable system, and perhaps have computers in each home. You may be asking what this has to do with surveillance. Think for a minute what actions you can take in our society or in any modern society without spending money. One cannot travel, buy food, or rent a motel room without it. If you gave a merchant, airline, or gas station a plastic card every time you spent money, your transaction could be recorded through a communication system to a central data base. Your funds would then be electronically transferred from your account to the merchant's. The computer could very easily also record the time of transaction, the day, and location. In fact a record could be kept of all of your movements. Through the cable TV system, particular programs you are watching on TV and when you watch them could be noted. You can see that a great deal of information could easily be obtained about almost all of your actions and movements.

You may now be thinking that such a system could never be implemented in this country. Certainly the technology is available for such a system and our society is moving rapidly toward such capabilities as electronic funds transfer, two-way cable systems, and home electronic shopping. Consider one actual case. In Columbus, Ohio, where the QUBE system is installed, a local movie theater owner was taken to court over an allegedly pornographic movie that was shown at his theater. Currently, Supreme Court guidelines state that a work is pornographic if it goes beyond the moral values and standards of the community in which it is being sold or shown. In this case, it just happened that the same movie had recently been shown on the local QUBE system. The local theater owner, in his defense, subpoenaed the records from QUBE to determine who watched the movie over the cable network. Of course, this was a brilliant move on his part, or on his lawyer's part, because if a significant number of people watched the movie, including supposedly outstanding citizens, the movie did not go beyond the community's moral values. But do you want judges, lawyers, and jurors reviewing the records of what you have watched on cable TV? Is this an invasion of your privacy? Fortunately, the judge in this case had the good sense to keep all names confidential.

Privacy Legislation

From the above examples, you can see some of the problems related to privacy. Computers could constantly monitor our financial transactions and the entertainment and goods we purchase via two-way cable systems. In addition to these threats to privacy, both governmental agencies and private businesses currently maintain huge data bases with information about private individuals. In the 1970s, there was substantial legislation passed that addressed privacy issues related to these data bases.

In the private sector, the primary piece of legislation governing privacy was the Fair Credit Reporting Act of 1970. Many lending agencies and credit bureaus maintain records concerning credit worthiness and individual financial transactions. The Fair Credit Reporting Act helps you to make sure that this data is correct. You have the right to access the data stored about you as well as the right to challenge and correct any inaccuracies. You should know, however, that institutions still have the right to maintain data concerning you; but it must be correct and they must allow you access to it.

Perhaps the greatest effect of privacy legislation has been on the operations of the federal government. There are four acts in this area. The first, the Freedom of Information Act of 1970, among other things allows individuals to access any information concerning themselves that may be stored in a federal government data base or file.

The Educational Privacy Act applies to educational institutions funded by the federal government. It applies to almost all educational institutions because almost all receive at least some federal funds. The act provides that a student's educational records may be accessed by both the student and his or her parents, and that information can be collected only by certain authorized individuals and distributed to only certain authorized individuals and agencies. The rights provided for under this act may be waived by the student.

The Privacy act of 1974 applies only to federal government agencies and provides that:

1. Information collected for one purpose cannot be used for other purposes unless an individual gives consent.
2. There must be no secret collections of data.
3. Individuals must have a right to access and correct erroneous data.

Agencies collecting data must ensure its accuracy and protect against its misuse.

The Right to Financial Privacy Act of 1978 addresses a threat to privacy existing within financial institutions. Currently, every check and credit card transaction that you make is recorded on microfilm by your bank and stored for five years. Prior to the Right to Financial Privacy Act of 1978, governmental investigative bodies such as the IRS and FBI could access these microfilm records and examine them without your knowledge. Obviously, a great deal of information can be collected from such records. The act provides that if an investigative body wishes to access personal financial data stored at a financial institution, they must notify the particular individual. This notification provides you with an opportunity to challenge their access in the courts.

In addition to federal laws, many individual states have passed their own privacy legislation. These laws are significant in that the federal legislation does not apply to most state institutions with the exception of educational institutions. Their provisions are usually similar to provisions of the Federal Privacy Act of 1974.

PERSONAL COMPUTERS

We have discussed personal computers in other sections of this book. However, it would be useful to summarize here the impact they are likely to have on society. Earlier in this chapter, we indicated that access to personal computer technology may differentiate between those who can use information to produce wealth and those who cannot.

One of the more significant questions posed by the use of personal computers is whether we will lose many of our current mental capabilities as the computer performs tasks for us. For example, most of the math that engineers learn in college and use in their day-to-day work can be performed by computer. Children are using the computer to complete their mathematics homework in elementary and secondary schools. Will this dependence upon the computer cause us to lose our mathematical abilities?

Perhaps the more significant question is whether it makes any difference if we lose a mental ability that can be purchased for a few hundred dollars or less? Certainly, as human beings have advanced, many capabilities formerly necessary to survival in earlier times have been lost. For example, there are very few people (if any) today who have the necessary skills to survive in a hunting and food gathering society without the use of modern firearms. This question of loss of skills is certainly an important controversy. Some say such losses will make no difference; others are very concerned about this possibility. The application essay at the end of this chapter further explores this area.

On a more positive note, there is no question that personal computers are going to make our lives more productive and take away some of the more humdrum, boring tasks that we currently have to perform. These electronic tools are going to become much more user-friendly. In fact, they are currently very easy to use for many nonprogrammers.

INTERNATIONAL DATA TRANSFERS

Most countries now restrict the movement of classified data outside of their country. But what about nonclassified data? Multinational firms have offices and factories in many different countries. On their large computer networks, data can move very quickly all the way around the world. Some countries, particularly in Europe, have been concerned about movement of data beyond their borders. This concern has brought about legislation restricting the international flow of data from some countries.

On what basis can a country justify such legislation? Remember, earlier in this chapter we argued that information is wealth. Many countries currently restrict the transfer of wealth or funds outside their borders. There are, of course, examples of strategically valuable information, such as engineering design data, or financial and economic data, whose movement could be restricted. Customer lists can be very valuable from a marketing standpoint, or a country may simply want to protect its citizens from unsolicited mail-order campaigns originating outside its borders.

Fundamentally, though, restrictions on international data transfers are a threat to the free movement of goods and ideas among countries. Such restrictions would also hamper a multinational corporation's ability to function smoothly. Most international economists would agree that such consequences would diminish international economic growth, particularly in a country that severely restricted international data transfers.

MANAGEMENT CASE 21-2

Midland Bank, a medium-sized bank in a Virginia city, has recently discovered that an employee has used the computer to embezzle $75,000 from the bank. The bank's management has decided to handle the case in the following manner. They will confront the employee with the evidence they have concerning embezzlement. If the employee will return to the bank a substantial portion of the $75,000, they will agree to dismiss the employee without calling in law enforcement officers and the case will be closed as far as the bank is concerned. They will also agree that the dismissal will be handled like a normal resignation and that the bank will give the employee favorable recommendations for any new job that he might pursue. The bank's primary rationale for this approach is that they cannot afford the adverse publicity that would ensue if the embezzlement was publicized in the newspaper. Public questions over the security of deposits might cause the bank to lose customers. Evaluate the bank's approach.

COMPUTER CRIME CASES

Another very interesting aspect of the computer's impact on society is computer crime. As shown by the cases below, several sensational computer crimes have been uncovered. However, most experts maintain that the number of computer crimes discovered represents only the tip of the iceberg. Most computer crime remains undetected. As discussed previously in chapter 19, a poorly controlled computer system provides almost unlimited opportunities for stealing funds or goods and then concealing the theft. The amount of money taken in an average armed robbery is very small in comparison to amounts taken through computer theft. Those who perpetrate a computer crime often are not prosecuted when caught. This occurs particularly in financial institutions because management feels that the institution would be embarrassed if the public learned of the crime. Management is also afraid that the public would lose confidence in the institution's ability to safeguard deposits.

One of the more interesting aspects of computer crime is the fact that almost no computer crimes have been uncovered by auditors. CPAs maintain that it is not their responsibility in an audit to uncover crime, since to do so would require prohibitively expensive procedures. However, most of the public feels that the detection of fraud is at least a part of the auditor's responsibility. This disagreement must somehow be resolved. As auditors become more competent in computer technology and use that technology as an audit tool, we may see more computer crime uncovered in the auditing process. To illustrate computer crime, three cases are presented below.

Equity Funding

The management of Equity Funding Life Insurance Company used the computer to perpetrate a major fraud against investors and creditors. The company generated bogus insurance policies with a total face value of over two billion dollars. These policies were then sold to reinsurers. Computer programs were rigged so that auditors could not easily access the files of nonexistent customers. The fraud was finally exposed when a former employee disclosed it, and the stockholders lost enormous amounts of money.

Pacific Bell

In this case, a teenager retrieved passwords, user manuals, and other confidential documents from trash cans outside the phone company's office. He then proceeded to steal equipment from supply centers. Using his knowledge of the company's computer system and a remote terminal, he would alter accounting records to show the theft as a bona fide use of equipment. The fraud was not discovered until an accomplice turned himself in.

Wells Fargo

Two employees of the Wells Fargo Bank collaborated with an account-holder to make fraudulent deposits to his account. Using the computerized interbranch settlement system, the bank employees would make offsetting entries to another branch's account. This entry would be rolled over every ten days so that no actual payment was demanded from the other branch. The criminals withdrew $21.3 million before the fraud was discovered when they made an improper entry.

SUMMARY

Information is wealth, and computers assist us in obtaining this wealth. Those who do not possess computer technology may end up being information poor because they lack the skills necessary to compete with others.

Working at home with a remote terminal might seem like an interesting option. It could, however, lead to boredom and social isolation.

Although automation does take away jobs temporarily, in the long run it creates more jobs. Moreover, it helps to raise society's standard of living.

Artificial intelligence aids experts in making better-informed decisions in areas like medicine and geology. These systems, however, do not replace human intelligence; rather, they complement it with the computer's immense memory and fast speed.

The computer can potentially be used to monitor most of our actions, thus robbing us of privacy. Recognizing this threat to our basic freedom, Congress has enacted several acts in recent years to protect the privacy of citizens.

The advent of personal computers could cause us to lose some of our basic skills. On the other hand, the personal computer will make life much more interesting by performing many routine chores for us.

Some countries are concerned about transborder flows of data, and have imposed certain restrictions on them. This could hamper world economic growth by restricting the free movement of information among countries.

Computer crime is a growing threat to society. The average take in a computer fraud is many times greater than in an armed robbery. Unfortunately, auditors have had little success in detecting computer fraud so far.

KEY TERMS

Information Services
Face-to-Face Contact
Electronic Shopping
Control
Automation
Worker Retraining
Artificial Intelligence
Expert Systems
Electronic Funds Transfer System
QUBE System
Privacy
Fair Credit Reporting Act
Freedom of Information Act
Educational Privacy Act
Privacy Act of 1974
Right to Financial Privacy Act
User-Friendly
International Data Transfers
Computer Crime

REVIEW QUESTIONS

1. Explain the phrase "information is wealth."
2. What are the advantages of working at home? What are the disadvantages?
3. Discuss some control problems that may be encountered when using data communication technology.
4. In the long run, how does automation create more jobs than it eliminates?
5. Is it possible for an artificial intelligence system to replace a human mind? If not, what functions can such a system perform?
6. Describe how computer technology could be used to monitor the actions of an individual.
7. How does computer technology constitute a threat to individual privacy?
8. What rights do you have under the Fair Credit Reporting Act of 1970?
9. List the major provisions of the Privacy Act of 1974.
10. What is the likely effect of personal computers on our basic mathematical skills?
11. What are the arguments for and against allowing free transfer of data across borders?
12. Why are victims of computer fraud often reluctant to report the crime?
13. How could Pacific Bell have prevented the computer fraud perpetrated against it?

DISCUSSION QUESTIONS

1. "Computerization will ultimately lead us to the point where we will only have to push buttons for everything. There will be no room for creativity or original thought." Discuss this statement.
2. Artificial intelligence systems are based on models of human thought processes. In what ways is such a system superior to traditional programming? Can you think of any applications of artificial intelligence other than those discussed in this chapter?
3. There is very little legislation or case law on the subject of computer crime. Discuss some of the problems a court would face when trying a case of computer fraud. Why is it difficult to use precedents from traditional criminal law?

RESEARCH PROJECTS

1. Write an essay on the pros and cons of working at home. Give your own preference and the reasons for it.
2. Interview a few secretaries who have switched from using traditional office equipment to computerized equipment, such as word processors and electronic mail. Prepare a report on their views on job security, retraining, and career prospects.

APPLICATION ESSAY

Our Computerized Future

(Reprinted with permission of Charles P. Lecht)

By Charles P. Lecht

At a recent meeting at IBI, during which Third World informatics requirements were discussed, a sincere attendee posed the following question: 'Are the benefits to be gained by the distribution of computer systems power to peoples everywhere not offset by the negative impact this distribution may have on skills development and education?' However sincere his concern, it reflected a major perceptual problem that must be overcome if we are to reap maximum benefit from the coming age of widespread computer systems power distribution. The attendee posing the question seemed like McLuhan's man looking forward through a rear-view mirror.

This paper deals less with philosophy than it does with technology. But lest you fear my tremendously optimistic forecast for our computerized future shows wanton disregard for human potential, I want to settle this issue right now. I deeply believe that the development of human potential is accelerated by swift and powerful technological innovation. And since, in my view, exponential growth in the scope of benign technology is subsumed in, and is but another expression of, the realization of human potential, it follows that nothing of consequence need be harmed by this process. To be sure, some trade-offs are always required, but the net effect will be positive.

What the lever was to the body, the computer system is to the mind. It is not difficult to imagine a time when people rebelled against the idea of augmenting bodily power by means of physical devices. Looking backwards through the lens of irreverent imagination, I can raise the ghost of an ancient conference of proto-Third World tribes during which someone, deeply in earnest, protests the use of levers as follows: 'If we distribute levers to all members of our tribe, won't their physical development be negatively impacted?' But history has provided no evidence to suggest that our bodies would have been any more powerful had we not had the benefits of mechanical leverage.

And, in my mind's eye, I can also see a time in the future when people will look back on this day and conclude that there was no evidence that our widespread use of computer and communications systems power did anything but enlarge human potential. (By computer and communications systems power, I do not mean electrical power; rather, I mean the power these systems provide to users to accomplish data processing and communications.) It is my belief that this widespread distribution is needed. It can provide us with a kind of leverage to increase the power of our minds so that we may come closer to achieving the human potential of which we dream. To me, this means a life wherein our physical needs are satisfied without the repetitive, enervating expenditure of physical effort, and we are free to get on with improving the spiritual and intellectual richness of our existence. Without widespread distribution of artificial

---

Charles Philip Lecht's involvement in informatics stretches back to 1951, making him an old-timer in a very young field. After twenty years as president of a world-wide consulting business, he has recently founded Lecht Sciences Inc. (LSI). Besides this, he has held a number of teaching posts, maintains a heavy schedule of speaking engagements and has authored five books, including **The Waves of Change** © C. Lecht.

intelligence (in which category I include artificial logic, artificial computational capability and artificial memory), the potential for improving human life will be limited by the relative scarcity of individuals capable of addressing it methodically, and by the sort of headway they are likely to make while compelled to work in isolation, their stride impeded by the muck and mire of general ignorance, misunderstanding and fear.

In the late 1970's, computer systems power (and the means for its delivery) matured to the point where it could be obtained virtually everywhere. Before this, the availability of such power was highly constrained. Obtaining it meant going to where it was (discrete computer centres).

I have often thought that the evolutionary process that brought us modern methods of computer systems power invocation and delivery was probably accidentally triggered by a Univac engineer. In the course of maintaining his Univac II, a task carrying along with it considerable danger of electrocution, he probably noticed that certain wrapped cables in the CPU could be unwrapped to allow the control panel to be removed from its housing. On doing so, he inadvertently created the first interactive remote terminal to trigger operation of a computer system through remotely pressed keys, switched toggles and pressed-button inputs.

By the time terminal technology came of age (in the 1960's), the length of wires and cables internal to the computer system reached twenty miles. I like to think of this as symbolic of things to come. As though under pressure in its confines, this massive net was at once to implode and to explode. Much of it was to be mapped onto a chip; some was to be stretched, seemingly bursting the seams of the system, to deploy itself across city and national boundaries. By the 1970's, our means of invoking and delivering computer systems power matured to the point where standard in-place communications (e.g., telephone lines) provided links between computer centres and users. And between computer systems. And between computer system components.

As the lines of communications companies became the arteries and veins of computer systems, the synthesis of communications and computer systems technologies occurred. Today, government, having assumed the burden of policing the activities of purveyors of both kinds of products and services, seems dumbfounded by this process. For example, the U.S. Justice Department, its fuses apparently blown, quit complaining about the (alleged) monopolistic practices of AT&T and IBM on the same day. As though the metamorphosis of each of these giants to encompass the business of the other, as synthesis took place, had induced stroke (or perhaps coma) in the Department, its operatives no longer seemed capable of telling one corporation from the other. This identity crisis was finessed with the government's usual grace: it lost its case against one and, invigorated by its triumph, proceeded to the next by dropping its charges against the other.

With both actions concluded, both corporations announced their plans to create massive networks of communications and computer systems, delivering their power in any and all forms to each and every place.

We are no longer required to be astonished that the 10,000-to-one price/performance improvement in computer systems power between the 1950's and today has shrunk both the physical size and the content of what we considered massive computer power before 1970. This means that processors, sometimes occupying 5,000 square feet or more of precious floor space and providing us with but a fraction of a

MIP (million instructions per second), have shrunk to the size of a silicon wafer which can pass through the eye of a needle. This has provided a new dimension to our capacity to obtain computer systems power. We no longer have to visit a computer centre or communicate with it from a terminal. The source of computer systems power has become small enough to make it practical to bring the computer system to us. And to carry it around.

The emergence of this new means of obtaining computer systems power occurred at the same time as did the means for mass producing it, which, in turn, led to incredible price reductions. By 1980, we really had our choice as to how we obtained computer systems power. From tiny packets carried in our pockets, to the employment of terminals to tap into massive repositories, to visiting computer centres, to immersing ourselves in these massive power sources: all has become commonplace.

From LSI (large-scale-integrated) silicon chips whose elements vanish into the microscopic, to massive networks, whose components span the world, and everything in between, the sources of computer systems power available to us today run the gamut from micro to macro.

These sources, by virtue of their having been combined with communications technology, may be tapped virtually at any time and at any place.

Master planners may orchestrate run-time combinations of heretofore unrelated, now symbiotic, processing configurations: an ad hoc synthesis not unlike that created by the conductor on his podium, eliciting symphonic harmony from widely disparate, essentially unrelated sounds. Some processing orchestrations do the brawny work, like carrying, storing and retrieving data; others bestow artificial intelligence.

The 1980's synthesis of computer technology and communications technology has provided us with a fantastic increase in our capacity to deliver artificial intelligence to the human brain. This kind of cognitive increase, however artificial, augments our natural endowment in much the same way that airplane instruments augment, even correct, our sensory perceptions. But it goes further than that. As the airplane provided us with an unnatural means of locomotion, so the power derived from synthesized computer and communications technologies provides us with unnatural means of information processing. There is no evidence that anyone could or would ever be able to manipulate megabytes of data flawlessly without the power provided by technology. And so it is finally revealed. Our operative capabilities, both physical and intellectual, can be extended and improved. And while continued evolutionary improvement might correct our deficiencies, we cannot afford to wait. From both the quantitative and qualitative standpoints, I suspect that computer and communications systems power augments our brain in vastly more ways than has the earlier distribution of physical power been capable of augmenting our body. And the synthesis of the means of physical and intellectual augmentation is already significantly underway, so that, by the end of this century, the two will start to work in as much (hopefully, more) symbiotic harmony as does our natural stuff, providing us with non-natural powers.

When this is accomplished, we will have achieved a breakthrough in the supply and demand equation, leading to efficiencies of a kind that cannot help but translate into a vastly improved life.

Some people have compared LSI (semiconductor computer chips) to oil in describing the role it will play in our next industrial revolution. If oil fueled the energy requirements of the last industrial revolution, LSI will as certainly power the next. Indeed, I see a connection between the increase in LSI embedded into every conceivable arena of production and the diminution of our need for oil. For example, if the means of production can be distributed and/or controlled by a widely dispersed industrial staff, our need to travel to our nominal places of employment will be greatly reduced.

And if the need to travel is greatly reduced, so, too, can the energy required to sustain our places of work be greatly reduced. Imagine our cities with increased productivity and decreased congestion.

But it does not stop there. As corporations disperse their operations to perform as master controllers in networks of contributing sources, the efficiencies to be gained exceed in scope and ramification the mere achievement of energy conservation. Gridlock is lessened everywhere.

Neither complete centralization nor complete dispersion of our means of production is in our future, but an ever-varying weave and degree of both. Those in corporate headquarters, inhabiting offices, those contributing (sometimes sporadically) from cottage industry environments, and everyone in between will see their lot greatly improved by the computerized future now within our grasp.

I can see headquarter habitats environmentally controlled by sensors which alter and adjust to maximize our physical, psychological, sociological and intellectual functioning. This obviously surpasses the mere adjustment of heat and light; it goes on to involve the adjustment of fundamental, intrinsically human barriers, including our own physical properties.

We see the first manifestations of this more clearly when we examine the needs of a space voyager. To accomplish anything meaningful in the far reaches of space, we must endure adjustments to everything, ourselves included.

I see an office in the corporate headquarters:

In the 1980's, on one wall a screen including all display technologies (e.g., movie screen, TV tube, liquid crystal, plasma).

In the 1990's, a screen for a wall.

In the 21st century, a holographic wall.

In the 1980's, our office continues to have paper.

In the 1990's, less paper.

In the 21st century, virtually no paper. There is a desk with little but a control panel on it.

In the 1980's, dictating equipment, a secretary and a word processor are close by.

In the 1990's, the secretary's job will be elevated to master of the office command and control center. Voice recognition equipment will produce copy either paperbound or in electronic media.

In the 21st century, paper will be employed, but only by desire, not by need, it having been replaced by electronic media, along with voice-recognized means of storage and retrieval. The concept of data will be broadened to include everything, ideational to material. Data will occur in space as broadcast (stored) signals to be retrieved on rebound from natural and artificial extraterrestrial bodies. From massive archival media to microscopic, cell-like caches, data will be stored and material and specifications will become virtually interchangeable.

With the elimination of the need for paper, the oxygen component of our environment should rise dramatically (as our forests are spared being fed to the memoranda mills). Our need for pens and pencils will be greatly diminished. Our arms will become freer and discover new purpose.

The quality of meetings should be greatly improved for they will be needed less frequently. And when they are needed, I foresee the following:

In the 1980's, teleconferencing via screen technology.

In the 1990's, the drama of two groups sitting at two tables in two locations which are at once one table in one location brought together by electronic synthesis.

In the 21st century, two tables, each pushed against a holographic wall bringing two groups together at one table in one room with diminished perception of dislocation.

In the 1980's, the telephone will still be our primary means of long-distance verbal communication.

In the 1990's, the need for a device physically plugged into a network will disappear, to be replaced by portable speaking and receiving systems.

In the 21st century, the need for a plugged-in device or a portable device will be replaced by the emergence of voice and image projection-reception systems invoked on demand and appearing in our minds, ultimately via LSI engineering techniques applied to the inmost machinery of the human cell—artificial neuronal interconnections. (More of that later.)

The executive inhabiting the corporate office will benefit enormously from this improved technology environment, his integration into which will produce a new dimension of freedom: the strain on his biological self will be diminished and his intellectual, creative and imaginative self can enjoy maximum play—both in the sense of latitude and of recreation. Time elapsed between conceptualization and realization will diminish.

The other side of the coin—perhaps we should say of the chip—is the means of distributing the products of our employment.

The immediate results of office work will remain bound in letters, memos, newspapers, books, reports, magazines, etc., in the 1980's, although more and more will be appearing on the screen.

As the requirement to create paper, to imprint it in some way, bind it and distribute it increases in cost, there is an increasing trend to avoid its usage. More and more will be delivered electronically.

Between the present day and the later 80's, a transition phenomenon bridging the publications production stage (as currently carried out) and the pure computerized delivery stage will emerge. Not surprisingly, it will involve a mixture of computerized delivery and conventional printing. Thus, in the 1980's, there will be an increasing trend to fashion the data to be published at headquarters, transmit it to the purchaser and print it at his home. The portability of paperbound media is a major factor in its longevity.

In the 1990's, innovation in electronic tablet technology should provide us with the means to eliminate paper as a publications medium while retaining its most valuable attribute: namely, portability. Until we can create a portable electronic tablet (within which a microprocessor will be embedded, integrating both logic and substantial memory), pure computerized delivery of reports, newspapers, books, etc., will be limited to our having to visit a terminal of some kind. It is hard to conceive of conventional publication formats as we now know them disappearing without some progress in the evolution of portability. How else could we sit under a tree in the summer breeze to read?

If broadcast technology improved to the point where we could indeed sit under a tree to read our favorite novel on a plasma screen, having invoked the book's contents in an on-demand mode, the issue of portability would be solved once and for all.

But information creation and distribution are far easier tasks than is the distribution of other products. So, while great strides will be made in instrumenting the blue collar-white collar means of production, the means of delivery of the material results will, perforce, lag far behind except in the pure information area. If data creation and delivery in the year 2000 is solved by informatics innovations involving both wire and wireless techniques, it is nevertheless hard to envision, for example, a panel on the wall of a consumer's residence which provides soup via cable, or broadcasts it directly from the factory. While there is no doubt that an economically viable process of production will be incredibly aided by, if not wholly consigned to, the technology of automation, from factory to office, somehow or other we will still have to find some means of bringing the hard products and the person who would use them together. I do not think it will ever be practical to distribute shoe factories in quite the same way as printing facilities.

Thus, the next big bottleneck to be overcome will be that of the means for delivering hard products. One fears that much of the increased efficiency to be gained through the electronic-office-cum-robot-factory scenario will be lost in the delivery problem. Even if teleportation were possible, its realization would lag far behind improvements in our means of production. Some breakthrough is needed to treat hard products as data. Could we be headed for a future where data and product are interchangeable on demand?

We are at once embedding LSI in ourselves at the same time as we embed ourselves in LSI. Microprocessor chips are invading not only inorganic tools, products, devices, etc., but also our very own biological selves.

The first manifestation of the invasion of our own biological selves by LSI is where it ought to be, namely, to correct physical limitations which should never have been. People with certain nervous conditions, organic insufficiencies or physical deformities which restrict normal performance will be the first target of LSI as embedded in human beings. LSI has for some time been embedded in devices which perform organic functions for living human beings; for example, in heart machines. At the moment, these are external. Heart machine technology is, however, improving to the point where it will be embedded.

The promise of LSI in improving vision, hearing and other vulnerable, crucial elements of our biology goes beyond correcting abnormal conditions. Its role in improving normal conditions is the most exciting. Imagine having an eye that can see in the dark or into our micro or macrocosmic worlds. Imagine hearing a cell move or the solar wind blow. Could it be that all devices that extend our normal cognitive powers are produceable as LSI? Are LSI cells?

We are already deeply committed to the creation of massive service networks through, in one way or another, most of the computer, communications and service companies of significance in the world. With short and long haul communications, wire and wireless, the globe is increasingly immersed in a sea of communications. And anchored at various points in this sea of communications are processing nodes. This combination of communications and processing defines a massive LSI within which we are becoming increasingly embedded. Consider it. If you accept the concept that the only thing differentiating an LSI embedded in us from the network within which we are ourselves embedded is size, some beautiful ideas result. In a sense, our future is to be suspended between the LSI within us and the networks external to us.

Yes, there are dangers implicit in this cosmos: but it is the opportunities that strike me as being of overriding interest. Communications between the microminiature LSI world and the macro LSI world, for example, can provide us with the means of internalizing holograms, endowing us with the means for effecting a form of travel without ever having to move from our seats. Captain Kirk's decomposition-recomposition machine, which suggests that we can be transformed into some kind of electronic stream, shot like puffed wheat to another location and reassembled, is far less likely than the concept I propose—to wit, that the other location can be brought to us via the massive informatics network, in which we are embedded, and recomposed in our minds via the LSI embedded within us.

Had it been suggested in the 1940's that large-scale-integrated networks with processing nodes could be printed through photolithographic methods on wafers so tiny that electron beam microscopes would be needed to see their elements, the most far-seeing of scientists would have called it science fiction, or something more rude. Yet, the massive new networks have gone exactly that route. The compression ratio of these networks in converting original format to LSI analogs is astounding. Is it not mind-boggling that systems of this size, logic and memory have now been compressed into LSI? They could now be housed within us.

How far can this compression go? Will the massive network of computer and communications devices now being spread over the world be capable of being so compressed that its processing power may ultimately reside on an LSI chip?

There is no doubt in my mind that we will see the power vested in these systems and others like them one day on chips. Technologies like gallium arsenide-based LSI or Josephson Junction Logic combined with improvements in silicon LSI wrapped in micro-refrigerators are starting to produce picosecond switching speeds. These small devices can produce the computing power of thousands of today's most massive machines. Their size: a cubic inch or two. How small can such systems become? Could they become the size of a cell and would it be reasonable to expect that, just as electro/chemical/mechanical technology has augmented the body in such a way as to improve its functioning, LSI will augment the cell to do likewise? Answers to questions such as these cannot, of course, be given with any certitude, but the trend is surely in this direction.

Bionic devices are clearly in our computerized future. But before they appear, computing devices created first of inorganic matter and later of organic matter will have emerged. We have just begun to explore biological computing devices. Research in this area will increase as the limits of inorganic technology are reached.

I am told that there is a cellular memory in all organic material. Of our body's sixty thousand billion cells, roughly one-half carry memories composed of data dating back to the primordial soup. If we could retrieve this memory, geneticists suggest that powers exercised by our progenitors and now lost to us could be revived. In this stream of genetic consciousness is locked the memory of how to fly and how to live under water, and perhaps even the secret of life; how it arose and why (or even whether) it ends with the death of the individual. In order to recall data from memory, we need proper I/O channels. Communications experts speak about 'handshaking,' a word conveying some form of cooperative relationship between the device extracting the data and the device containing it. In my mind's eye, I see LSI compressed to the size of a cell, see us communicating with it, and, through a series of as yet unexplored channels, bringing the data of past epochs back. If this can be done, our technological achievement will have surpassed that realizable through the agency of natural evolution, and the narrow bandwidths of our physical and intellectual being will have been so widened that we may ultimately leave even our technology behind us.

Discussion

1. Do you agree or disagree with Lecht's position that nothing of consequence will be harmed or lost by the distribution of computer power to people everywhere?
2. Is Lecht's analogy between the augmentation of human physical power and human intellectual power valid?

CHAPTER 22

INFORMATION SYSTEMS AND YOU

INTRODUCTION

Most of us realize that computer-based information systems have had and will continue to have a significant impact on our lives. However, many experts agree that this impact is just beginning. Computers will be more pervasive in the future than they are now. This chapter will first look at the effect of computers on professional careers, and then explore the various information systems careers available. We will also look at several professional information systems associations and certification programs. Finally, we will cover two suggested models for information systems education.

THE EFFECT OF COMPUTERS ON PROFESSIONAL CAREERS

There are very few careers, if any, that will not be affected by computers. Business professionals are presently relying very heavily on computers for their record keeping and information needs. Certainly those who know how to use computer technology effectively will have a competitive advantage over those who do not. As discussed in the previous chapter, artificial intelligence (expert systems) will affect even the most prestigious of careers, such as medicine, law, and accounting. These and other careers are based on information or expert knowledge. Computer systems may be able to provide much of this expert knowledge more effectively and at a lesser cost.

Most business professionals will find computers relieving them of many boring, time consuming, and repetitive details of their jobs. This will leave the more exciting, challenging, and interesting aspects of a professional business career for human beings to master. You will thus be much more productive in your career than your predecessors. Regardless of how sophisticated computer systems become, there will always be areas of knowledge and action that require human discretion.

Many experts have said that we are entering the information age because of computer-based systems. Large amounts of information will be almost instantly available to decision makers. A greater percentage of the work force will be employed as information workers. If decision makers are to employ this information productively, they must understand the methods by which it was produced. It is important that you not only understand information technology but also decision models, such as economic order quantity, linear programming, and others on which computer-based systems rely. It is not enough to simply take the information output from a computer system and rely on it for decision making without understanding the algorithms that produced the data. A decision maker must be able to decide if the information or recommendations supplied by the computer are reasonable. As business professionals, we cannot simply turn decision making over to the computer without understanding what is going on. In summary, the computer will provide us with a great deal of information, but we must still understand its underlying processes. Otherwise, the actual intelligence in the business world, the human mind, will have lost control. The real creative thinking and control must continue to be exercised by human beings. In your career, the computer is simply a very important tool that you are compelled to use effectively. Without doing so, you will probably lose the competitive business race.

MANAGEMENT CASE 22-1

Campbell Manufacturing Company is a large diversified manufacturer of industrial and consumer products located in the northeast. Campbell is considering a policy of encouraging personnel in user departments to transfer to the MIS department for a minimum period of two years and at the same time employees in the MIS department would be encouraged to transfer to user type jobs in marketing, finance, personnel, etc., also for a minimum of two years. Campbell's management feels that this cross-training will be very useful in the future, especially as users begin to develop applications themselves. Do you think this is a good policy? Would you be willing to make such a transfer if you were an employee?

INFORMATION SYSTEMS CAREERS

The largest impact of the computer revolution will be on information systems careers. The Bureau of Labor Statistics has predicted that by 1990 jobs for all information systems specialists will increase by 84 percent. In certain specialties, the expected increases are shown below:

systems analysts—an increase of 119 percent
programmers—an increase of 102 percent
computer operators—an increase of 116 percent
computer service technicians—an increase of 154 percent

The number of information systems specialists recruited is expected to be greater than in any other profession in the 1980s.

The primary reason for this increase is the declining cost of hardware and the subsequent increase in the number of computers. Once businesses and other organizations acquire computers, they quite naturally would like them to perform specific jobs. These jobs require software, which in turn creates a need for programmers and systems analysts. Someone must also operate the computer and service it.

It is interesting to observe that even with this large forecasted increase in jobs, information systems careers are not recession-proof. In the midst of the recession of 1982, the job market for entry level programmers without experience dried up. There was an oversupply of these individuals. At the same time, the market was still strong for programmers who had three to four years of experience. Figure 22-1 illustrates the relationships among primary careers in information systems. Some specific information systems careers are discussed below.

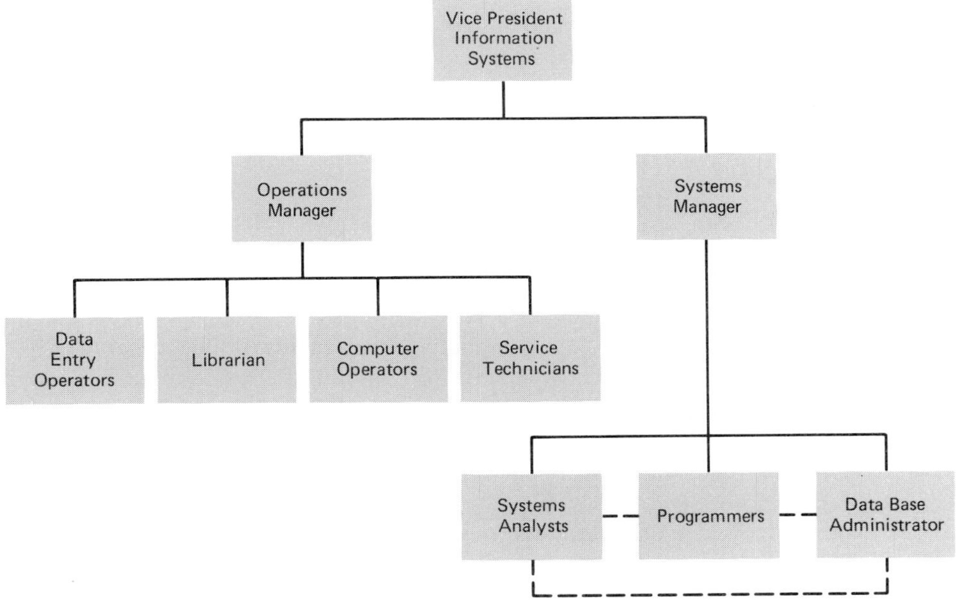

Figure 22-1 The Information Systems Department

Programmer

As discussed in previous chapters, there are two types of programmers: systems programmers and applications programmers. Systems programmers write and maintain systems software, such as operating systems, compilers, utilities, and data base management systems. These individuals normally have a degree in computer science. They quite often work for computer manufacturers and software houses. However, most large computer installations will have a few systems programmers, whereas most medium and small installations do not employ a full-time systems programmer.

By far, the greatest number of jobs in programming is for applications programmers. These individuals write programs to perform specific jobs for users, such as inventory control, accounts receivable, accounts payable, airline reservations, marketing analysis, and personnel information systems.

It is possible to obtain a job as an applications programmer without a four-year college degree. Individuals educated in technical schools and community colleges quite often become applications programmers. Many applications programmers, however, have college degrees in computer science, information systems, mathematics, or a host of other areas. Most employers prefer applications programmers to have had education in the computer area as well as in their application area. For example, if a programmer writes application programs in the accounting area, it helps to have accounting expertise. Marketing expertise would help in writing marketing applications. Many employers are therefore seeking applications programmers who have a broad business oriented degree with a major in information systems. In addition, applications programmers should have taken core business courses, such as accounting, finance, economics, business law, marketing, management, and quantitative methods.

Although the demand for programmers is projected to remain strong, the possibility certainly exists that new programming tools such as application generators will decrease the number of available jobs. Application development by users without programmers is likely to become much more prevalent in the future.

Systems Analyst

A systems analyst can be compared to an architect. His or her responsibility is to analyze and design application systems. In carrying out this responsibility, a systems analyst is heavily involved with the system development life cycle from analysis through implementation. Often the systems analyst is looked upon as an intermediary between users and programmers. Few analysts are highly skilled programmers. In fact, an analyst does not need to perform programming at all, although he or she should be familiar with several different business oriented languages. However, some firms have positions known as programmer/analysts. In this case, the systems analyst performs both programming and analysis functions and therefore must be competent in the programming area as well.

It is more important that the analyst have competence in the application area with which he or she is dealing. The analyst must deal directly with users and must understand their applications in order to design a new system. For these reasons, analysts sometimes have a formal education in areas such as marketing, economics, accounting, and management. But the best combination is to have an education in one of these application areas plus an information systems education. In fact, systems analysts are often employed by and report to the user organization rather than the information systems function. They analyze and design new systems and then turn the specifications over to the information systems organization for programming.

The job outlook for systems analysts is indeed bright. These types of individuals can initially pursue a career in systems analysis, and then decide whether to remain in the information systems organization or perhaps move into management in the application area in which they are trained. They are usually actively recruited by user organizations because of their computer expertise. Even if users develop many of their own applications in the future, they will need individuals with the expertise of systems analysts to guide them in the use of the new software, such as application generators and database management systems.

EDP Auditor

A subspecialty known as EDP auditor has developed within auditing. An EDP auditor is normally employed within the internal or external audit function. He or she has computer expertise and can therefore assist traditional auditors both in the review of computer controls and in the production of audit information through the use of computers. Currently, there is a very high demand for this type of individual, particularly within internal audit departments. In the long run, some maintain that traditional auditors will acquire the necessary computer expertise, and EDP auditors will no longer be necessary. However, it is doubtful that this will be the case. It is very difficult for one individual, an auditor, to have expertise in computer technology, generally accepted auditing standards, and generally accepted accounting principles. Furthermore, computer technology will continue to advance. There will always be a need for specialist EDP auditors who keep abreast of the latest computer technology and methods for controlling application systems based on that technology.

Data Processing Operations

There are several career areas within data processing operations, including data entry operator, librarian, and computer operator. A data entry operator keys data from source documents into computer readable form, usually on disk. Job openings in this area are expected to decline in the future. This is due primarily to source data automation where terminals, cash registers, and other devices capture data at the point of a business transaction. Data entry operators generally have only a high school diploma. There is no need for advanced education at the college level. The primary skill required is good typing abilities.

A librarian is responsible for storage of computer programs and data files, which are stored on tape or disk. The job entails keeping records of the use and storage of files. It also requires operating equipment that tests storage media (such as tape and disk) to assure that it will store data without error. A high school diploma is sufficient for this job.

Computer operators operate the computer equipment. Most only have a high school diploma. However, the operator must be familiar with the equipment and be able to make various types of devices operate properly. These include card readers, tape drives, disk drives, plotters, CPUs, and data switches. This job thus requires some technical training. In addition, the operator must be able to convey to programmers, systems analysts, and users the nature of problems that may occur in the execution of computer jobs.

Data Base Administrator

A data base administrator (DBA) is responsible for the design and control of a company's database. This is a management position. The individual must have a high level of technical data base expertise. He or she also must be able to communicate effectively with various user groups since the primary responsibility of this position is meeting the often conflicting needs of users. Other major responsibilities of the DBA are:

1. designing data bases
2. developing data dictionaries
3. designing and implementing procedures that will ensure the accuracy, completeness, and timeliness of data stored in the data base
4. mediating and resolving conflicts among users' needs for data
5. advising programmers, analysts, and users about the efficient use of the data base

Information Systems Consultant

An information systems consultant is very much like a systems analyst. This individual may be employed in an information center within a firm or by outside consulting agencies, such as management consulting or CPA firms. The role these individuals play can range from advising to hand holding when a user is trying to complete analysis, design, and implementation of a system. Many information systems consultants, particularly those employed by outside consulting agencies, hold advanced degrees, such as MBAs, Masters in Information Systems, or Masters of Accountancy. To be a successful consultant requires a special set of skills, including maturity, an ability to communicate effectively, a high level of technical knowledge both in computer systems and the application area, and the ability to both recognize problems and come up with solutions quickly without getting bogged down in details.

Information Systems Manager

In all the information systems career areas we have discussed, there are management positions. Typically, individuals start out in one of the career areas discussed and then move up to management positions in that area. In addition to technical expertise in the area, information systems managers need the same management skills essential to all management positions. These include the ability to communicate orally and in written form, the ability to plan, organize, and implement, and human relations skills so necessary for the supervisory function of management. Almost all information systems managers have a college education.

PROFESSIONAL ASSOCIATIONS

There are several professional associations in the computer and information systems field. Most have as their primary purpose the continuing education of computer professionals and the exchange of ideas in the information systems area. Some also offer professional certification programs which we will discuss in the next section. Many of these associations welcome student members. In fact some, like the Association for Computing Machinery, have local student chapters on many campuses.

AFIPS

The American Federation of Information Processing Societies (AFIPS), 1815 North Lynn Street, Arlington, Virginia 22209, (703) 558-3600, is a federation of information processing societies. Among the societies represented by AFIPS are the Data Processing Management Association (DPMA), The Association for Computing Machinery (ACM), the Institute of Electrical and Electronic Engineers (IEEE), the American Statistical Association (ASA), and the American Institute of Certified Public Accountants (AICPA). The primary activities of AFIPS are to sponsor the yearly National Computer Conference and exposition, and to represent its constituent professional societies in a similar international group (IFIPS).

DPMA

The Data Processing Management Association (DPMA), 505 Busse Highway, Park Ridge, Illinois 60068, (312) 825–8124, was founded as the National Machine Accountants Association. Its name was changed to DPMA in 1962. The Association has local chapters that hold monthly meetings, holds an annual data processing conference, sponsors an annual information systems education conference, publishes a monthly journal, *Data Management*, and sponsors various educational programs. This is a business oriented data processing association. Its membership is made up largely of practicing business data processing professionals.

ACM

The Association for Computing Machinery (ACM), 11 West 42nd Street, New York, NY 10036, (212) 869–7440, has as its primary objective the advancement of the science and art of information processing. It is the largest technical, scientific, and educational computing organization. As opposed to DPMA, ACM is primarily concerned with scientific computing and the academic pursuit of computer education. Many of its members are computer science faculty at universities. ACM has special interest groups (SIGs), which concern themselves with many different aspects of computing. For example, ACM members who have a special interest in small computers are members of SIGSMALL. There are other special interest groups in several areas, including Data Base, Computer Science Education, and Programming Languages. Active ACM chapters are located on many college campuses and in most cities.

ASM

The Association of Systems Management (ASM), 24578 Eardley Drive, Cleveland, Ohio 44118, (216) 243–6900, was founded in 1947 and is a national organization for individuals interested in the systems area. ASM publishes a monthly journal called *Journal of Systems Management* and has local chapters in most cities. It holds an annual conference and its membership is made up largely of systems analysts and information systems managers.

SIM

The Society for Information Management (SIM), 111 East Wacker Drive, Suite 600, Chicago, Illinois 60601, (312) 644–6610, was founded in 1968. Its members come from all areas of information systems, including information systems managers, business systems analysts, and educators. SIM holds an annual conference and also sponsors an annual international conference for information systems education. The latter has in recent years become an important annual conference for the exchange of papers and ideas among business information systems educators.

EDP Auditors Foundation

The EDP Auditors Foundation, 373 South Schmale Road, Carol Stream, Illinois 60187, (312) 653–0950, is a professional association of auditors who specialize in EDP auditing. It has local chapters in all major cities and holds an annual conference. In addition, it publishes a journal called *The EDP Auditor*. One of the most important activities of the EDP Auditors Foundation is sponsorship of the Certified Information Systems Auditor (CISA) exam. This will be discussed in the next section.

MANAGEMENT CASE 22-2

The Abbett Company is considering a policy which would require all of their computer professionals including EDP auditors to have an appropriate professional certification. Individuals within the systems development department could either hold the Certificate in Computer Programming or the Certificate in Data Processing. EDP auditors would be required to hold the Certified Information Systems Auditor designation. Abbett management believes that this policy would build a spirit of professionalism in the computer oriented staff. They feel that this is now lacking and to some extent, accounts for the high staff turnover they have experienced in these areas in the past. Do you think this is a good policy?

PROFESSIONAL CERTIFICATION PROGRAMS

There are several professional certification programs in the information systems area. Students planning careers in information systems should sit for those exams relating to their career interests. The best time to sit for these exams is during your senior year or shortly after you graduate, since contents of these exams are based on material learned in an undergraduate program. Of course, if receipt of certification requires work experience you cannot receive your certification until after you gain the required work experience. However, the rules allow you to take the exams prior to gaining work experience.

The CDP and CCP

The Certificate in Data Processing examination and the Certificate in Computer Programming examination are administered by the Institute for Certification of Computer Professionals (ICCP), 35 East Wacker Drive, Chicago, Illinois 60601, (712) 782–9437. This is a nonprofit organization established in 1973 with the purpose of testing and certifying computer professionals. As with AFIPS, ICCP is made up of several constituent societies. The CDP examination originated with DPMA but was turned over to ICCP in 1974. Candidates for the CDP exam must have at least five years of professional experience in the information systems area. In addition, they must pass a five-part exam, including parts on data processing equipment, computer programming and software, principles of management, quantitative methods, and systems analysis and design. The CCP is also a five-part exam and is designed to test the knowledge and skills required of a senior level programmer.

CISA

The Certified Information Systems Auditor exam is administered by the EDP Auditors Foundation, 373 South Schmale Road, Carol Stream, Illinois 60187, (312) 653–0950. This is a multiple choice exam covering the following general areas:

1. Application Systems Controls
2. Data Integrity
3. Systems Development Life Cycle
4. Application Development
5. System Maintenance
6. Operational Procedures Controls
7. Security Procedures
8. Systems Software
9. Resource Acquisition
10. Resource Management
11. Information Systems Audit Management

In addition to passing the exam, a minimum of five years practical experience in EDP auditing is required for certification.

INFORMATION SYSTEMS EDUCATION

Two professional organizations have been active in designing model curriculums for information systems education. Both ACM and DPMA published model curriculums in the early 1980s. Outlines of these curriculums are shown in Figures 22-2 and 22-3. As you can see, the course titles differ substantially in these two curriculums. The primary

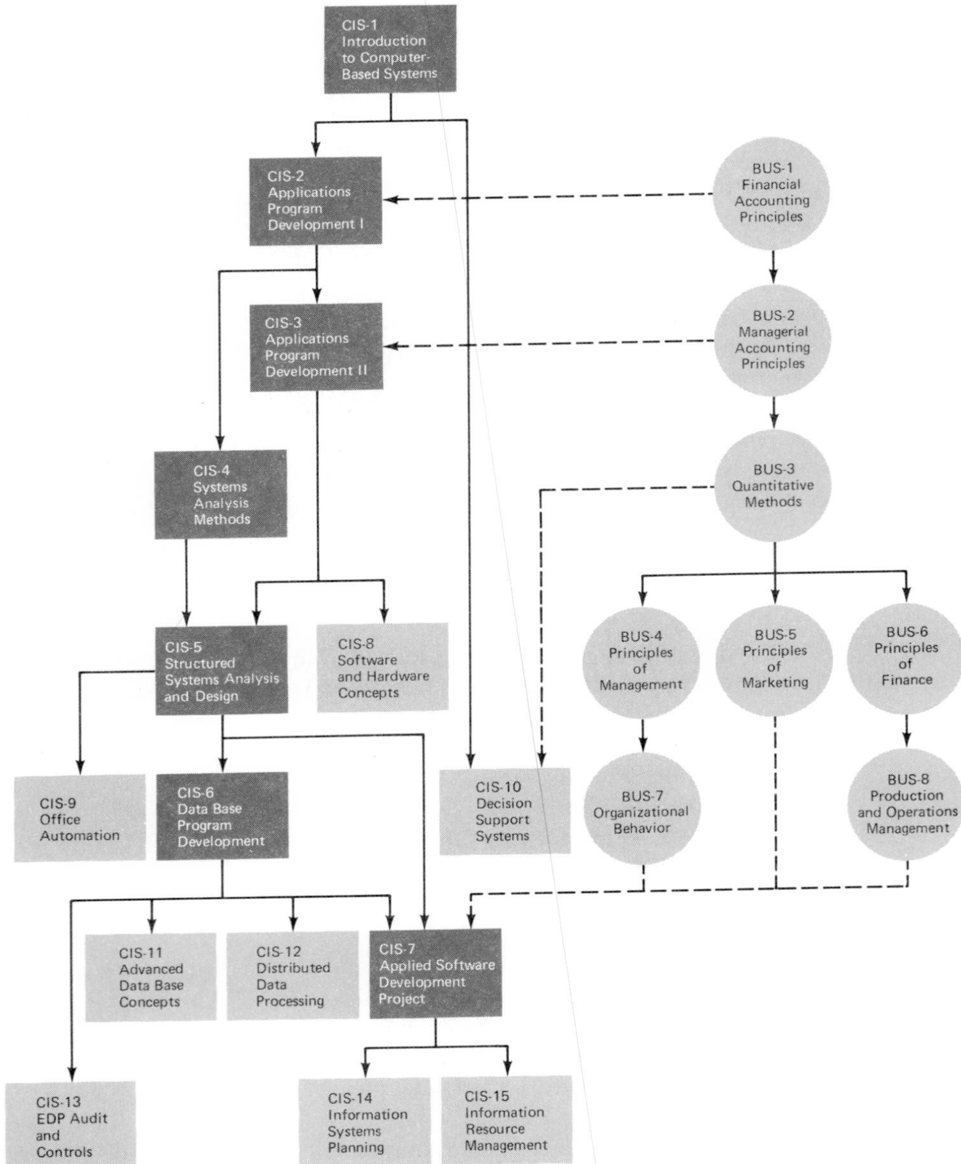

Figure 22-2 Structure of DPMA Model Curriculum for Computer Information Systems (From *DPMA Model Curriculum for Computer Information Systems.* Copyright and reprint permission granted. 1983. Data Processing Management Association Education Foundation. All rights reserved.)

difference between the two curricula is that the ACM curriculum has a more theoretical and conceptual basis, whereas the DPMA model curriculum is more practical and applied in nature. Another difference is that the DPMA model curriculum emphasizes that information systems education should be housed within colleges of business.

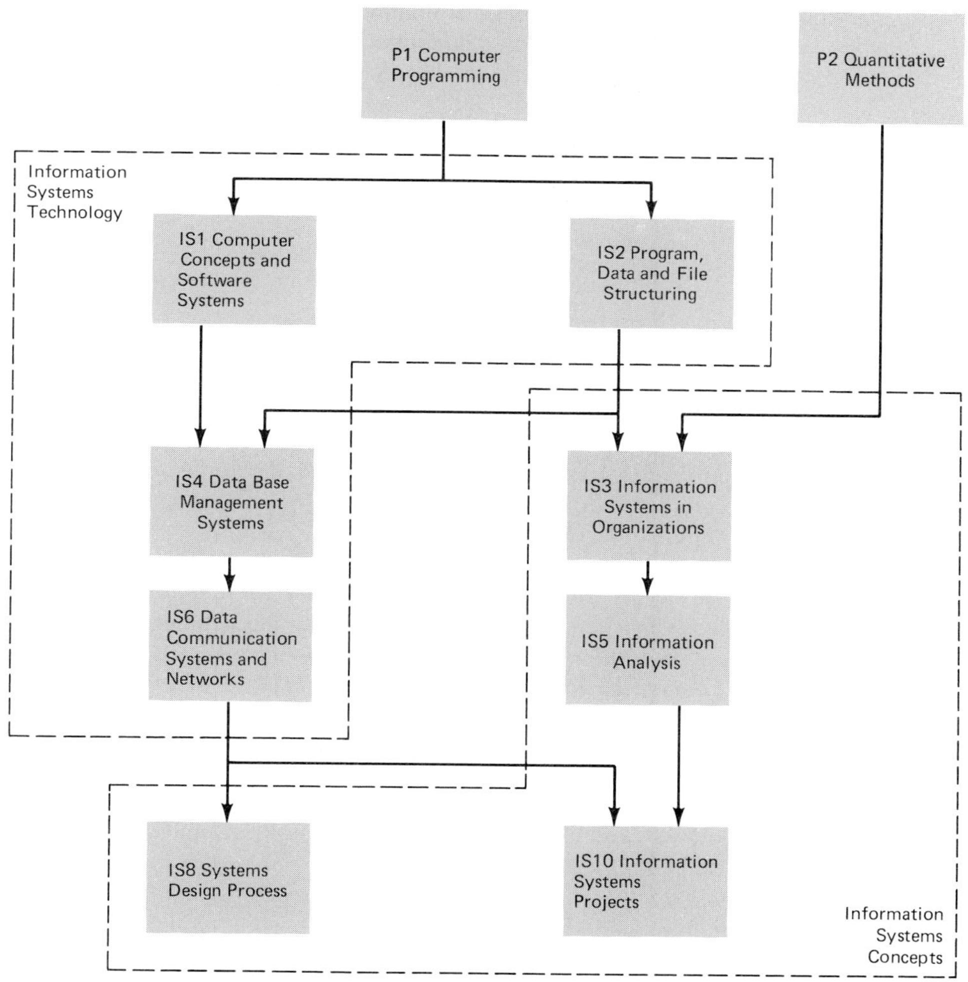

Figure 22-3 ACM Model Curriculum for Information Systems

It is rare that an information systems curriculum at a specific university or college exactly matches either of these two curricula. Model curricula are designed to be just that, models that are modified to fit the particular needs of a particular university or college. One does not have to follow these model curricula exactly to receive a very good information systems education.

SUMMARY

Most business professionals will now have to rely on computer-generated information to perform effectively in their jobs. However, in order to make informed and responsible decisions they must also understand the processes used by the computer in generating the information.

The Bureau of Labor statistics has predicted a large increase in information systems jobs during the 1980s. Careers in information systems may be categorized as follows:

1. Programmer
2. Systems Analyst
3. EDP Auditor
4. Data Processing Operations
5. Data Base Administrator
6. Information Systems Consultant
7. Information Systems Manager

There are many professional associations of data processing personnel. Some of the more prominent of these are:

1. American Federation of Information Processing Societies (AFIPS)
2. Data Processing Management Association (DPMA)
3. Association for Computing Machinery (ACM)
4. Association of Systems Management (ASM)
5. Society for Information Management (SIM)
6. EDP Auditors Foundation

Several kinds of professional certification exist in the data processing area. The Certificate in Data Processing, Certificate in Computer Programming, and Certified Information Systems Auditor are widely recognized qualifications for EDP personnel.

KEY TERMS

The Information Age
Information Workers
Decision Models
Algorithms
Systems Analysts
Programmers
Computer Operators
Computer Service Technicians
Programmer/Analysts
EDP Auditor
Application Generators
Internal Audit
External Audit
Data Entry Operator
Librarian
Data Base Administrator
Information System Consultant
Information System Manager
AFIPS
IFIPS
ACM
DPMA
ASM
SIM
EDP Auditors Foundation
CDP
CCP
ICCP
CISA
Model Curriculum

REVIEW QUESTIONS

1. Why is it important to understand the decision models used by computers?
2. What is the primary cause of the increase in demand for information systems specialists?

3. Distinguish between an applications programmer and a systems programmer.
4. What kind of educational background is needed for a career as an applications programmer?
5. Why would the use of application generators decrease the demand for programmers?
6. What is the difference between a programmer and a systems analyst?
7. Describe the functions of an EDP auditor.
8. Why is a librarian necessary in the data processing department?
9. Distinguish between a data base administrator and a data processing manager.
10. What skills are needed for a career as an information systems consultant?
11. Briefly describe each of the six professional associations discussed in this chapter.
12. What is the purpose of the CDP examination?
13. What do the initials CISA represent?
14. Is there any important difference between the model curricula suggested by the ACM and the DPMA?

DISCUSSION QUESTIONS

1. Some experts argue that tools like application generators and easy-to-use computer languages will greatly reduce the need for programmers in coming years. Does this mean that programming jobs will be the next victim of automation? If so, will it be possible to retrain computer programmers to do some other kind of productive work?
2. If you decide to build a career in the information systems area, which professional association(s) would you like to join? How would it (they) contribute to your professional development?
3. Professions such as medicine, law, and accounting have strict licensing requirements for practitioners. Why is there no such requirement in the information systems profession? Is such a requirement likely to be imposed in the future?

RESEARCH PROJECTS

1. Identify some software packages used by a professional group (architects, agronomists, etc.) and write a paper describing how the packages assist users in decision making. You can learn about specific software packages either by reading professional journals, or through personal contact with specialists in that area.
2. If your school offers a program in information systems, compare its curriculum with the model curricula suggested by ACM and DPMA. Identify the strengths and weaknesses of the program at your school. Copies of these model curricula are probably in your library or can be obtained from ACM and DPMA or from information systems faculty at your school.

MIS AND MANAGEMENT

Technician-To-Manager—More Than A Step Up

(Reprinted with permission from MIS Week, Jan. 19, 1983, p. 32)

By Rutrell Yasin

NEW YORK—The decision whether or not to take a technical career path or make that step into management is becoming a crucial one for the information systems professional as the MIS department emerges as a powerful force in the business world.

Too often a technician may move into management and discover that a whole new set of skills must be developed in order for him to be successful as a manager. In addition, many technicians are pushed into managerial positions but, in fact, would rather remain in technical areas and receive recognition, in the way of higher salaries and greater prestige, similar to their peers in management positions.

Davis Farmer, manager of technical planning and control in the information systems department at AFIA Worldwide Insurance in Wayne, N.J., thinks the DP professional labors under an "unnecessary conception." Since the managerial position has traditionally been one that has produced higher salaries, more status and prestige, DP people have been convinced that if they are not managers, they are failures, he said.

The DP field being relatively new, unlike other professions, has not yet evolved a set of standards or training arrangements for DP professionals, Farmer said, as he explained the wide spectrum of backgrounds among systems people working in his department at AFIA—the individuals range from those with formal education up to high school to those with Ph.D. degrees. Farmer noted that they must all interrelate.

Farmer said that one should look at two things when considering management development: (1) some people feel compelled to follow the management career path even though it is not in accord with their talents, and (2) one must look for the people who do want to be managers.

A manager has different attitudes and concerns than a technician, he said. A manager must understand the total operation of a company. "A project leader would not be asked to make a decision of whether or not his project should go on the back burner." Farmer noted, whereas a manager would have to make such a decision.

For the technically oriented person at AFIA, Farmer said he or she will develop a position as staff specialist in which the person will function as an in-house consultant. The position will emphasize technical and project-oriented assignments.

The typical staff specialist would probably come from the programmer analyst ranks and the position would be roughly equivalent to a project leader, Farmer said. But the function would allow for a more highly developed expertise.

Farmer added that no one would be forced to go into his area; rather, it is the company's way of showing personnel that there is another way. He noted that at AFIA, an attempt is made in the beginning of the recruitment process to find out how a person will fit in and whether or not that person's plans are consistent with the company's plans.

Since a major investment is being put into training, Farmer said they want it to be one that "benefits employee and employer." In addition, he expressed a concern that management training should start at the very bottom where the person can get the broadest experience. The emphasis should be on the company's needs and priorities, he added.

Addressing the topic of technician or manager at a meeting of the New York Chapter of the Association of Women in Computing, Geri Riegger, assistant vice president of operations at Blue Cross/Blue Shield of Greater New York, told the audience she assumed that the technical career path was the only one 20 years ago, and when she went into management she was not prepared for it.

She identified professional activities, such as programming, system programming and industry analysis, as technicians' jobs. When one talks about management, she said, one is talking about working through a group. A manager may manage various disciplines. "Many times you will find that you are managing something you don't know anything about," she added.

Some companies are establishing dual career ladders, she noted, wherein the corporation has established positions on a technical level equivalent with manager-level positions. However, opportunities on the managerial side tend to be greater.

Riegger attributes this to the corporate view that the manager is responsible for its bottom line and also to the ambivalence of the term "technical." From her experience, she said that she has found that "top management thought technicians were narrow, confined and couldn't speak English." She suggested changing the name of technician to "professional," especially in the computing field since it is relatively new and many people do not know that technicians are professionals.

If a person does decide to pursue the technical career path, Riegger said the person should become an expert in that field and, like Farmer, said that one can become a consultant in the technical area.

If one does decide to make the transition from technician to manager, Riegger said that person should stress activities that will prepare him or her for management positions. A first-line managerial position in which part of the activity is technical and part managerial would be a good training ground, she noted, but cautioned her audience, "don't use it as an extended technical job." The tendency here is for a person who has a staff of ten, for example, to end up doing all ten jobs.

In a project management position one could get excellent development for upper management, she added. The job involves "planning and communicating with management and also involves selling, taking corrective action and allocation of resources, money, time and people."

Like Farmer, she indicated the need for the person considering management positions to align his or her goals with the company's goals. One can spend a lot of energy and find that one's efforts are different from the corporate direction. "Lean more towards those goals you have in common with corporate goals," she said.

This raised the question of whether or not DP management was different from other kinds of management. "Yes and no," Riegger said. The newness of the field has caused the situation of a high level of risks. Riegger noted that DP management requires a great deal of "inventing disciplines where they don't exist."

In addition, the rate of change is ordinarily high because of technology. "One hundred things of change are going on at the same time." In the same respect, certain functions that are generic to general management apply to DP management. One needs to plan, to measure, to control multiple changes at one time.

"We need to communicate," Riegger said, "we don't need to look for esoteric ways of managing."

If a person needs exposure one should look for management positions in unorthodox places such as maintenance and operations. If the opportunity is offered, Riegger said, don't turn it down, even if the person is not fond of the area. If one finds the position does not work out, one can look for what is in technical areas.

James Webber, vice president of Omicron in Morris Plains, N.J., a group of corporate, MIS, data processing, office automation, and personnel/human resource executives from leading corporations who deal with people and technology issues, sees a trend with some enlightened companies to raise technical people on the same level with first or second managers backed up with equal money and equal prestige.

Webber indicated that in the general lifestyle of contemporary society, there is a recognition that there are other goals than managing people.

"Not every one wants to be a manager," Webber said, echoing Farmer's sentiments. A lot of people want to make more money and have an impact on their company but still remain technicians, he added.

Many companies have lost talented technical expertise because they had to move into management in order to get a higher salary. The subject of the technician moving to manager has been so prevalent in Omicron's interchange discussions that the organization has developed four interchanges on the "Transition to Management" for 1983.

The interchanges will address the development of communication skills, work on building productive project teams, and show participants how to increase their organizations' effectiveness in planning and implementing change. Webber said that management development is embedded in these interchanges because the senior technician is forced to argue, persuade and confront a group of his peers and sometimes, in turn, learn how to compromise.

At the moment, Webber said, most people in DP learn management by osmosis. An interchange like "Transition to Management" is also useful, according to Webber, because in many companies there are corporate management development units that provide management development. This is OK, Webber said, but there is a void for the DP person because a lot of it is not applicable to them, indicating there is a need for more specific things geared for the DP person.

"Like it or not," Webber observed, "DP people whether it is true or not, they at least perceive that they are different. In that sense perception is reality." Webber added that general management development would be a lot more palatable if it would attempt to tie in examples or case histories from the DP world.

Discussion

1. Why do technicians often have difficulty in making a successful transition to management positions?
2. What skills and background experience does a DP person offer when moving into general management?
3. Is DP management different from other kinds of management?

COMPREHENSIVE CASES

COMPREHENSIVE CASE 1

The Marrett Corporation Systems Planning Committee

James P. Ware

In early April 1980, Mike Ross was reflecting on the development of the Marrett Systems Planning Committee (SPC). Ross, Manager of Information Services (IS) for Marrett had been instrumental in getting the SPC established in 1979, and now he was wondering whether the group was developing rapidly enough. As of April 1980, the SPC had not yet formally adopted a planning and project approval system. However, the group was actively reviewing projects, and individual SPC members were playing an increasingly active role in developing and monitoring systems projects in their own departments. Although Ross was generally pleased with the SPC's positive acceptance in most parts of Marrett, he recalled with some frustration a comment made by the SPC's marketing representative, Pat Wheler at the time the committee had been formed. Wheler had been openly skeptical:

> I don't see why we need a *group* to manage Information Services. I don't have a committee telling *me* how to run my department!

In spite of Wheler's initial skepticism, Ross knew that the SPC was significantly different from an earlier group that he had worked with, the Systems Development Steering Committee (SDSC). The SDSC had almost universally been recognized as a hotbed of organizational politics and as highly ineffective. Now, as he reviewed the agenda for the upcoming SPC monthly meeting, Ross wondered what he should be doing to keep the positive momentum going, and to build the SPC into an effective, efficient planning body.

BACKGROUND ON THE MARRETT CORPORATION AND THE INFORMATION SERVICES FUNCTION

The Marrett Corporation was a well-known manufacturer of small gasoline and diesel engines. Marrett engines were used in a variety of commercial and consumer products,

---

including electrical power generators, pumps, lawnmowers, snowblowers, snowmobiles, and so on. With corporate headquarters in downtown Boston and operating facilities in several nearby towns, Marrett was a wholly owned subsidiary of the New England Power Products Company (NEPPCO). Other major NEPPCO subsidiaries included Manchester Marine (marine diesel engines), Marshfield Motors (small electrical motors used in power tools and appliances) and Soft Power, Inc. (a new division, focusing on solar energy units). Together this family of companies had generated operating profits of $37 million in 1979, and total sales of $683 million.

NEPPCO itself was a division of Universal Motors, Inc. (UMI), a multinational manufacturing conglomerate. UMI had acquired NEPPCO's predecessor company, the Boston Engine Corporation, in 1974. Boston Engine had been organized along major product lines, with several product-market divisions (consumer, industrial, marine, private label, etc.). In that organization, the corporate IS function had been handled by two departments. One group, Corporate Systems Support, had concentrated on corporate systems and common policies and procedures in areas such as documentation standards, IS and hardware planning, and system guidelines. The applications group, which provided systems development and data processing services to the various user divisions had been known as Divisional Information Services (DIS).

Mike Ross had been manager of DIS. Ross recalled that DIS had faced many of the user relationship problems that seem inevitable when a centralized IS department attempts to meet user demands in a decentralized, divisional organization:

> We actually took on a marketing orientation. I sent my staff to marketing seminars, and trained them to play down their technical role. We focused on user needs, and generated a terrific backlog of projects.

As a part of his efforts to build positive working relationships with the operating divisions, Ross had established a user committee known as the Systems Development Steering Committee, or SDSC. However, Ross had not had any real influence on who the SDSC members were; each user division had appointed its own representatives. Ross recalled that the assignment had not been considered highly desirable; the SDSC's efforts were often viewed with some suspicion, especially from divisions that were doing their own data processing. The SDSC had been intended as an opportunity for members to get together regularly to share applications problems and inform each other of systems development progress. However, the monthly meetings had involved more open conflict than discussion, and the Board had clearly become political. As one executive who had been a member of the SDSC recalled:

> The old SDSC had the wrong kinds of people. Most of them didn't care at all about DP, and those who did generally got anything they wanted. The SDSC had eleven members; we were lucky if seven showed up for a meeting, and three of those would never say a word. More often than not, those who did were in never-never land.

In March 1979, Boston Engine was substantially reorganized, and its name was changed to New England Power Products Company. The old product divisions were realigned and transformed into independent operating companies. Each new company inherited one or more of the Boston Engine product divisions. For example, Marrett became a gasoline and diesel engine company, combining operations from the old consumer and private label divisions. The two Boston Engine data processing departments (CSS and DIS) disappeared and were essentially combined to form the Information Services Department within the new Marrett Corporation. Mike Ross was named director of Information Services for Marrett, reporting to William F. Perry, newly appointed Senior Vice President of Finance and Administration. A simplified organization chart for the new Marrett Corporation appears in Exhibit 1.

Exhibit 1
The Marrett Corporation Systems Planning Committee
*Partial Organization Chart for Marrett Corporation**
(as of March 1979)

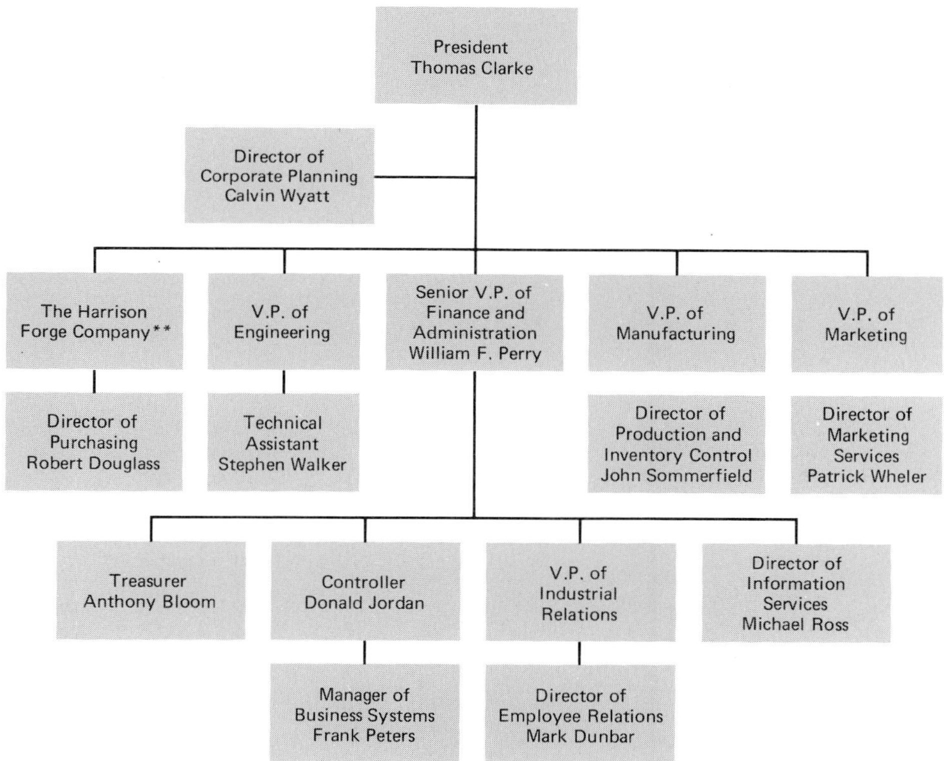

*Names and titles are shown for all individuals mentioned in the case.
**The Harrison Forge Company, technically an independent subsidiary, had been acquired some years earlier to manufacture engine blocks and other castings. Over time, the company had gradually taken over all of Marrett's purchasing functions.

The new organizational structure had several implications for Mike Ross and the Information Services Department. In the first place, the department moved up a level in status, since Perry was the only Senior V.P. within the new organization structure. Ross viewed this factor as a significant plus, even though Perry had never before been responsible for data processing (he did have extensive familiarity with the function, however; he had been corporate controller in the old Boston Engine organization).

A more important consequence of the reorganization was a significant change in the way Information Services worked with user departments. In Mike Ross's words:

> We no longer need marketing-oriented gimmicks to gain user acceptance. Now we're a functional department just like marketing, manufacturing, the controller, and so on. This is a major shift in department identity. Now we think of ourselves as staff support for selling engines—we're a key part of the company. Where DIS would work on meeting *user*-defined needs, now we go in and do the needs analysis, challenge the user's interest in acquiring a computer, and so on. In fact, what we do is a *business*-systems analysis.
>
> I really believe this reorganization has knocked out a lot of the user gamesplaying. Now it's clear that *we* do the data processing, and not the users.
>
> One of the first things Bill Perry did was to stress that our task is to be *proactive*, rather than *reactive*. He wants us to *lead* the other functions in how to use IS effectively.

FORMATION OF THE SPC

Several months after the March 1979 corporate reorganization, Perry and Ross began talking about establishing a new DP planning/steering committee. As a long-time DP user, Perry recalled how frustrating it had been to see the DP department set project priorities. Data processing had always reported to a financial person, and Perry believed that over 80% of the applications efforts had been financially oriented. Yet he knew there were many other kinds of needs going unmet all over the organization. Perry saw the SPC as a mini-Board of Directors:

> Their charter is not to run the day-to-day IS operations—that's Mike's job. Instead, I want the SPC to do IS planning for the whole organization. Beyond that, I want them to review the IS resource and help determine its optimum staffing level. The IS resource has to be used by *all* the functional areas in the company if it is to be fully effective.

Perry set out to make the SPC a mirror image of the company, with all major functional areas represented. He and Ross jointly determined the departments they wanted represented; they agreed that, whenever possible, each member should be a manager who reported directly to the vice president in his or her functional area. In addition, however, they hoped to get managers whom they felt would be supportive of Information Services efforts and compatible with each other. Perry met personally with each functional vice president to discuss the SPC's role in information systems planning, and to explore what manager from that area would become a member of the SPC. Although the VPs selected their own representatives, Perry made certain that his and

Ross's preferences were known. In a few instances Perry actually vetoed a VP's initial selections because he and Ross felt that individual would be a negative influence on the committee. The official memorandum announcing the SPC, describing its purpose and functions, and specifying membership conditions, is reproduced in part in Exhibit 2.

Exhibit 2
The Marrett Corporation Systems Planning Committee
Memorandum Announcing the Systems Planning Committee

Our CEO, Tom Clarke, has reviewed and endorsed the proposal to form a Systems Planning Committee.

The key elements that this group will deal with are:

—The I.S. resource is similar to the capital funds of the company, i.e., it must be planned and prioritized in tune with Marrett business needs.
—That there is a definite need, as well as benefit to be obtained, from the short and long range planning of the I.S. resource.
—There is a Marrett payoff through the exchange of functional needs, airing of problems and that we have the proper business influence "in touch" with the large dollar expenditures ($3,000,000) invested in I.S.
—And finally, that I.S. cannot be a successful influence without the cooperation and direction of such a group.

OBJECTIVES
The SPC group will serve as the interface between the I.S. development function and the operational business segments of The Marrett Corporation. Its primary objectives are to plan and prioritize the disposition of the I.S. resources in line with The Marrett Corporation business plan, to resolve resource conflicts in the master plan and monitor activities to insure proper interaction between functional departments.

DUTIES
—Participate in the annual planning process of the I.S. function.
—Prioritize the I.S. resource to follow the business plan.
—Monitor the progress of development projects with regard to changing business dynamics.
—Assist in the development of I.S. policies.
—Review and endorse major I.S. proposals.
—Serve as an education and information channel for all staff personnel with the member's functional area.

MEMBERSHIP
All members must hold a position that reports directly to a Marrett Corporation officer. He should maintain a departmental position which can fairly represent departmental needs while also being able to recognize and support needs that cross functional departmental lines.

Past systems experience is not a requirement. Emphasis is on an individual's ability

Exhibit 2 *(continued)*

to function as a team member, understanding of The Marrett Corporation's business needs, and an appreciation of the I.S. role in supporting the business functions.

Members are to be appointed by their respective functional officer. Membership is to be considered on a permanent, rather than rotating basis. Members are only replaced at the direction of the corporate executive committee. Members are expected to devote 10% of their position time to this responsibility.

LOGISTICS

The SPC will meet monthly with attendance expected to be of high priority. Meetings will take approximately 6 to 8 hours a session, with additional preparation time on the part of each member.

There will also be an annual 3-day planning session that members will be expected to participate in. This session will complement the annual 1 to 5 year business planning development function of Marrett.

There is some urgency in getting this project started and I would appreciate your early identification of your permanent representative. In the initial stages we will invite and expect active participation from several members of the old Systems Development Steering Committee to help in the transition.

W. F. Perry

The selection of an SPC chairman was a particularly difficult decision. Perry was clear from the beginning that Ross should not chair the SPC. For some time Perry considered establishing a rotating chairmanship, but finally rejected that as too impermanent. Ross estimated that the chairman might have to commit as much as 25% to 30% of his time to the SPC, especially during the first year, and it was difficult to find someone with that kind of time availability. Furthermore, Perry knew that they needed to find someone with a personal style that would fit the task—a dedicated, even-tempered approach, but willing to talk up the committee and its charter.

After some discussion the two men agreed that Frank Peters would be an excellent choice. Peters, 35 years old, had joined the old Boston Engine company in 1975 after six years with one of the Big 8 accounting firms. A CPA by background, Peters had become a computer audit specialist, and Perry (as controller) had hired him as manager of Systems Control to create a new internal computer-based systems planning and design group with an emphasis on audit requirements.

Following the March 1979 reorganization, most of Peters' department had been transferred to the Universal Motors corporate staff and relocated to New York. However, Perry had asked Peters to remain on his staff in Boston and appointed him director of Business Systems, where Peters had continued to work on several internal audit projects. In this position Peters was not a direct user of IS resources, and thus he had the added advantage of not bringing vested interests or biases to the SPC. In addition, Peters had been a member of the SDSC and shared Perry and Ross's desire not to repeat that experience.

Peters commented to the casewriter:

> The SDSC was far too involved in operating details. The group spent too much time trying to tell Mike how to do his job. It was overly concerned with individual project deadlines. I started out making it clear that the SPC would not be like that.

The other eight SPC members who were finally selected were as follows (office location is listed in parentheses following job title).

Tony Bloom, 35, Treasurer (Boston). Joined Marrett in 1975. Served on Boston Engine's corporate staff prior to the reorganization, and had been a member of the SDSC.

Bob Douglass, 43, Director of Purchasing (Boston). There were few computerized applications within Douglass's area, but Ross considered him basically supportive of the SPC's mission.

Mark Dunbar, 40, Director of Employee Relations (Brockton). With Marrett nine years, Dunbar had been with the old Boston Engine marine division. Dunbar had been project manager for a computerized employee information system several years earlier.

Don Jordan, 52, Controller (Boston). Had been with Marrett for over 20 years. Ross rated Jordan a solid supporter of the SPC, even though Jordan was not generally a strong advocate of computerized systems. As Ross put it, "Don is the *conscience* of the SPC; he makes us justify everything we do."

Jack Sommerfield, 36, Manager of Production and Inventory Control (Saugus). He had formerly been with the consumer engine division. Ross considered Sommerfield a "mover and shaker" in terms of accomplishing major system changes within manufacturing.

Stephen Walker, 60, Technical Assistant to the Vice President of Engineering (Brockton). Had been with Marrett about 10 years, and had worked in the Marrett Research Center prior to the reorganization.

Pat Wheler, 40, Director of Marketing Services (Saugus). Had been with the industrial division prior to the reorganization. Ross knew Wheler was skeptical about the SPC and suspected Wheler did not really want to serve on the committee.

Calvin Wyatt, 42, Director of Planning (Boston). Had joined Marrett in late 1978. Wyatt reported directly to Marrett's president, and was quite occupied with developing the planning process within the company.

Bill Perry's congratulatory memorandum to these eight men is reproduced in Exhibit 3.

SUMMER AND FALL 1979 SPC ACTIVITIES

Ross and Peters worked closely together to plan the SPC's initial meeting, to develop their concept of what the group's duties and responsibilities would be, and to define a set of operating procedures. The two men knew from the beginning that molding the

Exhibit 3
The Marrett Corporation Systems Planning Committee
Memorandun to Newly Appointed SPC Members

Congratulations on your appointment to The Marrett Corporation's Systems Planning Committee (SPC). You have been appoineted to this committee by the officer from your functional area because of your ability to fairly represent the needs of your function while also being able to recognize and support the needs of other functions. This trait is essential to the success of the SPC whose primary objectives are to:

—Plan and prioritize the disposition of the I.S. resources.
—Resolve resource conflicts.
—Monitor plan activities and insure proper functional interaction.

It is anticipated that the SPC will make a valuable contribution to the overall development and success of The Marrett Corporation. To insure the SPC's contribution is most meaningful will require your personal effort and contribution.

The first meeting of the SPC has been set for July 25, 1979, at the Park Plaza Hotel in downtown Boston. Mike Ross and Frank Peters are preparing an agenda which will be sent to you shortly.

Also, please mark your calendar for August 20th–22nd, 1979. A three-day SPC planning session is being set up for those days and your participation is essential.

W. F. Perry

---

group into an effective unit would not be a simple task. Among other problems, they knew that past experience with the SDSC were affecting many people's expectations about the SPC. Just as important, most of the members had not worked together before, and several came from parts of the company that had little or no experience with data processing. Peters commented:

> Initially, there were probably three or four subgroups that knew each other fairly well—but between subgroups there was almost no prior interaction. For example, Jack Sommerfield, who's now at Saugus, transferred there from Providence after the reorganization. Pat Wheler has always been at Saugus, but that was part of the old industrial division. Steve Walker's out at Brockton, but that has always been a separate facility.

These concerns led Peters to develop a plan for the first meeting that focused on helping the SPC members get to know each other and the new committee's basic tasks and responsibilities. The meeting, which took place in late July 1979, was kicked off by Bill Perry, who discussed his view of the SPC and why he felt it was an important effort. Peters then asked each member of the group to describe his own department—its size, organization, specific tasks, and so on. Finally, Mike Ross talked about his view of individual member responsibilities and gave a brief status report on current systems projects. Peters closed the meeting by describing plans for a 3-day off-site planning session at which the SPC would establish IS project priorities for 1980 in accordance with Marrett's 1980 business plans, which had already been developed. Bill Perry was mildly discouraged by the tone of the first meeting.

> I was very concerned. I didn't see very much commitment on the part of the members; they really seemed unresponsive. Mike and Frank did almost all the talking, and I wasn't sure how the rest of them were reacting.

Perry thought that perhaps his presence had been inhibiting, and he decided not to attend future meetings. Instead, he monitored the group's efforts by reading the monthly meeting minutes and talking individually with both Peters and Ross.

Peters and Ross were much more optimistic following the first meeting. They recognized that there was an air of cautiousness among the group, but felt that was to be expected. As Peters later recalled, "Mike said he expected the meeting to be a '6,' but he gave it an '8'."

The three-day planning session that Peters announced at the first SPC meeting was originally scheduled for late August. However, scheduling difficulties made the original dates impractical and the meeting was eventually rescheduled for October. The delay was a welcome one, however, as the SPC representatives generally found that their individual preparation for the planning meeting took longer than any of them had expected. Each representative was charged with compiling a list (with brief descriptions) of current and desired systems projects for his functional area.

The SPC had a special meeting in August to review a specific project that involved replacing a computer at the Brockton plant. Peters held the meeting in Brockton, to give the group an on-site exposure to the Brockton facility. In addition to reviewing the conversion project, the group also discussed procedures for developing their project priority lists. Peters provided the group with a set of guidelines outlining the types of projects to include and the information needed on each project. He also handed out a guide for the SPC representatives to follow as they interviewed other managers in their own areas.

Peters set a firm deadline of September 21 for all project proposals (and departmental priority rankings) to be submitted to him. That date would give him enough time to review the plans, clarify any questions, and distribute all the plans to all the members well in advance of the mid-October meeting.

Peters then suggested that the SPC meet for a half-day in mid-September to review everyone's progress on the information-gathering process. However, the group balked at this idea, and concluded they did not want to meet. Instead, they asked Peters to send out sample project descriptions as models, and indicated they would call him individually if they had any questions or problems. Peters chose not to push the issue, and acceded to the group sentiment.

Shortly after the August meeting Peters prepared a formal list of Operating Procedures for the SPC (reproduced in Exhibit 4), and distributed it along with the meeting minutes. About this same time Ross made a formal presentation about the SPC to all the members of the Information Services Department. He wanted to be certain that no one felt threatened or usurped by the SPC, and that everyone within IS understood fully the role that the SPC was intended to play.

Perry, Peters, and Ross all believed it was important for the SPC planning process to be tied as closely as possible to the Marrett corporate plans. By fall 1979 and 1980 business plans were well defined by functional area. (The company planning cycle

Exhibit 4
The Marrett Corporation Systems Planning Committee
Operating Procedures

1. The overriding concept of the SPC is that the Committee is a planning, prioritizing, and monitoring group. It is not a group for checking the status of the I.S. function.
2. Each SPC member is a permanent member of the Committee. His membership is not for a specified and limited period.
3. Each SPC member is expected to attend each meeting.
4. The SPC will meet on a regular basis. These regular meetings will be held once a month on the *third Wednesday* of each month.
5. The monthly meetings will generally be full-day sessions. Depending upon the agenda, however, the meeting may be only one-half day or may be longer than one day.
6. Special meetings may be called by the Chairman if a situation arises which cannot be properly handled as part of a regularly scheduled monthly meeting.
7. SPC meetings generally will be held "off-site" of company locations to avoid interruption by Secretaries, Bosses, telephones and other demands.
8. An agenda for each meeting will be mailed and will be received by members at least one week prior to the meeting date. SPC members are expected to contribute their input to the agenda.
9. A regular meeting location will be established so that the quality of meeting accommodations will be consistent.
10. Minutes of the meetings will be prepared and will be in the mail during the first Monday following the regular meeting date.
11. A three (3) day annual SPC planning meeting will be held to develop a recommended I.S. plan for the following three (3) years.
12. The SPC developed annual I.S. plan will be submitted to the Executive Committee for review and approval.
13. Monthly written reports from each member are required to be sent to the Chairman. The reports should provide a status for projects in the functional area that the member represents.
14. The SPC will, after appropriate review and discussion, take a position on I.S. policy items. When a written recommendation is issued, majority and minority viewpoints will be included. Such written reports will be given to W. F. Perry for review and decision making by the Executive Committee.
15. All projects for I.S. will be submited to I.S. only after the approval of the appropriate SPC representative.
16. Projects or activities of the SPC generally will not be accomplished through the use of subcommittees. However, I.S. resources will be available for detail fact gathering when the SPC has a need.

---

involved Executive Committee agreement on overall strategies by early June each year. These strategies were then converted into functional area business activity plans during the summer. By the end of each summer the corporate plans were reduced to annual budgets. Thus, by early fall each function had a clear definition of its targets and major activities for the coming year.)

Bill Perry commented on this planning process:

> I view the IS projects as *means* to the ends defined by our business strategy. The IS plans are based on the functional areas' definitions of what they need to accomplish their *business* goals. What's really powerful about this process is that the SPC may get several projects from different functional areas, all aimed at one general business strategy.

When Peters had collected all of the departmental systems plans he compiled them in a binder for distribution to all the SPC representatives. He also compiled and distributed all the functional area strategies—the first time, to his knowledge, that managers at this level of the company had seen each others' strategic plans. The SPC planning book—a solid four inches of functional business strategies and 53 detailed systems proposals—included a first-cut consolidated priority ranking that Peters prepared on his own. The book was sent out to everyone in mid-October.

THE OFF-SITE PLANNING MEETING

The planning meeting was held at a resort hotel in southern New Hampshire. The session began with cocktails and dinner on a Wednesday evening. Peters had asked the Marrett president to come to the dinner and give a kick-off speech, but the president cancelled out at the last minute (due to a sudden change in the scheduling of negotiations for an annual supply contract with one of Marrett's largest customers). Bill Perry gave the after-dinner speech instead. He reviewed the company's year-to-date financial performance (at a level of detail not normally shared with managers at this level), and stressed the importance of the SPC's task in helping to improve operating results.

On Thursday each SPC member in turn described his functional area's business strategy and summarized the key IS projects and needs within the area. This project review took all day, including a final hour after dinner. When the group finally broke up at 9:00 p.m. everyone was tired, but satisfied that they had a basic understanding of current and projected Information Services efforts throughout the company.

On Friday morning one of Ross's subordinates described in detail the Information Services Department's resources, covering both personnel and hardware. He also reviewed the projects currently being worked on. Following this session, each SPC member individually ranked all 53 projects. Then Ross and Peters split the group into two teams of five managers each (including themselves) and asked each team to produce a single ranking (the two men had previously determined the composition of the two teams, based on their assessments of personalities, experiences from the old SDSC, and their desire to avoid hostile clashes between dominant or outspoken individuals). The two teams spent several hours working independently to resolve individual differences in priority rankings. Then, at 3 p.m. on Friday afternoon, they presented their consolidated rankings to each other.

They discovered that the two independent rankings were relatively close, although there were several significant differences. What was most interesting, however, was the discovery that the two teams had developed slightly different approaches for establishing the rankings. In particular, one group had designed a two-stage process that began by first assigning each project request to one of three categories:

A. Necessary or required work; critical to the business.
B. Highly desirable.
C. Good ideas, but backburner in terms of urgency.

"A" projects were those that related directly to corporate strategy for 1980, or that were related to government regulations (and were thus not postponable), or those that promised an immediate high dollar return.

The second team found this approach helpful, and the total group quickly began discussing projects in terms of this category system. The group worked from 3 to 5 p.m. Friday afternoon attempting to resolve the conflicts between the two teams' independent rankings. However, even though the two lists were very close, they were unable to reach final agreement. Finally, at 5 p.m., Peters suggested they quit for the day and come back Saturday morning to resolve the remaining differences.

Bill Perry joined the group again on Saturday morning and sat in on their final session. He was generally pleased with what he saw, although he recognized that some SPC members were individually disappointed by how their own projects came out on the priority lists.

> This process clearly had to be done, and the group did a good job. Most importantly, they were allocating IS manpower resources to specific projects, and that forced them to push the lower priority projects out to future years. I know that made some of them unhappy; several people are pushing for expanding the IS resource. The thing I want now is for them to commit *user* manpower resources as well as IS resources.

The SPC members themselves seemed very satisfied with the planning session. One member called it a "three-day shirt-sleeve session with lots of sharing and participation—a good experience."

SPC ACTIVITIES IN 1980

As a follow-up to the planning meeting Peters and Ross made a formal presentation to the Marrett Executive Committee (the president and all the functional vice presidents) in late January 1980. The other SPC members attended the presentation but did not participate, except to respond to questions from Executive Committee members. When the president recognized how many IS projects were *not* going to get worked on during 1980 he offered to increase the IS budget. Ross turned down the offer, however, commenting, "I don't want more money yet—I'm having trouble spending what we have now."

Later, Ross commented to the casewriter:

> I don't want Information Services to be doing projects that don't have a business impact. Perry clearly wants us to spend our budget where it will have a significant effect. We're already growing as fast as we can, and I don't want to make promises I can't fulfill.

The SPC met on its regular monthly schedule through the winter and early spring of 1980. As planned, the meetings were normally held in a hotel a few blocks away from

Marrett's headquarters in downtown Boston. During this time period the group's attention was generally focused on reviewing progress on the major ongoing systems projects. However, Peters also tried to include one or two procedural issues on each agenda. Ross had adopted a formal project management system designed by a software consulting firm, and both he and Peters felt it was important for the SPC's project approval procedures to be consistent with the development phases of the project management system. However, Peters was moving very slowly in introducing formal procedures and documentation requirements to the SPC. He was reluctant to overload the members with paperwork, and he believed it was important for the group to participate actively in designing their own approval and monitoring procedures.

Several other more controversial issues were raised at various SPC meetings during this time period. On one occasion Peters brought up the chargeout system. There was a history of strong feeling about charging back IS costs to the users, much of it dating back to the old SDSC relationships (users had frequently complained that costs were too high). When Peters brought the subject up, Ross said, "If it's a factual problem we'll deal with it, but if it's an emotional issue, let's not involve everyone else." Peters suggested that a more comprehensive discussion of chargeout might be an appropriate agenda item for a future meeting, but several members said no, and the subject was dropped.

On another occasion Peters expressed some concern about attendance. Two members (Pat Wheler and Calvin Wyatt) had missed several meetings, and Peters was afraid their absences would affect the group's unity and credibility. However, the group seemed reluctant to discuss the subject, and in fact Peters sensed that those who *were* attending regularly felt indirectly and unjustly accused of lack of commitment. While Peters recognized the validity of this response, he remained frustrated about the problem. However, he did drop the subject at that point, concluding that a formal meeting was not the place to discuss it.

Peters and Ross also tried to include some form of "education" in each monthly meeting, though they were careful not to call it that. The SPC members were busy, pragmatic, results-oriented managers, and they seemed unwilling to commit to regular "educational" programs. There was just too much to do, too many immediate problems to solve and decisions to make. However, Peters and Ross got around this resistance by scheduling some kind of "informational" presentation for each SPC meeting. In April, for example, two managers (one from IS, one from the Treasurer's Department) were scheduled to report on a new cash management system. Though the report was basically a progress review, Peters and Ross knew that it would also provide useful general background on both cash management techniques and systems development work to the SPC members.

MEMBER VIEWS OF THE SPC

In April 1980, the casewriter spoke individually with several members of the SPC, asking for their assessment of the group's efforts and its impact on their departmental operations.

Tony Bloom, Treasurer, was generally very positive about the way the SPC was functioning. Bloom had been a member of the SDSC and was keenly aware of how differently the SPC was working out.

> This is a solid group of people. The members are higher in the organization than the old SDSC people. More important, these people are really on top of their own operations—and they don't want to look bad in front of each other. Each guy has his boss's ear, but they all wear an SPC hat.
>
> Given who we are, I think we make good business decisions. Nothing is sacred; people are willing to challenge each other and we're getting better each meeting. You have to remember that we didn't know each other well when the SPC began. I know there was a lot of feeling that the treasurer sat up in a white tower and didn't know other people's needs. Now, I can go to our meetings and hear other people's needs as well as tell them what I want.
>
> Basically, we're doing what we set out to do. Our purpose is effective resource utilization, and I think we're doing that pretty well.

Don Jordan, the Controller, was also positive about the need for the SPC. However, he was more ambivalent about how well the planning process was working out.

> I am pleased that our IS priorities are no longer being set by IS itself. The SPC is basically a good group trying to do the right thing for the company. But I'm not 100% confident of the judgments the group is making. The trouble is that we get a lot of "motherhood" projects that no one can argue against. And there's a lot of backscratching, too. You know, I'll support your project if you'll support mine.
>
> The trouble is, we don't always have good information on the project ideas. It's rarely a black/white situation. All the projects are *good* at some level. What worries me is when the needs outstrip the IS resources. I don't want to see IS turning down good projects. We ran out of resources very quickly this year, and a lot of important efforts are getting pushed into 1981.
>
> As an SPC member I do have one problem: I get all hell from my subordinates when I can't get a project approved. What is going to happen when I submit them again next fall and they get turned down again? Will my people react negatively and get discouraged? We had several high payback projects that got low priorities. It's a lot different than it was under the old organization, when we could get anything we wanted, as long as we paid for it. Maybe we should just allocate some part of the IS resource toward direct cash saving projects.
>
> What really gets me is poorly thought out proposals. Like last fall, we had one for "a better marketing information system"—that was the extent of the project definition. I ranked it 54th out of the 53 proposals we reviewed—but the group approved it.
>
> But, on balance, the SPC is the best solution for handling very touchy decisions. I can't think of a better way to do it, short of an all-knowing, benevolent dictator.

Jack Sommerfield, the manufacturing representative, was overseeing the largest current systems development project, a consolidated order entry and inventory control system. There were several other, smaller manufacturing systems projects in process as well. Sommerfield estimated that monitoring these efforts and attending SPC meetings was taking close to 25% of his time. Sommerfield stressed that the new manufacturing control system was *not* an IS project.

> It's a *manufacturing* project, not a systems project. If it's seen as an IS project I guarantee it will fail. We're not just allocating and measuring system people's time, but our *own* as well. In fact, we have actually hired three people who are doing nothing but manufacturing control systems. In manufacturing, the attitude is "screw systems, let's build engines." Of course, we see this new system as a competitive tool that will help us improve customer service and deliveries.
>
> What's unfortunate about the SPC is when key areas like marketing aren't involved like they should be. The SPC concept is right, but what matters is getting the right people involved. You have to have people who are willing to come to the meetings and spend time outside the meetings on systems projects. I know it's a lot of time to spend, but there are all kinds of personal benefits too. I never would spend any time on things like cash management systems or payroll systems if it weren't for the SPC. There's an important business payoff to that kind of learning, too. For example, the new manufacturing control system has all kinds of implications for Don Jordan, even though he doesn't yet realize what's in it for him.
>
> One concern I have is whether top management really understands the role and cost of information systems within Marrett. The SPC *needs* top management support, but I'm not sure they know what we've committed to. After Peters and Ross presented our plan to the Executive Committee in January, the president just accepted it. But I think there were too many vague things in that plan for them to take it as is. Will they support us when push comes to shove and we need more funding? I'm not sure they will.

The casewriter also attempted to talk with Pat Wheler, but was unable to schedule a meeting with him. Wheler reported that he was overwhelmed with work; his boss, the vice president of Marketing, had left the company in early 1980 and had not yet been replaced. Wheler was temporarily reporting directly to the president, and the entire marketing department was in a state of high uncertainty. Wheler also mentioned that at the time he had been asked to join the SPC he was already serving on "all kinds of committees—and that's not my style."

APRIL MEETING OF THE SPC

The April 1980 meeting of the SPC was held on Wednesday, April 23, at a hotel located just two blocks from Marrett's corporate headquarters in downtown Boston. Frank Peters opened the meeting by commenting that both Pat Wheler and Calvin Wyatt were absent and would miss the meeting because of other commitments. Peters also noted that Stephen Walker and Bob Douglass were not yet present, but were expected momentarily. Mark Dunbar expressed his personal concern that these kinds of absences and latenesses were reducing the SPC's effectiveness. Ten minutes of general discussion followed, and Dunbar's concern was clearly shared by everyone else present (Walker and Douglass arrived just as this discussion was ending). Peters indicated that he would discuss the group's concern privately with both Wheler and Wyatt.

The first item on the agenda was a report by Mike Ross on actual first-quarter manpower allocations versus plan. Most major projects were on schedule, though several were consuming more resources than planned. Ross stressed the importance of timely submission of detailed new project plans (those scheduled in October 1979) in order to stay on the 1980 timetable. But, basically, the core of the 1980 plan was being followed rather closely.

Tony Bloom and several of his subordinates then presented a detailed technical description of the new cash management system now in use. The system was the first major on-line system installed at Marrett, and it was now complete, operational, and largely successful (though still in shake-down period). Bloom mentioned that a post-implementation audit was planned but not yet underway.

Following a brief break for coffee, Frank Peters spent about fifteen minutes describing his ideas for project submission procedures and project status reporting guidelines. (A rough outline of Peters' proposals is included in Exhibit 5.) Peters distributed draft copies of a Service Request Form and a Progress Report Form, and asked for reactions. Discussion was relatively brief, as the SPC members had not seen the forms prior to the meeting. Peters concluded his presentation by commenting:

> Please look these over and give me some feedback within two weeks. Then we can adjust the forms. We can try using them for a while to see if they're workable. If not, we'll revise them. They're only tools.

Exhibit 5
The Marrett Corporation Systems Planning Committee
Project Submission Procedures Proposed at April 23 Meeting

SPC REPRESENTATIVE

A. Receives "sized" major project service from I.S. and asks himself the question:
   —Can project be held for submission at the annual SPC planning meeting?

B. If yes:
   —Hold project for submission at annual SPC planning session.

C. If no:
   —Contact SPC chairman to put project submission on agenda for next monthly SPC meeting.

D. Present project at SPC meeting utilizing the completed service request, cost estimates, and other pertinent information which will aid SPC in determining "worthiness" of project.

SYSTEMS PLANNING COMMITTEE

A. Is project being submitted as part of the SPC's annual planning?

B. If yes, review project, prioritize against other projects and either approve or reject project.

C. If approved, approval is to expand resources for the Systems Requirements phase only.
D. If no, then it must be a project submitted in a monthly meeting. Review project, evaluate its worthiness, determine if it should be added to SPC plan or rejected.
E. If added to SPC plan, determine its priority and adjust (modify) plan.
F. If a project submitted to SPC (either in annual planning or monthly meetings) is rejected, the SPC member takes this decision back to the appropriate manager with an explanation. The project is then either "dead" or it is revised or restructured for future submission to the SPC.

HOW IS A PROJECT SUBMITTED?

Functional Area

A. An individual has an idea (need) which involves using the I.S. Resource.
B. The individual takes his idea (need) to his manager.
C. The manager agrees the idea (need) is realistic and is worth pursuing.
D. The need is documented by the project initiator and his manager using a service request.
E. The service request is forwarded from the manager to the appropriate SPC representative.

SPC Representative

A. The SPC representative reviews the service request, and evaluates its merit in relation to other projects, asks questions, becomes familiar with the need.
B. The SPC representative may reject the project at this time and return it to the requesting manager.
C. The SPC representative may concur the project has merit. He will then sign the service request and forward it to I.S. for "sizing."

I.S.

A. I.S. receives service requests from SPC representatives (no one else) and assigns the request a project number.
B. I.S. performs a technical evaluation of the service request and sizes the project.
C. Is the request a minor project?
D. If yes, return copy of service request to SPC representative and begin work on project.
E. If no, then it must be a major project. Return a copy of the service request along with sizing and estimating data to the SPC representative. Do not begin any work on this service request unless the project is a government requirement or required for the continuation of the business per SPC representative.

Jack Sommerfield mentioned that he hoped both the projected and actual cost and man-hour data on the two forms would include user funding and personnel commitments as well as those coming from Information Services. Following a brief discussion it was decided to include user costs on several "test" projects to determine what kind of impact the data would have.

The remaining ninety minutes of the meeting were devoted to a review of the Consolidated Order Entry Project being managed by Jack Sommerfield, and to several new project requests. The SPC approved Tony Bloom's request to do a Requirements

Definition for an on-line credit management system, but rejected two enhancements to Bloom's existing cash management system. Don Jordan told Bloom that he could provide the needed information from existing independent reports. Bloom agreed to review the reports, but indicated he would resubmit his requests if he felt the reports were insufficient. Don Jordan then presented a request to modify a minor payroll system. The SPC approved a study of the project, although several members questioned the project's ROI and pointed out that the study had been all but rejected during the October 1979 planning session. The study was approved this time, however, because Jordan argued that the issue was not ROI but data accuracy. He maintained that a new system was essential for government reporting purposes.

Following discussion of several other minor support and conversion projects, the meeting was adjourned for lunch at 1:00 p.m.

MIKE ROSS'S CONCERNS

Following the meeting, Mike Ross spoke briefly with the casewriter regarding his feelings about the development of the Systems Planning Committee. Ross was generally pleased with the role being played by the committee; however, he did express several concerns:

> I guess the thing I really wonder about is whether the time and effort being put into this group is worth it, as far as the company is concerned. Have we saved ourselves a lot of problems? It's awfully hard to measure costs not incurred!
>
> As far as the future is concerned, my major question is, where do we go from here? I think the SPC is developing a good working pattern, but I'm not sure about what direction it should take from now on. How can we best build on the foundation we've got now?

COMPREHENSIVE CASE 2

General Foods Information Services Department

Leslie R. Porter

Ed Schefer, vice president of Information Services at General Foods, looked back at the accomplishments of his department over the past year with considerable satisfaction. Since June 1981 the number of personal computers had increased from 10, authorized on an ad hoc, informal basis, to more than 70 which were acquired under the new policy of personal computers.

Schefer realized that the success of the new policy depended on being able to strike an appropriate balance between encouraging managers to find profitable uses for personal computers and discouraging too rapid growth of what could be an expensive passing fad. ISD had taken specific steps towards achieving this balance. It had 1) set up the Personal Computer Placement Advisory Council, with the unanimous support of all functional units and divisions, to help the various departments find ways to use personal computers to their best advantage, 2) launched the Executive Development Program to acquaint senior managers with the potential opportunities of these new tools, and 3) opened a computer store just one week ago where managers and other employees of GF's functional units could experiment and familiarize themselves with personal computers before deciding to acquire one. The computer store also offered classes for interested employees in how to use the computer. While these achievements were substantial, Ed Schefer knew there was much left to do.

COMPANY BACKGROUND

Several food processing firms, notably Maxwell House Coffee and Jell-O, joined forces with the Post cereals business in the early twenties to form General Foods (GF). By 1982, with net annual sales well past the $8 billion dollar mark, GF was one of the world's leading producers of packaged grocery products, such as Sanka, Bird's Eye, Tang, Shake 'n Bake, and Gaines among others. Seventy percent of GF sales came from the U.S. market, but the international market was increasing in importance.

In the seventies, after an abortive attempt at diversification, General Foods settled into a period of slow, steady growth. By the end of the decade, the company was losing market share in its leading products, such as coffee, and faced a need to develop a more aggressive growth strategy to maintain its position of dominance for the future. In 1980 General Foods reorganized into four sectors, giving increased responsibility and authority to the sector management. (See Exhibit 1.)

Packaged Convenience Foods. Net sales of this sector, the largest of the four, account for 40 percent of GF total net sales. The sector has six product groups and four

---

Exhibit 1
General Foods Corporation
Corporate Management

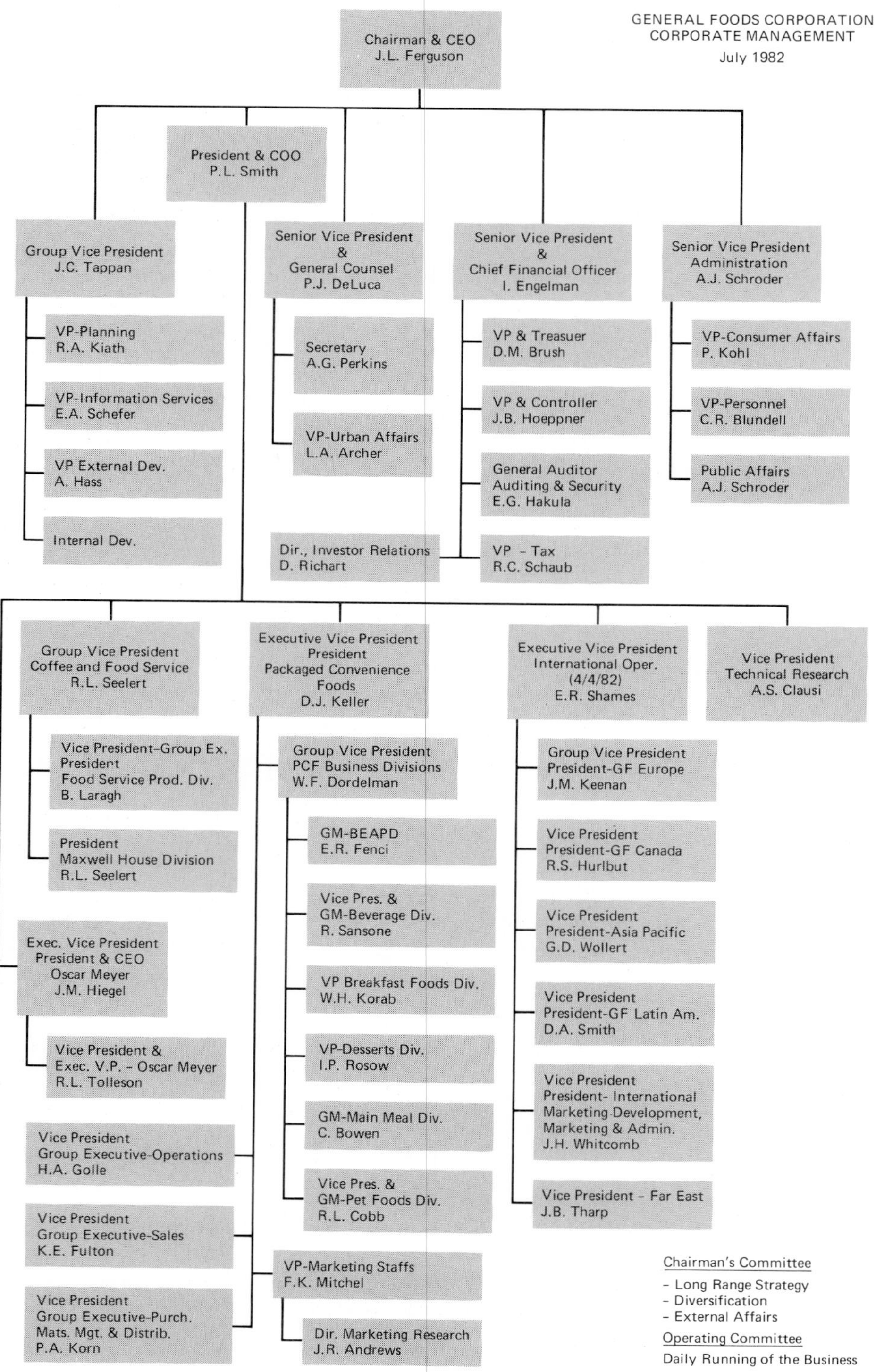
GENERAL FOODS CORPORATION
CORPORATE MANAGEMENT
July 1982
Chairman & CEO
J.L. Ferguson
President & COO
P.L. Smith
Group Vice President
J.C. Tappan
VP-Planning
R.A. Kiath
VP-Information Services
E.A. Schefer
VP External Dev.
A. Hass
Internal Dev.
Senior Vice President
&
General Counsel
P.J. DeLuca
Secretary
A.G. Perkins
VP-Urban Affairs
L.A. Archer
Senior Vice President
&
Chief Financial Officer
I. Engelman
VP & Treasuer
D.M. Brush
VP & Controller
J.B. Hoeppner
General Auditor
Auditing & Security
E.G. Hakula
Dir., Investor Relations
D. Richart
VP - Tax
R.C. Schaub
Senior Vice President
Administration
A.J. Schroder
VP-Consumer Affairs
P. Kohl
VP-Personnel
C.R. Blundell
Public Affairs
A.J. Schroder
Group Vice President
Coffee and Food Service
R.L. Seelert
Vice President-Group Ex.
President
Food Service Prod. Div.
B. Laragh
President
Maxwell House Division
R.L. Seelert
Exec. Vice President
President & CEO
Oscar Meyer
J.M. Hiegel
Vice President &
Exec. V.P. - Oscar Meyer
R.L. Tolleson
Vice President
Group Executive-Operations
H.A. Golle
Vice President
Group Executive-Sales
K.E. Fulton
Vice President
Group Executive-Purch.
Mats. Mgt. & Distrib.
P.A. Korn
Executive Vice President
President
Packaged Convenience
Foods
D.J. Keller
Group Vice President
PCF Business Divisions
W.F. Dordelman
GM-BEAPD
E.R. Fenci
Vice Pres. &
GM-Beverage Div.
R. Sansone
VP Breakfast Foods Div.
W.H. Korab
VP-Desserts Div.
I.P. Rosow
GM-Main Meal Div.
C. Bowen
Vice Pres. &
GM-Pet Foods Div.
R.L. Cobb
VP-Marketing Staffs
F.K. Mitchel
Dir. Marketing Research
J.R. Andrews
Executive Vice President
International Oper.
(4/4/82)
E.R. Shames
Group Vice President
President-GF Europe
J.M. Keenan
Vice President
President-GF Canada
R.S. Hurlbut
Vice President
President-Asia Pacific
G.D. Wollert
Vice President
President-GF Latin Am.
D.A. Smith
Vice President
President- International
Marketing Development,
Marketing & Admin.
J.H. Whitcomb
Vice President - Far East
J.B. Tharp
Vice President
Technical Research
A.S. Clausi
Chairman's Committee
- Long Range Strategy
- Diversification
- External Affairs
Operating Committee
Daily Running of the Business

functional support groups organized as a matrix. The functional support groups service not only the product divisions of Packaged Convenience Foods but also the two divisions of the Coffee and Food Services sector. Thus all the products sold by these two sectors as well as many of the products sold by the International Operations sector are produced in the 20 General Foods plants that report functionally through this sector. Each plant is operated as a cost center and may produce several GF products.

Coffee and Food Services. Coffee is viewed at GF as its flagship product and the company takes great pride in the fact that Maxwell House is the nations' largest selling coffee. This sector is also responsible for the Food Services Products Division, which deals with institutional clients who purchase many of GF's products.

International Operations. This sector is becoming increasingly important as GF strives to increase its sales volume. It is broken down into four geographical regions, with each region responsible for profits in the area it serves. In addition to the products GF manufactures in the United States, the international operation manufactures and sells products that are unique to the region served. While the regions share a marketing and development function, each region has its own administrative support function, such as personnel, with the heads of these having dotted-line relationships to their functional counterpart in the United States.

Oscar Mayer. Of the four sectors, Oscar Mayer is the most autonomous and least integrated into the GF corporation. With its headquarters in Madison, Wisconsin, Oscar Mayer has been left pretty much intact since it was acquired in May 1981. So far, it shares none of the corporate functional support resources, though the heads of its functional support units do have a dotted-line relationship with their counterparts at corporate headquarters in White Plains.

GF's corporate management was aware that changing its orientation towards growth would require more than a change in organizational structure. As James Ferguson, chairman and CEO, asserted:

> We are encouraging managers to take an aggressive stance, one that's oriented toward growth. All of us must be willing to take prudent risks to attain it.
>
> It boils down to what you might call the "culture" of a company. And we are changing our corporate culture—by articulating goals, increasing risk levels. By doing so, we have established the kind of environment in which aggressiveness and risk will be rewarded, recognizing that people may fail once in a while.
>
> The ultimate responsibility lies with the people running the business. We have told our various sectors: "You tell us how you can do your job better, and we'll support you." We find we are gaining their wholehearted commitment to this cultural change, because it's fun and rewarding to build a business.

To emphasize this change away from cost control to growth, GF added two new operating goals. First, each sector must meet its own specific growth targets to generate volume growth that is greater than the growth of the aggregate market. Second, each sector must accelerate its investments in new and existing businesses. These investments must add value to GF through incremental cash returns and growth in earnings.

INFORMATION SERVICES DIVISION

In the late 1970s GF became concerned about the effectiveness of its information services function. A review by external consultants reported:

> To a considerable extent, the facilities planning responsibility is fragmented throughout the various information services organizations within the corporation. As is frequently the case when facilities planning is performed and controlled on a decentralized basis by people who have other full-time responsibilities, facilities decisions appear to be made on a reactive rather than on a carefully planned basis. The overall results of the decentralized planning process is a diverse picture of hardware, facilities plans of varying quality, unnecessarily high costs to satisfy processing requirements, and significant barriers to the use of common systems. As was found in the project team's review of the existing systems plans, there is no comprehensive corporate facilities plan which defines the long-range strategic direction that the company plans to follow in providing operational support for its future information requirements.

The study concluded that GF ranked relatively low in its adoption of information systems technology when compared to other major consumer goods companies of similar size and sophistication.

In 1978 GF had 16 data centers located throughout the country. Two were in the corporate offices, one at Battle Creek (360/65) and the other in White Plains (360/65, 370/158). In addition, each of the SBUs and plants had some data processing capability. The Distribution, Sales and Service Division had four regional centers, each with either an IBM 370/138 or 370/125. Food Products Divison had a 370/138 in Dover and the plants had System 34s. Pet Foods, Beverage and Breakfast Foods, and Maxwell House all had some degree of data processing support in their plants.

Along with the proliferation of equipment throughout GF went a proliferation of applications and approaches to the applications. The marketing function had 26 different systems for sales tracking and analysis, 13 systems related to call reporting, and 10 systems for sales forecasting. The main reasons given for this proliferation of duplicate systems were incompatibility of hardware and a general lack of communication about what other divisions were doing.

Despite this large number of installed systems, few aids were provided to managers to help them in increasing sales or reducing costs. Interviews with users indicated that the information they received was often neither timely nor useful.

- I know the information is available in our current systems but I can't get it in the format (or within the time frame) that I need it.
- This report has information which I consider critical, but it is so difficult to dig it out from the details, that it's not worth the effort.
- Yet, I get that voluminous report once a month. My secretary files the new one, throws away the old one, and I seldom, if ever, reference it.
- We collect the data on a daily basis, but when I see it in a report, it's ten days old and no longer actionable.

- If we could state plant costs on a comparable basis, we could make those decisions with more confidence.
- That other function collects the information at the level of detail we need it, but we don't have access to the detail.

Expenditures for data processing had grown to over $35 million by 1978. The report on the information services function concluded that a real need existed for more centralized control of this resource and anticipated three primary advantages. First, large savings could accrue from centralizing the hardware in White Plains and distributing the processing capability only to those plants that had unique needs for local processing. Further, these plants that required local processing capability should all use the same hardware to facilitate the sharing of software. Second, centralized control of software development would bring significant savings by eliminating duplication in projects and providing more cost effectiveness through a larger development group. Third, centralizing would allow those responsible for information resources to focus on software that would support the strategic objectives of the corporation as a whole. Jim Tappan, group vice president with responsibility for Planning & Development as well as Information Services, saw ISD supporting the corporate strategic objectives in two ways. First, by providing better and more timely information, ISD would support the goal of building GF's base businesses. Second, ISD needed to take an active role in helping the divisions and functional departments meet their strategic objective of controlling and reducing corporate administrative costs.

By 1982, the ISD budget had grown to over $50 million, and most of the recommendations arising from the 1978 review had been implemented. Information Services Department was now a centrally directed function, with a corporate staff that managed business information systems for the Coffee and Food Services sector, Packaged Convenience Foods sector, the domestic divisions, and all corporate functions. In addition, it had the responsibility for coordinating the International Operations' systems activity worldwide. Oscar Mayer at the time still had its own MIS function.

ISD had the responsibility not only for data processing, but also management science and telecommunications support. To provide this as well as the systems development support, ISD was divided into five groups (see Exhibit 2).

Business Systems and Client Service. This group is the focal point for ISD's support of clients. It is composed of two units, Business Systems and Client Services. Business Systems is responsible for identifying opportunities to improve business performance by strengthening the business systems, for developing an integrated portfolio of strategic systems and a practical implementation plan for that portfolio, and for satisfying division and sector systems needs.

Business Systems staff include among their roles: assuring commonality of business information, translating business solutions into data processing designs, determining the feasibility and economic practicality of systems solutions to business problems, and providing overall project management to most systems projects.

Client Services is staffed by Client Service managers, each assigned to a sector or a division, and each responsible for assisting the client in developing and executing systems plans. The Client Services managers helps his or her client to identify business problems, explore alternatives and determine which are the most appropriate systems

Exhibit 2
General Foods Information Services Department

GENERAL FOODS CORPORATION

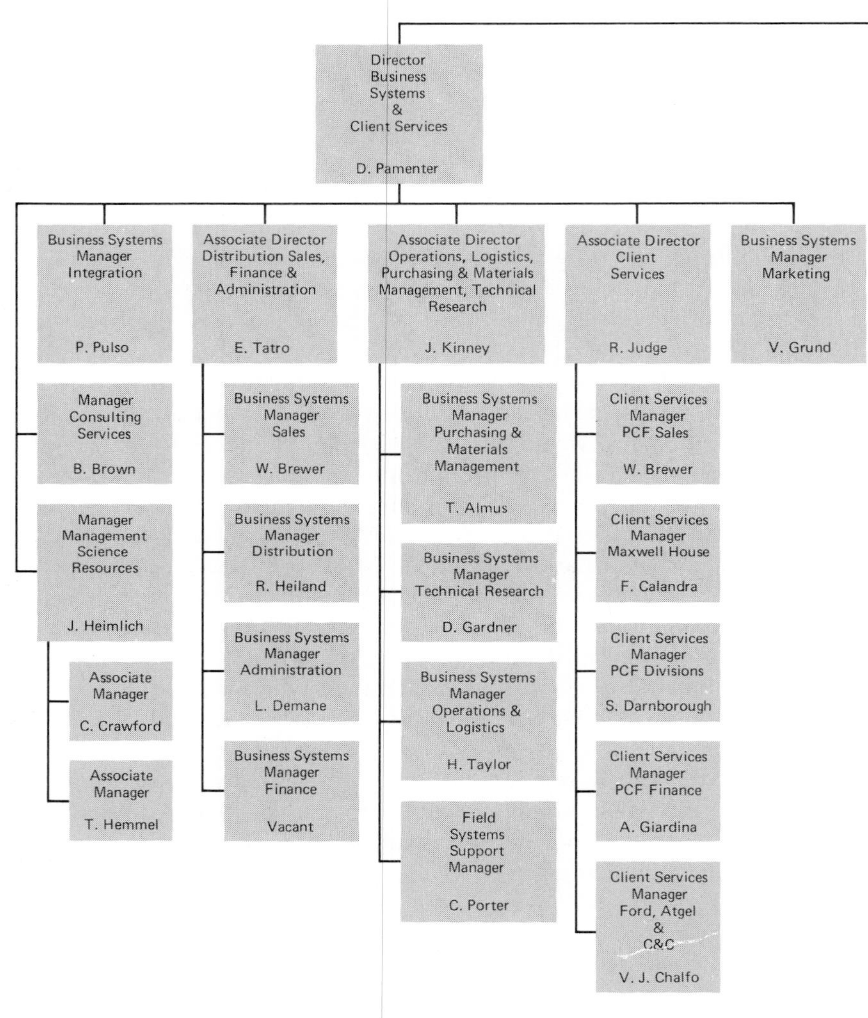

Exhibit 2 (*continued*)

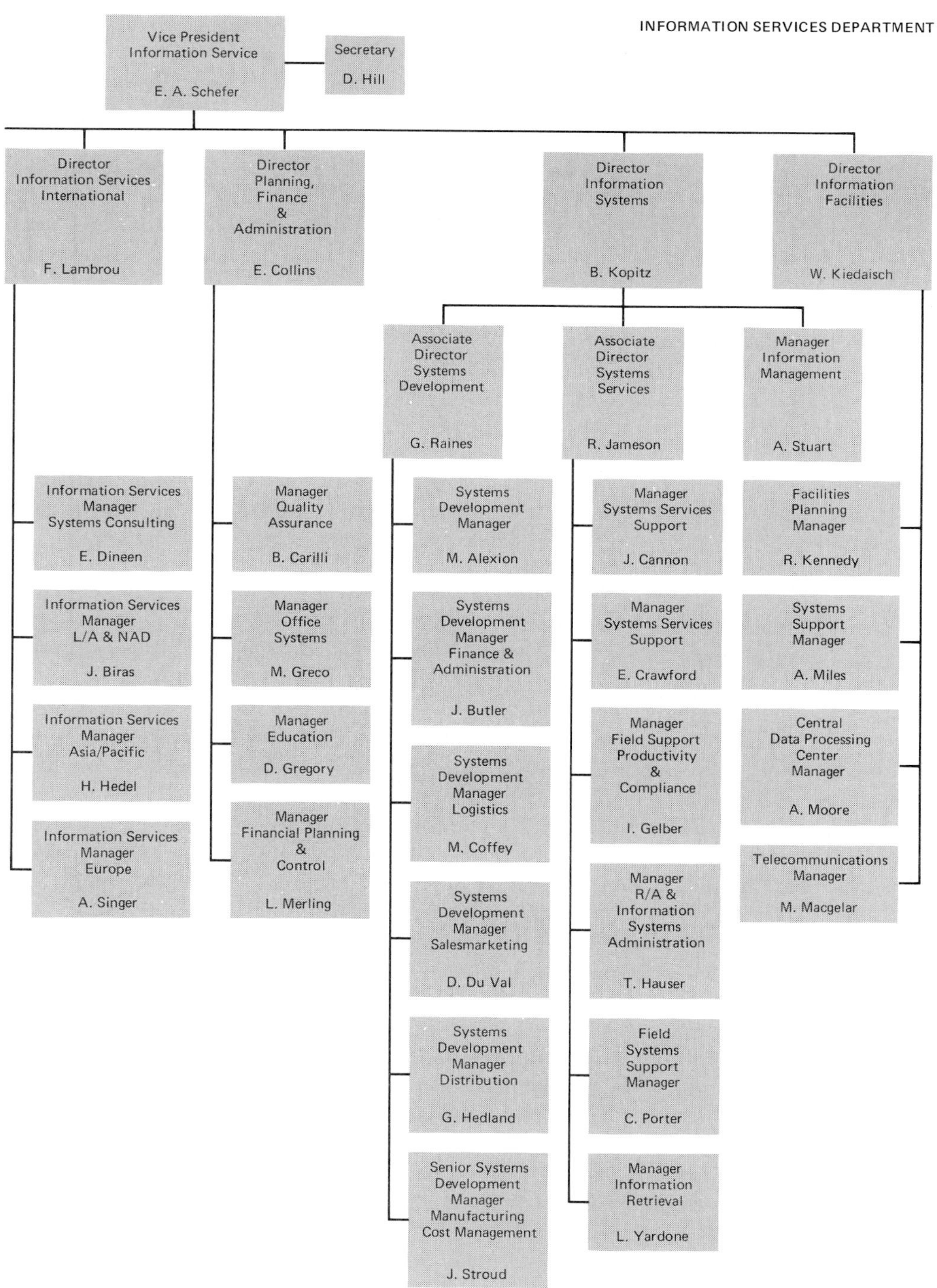

INFORMATION SERVICES DEPARTMENT
Vice President Information Service E. A. Schefer
Secretary D. Hill
Director Information Services International F. Lambrou
Director Planning, Finance & Administration E. Collins
Director Information Systems B. Kopitz
Director Information Facilities W. Kiedaisch
Associate Director Systems Development G. Raines
Associate Director Systems Services R. Jameson
Manager Information Management A. Stuart
Information Services Manager Systems Consulting E. Dineen
Information Services Manager L/A & NAD J. Biras
Information Services Manager Asia/Pacific H. Hedel
Information Services Manager Europe A. Singer
Manager Quality Assurance B. Carilli
Manager Office Systems M. Greco
Manager Education D. Gregory
Manager Financial Planning & Control L. Merling
Systems Development Manager M. Alexion
Systems Development Manager Finance & Administration J. Butler
Systems Development Manager Logistics M. Coffey
Systems Development Manager Salesmarketing D. Du Val
Systems Development Manager Distribution G. Hedland
Senior Systems Development Manager Manufacturing Cost Management J. Stroud
Manager Systems Services Support J. Cannon
Manager Systems Services Support E. Crawford
Manager Field Support Productivity & Compliance I. Gelber
Manager R/A & Information Systems Administration T. Hauser
Field Systems Support Manager C. Porter
Manager Information Retrieval L. Yardone
Facilities Planning Manager R. Kennedy
Systems Support Manager A. Miles
Central Data Processing Center Manager A. Moore
Telecommunications Manager M. Macgelar

solutions, and arranges for support from other areas of Information Services in achieving solutions. The Client Services unit provides feedback from the business units, which helps to insure the practicality and effectiveness of the department's services.

Information Systems. This group is responsible for working closely with business systems in the design, programming, and implementation of systems. It consists of three professional technically oriented units: Systems Development, System Services, and Information Management.

Systems development has primary responsibility for technical design, programming, and implementation of large-scale systems which have been identified as strategically important and as supporting the major business thrusts of the corporation.

Systems Services has responsibility for the support of all currently operating GF systems and for the development of others such as process control applications, the management of field data centers at manufacturing locations, and support of time-sharing applications.

Information management focuses on the integration and management of the corporation's data. Included in its responsibilities are data base design, data resource management, and support and performance monitoring of the GF data base environment.

Information Systems presently employs over 300 programmers and other professionals. Approximately 150 of these professionals are permanently located in the 17 plants that have data processing capability, while the remaining 150 are split more or less evenly between new System Development and Systems Services.

Information Facilities. This group has functional responsibility for GF information processing facilities and provides a service-oriented operation across the corporation. The group manages the corporate data processing center and all voice and data network facilities. Within this group are specialists in hardware, systems software, and telecommunications.

In 1982 the equipment at GF included an IBM 370/158 and a 3033 operating in an MVS environment supporting their transaction-oriented systems. GF's general purpose time-sharing needs are met with two IBM 4300s running CMS. At that time 17 of their 23 plants supported local processing and the sending and receiving of data with System 34s which were to be replaced with System 38s. While these machines were owned by the plants, the staff (7 to 9 supporting operations, data entry and programming), as discussed earlier, reported to information services.

In addition, 18 of the 20 distribution centers have IBM Model 34s for order entry. These machines have no support staff at all. There are also four regional centers, one of which has an IBM 370/138 and the remaining three have IBM 370/135s. These machines were scheduled to be replaced with System 34s.

Finance, Planning and Administration. This group is responsible for developing the department's strategic and financial plans, operating policies and procedures, and standards; for assurance that all systems developed conform to standards; and for training and development programs to help increase the skills of all information services people.

It is also in charge of developing office systems for the corporation (automating secretarial/clerical activities, electronic mail communications, work simplification studies, and other projects).

International. This is a complete systems management function responsible for coordinating all International Operations systems activities and for integrating International Operations plans and objectives into overall Information Services strategy. It also assists in the transfer of technology and applications between the systems organizations of GF's domestic operations and the various GF international companies.

PERSONAL COMPUTERS

While the recommendations for centralizing information services were being implemented, Ed Schefer had become increasingly concerned about determining the appropriate role for personal computers with General Foods. Towards this end, he participated in numerous discussions on their role with the research board as well as other industry groups. In the summer of 1980, Ed acquired a Radio Shack Model III to be used by the ISD staff to determine their overall potential. But the following summer, significant interest in personal computers was clearly evident within the user departments of GF. ISD had installed one as an experiment six months earlier in the Food Service Products Division which had already achieved productivity gains through the use of its spread sheet program. In June, Sal Andreoli had returned from a tax conference where he met an old friend who had an Apple computer. Sal knew that the system he had, which ISD had charged him $11,000 for development, and was costing him $300 to $400 per month to run, was not meeting his needs. Rather than spend another $13,000 estimated by ISD as necessary to redo the system, Sal felt he should spend only $7,000 to try an Apple computer. His friend had assured him that the applications were straightforward and even offered to come and set them up for him in an afternoon. After ISD had received Sal's proposal to forego the new system in favor of acquiring an Apple, they met with Sal on numerous occasions to make absolutely certain he understood both the limitations of the Apple as well as the potential problems he could expect to encounter.

Up to this time, ISD had been hesitant about taking a position on personal computers because it was not clear how they would fit in. However, with the success of the food services experiment and pressures from other departments, Ed Schefer decided it was time for ISD to develop its policy on this issue. The first problem Ed faced, however, was where to assign responsibility for personal computers. Bill Kiedaisch, director of information facilities (see Exhibit 2) felt that personal computers were primarily another piece of hardware and therefore, that information facilities should have responsibility for their dissemination and control. However, Bernie Kopitz, director of information systems, felt that since the use of these devices was primarily software driven, responsibility for them should fall under his group. Ed, however, felt strongly that the approach taken should focus on the users rather than the technology; consequently the responsibility for personal computers should be located in the ISD marketing area, that is, client services. To this end he asked Bob Judge, associate director of client services, to synthesize the information collected to date and come up with a proposal for General Foods.

Bob Judge's proposal stated that ISD should aggressively support the introduction of personal computers, basically in three areas. First, they were useful as a stand-alone productivity tool to help people do their jobs better. Second, as a prototyping tool, they could be used to develop working models of large systems. Thus, ISD could work with users to create the models of a desired system, get the bugs out, and make certain that the system met the users' needs. This would have a beneficial impact both in the user departments and in ISD. Third, a personal computer could serve as an intelligent terminal to access data on the mainframe. The concern, therefore, should not be on the number of personal computers placed but where they are placed. In an inappropriate location they could be counterproductive because of all the distraction available for these machines. For this reason, Bob felt that it was important to have top management involved in their placement. In addition, Bob proposed setting up an area in GF where the potential user could come and work with personal computers to gain a better understanding of what they could and could not do. Schefer agreed with Bob's proposals and authorized him to implement them.

Bob first secured the involvement of senior management. He met with the heads of every functional unit and every division to explain what ISD was doing and to get from each person the name of a unit or division representative to serve on the Personal Computer Placement Advisory Council (PCPAC). The PCPAC would meet once a quarter to recommend policies with regard to personal computers, thus providing a forum for dissemination of information back to the individual units and divisions. In addition, the signature of the unit's representative on PCPAC would be required for any placement request submitted to ISD for a personal computer, and this, it was felt, would provide the unit head or division president with an assurance that in his area the acquisition program was being controlled. All the unit heads and division presidents agreed, and within a week each had provided the name of the appropriate individual. While in some cases this individual was the unit head or division president himself; in other cases the person nominated was a person in a responsible management position—usually on the staff of the unit head or division president.

In addition to the creation of PCPAC, Bob felt it was very important to raise the overall level of understanding at GF as to the capability of the personal computer, especially with senior management. It was generally accepted that there was a growing gap in senior management's awareness of the potentials of system technology. Bob felt it was important to the future of GF that the top management of the company understand not only the capabilities of these machines but, more important in the broader context, how these systems could have an impact on the functions they manage. To facilitate this Bob proposed establishing the Executive Development Program. In this program the functional heads and division heads would be loaned a personal computer to take home for 120 days and given a structured set of exercises to follow, to build their confidence with the device. The final project required the participant to put up two applications; one from his job, and one from his home.

Lastly, Bob proposed the creation of a computer store within GF. This store would provide interested employees hands-on experience in working with one of three personal computers. He decided that the store should stock Apple IIs, IBM personal computers, and Radio Shack Model IIIs. It would also stock a wide array of software to support the business functions. The store would provide classes in the morning for interested employees to better prepare them to use these devices. GF negotiated favorable purchasing contracts at a number of computer stores in the area and also arranged that GF's employees could purchase personal computers for their own use at the same discount.

In October, Sal Andreoli's tax department received its Apple Computer, and by the following spring every group within the tax department had some applications on the Apple, using either Visicalc or a DB Master, a data base package. In fact, the Apple was being used over 160 hours a month and it was usually necessary to reserve it in advance. As Sal pointed out:

> These things are really cost efficient because they remove all that grunt work from a person's job. I feel I'm using my job time better. I look at it as a job enrichment for those who work for me, for their jobs are becoming more meaningful. People are staying late or coming in early just to get access to the computer because it means that much to them.

By the end of June, the proposals defined in General Foods' strategy statement for implementing GF/ISD's policy on personal computers (Exhibit 3) were almost completely implemented. PCPAC's representatives had approved the purchase of over 70 personal computers. Twenty of GF's senior management were involved in the Executive Development Program and each had a personal computer at home. All were enthusiastic about the opportunity of gaining exposure to this new technology and were convinced that there were many applications for it in the various functions that reported to them. Andrew Schroder, senior vice president—administration, felt that the personal computer helped address a number of issues. Schroder noted:

> I'm not a financial executive. My responsibilities are government relations, consumer affairs, public relations, and corporate personnel. I picked up my computer last Friday and have only worked on it over this past weekend. So far I'm halfway through the chicken farm exercise which involves setting up tables for dealing with inventory issues. I'm about at the point where I wonder whether this is really what I, in my particular capacity, need. However, I'm beginning to get some feel for how one goes about interacting with a computer and I think that will be helpful. Whether I need to get very much further with the chicken farm exercise is another question.
>
> There are some principles here which I would certainly support. One of the issues I've felt strongly about is what we in General Foods are doing about making certain that the learning experience doesn't stop when an individual enters the workplace. So in the broadest form, what this is, is an opportunity for us to continue learning. This would avoid putting ourselves in the unfortunate situation where massive learning has been acquired by our newer entries but is not being understood by the more senior levels of our organization.
>
> A second issue which is applicable to my function, is learning first hand what are the capabilities of personal computers in terms of managing the knowledge mass that we have got to handle in our part of the business. I can't think of any more interesting issue of technology, new technology,

bursting onto the scene than the notion of the personal computer which provides the capability in the office or in one's home of keeping pace with this information. Again, a chicken farm exercise must not be an end in itself but a means to something else. I see the exercises as a means to understanding the computer as a tool for monitoring more effectively the news, either media or congressional events. I'm going to be increasingly interested in ways that it can be harnessed for my particular purposes. Putting together a P&L for hypothetical business again had better be a means to some other more appropriate end, for as an end in and of itself it is going to grow old very quickly.

Exhibit 3
General Foods Information Services Department
Strategy for Implementing GF/ISD Policy
Personal Computing

I. *TOP DOWN DIRECTION*

GF management will set the direction on placement of personal computers in their respective units. Information Services will support all Unit Heads in this process by implementing and managing the on-going aspects of our Executive Development Program on personal computing.

Executive Development Program

Designed to:
A. Inform Unit Heads of the current technology, capabilities and trends from a business perspective.
B. Review the GF/ISD process for providing appropriate guidance and support to assist users in the effective use of this technology.
C. Involve senior management in determining the extent to which their organizations should pursue the personal computing option.
D. Assist Unit Heads in selecting an appropriate delegate to act as that Unit's representation on the Advisory and Placement Council.

Advisory and Placement Council

The Personal Computer Advisory Council will meet on a quarterly basis for the purposes of constructively reviewing and discussing policies, processes, activities and uses of personal computers across GF. The activities of this group will result in periodic reports to senior management on the status of personal computers in the company.

The council is a forum to foster understanding within GF and to insure consistent communication of policies progress and plans. The make-up of the group will consist of representatives from each functional area and division appointed by the unit head.

II. *FACILITY SUPPORT*

Information Services will maintain a support facility that will assist Units in the placement and use of personal computers. The facility will consist essentially of the following:

A. *Personal Computer Center*
   1. A facility designed to serve the units educational needs, demonstrate equipment (current Apple, IBM, TRS-80), software and selected applications, and

Exhibit 3 (*continued*)

counsel users and potential users on the myriad of tools and packages available.

2. This center will provide GF Units with a single contact and coordinating point for obtaining purchases at the best possible price, ensuring maintenance and service contracts are in order, and provide trouble shooting/problem solving service to the Units.

B. *Loan Program*
Accompanying the Executive Development Program is a loan program of personal computers for up to 120 days. This program is managed through the computer center and is designed to increase management's awareness and understanding of how technology based information processing and tools can impact their operation, via hands-on activity.

GF POLICY ON PERSONAL BUSINESS COMPUTERS

POLICY STATEMENT
It is the policy of General Foods to promote the effective use of technology based productivity tools—namely, personal computers through an active program of coordination and support. This responsibility resides in Corporate Information Services and:

1. Recommends policy and strategy to senior GF management.
2. Supports all GF Units in identifying the appropriateness of personal computers for specific needs.

It is also the policy of General Foods that each Unit is responsible for determining the business justification for personal computers in their organization.

DEFINITION
Personal computers are technology based information tools, sometimes referred to as "micro" computers which are usually desk top sized and cost less than $7,500 to purchase.

CORPORATE INFORMATION SERVICES
A. *Consulting and Advisory Role*
Corporate Information Services will maintain a current knowledge of the state-of-the-art technology and developing trends relating to personal computers, and will help potential or current users by:

1. Assisting GF business units and functions in determining the appropriate use of personal computers as productivity and decision making aids.
2. Assisting clients in the actual use of those tools through education and training programs appropriate to individual area needs.
3. Providing support in determining the appropriate hardware and software to meet needs at minimum cost.

B. *Concurrence Role*
Corporate Information Services Personal Computer Center will be the central facility for concurring on the purchase and placement of personal computers to en-

Exhibit 3 (*continued*)

sure that:

1. Hardware and software is obtained at the lowest cost.
2. Adequate service is negotiated and provided when required.
3. Users of personal computers are informed of new developments.
4. Information Services overall strategies and support resources remain tuned to the developing activity in the individual units.

This will enable ISD to maintain a central inventory of equipment and software in order to facilitate sharing of experience, software developments, etc.

USER AREA RESPONSIBILITY
Decision authority on use and placement of personal computers resides with the unit head and is based on the units assessment of business justification and assurance that its usage is consistent with the units mission. The user will be responsible for equipment operation and physical security.

ACCOUNTING CONSIDERATIONS
Accounting Financial Policy No. 28 requires that all costs related to the purchase of Personal Computers be expensed at the time of purchase. Control of these expenditures will be through the normal budget process.

June 7 was the opening day of Bob's Byte Boutique, as Bob's computer store had become affectionately called. The store had a classroom with ten Radio Shack Model IIIs and a large screen TV. Because Bob had chosen to restrict the class size so that each student had a machine to work with, each class could only accommodate eight students. The classes were so successful that they quickly became booked up for two months in advance. Bob charged the student's sponsoring department $25 a student. The charge was intended to provide a minimum amount of inconvenience—thereby, it was hoped, limiting the enrollment to those who had a serious interest. Further, it had been hoped that those who enrolled in the class would feel obliged to attend, given that their department was going to be charged whether they came or not. The computer store was open from 12 noon to 4:30 p.m. for anyone to come and experiment at no charge.

While everyone in ISD management was extremely supportive of Bob Judge's effort in raising the general level of computer literacy within General Foods there was some disagreement as to what would be the total potential benefits. For instance, Bernie Kopitz and Bill Kiedaisch both felt that the interest in personal computing was based, to a large extent, on a general misunderstanding as to the capabilities of the machines, and that this provided an excellent educational opportunity which alone could justify the expense. As Ed Collins, director of Planning, Finance, and Administration said:

> The installation of these 70 or so personal computers provided an excellent cost effective opportunity which was well worth the investment of $350,000. Even if you assumed two dollars of personal time for one dollar of computer cost, the cost to GF was only one hundredth of one percent of GF's net revenue. Besides, very few new individual systems could be developed for under $350,000.

Bill Kiedaisch emphasized the importance of this educational aspect of GF's personal computer policy as follows:

> The person coming in the door who says "Gee, I've never had a computer before but now I can use it," sees a lot of potential benefit that probably will not materialize. People like CMS with its broad range of software; capability to share data; and this is what they need to solve their problem. They can use vehicles like Visicalc but eventually they are going to say "How do I get the general ledger data into my Visicalc model, massage it, and put it back"? This opens up the whole broad issue of centralized data management. Further, there is just as much discipline required in programming a personal computer as there is in programming a Cray computer. As people bump against these limitations they are going to take a different point of view and eventually these things are going to collect dust. However, we have to let the people get hands-on experience if they are going to begin to understand the benefits and the limitations of personal computers. That's what we are looking to achieve.

Bernie Kopitz added for emphasis:

> A minority of these computers will stick to the ribs but the majority will fall off and collect dust. That's what is really underlying our basic philosophy in setting up the computer store. Let them try it and get it out of their systems rather than going out and buying a computer for anyone who is interested. Just because their sixth grade child can sit at a micro and program it, they come in here and say, "I can do everything for myself with only a one-time cost of a few thousand dollars. I don't have to pay you to do what I need. I'm going to try it." We give them one of these things to try for awhile and most of them will come back. They will realize they can't do everything they want.

In discussions with ISD's senior management several concerns were raised on the introduction of personal computers. First, Bill Kiedaisch felt that rather than being a productivity aid the personal computer could actually be counterproductive:

> As far as productivity is concerned, this is where I feel we have the biggest trap. Unless you have a vehicle like Visicalc where a person sits down and become productive immediately, who knows how much time managers waste trying to program these things. You can't take a guy who is supposed to be forecasting sales and let him get enamored with the hardware and software. He's not going to be doing his job.

Another problem of concern often expressed was the potential for departments to become operationally dependent on systems developed on their personal computers. These systems are not likely to be adequately documented, and thus when the person who developed them is promoted, or worse, leaves GF, there is the danger that the department could not function at its full effectiveness. While ISD strongly discourages the development of such systems, they believe once the user has the machine it is really out of ISD's hands. As Bernie stressed:

> Let him not back up his system, let him not document it, that's his prerogative. That's how he saves his money. If he wants all those things, he may as well pay us to do it.

As Bill pointed out earlier, there was also the problem of data security and access. To cope with the problem of data access, in general, ISD had already formed the Data Access Center as part of the Information Management group. This center is staffed with people who are responsible for providing data from any of GF's data bases in whatever form the user needs it, in a timely manner. This data could be provided in printed reports or in files in the data interchange format (DIF) which can be accessed by personal computers. The Data Access Center, with its extensive data dictionary, provides the interface between the data and the users. It is at this point that ISD managers feel that they can at least control who has access to what data. Further, it is ISD policy that all updates to this data be done on GF's mainframe. Thus, a user who needs to work with the most current data can simply download the data from the mainframe to the personal computer. This approach limits the user's responsibility for the security of the data, as the files of record are the data files stored on the mainframe.

Ed Schefer was well aware of the potential problems, such as data and program security, inappropriate use of management and employee time, and excessive expenditure of corporate funds for something that ultimately would not be used. But he felt that the significant potential for productivity gains made it essential to pursue the opportunities presented by personal computers. He hoped that this policy would serve to strengthen the relationship between users and ISD. Further, he hoped that this relationship would give ISD the credibility needed to provide the kind of guidance that would prevent users from falling into any of the potential pitfalls.

COMPREHENSIVE CASE 3

Heidelberg Chemicals

Andrew Grindley

> "I guess I'm on the Steering Committee to protect the interests of the Agrichemicals Division. We can't seem to get service out of the Data Processing Department and although it has not hurt us much yet, we have had to do some manual data manipulation because we could not get our systems changed. We would like eventually to have our program modified to let us get the reports we need by entering the data in the same form as we receive them. But the systems people have been too busy developing the on-line system for the Industrial Division; they haven't had time for us. At the monthly Steering Committee meetings I keep pressing for more service for Agrichemicals."

Ms. Fabian was not complaining. She was simply responding to the question of why she was on the Data Processing Steering Committee. She was an operations analyst in the Agrichemicals Division of Heidelberg Chemicals Inc. and was responsible for preparing reports for management and for government bodies on the chemicals purchased and sold for various agricultural purposes. These chemicals included fertilizers, animal food additives, veterinary supplies, pesticides and insecticides.

THE COMPANY

Heidelberg Chemicals, Inc. was a wholly-owned subsidiary of a German chemical firm. Located in Boston, it sold approximately $30 million in chemicals each year. The company did no manufacturing although it did some blending and packaging of products which it purchased in bulk.

The German parent also owned another company, Pennsylvania Chemicals, Inc. which sold approximately $100 million per year. A second kindred company of Heidelberg's, Bedford Dye Inc., was located in New Bedford, Mass. and did much of the chemical manufacturing for small firms such as Heidelberg. The total of the sales of all three American subsidiaries represented approximately 6% of the worldwide sales of the 80 affiliated companies.

Heidelberg Chemicals Inc. was managed as two operating divisions, Industrial Chemicals and Agricultural Chemicals, usually referred to as Agrichemicals. 1979 sales of the Industrial Division amounted to $12 million and for the Agricultural Division, $18 million. A third division, Administration, cut across both of the other two and was responsible for all financial and administrative matters for the whole company.

The two operating divisions performed mainly a marketing function but they also took responsibility for warehousing their products and some blending and repackaging.

Case material of the Western School of Business Administration is prepared as a basis for classroom discussion. This case was prepared by Professor Andrew Grindlay.

Each of the three divisions was headed by a Vice President who, as one of his many duties, sat on the Data Processing Steering Committee.

COMPUTING AT HEIDELBERG CHEMICALS

The company got started in processing data in 1960 on unit record equipment rented from IBM. Mr. George Lake was retained at that time to run the equipment and to supervise the newly-hired keypunch operators. Later, the unit record machines were replaced by an IBM 360/20 card system which in 1971 was replaced by a Univac 9300 and in February 1980, by a Univac 90/30 computer. It had 160,000 bytes of memory, six disk drives, a card reader, a printer, and a video terminal which was located in the computer room and used by the programmers.

Over the years systems had been developed for all three divisions of the company by programmers who had been hired by Mr. Lake. One of them, Mr. Don Patton, joined the firm in 1968 as a programmer/trainee and as he had had no training or experience in computing, was sent on IBM courses to learn RPG and COBOL. In 1970 he was made Systems and Programming Manager, reporting to Mr. Lake who in turn reported to the Vice President, Administration.

About two thirds of the programs in use were written in RPG, a simple, easy-to-use language with rather limited capabilities, and the remainder in COBOL, a more powerful but more difficult language. The company payroll was not processed on Heidelberg Chemicals' computer. Instead it was done by one of the large banks at an agreed price per check.

Data Processing grew within the Heidelberg Company and in 1974 Mr. Robert MacDonald was employed as Vice President, Administration, and given responsibility for the systems and data processing. In 1979 there were eight people in the department; Mr. Lake, Mr. Patton, a programmer/analyst, a programmer, a supervisor of data entry and control, two data entry clerks, and a computer operator. The supervisor of data entry and control also served as backup computer operator. About 60% of the time of the two programmers was used to maintain and enhance existing programs.

Shortly after he was appointed Mr. MacDonald received a letter from the data processing manager at the parent company in Germany outlining the company's policy on computing. It was policy, the letter said, to charge out all system development and all computer operations costs to the operating divisions. Further, within two years annual systems and data processing costs including a space charge of 15% of actual expenditures should be held to no more than 1% of sales. Finally, Mr. MacDonald was urged to meet with his counterparts from the two other U.S. subsidiaries, both of which had machines of their own, to explore the possibility of the joint use of a single computer.

On receiving the letter and having had no experience in systems and data processing, Mr. MacDonald formed a Steering Committee to help him to manage it. He asked the other two Vice-Presidents to serve, along with Mr. Lake, Mr. Patton, Mr. Tom Hill, who was the Industrial Chemicals Marketing Research and Planning Director, and Ms. Judy Fabian, the operations analyst in the Agrichemicals Division. Mr. MacDonald was chairman. At one of the early meetings Mr. MacDonald presented to the Committee a statement outlining the role of data processing in the company. This statement had been drafted initially by Mr. MacDonald and presented to the firm's Management Committee (the President and the three Vice Presidents). The Management Committee saw two different drafts of the statement before approving the third one. This final version was presented to the Steering Committee in December, 1974 and approved without change. (See Appendix I for the statement as finally approved.)

At the meetings of the Steering Committee, Mr. Patton customarily presented progress reports on the various systems under development and on maintenance and enhancements to existing programs. Other members suggested new systems or modifications to old ones; the Committee decided on priorities and recommended additional resources where appropriate. For example, in 1978 when Mr. Patton and Mr. Lake thought it was time to replace the Univac 9300 computer they presented a proposal to the Steering Committee which authorized Mr. Lake to issue a Request for Proposal (R.F.P.) to computer vendors. When he and Mr. Patton had selected the Univac 90/30 from the several proposed, the Steering Committee approved the acquisition and the Vice President of administration wrote to the parent organization in Germany for authorization. The main reason given to justify the new equipment was that the Industrial Chemicals Division had asked Mr. Lake to develop an on-line order entry system for them which would require a computer with greater capabilities than the one they had. In addition, the existing computer was becoming unreliable and was taking longer to repair when it did fail. In 1977, for example, it was unavailable during scheduled operating hours for a total of 345 hours.

The data processing officials at the parent company wrote a long letter to Mr. MacDonald asking for additional information. They wanted to know the reasons for the 345 hours of downtime in 1977 and also requested a project plan for the development of the on-line order entry system. They wanted to know, too, why Heidelberg had rejected the IBM System 34 in favor of the Univac 90/30. They pointed out that an affiliated company, Bedford Dye, Inc., had a small System 34, tended by one person, and strongly urged Mr. MacDonald to try to work with both Bedford Dye and Pennsylvania Chemicals to coordinate their data processing activities and perhaps share computing resources. They also wanted to review any final contract with a computer vendor before it was signed by Heidelberg and urged Mr. MacDonald to try to negotiate more flexible terms for a broken contract, a lower price, a maintenence guarantee, and a provision whereby Heidelberg would incur no maintenance charges for the first three months of the installation.

There followed a period of several months of negotiations between the data processing officials in Germany, Mr. MacDonald and Univac with Mr. Lake and Mr. Patton providing most of the contact with Univac. Finally the order was placed and the contract signed.

THE ON-LINE ORDER ENTRY SYSTEM

Under the order entry procedure then in use, when a customer telephoned an order to Heidelberg Chemicals, a clerk at the order desk searched through a tub file of cards to find the customer's card to get credit and shipping information and then searched through an inventory tub file to learn if the required products were in stock. As there were approximately 1,000 items in stock it usually took a few seconds to find the correct card before being able to accept the customer's order. The card showed not only the quantity on hand but also the price and other relevant product information. After accepting the customer's order the clerk wrote the quantities in pencil on the appropriate cards, and then prepared a shipping order. Later, after the goods were shipped, this order was returned to the order desk where another clerk went back to the inventory cards and wrote in pen the actual quantities shipped and a new balance on hand. When a shipment was received from a supplier, the card was updated. If, on scanning the inventory card, the order clerk discovered that they were out of an item, before telling a customer she checked a third tub file containing purchase orders, to be able to tell the customer when a new supply was expected. While this procedure sometimes took only a few seconds, it occasionally kept the customer waiting on the telephone for several minutes. An on-line order entry system, the Vice President of Industrial Chemicals felt, would reduce the average time it took a customer to place an order.

Six clerks worked in the order desk area answering the telephones, checking card files and updating records as goods were shipped or received. They enjoyed their work and thought the system worked well. When asked if they thought a computerized system would improve things, in unison they say "no." Several suppliers they occasionally called had computerized systems and the clerks reported that these calls invariably took longer than calls to non-computerized suppliers.

A video display terminal had been purchased by the Company in anticipation of the development of an On-Line Order Entry System and had been located in the room where the six clerks worked. Although it had a plastic cover over it and was not yet being used, the clerks viewed the terminal as a threat to their customary way of doing things. They had been told that a new system was being developed but they had not been told how it would be used or what the effect on them would be. They had heard in the employee cafeteria that one of the arguments used to justify the development of the On-Line System was the plan to eliminate one and perhaps two of the six jobs.

To develop the On-Line Order Entry System, Mr. Lake and Mr. Patton had visited Pennsylvania Chemicals Inc., a much larger but similar company to learn how orders were processed there. They learned that Pennsylvania Chemicals had spent a half million dollars for the design of an on-line order entry system and was in the process of writing the programs to make it run on a large IBM 370/158 computer. This machine was several times larger and faster than the Univac 90/30 at Heidelberg Chemicals. Mr. Lake and Mr. Patton decided, however, that with the design specifications developed for Pennsylvania Chemicals they would be able to draw flow diagrams and write the programs for an on-line order entry system of their own. It would not be as large nor as complex as the other company's but they would still require an additional 230,000 bytes of memory on their Univac. The Steering Committee authorized the additional memory at a rental of $10,000 per year, as well as two video display terminals which would cost $3,000 each to purchase. There would be no additional cost for programming because Mr. Patton and one of the programmer/trainees who was already on staff would do the necessary work. To speed up the work, Mr. Patton decided not to draw flow diagrams but to write the COBOL code directly from the detailed specifications provided by Pennsylvania Chemicals.

THE STRUCTURE OF THE ON-LINE ORDER ENTRY SYSTEM

When complete the On-Line Order Entry System would consist of five Modules:

1. The Purchase Order module would allow the direct entry of all purchase orders to a Purchase Order file containing complete information on all orders which had been placed on suppliers and which had not yet been delivered.
2. The Customer File module would allow the Customer file to be updated with new information on address changes, credit information, sales, balance outstanding and unfilled orders.
3. The Product module was designed to introduce into the Product file new information about the products, both raw material and finished goods, carried by the company. This included chemical composition, names of suppliers, product code number and other information that would be used in a sales catalogue carried by a salesman.
4. The Formulation module maintained the Formulation file which contained complete information on the ingredients of all of the end products blended by the company.
5. The Inventory module was to keep a running count of all items stocked, showing both the quantities on hand and quantities on order but not yet delivered.

Some of the information to be used by the new on-line system was already stored in the computer files but these files would be converted to use the file structure required of the information management system provided with the Univac 90/30. Mr. Patton said he planned to write a program to make the conversion. He also planned to run the new on-line system in parallel with the manual system for a few months until he was sure the new one worked properly, at which time the manual system with all its tub files would be abandoned.

EXISTING SYSTEMS

The Univac 90/30 was used for two main purposes. The first was to provide analysis of sales information to the marketing people in both of the operating divisions of the company. The Division Vice Presidents received monthly reports giving sales by product, by salesman, by customer and for the whole division. Costs were also provided as were net profit figures.

The other major use of the Univac was to transmit data on the price and chemical composition of the various raw ingredients of the Agrichemical products to a computer in Rochester, New York. Also sent was information on the finished products to be sold by the Agrichemicals Division. The computer in Rochester, owned by a computer service firm, processed the data in what was called an optimizing model and returned to Heidelberg Chemicals' Univac the most economical mix of ingredients to meet the product specifications. The model was written in the FORTRAN language and required a much larger computer than the Heidelberg machine. The total cost of this service was $7,000 per year.

The procedure used to access the Rochester computer started in the Agrichemicals Division office where a clerk prepared sheets containing the pertinent information. These sheets were then taken to the computer room at Heidelberg Chemicals where a keypunch operator prepared punched cards which were read by a card reader and the information stored on one of the Univac's disks. Later Ms. Fabian sat at a video display terminal in the Agrichemicals Division office and called the information which had been on cards onto the screen of the terminal, correcting errors and changing the way it was organized. When she was satisfied that the information was correct, she typed a command on the keyboard of the terminal and the entire file was transmitted by telephone line to Rochester where it was stored on a disk awaiting its turn to be processed. Later, when the processing was complete, the results were returned by telephone line to the Univac and were printed on the system's line printer.

Ms. Fabian, who was responsible for this use of the computer by the Agrichemicals Division, said that the service was excellent. The computer at Rochester gave her fast turnaround and had not had a malfunction in all the time she had used it. Occasionally the telephone connection between the two computers was troublesome but other than that the system seemed to work well.

The one thing she did not think very good was the fact that she had to perform an edit function on the data before they were sent to Rochester. She had asked George Lake if he would have a programmer modify the program on the Univac which created the file from cards so the data would be in the correct format and sequence for Rochester but Mr. Lake said he did not have any people available to do it right then. He suggested she wait until the On-Line Order Entry System for the Industrial Chemicals Division was complete. Ms. Fabian offered to make the change herself because although she had never learned RPG she had taken a course in FORTRAN and believed that by studying the manuals she could learn enough about RPG and the Univac's operating system to make the necessary changes. Mr. Lake declined her offer to help.

THE CHARGEOUT SYSTEM

At the beginning of each year Mr. Lake estimated the usage of the computer for the year and calculated a price per CPU hour which would cover his total computer cost. People and data entry machines located in the area occupied by the operating divisions were paid for directly by those divisions.

Mr. Patton and his two programmers kept track of the time they spent on the development of new systems and where a system could be identified with a division, their time was charged to that division. In 1980, the rates charged the divisions were:

Computer Time	$429.59 per CPU hour
Data Entry	18.11 per hour
Systems & Programming	29.94 per hour

Each month Mr. Lake sent a list of divisional charges to the accounting office which adjusted them proportionally to make the total charged to the three divisions equal to the total of all expenditures incurred to operate the data processing department.

When asked about the effect of this charging out on the division decision makers, Mr. Lake was unsure of any. He said that no user manager had ever come to him to ask why the charges were what they were although occasionally at a Steering Committee meeting someone would say something like, "With all this money I am paying for data processing, why can't I get better service?" Mr. Lake went further to say that the only reason he knew of for having a chargeout system was because the parent company in Germany wanted them to.

THE WORD PROCESSOR

Because the Agrichemicals Division was required to submit numerous reports to various government bodies, the Manager of Quality Assurance and Reports, Mr. Dwight Ladd, requested approval to get a word processing system. The request was forwarded by the Vice President of Agrichemicals to the President who sent it to Mr. MacDonald for action. Mr. MacDonald was not opposed to the idea of a word processor; indeed he had for some time been thinking of getting one for the entire company. He was a little reluctant to order one for just one division however. He was also concerned about the organizational authority over the proposed machine. He had an office manager who looked after typewriters, photocopiers, stationery, etc., and he wondered if this man should be asked to take responsibility for the word processor. After all, it was just a big brother to the typewriters with storage capability, of which the company had many, all in the jurisdiction of the office manager.

He thought too that perhaps Mr. Lake, Manager of the Data Processing Department, should be asked to take responsibility for it. Although no decision had been made on which word processor was to be purchased, Mr. MacDonald knew that some models were stand-alone while others, for about the same price could be coupled to the Univac, providing for greater capability. It somehow seemed that if it were to be coupled to the computer it should be the responsibility of the Data Processing Department.

Finally, he considered the possibility of letting the Agrichemicals Division take responsibility for it; it was they who requested it and they would be the major users. Further if it "belonged" to Agrichemicals, it would not show up on the financial statements as data processing; Mr. MacDonald was having trouble keeping data processing expenditures below the 1% of sales target set by the parent organization. While he was contemplating the question, his secretary placed his afternoon mail on his desk and right on top was a memorandum from the Vice President of the Agrichemicals Division explaining that he had seen a demonstration of a word processor connected to a Univac 90/30 with the same configuration as Heidelberg Chemicals and he wanted permission to lease one for five years at $15,000 per year out of Agrichemicals' funds. It had 2,000 bytes of storage, a printer, two diskette drives and two video terminals. Although it would be the responsibility of the Agrichemicals Division, the Vice President said he would be willing to make it available to the other two divisions.

Appendix I

Heidelberg Chemicals Inc.

The Computer Services Department Mission

The mission is intended to develop and maintain a systematic approach in the provision of EDP services with which the "USER" will concur and identify.

1.0 *OBJECTIVES OF EDP DEPARTMENT*

1.1 Prime Objective:

To satisfy the Company's need for management decision making and monitoring tools through the provision of timely, accurate and usefully presented information.

1.2 Secondary Objective:

To maintain optimum operational efficiency in the areas of:

—hardware utilization

—technology (software development, upgrading and maintenance)

—personnel (capability and upgrading)

1.3 These objectives must be achieved at an optimum cost-benefit to the Company measuring up to the HEIDELBERG GROUP standards if possible and desirable.

2.0 *RESPONSIBILITY*

It will be the responsibility of Company management (through the Management Committee) to oversee the benefits of EDP and approve priorities. The operational aspects remain the responsibility of the Administration division.

3.0 *USER NEEDS*

The Company makes use of computer services through satisfying various USER needs. USER needs are:

(a) To identify the business environment based on information which the USER has generated.

(b) Receive timely, accurate and useful information regarding the USER's position relative to past performance, current objectives, and future plans. This information will be useful for the USER to:

—take advantage of opportunities

—act promptly on problem areas

—manage day-to-day operations efficiently and effectively

—make future plans

4.0 *COMPUTER SERVICES DEPARTMENT NEEDS*

The satisfactory provision of services to the USER is the specific responsibility of the department through the use of specialized personnel and equipment. To service USER needs, the department must be able to identify its operations according to the following functions:

(a) new applications

(b) maintenance/review of existing applications, basic data, programs and internal computer systems

(c) on-going operations (production of established applications for the USERS)

To obtain maximum efficiency, the EDP resource (personnel and equipment) must be coordinated with USER needs by means of:

(a) an annual EDP operating plan. This must be completed in sufficient detail in order to develop an operating budget for the coming year.

(b) five-year resource plans to accommodate long-term requirements. These plans would be revised annually at the completion of the annual operating plan.

5.0 *PLANNING AND RESPONSIBILITIES*

In order to arrive at these plans, the following requirement responsibilities are necessary.

(a) It will be the USER's responsibility to develop a list of required projects specifically for the following year and generally for the next five years.

(b) It will be EDP's responsibility to further develop with the USER an agreed upon detailed description of current proposed projects as specified by procedures.

(c) It will be EDP's responsibility to secure such a list in a timely fashion and match time/cost requirements with current capabilities.

(d) The USER's needs will be coordinated through an EDP steering committee.

(e) The proposed project list will be reviewed for overall priority and finalized by the Management Committee for inclusion into an operating plan.

(f) It will be EDP's responsibility through the EDP steering committee to develop and secure agreement on a project timetable within the limits of EDP capacity.

(g) The EDP steering committee will be responsible for reviewing the progress of projects and/or operations from the USER's point of view as specified by procedures.

(h) It will be an Administration division responsibility to plan and provide the requirements of EDP facilities and manpower for the short and long term needs of the Company.

(i) It will be the EDP manager's responsibility for efficient and effective operations in all aspects of that department.

(j) The Administration division will develop costs of the various elements of (a) established EDP productions (b) new project developments costs and (c) maintenance costs.

(k) It will be an Administration division responsibility to develop an equitable EDP cost charge out system and monitor it with the USERS.

COMPREHENSIVE CASE 4

MIS Project Management at First National Bank

Harold Kerzner

During the last five years First National Bank has been one of the fastest growing Banks in the midwest. The Holding Company of the Bank has been actively involved in purchasing small banks throughout the state of Ohio. This expansion and the resulting increase of operations has been attended by considerable growth in numbers of employees and in the complexity of the organizational structure. In five years the staff of the Bank has increased by 35% and total assets have grown by 70%. FNB management is eagerly looking forward to a change in the Ohio Banking Laws that will allow state-wide banking.

ISD HISTORY

Data processing at FNB has grown at a much faster pace than the rest of the Bank. The systems and programming staff grew from twelve in 1970 to over seventy-five during the first part of 1977. Due to several future projects the staff is expected to increase by 50% during the next two years.

Prior to 1972, the Information Services Department reported to the Executive Vice-President of the Consumer Banking and Operations Division. As a result, the first banking applications to be computerized were in the Demand Deposit, Savings and Consumer Credit Banking areas. The computer was seen as a tool to speed-up the processing of consumer transactions. Little effort was expended to meet the informational requirements of the rest of the Bank. This caused a high-level conflict since each major operating organization of the Bank did not have equal access to systems and programming resources. The management of FNB became increasingly aware of the benefits that could accrue from a realignment of the Bank's organization into one that would be better attuned to the total information requirements of the corporation.

In 1972 the Information Services Division (ISD) was created. ISD was removed from the Consumer Banking and Operations Division to become a separate Division of the Bank reporting directly to the President of the Bank. An organization chart depicting the Information Services Division is shown in Exhibit I.

PRIORITIES COMMITTEE

Also during 1972 the Priorities Committee was formed. It consists of the chief executive officer of each of the major operating organizations whose activities are directly affected by the need for new or revised information systems. The Priorities Committee

---

This case was prepared by Donald W. Lisk under the direction of Associate Professor Harold Kerzner as a basis for class discussion rather than to illustrate either effective or ineffective handling of an administrative situation.

Exhibit I
Information Services Division Organization Chart

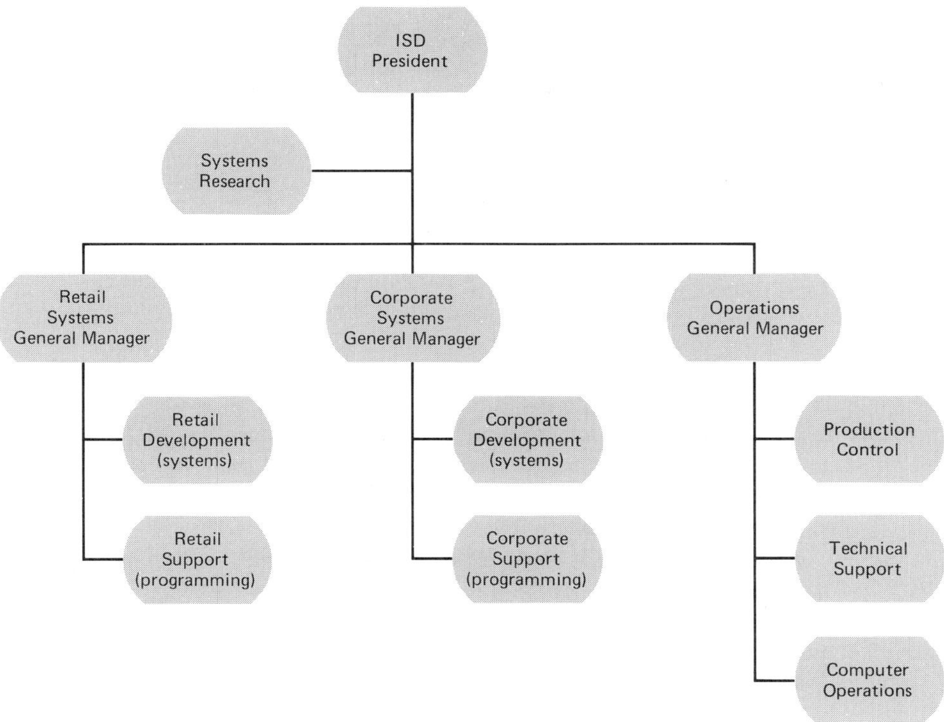

was established to insure that the finite resources of systems and programming personnel and computer hardware are expended only on those information systems that can best be cost justified. Divisions represented on the Committee are included in Exhibit II.

The Priorities Committee meets monthly to reaffirm previously set priorities and rank new projects that have been introduced since the last meeting. Bank policy states that the only way to obtain funds for an information development project is to submit a request to the Priorities Committee and have it approved and ranked in overall priority order for the Bank. The process of placing potential projects in ranked sequence is performed by the senior executives using conventional business skills. The primary document used for Priorities Committee review is called the project proposal.

THE PROJECT PROPOSAL LIFE CYCLE

When a User Department determines a need for the development of or enhancement to an information system, it is required to prepare a draft containing a statement of the

Exhibit II
First National Bank Organization Chart

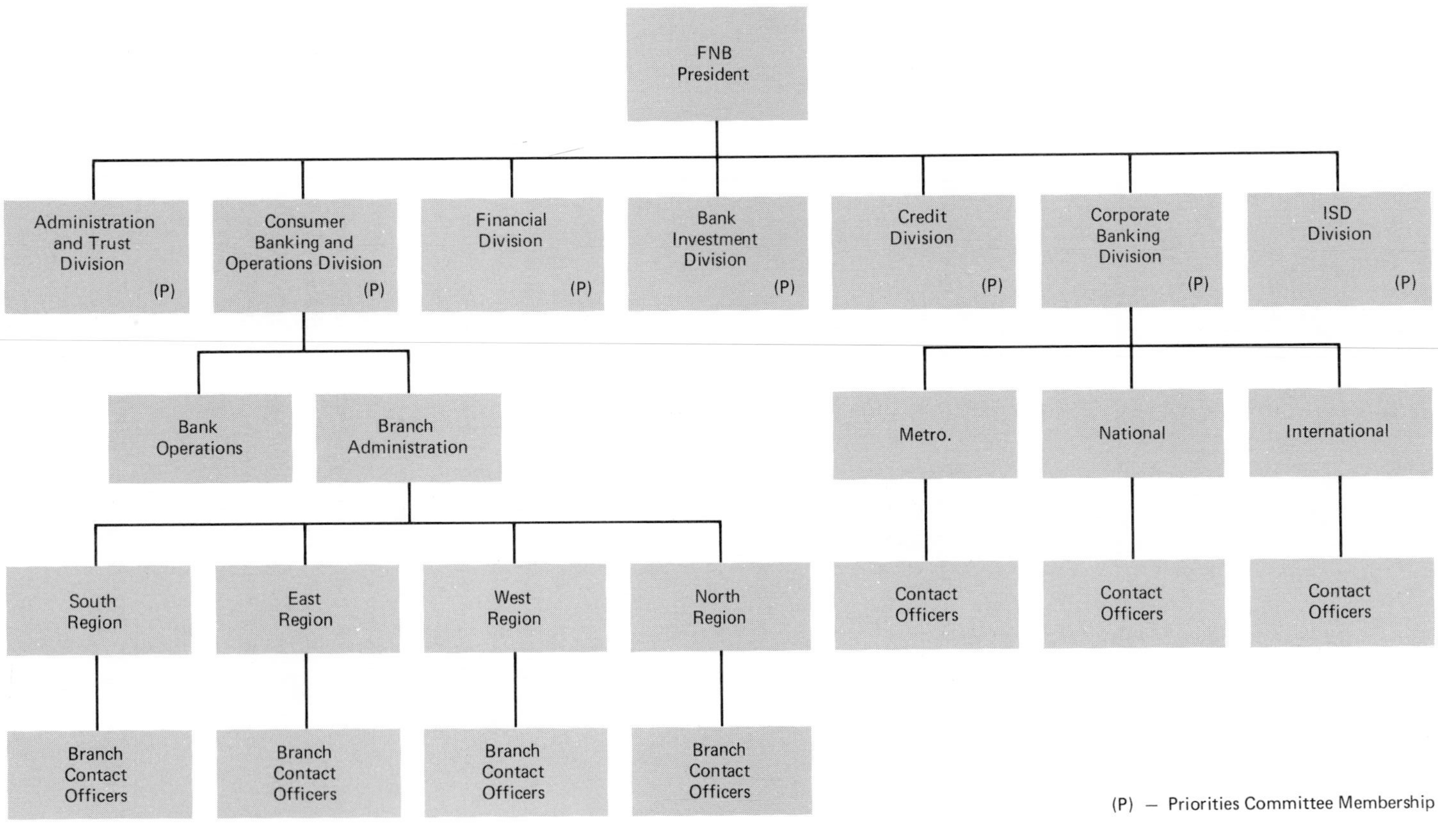

FNB President

Administration and Trust Division (P)
Consumer Banking and Operations Division (P)
Financial Division (P)
Bank Investment Division (P)
Credit Division (P)
Corporate Banking Division (P)
ISD Division (P)

Bank Operations
Branch Administration

Metro.
National
International

South Region
East Region
West Region
North Region

Contact Officers
Contact Officers
Contact Officers

Branch Contact Officers
Branch Contact Officers
Branch Contact Officers
Branch Contact Officers

(P) — Priorities Committee Membership

problem from its functional perspective. The problem statement is sent to the president of ISD who authorizes Systems Research (see Exhibit I) to prepare an impact statement which includes a general overview from ISD's perspective of:

—Project Feasibility
—Project Complexity
—Conformity with Long-range ISD Plans
—Estimated ISD Resource Commitment
—Review of Similar Requests
—Unique Characteristics/Problems
—Broad Estimate of Total Costs

The problem statement and impact statement are then presented to the Priorities Committee members for their review. The proposals are preliminary in nature, but they permit the broad concept (with a very approximate cost attached to it) to be reviewed by the Executive Group to see if there is serious interest in pursuing the idea. If the interest level of the Committee is small, then the idea is rejected. However, if the Priorities Committee feels the concept has merit, they authorize the Systems Research group of ISD to prepare a full scale project proposal which contains:

—A Detailed Statement of the Problem
—Identification of Alternative Solutions
—Impact of Request On:
  —User Division
  —ISD
  —Other Operating Divisions
—Estimated Costs of Solutions
—Schedule of Approximate Task Duration
—Cost/Benefit Analysis of Solutions
—Long Range Implications
—Recommended Course of Action

After the project proposal is prepared by Systems Research the User Sponsor must review the proposal and appear at the next Priorities Committee meeting to speak in favor of the approval and priority level of the proposed work. The project proposal is evaluated by the Committee and either dropped, tabled for further review, or assigned a priority relative to ongoing projects and available resources.

The final output of a Priorities Committee meeting is an updated list of project proposals in priority order with an accompanying milestone schedule that indicates the approximate time span required to implement each of the proposed projects.

The net result of this process is that the systems development priority setting is done by a cross-section of executive management; it does not revert by default to Data Processing Management. Priority setting, if done by data processing, can lead to misunderstanding and dissatisfaction by sponsors of the projects that did not get ranked highly enough to be funded in the near future. The project proposal cycle at FNB is included in Exhibit III. Once a project has risen to the top of the ranked priority list, it is assigned to the appropriate Systems Group for systems definition, system design and development, and system implementation.

Exhibit III
The Project Proposal Cycle

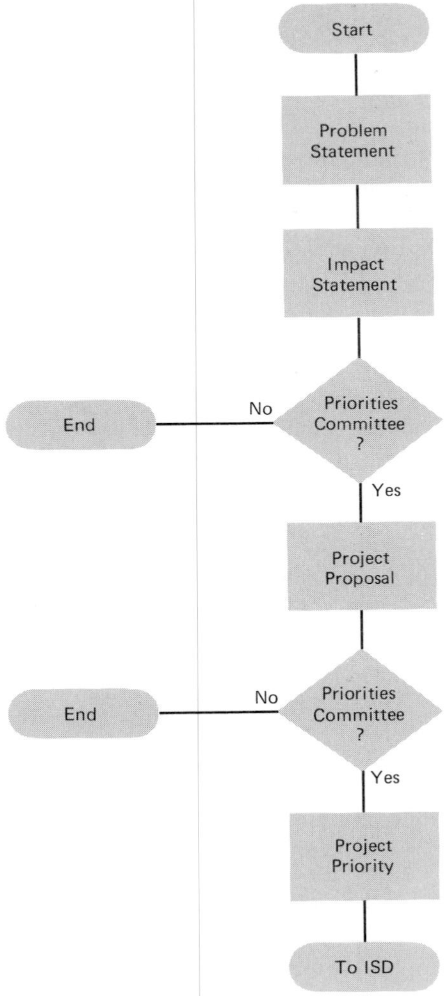

The time spent by Systems Research in producing impact statements and project proposals is considered to be overhead by ISD. No Systems Research time is directly charged to the development of information systems.

PROJECT LIFE CYCLE

As noted before, the systems and programming staff of ISD has increased in size rapidly and is expected to expand 50% during the next two years. As a rule most new employees have previous data processing experience and training in various systems methodologies. ISD management recently implemented a Project Management System which was dedicated to providing a uniform step-by-step methodology for the development of Management Information Systems. All project work is covered by tasks which make up the Information Project Development Life Cycle at FNB. The subphase used by ISD in the Project Life Cycle are:

1. Systems Definition
   A. Project Plan
   B. User Requirements
   C. Systems Definition
   D. Advisability Study
2. Systems Design and Development
   A. Preliminary Systems Design
   B. Subsystems Design
   C. Program Design
   D. Programming and Testing
3. System Implementation
   A. System Implementation
   B. System Test
   C. Production Control Turnover
   D. User Training
   E. System Acceptance

PROJECT ESTIMATING

The Project Management System contains a list of all normal tasks and subtasks (over 400) to be performed during the Life Cycle of a Development Project. The Project Manager must examine all the tasks to determine if they apply to his project. He must insert additional tasks if required and delete tasks which do not apply. The Project Manager next estimates the amount of time (in hours) to complete each task of each subphase of the Project Life Cycle.

The estimating process of the Project Management System uses a "moving window" concept. ISD management feels that detailed cost estimating and time schedules are only meaningful for the next subphase of a project, where the visibility of the tasks to be performed is quite clear. Beyond that subphase a more summary method of estimating is relied upon. As the project progresses, new segments of the project gain visibility. Detailed estimates are made for the next major portion of the project and summary estimates are done beyond that until the end of the project.

Estimates are performed at five intervals during the Project Life Cycle. When the project is first initiated the funding is based on the original estimates, which are derived from the list of normal tasks and subtasks. At this time, the subphases through the advisability study are estimated in detail and summary estimates are prepared for the rest of the tasks in the project. Once the project has progressed through the advisability study, the preliminary systems design is estimated in detail and the balance of the project is estimated in a more summary fashion. Estimates are conducted in this manner until the system implementation plan is completed and the scope of the remaining subphases of the project are known. This multiple estimating process is used because it is almost impossible at the beginning of many projects to be certain of what the magnitude of effort will be later on in the Project Life Cycle.

FUNDING OF PROJECTS

The project plan is the official document for securing funding from the sponsor in the User Organization. The project plan must be completed and approved by the Project Manager before activity can begin on the User requirements subphase (1B). An initial stage in developing a project plan includes the drawing of a network that identifies each of the tasks to be done in the appropriate sequence for their execution. The project plan must include a milestone schedule, a cost estimate and a budget request. It is submitted to the appropriate General Manager of systems and programming for review so that an understanding can be achieved of how the estimates were prepared and why the costs and schedules are as shown. At this time the General Manager can get an idea of the quantity of systems and programming resources required by the project. The General Manager next sets up a meeting with the Project Manager and the User Sponsor to review the project plan and obtain funding from the User Organization.

The initial project funding is based on an estimate that includes a number of assumptions concerning the scope of the project. Once certain key milestones in the project have passed, the visibility on the balance of the project becomes much clearer and re-estimates are performed. The re-estimates may result in refunding if there has been a significant change in the project. The normal milestone refunding points are as follows:

1. After the Advisability Study (ID)
2. After the Preliminary Systems Design (2A)
3. After the Program Design (2C)
4. After Systems Implementation (3A)

The refunding process is similar to the initial funding with the exception that progress information is presented on the status of the work and reasons are given to explain deviations from project expenditure projections. A revised project plan is prepared for each milestone refunding meeting.

During the systems design and development stage, design freezes are issued by the Project Manager to Users announcing that no additional changes will be accepted to the project beyond this point. The presence of these design freezes is made visible at the beginning of the project. Following the design freeze no additional changes will be accepted unless the project is re-estimated at a new level and approved by the User Sponsor.

SYSTEM QUALITY REVIEWS

The key element in insuring User involvement in the new system is the conducting of quality reviews. In the normal System Cycle at FNB, there are ten quality reviews, seven of which are participated in jointly by Users and Data Processing personnel, and three of which are technical reviews by Data Processing personnel only. An important side benefit of this review process is that users of a new system are forced to become involved in and are permitted to make a contribution to the systems design.

Each of the quality review points coincides with the end of a subphase in the Project Life Cycle. The review must be held at the completion of one subphase to obtain authorization to begin work on the tasks of the next subphase of the project.

All tasks and subtasks assigned to members of the project team should end in some "deliverable" for the project documentation. The first step in conducting a quality review is to assemble the documentation produced during the subphase for distribution to the Quality Review Board. The Quality Review Board consists of between 2 and 8 people who are appointed by the Project Manager with the approval of the Project Sponsor and the General Manager of Systems and Programming. The minutes of the Quality Review meeting are written either to express "concurrence" with the subsystem quality or to recommend changes to the system that must be completed before the next subphase can be started. By this process the system is fine tuned to the requirements of the members of the Review Group at the end of each subphase in the system. The members of the Quality Review Board charge their time to the project budget.

Quality Review points and Review Board make-up are as follows:

Review	Review Board
User Requirements	User Oriented
Systems Definition	User Oriented
Advisability Study	User Oriented
Preliminary Systems Design	User Oriented
Subsystems Design	Users & D.P.
Program Design	D.P.
Programming & Testing	D.P.
System Implementation	User Oriented
System Test	User Oriented
Production Control Turnover	D.P.

To summarize, the quality review evaluates the quality of project subphase results including design adequacy and proof of accomplishment in meeting project objectives. The Review Board authorizes work to progress based upon their detailed knowledge that all required tasks and subtasks of each subphase have been successfully completed and documented.

PROJECT TEAM STAFFING

Once a project has risen to the top of the priority list, the appropriate manager of Systems Development appoints a Project Manager from his staff of analysts. The Project Manager has a short time to review the project proposal created by Systems Research before developing a project plan. The project plan must be approved by the General Manager of Systems and Programming and the User Sponsor before the project can be funded and work started on the User requirements subphase.

The Project Manager is "free" to spend as much time as required in reviewing the project proposal and creating the project plan; however, his time is "charged" to the project at a rate of $26 per hour. The Project Manager must negotiate with his "boss," the manager of Systems Development to obtain the required systems analysts for the project starting with the User requirements subphase. The Project Manager must obtain programming resources from the manager of Systems Support. Schedule slippages caused by a lack of systems or programming resources are to be communicated to the General Manager by the Project Manager. All ISD personnel working on a project charge their time at a rate of $26 per hour. All computer time is billed at a rate of $64 per hour.

There are no User Personnel on the project team; all team members are from ISD.

CORPORATE DATA BASE

John Hart had for several years seen the need to use the computer to support the Corporate Marketing effort of the Bank. Despite the fact that the majority of the Bank's profits were from corporate customers, most information systems effort was directed at speeding up transaction handling for small unprofitable customers.

Mr. Hart had extensive experience in the Corporate Banking Division of the Bank. He realized the need to consolidate information about corporate customers from many areas of the Bank into one "Corporate Data Base." From this information Corporate Banking Services could be developed to not only better serve the corporate customers, but also to contribute heavily to the profit structure of the Bank.

The absence of a Corporate Data Base meant that no one individual knew what total banking services a corporate customer was using, because corporate services are provided by many banking departments. It was also impossible to determine how profitable a corporate customer was to the Bank. Contact Officers did not have regularly scheduled calls. They serviced corporate customers by the "seat of their pants" or "gut feel." Unfortunately many customers were "sold" on a service because they walked in the door and requested it. Mr. Hart felt that there was a vast market of untapped corporate customers in Ohio who would purchase services from the Bank if they were contacted and "sold" in a professional manner. A Corporate Data Base could be used to develop corporate profiles to help Contact Officers sell likely services to corporations.

Mr. Hart knew that data about corporate customers was being processed in many departments of the Bank, but mainly in the following divisions:

—Consumer Banking and Operations
—Corporate Banking
—Financial
—Credit

He also realized that much of the information was processed in manual systems, some was processed by time-sharing at various vendors and other information was computerized in many internal information systems.

The upper management of FNB must have agreed with Mr. Hart because in December of 1976, the Corporate Marketing Division was formed with John Hart becoming its Executive Vice-President. Mr. Hart was due to retire within the year but was honored to be selected for the new position. He agreed to stay with the bank until "his" new system was "off the ground." He immediately composed a problem statement and sent it to the President of ISD. Systems Research compiled a preliminary impact statement. At the next Priorities Committee meeting a project proposal was authorized to be done by Systems Research.

The project proposal was completed by Systems Research in record time. Most information was obtained from Mr. Hart. He had been thinking about the systems requirements for years and possessed vast experience in almost all areas of the Bank. Other User divisions and departments were often "too busy" when approached for information. A common reply to a request for information was "the project is John's baby; he knows what we need."

The project proposal as prepared by Systems Research recommended the following:

—Interfaces should be designed to extract information from existing computerized systems for the Corporate Data Base (CDB).
—Time-sharing systems should be brought in-house to be interfaced with the CDB.
—Information should be collected from manual systems to be integrated into the CDB on a temporary basis.
—Manual systems should be consolidated and computerized, causing a potential reorganization of some departments.
—Information analysis and flow for all departments and divisions having contact with corporate customers should be coordinated by the Corporate Marketing Division.
—All Corporate Data Base analysis should be done by the Corporate Marketing Division staff using either a user controlled report writer or interactive inquiry.

The project proposal was presented at the next Priorities Committee meeting where it was approved and rated as the highest priority MIS Development Project in the Bank. Mr. Hart became the User Sponsor for the CDB project.

The project proposal was sent to the manager of Corporate Development who appointed Jim Gunn as Project Manager from the staff of analysts in Corporate Development. Jim Gunn was the most experienced Project Manager available. His prior experience consisted of successful projects in the Financial Division of the Bank.

Jim reviewed the project proposal and started to work on his project plan. He was aware that the Corporate Analyst group was presently understaffed but was assured by his manager, the manager of Corporate Development, that resources would be available for the User requirements subphase. He had many questions concerning the scope of the project and the interrelationship between the Corporate Marketing Division and the other users of Corporate Marketing Data. But each meeting with Mr. Hart ended with the same comment, "this is a waste of time. I've already been over this with Systems Research. Let's get moving." Jim also was receiving pressure from the General Manager to "hurry-up" with the project plan. Jim therefore quickly prepared his project plan which included a general milestone schedule for subphase completion, a general cost estimate and a request for funding. The project plan was reviewed by the General Manager and signed by Mr. Hart.

Jim Gunn anticipated the need to have four analysts assigned to the project and went to his manager to see who was available. He was told that two junior analysts were available now and another analyst should be free next week. No senior analysts were available. Jim notified the General Manager that the CDB schedule would probably slip due to a lack of resources but received no response.

Jim assigned tasks to the members of the team and explained the assignments and the schedule. Since the project was understaffed, Jim assigned a heavy load of tasks to himself.

During the next two weeks the majority of the meetings set up to document User requirements were cancelled by the User departments. Jim notified Mr. Hart of the problem and was assured that steps would be taken to correct the problem. Future meetings with the users in the Consumer Banking and Corporate Banking Divisions became very hostile. Jim soon discovered that many individuals in these Divisions did not see the need for the Corporate Data Base. They resented spending their time in meetings documenting the CDB requirements. They were afraid that the CDB project would lead to a shift of many of their responsibilities and functions to the Corporate Marketing Division.

Mr. Hart was also unhappy. The CDB team was spending more time than budgeted in documenting User requirements. If this trend continued, a revised budget would have to be submitted to the Priorities Committee for approval. He was also growing tired of ordering individuals in the User departments to keep appointments with the CDB team. Mr. Hart could not understand the resistance to his project.

Jim Gunn kept trying to obtain analysts for his project but was told by his Manager that none were available. Jim explained that the quality of work done by the junior analysts was not "up to par" due to lack of experience. Jim complained that he could not Subphase was scheduled for next month making it extremely critical that experienced analysis tasks himself. He also noted that the Quality Review of the User Requirements Subphase was scheduled for next month making it extremely critical that experience analysts be assigned to the project. No new personnel were assigned to the project. Jim thought about contacting the General Manager again to explain his need for more experienced analysts, but did not. He was due for a semi-yearly evaluation from his Manager in two weeks.

Even though he knew the quality of the work was lacking, Jim was determined to get the project done on schedule with the resources available to him. He drove both himself and the team very hard during the next few weeks. The Quality Review of the User Requirements Subphase was held on schedule. Over 90% of the assigned tasks had to be redone before the Quality Review Board would sign-off on the review. Jim Gunn was "removed" as Project Manager.

Three senior analysts and a new Project Manager were assigned to the CDB project. The project received additional funding from the Priorities Committee. The User Requirements Subphase was completely redone despite vigorous protests from the Consumer Banking and Corporate Banking Divisions.

Within the next three months the following events happened:

—The new Project Manager resigned to accept a position with another firm.
—John Hart took early retirement.
—The CDB project was "tabled."

GLOSSARY

SOURCES

1. ANSI definitions are preceded by an asterisk. An asterisk to the left of the term indicates that the entire entry is reproduced with permission from American National Standards Committee X3 Technical Report *American National Dictionary for Information Processing Systems X3/TR-1-82,* copyright 1982 by the Computer and Business Equipment Manufacturers Association (CBEMA), copies of which may be purchased from CBEMA, 311 First St. NW, Washington, D.C. 20001. Where definitions from other sources are included in the entry, ANSI definitions are identified by an asterisk to the right of the item number. The symbol "(ISO)" at the beginning of a definition indicates that it has been discussed and agreed upon at meetings of the International Organization for Standardization, Technical Committee 97/Subcommittee 1, and has been approved by ANSI for inclusion in the *American National Dictionary for Information Processing.* The symbol "(SC1)" at the beginning of a definition indicates that it is reprinted from an early working document of ISO Technical Committee 97/Subcommittee 1 and that agreement has not yet been reached among its members.
2. Definitions from *Data Processing Glossary,* IBM Publication C-20-1699-5 (October 1977) are indicated by (IBM) prior to the definition.
3. If no source is indicated the definition is the author's.

abacus An ancient Chinese device which used beads strung on wires for arithmetic computations.

***absolute address** An address that is permanently assigned by the machine designer to a storage location.

access controls The controls that limit access to program documentation, program and data files, and computer hardware.

***access time** (ISO) The time interval between the instant at which an instruction control unit initiates a call for data and the instant at which delivery of the data is completed.

accounts payable system A computer system that helps provide control over payments to suppliers, issues checks to these suppliers, and provides information necessary for effective cash management.

accounts receivable system A computer system used for billing customers, maintaining records of amounts due from customers, and generating reports on overdue amounts.

***accuracy** (1) (ISO) A quality held by that which is free of error. (2) (ISO) A qualitative assessment of freedom from error, a high assessment corresponding to a small error.

acoustic coupler (IBM) A type of data communication equipment that permits use of a telephone handset as a connection to a telephone network for data transmission by means of sound transducers. See modem.

ad hoc approach A system development approach directed toward solving a particular problem without considering other related issues.

***address** (1) (ISO) A character or group of characters that identifies a register, a particular part of storage, or some other data source or destination. (2) (ISO) To refer to a device or an item of data by its address.

advanced information system/net 1 A data switching network that can connect various devices made by many different computer manufacturers.

airline reservation system (IBM) An online application in which a computing system is used to keep track of seat inventories, flight schedules, and other information required to run an airline. The reservation system is designed to maintain up-to-date files and to respond, within seconds or less, to inquiries from ticket agents at locations remote from the computing system.

algorithm Synonym for program.

alphabetic character (IBM) A letter or other symbol, excluding digits, used in a language.

***alphanumeric** Pertaining to a character set that contains letters, digits, and usually other characters, such as punctuation marks. Synonymous with alphameric.

American National Standards Institute (ANSI) (IBM) An organization for the purpose of establishing voluntary industry standards.

***analog computer** (1) (ISO) A computer in which analog representation of data is mainly used. (2) A computer that operates on analog data by performing physical processes on these data. (3) Contrast with digital computer.

answerback (IBM) The response of a terminal to remote control signals. See also handshaking.

anticipation check A control based on the fact that certain fields in an input record should always be non-blank or that an input record is expected for each master file record.

APL (a programming language) (SC1) A programming language with an unusual syntax and character set, primarily designed for mathematical applications, particularly those involving numeric or literal arrays.

application controls Controls applied directly to the individual computer application: (1) input controls, (2) processing controls and (3) output controls.

application development by users The development of application programs by users, with only limited support from programmers and system analysts.

application generator A software system that generates computer programs based on the user's needs. Actually, an application generator consists of a large number of precoded modules that perform various functions. The user merely specifies the functions needed for his or her application and the system invokes the appropriate modules and runs them.

application program (IBM) A program written for or by a user that applies to a particular application.

application programmer A programmer who writes and maintains application programs. Contrast with system programmer.

arithmetic proof checks A control that verifies the results of mathematical operations.

***arithmetic-logic unit** (ISO) A part of a computer that performs arithmetic operations, and related operations.

***array** An arrangement of elements in one or more dimensions.

***artificial intelligence** The capability of a device to perform functions that are normally associated with human intelligence, such as reasoning, learning, and self-improvement.

***ASCII** American National Standard Code for Information Interchange. The standard code, using a coded character set consisting of 7-bit coded characters (8 bits including parity check), used for information interchange among data processing systems, data communication systems, and associated equipment. The ASCII set consists of control characters and graphic characters. (The ASCII-8 code contains 8 bits without the parity bit).

***assemble** To prepare a machine language program from a symbolic language program by substituting absolute operation codes for symbolic operation codes and absolute or relocatable addresses for symbolic addresses.

***assembler** (ISO) A computer program used to assemble. Synonymous with assembly program.

***assembly language** A computer programming language whose statements may be instructions or declarations. The instructions usually have a one-to-one correspondence with machine instructions.

***assembly program** (ISO) Synonym for assembler.

assignment statement A program statement that performs some computations and assigns the resulting value to a variable.

assumed decimal point (IBM) In COBOL, a decimal point position that does not involve the existence of an actual character in a data item. It does not occupy an actual space in storage.

audit trail A permanent record of the transactions executed by a computer system.

asynchronous transmission A data transmission method in which each byte is transmitted separately.

***auxiliary operation** An offline operation performed by equipment not under control of the processing unit.

availability The descriptive quality pertaining to how quickly a computer system can respond to high priority jobs.

***background processing** (1) (ISO) The execution of lower-priority computer programs when higher-priority programs are not using the system resources. (2) Contrast with foreground processing.

backup file A file which contains redundant copies of current files or the only copy of non-current files which are used to reconstruct current files in case current files are partially or totally destroyed.

***balanced error** (ISO) A set of errors the distribution of which has the mean value zero.

base register A register in the CPU which is used as a reference point to specify all other storage locations for the program.

BASIC (beginner's all-purpose symbolic instruction code) (SC1) A programming language with a small repertoire of commands and a simple syntax, primarily designed for numerical applications.

batch (IBM) An accumulation of data to be processed.

batch-direct The processing method where changes and inquiries to the file are batched and processed periodically under a direct access file organization method.

batch mode synonymous with batch processing.

***batch processing** (1) The processing of data or the accomplishment of jobs accumulated in advance in such a manner that each accumulation thus formed is processed or accomplished in the same run. (2) The processing of data accumulated over a period of time. (3) Loosely, the execution of computer programs serially. (4) Pertaining to the technique of executing a set of computer programs such that each is completed before the next program of the set is started.

batch-sequential processing The processing method where changes and inquiries to the file are batched and processed periodically under a sequential file access method.

batch-serial execution A method of data processing where each program is executed in the order in which it was read into the system, only one program is executed at a time.

batch total The sum resulting from the addition of a specified numeric field from each record in a batch of records which is used for control and checking purposes. See control total and hash total.

***baud** A unit of signaling speed equal to the number of discrete conditions or signal events per second.

benchmark program A sample program which is representative of at least part of the buyer's primary computer workload and which is executed on alternative computer configurations to provide information useful in making a computer acquisition decision.

***binary** (ISO) Pertaining to a selection, choice, or condition that has two possible values or states.

***binary digit (Bit)** (1) (ISO) Synonym for bit. (2) In binary notation, either of the characters 0 or 1.

binary number system A number system that uses only the digits 0 and 1, rather than the ten digits in the decimal system. This system is used to represent electronic computer design since its two digits are used to represent the two conditions (on-off) that are present in electronic components.

binary representation synonymous with binary number system.

***binary search** (ISO) A dichotomizing search in which, at each step of the search, the set of items is partitioned into two equal parts, some appropriate action being taken in the case of an odd number of items.

***bit** (1) (ISO) In the pure binary numeration system, either of the digits 0 and 1. Synonymous with binary digit. (2) (ISO) Deprecated term for binary element.

***block** (1) (ISO) A string of records, a string of words or a character string formed for technical or logic reasons to be treated as an entity. (2) A collection of contiguous records recorded as a unit. Blocks are separated by interblock gaps and each block may contain one or more records.

blocking factor (ISO) The number of logical records in each block.

block format The format of each individual message sent through a communication system. This includes control characters to mark the beginning and end of the message, and error detection characters.

bootstrap A term used with microcomputers to indicate starting the computer up and causing the operating system to commence operation. See initial program load.

bottleneck A slowdown in one part of the system that can cause the whole system to operate below capacity.

bottom-up approach A system development approach that leads to the creation of many independent information systems within individual departments. These are later integrated into one large system.

boundary The area that separates one system from another.

bpi (IBM) Bits per inch.

bps Bits per second.

***branch** (1) (ISO) In the execution of a computer program, to select one from a number of alternative sets of instructions. (2) A link between a parent node and a child node in a tree structure.

broadband (high speed channel) (1) (IBM) A communication channel having a bandwidth greater than a voice-grade channel, and therefore capable of higher-speed data transmission. (2) A channel of voice grade and used where data must be transmitted at high speed.

bubble storage A non-volatile memory device which stores data by polarizing microscopic bubbles in a crystalline substance.

***buffer** A routine or storage used to compensate for a difference in rate of flow of data, or time of occurrence of events, when transferring data from one device to another.

***bug** A mistake or malfunction.

bundling The selling of hardware and software together as a package.

***burst** (1) In data communication, a sequence of signals counted as one unit in accordance with some specific criterion or measure. (2) To separate continuous-form paper into discrete sheets.

bus A communication link that connects the CPU to its peripheral devices.

by-product data entry The capture of data as a by-product of some other operation which is traditionally not part of a data entry operation.

byte (1) *(ISO) A binary character string operated upon as a unit and usually shorter than a computer word. (2) (IBM) The representation of a character.

calculate To perform one or more arithmetic functions including addition, subtraction, multiplication and division.

***calculator** (ISO) A data processor, especially suitable for performing arithemetical operations, that requires frequent intervention by a human operator.

***call** (ISO) The action of bringing a computer program, a routine, or a subroutine into effect, usually by specifying the entry conditions and jumping to an entry point.

card code (IBM) The combinations of punched holes that represent characters (for example letters, digits) in a punched card.

***card column** (ISO) A line of punch positions parallel to the shorter edges of a punch card.

***card deck** (ISO) A group of related punched cards.

***card punch** (1) A device that punches holes in a card to represent data. (2) (ISO) Deprecated term for keypunch.

***card reader** (1) (ISO) A device that reads or senses the holes in a punched card, transforming the data from hole patterns to electrical signals. (2) An input device that senses hole patterns in a punched card and translates them into machine language. Synonymous with punched card reader.

card sorter (ISO) A device that deposits punched cards in pockets selected according to the hole patterns in the cards.

catalog (1) (ISO) A directory of locations of files and libraries. (2) (IBM) The collection of all data set indexes that are used by the control program to locate a volume containing a specific data set. (3) (ISO) To enter information about a file or a library into a catalog.

cataloged data set (IBM) A data set that is represented in an index, or hierarchy of indexes, in the system catalog; the indexes provide the means for locating the data set.

cathode ray tube (CRT) (IBM) An electronic vacuum tube, such as a television picture tube, that can be used to display graphic images or data.

***central processing unit (CPU)** (ISO) A unit of a computer that includes circuits controlling the interpretation and execution of instructions. Synonymous with central processor.

***chained list** (ISO) A list in which the items may be dispersed but in which each item contains an identifier for locating the next item.

chaining (IBM) A system of storing records in which each record belongs to a list or group of records and has a linking field for tracing the chain.

channel (1) *A path along which signals can be sent, for example, data channel, output channel. (2) (IBM) A device that connects the processing unit and main storage with the I/O control units.

***character** A letter, digit, or other symbol that is used as part of the organization, control, or representation of data. A character is often in the form of a spatial arrangement of adjacent or connected strokes.

***character printer** (ISO) A device that prints a single character at a time, e.g., a typewriter. Synonymous with character-at-a time printer, serial printer. Contrast with line printer.

***character set** An ordered set of unique representations called characters, e.g., the 26 letters of the English alphabet, boolean 0 and 1, the set of symbols in the Morse code, and the 128 ASCII characters.

character string (1) *(ISO) A string consisting solely of characters. (2) (IBM) A connected sequence of characters.

***check bit** A binary check digit, e.g., a parity bit.

check digit An extra digit in identification codes, such as part numbers, so that the validity of the code can be determined by performing an arithmetic operation on the code.

checkpoint (1) (ISO) *A place in a computer program at which a check is made or at which a recording of data is made for restart purposes. (2) (IBM) A point at which information about the status of a job and the system can be recorded so that the job step can be later restarted.

checkpoint/restart facility (IBM) A facility for restarting execution of a program at some point other than at the beginning, after the program was terminated due to a program or system failure. A restart can begin at a checkpoint or from the beginning of a job step, and uses checkpoint records to reinitialize the system.

chief programmer team An organizational structure often used for programming projects. A small group consisting of a chief programmer, assistant programmers, a librarian and a back-up programmer working independently on a programming task with very little supervision.

classical system development A traditional system development methodology. It has five phases: feasibility study, analysis, design, coding, and testing.

classification The identification of an item of data with a certain category. For instance, a sales transaction may be classified as cash or credit.

***clear** (1) (ISO) To put one or more storage locations or registers into a prescribed state, usually that denoting zero.

***closed shop** (1) Pertaining to the operation of a computer facility in which most productive problem programming is performed by a group of programming specialists rather than by the problem originators. The use of the computer itself may also be described as closed shop if full-time trained operators, rather than user/programmers serve as the operators. (2) Contrast with open shop.

clustered system A data entry system in which several keyboards are connected to one or two magnetic storage devices.

COBOL (Common business-oriented language) (SC1) An English-like programming language designed for business data processing applications.

CODASYL (IBM) Conference on Data Systems Languages.

code (1) *(ISO) A set of unambiguous rules specifying the manner in which data may be represented in a discrete form. Synonymous with coding scheme. (2) *A set of items, such as abbreviations, representing the members of another set. (3) (IBM) Loosely, one or more computer programs, or part of a computer program. (4) (ISO) To represent data or a computer program in a symbolic form that can be accepted by a data processor. (5) (IBM) To write a routine.

code comparison A comparison of two different versions of a program to detect any fraudulent code.

code inspection A review of program code by a review team. The programmer walks the reviewers through the code who check it for compliance with design specifications.

***coder** A person who writes but does not usually design computer programs.

coding scheme A set of symbols that represent alphabetic and numeric information within the computer.

cohesion A measure of the strength of association between the internal functions of a given module.

***collator** (ISO) A device that collates, merges, or matches sets of punched cards or other documents.

***command** (1) A control signal. (2) Loosely, an instruction. (3) Loosely, a mathematical or logic operator. (4) Deprecated term for instruction.

communication protocol A set of rules governing the flow of data through a communication system.

communications processor A device that converts data to a standard protocol before transmitting it over communication lines, and decodes received data for the computer's own use.

compare To examine two pieces of data to determine whether they are equal or one is greater than the other.

compatible (IBM) Pertaining to computers on which the same computer programs can be run without appreciable alteration.

***compile** (1) (ISO) To translate a computer program expressed in a problem-oriented language into a computer-oriented language. (2) To prepare a machine language program from a computer program written in another programming language by making use of the overall logic structure of the program, or generating more than one computer instruction for each symbolic statement, or both, as well as performing the function of an assembler.

***compiler** (ISO) A computer program used to compile. Synonymous with compiling program.

***computer** (ISO) A data processor that can perform substantial computation, including numerous arithmetic or logic operations, without intervention by a human operator during the run.

***computer architecture** The specification of the relationships between the parts of a computer system.

computer assisted instruction (CAI) (IBM) A data processing application in which a computing system is used to assist in the instruction of students. The application usually involves a dialog between the student and a computer program which informs the student of mistakes as they are made.

computer fraud Illegal use of computer facilities to misappropriate corporate resources. This includes unauthorized changes to both software and hardware systems.

computer graphics (SC1) That branch of science and technology concerned with methods and techniques for converting data to or from graphic display via computers.

computer operator An employee who monitors the performance of the CPU and storage devices. He or she performs most of the human functions necessary to keep the system running.

***computer output microfilm (COM)** (1) (ISO) Microfilm that contains data that is received directly from computer-generated signals. (2) To place computer-generated data on microfilm.

***computer program** A series of instructions or statements, in a form acceptable to a computer.

computer service technician A trained technician who is responsible for the repair and maintenance of hardware devices.

***concurrent** (1) (ISO) Pertaining to the occurrence of two or more activities within a given interval of time. (2) Contrast with consecutive, sequential, simultaneous.

connection A link between two modules showing which module calls the other.

***consecutive** (1) (ISO) Pertaining to the occurrence of two sequential events without the intervention of any other such event. (2) Contrast with concurrent, sequential, simultaneous.

***console** A part of a computer used for communication between the operator or maintenance engineer and the computer.

consultant An EDP expert who assists users in developing and debugging their own applications.

control The process of comparing actual results to planned results.

control data Data that is used by the program solely for making processing decisions.

control group The group of personnel separated from computer operations which maintains input-output controls and reviews output prior to distribution to users.

***control program** (ISO) A computer program designed to schedule and to supervise the execution of programs of a computing system. See operating system.

control program for microcomputers (CP/M) A popular operating system for personal computers.

control statement A statement that regulates the order of execution in a program, e.g., an IF statement.

control total (IBM) A sum, resulting from the addition of a specified field from each record in a group of records, that is used for checking machine, program, and data reliability.

control unit (1) A subsystem contained within the transformation process of every information system. A control component selects, interprets, and executes programmed instructions so that the system can function. In total, it controls the actions of a system. (2) That part of the central processing unit that decodes program instructions and directs the other components of the computer system to perform the task specified in the program instruction.

conversational mode (ISO) A mode of operation of a data processing system in which a sequence of alternating entries and responses between a user and the system takes place in a manner similar to a dialog between two persons. Synonymous with interactive mode.

conversion (IBM) (1) The process of changing from one method of data processing to another. (2) The process of changing from one form of representation to another; e.g., to change from decimal representation to binary representation.

***copy** (ISO) To read data from a source, leaving the source data unchanged, and to write the same data elsewhere in a physical form that may differ from that of the source, e.g., to copy a file from disk storage onto magnetic tape.

core storage (1) *A magnetic storage in which the data medium consists of magnetic cores. (2) Deprecated term for primary storage.

couple A data item that moves from one module to another.

coupling The level of interdependence between modules.

CP/M See control program for microcomputers.

CPU time (IBM) The amount of time devoted by the processing unit to the execution of instructions. Synonymous with CPU busy time.

***CRT display** See cathode ray tube.

***cryogenics** The study and use of devices utilizing properties of materials near absolute zero in temperature.

cursor (IBM) A movable spot of light on the screen of a display device, usually indicating where the next character will be entered.

***cycle** An interval of space or time in which one set of events or phenomena is completed.

cycle time (ISO) The minimum time interval between the starts of successive read-write cycles of a storage device.

cylinder (1) (ISO) In a disk pack, the set of all tracks with the same nominal distance from the axis about which the disk pack rotates. (2) (IBM) The tracks of a disk storage device that can be accessed without repositioning the access mechanism.

daisy wheel printer A high quality printing device that uses a print wheel and a typewriter-like ribbon to print text and data.

DASD (IBM) Direct access storage device.

***data** (1) (ISO) A representation of facts, concepts, or instructions in a formalized manner suitable for communication, interpretation, or processing by humans or automatic means. (2) Any representations such as characters or analog quantities to which meaning is, or might be, assigned.

data acquisition (IBM) The process of identifying, isolating, and gathering source data to be centrally processed.

***data bank** (1) (ISO) A set of libraries of data. (2) A comprehensive collection of libraries of data. For example, one line of an invoice may form an item, a complete invoice may form a record, a complete set of such records may form a file, the collection of inventory control files may form a library, and the libraries used by an organization are known as its data bank.

***data base** (1) (ISO) A set of data, part of the whole of another set of data, and consisting of at least one file, that is sufficient for a given purpose or for a given data processing system. (2) A collection of data fundamental to a system. (3) A collection of data fundamental to an enterprise. The terms data base and data bank are often used interchangeably.

data base administrator The person responsible for coordinating the data base including provisions for data security.

data base approach A system development approach that emphasizes the development of a common data base in a computerized environment.

data base machine A computer dedicated entirely to the use of a data base management system.

data base management system (DBMS) A systems program which serves as an interface between applications programs and a set of coordinated and integrated physical files called a data base.

data cartridge (IBM) The storage medium of the mass storage system, consisting of a container with magnetic media wound around a spool inside it. All data cartridges within the mass storage facility are online.

data cell (IBM) A direct access storage volume containing strips of tape on which data is stored.

data communication (1) *The transmission and reception of data. (2) The transfer of data from one device in an information system to another. (3) The transmission of data from one physical location to another.

data definition language A language that is used to define the relationship between the logical and physical views of a data base.

data definition (DD) statement (IBM) A job control statement that describes a data set associated with a particular job step.

data dictionary A dictionary which defines the meaning of each data item stored in a data base, and describes interrelationships among them.

data editing synonymous with editing.

data entry The process of entering data into a computer system in order to communicate with it.

data entry operator An employee who keys data from source documents into computer readable form like disk or tape.

data flow diagram A graphic representation of the movement and transformations of data within an organization.

data independence A lack of dependence between the physical structure of data storage and the structure of application programs.

***data management** The function of controlling the acquisition, analysis, storage, retrieval, and distribution of data.

data manipulation language A language that is used to define operations on a data base like retrieval, sorting, and updating of records.

***data medium** The material in or on which data is stored.

data processing The capture, storage and processing of data to transform it into information that is useful for decision making.

data redundancy The situation where identical data is stored in two or more files.

data set (IBM) The major unit of data storage and retrieval in the operating system, consisting of a collection of data in one of several prescribed arrangements and described by control information to which the system has access. Synonymous with file. See file.

data set name (DSN) (1) (IBM) The term or phrase used to identify a data set. (2) The name of an individual file on a volume, also referred to as the internal label.

data set organization (IBM) The arrangement of information in a data set; for example, sequential organization or virtual storage organization. Synonymous with file organization.

data structure diagram A graphical representation of the logical relationships between various data files.

data switch A device similar to a telephone exchange, which can establish a data communication link between any two devices connected to it.

data type The category that a data item belongs to, e.g., numeric, alphabetic, etc.

***debug** (ISO) To detect, to trace, and to eliminate mistakes in computer programs or in other software. Synonymous with checkout.

decimal number system A system that represents numbers in terms of the powers of ten, that is, units, tens, hundreds, etc. This is the system we normally use in our everyday lives.

decision model A formula or set of formulas that assist in making a decision based on given input values.

***decision table** (1) (ISO) A table of all contingencies that are to be considered in the description of a problem, together with the actions to be taken. (2) A presentation in either matrix or tabular form of a set of conditions and their corresponding actions.

decision tree A graphic representation of all contingencies to be considered, together with the actions that must be taken for each one of them.

***decollate** To separate the plies of a multipart form or paper stock. Synonymous with deleave.

default (IBM) An alternative value, attribute, or option that is assumed when none has been specified.

default option See default.

***delimiter** A flag that separates and organizes items of data. Synonymous with punctuation symbol, separator.

demand listing A report generated only when a user requests it. Typically used to fill irregular needs for information.

***density** See recording density.

***destructive read** (ISO) A reading that also erases the data in the source location.

device (IBM) A mechanical, electrical, or electronic contrivance with a specific purpose.

device controller A part of the CPU which manages communications between the CPU and peripheral devices.

dial-up terminal (1) (IBM) A terminal on a switched line. (2) A terminal which is connected to the computer by dialing the computer system over a telephone line. See hardwired-terminal.

***digit** (1) (ISO) A graphic character that represents an integer, e.g., one of the characters 0 to 9. (2) (ISO) Synonymous with numeric character.

***digital computer** (ISO) A computer in which discrete representation of data is mainly used.

digit analysis A method for choosing certain digits in a record key to use for addressing purposes.

direct access (1) (ISO) The facility to obtain data from a storage device, or to enter data into a storage device in such a way that the process depends only on the location of that data and not on a reference to data previously accessed. (2) (IBM) Contrast with sequential access. (3) The file organization that enables a record to be located and retrieved by the CPU without a large amount of searching.

direct access storage device (DASD) (IBM) A device in which the access time is effectively independent of the location of the data. Synonymous with immediate access storage.

direct conversion A method of converting to a new information system, such that the old system is discontinued one workday and the new system is started the next day.

direct file organization A file organization that allows direct access to a record without sequentially examining a large number of other records.

disaster controls Controls that minimize the risk of loss due to natural and man made disasters like flooding, fire, and hurricanes.

disk (IBM) Loosely, a magnetic disk unit.

disk drive A device that houses a disk or diskette while it is in use. It contains a motor and one or more magnetic heads to read and write data on the disk.

diskette Synonymous with floppy disk.

display (1) *(ISO) A visual presentation of data. (2) (IBM) To present a display image on a display surface. (3) (IBM) Deprecated term for display device.

distributed data base A data base that resides on two or more separate computers simultaneously. The data base may either be partitioned between the two computers or replicated at both locations.

distributed data processing The concept of distributing the load of data processing through the installation of computers at a company's remote locations, so the local data processing needs are handled by the remote location's own local computer.

document (1) *(ISO) A data medium and the data recorded on it, that generally has permanence and that can be read by man or machine. (2) To record information to provide support or proof of something.

documentation (1) *(ISO) The management of documents which may include the actions of identifying, acquiring, processing, storing, and disseminating them. (2) A collection of documents which support and explain a data processing application.

documentation standards Specific procedures for system documentation including flowcharting conventions, coding conventions, and documentation revision procedures.

DOS (IBM) Disk operating system.

***dot matrix printer** (ISO) A printer in which each character is represented by a pattern of dots.

downtime The time interval during which a functional unit is inoperable due to a fault.

DP operations department MIS personnel who are responsible for managing the day-to-day operations of data processing facilities.

***drum printer** A line printer in which the type is mounted on a rotating drum that contains a full character set for each printing position.

***dump** (1) (ISO) Data that have been dumped. (2) (ISO) To write the contents of a storage, or of part of a storage, usually from an internal storage to an external medium, for a specific purpose such as to allow other use of the storage, as a safeguard against faults or errors, or in connection with debugging.

***duplex** In data communication, pertaining to a simultaneous two-way independent transmission in both directions. Synonymous with full duplex.

duplex transmission (SC1) Data transmission over a data circuit in both directions at the same time.

***duplicate** (ISO) To copy from a source to a destination that has the same physical form as the source, e.g., to punch new punched cards with the same pattern of holes as an original punched card. Synonymous with reproduce.

***duplication check** A check based on the consistency of two independent performances of the same task.

***dynamic dump** (ISO) Dumping performed during the execution of a computer program, usually under the control of that computer program.

***EAM** See electrical accounting machine.

***EBCDIC** Extended binary-coded decimal interchange code. A coded character set consisting of 8-bit coded characters.

echo check (1) *A method of checking the accuracy of transmission of data in which the received data are returned to the sending end for comparison with the original data. (2) A hardware control that verifies that a device has been activated to carry out an operation which it has been instructed to perform.

edit (1) *(ISO) To prepare data for a later operation. Editing may include the rearrangement or the addition of data, the deletion of unwanted data, format control, code conversion, and the application of standard processes such as zero suppression. (2) To examine data for error conditions.

edit directed I/O Input or output of formatted data.

EDP auditor An auditor who specializes in auditing computer-based information systems.

electromechanical computer A machine that performs computations through the mechanical movement of its parts.

***electrical accounting machine (EAM)** Pertaining to data processing equipment that is predominantly electromechanical such as a keypunch, mechanical sorter, collator, and tabulator.

***electronic data processing (EDP)** (ISO) Data processing largely performed by electronic devices.

electronic digital computer A device that processes digital data through the flow of electrical signals in its circuits.

electronic funds transfer system A computerized system that can transfer money from one point to another immediately, using data communication lines.

electronic mail The transmittal of messages between computer users over a data communication network.

electronic shopping Selecting merchandise and ordering it through a remote terminal installed in your home.

embedded pointer A field within a record which contains the address of a related record.

***emulate** (1) To imitate one system with another, primarily by hardware, so that the imitating system accepts the same data, executes the same computer programs, and achieves the same results as the imitated system. (2) Contrast with simulate.

encoding Storage of data in coded form. It may not be accessed by a user who does not know the code.

***end-of-tape marker (EOT)** A marker on a magnetic tape used to indicate the end of the permissible recording area, e.g., a photo reflective strip, a transparent section of tape, a particular bit pattern.

end user The person who ultimately uses the computer's output.

entry controls Controls over entry to areas where computer equipment like CPUs and storage devices are installed.

***erasable storage** (1) (ISO) A storage device whose contents can be modified. (2) Contrast with read-only storage.

***erase** (ISO) To remove all previous data from magnetic storage by changing it to a specified condition; that may be an unmagnetized state or a predetermined magnetized state.

ergonomics A field of study devoted to understanding the effect of the work environment on workers.

***error** (1) (ISO) a discrepancy between a computed, observed, or measured value or condition and the true, specified, or theoretically correct value or condition. (2) (ISO) Deprecated term for mistake.

error correction input An input that corrects an error condition resulting from other types of inputs.

error handling Procedures for detecting errors in input data, and ensuring that they are corrected before the data is processed.

***error message** An indication that an error has been detected.

error recovery The ability of a system to continue operating normally after the user has made an input error.

exception (IBM) An abnormal condition such as an I/O error encountered in processing a data set or a file.

exception report A report generated only if an activity or system gets out of control and requires human attention.

executable statement A program statement that instructs the computer to perform a certain action.

execute (SC1) To perform the execution of an instruction or of a computer program.

execution time (IBM) The time during which an instruction is decoded and performed.

expert systems Systems that possess artificial intelligence.

extract (1) *(ISO) To select and remove from a set of items those items that meet some criteria, e.g., to obtain certain specified digits from a computer word as controlled by an instruction or a mask. (2) (IBM) To remove specific items from a file.

face-to-face contact Direct interaction among human beings. Some people fear that this kind of contact may be reduced due to the spread of data communication systems.

facilities management vendor A firm that specializes in managing, staffing and operating computer installations for its customers.

***fault** (ISO) An accidental condition that causes a functional unit to fail to perform in a required manner.

feasibility study The first step in classical system development. At this step the system analyst identifies the objectives of the present system and determines whether a new system would be cost-effective.

***fetch** To locate and load a quantity of data from storage.

fiber optics A laser-based data communication technique which transmits data over glass fibers by means of light waves (Photonic (light-based) mode of data transmission).

***field** (1) (ISO) In a record, a specified area used for a particular category of data, for example, a group of bytes in which a wage rate is recorded. (2) A group of adjacent card columns on a punch card.

file (1) (ISO) A set of related records treated as a unit, e.g. in stock control, a file could consist of a set of invoices. (2) A collection of related records.

file activity The proportion of master file records that are actually used or accessed in a given processing run of the file or during a given period of time.

***file layout** (ISO) The arrangement and structure of data or words in a file including the order and size of the components of the file.

file maintenance inputs All changes to files which are not originated by business transactions.

file protected (IBM) Pertaining to a tape reel with the write-enable ring removed or a floppy disk with the file protect notch covered with tape.

file protection ring A plastic ring that must be inserted into a reel of magnetic tape before it can be written on. (An alternative is a no-write ring which prevents the file protection ring from being inserted and therefore, prevents files from being written on when it is inserted in a reel of tape.)

file query The retrieval of some specific information from a file.

file volatility The number of additions and deletions to a file in a given period of time.

fine tuning Removing bottlenecks and reallocating work among system resources, in order to obtain maximum output from the given resources.

fire controls Controls that minimize the risk of losses from fire. These include both emergency procedures and preventive measures.

fixed-form (IBM) Pertaining to entry of data or the coding of program statements in a predefined format. Contrast with free-form.

fixed-length record (IBM) A record having the same length as all other records with which it is logically or physically associated. Contrast with variable-length record.

***flag** (1) Any of various types of indicators used for identification, e.g., a word mark. (2) A character that signals the occurrence of some condition, such as the end of a word. (3) (ISO) Deprecated term for mark.

flat file A file containing only fixed-length records of equal length.

floppy disk A data storage medium that is a 5¼ or 8 inch disk of polyester film covered with a magnetic coating.

flowchart (1) *(ISO) A graphical representation for the definition, analysis, or method of solution of a problem, in which symbols are used to represent operations, data, flow, equipment, etc. (2) *Contrast with block diagram. (3) See data flowchart, program flowchart, control flowcharting, system flowchart and block diagram.

***flowchart symbol** (ISO) A symbol used to represent operations, data, flow, or equipment on a flowchart.

***fold** To compact data by combining parts of the data, e.g., to transform a two-word alphabetic key into a one-word numeric key by adding the numeric equivalents of the letters.

***font** A family or assortment of characters of a given size and style, e.g., 9 point Bodoni Modern.

***foreground processing** (1) (ISO) The execution of a computer program that preempts the use of computer facilities. (2) Contrast with background processing.

***format** (ISO) The arrangement or layout of data in or on a data medium.

***FORTRAN (Formula Translation)** A programming language primarily used to express computer programs by arithmetic formulas.

free-form (IBM) Pertaining to entry of data or the coding of statements without regard for predefined formats. Contrast with fixed-form.

front-end processor A computer configuration where the minor jobs or communication tasks are handled by a mini-CPU, allowing the main CPU to handle all batch jobs and programs the front-end processor cannot handle.

functional specification document An outline of the proposed new system. This may include a problem description, assumptions, performance requirements, and a system flowchart.

functional information system A set of application systems that satisfy the information needs within a functional area of the business.

functional primitive The lowest level of a data flow diagram where the actual processing of data is described.

Gantt chart A graph where output activities are plotted as bars on a time scale. This chart was developed by Henry L. Gantt in 1917. These charts indicate who is assigned responsibility for completing certain tasks, the estimated or planned dates jobs are to be started and completed, and the actual dates particular tasks have been started and completed.

general controls Overall managerial controls applied to all software, hardware, and personnel involved in the information system.

generalized module A precoded module that performs some commonly used function. It may be used by many different users for a variety of purposes.

generations Distinct categories of computer systems developed during different periods since the dawn of the computer age in the 1940s.

grandparent-parent-child backup A file backup system in which the current version of the file and the two previous versions are always retained.

graphics (IBM) See computer graphics.

graphics language A computer language that may be used to retrieve data from files or data bases and display it graphically.

***half-duplex** (1) In data communication, pertaining to an alternate, one way at a time, independent transmission. (2) Contrast with duplex.

handshaking (IBM) Exchange of predetermined signals when a connection is established between two data set devices. See also answerback.

hard copy (1) (SC1) In computer graphics, a permanent copy of a display image that can be separated from a display device, for example, a display image that is recorded on paper. (2) (IBM) A printed copy of machine output in a visually readable form; for example, printed reports, listings, documents, and summaries. Contrast with soft copy.

hardware study An analysis of hardware requirements for an information system. It normally leads to a tentative selection of equipment.

hardwired terminal A terminal which is directly wired to the computer. See dial-up terminal.

***hash total** The result obtained by applying an algorithm to a set of data for checking purposes, e.g., a summation obtained by treating data items as numbers.

hashing An addressing scheme which divides the record key by a large prime number and uses the remainder as the record's relative address.

***head** (ISO) A device that reads, writes, or erases data on a storage medium, e.g., a small electromagnet used to read, write, or erase data on a magnetic disk, drum or tape.

header label (IBM) A file or data set label that precedes the data records on a unit of recording media.

header record (1) (IBM) A record containing common, constant, or identifying information for a group of records that follows. Synonymous with header label. (2) The first record stored on magnetic tape or disk that contains information about the file such as the data set name, logical record length and block-size.

***heuristic method** (ISO) Any exploratory method of solving problems in which an evaluation is made of the progress toward an acceptable final result using a series of approximate results.

hexadecimal representation A number system used to represent data internally in a computer and for memory dumps. The digits of a hexadecimal number represent powers of sixteen.

hierarchical structure A distributed system design where a superior/subordinate relationship exists between distributed computer installations.

***high level language** (ISO) A programming language that does not reflect the structure of any one given computer or that of any given class of computers.

history file (1) (IBM) A file in which a record is kept of jobs or transactions. (2) A file in which a record is kept of noncurrent master file data.

***hit** (1) A comparison of two items of data that satisfies specified conditions. Contrast with match. (2) A transient disturbance to a communication medium.

***Hollerith card** A punch card characterized by 80 columns and 12 rows of punch positions.

horizontal network A distributed system design where each local installation is equal and has the capability of communicating with all other installations (synonymous with ring network).

host computer (IBM) (1) The primary or controlling computer in a multiple computer operation. (2) The primary or controlling computer in a data communication system.

***housekeeping operation** (ISO) An operation that facilitates the execution of a computer program without making a direct contribution. For example, initialization of storage areas; the execution of a calling sequence. Synonymous with overhead operation.

human factors The positive and negative behavioral implications of introducing EDP systems into the workplace.

hybrid configuration A ring structured communication network where each node on the ring is also the center of a star network.

***idle time** (ISO) Operable time during which a functional unit is not operated.

immediate-direct processing The immediate processing of transactions and inquiries with direct access files.

immediate mode A mode of processing under which transactions are processed to update the master file shortly after they occur.

***impact printer** (ISO) A printer in which printing is the result of mechanical impact.

implementation A phase in the system development cycle when coding, testing and manual procedure development are done.

***index** (1) (ISO) In programming, a subscript, of integer value, that identifies the position of an item of data with respect to some other item of data. (2) (ISO) A list of the contents of a file or of a document, together with keys or references for locating the contents. (3) A symbol or a numeral used to identify a particular quantity in an array of similar quantities. For example, the terms of an array represented by X1, X2, . . . , X100 have the indexes 1, 2, . . . , 100 respectively.

index area A part of an ISAM file that stores the indexes necessary for retrieving data records.

indexed sequential access method (ISAM) A file organization where records are stored sequentially, yet direct access may be made to individual records in the file through an index of records' absolute addresses.

index file A file used to indicate the address of records stored on secondary storage devices.

information (1) *(ISO) The meaning that a human assigns to data by means of the known conventions used in their representation. (2) Data processed by humans to reduce uncertainty.

information rich Those people who have access to modern information technology.

information center A service department in an organization that assists users in developing their own computer applications.

information response The information provided by the computer after processing input data.

***information retrieval (IR)** (1) (ISO) The action of recovering specific information from stored data. (2) (ISO) Methods and procedures for recovering specific information from stored data.

information services Businesses that maintain large data bases on various subjects. For a price, a customer can tap the data base and retrieve information that is of interest to her or him.

information system consultant An individual who assists users with various problems ranging from simple trouble shooting to complete system design and implementation.

information system manager An MIS professional who is responsible for managing the entire EDP department, or some part of it.

information system master plan An outline of the overall strategy for implementation of the information system.

information workers People who create, process, and use substantial amounts of information as a normal part of their jobs.

***initialize** To set counters, switches, addresses, or contents of storage to zero or other starting values at the beginning of, or at prescribed points in, the operation of a computer routine.

initial program load (IPL) (IBM) The initialization procedure that causes an operating system to commence operation.

ink jet printer (IBM) A non-impact printer in which the characters are formed by the projection of a jet of ink onto paper.

input synonymous with input data.

***input area** An area of storage reserved for input. Synonymous with input block.

input controls Controls that ensure that all inputs are authorized, accurate, and are properly converted to machine readable format.

***input data** (1) (ISO) Data being received or to be received into a device or into a computer program. Synonymous with input. (2) Data to be processed.

input/output statement A program statement that causes the computer to either read input data or produce output.

input stream (IBM) The sequence of job control statements and data submitted to an operating system on an input unit especially activated for this purpose by the operator. Synonymous with input job stream, job input stream.

***input unit** (ISO) A device in a data processing system by which data can be entered into the system.

inquiry (IBM) A request for information from storage; for example, a request for the number of available airline seats, or a machine statement to initiate a search of library documents. Synonym for query.

inquiry and transaction processing (IBM) A type of teleprocessing application in which inquiries and records of transactions received from a number of terminals are used to interrogate or update one or more master files maintained by the central system.

***instruction** (ISO) In a programming language, a meaningful expression that specifies one operation and identifies its operands, if any.

instruction time (I-time) (IBM) The time during which an instruction is fetched from the main storage of a computer into an instruction register. See also execution time.

integrated circuit A device that contains transistors that are deposited photochemically on a chip of silicon material. These devices have greatly increased the speed of computers while sharply reducing their size.

integrated word processing/data processing The combination of word processing and numeric data processing capabilities into one integrated system. Such systems are used to produce management reports which require both text and numbers.

intelligent terminal (1) (IBM) Deprecated term for programmable terminal. (2) A terminal which contains a microprocessor and is therefore, capable of performing some data processing by itself without recourse to the central computer.

interactive (IBM) Pertaining to an application in which each entry calls forth a response from a system or program, as in an inquiry system or an airline reservation system. An interactive system may also be conversational, implying a continuous dialog between the user and the system.

interactive data entry The process of entering data directly into the computer through a data entry terminal.

interblock gap (1) (ISO) The space between two consecutive blocks on a data medium. (2) *An area on a data medium to indicate the end of a block or physical record.

***interface** (1) A shared boundary. An interface might be a hardware component to link two devices or it might be a portion of storage or registers accessed by two or more computer programs. (2) The inputs and outputs that move from one module to another in a software system.

internal storage (1) (ISO) Storage that is accessible by a computer without the use of input/output channels. (2) (IBM) Deprecated term for main storage.

international data transfer The movement of data across national boundaries through data communication networks.

***interpret** (ISO) To translate and to execute each source language statement of a computer program before translating and executing the next statement.

interrupt (ISO) A suspension of a process, such as the execution of a computer program, caused by an event external to that process, and performed in such a way that the process can be resumed.

invalid code checks A control that verifies codes contained by input records to assure that they are valid.

inventory system Computer equipment and programs used to monitor inventories and minimize inventory costs.

***inverted file** (1) A file whose sequence has been reversed. (2) In information retrieval, a method of organizing a cross-index file in which a keyword identifies a record; the items, numbers, or documents pertinent to that keyword are indicated.

***I/O** Input/output.

***IPL** See initial program loader.

ISAM (IBM) See indexed sequential access method.

***ISO** International Organization for Standardization.

job (1) *A set of data that completely defines a unit of work for a computer. A job usually includes all necessary computer programs, linkages, files, and instructions to the operating system. (2) (IBM) A collection of related problem programs, identified in the input stream by a JOB statement followed by one or more EXEC and DD statements.

***job control language (JCL)** A problem-oriented language designed to express statements in a job that are used to identify the job or describe its requirements to an operating system.

kernel program A sample program of small size executed on alternative computer configurations to provide information useful in making a computer acquisition decision.

key (1) *(ISO) One or more characters, within a set of data that contains information about the set, including its identification. (2) (IBM) To enter information from a keyboard.

key-entry (IBM) Pertaining to the input of data manually by means of a keyboard.

key-to-disk data entry The process of recording data on disk before inputing it to the computer.

key-to-diskette data entry The process of recording data on diskettes before inputing it to the system.

key-to-tape data entry The process of recording data on magnetic tape before inputing it to the computer.

key verifier A machine that verifies that data which has been key punched, was key punched correctly.

***keypunch** (ISO) A keyboard-actuated device that punches holes in a punch card or punched card. Synonymous with keyboard punch.

keyword A special word in a programming language that tells the computer which operation to perform.

label (1) *(ISO) One or more characters, within or attached to a set of data, that contains information about the set, including its identification. (2) *(ISO) In computer programming, an identifier of an instruction. (3) (IBM) An identification record for a tape or disk file. (External labels are written on paper on the outside of a physical volume. Internal labels are stored in computer readable form on the storage medium itself.)

language translator (IBM) A general term for any assembler, compiler, or other routine that accepts statements in one language and produces equivalent statements in another language.

laser printer A high quality non-impact printer that is capable of producing a wide variety of type fonts.

laser storage A memory device which makes use of laser beams for storing data. These laser beams form microscopic patterns to represent characters on various surfaces.

***leader** The blank section of tape at the beginning of a reel of tape.

leasing A contract arrangement which binds the user of a system to rent it over a relatively long period of time. However it typically costs less than a rental arrangement.

***left-justify** (1) (ISO) To shift the contents of a register, if necessary, so that the character at the left-hand end of the data that has been read or loaded into the register is at a specified position in the register. (2) (ISO) To control the printing positions of characters on a page so that the left-hand margin of the printing is regular.

***letter** (ISO) A graphic character, that, when used alone or combined with others, represents in a written language one or more sound elements of a spoken language, but excluding diacritical marks used alone and punctuation marks.

***level** (ISO) The degree of subordination of an item in an hierarchical arrangement.

***level number** (ISO) A reference number that indicates the position of an item in a hierarchical arrangement. Synonymous with rank.

leveled data flow diagram A hierarchically partitioned data flow diagram. Each level describes in more detail the data flows shown in the level above it. Increased partitioning at lower levels keeps the diagrams of manageable size.

librarian An MIS employee who is responsible for the storage of program and data files. These files are normally stored on tape or disk.

***library** (1) A collection of related files. For example, one line of an invoice may form an item, a complete invoice may form a file, the collection of inventory control files may form a library, and the libraries used by an organization are known as its data bank. (2) A repository for demountable recorded media, such as magnetic disk packs and magnetic tapes.

***library routine** A proven routine that is maintained in a program library.

limit/reasonableness check See reasonableness checks.

***line printer** (1) (ISO) A device that prints a line of characters as a unit. Synonymous with line-at-a-time printer. (2) Contrast with character printer, page printer.

linkage editor (ISO) A computer program used to create one load module from one or more independently-translated object modules or load modules by resolving cross references among the modules.

link edit (IBM) To create a loadable computer program by means of a linkage editor.

linking Synonymous with link-editing.

***list** (1) (ISO) An ordered set of items of data. (2) To print or otherwise display items of data that meet specified criteria. (3) (ISO) Deprecated term for chained list.

list directed I/O Input or output of unformatted data. The computer uses a default format for this kind of I/O.

load (1) (ISO) In computer programming, to enter data into storage or working registers. (2) (IBM) To bring a load module from auxiliary storage into main storage for execution.

load module (ISO) A program unit that is suitable for loading into main storage for execution; it is usually the output of a linkage editor.

load module library (IBM) A partitioned data set that is used to store and retrieve load modules. See also object module library, source module library.

local data Data that is only used by one computer in a distributed data processing environment.

***location** Any place in which data may be stored.

logical file A file as conceptualized logically by the user. A logical file may or may not physically exist.

logical model A model of a system which emphasizes what is to be done, rather than who or what does it.

logical record (1) *A record independent of its physical environment. Portions of the same logical record may be located in different physical records, or several logical records or parts of logical records may be located in one physical record. (2) (IBM) A record from the standpoint of its content, function, and use rather than its physical attributes; that is, one that is defined in terms of the information it contains.

logical view Representation of the data in a data base in a format that is meaningful to the applications programmer.

logoff (IBM) The procedure by which a user ends a terminal session.

logon (IBM) The procedure by which a user begins a terminal session.

machine cycle The time required by the CPU to perform one machine operation.

***machine language** (1) A language that is used directly by a machine. (2) (ISO) Synonym for computer language.

machine operation The smallest unit of processing done by a computer, e.g., adding 0 to 1.

***machine-readable medium** A medium that can convey data to a given sensing device. Synonymous with automated data medium.

macro instruction A set of program statements that may be invoked simply by a one line reference to the set.

magnetic card (ISO) A card with a magnetizable surface layer on which data can be stored by magnetic recording.

magnetic core storage See core storage.

***magnetic disk** (ISO) A flat circular plate with a magnetic surface layer. Synonymous with disk.

magnetic disk unit (ISO) A device containing a disk drive, magnetic heads, and associated controls.

magnetic drum A cylindrical data storage device used in early computer systems.

***magnetic ink character recognition (MICR)** (1) Character recognition of characters printed with ink that contains particles of a magnetic material. (2) Contrast with optical character recognition.

***magnetic storage** A storage device that utilizes the magnetic properties of certain materials.

magnetic strip (IBM) A strip of magnetic material on which data, usually identification information, can be recorded and from which the data can be read.

magnetic tape (1) (ISO) A tape with a magnetizable surface layer on which data can be stored by magnetic recording. (2) *(ISO) A tape with a magnetic surface layer. (3) *A tape of magnetic material used as the constituent in some forms of magnetic cores.

magnetic tape drive See tape drive.

magnetic thin film storage (ISO) A magnetic storage in which data are stored by magnetic recording in a film of molecular thickness, coated on a substrate.

mainframe (1) *Synonym for central processing unit. (2) A large computer system that typically has over a hundred K bytes of primary storage.

***maintainability** (ISO) The ease with which maintenance of a functional unit can be performed in accordance with prescribed requirements.

maintenance Correction of errors discovered in programs, and updating the programs to satisfy changed requirements.

man-machine boundary The line of demarcation between manual operations and computerized functions.

management controls Control mechanisms that ensure proper management of EDP facilities in accordance with organizational objectives.

management information system (MIS) (1) *(ISO) Management performed with the aid of automatic data processing. (2) *An information system designed to aid in the performance of management functions. (3) A system for providing information for decision making; an automated system which uses a computer to process data.

***manual input** (1) The entry of data by hand into a device. (2) The data entered as in (1).

mass storage (ISO) Storage having a very large storage capacity.

***master file** (ISO) A file that is used as an authority in a given job and that is relatively permanent, even though its contents may change. Synonymous with main file.

master-slave relationship A hardware setup in which a peripheral device is completely under the control of a CPU.

***match** (1) A comparison to determine identity of items. (2) Contrast with hit.

mega (M) (IBM) Ten to the sixth power, 1,000,000 in decimal notation. When referring to storage capacity, two to the twentieth power, 1,048,576 in decimal notation.

***memory** (ISO) Deprecated term for primary storage.

memory management system A systems program that allocates scarce primary storage to application programs. It attempts to allocate memory space among competing users in a fair and optimal manner.

memory fragmentation Small blocks of noncontiguous, unused primary storage. These blocks are created in a multiprogramming system because programs of different sizes enter and leave the system at different times and do not necessarily occupy contiguous memory space.

memory module Extra memory devices that may be added to the basic hardware of a personal computer in order to expand primary storage.

***merge** (1) (ISO) To combine the items of two or more sets that are each in the same given order into one set in that order. (2) See balanced merge. (3) See also collate.

***MICR** Magnetic ink character recognition.

microcoding (microprogramming) The technique of placing programs in hardware devices (like ROM). This is often used for systems programs like operating systems.

microcomputer The smallest of computer systems, typically having between 4K and 256K of primary storage.

microfiche (SC1) Microform whose medium is film, in the form of sheets that contain microimages arranged in a grid pattern. The microfiche usually contains a title that can be read without magnification. Microfiche with images reduced by a very high reduction factor usually are named ultrafiche.

microfilm (SC1) Microform whose medium is film, in the form of rolls, that contains microimages arranged sequentially.

microform (SC1) Any medium that contains microimages; for example, microfiche, microfilm.

microsecond (IBM) One-millionth of a second.

millisecond (IBM) One-thousandth of a second.

minicomputer A medium-sized computer system that typically has less than 100K, but greater than 32K of primary storage.

***MIS** Management information system.

***mistake** (1) A human action that produces an unintended result. (2) Contrast with error and fault.

mnemonic An abbreviated name.

modem (Modulator-demodulator) (SC1) A functional unit that modulates and demodulates signals. One of the functions of a modem is to enable digital data to be transmitted over analog transmission facilities.

***modularity** The extent to which a system is composed of modules.

***module** (1) A program unit that is discrete and identifiable with respect to compiling, combining with other units, and loading, e.g., the input to, or output from, an assembler, compiler, linkage editor, or executive routine. (2) A packaged functional hardware unit designed for use with other components.

monitor (1) (ISO) A functional unit that observes and records selected activities within a data processing system for analysis. (2) (IBM) Software or hardware that observers, supervises, controls, or verifies the operations of a system.

***monitor program** (ISO) A computer program that observes, regulates, controls, or verifies the operations of a data processing system. Synonymous with monitoring program.

MS-DOS (Microsoft Disk Operating System) An operating system used on personal computers, especially the IBM PC.

multiplexing (IBM) The division of a transmission facility into two or more channels either by splitting the frequency band transmitted by the channel into narrower bands, each of which is used to constitute a distinct channel (frequency-division multiplexing), or by allotting this common channel to several different information channels, one at a time (time-division multiplexing).

multiprocessing (1) (ISO) A mode of operation that provides for parallel processing by two or more processors of a multiprocessor. (2) The processing of a single program by two or more CPUs.

multiprogramming (1) *A mode of operation that provides for the interleaved execution of two or more computer programs by a single central processing unit. (2) The capability of a computer CPU to execute two or more programs concurrently.

nanosecond (IBM) One-thousand-millionth of a second.

natural program break A break in a program such as a request for I/O, that enables systems under multiprogramming to rotate programs.

***nest** (1) (ISO) To incorporate a structure or structures of some kind into a structure of the same kind. For example, to nest one loop (the nested loop) within another loop (the nesting loop); to nest one subroutine (the nested subroutine) within another subroutine (the nesting subroutine). (2) To embed subroutines or data in other subroutines at a different hierarchical level such that the different levels of routines or data can be executed or accessed recursively.

network (IBM) In data communication, a configuration in which two or more terminal or processor installations are connected.

network structure The data structure which allows a many-to-many relationship among the nodes in the structure.

***node** (1) The representation of a state or an event by means of a point on a diagram. (2) In a tree structure, a point at which subordinate items of data originate. (3) A CPU, terminal, or other device on a communication network.

***noise** Loosely, any disturbance tending to interfere with the normal operation of a device or system.

non-impact printer (ISO) A printer in which printing is not the result of mechanical impacts; for example, thermal printers, electrostatic printers, photographic printers.

non-recurring costs The initial costs which are not expected to arise in years subsequent to the initial installation of a computer system.

***nondestructive read (NDR)** (ISO) A read process that does not erase the data in the source. Synonymous with nondestructive readout.

nonprogrammable decision A decision related to an ill-defined or unstructured problem.

***number** (1) A mathematical entity that may indicate quantity or amount of units. (2) Loosely, a numeral.

***numeric** (ISO) Pertaining to data or to physical quantities represented by numerals. Synonymous with numerical.

numeric/alphabetic checks A control that assures that input record fields that should contain only numeric characters do not contain alphabetic characters or vice versa.

***object code** Output from a compiler or assembler which is itself executable machine code or is suitable for processing to produce executable machine code.

object module (IBM) A program unit that is the output of an assembler or a compiler and is suitable for input to a linkage editor.

***object program** (1) (ISO) A fully compiled or assembled program that is ready to be loaded into the computer. (2) Contrast with source program. (3) Synonymous with target program.

objectives Desired goals which have not been met yet.

office automation The increasing use of EDP systems to perform routine office chores and improve productivity.

offline (1) (ISO) Pertaining to the operation of a functional unit without the continual control of a computer. (2) A peripheral device or file that is not in direct communication with the CPU.

***offline storage** Storage not under control of the central processing unit.

online (1) (ISO) Pertaining to the operation of a functional unit that is under the continual control of a computer. The term "online" is also used to describe a user's access to a computer via a terminal. (2) A computer system, peripheral device, or file, such as a terminal or disk drive, that is in direct communication with the CPU.

online direct access system A computer system which has several terminals in direct communication with the CPU which is in turn in direct communication with direct access files.

***online storage** Storage under the control of the central processing unit.

online system (IBM) A system in which the input data enters the computer directly from the point of origin or in which output data is transmitted directly to where it is used.

***open shop** (1) Pertaining to the operation of a computer facility in which most productive problem programming is performed by the problem originator rather than by a group of programming specialists. The use of the computer itself may also be described as open shop if the user/programmer also serves as the operator. (2) Contrast with closed shop.

***operand** (1) (ISO) An entity to which an operation is applied. (2) That which is operated upon. An operand is usually identified by an address part of an instruction.

***operating system** (ISO) Software that controls the execution of computer programs and that may provide scheduling, debugging, input/output control, accounting, compilation, storage assignment, data management, and related services.

***operation** A program step undertaken or executed by a computer, e.g., addition, multiplication, extraction, comparison, shift, transfer. The operation is usually specified by the operator part of an instruction.

***operation code** (ISO) A code used to represent the operations of a computer.

operational decision A decision on how to carry out specific tasks effectively and efficiently.

operator message (IBM) A message from the operating system or a problem program directing the operator to perform a specific function, such as mounting a tape reel, or informing him of specific conditions within the system, such as an error condition.

opscan Synonymous with optical scanner.

***optical character recognition (OCR)** The machine identification of printed characters through use of light sensitive devices.

optical reader (IBM) A device that reads hand written or machine printed symbols into a computing system.

***optical scanner** (ISO) A scanner that uses light for examining patterns and reading them into a computing system.

order processing system A computer system that initiates shipping orders, keeps track of backorders, and produces various sales analysis reports.

origination The creation of raw data as a result of a business event or transaction.

***output** (ISO) Pertaining to a device, process, or channel involved in an output process, or to the data or states involved in an output process.

output controls Controls that help assure the accuracy of computer results and ensure proper distribution of output.

***output unit** (ISO) A device in a data processing system by which data can be received from the system.

overflow area The area of an ISAM or other direct access file which contains record additions that cannot be inserted in the prime area during periods between file reorganizations.

***pack** (ISO) To store data in a compact form in a storage medium by taking advantage of known characteristics of the data and the storage medium, in such a way that the original data can be recovered, for example, making use of bit or byte locations that would otherwise go unused.

packaged design A package including the structured specifications of data flow diagrams, data dictionary, and module descriptions including pseudocode, structured English, decision tables, decision charts, and sometimes program flowcharts.

packed decimal (IBM) Representation of a decimal value by two adjacent digits in a byte. For example, in packed decimal, the decimal value 23 is represented in one eight-bit byte by 0010 0011.

page (ISO) In a virtual storage system, a fixed-length block that has a virtual address and that can be transferred between real primary storage and auxiliary storage.

page-in (IBM) In virtual storage systems, the process of transferring a page from external (secondary) page storage to real (primary) storage.

page-out (IBM) In virtual storage systems, the process of transferring a page from real (primary) storage to external (secondary) page storage.

page printer (IBM) (1) A device that prints one page as a unit, e.g., cathode ray tube printer, film printer, xerographic printer. Synonymous with page-at-a-time printer. (2) Contrast with character printer, line printer.

paging (1) (ISO) The transfer of pages between real storage and auxiliary storage. (2) *A time sharing technique in which pages are transferred between primary storage and auxiliary storage. Synonymous with page turning.

parallel conversion A method of converting to a new system whereby both the old and the new systems operate concurrently until management is satisfied that the new system will perform satisfactorily.

***parallel processing** The simultaneous execution of two or more processes in a single unit.

parameterized application package Prewritten application programs that the user can modify to suit his or her own requirements. The modification is done simply by specifying values for certain parameters.

***parity bid** A check bit appended to an array of binary digits to make the sum of all the binary digits, including the check bit, always odd or always even.

***parity check** A check that tests whether the number of ones (or zeros) in an array of binary digits is odd or even. Synonymous with odd-even check.

partitioned data set (PDS) (IBM) In OS/360 and OS/VS, a data set in direct access storage that is divided into partitions, called members, each of which can contain a program or part of a program. Each partitioned data set contains a directory (or index) that the control program can use to locate a program in the library. Synonymous with program library.

partitioning Decomposing a data flow diagram into smaller, more detailed diagrams.

partitions Blocks of storage space in primary memory. Parts of programs are stored in these blocks in a multiprogramming environment.

PASCAL A block structured high level computer language, named after a pioneer computer scientist Blaise Pascal.

***pass** One cycle of processing a body of data.

password (IBM) (1) A unique string of characters that a program, computer operator, or user must supply to meet security requirements before gaining access to data. (2) In systems with time sharing, a one-to-eight character symbol that the user may be required to supply at the time he logs on the system. The password is confidential, as opposed to the user identification.

***patch** To modify a routine in a rough or expedient way.

payroll register A report which provides a recap of payment transactions for each employee and serves as an important part of the audit trail of the system.

payroll system A computer system that assists in the preparation of salary checks, maintains payment records, and provides management reports related to payroll activities.

peripheral device Synonymous with peripheral equipment.

***peripheral equipment** (ISO) In a data processing system, any equipment, distinct from the central processing unit, that may provide the system with outside communication, storage, input/output, or additional facilities.

personal computer A microcomputer that is small enough to sit on a desk top and may be used by a person with very little technical expertise.

PERT-CPM Scheduling methods using networks consisting of activities that consume resources and take time and events which mark the beginning and end of the activities. These methods allow the minimum amount of time in which a project can be completed and the critical path to be determined.

phased conversion A method of converting to a new system whereby the old system is gradually phased out, and the new gradually phased in at the same time.

physical file A collection of records that are physically located contiguous to one another. Contrast with logical file.

physical record (1) (ISO) A record whose characteristics depend on the manner or form in which it is stored, retrieved, or moved. A physical record may consist of all or part of a logical record. (2) Records which physically exist. Contrast with logical record.

physical view Representation of the data in a data base in terms of physical characteristics like location, field length, and access method.

picosecond (IBM) One trillionth of a second. One thousandth of a nanosecond.

pilot conversion A method of converting to a new system where the new system is introduced in some selected departments. If it functions satisfactorily, then it is extended to the whole organization.

planning Planning is part of the process of management decision making. Planning involves identifying the alternatives from which to choose, selecting the criteria to be used in choosing an alternative, and selecting the plan of action to be implemented for the problem.

plug-compatible A hardware unit produced by one manufacturer that can directly replace units produced by another manufacturer.

***pointer** An identifier that indicates the location of an item of data.

point-of-sale (POS) data entry Immediate entry of sales transactions to the computer through a cash register which is connected to the computer.

polling A process by which the CPU addresses different terminals in turn to check if they have any input data for transmission to the CPU. A single line links all these terminals to the CPU.

portability (1) (IBM) The ability to use data sets or files with different operating systems. Volumes whose data sets or files are cataloged in a user catalog can be demounted from storage devices of one system, moved to another system, and mounted on storage devices of that system. (2) The ability to move programs from one computer to another without modification.

***position** (1) (ISO) In a string, each location that may be occupied by a character or binary element and that may be identified by a serial number. (2) See bit position, punch position, sign position.

post (IBM) To enter a unit of information on a record. (2) To note the occurrence of an event.

post-implementation audit Usually consists of two steps: (1) an evaluation of a new system using the objectives stated during the systems investigation phase, and (2) a review and evaluation of the systems development cycle.

power controls Controls that prevent damage to the system from voltage fluctuations and power breakdowns.

***precision** (1) (ISO) A measure of the ability to distinguish between nearly equal values. (2) The degree of discrimination with which a quantity is stated. For example, a three-digit numeral discriminates among 1000 possibilities.

prespecified computing EDP applications for which processing requirements can be determined ahead of time and programmed in the conventional manner.

primary key A field in a record whose value uniquely identifies the record. For instance, I.D. number may be a primary key for a file or data base pertaining to students at a university.

primary storage (1) (ISO) Program-addressable storage from which instructions and other data can be loaded directly into registers for subsequent execution or processing. (2) (IBM) Contrast secondary storage. (3) (ISO) Deprecated term for internal storage.

prime area The area of an ISAM or other direct access file containing all the records of the file after the file is initially created or reorganized.

printer (IBM) A device that writes output data from a system on paper.

priority (IBM) A rank assigned to a task that determines its precedence in receiving system resources.

priority scheduler (IBM) A form of job scheduler that uses input and output work queues to improve system performance.

problem oriented language A high level language which the user can use to describe a problem. The compiler automatically generates the procedures necessary to solve the problem.

***procedure-oriented language** (ISO) A problem-oriented language that facilitates the expression of a procedure as an explicit algorithm; for example, FORTRAN, ALGOL, COBOL, PL/I. Synonymous with procedural language.

***process** (1) A course of events occurring according to an intended purpose or effect. (2) A systematic sequence of operations to produce a specified result. (3) To perform operations on data.

***process control** Automatic control of a process in which a computer is used for the regulation of usually continuous operations or processes.

processing program A systems program that assists a user in developing and using application programs. Examples are: compilers, librarians and utility programs.

processing controls Controls that increase the integrity of processing.

***program** (1) (ISO) A series of actions designed to achieve a certain result. (2) Loosely, a routine, (3) (ISO) To design, write and test computer programs. (4) Loosely, to write a routine.

program documentation The documentation relating to individual programs.

***program flowchart** (ISO) A flowchart representing the sequence of operation in a computer program. Synonymous with program flow diagram.

program library (1) *(ISO) An organized collection of computer programs that are sufficiently documented to allow them to be used by persons other than their authors. (2) *A collection of available computer programs and routines. (3) (IBM) Synonym for partitioned data set. (4) A file containing the production copy of both applications and systems programs.

program segmentation Breaking a program into small segments which will fit small, noncontiguous blocks of space available in primary storage.

program stubs Dummy modules that are called by the parent module during the testing phase. This allows testing of the parent module before the lower level modules are written.

programmable decision A decision that is made within the guidelines of an established policy.

programmer A person who designs, writes, and tests computer programs.

programmer/analyst An MIS professional who performs both programming and systems analysis functions.

***programming** (ISO) The designing, writing, and testing of computer programs.

***programming language** (ISO) An artificial language established for expressing computer programs.

***programming language one (PL/1)** A programming language designed for use in a wide range of commercial and scientific computer applications.

project management approach A system development approach where each application development project is assigned to a project team.

protect To safeguard data from unauthorized changes on destruction.

protected field (IBM) On a display device, a display field in which the user cannot enter, modify, or erase data from the keyboard. Contrast with unprotected field.

pseudocode A description of program logic using English language sentences, instead of the statements of a computer language.

prototype An experimental version of a user developed application.

***punched card** (1) A card punched with hole patterns. (2) See Hollerith card.

QUBE system A combination of cable TV and a computer system which allows viewers to respond to broadcast messages through a keyboard.

query (SC1) In interactive systems, an operation at a terminal that elicits a response from the system.

query language A high level computer language used to retrieve specific information from a data base.

queue (IBM) A line or list formed by items in a system waiting for service; for example, tasks to be performed or messages to be transmitted in a message switching system.

***radix** (1) (ISO) In a radix numeration system, the positive integer by which the weight of the digit place is multiplied to obtain the weight of the digit place with the next higher weight, e.g., in the decimal numeration system the radix of each digit place is 10. (2) Deprecated term for base.

radix transformation An addressing scheme under which the record key is converted to a nondecimal basis and used as the relative address for the record.

random access (ISO) Deprecated term for direct access.

random access memory (ISO) Deprecated term for direct access storage.

random addressing Synonymous with direct addressing.

randomizing (IBM) A technique by which the range of keys for an indirectly addressed file is reduced to smaller ranges of addresses by some method of computation until the desired address is found.

***random number** (1) (ISO) A number selected from a known set of numbers in such a way that the probability of occurrence of each number in the set is predetermined. (2) A number obtained by chance. (3) One of a sequence of numbers considered appropriate for satisfying certain statistical tests or believed to be free from conditions which might bias the result of a calculation.

***range** (1) (ISO) The set of values that a quantity or function may take. (2) The difference between the highest and lowest value that a quantity or function may assume. (3) (ISO) Deprecated term for span.

raw data (IBM) Data that has not been processed or reduced.

***read** (ISO) To acquire or interpret data from a storage device, from a data medium, or from another source.

read-only memory (ROM) (ISO) Deprecated term for read-only storage.

read-only storage (ROS) (ISO) A storage device whose contents cannot be modified, except by a particular user, or when operating under particular conditions; for example, a storage device in which writing is prevented by a lockout. Synonymous with fixed storage.

read/write head (ISO) A magnetic head capable of reading and writing.

real storage (ISO) The primary storage in a virtual storage system. Physically, real storage and primary storage are identical.

realtime system A computer system with the capability of immediately capturing data concerning ongoing events or processes and providing information necessary to manage these ongoing events.

***realtime input** (ISO) Input data received into a data processing system within time limits that are determined by the requirements of some other system or at instants that are so determined.

***realtime output** (ISO) Output data delivered from a data processing system within time limits that are determined by the requirements of some other system or at instants that are so determined.

***realtime processing** (ISO) The manipulation of data that are required or generated by some process while the process is in operation; usually the results are used to influence the process, and perhaps related processes, while it is occurring.

reasonableness checks Program controls that monitor the values of input data and make sure that they are within proper limits. For instance, a reasonableness check would trap a time card that showed 150 hours worked in one week.

record (1) *(ISO) A collection of related data or words, treated as a unit; for example, a stock control, each invoice could constitute one record. (2) A collection of adjacent data fields relating to some specific entity. Analogous to a file folder in a manual file.

***record layout** (ISO) The arrangement and structure of data or words in a record, including the order and size of the components of the record.

***recording density** The number of bits in a single linear track measured per unit of length of the recording medium.

recurring costs The costs expected to continually arise throughout the life of the computer's installation.

redundancy The difference between the maximum number of bits of information that could be transmitted by a set of signs if they were equally probable and the number actually transmitted expressed as a percentage of the maximum.

redundancy check (1) (ISO) A check using extra (redundant) data systematically inserted for that purpose. (2) A control imposed by the performance of a task by two hardware units independent of each other.

reel (ISO) A cylinder with flanges on which tape may be wound.

***register** (ISO) In a computer, a storage device, usually intended for some special purpose, capable of storing a specified amount of data such as a bit or a word.

***relative address** (ISO) An address expressed as a difference with respect to a base address.

relational model A logical view of a data base which treats all data as if it were stored in the form of tables.

relevance The usefulness of data for decision making purposes.

remote (IBM) In data communication, pertaining to devices that are connected to a data processing system through a data link.

remote job entry (RJE) (ISO) Submission of a job through an input unit that has access to a computer through a data link.

report Management information printed on a hard copy medium like paper.

report generator A high level language that can be used to produce reports in almost any format.

report program generator (RPG) (IBM) A processing program that can be used to generate object programs that produce reports from existing sets of data.

request for proposal A document that specifies the requirements for equipment and software to be purchased.

***rerun** (1) (ISO) A repeat of a machine run from its beginning, usually made desirable or necessary by a false start, by an interruption, or by a change. (2) (ISO) To perform a rerun.

reserved words Words in a program that have a special meaning for the compiler. The user may not use them for any other purpose.

resident (1) (ISO) Pertaining to computer programs that remain on a particular storage device.

resident supervisor That part of the operating system which is used most often, and is continuously stored in primary storage.

resource (IBM) Any facility of the computing system or operating system required by a job or task, and including main storage, input/output devices, the processing unit, data sets, and control or processing programs.

resource allocation (ISO) The assignment of the facilities of a data processing system for the accomplishment of jobs; for example, the assignment of main storage, input-output devices, files.

resource management Synonymous with resource allocation.

response (IBM) An answer to an inquiry.

response time (1) *(ISO) The elapsed time between the end of an inquiry or demand on a data processing system and the beginning of the response, e.g., the length of time between an indication of the end of an inquiry and the display of the first character of the response at a user terminal. (2) The elapsed time between submission of a command on a remote terminal and the completion of that command as evidenced by a message on the terminal screen or printer.

***restart** (ISO) The resumption of the execution of a computer program using the data recorded at a checkpoint.

retrieve To move data from secondary storage to the CPU so that it may be processed.

rewind (IBM) To return a magnetic or paper tape to its beginning.

right-justify (1) (ISO) To control the positions of characters on a page so that the right-hand margin of the printing is regular. (2) To align characters horizontally so that the right-most character of a string is in a specified position.

ring configuration A communication network in which several CPUs are connected in a circular pattern. Each computer can communicate with either one of its neighbors in the circle.

rigid disk A hard flat circular plate coated with magnetic material, used as a secondary storage device in most mainframe computers.

***RJE** (ISO) Remote job entry.

robot A mechanical device that operates under the control of a computer.

***rollback** A programmed return to a prior checkpoint.

***roll-in** To restore in main storage, data or one or more computer programs that were previously rolled out.

***roll-out** To transfer data or one or more computer programs from main storage to auxiliary storage for the purpose of freeing main storage for another use.

routine (1) * (ISO) An ordered set of instructions that may have some general or frequent use. (2) A computer program.

***row** (1) A horizontal arrangement of characters or other expressions. (2) Contrast with column.

RPG See report program generator.

***run** (ISO) A single performance of one or more jobs.

sabotage controls Controls that reduce the risk of sabotage in EDP operations.

SC1 (IBM) Subcommittee 1; a subcommittee of ISO Technical Committee/97, responsible for the development of an international vocabulary for data processing.

***scan** To examine sequentially, part by part.

schema The logical structure of a data base.

scheduled listing A report that is produced at a regular interval like a week, a month, or a year.

scratch (IBM) To erase data on a volume or delete its identification so that it can be used for another purpose.

scratch file (IBM) A file used as a work area.

***search** (ISO) The examination of a set of items for one or more having a given property.

secondary storage (1) *(ISO) A storage device that is not primary storage. (2) *Storage that supplements another storage. (3) (IBM) Data storage other than primary storage; for example, storage on magnetic tape or direct access devices. Synonymous with external storage, secondary storage. (4) *Contrast with primary storage.

***sector** (ISO) That part of a track or band on a magnetic drum, a magnetic disk, or a disk pack that can be accessed by the magnetic heads in the course of a predetermined rotational displacement of the particular device.

seek time (IBM) The time that is needed to position the access mechanism of a direct access storage device at a specified position. See also access time.

***segment** (1) (ISO) A self-contained portion of a computer program that may be executed without the entire computer program necessarily being maintained in internal storage at any one time. (2) (ISO) To divide a computer program into segments.

segregation of functions Dividing up the workload among employees such that the work of one becomes a check on the work of others.

semantic gap A lack of correspondence between a problem definition and the computer code written to solve it.

semantic error An error in the logic of the program, as opposed to syntax errors.

***semantics** (1) (ISO) The relationships of characters or groups of characters to their meanings, independent of the manner of their interpretation and use. (2) The relationships between symbols and their meanings.

semiconductor An electronic circuit which can be reproduced photographically in a miniaturized form on silicon wafers.

***sequence** (1) (ISO) A series of items that have been sequenced. (2) An arrangement of items according to a specified set of rules e.g., items arranged alphabetically, numerically, or chronologically. (3) (ISO) Deprecated term for order. (4) (ISO) Synonym for collating sequence.

sequence checks A control that verifies that input records are in ascending order by record key field.

***sequential** (1) Pertaining to the occurrence of events in time sequence, with no simultaneity or overlap of events. (2) Contrast with concurrent, consecutive, simultaneous.

sequential access (IBM) (1) An access mode in which records are obtained from, or placed into, a file in such a way that each successive access to the file refers to the next subsequent record in the file. The order of the records is established by the programmer when creating the file. (2) Contrast with direct access.

sequential file organization A file organization with all records typically ordered in ascending order by record key.

serial access (ISO) Synonym for sequential access.

***serial processing** (1) Pertaining to the sequential or consecutive execution of two or more processes in a single device such as a channel or processing unit. (2) Contrast with

service bureau A company which provides batch computer processing service on an as-needed basis and charges for the service based on an hourly rate.

session (IBM) The period of time during which a user of a terminal can communicate with an interactive system; usually, the elapsed time from when a terminal user logs on the system until he logs off the system.

***set** (1) (ISO) A finite or infinite number of objects of any kind, of entities, or of concepts, that have a given property or properties in common. (2) (ISO) To cause a counter to take the state corresponding to a specified number. Contrast with reset. (3) (ISO) To place a storage device into a specified state, usually other than denoting zero. Contrast with reset.

***setup** An arrangement of data or devices to solve a particular problem.

shared data Data that is used by two or more computers concurrently in a distributed data processing system.

***sign bit** (ISO) A bit or a binary element that occupies a sign position and indicates the algebraic sign of the number represented by the numeral with which it is associated.

***significant digit** (ISO) In a numeral, a digit that is needed for a given purpose; in particular, a digit that must be kept to preserve a given accuracy or a given precision.

***sign position** (ISO) A position, normally located at one end of a numeral, that contains an indicator denoting the algebraic sign of the number represented by the numeral.

simple direct file organization A direct file organization that uses the record key to directly compute the record's relative address.

simplex transmission (SC1) Data transmission over a data circuit in one pre-assigned direction only.

***simulate** (1) (ISO) To represent certain features of the behavior of a physical or abstract system by the behavior of another system, e.g., to represent physical phenomena by means of the operations performed by a computer or to represent the operations of a computer by those of another computer. (2) To imitate one system with another, primarily by software, so that the imitating system accepts the same data, executes the same computer programs, and achieves the same results as the imitated system.

***simulation** (ISO) The representation of certain features of the behavior of a physical or abstract system by the behavior of another system; for example, the representation of physical phenomena by means of operations performed by a computer or the representation of operations of a computer by those of another computer. Contrast with emulation.

***simultaneous** (ISO) Pertaining to the occurrence of two or more events at the same instant of time. (2) See also concurrent, consecutive, sequential.

skeleton application program A simple program developed as a model for an actual application. The skeleton program includes only the most essential capabilities needed in the actual application.

***snapshot dump** (1) (ISO) A dynamic dump of the contents of one or more specified storage areas. (2) A selective dynamic dump performed at various points in a machine run.

°**snapshot program** (ISO) A trace program that produces output data only for selected instructions or for selected conditions.

soft copy (SC1) Information that is displayed without making a printed copy; for example, information displayed on a CRT display device.

***software** (ISO) Computer programs, procedures, rules, and possibly associated documentation concerned with the operation of a data processing system.

software directory A reference book that lists a large number of software packages and describes their major characteristics. Typically software directories are written for specific application areas like accounting, finance, etc.

software monitor A software system that monitors the performance of various system devices.

***sort** (1) The operation of sorting. (2) (ISO) To segregate items into groups according to specified criteria. Sorting involves ordering, but need not involve sequencing, for the groups may be arranged in an arbitrary order. (3) To arrange a set of items according to keys which are used as a basis for determining the sequence of the items, e.g., to arrange the records of a personnel file into alphabetical sequence by using the employee names as sort keys.

***sort key** A key used as a basis for determining the sequence of items in a set.

sound synthesizer An acoustic device which, when connected to a computer, can produce many different voice and musical sounds.

source code Synonymous with source program.

source-data automation The capture of data, in computer-readable form, at the place and time of an event.

***source language** (ISO) A language from which statements are translated into machine language.

source module (IBM) The source statements that constitute the input to a language translator for a particular translation.

source module library (IBM) A partitioned data set that is used to store and retrieve source modules. See also object module library, load module library.

***source program** (1) (ISO) A computer program expressed in a source language such as COBOL or FORTRAN. (2) Contrast with object program.

speed The number of machine operations performed by a CPU in one second.

specification statement A passive statement in a program which describes data characteristics to the computer, but does not make it perform any action.

specification form A form used to specify computations, input file format, and report format in RPG.

spooling (Simultaneous peripheral operation online) (ISO) The use of auxiliary storage as a buffer storage to reduce processing delays when transferring data between peripheral equipment and the processors of a computer.

spreadsheet A program that allows the user to create a large two-dimensional table on the computer's screen, and to manipulate the data in the table in many different ways.

stacked job processing (IBM) A technique that permits multiple job definitions to be grouped (stacked) for presentation to the system, which automatically recognizes the jobs, one after the other. More advanced systems allow job definitions to be added to the group (stack) at any time and from any source, and also honor priorities.

stand-alone (IBM) Pertaining to operation that is independent of another device, program, or system.

stand-alone key-to-rigid disk A data entry setup consisting of a minicomputer with disk storage which supports a number of online CRT terminals.

star configuration A communication network in which several microcomputers are connected to one central CPU.

***statement** (1) (ISO) In a programming language, a meaningful expression that may describe or specify operations and is complete in the context of that programming language. (2) In computer programming, a symbol string or other arrangement of symbols. (3) (ISO) Deprecated term for instruction.

statistical multiplexor A multiplexing device that allocates transmission time to different terminals in proportion to their volume of data I/O.

storage The process of retaining data, program instructions, and output in machine readable form.

storage fragmentation (IBM) Inability to assign real storage locations to virtual addresses because the available spaces are smaller than the page size.

***store** (1) (ISO) To enter data into a storage device or to retain data in a storage device. (2) (ISO) In computer programming, to copy data from registers into internal storage.

stored program A set of instructions residing in the computer's memory that may be executed without human intervention.

***stored program computer** (ISO) A computer controlled by internally stored instructions that can synthesize and store instructions, and that can subsequently execute these instructions. Synonymous with programmed computer.

strategic decision-making Involves making decisions at the upper or strategic level of the organization. These decisions affect the future of the organization and are made in an environment of uncertainty. Strategic decisions involve establishing goals, policies, and long term resource allocations.

***string** (ISO) A linear sequence of entities such as characters or physical elements.

structure chart A graphic representation of the hierarchical relationships between various modules.

structured analysis A system analysis methodology used in structured system development. A structured analysis moves from a study of the existing system to its logical model. Then the logical model of the new system is created and developed into a new physical system.

structured design Development of the logic of program modules and their interfaces.

structured programming An approach to computer programming which restricts the flow of control to three basic constructs: sequence, loop, and conditional.

structured English A tool used for describing program logic in English-like terminology. It uses the vocabulary of English combined with the logical constructs of a programming language to make the logic understandable to human beings.

structured system development A system development methodology based on three major principles: partitioning into small modules, specification of interfaces between modules, and specification of processes within the modules.

***subroutine** (1) (ISO) A sequenced set of statements that may be used in one or more computer programs and at one or more points in a computer program. (2) A routine that can be part of another routine.

subschema The logical view of that part of a data base that is of interest to a particular application.

subsystem (1) (IBM) A secondary or subordinate system, usually capable of operating independently of, or asynchronously with, a controlling system. (2) A part of the total system. All subsystems combine to comprise the system.

summarize To aggregate data into totals and condensations which are more meaningful than the raw data.

summary file A file containing data extracted and summarized from other files.

***supervisory program** (ISO) A computer program, usually part of an operating system, that controls the execution of other computer programs and regulates the flow of work in a data processing system. Synonymous with executive program, supervisor.

survey Collection of information to decide whether there are feasible ways of improving on the current system, and to identify the constraints on the project.

suspense file A file of input records in which errors have been detected.

***symbolic language** A programming language that expresses addresses and operation codes of instructions in symbols convenient to humans rather than in machine language.

synchronous transmission A data transmission method in which a long stream of bytes is transmitted without interruption. This method is economical for complex, high speed equipment which processes large volumes of data.

***syntax** (1) (ISO) The relationship among characters or groups of characters, independent of their meanings or the manner of their interpretation and use. (2) The structure of expressions in a language. (3) The rules governing the structure of a language.

***system** (ISO) In data processing, a collection of men, machines, and methods organized to accomplish a set of specific functions.

systems analysis (1) (IBM) The analysis of an activity to determine precisely what must be accomplished and how to accomplish it. (2) The evaluation of the set of alternatives in a system with a set of criteria.

systems and programming group MIS personnel who develop or acquire applications software systems.

systems development cycle The different phases that a typical computer-based information system goes through.

systems development controls Control procedures to manage the systems development, system documentation, and program maintenance functions.

systems documentation The documentation of the system that provides an overview of the system's features.

systems flowchart A flowchart providing an overall view of the inputs, processes, and outputs of a system.

system library (IBM) A collection of data sets or files in which the various parts of an operating system are stored.

system management facilities (SMF) (IBM) An optional control program feature of OS/360 and OS/VS that provides the means for gathering and recording information that can be used to evaluate system usage.

system network architecture (SNA) A data communication system used to connect various IBM devices.

system output device (IBM) A device assigned to record output data for a series of jobs.

systems programmer (IBM) A programmer who plans, generates, maintains, extends, and controls the use of an operating system with the aim of improving the overall productivity of an installation. Contrast with application programmer.

system residence volume (IBM) The volume on which the nucleus of the operating system and the highest-level index of the catalog are located.

system resource (IBM) Any facility of the computing system that may be allocated to a task.

systems software A set of programs that controls the use of hardware and software resources. These programs allocate system resources to application programs, based on their needs and their priorities.

systems software group MIS personnel who install and maintain systems software such as operating systems.

table A two dimensional data structure used as a logical model in relational data base management systems.

tactical decision-making Involves making decisions at the middle or coordinating level of the organization. The decisions are made primarily to reach the present goals of the organization. A common decision on this level involves resource allocation for the present needs of the organization.

***tag** (ISO) One or more characters, attached to a set of data, that contains information about the set, including its identification.

***tape drive** (1) (ISO) A mechanism for controlling the movement of magnetic tape. This mechanism is commonly used to move magnetic tape past a read head or write head, or to allow automatic rewinding. Synonymous with tape deck, tape transport. (2) (ISO) Deprecated term for tape unit.

technical support staff MIS personnel who are responsible for hardware maintenance and establishing data processing standards.

***temporary storage** In computer programming, storage locations reserved for intermediate results. Synonymous with working storage.

terminal (1) *A point in a system or communication network at which data can either enter or leave. (2) (IBM) A device, usually equipped with a keyboard and some kind of display, capable of sending and receiving information over a communication channel.

text handling The processing of textual data by computer, as opposed to numeric data. Also, see word processing system.

test data Hypothetical data used to test a new program for errors. Test data should be comprehensive enough to cover all possible types of valid and invalid inputs so that program performance may be observed under all circumstances.

thrashing (IBM) In virtual storage systems, a condition in which the system can do little useful work because of excessive paging.

throughput (ISO) A measure of the amount of work performed by a computer system over a given period of time, e.g., jobs per day.

time slice (IBM) An interval of time on the central processing unit allocated for use in performing a task. Once the interval has expired, central processing unit time is allocated to another task; thus a task cannot monopolize processing unit time beyond a fixed limit.

timeliness The speed with which data is provided to the user for decision making purposes.

timesharing (1) (ISO) A mode of operation of a data processing system that provides for the interleaving in time of two or more processes in one processor. (2) (IBM) A method of using a computing system that allows a number of users to execute programs concurrently and to interact with the programs during execution. (3) (ISO) Deprecated term for conversational mode.

timesharing service A service firm that rents out computer time to its customers. The customer typically accesses the CPU through a remote terminal located at its place of business.

top-down approach A system development approach which calls for the development of an integrated information system based on the objectives of the business.

trace (1) *A record of the execution of a computer program; it exhibits the sequences in which the instructions were executed. (2) (IBM) To record a series of events as they occur.

track (ISO) The path or one of the sets of paths, parallel to the reference edge on a data medium, associated with a single reading or writing component as the data medium moves past the component.

trailer label The last record in a file on magnetic tape which contains control information such as a count of the number of records in the file.

transaction analysis The derivation of a structure chart from the transaction center data flow diagram.

transaction center data flow diagram A data flow diagram characterized by parallelism of data flows.

transform analysis The derivation of a structure chart from a transform type of data flow diagram.

transform data flow diagram A linear data flow diagram where all data flows through a single, clearly identifiable stream.

transform description A description of how data is to be processed at the lowest levels of a data flow diagram.

transistor A semiconductor device that performs switching functions in an electronic circuit.

translation Generation of object code from source code.

***translator** (ISO) A computer program that translates from one language into another language and in particular from one programming language into another programming language. Synonymous with translating program.

***transmit** To send data from one place for reception elsewhere.

tree structure A hierachical data structure, characterized by a top node called a root, and nodes having a one-to-many relationship.

turn-around document A document which can be sent out to human users and is also readable by the computer when it is returned. The remittance advice on a punched card that comes with utility bills is a common example of a turn-around document.

turnaround time (1) (ISO) The elapsed time between submission of a job and the return of the complete output. (2) The elapsed time between submission of a batch job and the availability of output.

unbundling The selling of hardware and software separately.

unit record (IBM) A card containing one complete record; a punched card.

universal product code (UPC) A bar-coded symbol printed on the package of a consumer product. This is detected by an optical reader and is used by the computer to identify and price the product.

***unpack** (ISO) To recover the original form of the data from packed data.

unprotected field (IBM) On a display device, a display field in which the user can enter, modify, or erase data from the keyboard. Contrast with protected field.

update (IBM) To modify a master file with current information according to a specified procedure.

user (IBM) Anyone who requires the services of a computing system.

user-driven computing EDP applications for which users do not always know what information they will need and when. It is often necessary to modify the programs on short notice in such systems.

user-defined words Words in a program that have been defined by the programmer to have specific meanings.

user exit A point in an application generator program at which a user exit routine may be given control.

user exit routine (IBM) A routine written by a user to take control at a user exit of a program supplied by IBM.

user friendly systems Software systems that make it easy for noncomputer oriented people to use computers.

***utility program** (1) (ISO) A computer program in general support of the processes of a computer; for instance, a diagnostic program, a trace program, a sort program. Synonymous with service program. (2) A program designed to perform an everyday task such as copying data from one storage device to another.

vacuum tube Glass covered instruments that were used to regulate the flow of electrons through the circuits of early computer systems.

***validation** The checking of data for correctness, or compliance with applicable standards, rules, and conventions.

validity checks A hardware control that monitors the bit structure of bytes to determine whether the combination of the on and off bits represent a valid structure within the character set of the computer.

variable-length record (1) (IBM) A record having a length independent of the length of other records with which it is logically or physically associated. Contrast with fixed-length record. (2) *Pertaining to a file in which the records are not uniform in length.

vendor support Services provided by the seller of a hardware or software system. These typically include training, repair and maintenance, installation, testing, consulting and backup arrangements.

verifiability The ability to confirm the accuracy of data. Accuracy may be confirmed by comparing with other data of known accuracy or tracing back to the original source.

***verify** (1) To determine whether a transcription of data or other operation has been accomplished accurately. (2) To check the results of entry of data.

very high level programming language Simple-to-use programming languages which allow the user to develop applications in a much shorter time period than regular programming languages. These languages make heavy use of default options to make the user's task less burdensome.

virtual storage (ISO) The storage space that may be regarded as addressable main storage by the user of a computer system in which virtual addresses are mapped into real addresses. The size of virtual storage is limited by the addressing scheme of the computing system and by the amount of auxiliary storage available, and not by the actual number of main storage locations.

voice recognition system A hardware or software device which can interpret the patterns of an individual's speech thereby enabling voice input to a computer.

volatile storage (ISO) A storage device whose contents are lost when power is removed.

volume (1) (ISO) A certain portion of data, together with its data carrier, that can be handled conveniently as a unit. (2) (ISO) A data carrier that is mounted and demounted as a unit, for example, a reel of magnetic tape, a disk pack. (3) (IBM) That portion of a single unit of storage that is accessible to a single read/write mechanism, for example, a drum, a disk pack, or part of a disk module.

Winchester disk A rigid disk often used with microcomputers.

window (1) (SC1) In computer graphics, a bounded area within a display image. (2) One of two or more bounded areas within the display of a CRT terminal that allows two or more applications to be displayed simultaneously.

***word** (1) (ISO) A character string or a binary element string that it is convenient for some purpose to consider as an entity. (2) A character string or a bit string considered as an entity.

word processing system A computer system that stores and processes text data. These systems typically include powerful editing and text formatting capabilities.

word size A measure of the amount of data the CPU can process simultaneously.

work file (IBM) A file used to provide storage space for data that is needed only for the duration of a job.

***working storage** (ISO) Synonym for temporary storage, working space.

workload model A set of one or more computer programs which are representative of the buyer's planned computer workload. These are typically executed on alternative computer configurations to provide information which is useful in making an acquisition decision.

***write** (ISO) To make a permanent or transient recording of data in a storage device or on a data medium.

write-enable ring (IBM) A device that is installed in a tape reel to permit writing on the tape. If a tape is mounted without the ring in position, writing cannot occur; the file is protected.

write-read checks A control similar to redundancy checks, as data is written on magnetic tape or disk, it passes through a read head, which reads the data and compares it to the data which should have been written.

***zerofill** (ISO) To character fill with the representation of the character zero. Synonymous with zeroize.

***zero suppression** (ISO) The elimination from a numeral of zeros that have no significance in the numeral. Zeros that have no significance include those to the left of the nonzero digits in the integral part of a numeral and those to the right of the nonzero digits in the fractional part.

INDEX

†